TORONTO BAY

Toronto Island, 1977

PART II STUDY

Central Waterfront
Planning Committee

CITY OF TORONTO PLANNING AND
DEVELOPMENT DEPARTMENT

Job No: 07097-50   August, 1977

More Than an Island

More Than an Island

A History of the Toronto Island

SALLY GIBSON

IRWIN PUBLISHING
Toronto   Canada

Canadian Cataloguing in Publication Data

Gibson, Sarah Duane Satterthwaite, 1946–

More Than an Island
Includes Index

ISBN 0-7720-1446-9

I. Toronto Islands (Ont.)—History. I. Title.

FC3097.52.G52   1984   971.3'541   C84-098241-0
F1059.5.T686T68   1984

Designed by Robert Burgess Garbutt
Typeset by Alpha Graphics Limited
Printed in Canada by T.H. Best Printing Company Limited

1 2 3 4 5 6 7 8 THB 91 90 89 88 87 86 85 84

Published by Irwin Publishing Inc.

*Abbreviations
for Picture Credits*

AC: author's collection
CI: *Centre Islander*
CTA: City of Toronto Archives
CTA:GM: City of Toronto Archives, *Globe and Mail* Collection
CTA:JC: City of Toronto Archives, James Collection
CTA:TIA: City of Toronto Archives, Toronto Island Archives Collection
CWM/NMM/NMC: Canadian War Museum/ National Museum of Man/National Museums of Canada
MTLB: Metropolitan Toronto Library Board
OA: Ontario Archives
PAC: Public Archives of Canada
PAC,DND: Public Archives of Canada, Department of National Defence Collection
PAC,NMC: Public Archives of Canada, National Map Collection
RCYC: Royal Canadian Yacht Club
RCYC   Annals: *Annals of the Royal Canadian Yacht Club, 1852–1937* by C. H. J. Snider
ROM: Royal Ontario Museum
SDG: S. D. Gibson
THB: Toronto Historical Board
THC: Toronto Harbour Commission
TIA: Toronto Island Archives
TTC: Toronto Transit Commission
WIW: *Ward's Island Weekly*
YUA:TC: York University Archives, *Telegram* Collection

This book was published with the assistance of a grant from the Toronto Sesquicentennial Board in honour of the 150th anniversary of the City of Toronto.

To Douglas

Contents

Preface   ix

1   The Early Days: Indians, Explorers and Traders   2

2   The Establishment of York: "My Favourite Sands"   12

3   Little York in War and Peace   26

4   Development of the Peninsula   38

5   Toronto Island in the Age of Ned Hanlan   64

6   The Island of Hiawatha   86

7   Edwardian Heyday   120

8   For King and Island   152

9   The Sandy Thirties   180

10   War, Winter and Waffling   204

11   The Metro Bulldozer   236

12   "We Shall Fight Them on the Beaches..."   264

Notes   297

Index   311

Preface

I never fully appreciated William Blake's well-known phrase, "To see a World in a Grain of Sand," until I was midway through my ten-year study of Toronto's own sandbar, the Toronto Island. The more I learned about Island history, the more I learned about wider history, not only the history of Toronto or Ontario, but of Canada and even beyond. Great events— like waves of immigration or depressions or world wars—began to take on much greater meaning as I saw their direct effects on particular people in a particular place. What had started as a relatively "insular" history, therefore, evolved into a more ambitious project: to give not only a detailed history of the Toronto Island, but to provide a window on the larger world.

Every place has a rich history to reveal, should anyone care to uncover it. But few places in Canada can boast of a more dramatic or colourful history than this small island (or cluster of islands, as it is in physical reality, if not in common parlance) that has harboured a small, separate community in the shadow of our largest city. Duels, shipwrecks, fires, daring rescues, whimsical amusements, sporting triumphs and murders have all taken place here. Fishermen and princes, fur traders and war pilots, tunnel diggers and high-wire walkers, sports heroes and enemy soldiers, the elite and the ordinary— all have made their way to the Island's shores and made their contribution to our history.

In 1882, local historian G. Mercer Adam wrote, "What 'the mountain' is to the Montrealer, 'the island' is to the people of Toronto." As this implies, the Toronto Island has long exercised a geographic and imaginative hold on the city's residents and visitors. In an area with few spectacular geographic features, the Island (or Peninsula, as it was in its infancy) understandably became the focal point of the maritime settlement that grew across the bay. This geographic prominence was especially strong in the early days when everyone came by boat—by

canoe, by *bateau*, by sailing ship and by steamship. But its importance continued into the railway and automobile ages, in part, perhaps, because this island shares the aura common to all islands as a special, exciting, mysterious, even exotic place. Certainly, few places in Toronto have inspired such intense interest and loyalty among residents and mainlanders alike. Few places have been the subject of more plans—or more grandiose plans. And few places have been the focus of greater controversy, especially in more recent years, when confrontations over the Island's future have inspired national media attention.

My own involvement with the Toronto Island began in 1973, at the peak of one of these controversies. I was hired by the City of Toronto to write a report about the future of the threatened community, which by then had been reduced from over six hundred houses and several thousand residents, to two hundred and fifty houses and seven hundred defiant residents. In due course, this report recommended that the community should be allowed to remain, and not be destroyed by Metropolitan Toronto in order to create about thirty-three more acres of parkland.

The report did not have much effect on Metro Council, which voted, again and again, to remove the community; but it had some effect on City Council, and a very profound effect on me. So much so, that I devoted the next several years to writing my doctoral dissertation on "sense of place" and "defence of place," using the Islanders and the Island as a splendid example of what happens when people who are deeply attached to a particular place are threatened with expulsion. In the course of preparing my dissertation, I dipped into the Island's earlier history and became convinced that a fascinating history could, and should, be written.

After receiving my Ph.D., I turned to this project. Like a medieval scholar poring over yellowing church records and estate managers' wool tallies in order to recreate life in a fourteenth-century parish, I have spent countless hours sifting through a hundred and fifty years of assessment rolls and council minutes, in an effort to bring to life the history of this special, clearly-defined place. I have combed through countless articles in both mainland and Island newspapers. I have found myself in strange places, like the Necropolis on one sunny Halloween afternoon, looking for a tombstone which might have some needed dates carved on it; or the Metro Police Museum on another sunny afternoon, surrounded by sawed-off shotguns and other criminal memorabilia, looking for photographs of a murder victim. And my search for further facts and illustrations has led me as far afield as the Glenbow in Calgary and the Smithsonian in Washington.

Unlike the medievalist, however, I have also been able to watch recent events unfold, and have talked to the people involved. I have attended and recorded dozens of meetings both on and off the Island. I have interviewed a score of politicians on both sides of the recent controversy. And, most enjoyable of all, I have spent many hours talking to dozens of past and present Islanders, who willingly shared their knowledge of and affection for the Island. I thank them one and all for being so generous with their time and observations. Their contributions are obvious throughout the text.

Many others must also be thanked. I would like to acknowledge the help of the following groups and institutions, with special thanks to the individuals named: the Alberta–Glenbow Foundation; the Art Gallery of Ontario; the City of Toronto Archives (Scott James, Victor Russell, Linda Price, Karen Teeple, Pam Wachna, Elizabeth Cuthbertson and former archivist James Fraser); the Canadian War Museum (Hugh Halliday); Clarkson Gordon (Ed Phillips); Confederation Life; the *Globe and Mail* (librarian Jocelyn Currie); the Marine Museum (Peter Styrmo and former curator Alan Howard); the McCord Museum (Stanley Triggs); the Metropolitan Toronto Library Board (the staff of the Baldwin Room); the Metropolitan Toronto Police Museum; the National Gallery (Greg Spurgeon); the Ontario Archives (Ken MacPherson); the Public Archives of Canada (Joy Houston of the National Photography Collection and Ed Dahl of the National Map Collection); the Royal Canadian Yacht Club (archivist Jill Cuthbertson); the Royal Ontario Museum; the Smithsonian Institution; the *Star* (John Honderich and librarian Carol Lindsay); the *Sun* (librarian Julie Kirsch); the Thomas Fisher Rare Book Library; the Toronto Harbour Commission (Linda Penstone-Parsley and Don Berry); the Toronto Island Archives (Peter Holt); the Toronto Island Residents Association; the Toronto Transit Commission (Ted Wickson); and the York University Archives (David Hughes).

My thanks are due to the following people for allowing me to reproduce pictures from their private collections: David Amer, Val Fiedler, Mrs. James A. Grant, William and Elizabeth Kilbourn, Frank P. Oster, Joyce and George Robinette, Al and Luise Schoenborn, Eleanor Sinclair and Betty Stark.

I would like to thank the following people who gave special help on a variety of matters: Elizabeth Amer, for warm hospitality and miscellaneous deeds of derring-do; Peter Atkinson and Eldon Bennett, for advice about the Island's tangled legal history; Andrew Johnston, for information about Babe Ruth and the Island theatre; Shirley Morris, for graciously sharing her detailed research on John George Howard; Maureen Smith, for information about the Island School and the history of the Toronto Island Residents Association; and Christopher Varley, for details about Frederick Varley.

I would like to acknowledge the support of the Ontario Arts Council, and am grateful to the Social Sciences and Humanities Research Council of Canada for financial assistance during the long period of researching and writing this book. I also thank the City of Toronto's Sesquicentennial Committee for a grant to help Irwin Publishing Inc. publish the book in fitting fashion.

At Irwin Publishing I would especially like to thank John Pearce, who has seen this project through from beginning to end with enthusiasm and astonishing good humour; and Rick Archbold, freelance editor extraordinaire, whose sharp eye, sharp pen and diplomatic manner have all been most appreciated.

On the domestic front, I would like to thank Meg and Katie, who accompanied me on many a journey to the Island and who made the completion of each stage of the long book-creating process an occasion for family celebration. Above all, I want to thank Douglas, who gave practical and moral support throughout, and to whom I dedicate *More Than an Island*.

SALLY GIBSON
Mainland Toronto
April 1984

More Than an Island

1

The Early Days: Indians, Explorers and Traders

On a day long before the coming of the white man [the Great Spirit] was in a mood of anger and, as he often expressed himself forcefully, the winds that day came with a terrific roar, laid the forests flat as matchsticks, whipped the waves as tall as treetops on Lake Ontario and made the earth tremble with their violence...

There was no island then off the northern shore of Lake Ontario but when the sinking and upheaval finished and the storm had ended an island had been formed and that island is now Toronto Island.[1]

In this dramatic fashion, Mohawk Indians used to pass on their legend of the Island's birth. The more widely accepted version, which speaks of the incremental build-up year by year of eroded material swept westward from the Scarborough Bluffs, may be more accurate but lacks the element of surprise.

What is surprising, however, about the Toronto Island's history in the early days is that the Island lay in an area called many names, but not always Toronto, and that it was a peninsula, not an island. By the time the town of York was established in 1793, this peninsula stretched about five-and-a-half miles westward from the mouth of the meandering Don River to form one of the best-protected natural harbours on the north side of Lake Ontario. The peninsula created the harbour; and the excellent harbour was what led Governor Simcoe to create the town that became Toronto. But long before the town of York was founded, the area around what was to become the Toronto Island was known to Europeans. From the sketchy records a long and colourful history can be deduced, stretching back to the seventeenth century, when Shakespeare was still alive.

The first character to step on the scene was suitably Shakespearean, bound for a tragic end at the hands of the Indians whose life he had adopted as a teenager. Étienne Brûlé was still a young man in September 1615 when, guided by a dozen Hurons portaging two canoes, he broke through the glow of early autumn foliage to become the first white man to look upon the future site of Toronto—and the Toronto Peninsula. From the mouth of the Humber River, at the foot of the twenty-eight-mile-long Toronto Carrying Place along the Humber, which linked the great inland seas we now call Lake Ontario and Lake Huron via Lake Simcoe, Brûlé could see an impressive panorama before him. To his right and left, the primeval forest clothed the shores of Humber Bay in tones of red, orange, gold and evergreen; before him the waters of the great lake swept away to the horizon; and, some six miles to the east, a thin line of trees marking the Peninsula curved off into the distance.

Brûlé was a man born to follow beckoning shorelines, but on this occasion he did not have time to linger and explore the area. His commander, Samuel de Champlain, was on a wide-ranging exploratory, religious and, as it turned out, unsuccessful military expedition far from his Quebec City base. The leader of New France had dispatched Brûlé from Lake Simcoe to enlist the aid of the Andaste Indians who lived south of Lake Erie in his current campaign against the Iroquois. So Brûlé, the tough, independent Frenchman who had alienated his countrymen by going native and actually living among the Indians—but who had also proved useful to them as a guide and interpreter—immediately left the Toronto area and continued westward to complete his mission.

As the French opened up the interior of the continent gathering furs and spreading the gospel, missionaries, traders and explorers passed

(Left) *Lake Ontario still produces storms that recall the words of the Indian legend of the Island's creation: "The waters of the Lake rose and fell. It had never before been known to make such a sound as it hissed and bubbled and slapped and tore at the land....The Great Spirit was indeed angry."* [SDG]

(Above) *Etienne Brûlé, Champlain's envoy to the Andastes, halts briefly with his Huron escort at the mouth of the Humber River in September 1615 to look east toward the Toronto Peninsula.* [PAC (C-73635)]

up and down the narrow footpath along the east side of the Humber on their journeys between the lakes. During the period of bloody unrest in mid-century, when the Iroquois

> Infesting lake and stream, forest and shore,
> Were trapping soldiers, traders, Huron guides...[2]

the Jesuit Father Jean de Brébeuf may have plodded barefoot along this pathway on his journeys back and forth to Sainte Marie, his pallisaded mission among the Georgian Bay Hurons. After the 1673 establishment of Fort Frontenac at Cataraqui (Kingston) in the east and of the mission/fort of Michilimackinac

at the northern meeting of Lakes Michigan and Huron, other blackrobed Jesuits, undeterred by the grisly martyrdom of "Brébeuf and His Brethren," certainly passed this way. As they paddled their canoes or sailed their small brigantines along the northern side of Lake Ontario, hugging the shore for protection, they became intimately familiar with its coastline. The future Scarborough Bluffs must have been a sought-for landmark, soon followed by the Peninsula. On a fine sunny day the first sight of these well-known "trees in water"[3] in the distance must have been welcome. On a stormy day, however, its appearance must have summoned up the last reserves of energy as the travellers prepared to battle their

way against wind and water around this one last obstacle before coming to rest in the haven of Humber Bay, their lake journey at an end.

The bloody wars between the Hurons to the north (aided by the French) and the Iroquois to the south (aided by the Dutch and later by the English) for control of the rich beaver territory lying north of Lake Ontario rendered the large area around the Peninsula unsafe and unsettled. No doubt during that time rival parties of Huron and Iroquois warriors stalked one another along this same Toronto Carrying Place. Again the no man's land of the Peninsula would have been a familiar beacon to invading Iroquois paddling their large war canoes across the lake, and the whole area around the mouth of the Humber would have been familiar to both sides.

It was only around 1675, after the Hurons had been pushed away and the Iroquois had gained control, that the first Indian settlement was built in the Toronto area—the Seneca village of Teiaiagon. This pallisaded enclosure was probably located at what would later be called Baby Point, on a high hill overlooking the Humber River and the Toronto Carrying Place. Although there are no Indian records describing daily life at Teiaiagon, it is certain that its residents knew the surrounding area well and no doubt fished and hunted off the Peninsula, returning home with their canoes heavily laden with whitefish and herring, wild ducks and pigeons.

European visitors to Teiaiagon—especially insatiable explorers like Hennepin, Jolliet and LaSalle—would also have become familiar with the nearby lakeshore and the Peninsula. Father Louis Hennepin, a Franciscan friar who apparently had a thirst for adventure and glory as well as for saving souls, provides us with not only the first tourist account of Niagara Falls ("a vast and prodigious Cadence of Water which falls down after a surprizing and astonishing manner"), but also with the first written reference to Teiaiagon. In November of 1678 Hennepin left Fort Frontenac for Niagara, where he expected to meet LaSalle and join his expedition to the West. Because the "Winds and the Cold of Autumn were then very violent,"[4] he sailed in a small

ten-ton brigantine along the north shore of Lake Ontario. After rounding the Peninsula, he arrived safely in the icy Humber Bay. But, "the wind turning then contrary," he was "oblig'd to tarry there" aboard ship for nearly three weeks until December 15.

Louis Jolliet, that restless man of many talents, also preceded LaSalle to the Toronto Carrying Place, just as he preceded him to the upper Mississippi. Although Jolliet remains a shadowy historical presence because of his unfortunate

habit of losing his records in rapids, he may have provided the information used to make what appears to be the first map with the Toronto Peninsula (or Island) clearly marked on it.

As for LaSalle, his first recorded visit to Teiaiagon and the Carrying Place was in 1680. On August 10 he set sail from Fort Frontenac for Michilimackinac with a party of twenty-five men, including carpenters to complete the vessel that he planned to use to descend the Mississippi. He, like Hennepin before him and countless

A detail from Claude Bernou's map of c. 1680, probably the first map to show the Indian village of Teiaiagon ("Teyeyagon") and the Toronto Island. Either Jolliet or La Salle was the likely source of information for the map. [PAC, NMC copy of original in Paris, Bibliothèque Nationale, SHM, Rec. 67, no. 47.]

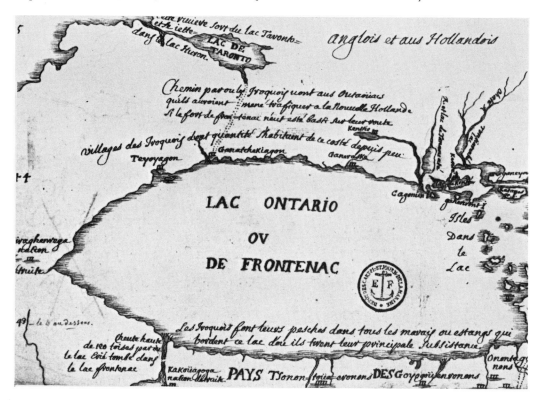

visitors after him, hugged the northern shore of the lake and steered around the Peninsula to the mouth of the Humber. Unlike Hennepin, LaSalle chose to remain ashore in Teiaiagon while his baggage was being hauled over the rugged portage along the Humber to Lake Simcoe and undoubtedly the great explorer took advantage of the opportunity to investigate the surrounding area. The following year, 1681, LaSalle travelled to and from Fort Frontenac via Teiaiagon and the Toronto Carrying Place, and even spent part of his fifteen-day visit that August writing a letter from the village—the first case of a Toronto postmark.

Fur traders too, tough, anonymous men, rounded the Peninsula and passed along the Toronto Carrying Place in those early days. It is sobering to think of the sweat and blood expended simply to keep the dandies of Europe fashionably attired in a natty, beaver felt cocked hat or a foppish ''Paris Beau'' top hat. But ''style'' has always meant ''profit.'' So the Toronto Carrying Place, which lay astride a peripheral—but still profitable—route to the interior, attracted its share of those pursuing the soft underfur of the buck-toothed beaver.

During this period, a shadowy train of buckskinned *coureurs de bois*, many of whom had left the routine of the Quebec family farm for the adventure of the forest, packed their loads of pelts along this route. And parties of tireless *voyageurs* paddled their company's huge freight canoes back and forth between Fort Frontenac

For decade after timeless decade, voyageurs, like those depicted here by Frances Ann Hopkins in a fog on Lake Superior, paddled their freight canoes laden with cargo and distinguished passengers past the Toronto Peninsula. [Glenbow—Alberta Foundation]

and the interior. On good days, they could easily round the Peninsula before heading up the Humber; but in foul weather it was easier to carry their boat and ninety-pound bales of goods across its narrow neck—used ''since time immemorial'' as a portage point[5]—and to continue along the sheltered Toronto Bay to the Humber. Theirs was but a small taste of the awful labour

that lay in store generations later for the men of the North West Company who had to drag their heavy, awkward *bateaux* across the Peninsula and then haul them inch by inch up primitive Yonge Street.

In 1720, frustrated by the sight of fur-laden Indian canoes heading toward the southern shore of the lake to trade with the English, the French

established the first European settlement at Toronto, which they called the Magasin Royal. By this time, the Iroquois had left the area and the Mississaugas were well entrenched at the western end of the lake. They had established villages from the mouth of the Niagara River around to the mouth of the Rouge River east of Toronto. The most important of these were at

Long before the white man came, Indian fishermen off the Peninsula had speared salmon lured by the light of birch bark or pine knot torches. This practice later fascinated young Paul Kane who grew up at York in the 1820's—"In my boyish days I have seen as many as 100 light-jacks gliding about the Bay of Toronto and have joined in the sport"—and no doubt informed his painting of this traditional scene, Spearing Salmon By Torchlight at Fox River c. 1845.   [ROM]

Toronto—one on the site of the Senecas' Teiaiagon and, it appears, another one across the river on the west side of the Humber. The Mississaugas, like their predecessors, became familiar with the coastline. No doubt they soon established the tradition—recorded by later observers like Mrs. Simcoe and Paul Kane—of night fishing off the Peninsula. Blazing torches would attract the salmon to the surface where waiting spearmen skilfully struck, then hauled them into their canoes. Dousing their torches, the fishermen would then turn homeward to the mouth of the Humber past the Peninsula's black profile, the silence broken only by the soft "silver drip of the regular paddles falling in rhythm."[6]

Unfortunately for the French, the Mississaugas also took to paddling their canoes southward to trade with the English. The English traders from Orange (Albany) were always glad to exchange rum for furs, and the exchange was mutually agreeable.

In order to staunch this flow of fur, the French established fortified trading posts at Niagara (which grew into a large fort), at Quinte and at Toronto (probably on the old Teiaiagon site). This wooden blockhouse was manned by a small staff and was stocked with everything from buttons and shirts to tobacco and powder and shot. For several years these French posts were extraordinarily successful—the Mississaugas traded at home and other Indians as well as unpatriotic *coureurs de bois* were intercepted on their way south. The English profits at New York declined almost by a half. But the English in turn retaliated by building a fortified stone house at Oswego at the southeastern corner of Lake Ontario (the first permanent English settlement on the lakes) and recaptured a major share of the trade, so that French profits in 1725 were only a third of those in 1724.

The Toronto post languished. In the period between 1730 and 1750 there is no record of a regular post and Toronto was once again merely a way station for Indians bound for Oswego and for *voyageurs* passing along the Toronto Carrying Place. These homeward-bound Frenchmen frequently camped at the mouth of the Humber before setting off around the Peninsula on their prescribed journey along the northern shore of the lake. The French authorities had adopted the bureaucratic ruse of issuing licenses to traders to go into the upper country on the condition that they travel only along the *northern* side of the lake, well away from the temptations of the English trading points.

In this period, the Peninsula appears fleetingly in the diary of one Chaussegros de Léry. In June 1749 de Léry accompanied a group of traders and settlers headed by Captain de Sabrevois, who was on his way from Montreal to take command at Detroit. Among the captain's baggage was a preciously tended vine with which he hoped to start a delicious and profitable vineyard (Château Detroit, perhaps). On June 29 the group came ashore at the mouth of the Rouge River and, embarking again at about midnight, they paddled under a starlit sky across the calm, dark lake to the Peninsula, where they arrived about dawn. The fact that they breakfasted as the sun rose over the lake before continuing on their way establishes de Léry's party as the first recorded picnickers on the Toronto Island.

The tug of war between the French and the English for control of the fur trade—and of the North American continent—came to a head in the 1750s. The part played by Toronto in this great struggle was, in the admirably concise words of historian Percy J. Robinson, "entirely insignificant." It was a minor outpost in a string of forts and posts that at one time stretched from the Gulf of St. Lawrence to the Gulf of Mexico. But it was this broader struggle that brought French soldiers to the shores of Humber Bay and the nearby Peninsula.

In order to recapture some of the trade being lost to the English and bring about the destruction of Chouaguan (Oswego) by peaceful means, the French decided to reestablish a post at Toronto in 1750. The Chevalier de Portneuf, an ensign at Fort Frontenac, was ordered to Toronto with a sergeant and four soldiers to build the fort. Called Fort Toronto and probably located near the mouth of the Humber, Portneuf's fort was no more than a small, stockaded trading post. But by the end of its first summer of operation, it had proved so successful that the French decided to build a second, larger post. On August 20, 1750, the Governor of New France, the Marquis de la Jonquière, wrote to Paris to the Minister of Marine (who was responsible for the colonies) for permission to build a new fort, not on the old site but further east, "on the point of the bay formed by the peninsula" (this was slightly west of the modern location of the Western Gap). He was shrewd enough to suggest that it should be named Fort Rouillé after the minister. So, between September 1750 and the following spring, Fort Rouillé rose on an elevated spot (out of cannon shot from the lake) overlooking Toronto Bay and the Peninsula to the east and Humber Bay away to the west. Although according to a contemporary observer it was "very well built, piece upon piece," this 180-foot-square structure was still deemed "only useful for trade" not war, and this was certainly its main function.

Little is known about life at the fort. The small garrison (which numbered only eight in 1754—one officer, two sergeants, four soldiers and one storekeeper) was drawn from the Compagnies de la Franche Marine. The soldiers must have been startled out of their boredom in February 1754 by the mirage-like sight of a procession of soldiers skating in single file "drawing seven or eight sledges one after the other with men on them," rounding the point of the Peninsula and entering Toronto Bay.[7] They were on their way from Montreal to Niagara and had skated much of the way along the north shore of Lake Ontario, thus confirming that skating on Toronto Bay has a long and honourable history.

Early in 1756, as the French-English struggle became more intense, the French residents of the Toronto area did play a minor part. They sent a contingent of thirty Mississaugas to join an expedition to harass the hated Oswego in May. (Oswego fell in July to the new French commander, Montcalm, in his first North American encounter.) But overall the small post was at the mercy of events unfolding elsewhere. In 1758 the English attacked Fort Frontenac, which they captured and destroyed. They then laid siege to Niagara, which capitulated in less than a month on July 25.

The imminent fall of Fort Niagara spelled the end for Fort Toronto. Two canoes from Niagara managed to slip by the besiegers and reach the French schooner *Iroquoise*, commanded by René-Hypolite LaForce, lying at a safe distance off Niagara. LaForce immediately weighed anchor and sailed across the lake, past the Peninsula, to bring word to the anxious garrison at Fort Rouillé. The fort's commander, Captain Douville, had no choice but to follow his orders from Governor Vaudreuil; he burned his fort and retreated with his fifteen soldiers to Montreal. For the last time, a party of French soldiers rounded the Peninsula and set off to the east. By the time

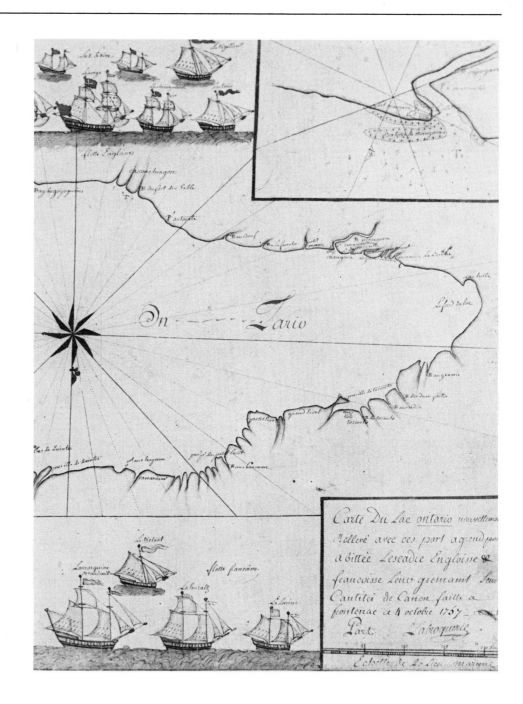

(Above) *Innumerable trading parties like this one rounded the presqu'île and stopped at palisaded Fort Rouillé in the 1750's to barter furs for cloth, bread and eau-de-vie.* [PAC (C-14253)]

(Left) *Naval officer Pierre Boucher de Labroquerie portrayed the French view of Lake Ontario, looking southward across the water in 1757. Fort Toronto (or Rouillé), protected by an impressively exaggerated "pre ille de toronto," is shown in the lower righthand part of the map; meanwhile, the enemy British fleet rules the waves on the top and the friendly French fleet floats along the bottom.* [PAC, NMC copy of the original in the British Library, King's Maps.]

the British party dispatched by Sir William Johnson, now in command at Fort Niagara, reached Toronto on July 28, the fort was "simply a confused mass of charred timber with a low chimney-stack of coarse brick surrounded by a shattered flooring of broad flagstones from the adjoining beach."[8] The French military presence in Toronto was at an end.

The English continued to press the French until Wolfe finally defeated Montcalm on the Plains of Abraham at Quebec City in September 1759 and the British fleet ensured the victory

the following spring. The Treaty of Paris in 1763 formalized the fact that North America belonged to the English Crown. George III, like the rest of his subjects, may have showed little interest in settling Toronto for nearly thirty years, but trade with the Indians continued, and memorable characters began to appear on the local scene with increasing frequency.

Major Robert Rogers was the controversial leader of Rogers' American Rangers, who had learned guerrilla warfare tactics from the Indians and used them to good effect for the

British in the recent conflict. After the war was over, Rogers loaded two hundred of his green-coated Rangers into fifteen whale boats and set off from Montreal to take formal possession for the English of the abandoned French forts in the west. On September 30, 1760, having left the ruins of Fort Frontenac behind, he complained in his *Journal* that "[m]any points extending far into the water occasioned a frequent alteration of our course." One of the most prominent of these inconvenient points was the Toronto Peninsula, which he rounded on the evening of September 30 without further comment.

The war between the British and their rebellious American colonists did not affect the Toronto area directly. But Captain Walter Butler—son of another famous American Ranger, Lieutenant Colonel John Butler—was forced to interrupt his harrying of American settlers on their western frontier south of the lakes to travel through Toronto. At the height of the war, the bureaucracy of the British army had triumphed yet again and he was required to travel all the way to Quebec with the pay lists and accounts of his regiment. After the unpleasantness of the Cherry Valley massacre, where his Indian allies had got out of hand, even such a pointless expedition perhaps had its charms for Butler. After an unsettling night on March 11, when his tent was blown down, Butler set off with the early morning light. By midday, the party had reached the "noble Bay" formed by "a long neck or Point of Land running 7 or 8 miles into the lake," which was "filled with All sorts of Wild Fowl," even in the month of March. He, like Rogers, was faced with the problem of getting around this protruding Peninsula. Unlike Rogers, Butler was travelling from west to east with an unfavourable wind. He adopted the taxing but effective ploy of dragging the boat across the narrow neck of the Peninsula, which he described in his *Journal:*

> Two Messessaugoes [sic] came to me & informed me a number of them lived up this River [the Credit]. Gave them Bread, put off at 12; row'd to the Bottom of the Bay Above Toronto, hoisted sail, found the wind too high to go round Long Point forming the Basin or Bay, below Toronto, Continuing sailing down the Bay to the Carrying Place, unloaded the Boat, Hauled her over and Loaded again in an hour and a half, row'd from this to the beginning of the high Lands, Encamp'd on the Beach & Secured the Boat.⁹

This account makes clear that portaging across the Peninsula was common enough by 1779 for there to be a special spot designated as ''the Carrying Place'' where travellers could break their journey, and their backs.

Military men made brief appearances, but shortly after the fall of Fort Toronto traders were again coming to Toronto, and staying. A Monsieur Baby of Detroit (whose son gave birth to the estate at Baby Point) appeared in the summer of 1762 and was followed by other traders, both French and English. One of the most interesting of these was a Frenchman from Montreal called St. Jean Baptiste Rousseau, who established a trading post at the mouth of the Humber around 1770. Rousseau, of course, knew the area well; indeed, he knew it so well that he could pilot ships into Toronto Harbour without being caught by the sandy fingers of the Peninsula. His house on the Humber (sometimes called St. John's River in his honour) was well known to *coureurs de bois* traversing the Toronto Carrying Place and to other prominent visitors who passed through, such as Frobisher of the North West Company and Chief Joseph Brant.

Brant was the famous Mohawk Chief who remained loyal to the British during the American War of Independence and whose duties during that war brought him past Toronto and the Peninsula.¹⁰ His loyalty cost him dearly. He and his people joined the Loyalist trek northward, where they settled along the Grand River in Upper Canada. After the war Brant undoubtedly was able to enjoy more leisurely visits to the Toronto area. His daughter, Margaret Clyne, married Rousseau in 1787 and Brant must have visited the Rousseau household more than once. It is easy to imagine Brant and his friend Rousseau hunting the migrating geese or the wild pigeons that sometimes darkened the air over the bay and Peninsula.

After the American Revolutionary War, a number of Frenchmen who had suffered severe losses or rendered particular services to the British Crown applied for grants of land in the Toronto area as recompense. Captain Jean Baptiste Bouchette had saved the life of Sir Guy Carleton

In August 1788, Lord Dorchester arrived in Toronto to complete the Toronto Purchase negotiated the previous year. Barrels of cloth, ribbon, knives, guns, shot, tobacco, laced hats, fish spears, brooches, earbobs and sundry goods were duly delivered to the Mississauga Indians gathered on shore. According to early maps, the Toronto Purchase included the Toronto Peninsula, but modern day Mississaugas have disputed this claim. [Confederation Life Collection]

during the fall of Montreal in 1775 by navigating his lordly companion safely through the American lines to Quebec City—disguised as a lowly, tongue-tied Canadien sailor. In Quebec Carleton was able to rally the British and eventually to repel the Americans from Canada. Bouchette now approached Carleton who, as Lord Dorchester and Governor General of Canada, was in a position to help him. René-Hypolite LaForce (who, before readjusting his loyalties, had commanded the *Iroquoise*, the last vessel to fly the French flag on Lake Ontario) and Sieur de Rocheblave also approached Dorchester. De Rocheblave, who wanted to be given a large tract of land as well as a monopoly over the Toronto Carrying Place, was the most persistent. The Peninsula had a special place in his plans. In one of several petitions to Dorchester (May 25, 1787) he asked for the ''small island laying between the said old settlement and same Bay on which to keep some animals.'' This is the first record of anyone intending to farm on the Peninsula.

Dorchester was favourably disposed toward such requests, but his good favour was never translated into tangible land grants. Meanwhile, Benjamin Frobisher and the Montreal fur traders were also lobbying vigorously for land to ensure a safe British route to the interior. (Other traditional routes passed close to the uneasy border with the Americans.) Dorchester was impressed enough by their forceful approaches to take the first steps toward establishing a formal settlement at Toronto. In September 1787 British officials met with three Mississauga chiefs in the Bay of Quinte to begin negotiations for the Toronto Purchase, which included the Toronto Peninsula.

The following August surveyor Alexander Aitken arrived in Toronto Bay aboard the square-

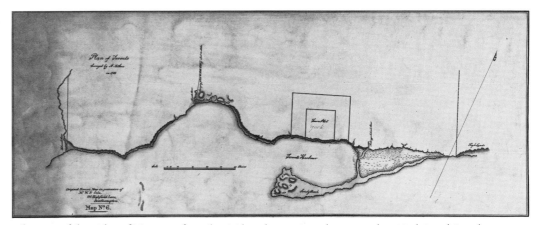

This copy of the "Plan of Toronto," from the "Tobicoak River" in the west to the "High Lands" in the east, reflects Alexander Aitken's survey conducted under the stern surveillance of Chief Wabukanyne in August 1788. [PAC, NMC]

sailed *Seneca* to make the first survey of the area. A few days later Lord Dorchester (accompanied by Sir John Johnson, Superintendent of Indian Affairs, and Colonel Butler of Butler's Rangers) arrived from Niagara to complete the purchase. By then, Aitken had built a shelter to protect the 149 barrels of provisions and diverse presents for the Indians and was proceeding to make his survey under the watchful eyes of the Mississauga chiefs, who seemed inclined to dispute his passage, following him and staring as he worked. Backed by the military presence of Colonel Butler, Aitken gained some ground and was able to proceed with his task of establishing the boundaries of the purchase. But after the Dorchester party left, poor Aitken was on his own—scrambling up and down ravines and creek banks, gingerly carrying instruments and nervously taking sightings all under the implacable gaze of the stern Chief Wabukanyne. He was finally forced to give up when the unyielding Wabukanyne had ''cautioned me against crossing it [the Etobicoke creek]'' for ''I

[was] left without any one to settle any disputes that might arise between me and the Indians.'' (Wabukanyne was perhaps wise to be suspicious of invading white men: in 1796 he was murdered on the beach in front of York by a drunken soldier who was later released for lack of evidence.) In any event, Aitken had made a fairly complete survey and as instructed had, with the mathematical precision of his profession, laid out a rectangular town site. It lay directly ''opposite the middle of the Harbour'' rather than near the old Fort, which, he felt, would have been ''too near the Point'' of the Peninsula.

Of this Peninsula he seems to have had a low opinion: ''As for the Peninsula which forms the Harbour it is not fit for any kind of cultivation or improvement.'' This was perhaps the first but certainly not the last unfavourable comment about the Toronto Island.

With the completion of the Toronto Purchase and the first survey of the area, the stage was set for the arrival of two great admirers of the Peninsula.

2

The Establishment of York: "My Favourite Sands"

The martial trumpets blared and the drums thumped resoundingly from the open deck as the eighty-ton *Mississaga* pulled slowly away from the mouth of the Niagara River. It was the evening of July 29, 1793, and Upper Canada's first lieutenant governor, Colonel John Graves Simcoe, was embarking on his historic voyage across the lake to establish the town of York on Toronto Bay. He was accompanied by his young wife Elizabeth, their two smallest children, a handful of aides and the rest of his own beloved regiment, the Queen's Rangers.[1] As the lights of Fort Niagara and the fifty or so log cabins and frame cottages that comprised the temporary capital of Newark receded into the distance, Simcoe's thoughts must have turned toward the daunting task before him: to hew a military stronghold and a "capital city" out of the raw wilderness.

The lieutenant governor was already familiar with the Toronto area. The previous May he had travelled around the head of the lake from Niagara to Toronto in a *bateau* (a sort of oversized rowboat, powered by oars and/or a sail). Shortly after that visit, he declared to Alured Clarke, his opposite number in Lower Canada, that the bay formed by the Peninsula was "the best Harbour on the Lakes." As a military man his interest in Toronto was more than an aesthetic one. His first concern was the defence of the province. And this Peninsula played an important part in his plans—indeed, was a major factor in his decision to build the town that became Toronto, as he wrote to Clarke:

> I found it to be without Comparison the most proper situation for an Arsenal in every extent of that word that can be met with in this Province. The Spit of Sand which forms its entrance is capable of being so fortified with a few heavy Guns as to prevent any Vessel from entering the Harbour, or from remaining within it. From the diversity of the Sand Banks any small point of ground is sufficiently strong to be selected for the present purposes....

He began to refer to the western tip of the Peninsula somewhat grandly as Gibraltar Point. It was not that the three-foot-high sandbank bore any striking physical similarity to its distinguished namesake. Rather, he chose the name because, as his wife noted, he felt it could be "fortified so as to be impregnable." He therefore planned to build a well-armed blockhouse and a storehouse there.

But no blockhouse, storehouse or any other building on the Peninsula met the eyes of the governor's party on the July morning when they woke to catch their first glimpse of the harbour and the densely forested north shore of Lake Ontario, where a detachment of Queen's Rangers was already hard at work clearing the forest and establishing a camp. Apart from the addition of the Queen's Rangers, the view that presented itself on this midsummer morning undoubtedly appeared very similar to the one recorded by Lieutenant (later Surveyor General) Joseph Bouchette, who had prepared the first survey of Toronto Harbour some months earlier:

> I still distinctly recollect the untamed aspect which the country exhibited when first I entered the beautiful basin, which thus became the scene of my early hydrological operations. Dense and trackless forests lined the margin of the lake, and reflected their inverted images in its glassy surface. The wandering savage had constructed his ephemeral habitation beneath their luxuriant foliage—the group then consisting of two families of Messassagas [sic],—and the bay and neighbouring marshes were the hitherto uninvaded haunts of immense coveys of wild fowl: indeed they were so abundant as in some measure to annoy us during the night.[2]

Like many gently-reared Englishwomen of her time, Mrs. Simcoe was an accomplished artist, always on the look-out for striking "scenes" to record. Setting up her easel near the mouth of the Don River and facing westward, Mrs. Simcoe painted a scene which was described in 1807 by traveller George Heriot:

> The left side of the view comprehends the long peninsula which incloses (sic) this sheet of water, beautiful on account of its placidity and rotundity of form...

[MTLB]

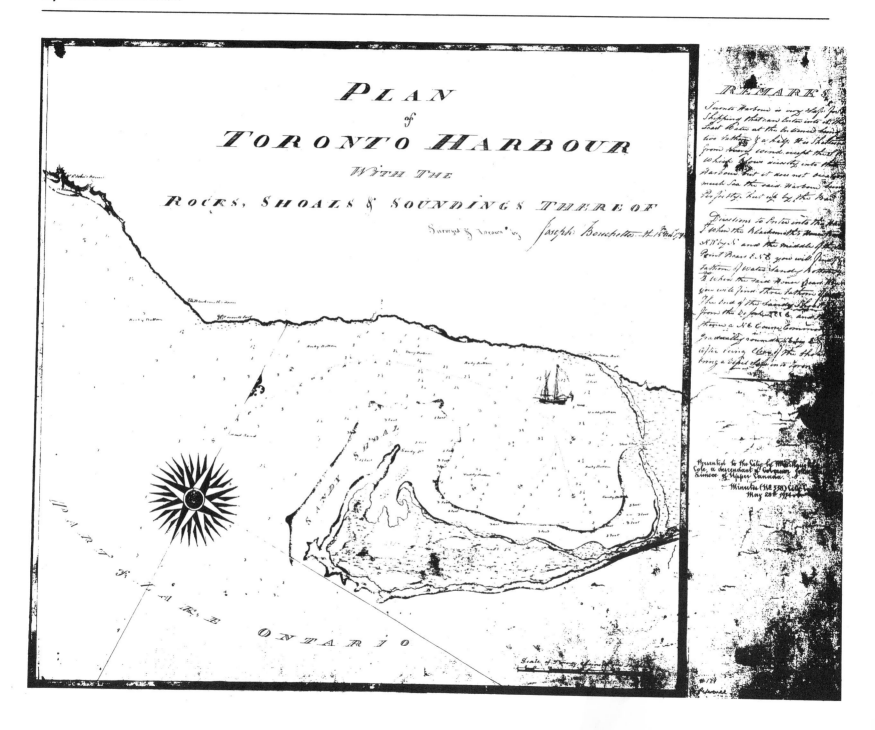

(Above) *After Joseph Bouchette freed the* Onondaga *from her icy prison off Gibraltar Point (above), this same ship was nearly the death of Mrs. Simcoe in May 1795. Describing her harrowing re-entry into York Harbour, when the Captain was "supposed not to be sober," she commented, "I was unusually frightened having dreamt twice following the other night that I was lost in the* Onondaga. *My servant came several times to tell me we were going to the bottom. I told her to shut the door & leave me quiet, for the motion of the Vessel made me sick."* [Rowley W. Murphy/CI/MTLB]

(Left) *Eighteen year old Joseph Bouchette produced this survey of the Toronto Harbour for Lt. Governor Simcoe in November 1792. His "Remarks" accompanying the map describe the virtues of the harbour: "Toronto Harbour is very Safe for the Shipping that can Enter into it. The Least Water at the Entrance being two Fathoms and a half. It is Sheltered from every wind except the SW which Blows directly into the Harbour, but it does not occasion much Sea, the said Harbour being perfectly Shut up by the Bar."* [CTA]

On this occasion, the *Mississaga*, with the governor and his companions, was piloted past the treacherous sandy shoals, which stretched from the western tip of the Peninsula into Toronto Harbour itself, by none other than St. Jean Baptiste Rousseau, the French fur trader who had been living at the mouth of the Humber for many years. Historian Percy Robinson commented acidly on this event: "The last Frenchman of Toronto was to welcome a governor who proceeded at once to wipe out all the traditions of the French regime."

These sandy shoals were to be the scene of near disaster and ultimate triumph for young Lieutenant Joseph Bouchette, son of Dorchester's saviour, Captain Jean Baptiste Bouchette. The fourteen-gun schooner *Anandoga* (or *Onondaga*) became grounded on these shoals off the Peninsula by rough weather in December 1793. After being iced in place for a couple of months, she was finally freed by Lieutenant Bouchette and his straining men in February 1794. According to Dr. Henry Scadding's *Toronto of Old*, Bouchette then sailed her triumphantly to Niagara (or

Newark) where he was greeted by the cheers of the garrison and local populace. He was soon promoted and immodestly went on to commemorate his exploit on his later maps of York Harbour.

Safely moored in the Toronto Bay, the Simcoes rowed ashore on July 30, 1793, and chose a spot (near the foot of present day Bathurst Street east of what is now known as Old Fort York) on which to erect their famous "canvas house." This was a thirty-foot tent on a wooden frame and platform, which they had purchased from the estate of the renowned explorer Captain James Cook. Legend has it that this much-travelled tent had been erected on Botany Bay, Australia, prior to being erected on Toronto Bay with its splendid view of the lake and Peninsula.

Since this was Elizabeth Simcoe's first visit to the area, her husband was eager to show her the site he had chosen for the future town. They went in a boat two miles to the "bottom of the Bay & walked through a grove of fine Oaks" where the town would be built. From this point Mrs. Simcoe looked across to the Peninsula and recorded her first, enthusiastic comment: "A low spit of Land covered with wood forms the Bay & breaks the Horizon of the Lake which greatly improves the view which indeed is very pleasing. The water in the Bay is beautifully clear & transparent."

With characteristic energy, Governor Simcoe set about establishing what he hoped would be only a temporary capital. He assigned Alexander Aitken, the intrepid surveyor of the Toronto Purchase, to survey a town site as close as possible to the Don River (that is, further east than his 1788 plan and much more modest in scale). Simcoe and his council made grants of land. He travelled up the Humber and the Toronto Carrying Place and back down an Indian trail along the Don River. He began work on two great roads—Dundas Street, which was to run west to the future town of London, and Yonge Street, which was to run northward to open the rich hinterland and to attract the rich northwest fur trade. He began fortifying the area. And he continued squabbling with Governor General Lord Dorchester, who disapproved of his choice of site for a new capital as well as of a number of other matters.[3]

Meanwhile, with equal enthusiasm Elizabeth Simcoe began to explore her new home "amid the beat of Drums & the crash of falling trees." She was an observant amateur botanist, a skilled artist and a keen naturalist (she was particularly interested in a couple of live rattlesnakes that soldiers clearing Dundas Street had captured and sent to her in a barrel—apparently without ironic intent). She was also an indefatigable diarist who even wrote entries in her diary to her four daughters in England while she was being tossed about on the high seas. As a consequence she has left us an invaluable eyewitness account of the earliest days in York.

A few days after her arrival, she made her first visit to the Peninsula:

> We rode on the Peninsula so I called the spit of sand for it is united to the mainland by a very narrow neck of ground. We crossed the Bay opposite the Camp, & rode by the Lake side to the end of the Peninsula.

> We met with some good natural meadows & several Ponds. The trees are mostly of the Poplar kind covered with wild Vines & there are some fir. On the ground were everlasting Peas creeping in abundance of a purple colour. I was told they are good to eat when boiled & some pretty white flowers like lillies of the Valley.

This was the first of many visits she made to her "favourite sands." Sometimes she walked

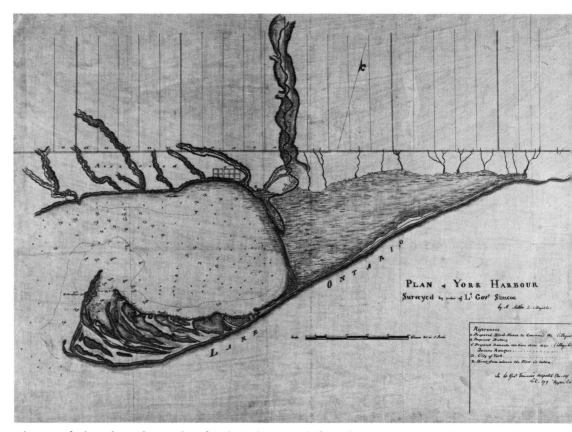

This copy of Alexander Aitken's "Plan of York Harbour," made for Lt. Governor Simcoe in the summer of 1793, shows the actual lay-out of the "City of York" (which was smaller, and placed closer to the Don River than his ambitious 1788 version), as well as "Gibraltar Point" at the western tip of the Peninsula. [PAC, NMC]

with the governor and, like later generations of Torontonians, had a picnic. Sometimes she rode alone for exercise, sometimes with her family and sometimes in the company of Lieutenant Thomas Talbot—later to be the founder of the immense Talbot settlement along the northern shore of Lake Erie. On September 16, 1793, she and Lieutenant Talbot informally inaugurated horse racing on the Peninsula (a popular pastime in the early part of the nineteenth century) and during the winter she used to admire "Mr. Talbot skait"—the first gay blade in York.

Sometimes she enjoyed being paddled across the bay in an enormous birch-bark canoe, "such as is used by the North West Company to transport their goods to the Grand Portage," to dine on the Peninsula. These outings were not unbearably rustic. A small table was brought so that she could disembark without getting her feet wet when the fragile canoe was brought to rest some distance from dry land. And the interior of the canoe (paddled by up to a dozen canoeists) had room for four or five passengers "to sit very commodiously in the center under an awning." Sometimes she would gather her paper and watercolours and set off on an expedition to capture natural views so different from the domesticated countryside of her Devonshire home. Sometimes, like later generations, she enjoyed dashing across the ice in carioles (horse-drawn sleighs) and even on horseback, although the latter amusement could be hazardous. Once while crossing the bay her horse slipped; she unceremoniously threw herself off (thinking there was a hole in the ice) and thwacked the horse's flank with her crop to prevent his rolling on top of her. She was shaken but unhurt. Her energy and curiosity also impelled her to join ice-fishing and nighttime salmon-spearing expeditions on the bay. And always she recorded news of the plants and wildlife around her. She described the wild grape vines, whose fruit, some soldiers cutting Dundas Street had discovered, made "tolerable Wine." She noted the groves of "fine Oaks" on the bay, the dark spruce hemlock along the Humber, the meadow grass on the Peninsula (although her pyromaniacal tendencies occasionally got the better of her, as she set fire to various trees, meadows and swamp rushes—all to "pretty effect") and an assortment of previously unfamiliar species. She observed the flights of "wild Pidgeons," the annual migrations of wild ducks and geese, the soulful sound of the enormous loons on the bay, "which make a noise like a man hollowing in a tone of distress," and the appearance of bald eagles near the site

chosen for their retreat, Castle Frank, on a hill overlooking the Don River. The Simcoes, it seems, also initiated the Toronto cottage tradition and, after Castle Frank was built, Mrs. Simcoe went less frequently to the Peninsula for exercise.

August 24, 1793, was a memorable day in the history of little York. Almost a month after his arrival the governor received news that the Duke of York had "distinguished himself in an action at Famars by which the French were dislodged & driven out of Holland." With all the ceremony he could muster in the wilderness, Simcoe used this as a suitable occasion to name the town after the duke. He ordered a royal salute to be fired; the soldiers, drawn up in ranks, fired out toward the bay; while the *Mississaga* and *Onondaga*, with the Peninsula stretching behind them as a backdrop, boomed out a response.

Simcoe's receiver general, Peter Russell, loyally shared the governor's enthusiasm for the harbour and the Peninsula (but not for spending the winter in a tent or sharing "the Misery in which they live"). Declaring that he was "charmed with the Situation of the proposed City of York in the Bay of Toronto," he described the military advantages of the Peninsula in a letter of September 16, 1793. "There is a very secure Situation for Batteries & an inclosed [sic] work to cover them" which, with the mainland Battery, could "perfectly scour every part of the Bay should Boats with Troops happen to pass into it." Furthermore, he noted, "Amongst these sand Peninsulas are also excellent Coves for the reception of small Craft" and places where wharfs could run out to deep water to provide safe winter anchorage. He was also impressed by the recreational value of the Peninsula, as he wrote his sister Elizabeth, noting that "the Air on the opposite side is clear & healthy & a hard Sand of several Miles to ride or drive a Carriage on" forms the outer edge of the "Beautiful Bason." In short, Russell was "greatly pleased with the beauty & Defensibility of the Situation."

Later visitors to York were not so impressed

August 24, 1793. "It was a damp day & from the heavy atmosphere the Smoke from the Ships' Guns ran along the water with a singular appearance," Mrs. Simcoe wrote in her diary on the occasion of the naming of York, which she commemorated in this painting. [MTLB]

by the suitability of these sandbanks as foundations for military works. For example, in 1826 Sir James Carmichael Smyth wrote a Report on Defence to the Duke of Wellington in which incredulity and irritation combine:

> Our first idea upon seeing York, was to have proposed to occupy Gibraltar point. Upon examining the ground, however, it appeared to be composed of nothing but sand. The deep water and entrance into the Harbour, is moreover close to the mainland. We caused an excavation of 3 feet to be made, and on returning to it next day, it was full of water. Of course, therefore, nothing of a permanent nature can be constructed on this point.

Other critics were less restrained in their comments about the Upper Canadian version of Gibraltar. A Lieutenant Francis Hall visited York shortly after the end of the War of 1812 and snorted: "Before the city a long flat tongue of land runs into the lake, called Gibraltar Point, probably from being very *unlike* Gibraltar. York [is] wholly useless as either a port or a military post...."[4] And George Ramsay, Earl of Dalhousie, echoed these sentiments when he visited Upper Canada in 1819. The Lieutenant Governor of Nova Scotia showed typical Maritimer's disdain when he scoffed in his journal, "The opposite of the bay called Gibraltar, as a joke I suppose, is so low as to be flooded in bad weather." He left with a low opinion of both York and the Peninsula.

Simcoe may have given Gibraltar Point its grand name, but he was only able to accomplish a small part of his grand plans. During his brief tenure he did see the raising of the first buildings on the Peninsula—a couple of storehouses (in 1794 or '95). Their location far across the bay was a fine gesture but an inconvenient one, as a group of soldiers discovered to their cost in February 1796. While they were crossing the bay to get to the storehouses, Mrs. Simcoe reported, their boat was driven into the ice by a strong east wind. They sat cooling their heels among the ice floes until eight o'clock that night, when a rescue boat made its way through the darkness and was finally able to extricate them.

Later in 1796 the Simcoes decided to return to England. The governor was frustrated and debilitated by his experiences in Upper Canada and was not unhappy to leave. But his wife felt otherwise. She had had many exciting and happy experiences and was sad to be leaving. So, on July 21, 1796, Elizabeth Simcoe stood on the deck of the *Onondaga*, sketched York and the Peninsula for the last time and watched through tear-reddened eyes her "favourite sands" recede forever into the distance.

In Simcoe's absence Peter Russell took over as administrator of the province. He carried out and enlarged upon some of his superior's plans. For example, he expanded the town by adding a "New Town" to the west of the "Old Town"; he oversaw the construction in 1796 of the first parliament buildings, which overlooked the bay at the foot of what is now Berkeley Street; he presided over the first parliament in York in 1797; he hired Asa Danforth to cut a road

"Cried all the day," Mrs. Simcoe noted in her diary on July 21, 1796, the day she left York to return to England. "Little wind, soon became calm," she noted, which enabled her to make this final sketch of York beyond the storehouses on Gibraltar Point. [PC (C-13927)]

eastward to Kingston; and he had a vessel, the *Toronto*, built for the use of the civilian government in 1799.

Russell himself moved from Niagara to York in 1797—rounding Gibraltar Point in a storm that soaked both him and his belongings. Nevertheless, his spirits were not permanently dampened. Russell was well pleased with his new, expensive house, which had been designed for him by William Berczy, one of the builders of Yonge Street. Like most of the early houses of York, Russell Abbey looked out over the bay toward the Peninsula, and Russell appreciated his view. He wrote to his friend, Chief Justice of Lower Canada William Osgoode, on September 28, 1798, "I have a very comfortable house near the Bay, from whence I see everything in the harbor & entering it...." His devoted sister and companion, Elizabeth Russell, seemed to be equally pleased. She wrote to a friend the following January about the house and the attractions of the bay and the Peninsula:

We have a good House which my Brother has built at a very great expense in a most charming situation in front of the Town with a most Beautiful Bay before us and but a few yards from our door on which in the summer there is charming Fishing and rowing or sailing, particularly up a river called the Don, and in the winter it is all Froze and an amazing thickness, it is Delightful Slaying [sic] on the Ice on which about a mile & quarter we go across the Bay to the opposite side to the Lake (Ontario) on the sands of which there is charming riding or driving to the Length of eight miles.

The Russells were quite typical in the importance they ascribed to their view of the bay. Indeed, for all the residents of York and Toronto right up to the time when the railways and then the highways cut the city off from the waterfront, the lake with its harbour and its island was a source of endless fascination, "its sound, its aspect, its condition being matters of hourly observation," as Henry Scadding wrote eighty years later in *Toronto of Old*. The town, of course, sprang up on the shore of the lake and its face was turned toward the water.

In the early years virtually all communication was by water. At first there were no roads at all linking the little community to other population centres. Only "dense and trackless forests" lay between York and Niagara and Kingston. Even later, after major roads were cut through the forests, little York was still isolated during the rains of spring and fall that turned the primitive highways into muddy, impassable marshes. People, letters and goods still arrived most expeditiously by water.

Perhaps even more important than this, the lake was the great natural element dominating York. The lake and the Peninsula, like the mountain in Montreal, provided the focus for the town. And, not surprisingly, residents made a point of building houses so that they could gaze out over the water.

Under Administrator Russell's aegis, a blockhouse and guardhouse, as well as protection

Elisabeth Frances Hale's view of Palace (Front) Street in 1804 shows that from the beginning, York's residents took advantage of their waterside location to look out toward the bay, the peninsula and the lake beyond. [PAC (C-40137)]

T. W. McLean's engraving for Toronto's 100 Years, published in 1934, is one possible version of the two-storey, squared pine log Blockhouse, which was standing at Gibraltar Point by the end of 1799.

(Below) Lt. Sempronius Stretton painted this artfully busy version of life at York Barracks in May 1804. A party of redcoats like those practising the Canada goose-step beyond the Blockhouse left Fort York and crossed over to the Peninsula to arrest Ogetoni-cut. [PAC (C-14905)]

for two "gun-row boats," were finally added to the storehouse on Gibraltar Point. According to a list of government property at the end of 1799, the storehouse and blockhouse were "built of Square Logs and are weather-boarded, and have Loopholes in the second Story" (no mention of armament was made) and the guardhouse of frame construction was "upwards of 30 feet long divided into two apartments on the first floor with a Fire place in each." Founder of the *Telegram* and keen local historian John Ross Robertson later suggested that one or two twenty-four-pounder cannon were mounted on the roof, but this seems unlikely, as later events

would suggest. In any event, with or without twenty-four-pounders, a small military establishment was located on the tip of the Peninsula by 1799.

Although Toronto at this time had promise, it was still "just emerging from the woods," as one resident commented in 1801.[5] Just how unimpressive the new town was can be gathered from the fact that two important Canadians passed by without deigning to visit the straggling little collection of log houses on muddy streets, preferring instead to break their journey at the Peninsula. These typical Montrealers were the famous fur trader and explorer Sir Alexander Mackenzie and his powerful partner in the North West Company, William McGillivray, who were on their way from Montreal to Michilimackinac in May 1799. They made rapid progress along the north shore of Lake Ontario—their tireless *voyageurs* paddling steadily throughout the night and resting only five minutes every two hours to smoke their traditional pipes. The splashes of their paddles disturbed the salmon and the surface of the lake for yards around the huge canoe was alive with the silver flashes of salmon leaping out of their way. George Landmann, a young engineer in the party, described the flight of the salmon, and continued:

> Shortly after sunrise we arrived at Gibraltar Point, a low and extended slip of land forming the Bay of York or Toronto....We were all very much tired; the tent was pitched, and we lay down for a couple of hours whilst the kettle should be placed on the fire to cook the day's provision.
>
> After making a good breakfast, we embarked without crossing to the town.[6]

In August 1799, General Peter Hunter took up his post as lieutenant governor. His speech upon arriving at York Harbour aboard the *Speedy* was a model of brevity: "Gentlemen—Nothing that is within my power shall be wanting to contribute to the welfare of this colony."[7] His appearances in York were also brief—because of his military duties he spent most of his time away from the capital. His only contribution to the development of the Peninsula seems to have been the introduction of a flock of goats "for the sake," Dr. Scadding suggested, "of the supposed salutary nature of whey goats' milk."

They were apparently among the casualties of the War of 1812, having been dispersed when land access to the Peninsula was cut off—or possibly liberated by the invading Americans.

There is no record of any permanent Indian settlements on the Peninsula, but Indians certainly raised what Joseph Bouchette had called their "ephemeral habitations" from time to time on its sandy shores. The Indians appear to have been the first to recognize its value as a health resort.

The schooner Speedy *brought General Peter Hunter to York in 1799 and took Ogetonicut, with "many of the leading inhabitants of York," to the bottom of Lake Ontario in October 1804.* [C. H. J. Snider/MTLB]

In September 1793, for example, Governor Simcoe remarked to the Duke of Richmond that "the Sandy Peninsula is so healthy, as that the native Indians have requested permission to encamp upon it with their families at the Sickly Season." And Mrs. Simcoe, who had enjoyed the "peculiarly clear & fine" air on these sands, echoed her husband's comments about its supposed curative powers. She certainly had found evidence of Indian presence during her rambles over the Peninsula. On one occasion she discovered an Indian grave, which was marked by a small pile of wood, a bow and arrow and a dog skin hung nearby—mute evidence that the air on the Peninsula was not invariably salubrious and health-giving. Surveyor General (and man of property at York) David W. Smith later spread the news of the Peninsula's healthy atmosphere to a wider audience. In his 1799 *Gazetteer of the Province of Upper Canada* he observed: "The long beach or peninsula, which affords a most delightful ride, is considered so healthy by the Indians that they resort to it whenever indisposed, and so soon as the bridge over the Don is finished, it will, of course, be generally resorted to...."

The Indians, like the white settlers, hunted and fished on the Peninsula, trapping muskrat among its reeds, dredging giant turtles out of its muddy ponds, spearing fish in its shallow lagoons and shooting duck and geese and other fowl fattened on its wild rice. Although no Indians resided in the town of York at this period, they certainly appeared at its fish market on the gravelly beach below Palace (Front) Street and at its main market (an open field where the present St. Lawrence Hall now stands) to sell their fish and game, as well as wild berries and hand crafts like leather moccasins.

Sometimes Indians came to York and the Peninsula for other reasons. In the spring of 1804 a long procession of Chippewas led by their Chief Wabbekisheco paddled eastward from Annis Creek near Oshawa and set up camp at Gibraltar Point. The previous year a white man had killed one of their tribe, Whistling Duck, whereupon the slain Indian's brother, Ogetonicut, had allegedly taken revenge by killing a white fur trader, John Sharpe. Lieutenant Governor Hunter had apparently promised that Whistling Duck's white murderer would be punished. But after a year had elapsed without any action being taken, the Indians came to York to seek justice. This proved to be a mistaken quest. A party of soldiers from Fort York descended on the camp on the Peninsula, arrested the unfortunate Ogetonicut and forced him to return with them to the mainland, where he languished in York's first jail until fall.

It was decided that the Indian (but not the white man) would have to be tried at Presqu'ile on the Bay of Quinte. So, on October 7, 1804, Ogetonicut and many of the leading citizens of York set out for Presqu'ile in the *Speedy*. When they left York Harbour the wind was moderate. By the middle of the night, however, a violent autumn storm had arisen and the *Speedy* went down without a trace somewhere off Presqu'ile. No one survived. But at least one person profited from the tragedy, D'Arcy Boulton, Sr. When the *Speedy* went down, a significant part of the legal establishment of Upper Canada went down with her so Boulton decided that this was an opportune moment to move to York, where in time he became one of the founding members of the Family Compact.

In 1809 a major landmark was finally completed on the Peninsula: the Lighthouse. It was located on the southern or lake shore less than twenty-five feet from the water at a spot now known inaccurately as Gibraltar Point. According to historian Edwin Guillet, Hunter's successor, Lieutenant Governor Francis Gore, travelled to the Peninsula on April 6, 1808, and personally chose the location. (John Ross Robertson, however, suggested that it had actually been started earlier in 1806.) In any event, huge blocks of stone were transported from Queenston aboard the *Mohawk* to construct the Lighthouse, the first stone building in York. It was made hexagonal in shape with walls six feet thick at the base. From 1809 to 1832 it rose seventy feet into the air. In 1832 another twelve feet were added, giving it a total height of eighty-two feet. The earliest keepers, J.P. Rademuller, William Halloway, then James Durnan, lived in a two-room frame house located nearby. They were the first civilian residents on the Island.

By August 1809 the *Upper Canadian Gazette* proudly announced that the Lighthouse was sufficiently complete "to be applied to its original purpose" and for nearly one hundred and fifty years its beacon guided vessels travelling on Lake Ontario. Unfortunately its record was not unblemished. In the winter of 1811-12 the yacht *Toronto* was wrecked on the southern shore of the Peninsula, apparently through the skipper's confusion about the position of the light. "Her skeleton," Dr. Scadding noted in 1873, "was long a conspicuous object, visited by ramblers on the Island." For many years the Lighthouse remained the best known landmark in Toronto, the first building that visitors could see when they approached the city from the lake and the last that lingered in sight when they left.

From David Smith's 1799 *Gazetteer* onward, comments and complaints about providing adequate access to the Peninsula were plentiful. In the early years, Peninsula-bound residents of York had to cross the Don River, which of the town in a walk or a ride to the Island,'' as residents of York frequently referred to the Peninsula in defiance of geography if not of psychology. (The sandbar may have been physically a peninsula, but its remoteness and relative inaccessibility made it mentally an island.) Residents, however, were cautioned not to ''draw sand or pass with loaded waggons or carts over the new bridge or Float.''[9] By 1808 residents were once again high and dry on the wrong side of the Don, cut off from the Peninsula. Noting that lives had been lost for want of a bridge, the editors of the *Upper Canada Gazette* appealed on April 1 to the public spirit and self-interest of York's residents to donate money toward building a new bridge:

> When completed the peninsula will answer every purpose of an extensive common to the owners of cattle; to those who may use it for purposes of recreation, it furnishes a most delightful walk or ride, as a race ground or a place for field exercise, we know not its equal; the sportsman will find constant and easy access to the best shooting ground, and the convalescent might find health in an occasional excursion to the opposite beach.

The lieutenant governor's wife, Mrs. Gore, apparently set a sterling example by donating a liberal sum. Eventually a new bridge was erected and residents had relatively free access to the Peninsula until the War of 1812 when, as a defensive measure, the Upper Canadian military establishment literally burned its bridges behind it in the retreat toward Kingston.

The Peninsula and the bay that it embraced were naturally the focus of much of the outdoor recreation life of York's early residents, both civilian and military. Sportsmen of the era were almost obsessively enthusiastic about guns and shooting. And when they were not busy shooting

The government yacht Toronto *is shown here under full sail around 1810, a year before she was wrecked near this spot. She failed to benefit from the recently built Lighthouse, whose steady beacon consumed about two hundred gallons of sperm whale oil each year.*   [C. H. J. Snider/MTLB]

emptied into the bay between the townsite and the Peninsula. (After the War of 1812 their problems were doubled—they had to cross the Big Don and the Little Don, which had grown up as a result of defensive measures taken by the military.) The Don appears to have always been a recalcitrant river. Normally a relatively

tame meandering stream, it became swollen and uncooperative after the spring rains and runoff and it had a history of sweeping away the various fragile bridges thrown up by York residents eager to enjoy their Peninsula. As early as 1806,[8] a floating bridge was precariously stretched over the Don ''to accommodate the inhabitants one another in wars or duels, they hastened off into the forests or across to the Peninsula to blaze away at the great variety of animals and birds hidden there. The young Heward brothers, for example, who were characterized by Dr. Scadding as "mighty hunters," could test their "sportsman skill on the Island just across the bay where the black-heart plovers [like Ward's Island tenters of another era] were said always to arrive on a particular day, the twenty-third of May, every year." Another favourite pastime of young gentlemen of this era was horse racing, and the Peninsula provided the residents of York with their first racecourse—a straightaway where up to twelve horses could pound headlong down the hard-packed sands while gentlemanly wagers hung in the balance.

In addition to the more conventional sporting activities—like swimming, sailing, fishing, hunting, picnicking, riding, walking, skating, curling and carioling—the bay and Peninsula provided more exotic fare. In 1801 Provincial Secretary William Jarvis introduced a Canadian version of that popular old English sport of fox hunting. At noon on a frosty February day Jarvis unbagged a fox near the centre of the frozen bay, turned loose the hounds and in the

In the predawn hours of April 3, 1812, Dr. William Warren Baldwin signed his will at this blockhouse near the foot of Berkley Street, on his way to face Attorney General John Macdonell in a duel on the Peninsula. [MTLB]

hallooing company of a number of friends tore off on horseback in slippery pursuit of ''poor Reynard.'' Naturally, the *Upper Canada Gazette* duly reported, their sporting endeavours were admired by ''the beau monde of both sexes in carioles and sleighs.''

The Peninsula, however, was also the focus of more sombre activities. Before dawn on April 3, 1812, Dr. William Warren Baldwin (a man of many talents—doctor, lawyer, architect, political reformer and advocate of ''responsible government'') arose after a night of fitful sleep, to prepare to fight a duel with John Macdonell at a remote spot on the Peninsula. Macdonell, the newly appointed attorney general (a post which Baldwin had hoped to obtain) had given offence to Baldwin by using ''expressions so wanton and ungentlemanly''[10] in some insignificant court encounter that Baldwin through the mediation of Lieutenant Thomas Taylor demanded an apology for the ''offensive words.'' Macdonell refused, so Baldwin demanded satisfaction. Baldwin's second, Lieutenant Taylor, and Macdonell's second, Duncan Cameron, met to arrange the details.

Early on the appointed April day, Baldwin slipped unnoticed out of his house at Palace and Bay Streets and turned left past the shadowy hulk of the *Sir Isaac Brock*, the giant ship that was being built right outside his front door. He walked with Taylor eastward, past Cameron's still-dark house, along the margin of the bay to the town blockhouse near the brick Parliament Building. There he paused briefly to sign the short will he had prepared the previous night. While they continued around the bay, striding through the early morning mist off the Don Marshes, they could spy Macdonell and Cameron in the distance, crossing the bay in a sleigh. At the appointed spot the four gentlemen met for their 6 A.M. rendezvous as the sun rose over Lake Ontario. The formalities were explained, pistols chosen and the combatants placed back to back.

When they turned to face one another and the signal to fire was given, Macdonell simply stood with his arms at his side. Baldwin levelled his gun, paused, then turned his aim aside, sending the bullet flying harmlessly out over the Peninsula. As the report set the birds screeching into the air the two men shook hands. They were not friends when they returned to the mainland but at least both were alive, and they were no longer sworn enemies.

For Macdonell, however, this incident provided only a brief reprieve. Six months later on October 13 he lay dead with his commander, General Sir Isaac Brock, in a bloody field at Queenston Heights.

3
Little York: In War and Peace

At about five o'clock on the evening of April 26, 1813, an alert observer on the Scarborough Bluffs sighted the sails of the American fleet. The war was coming to Little York.

Before that fateful sighting the war had seemed a little remote. Not so remote, of course, as the Napoleonic Wars in Europe and the attendant naval blockade that had helped to cause the war in the first place. Some Americans, irritated by the blockade, were even convinced that Canadians were eager to join them in a war of liberation to throw off the yoke of British imperialism. They were sadly mistaken, of course, and the war they declared in 1812 became a "Holy War in Ontario's history...the breeding-place of Canadian heroes."[1]

The greatest of these heroes was Major General Isaac Brock, who was administrator and chief of military operations in Upper Canada. When first news of the war reached him in Little York (civilian population barely 700) on June 27, 1812, he set off immediately with a detachment of York troops for the Niagara frontier where an American attack might be expected. York's waterfront was no doubt lined with patriots and anxious relatives eager to watch the twelve-gunned transport ship, the *Simcoe*, clear Gibraltar Point and head off to war.

In fact Brock's initial visit to the frontier was brief. But over the next few months he was a whirlwind of activity, engaged in sharp actions as commander of a force that included members of the York Volunteers and chafing under the news of an armistice. The ceasefire ended in September and early on the morning of October 13, Brock was wakened at his post in Fort George near Newark by the sound of guns booming across the border. The Americans had landed at Queenston. Riding hell for leather toward Queenston, he arrived just as the American

forces appeared at the top of the heights. The Americans charged toward the British battery halfway down the slope and took it. Rallying his men, Brock led the counter charge up the slippery escarpment—but was felled by an American rifleman and died, allegedly with the stirring words "Press on the York Volunteers" on his lips—a myth gladly promulgated by York's residents.

Although Brock became the hero, Major General Sir Roger Sheaffe, who assumed command, saved the day—taking hundreds of prisoners and regaining control of the vital Niagara peninsula. The following evening (October 14) the *Simcoe*, her deck crowded with American prisoners, was sighted off the Peninsula. The captain was greeted by cheers from the waiting crowd when he announced the victory at Queenston Heights—and by stunned silence when he broke the news of Brock's death.

The winter of 1812-13 was a severe one in York. By January four feet of snow lay on the ground and the lake was frozen as far as the eye could see. Indian allies had gathered together and were encamped in the surrounding woods, which echoed with their "war dances" and "savage yells," according to resident Thomas G. Ridout. The anxious citizens of York distracted themselves by engaging in an orgy of patriotic activity. The good ladies, for example, decided to sew a set of regimental colours (designed by Dr. Baldwin's youngest sister, the artistic Mary Warren Baldwin) for the 3rd York Militia, to celebrate their participation in the victories of Detroit and Queenston Heights. The Colours were presented in January 1813 at a service in St. James Church, presided over by a recent immigrant to York, the ambitious Anglican Scot, the Reverend Dr. John Strachan.

Meanwhile on the waterfront, the *Sir Isaac*

(Above) *After lying off the Peninsula during the night of April 26, 1813, the American fleet continued on past the Lighthouse to land troops about two miles west of Fort York. Owen Staples' over-enthusiastic interpretation (there were, for example, fourteen, not sixteen, American ships) nevertheless captured the sweep of the action directed from Commodore Chauncey's impressive flagship, the 24-gun Madison (third from right.)* [MTLB]

(Right) *With the line of the Peninsula behind her and Dr. Baldwin's house before her, the 30-gun Sir Isaac Brock was under construction when the Americans attacked York on April 27, 1813.*
[C. H. J. Snider/MTLB]

Brock was slowly nearing completion. At thirty guns she was designed to be the largest ship on Lake Ontario and would, it was hoped, give the British forces control of the lake. From his writing desk at his front window, Dr. Baldwin could follow the ship's progress, for it was, as he wrote a friend in April, "on a stock just by my door.''[2] Unfortunately for York the building of the *Brock* (which the Americans knew and feared) ensured that the provincial capital would be attacked as soon as the ice broke; even more unfortunately the town's completely inadequate defences virtually ensured that it would be captured.

When the American ships were first sighted on this fateful spring day in 1813, they were, according to invading Colonel Cromwell Pearce's account, about ''25 miles South of York Light-House''—that landmark for friend and foe alike. The spectator on the Scarborough Bluffs hurried to the Garrison, where the alarm gun was sounded. As the alarm boomed around the bay, in the words of the Reverend Dr. Strachan, ''all [was] hurry and confusion.'' Militia men from outlying areas, like farmer Ely Playter who had just arrived at home from the Garrison, turned around and headed back toward town. Military and civil leaders held hastily convened meetings. And some elderly men and women and children moved off to seek security in the countryside. Among these last was Dr. Baldwin's sister, the artistic Mary, who had seen the approaching American fleet and observed with somewhat misplaced aesthetic appreciation, ''Nothing could equal the beauty of the fleet coming in, it preserved the form of a crescent, while the sails were white as snow.''[3]

The previous day the fourteen American ships carrying about seventeen hundred soldiers had cleared Sackett's Harbour at the eastern end of the lake, where they had wintered. Blown by a favourable east wind, they had travelled along the south shore of the lake and past the mouth of the Niagara River. Then, with heavy swells (and soldiers' stomachs) rising, they headed north toward the Lighthouse at York, which they sighted at sunset. After dark they furled their

sails and anchored south of the Peninsula. While York's residents were anxiously preparing for the morrow, the American officers were gathering aboard Commodore Isaac Chauncey's new, twenty-four-gun flag ship, the *Madison*, to go over the final plan of attack.

The night was a short one for both sides and much time was spent by both anxiously peering over the dark line of the Peninsula separating them. The Reverend Dr. Strachan—the ''pugnacious ex-Presbyterian who would have made an excellent general''[4]—rose at 4 A.M. and immediately rode off to the Garrison west of the town. With the aid of a glass he could see the American ships, ''decks thickly covered with troops,'' preparing to launch their attack. The soldiers at the fort could look through their gun embrasures and catch glimpses of the enemy lurking behind the Peninsula. Similarly, Ely Playter, who had spent the night on the floor of General Sheaffe's residence, ''could see the American fleet when it came light—opposite the Tellegraft [Lighthouse].'' And from his bedroom window on Palace Street John Beikie ''at the peep of day'' could just discern ''the whole Yankie fleet...off the Light House.''

General Sheaffe had only about 700 men (about 300 regulars, 300 relatively untested militiamen, about 100 Indians and a handful of dockhands) to resist an attack by a force more than twice its size, composed almost entirely of trained soldiers. Furthermore, the American artillery far outweighed the tiny complement that the defenders could muster. As the sun rose, the American flotilla weighed anchor, sailed westward past the Peninsula and headed toward the point where the old French Fort Rouillé had once stood. It was at this moment that the soldiers of the Garrison got their first good look at the enemy fleet. Isaac Wilson, with Mary

Baldwin's detached sense of aesthetics, described the scene: ''The first time I saw them they were passing close to the point of land that forms the Bay of York which you may see in Thos. Stanton's maps. There were 15 sail [actually 14] and they had a very pretty appearance it being a clear still morning.''

The wind, however, came up and blew the Americans further westward than they had planned. While their ships laid down a covering fire of grapeshot, the blue-coated American troops swarmed ashore about two miles west of the British fort, at what is now Sunnyside Beach. Major Givens and his Indians were the first to oppose the landing; a group of fewer than a hundred regulars soon joined them, but the militia, floundering around in a nearby ravine, failed to arrive. It was a short but bloody encounter. British casualties were high and by 10 A.M. over a thousand Americans had landed. The noted explorer, Brigadier General Zebulon Pike, took command and headed eastward toward the fort. Meanwhile, Commodore Chauncey took his ships back toward the mouth of York Harbour and pounded the British fortifications with murderous effect from a position between the point of the Peninsula and Fort York. The guns at the fort tried to answer the American barrage, but their range was simply too short and the cannon balls fell harmlessly into the lake.

By this time (about noon), after a British mobile magazine had accidentally exploded, killing and wounding another 35 of their men, Sheaffe decided that his position was untenable. Rather than risk losing the rest of his precious regulars, he gave the order to retreat to Kingston—probably a wise decision, but one for which Strachan and the citizens of York never forgave him. He gave orders for the main powder magazine to be exploded. When this was done the horrendous explosion shook houses throughout the town and a balloon-shaped cloud of smoke drifted out over the lake. The explosion—and the resulting rain of stones and debris—devastated the nearby American force, killing 38 men outright, including General Pike, and wounding over 200 more. Proceeding through the town unaware of the devastation in his wake, Sheaffe gave orders for the unfinished *Sir Isaac Brock* to be set on fire to at least deny its use to the Americans. He told Colonel Chewett and Major William Allan (of the militia) "to make the best conditions they could With the enemy for the town." And he burned the Don Bridge as he left.

The Reverend Dr. Strachan and his protégé Captain John Beverly Robinson (who was also the Attorney General of Upper Canada) joined the military leaders in their negotiations with the Americans. By four in the afternoon the terms of surrender had been agreed upon (militia to surrender and be paroled, military and naval stores to be surrendered, private property of townspeople to be protected), but not signed and therefore not in force. The following day an enraged Strachan "went toward a full day of badgering and verbal sniping."[5] Whether Strachan really saved York from being set on fire (General Dearborn, furious about the death of General Pike and the destruction of the *Brock*, had apparently threatened to make the town smoke) and whether his verbal aggression did induce Dearborn to sign is relatively unimportant. The Americans did sign and Strachan was given credit for having stood up to the Americans in defence of the town and of a British Upper Canada. From this time on Strachan's star was on the rise—until, after the war, it shone above all the rest.

The Americans stayed for several days in York. In addition to destroying obvious military targets, they also burned the Parliament Buildings— a deed which later gave the British a convenient excuse for burning the White House in Washington. And they did engage in some looting, although by modern standards the troops were remarkably restrained. Finally, to the great relief of the local citizenry, they boarded their ships on May 2, only to languish for several days in the harbour waiting for a storm to subside before leaving.

What role did the Gibraltar Point Blockhouse

This 1816 map shows the location of the Gibraltar Point Blockhouse, the storehouses, the Lighthouse and the Lighthouse Keeper's cottage on the Peninsula; the landing spot of the invading Americans; the rebuilt Fort York; and the location of both the Sir Isaac Brock *and the Parliament buildings, which were burned during the invasion.* [MTLB]

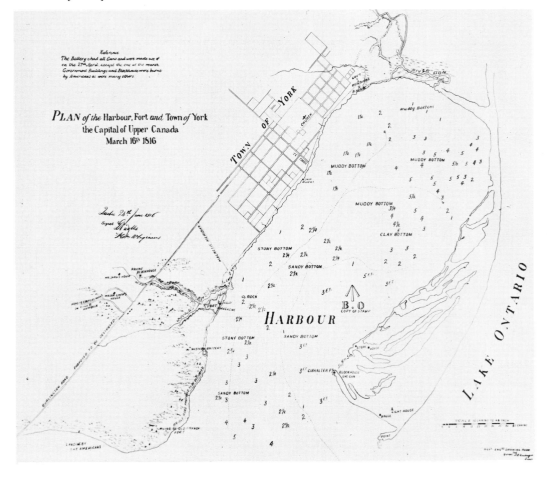

Mrs. William Dummer Powell kept a sharp eye on the lake from this house, located on the site of the present day Royal York Hotel. On June 12, 1813, before the second American visit, her view was marred. "...a Boat is just coming round the point [of the Peninsula]," she wrote her husband, the Chief Justice. "I sicken at the Idea of its being 13 Stripes...." With relief, she discovered that, this time, the boat was British. [MTLB]

play in the defence of York? That remains a mystery. The most significant thing about the Blockhouse is that like Sherlock Holmes' celebrated dog it did not bark. Stories about the Blockhouse vary. But whether it was unarmed, unmanned, or simply inefficient, the Blockhouse seems to have been completely uninvolved. There seems to be no record of its having participated in the battle on its doorstep. But perhaps the best testimony to its insignificance is the fact that the Americans did not even bother to set fire to it when they destroyed the other remaining military buildings. (They corrected this omission when they returned briefly on July 31, 1813.) So Governor Simcoe's vaunted Gibraltar Point fortifications were unable to protect the fort and the little town of York in the hour of their greatest need.

York was relatively uninvolved in the rest of the war. The loss of the *Brock* and the large number of supplies destroyed or captured there had a markedly detrimental effect on the British cause. Indeed, the later reverses on Lake Erie were at least partly attributable to the lack of supplies. But apart from the unwelcome return of the Americans on July 31, York's citizens remained at least one step removed from the hostilities. The fort was rebuilt and expanded at the site now known as Old Fort York. The town served as a hospital and hundreds of casualties were sent back from the front for care and recuperation, with the ships carrying wounded soldiers sometimes being met by crowds on the shore.

York's twice-bitten citizens, however, remained apprehensive lest they be invaded again by the dreaded Yankees and scores of eyes were constantly scouring the horizon beyond the Peninsula for signs of an approaching enemy fleet. Fortunately no enemy again landed, but as reminders of the war, York's citizens could often hear cannonading in the distance and could watch naval battles being waged off on the horizon, too far away to discern which ships were whose. In December 1813, they could even see the town of Niagara burning across the lake. Many spectators apparently lined the waterfront that cold winter night to gaze at the unnatural orange glow staining the southern sky behind the black silhouette of the Lighthouse. The war, in short, was never far from their minds. Even an east wind (such as the one that had blown the Americans toward York in April 1813) was enough to put them "in great fear," as Dr. Baldwin wrote in July 1814. In fact, his friend Miss Elizabeth Russell became so upset when the east wind blew, he noted, "that it appear[ed]

like mental derangement.'' She, like some other residents, went to the country for relief. Finally news of peace reached York on February 15, 1815, and, as the *York Gazette* noted on April 15, ''The wild duck revisit our waters since peace was made.''

In 1815, York was still ''a small and undistin-guished village.''[6] It had a population of only about 700, contained about 110 houses and 20 stores, and could boast few public buildings of any consequence. But great social and physical changes were to occur over the next two decades.

On June 6, 1817, the sidewheeler *Frontenac*

chugged around the Peninsula and into the harbour, the first steamship to land at York. With her long black hull, splashing paddle wheel, single smoking stack and three masts—just in case the steam should prove to be less reliable than predicted—she must have been an object of intense curiosity to spectators along the waterfront. Although one day the *Frontenac*'s descendants would take over water travel, the waterfront that day was still dominated by graceful schooners and other sailing ships, whose number increased along with York's population and importance as a commercial centre. For many years, the

arrival of each ship was signalled to the mainland by flags raised at the Lighthouse on the Peninsula.

There were other curious sights in York during this period. One of the most curious must have been the North West Company *bateaux* being hauled up primitive Yonge Street on wagons. From York's earliest days there had been great hopes of attracting the fur trade. Lieutenant Governor Simcoe laid out Yonge Street to Lake Simcoe not only to open the agricultural hinterland but also to attract this fur trade. The North West Company was interested—but not committed to the idea of using the Yonge Street route. In 1798 the Company voted £12,000 ''toward making Yonge Street a better road''[7] and even Simon McTavish of the North West Company came to York to investigate the situation. Before the War of 1812, however, little use was made of the route[8] while, in the best tradition of Canadian capitalism, the Company tried to wheedle large land grants out of the Upper Canadian government in exchange for using the Niagara-Detroit route to Lake Superior.

During and after the war, until it merged with the Hudson's Bay Company in 1821, the North West Company did indeed use Yonge Street. One local resident, Isaac Wilson, who obviously had survived the ''very pretty'' attack by the Americans in 1813, now complained in August 1815 about the scarcity and high cost of labour in York because of ''the high wages that are given for people with waggons to carry goods through the country to the Lakes for the North West Company to trade with the Indians.'' And Dr. Henry Scadding reported talking to eyewitnesses who had seen "brigades of North West Company boats en route to Lake Huron" using one of two routes: first travelling up the Don to a tributary which crossed Yonge Street and second placing the boats on wagons (or "trucks") pulled by oxen from the bay, along the line of Yonge Street, up "Gallows Hill" (near present-day Rosedale subway station) with the aid of a capstan and on into the hinterland. Whichever route was used, Dr. Scadding suggested, the boats were "shifted across from the Lake into the harbour at the 'Carrying-place'—the narrow neck or isthmus a little to the west of the mouth of the Don proper" where the Eastern Gap now is. As in the previous centuries, the Peninsula portage must have provided a welcome shortcut for weary *voyageurs*.

In December 1821 the vexed question of bridges to the Peninsula was again raised. By this time citizens of York were feeling "deprived of their former intercourse with that place, which not only afforded a pleasant ride and other conveniences to many, but also the pasturage of Cattle which was found a great accommodation to the Inhabitants in general." They therefore petitioned the new lieutenant governor, Sir Peregrine Maitland, who had arrived in 1818, for permission to build "the necessary Bridges."[9] Permission was apparently granted, since a subscription to pay for the bridges was begun in 1822, many of the most prominent citizens contributing. Mr. Edward Angell (unwisely) built the bridges before the full amount of money had been raised. But by September 1827 the *Upper Canada Gazette* was again forced to report that "the Don Bridge near this Town is again in an impassable state" and residents had to use the "temporary floating bridge" erected by an enterprising businessman who charged a

toll. According to Dr. Scadding, York's residents "continued to regret the inaccessibleness of the peninsula" and its many pleasures, until the following decade when new bridges and, more importantly, ferry boats were made available.

Simcoe's enchantment with the Peninsula and the harbour may have blinded him to some of the natural health hazards associated with his town site near the extensive Don Marshes. A Mr. E. A. Talbot visited York in 1822 and noted that in wet weather the streets of York were, if possible, even muddier than those of Kingston. He went on to suggest that "the situation of the town is very unhealthy; for it stands on a piece of low marshy land, which is better calculated for frog-pond or beaver-meadow than for the residence of human beings."[10] As a result, town residents (but not the soldiers of the Garrison, who were on higher, drier ground several miles to the west) were subject to "agues and intermittent fevers." The cause, however, was not the "miasma" of the marsh, as contemporaries believed, but the mosquitoes it nourished. Boat trips to the Peninsula provided much-needed relief from the mosquitoes and miasma of the mainland.

Another health hazard appeared in this decade in the unwelcome form of smallpox. Although, fortunately, smallpox never reached epidemic proportions, an officer at the Garrison (where a case had appeared among some Irish immigrants who lived there) was moved to suggest on August 2, 1822, that the best way to prevent its spread would be to isolate the patients. He wondered if "the block house on the opposite side of the Bay would answer."

Nor was all well with the body politic at this time. The new lieutenant governor was not the man to reject a system based on position and privilege, however unpopular it might be. Sir

Peregrine Maitland had the Regency good looks calculated to stir the blood of a duke's daughter; and indeed Lady Sarah Lennox was moved to elope with him. When his father-in-law the Duke of Richmond recovered from the shock and was appointed governor-in-chief of the British Colonies in North America, Sir Peregrine was given his post in Upper Canada.

During his tenure (1818-1828), his principal advisor, the Reverend Dr. Strachan, who had haggled with the Yankees at the surrender of York, probably reached the apogee of his power. At the same time, the seeds of radical opposition were firmly planted by another recent Scottish immigrant to York (1824)—William Lyon Mackenzie. Maitland was High Tory, High Anglican and high handed, as were Strachan and the Family Compact he dominated—that relatively small group of men, like the Robinsons, the Boultons and the Jarvises, who came to believe that they should rule by a local extension of the principle of divine right. They gave Mackenzie plenty of ammunition.

As the Strachan group went about its business running the province, Mackenzie established a radical outpost overlooking the bay. He set up his *Colonial Advocate* office on Palace Street in the former cottage of another reformer, William Willcocks. The fiery-haired, fiery-eyed, fiery-tongued little Scotsman probably had little time to relax and enjoy the view. He was busy launching attacks in his newspaper against the men of privilege and stirring up trouble in the only elected body in the province, the relatively powerless legislative assembly, to which he was first elected with a short-lived Reform majority in 1828. His journalistic attacks did not stop at matters of policy but became personally abusive.

Finally, on June 8, 1826, when Mackenzie

was away in Queenston, some of the well-bred (but not well-behaved) young sons of privilege decided to teach him a lesson. As the sun was setting west of Gibraltar Point, fifteen well-dressed young bloods led by Samuel Peters Jarvis marched to the *Advocate* office, broke down the door, destroyed the press and dumped the type into the bay from, appropriately enough, Allan's Wharf at the foot of Frederick Street (Allan was one of the prime targets of Mackenzie's invective). Ironically, their actions saved Mackenzie's newspaper. The court settlement he was awarded by Chief Justice William Campbell (whose nephew was one of the offenders) enabled him to pay off his debts and to churn out more attacks. In his political career, he inspired so much animosity that the Tory-dominated legislative assemblies of 1831 to 1833 regularly expelled him and called by-elections; whereupon his loyal farming constituents north of York just as regularly voted him back in.

During this postwar period York was growing rapidly, but the Peninsula remained relatively remote and unchanged. (The only permanent residents continued to be the lighthouse keeper and his family, who were occasionally visited by Indians.) But across the bay the situation was very different. Commercial opportunities expanded so that by 1834 there were 100 stores and the first bank. The population was swollen by massive emigration from Britain in the 1820s and 1830s until by 1834 it exceeded 9,000. And the physical fabric of the community changed dramatically. Many new and improved public buildings were created—like the twice rebuilt Parliament Buildings overlooking the bay between Graves and John Streets; and, along King Street, the new Upper Canada College, the courthouse, the jail, the City Hall-and-Market and the refurbished St. James Church which seemed to grow with the status of its rector, Dr. Strachan.

At the same time, men of wealth and position built suitably impressive private residences to reflect their status. Palace Street (now Front Street), with its cool breezes and splendid view of the bay, Peninsula and lake, became a fashionable residential area. All over the little town 1818 was a year of architectural importance, the year of the Great Houses. Strachan built his lavish Palace, which outshone the nearby lieutenant governor's house. (Legend has it that the magnificence of this residence inspired Strachan's brother James from Aberdeen to exclaim, "I hope it's a' come by honestly, John.") D'Arcy Boulton, Jr., son of the lawyer who had so profited from the loss of the *Speedy*, built his coolly elegant Georgian residence the Grange at the head of John Street on a park lot in what was still the country. And in the same year York's first civilian doctor, self-taught lawyer and political reformist, Dr. William Warren Baldwin, built his beloved Spadina away atop the Davenport Hill. Each had an unobstructed view of the lake. Even Dr. Baldwin, from the spacious lawn in front of his "very commodious house in the country," could look out through the opening he had had specially cleared over the roofs of the growing town three miles away to

While performing his vice-regal duties, Sir Peregrine Maitland found time to absorb and sketch some of the natural beauties of York. One drawing of the Toronto Harbour in 1820, with its Peninsula and distinctive Lighthouse, later formed the basis for this sepia lithotint. [MTLB]

Visiting Indians cook among romantically stylized foliage on the Peninsula, the steamer Queenston *shows the flag, and a much expanded town stretches along the margin of the bay in this aquatint based on James Gray's drawing of* York From Gibraltar Point *in 1828.*   [MTLB]

(Below) *From the well-known Dr. Baldwin atop Davenport hill to this unknown artist closer to the water, York residents liked to admire the Peninsula and "the vessels passing up and down the bay." This 1829 drawing points to the importance of "the Peninsular route," not to mention "Jane" and "Johnny" and "Graham."*   [PAC (C-104491)]

view the lake, the Peninsula and "the vessels passing up and down the bay. "Other equally impressive houses followed—like Henry John Boulton's Holland House, Dr. Baldwin's own town house, William Allan's Moss Park and so on—all with clear views of the lake and the Peninsula.

The bay and the Peninsula continued to be the focus of outdoor recreation. In summer Upper Canada College boys used to swim, rent boats from "Fisty" Masterson (whose earlier money-making schemes had apparently included smuggling) and drag long, heavy planks across the shore in order to paddle off toward the Peninsula (with frequent not unwelcome dunkings in the bay). In winter they liked to skate on the frozen bay, no doubt encouraged by the stylish example of their headmaster, who was said to be the best skater in York. On occasion, however, permission to skate was cancelled—as happened when some pranksters set fire to the marsh. The culprits were never caught.

Sportsmen—like their quarry—continued to flock to the Peninsula. In fact, the Peninsula was so much the preserve of sportsmen that they were surprised to see anyone else splashing through the marshes en route. Dr. Scadding tells

James Worts' account books recorded that his windmill tower was finished on November 26, 1831 and required 105,000 bricks, 216 bushels of lime and 100 loads of sand (probably excavated from the nearby Peninsula). The Gooderham-Worts windmill, shown in Thomas Young's view of Toronto in 1834, became a familiar landmark on the bay. [Clarkson Gordon]

the story of Mr. James Beaty, his duck gun under his arm, encountering a recent immigrant to York, Mr. James Worts, who was "rambling apparently without purpose in the bush" near the mouth of the Little Don. When asked what on earth he was doing out there without a gun, Mr. Worts revealed that, of all strange things, he was looking for a place to build a windmill. In 1831-32 the quixotic Mr. Worts did build his windmill near the mouth of the Don and was soon joined by his brother-in-law William

Gooderham. In 1834 Gooderham carried on the business after poor Worts drowned himself in the well of the mill because of his wife's death in childbirth. The Gooderham and Worts windmill, with its circular red brick tower and long arms, became a familiar landmark on the bay and the foundation of the Gooderham-Worts distilling fortune.

Officers of the Garrison were always welcome additions to the polite society of York. Dr. Walter Henry of the 66th, which was ordered to

York in May 1833 for a brief stay, observed candidly that perhaps their band, which played two evenings a week for the general public, had something to do with their becoming "favourites."

Dr. Henry put his hunting knowledge of the Peninsula to good effect when treating the elderly chief justice, William Campbell, who was lying on his sickbed in his elegant brick house overlooking the bay along the length of Frederick Street. (The house has since been moved by the Advocates' Society to Queen Street at University Avenue.) Dr. Henry tells the story:

> My worthy patient became very weak towards the end of the year—his nights were restless—his appetite began to fail, and he could only relish tid bits. Medicine was tried fruitlessly, so his Doctor prescribed snipes. At the point of the sandy peninsula opposite the barracks, are a number of little pools and marshes, frequented by these delectable little birds; and here I used to cross over in my skiff and pick up the Chief Justice's panacea. On this delicate food the poor old gentleman was supported for a couple of months, but the frost set in—the snipes flew away, and Sir W____ died.[11]

Ordinary soldiers, of course, had less time—and less money—than their superiors for entertainment. Their main leisure activity seems to have been drinking. The night sentry was posted later than usual on pay day because the men were positively expected to get drunk and to have trouble finding their way back to the fort. Drinking of this sort was apparently behind the incident that has become the best known Island legend. It occurred against the appropriately Gothic backdrop of the peninsular Lighthouse. On a cold January night in 1815 a party of soldiers from the Garrison apparently visited their friend, the first Lighthouse Keeper, J. P. Rademuller. When he saw that his guests were becoming too drunk, the legend goes, the usually generous gentleman refused to produce more liquor. Thereupon the enraged soldiers beat the "inoffensive and benevolent"[12] Rademuller to death with their heavy belts and made good their escape along Blockhouse Bay.

Whether this version of the tale is accurate is impossible to know since the perpetrators of the "barbarous and inhuman"[13] murder were

never found. But the story has entertained generations of Island residents, and has caused small boys and girls to give the Lighthouse a wide berth on many a dark and stormy night.

In 1832 death on a grander scale came to York and the Peninsula narrowly missed becoming the Grosse Ile or Ellis Island of Little York. On June 8, 1832, the steamship *Great Britain* dropped anchor in the harbour, bringing among its passengers the first case of cholera to reach York. The immigrant ships had already done their deadly work in Quebec and Montreal where hundreds were dying. By the time the epidemic had run its course in York that long, hot summer, the town had almost literally been decimated. Out of a population of 5,505, over 500 cases had been reported and 205 deaths had been attributed to the disease.

The sanitary conditions of York at the time were appalling. Drinking water was drawn from the closest and therefore filthiest parts of the bay (referred to in a contemporary news report as "carrion broth" because of all the dead animals in it[14]). Throughout the town stagnant pools of water "green as a leek,"[15] rotting vegetables, filthy privies, open drains and so on produced a situation almost beyond the hope of control. Add to this the influx of 11,000 immigrants who landed at York in the summer of 1832 alone, and it is clear that the town faced an impossible situation. Immigrant sheds were hastily built on the shore near Rees's Wharf at the foot of Graves Street, where many of the immigrant ships landed, and in the yard of the York Hospital. The conditions in these overcrowded sheds must have been truly hellish—dark, dirty, hot and foul with the stench of death.

Now-archdeacon Strachan worked heroically and fearlessly during the summer epidemic to minister to the sick and dying. But he and his near neighbour Chief Justice William Dummer Powell were clearly motivated more by self-interest than altruism when they suggested to Lieutenant Governor John Colborne on May 24,

Lighthouse Keeper Rademuller lived in the shuttered pioneer cottage in this 1908 photograph. Built around 1808 of three inch planks joined by nails from the blacksmith's forge at Fort York, it was occupied by Rademuller until his death in January 1815. The murdered Rademuller was succeeded by Keeper Holloway who was, according to John Ross Robertson, "always friendly with the officers" who hunted duck and snipe nearby. His stout wife kept a dun brown cow, dispensed bread and cheese to hungry hunters, and was once saved from drowning by Bishop Strachan's son James. [MTLB]

In Frederic Waistell Jopling's energetic drawing, dogs bark, horses gallop, bands play, handbells ring and a coven of "Torontonians" prances around a rousing bonfire on the edge of the bay to celebrate the incorporation of the City of Toronto on March 6, 1834. [MTLB]

1833, that the offensive immigrant sheds be removed. They complained that the sheds (which their own houses happened to overlook) were "a great nuisance to all the neighbourhood," being "receptacles for drunkeness and vice, and surrounded by every kind of filth." If action was not taken, "the whole space under the Bank [of the shore] will be covered with the meanest sort of buildings, and render it impossible for decent people to walk in front of that part of the Town." Well, harrumph. The undeniably "decent" Powell helpfully suggested in an accompanying letter "that the Sheds for reception of the Emigrants should be erected on the Peninsular in front of York uninhabited except for the Keeper of the Light House, and a Ferry established and supported by the Town or even private Subscription, to avoid the chance of Infection and the many Evils of a Town Residence of the newly imported Paupers." Presumably he meant that they should be located on the far side of the Peninsula, so that they would not mar his beautiful view. Fortunately for its later development, an immigrant reception post and quarantine area like Grosse Ile was not built on the Peninsula. Immigrants who would have suffered at either location continued to suffer on the mainland.

The cholera epidemic of 1832 was one of the many problems that overtaxed the town's system of government beyond endurance. In March 1834, therefore, Little York became the City of Toronto, with its own elected mayor and city council.[16] Irony of ironies, the first mayor elected by the council was none other than William Lyon Mackenzie.

At the time of Toronto's incorporation, the Peninsula a mile and a half across the bay still seemed wild and full of dangers to some timorous residents. Mrs. Durnan was very much frightened when she learned in 1832 that her son James was about to become the keeper of the Lighthouse. She wondered aloud, nervously, "Are there Indians on the Island and do people who live there wear clothes?"[17] The hotel owners who would follow Durnan to the Peninsula would have greater dangers to contend with—frolicking Torontonians.

4
Development
of the Peninsula

In the fall of 1833 Michael O'Connor proudly announced the opening of his hotel, the Retreat on the Peninsula, and ushered in the resort era of the Toronto Peninsula. O'Connor, appropriately enough, was a veteran of the Peninsular War against Napoleon in Spain, where he had suffered through the famous Corunna retreat led by Sir John Moore, before emigrating to Canada in the postwar rush. O'Connor hoped to attract "Sportsmen, Parties of pleasure, and individuals who may wish to inhale the Lake breeze" from as far away as Montreal, Kingston and Niagara, as well as to reminisce over his "particularly selected" wines and liquors with old comrades in arms "whose recollection of the Spanish Peninsula will ever be dear to their memory, as recorded in the pages of British History."[1]

O'Connor's liquor license might have been a great attraction, but his placement at "the Narrows" next to Benjamin Knott's Blue and Poland Starch Factory must have been a distinct disadvantage—its noisome location perhaps attractive only to Toronto's stuffed-shirts. In any event, Knott seems to have been the Peninsula's first real entrepreneur. After complaints from the York Board of Health, Knott had decided to transfer his soap and starch factory from the town to the Peninsula, where it would be "convenient to the Lake for pure water and to the Bay for shipping and receiving stock."[2] Knott soon built the Peninsula's first and only factory, churned out candles and starch as before, provided employment for Peninsula potato farmers and welcomed visitors from the distant shores of the mainland. Brewers William and Thomas Helliwell, for example, rowed across the bay after church in July 1833, braving a downpour that they fended off with the help of their trusty "umberelows,"[3] to visit Knott and "the Island"— as they, like others, persisted in calling the

Peninsula. Not content to live by starch alone, Knott seems to have been the builder of the hotel, which he leased to O'Connor and later proprietors.[4] In any case, the hotel was built and patrons were sought. Knott and O'Connor solved the perennial problem of providing ready access to the Island playground by operating the first of many eccentric boats to churn through the waters between the town and the Island: the "horse boat," which O'Connor named *Sir John of the Peninsula*, presumably in honour of Sir John Moore who lay buried in Spanish soil "alone with his glory."[5] This first Island ferry boat was powered by two teams of two horses walking on treadmills which turned side paddle wheels. Visitors had to regard "getting there" as half the fun since each trip across the eastern end of the bay lasted some thirty to forty minutes, presumably depending on the state of the weather and the humour of the horsepower. According to Knott's ad in the *Canadian Freeman*, the "commodious and safe" *Sir John of the Peninsula* was scheduled to make her maiden voyage on September 9, 1833, and by early October "the team boat" was making three daily trips from the wharf at the foot of Church Street to the Peninsula. She even made regular trips on Sunday

Captain R. H. Bonnycastle's chatty map of 1833 does not show O'Connor's hotel or Knott's soap and starch factory at the narrows of the Peninsula. This detail, however, does show the route of the first horse boat, the "ruined bridge" over the Don River which prevented local residents from riding to the Peninsula, the "lofty windmill" at the angle of the bay, the "white and herring" fishing grounds south of the Peninsula, the Lighthouse, the location of the now-demolished Gibraltar Point Blockhouse and its namesake, Blockhouse Bay. [PAC, NMC]

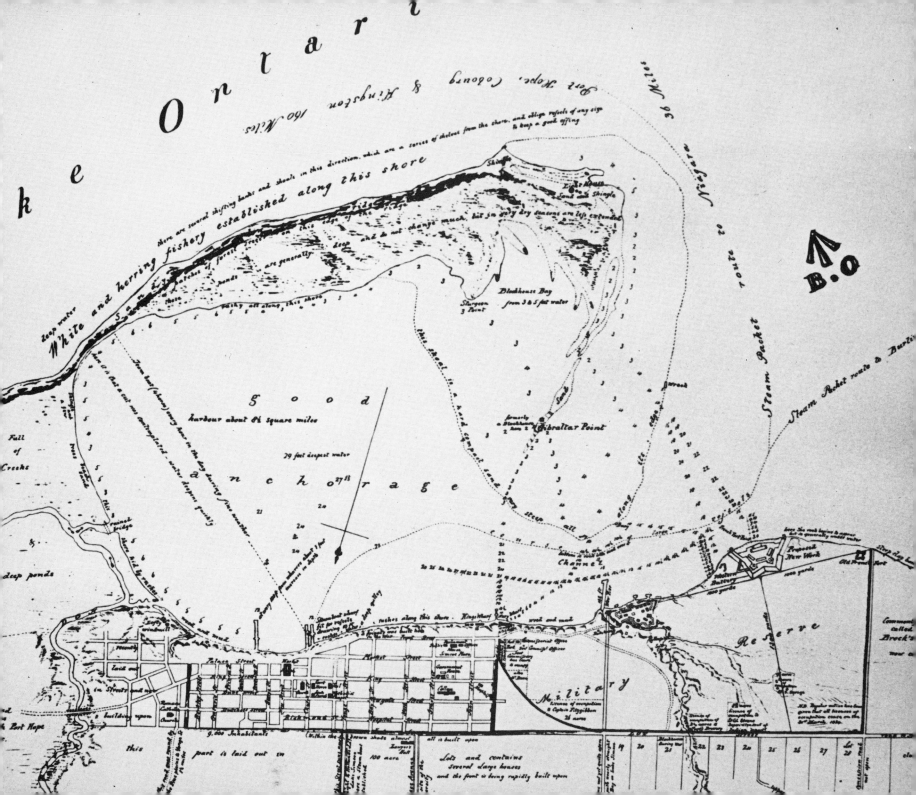

(though, of course, ferry services were interrupted between nine and one to allow patrons to attend church services).

Unfortunately for O'Connor, his New World peninsular venture was not a success. In the summer of 1834 the dreaded cholera once again swept through Toronto, reaching epidemic proportions in the oppressively sultry month of August. Those two arch political foes, Mayor William Lyon Mackenzie and Archdeacon John Strachan, showed equal courage in combatting the disease. According to biographer William Kilbourn, Mayor Mackenzie "threw himself into the relief work as furiously as if he were fighting the whole Family Compact single-handed"— sometimes even driving the cholera cart himself. And according to the *Patriot* of August 19, the dour Archdeacon made "regular and constant" trips between his Front Street home and the special cholera hospital set up in the east wing of the new Parliament Building overlooking the bay. All to little avail. Pestilence-ridden immigrant sheds again lined the lakeshore below the grassy promenade, residents fled the town for the supposed safety of the countryside, and Potters Field again received its grim burden. Many Toronto residents, unable to flee to the country, scurried instead to the Peninsula "to enjoy the salubrity and freshness of Air."[6] But not enough of them came to save O'Connor. At the end of August Benjamin Knott placed an ad in the *Advocate* to rent his "lately erected" "large and commodious Hotel" on the Peninsula, though only someone "fully qualified to conduct a first rate Hotel" need apply, he emphasized.

On New Year's Day 1835 the new proprietors, Messrs. Anderton & Palin, placed a florid ad for their Peninsula Hotel, which they hoped would form "a pleasant and healthy retreat for individuals and families desirous of changing

Messrs. Gooderham, Palin and Anderton were among those who petitioned City Council in 1835 to improve the road to the windmill and the Peninsula beyond. Owen Staples painted this rutted route, and the more comfortable horse boat in the distance. [CTA]

the air of the City for the salubrious atmosphere of the Island." They promised heat, "comfortable furniture," "a larder stocked with game in season" (presumably caught on the Island or in the Marsh), "choice Wines with prompt attention" and "a handsome Ball Room for those parties desirous of dancing."[7] Anderton & Palin's partnership, however, barely survived the winter, hardly the most auspicious time to open what was primarily a summer retreat. In May 1835 Anderton fled the sandy soil of Toronto's Peninsula for the greener tourist pastures of Niagara Falls where he opened the Pavilion Hotel. Palin soldiered on alone.

Meanwhile, in the spring of 1835, a number of Torontonians became concerned about the state of the harbour (a perennial Toronto obsession). A group of prominent citizens began to lobby for a canal to be cut across the neck of the Peninsula to drain the marsh, flush out the increasingly fetid bay water and provide a convenient new entrance to the harbour for the boats approaching from the east. "Friends of the Cut" held a well-attended public meeting at the Commercial Hotel on March 3 and asked the government to appoint an engineer to report on the project. City Council members respectfully waited on Lieutenant Governor Sir John Colborne, who readily appointed Captain (later Sir) Richard H. Bonnycastle of the Royal Engineers. But little came of Bonnycastle's hastily prepared report of March 12, which recommended cutting ''a small canal at the Narrows.''

Transportation to the Island had become an issue and several real improvements were made in the spring of 1835. At the time the only public ferry was the picturesque but pokey horse boat, and there was no land access at all—a fact regretted by ''every inhabitant of [Toronto] able

to indulge in the luxury of a carriage, or a saddle horse, or given to extensive pedestrian excursions.''[8]

That year, George Heathcote completed the first steam ferry, the *Toronto*. She was 62 feet long, 13 feet across the beam, and was driven by a 14-horsepower engine. According to the *Patriot* of October 9, she was ''composed of the best seasoned materials, having a commodious

Thomas Roy worked with Captain Bonnycastle on a proposal in March 1835 to improve the state of Toronto Harbour, where "noxious stuff...offensive to the sight, to the smell, and to the health of the inhabitants" was allowed to collect and float about on the "still waters" of the bay. Roy's map shows the "proposed canal" across "the Narrows or Portage" near Knott's starch factory and the hotel, as well as the much ballyhooed new bridges across the Don River. [PAC, NMC]

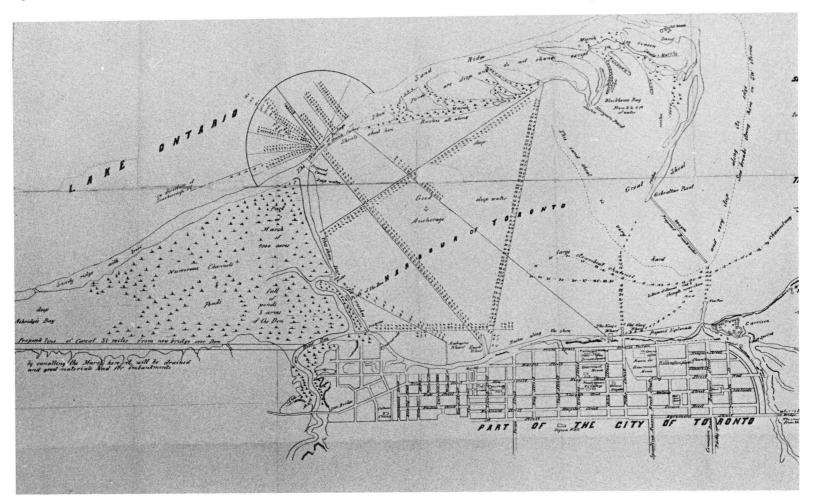

deck cabin with fittings, and in every respect adapted for the comfort and accommodation of passengers.'' The *Toronto* ran throughout the summer but ran out of steam later in the year when she was taken off the route and sold. The ferry system reverted to real horses rather than steam horses; perhaps they were still more reliable.

Meanwhile, during that spring of 1835, through the good offices of Lieutenant Governor Colborne, the military was busy rebuilding the Don bridges and improving the road to the Peninsula.⁹ This project was popular, but not universally so. On March 9 John Scadding (father of Dr. Henry Scadding), brewer Thomas Helliwell and other residents and businessmen along the Don River complained to City Council that the new bridges would be ''a great grievance and nuisance'' to them. They were worried that the clearance would be too small (only four feet) and passageway too narrow (only fourteen feet between the piers) to enable them to continue with their traditional activities—such as floating timber down the river, using boats in summer and horse-drawn sleighs in winter to haul their goods and taking boats rigged with tall jack lanterns to the bay for night fishing.

Whether any alterations in the plans were made is unknown. But to the joy of most Torontonians the bridges were completed and handed over to the City with great pomp and circumstance on August 22, 1835. Two processions converged on the site. Captain Bonnycastle accompanied by the Toronto Artillery Corps and the band of the 15th Regiment proceeded to the new bridges. The Royal Standard was hoisted and a twenty-one-gun salute boomed out across the bay and marsh (no doubt the wild fowl nesting in the area thought Armageddon had arrived in the form of cannon-bearing sportsmen). Meanwhile, a solemn procession of City Councillors, led by Mayor Sullivan resplendent in his

John George Howard painted this Dickensian view of skating, and carioling and body-checking on the bay in 1835.   [THB/MTLB]

scarlet coat of office, wound its way from City Hall along the lakeshore road to the first bridge. Captain Bonnycastle stepped forward to officially transfer the bridges, "which [had] been erected for the benefits of the inhabitants that they may in all times to come be enabled to enjoy the salubrious air of the Peninsula."[10] The mayor graciously accepted the bridges and proceeded with his council members to celebrate the occasion at the Peninsula Hotel, where Palin no doubt provided an ample luncheon of "comfortable refreshments," washed down by the "best Wines and Liquors."[11] The well-fed mayor and corporation then swaggered home aboard the ferry.

Residents' joy in the new bridges was no doubt tempered when City Council erected a toll house and began collecting tolls, which ranged from twopence for a saddle horse to sixpence for every four-wheeled pleasure carriage drawn by two or more horses.[12] To add insult to injury the new bridges were first damaged then swept away altogether a few years later.

Palin meanwhile was enjoying great success, even thanking the gentry and inhabitants of Toronto "for the liberal support" they had shown him. The *Toronto*, he noted in his ad dated September 4, 1835, was making regular hourly trips from McDonald's Wharf at the foot of Church Street. This together with the new bridges (for the time being) rendered "the Peninsula one of the most inviting and healthy rides near the City." In addition to the usual blandishments, Palin offered "Cold and Warm Baths for ladies and gentlemen, on the newest principle so strongly recommended by the medical profession for health and recreation." In a city with little indoor plumbing this must have been a treat indeed. The hospitable Palin continued to operate the Peninsula Hotel for several more years before disappearing from the scene.

During this period the political temperature of Toronto and Upper Canada generally was rising, reaching the boiling point in the Rebellion of December 1837. The "Reformers" won the provincial election of October 1834 and William Lyon Mackenzie once again turned his attention to the legislative assembly. He and his compatriots compiled a massive report of grievances, which comprised his "last great arraignment of the Compact from his place in the Assembly."[13] A copy of this report found its way across the Atlantic into the hands of King William IV and his Whig secretary of state for the colonies, Lord Glenelg. Characterized by William Kilbourn as a "ditherer" who summoned his resolution for one last drastic act before relapsing into "a state of agitated paralysis," Glenelg abruptly dismissed Lieutenant Governor Colborne and then proceeded to make one of the more unfortunate appointments ever made by a colonial secretary, the romantic and adventuring, but haughty and inflexible, Sir Francis Bond Head.

Bond Head was altogether unsuited by experience and temperament to manage the delicate situation in the colony. Given instructions to proceed cautiously, he was a man who seemed to regard appeasement and compromise as surrender. Among his previous accomplishments was being the first Englishman to gallop across the Argentinian pampas to the Andes and back in less than a week (thus earning himself the title Galloping Head) and learning the delicate art of lassoing. His skill with this rope so impressed William IV that the King knighted him. But of politics and diplomacy he knew little and accomplished less as he galloped headlong into disaster.

Sir Francis arrived in Toronto in the dreary month of January. Colborne quietly slipped off to Lower Canada to turn his full attention to

military matters while Head was astonished to be greeted by the Radical portion of Toronto cheering and waving banners proclaiming "Sir Francis Bond Head, A Tried Reformer." But Head was neither a reformer nor a politician. "I was no more connected with human politics than the horses which were drawing me," he later confided to his diary. Sir Francis's lack of political horse sense was to prove disastrous.

Toronto had no pampas or distant Andes to offer, but it did have the Peninsula. Over the next few months, as he precipitated one political crisis after another, Galloping Head enjoyed escaping across Colborne's bridges to speed along the sandy lakeshore toward the Lighthouse, where Keeper James Durnan and his family still lived in the small plank cottage built for the first keeper in 1808. But not for much longer. After a tour around the Lighthouse and Durnan's primitive cabin in the summer of 1836, Sir Francis finally said, "Durnan, this is not a very comfortable home for you to live in; if you'll get up a petition to have it improved, I'll sign it and see that you get what you want." And so, according to John Ross Robertson, another Island landmark was born—the new lightkeeper's cottage.

Meanwhile, Toronto and its harbour were growing apace. Between 1834 and 1841 some eight new wharfs were built and the population increased from about 9,000 in 1834 to over 18,000 in 1844. Not all commercial enterprise on the waterfront, however, was devoted to shipping and ancillary activities. In the summer of 1836 John Cull made a splash when he built his famous "Royal Floating Baths" at the foot of Frederick Street. This remarkable edifice was 110 feet long, 21 feet wide and contained 10 warm and 10 cold baths, as well as "Vapour and Shower Baths." One end, naturally, was "exclusively appropriated for Ladies" who had a private entrance to more effectively guard their modesty. From the 80-foot promenade deck "with a dome roof and trellis-work guards all around," patrons could gaze out across the bay to the Peninsula and the sparkling lake beyond. Those exhausted from the efforts of their exercise could withdraw to the "elegant drawing room" adjoining the promenade.[14] By the 1840s, however, the only patrons of the baths seemed to have been the Baptists, who changed their clothes there before entrusting their souls to God and their bodies to the noxious waters in this corner of the bay.

In spite of such amenities, Toronto had her critics, none more caustic than author-artist Anna Jameson. Mrs. Jameson arrived on a cold forbidding day in December 1836 to join her husband Vice Chancellor Robert Jameson. Her introduction to the city was inauspicious: she stepped off the steamboat and sank ankle-deep in mud and ice. If she took any notice of John Cull's splendid baths through the descending gloom, she did not record it. She stumbled tearily through the driving sleet and along the "dreary, mirey ways" to her new home at Brock and Newgate (Adelaide) Streets. This house was "ill provided with defenses against the cold"—even her writing ink used to freeze—but it did at least provide a welcome "glimpse of the bay," which would provide some comfort in the cold and lonely months to come.[15]

She was less than enthusiastic about Toronto, which she described as

> a little ill-built town on low land, at the bottom of a frozen bay, with one very ugly church, without tower or steeple [St. James]; some government offices, built of staring red brick, in the most tasteless, vulgar style imaginable; three feet of snow all around; and the grey, sullen, wintry lake, and the dark gloom of the pine

forest bounding the prospect; such seems Toronto to me now [December 20, 1836]. I did not expect much; but for this I was not prepared.

As the wife of Vice Chancellor Robert Jameson, Mrs. Jameson had certain social chores to perform. Among these was attending the prorogation of the legislative assembly (elected the previous summer) in March 1837. Noting that Lieutenant Governor Head was "enthusiastically cheered" when he arrived—"a circumstance rather unusual of late"—she went on to describe the wintry lakeside tableau in front of the red brick Parliament Buildings:

> The snow-expanse was all around, and, between the shore of the frozen bay and the line of building, the space was filled by sleighs of all shapes and sizes, the horses curveting and kicking up the snow, and a crowd of some hundred people in all manner of strange defences against the piercing frost, intermingled with military costumes, and a few Indians lounging by in their blanket-coats and war-plumes.

The Jamesons soon moved to a new house at Front Street west of Spadina Avenue on the bank of the lake, overlooking a splendid vista—"… we command, at one glance, the entrance to the bay, the King's Pier, the lighthouse, and beyond, the whole expanse of Lake Ontario to the Niagara shore." Mrs. Jameson hated the long, interminable winter, although she liked viewing the full moon over the icy bay "which glittered like a sheet of silver" and revelled in sleighing to Niagara Falls, as well as across the bay before her. So she like other Torontonians warmly greeted the first true harbingers of a Toronto spring: the ice in the bay groaned, cracked and miraculously disappeared in the space of twelve hours and the first steamboat of the season churned past her window into the harbour "with flags and

streamers flying" to be greeted by "the cheers of people" who had hurried down to the lake as she "swept majestically into the bay."

As far as the Peninsula was concerned, Anna Jameson was not overwhelmed by its natural beauty:

> The opposite side of the bay is formed by a long sandbank, called the "island," though, in fact, no island, but a very narrow promontory, about three miles in length and forming a rampart against the main waters of the lake. At the extremity is a light-house, and a few stunted trees and underwood. This marsh, intersected by inlets and covered with reeds, is the haunt of thousands of wild fowl, and of the terrapin, or small turtle of the lake; and as evening comes on, we see long rows of red lights from the fishing boats gleaming along the surface of the water, for thus they spear the lake salmon, the bass, and the pickereen.

But like many Torontonians and Islanders she became increasingly fascinated and enchanted by the many moods of Lake Ontario itself, which became "like the face of a friend" to her.

While Mrs. Jameson made a northward tour through Indian country to Lake Huron in 1837, William Lyon Mackenzie and his followers prepared for rebellion. The time seemed ripe. Toronto and its hinterland were plunged into a deep economic depression and Governor Head, with his newly won Tory majority, was triumphant and uncompromising. During the summer Mackenzie darted around the countryside organizing his loyal rural followers. Farmers beat their ploughshares into swords or, more accurately, pikes and began drilling, using umbrellas and walking sticks when muskets were unavailable. Then, in an unwise act of bravura, Sir Francis (who for some reason refused to entertain the notion that anyone in his realm of Upper Canada would be so unhappy or so unloyal as to rebel) sent all his troops to Colborne in Lower Canada, which *was* expecting trouble.

Finally, in early December 1837 the tragi-comic opera of a rebellion was played out in the gardens, fields and streets of Toronto. While Mackenzie roused his farmers' army north of the city and Colonel James Fitzgibbon dashed around madly (some used the word deliberately) to organize the defence of the town, Head dithered and delayed. His most decisive act in the early part of the rebellion seems to have been to send his wife and family, along with that of Chief Justice Robinson, to the safety of a small steamer in the bay. "He had his family out in the Bay," Mackenzie later wrote scornfully, "as if they were china, while other folks' families, being but brownware, had to run all risks ashore."[16] More "china" followed. When the rebels set fire to Dr. Horne's house across the ravine, Sheriff Jarvis's wife Mary decided it was time to flee "Rosedale" and also seek the safety of the bay. She bundled her two sick children into the carriage waiting behind the house and, avoiding Yonge Street, made her way down to Front Street and the steamer. (Her daughter, Fanny Jarvis, who was seven at the time, later recalled that "one gentleman of Toronto was found hiding in the steamer—the only one on board."[17] She did not reveal his name.) From the deck of this little steamer, those who dared look could have watched some of the strange advances and retreats along Yonge Street during the next few days.

"Sometimes a thunder-squall from the west sends the little sloops and schooners sweeping and scudding into the harbor for shelter," wrote Anna Jameson, who sketched this view of the Peninsula in 1837. [Thomas Fisher Rare Book Library]

The decisive moment came in the wintry twilight of Tuesday, December 5. With his family now safe in the bay, Sheriff Jarvis and twenty-seven riflemen skirmished with Mackenzie's men in William Sharpe's vegetable patch (now Maple Leaf Gardens). They put the rebels to flight and, unknowingly, broke the back of the rebellion. Late that same night the hearty Allan Napier MacNab, guided by the beacon atop the Gibraltar Point Lighthouse, navigated past the Peninsula and steamed into the harbour with sixty men from Gore, the district surrounding Hamilton. Sir Francis effusively declared him to be the saviour of the city.

The "battle" of Thursday December 7 at Montgomery's farm north of the city marked the inglorious end of the rebel cause and Mackenzie fled toward the border with a £1,000 price on his head. Canadians would have to wait a few years for the resurrection of what Sir Francis called "that perfidious enemy, responsible government."[18] Meanwhile, the ground work had been laid for the rise of that "wild and rabid Toryism of Toronto" which Charles Dickens deplored after his visit in 1841.[19]

Mackenzie reached the safety of Navy Island in the Niagara River, where he set up a provisional government and attracted a number of American supporters. Toronto, meanwhile, spent an uneasy winter. The Queen's Rangers mounted a guard over the docks along the bay and patrolled the streets at night; visiting and merry-making was much reduced over the holiday season; even skaters and carioles on the bay kept a sharp eye out, fearing an over-ice attack by the rebels.

Meanwhile, Sir Francis Bond Head was replaced by Sir George Arthur, whose experience as governor of Van Diemen's Land came in handy as he meted out severe "justice." Despite public outcry two popular rebels, Lount and Matthews, were hanged in April, while many others were run to ground and imprisoned. One such group was marched in chains down Yonge Street on June 8, 1838, to the wharf where a steamer was waiting to take them away. Rebel Thomas Sheppard recalled the melancholy departure, with families standing on shore, watching the steamer round the Peninsula and disappear into the distance:

> The mothers and wives of the rebels crowded around to see the last of us as they thought. I tell you it was a hard parting with the old folks, who stood there on the wharf looking after the steamer until we were out of sight. At Kingston we were marched to Fort Henry, where we were supposed to stay until Her Majesty was ready to give us a free passage to Van Dieman's land.[20]

While "patriots" made attacks across the border from the United States, Britain sent out reinforcements, improved local defences (e.g., built blockhouses around the city and somewhat later a new fort, which afterwards became Stanley Barracks) and appointed the haughty but brilliant Lord Durham as governor-in-chief of British North America.

Queen Victoria's coronation on June 28, 1838, provided one bright spot. Amidst reports of border raids and even fears of attack by sea (schooners had been sighted off the Scarborough coast but it was unclear whether arms or simply contraband had been landed), Torontonians and loyal citizens across the province prepared for the festivities. The streets were decorated with flags and banners and evergreens. Steamers entering the harbour, including the new *Queen Victoria* on her maiden voyage from Niagara, were similarly festooned and all ships in the harbour had their colours hoisted. At noon a royal salute was fired out over the lake from the Garrison and a *feu de joie* was fired by the troops. At night the town was aglow with a "general illumination" and rockets and other splendid fireworks were set off over the bay to the general delight and applause of all present.

The arrival of Lord Durham provided the other highlight of 1838 and the excuse for the largest waterfront reception yet seen in Toronto. On July 18 he deigned to visit the capital of Upper Canada for one whole day and night. Encouraged by an official civic holiday, twelve thousand loyal Torontonians waited by the water for the governor-in-chief to arrive, only to find that his lordship was "indisposed" and had instructed the captain of the *Cobourg* to linger in Humber Bay. Finally his lordship and Lady Durham landed and proceeded through the city's streets receiving loyal addresses at every possible location.

The next day a similar fate awaited the distinguished visitors. Hook and Ladder companies, saintly patriotic societies and government officials lined the streets and the wharfs to bid them a full-throated farewell. It is only appropriate that this lightning tour of Toronto ended amidst the booming of cannon from the Garrison and the sound and fury of a terrific summer thunderstorm.

As Durham safely rounded Gibraltar Point, Lighthouse Keeper James Durnan was perhaps watching the grand but stormy departure from his shining perch high above the lake. By this time there were still few permanent residents on the Peninsula—Durnan and his family and a few fishermen, who were visited by the occasional Indian. Although his mother had feared for his safety in this wild spot when he took up the job, Durnan had discovered that these Indians were far from dangerous, as James's son and successor later told John Ross Robertson:

After the uncertainties of Mackenzie's 1837 rebellion, Torontonians were delighted to show their loyalty to the crown by celebrating Victoria's coronation on June 28, 1838 in right royal style. Here the Queen's Rangers parade at Fort York before booming a salute out toward the Peninsula in the distance. [Confederation Life Collection]

[F]rom 1834-40, there was an occasional camp of Indians at the birch tree ridge, a little east of Blockhouse Bay. These children of the forest were fond of milk, and often came to the lightkeeper's door and asked for a pitcher full and were seldom refused, if there was milk to spare. On one occasion two of them—a man and a squaw—walked into the living room of the cabin to make their usual request, and just as they entered the room they saw that the family were at morning worship. Without a word they dropped upon their knees and bowed their heads until the service was finished, and then got a quart of milk.

Lord Durham's legacy was the Act of Union in 1840, which officially united Upper and Lower Canada. The legacy of his successor Charles Poulett Thompson (later Lord Sydenham), who visited Toronto as rarely as he could, was the transfer of the capital from Toronto to Kingston. Torontonians were not amused, but they had little choice in the matter. And one government department after another lumbered down to the wharfs in the spring of 1841 to move to the new capital.

The harbour was expanding steadily throughout this pre-railroad era. The lakefront was alive with the sounds of swearing stevedores and of

Coke Smyth, drawing instructor to Lord Durham's two daughters, created a tranquil view of the "Entrance to Toronto" in 1838, quite unlike the reality that attended his master's visit aboard the Cobourg. [Clarkson Gordon]

whistling steamships. Newcomers like Peter and George Brown, who arrived aboard the new *Chief Justice Robinson* in the summer of 1843 to found a newspaper, could not help but be impressed by the bustle and prosperity of the lakeside town.

There were, admittedly, a few problems. Sir Richard H. Bonnycastle was impressed by Toronto's "splendid harbour" protected by "a long horn of sand ... in a sort of sickle shape,"[21] but was less than enchanted by the "narrow decaying pier" where he landed and was most annoyed by the jostling and pestering of carters and hotel employees seeking business. Not only were some of the wharfs rotten and dangerous,

but slimy, noxious weeds polluted the bay water and brawling dockside toughs occasionally made the area unsafe for law-abiding citizens. There were other hazards. Sometimes a gale would sweep off the lake, tearing some boats from their moorings and driving others aground. On other occasions steamers competing for space in the crowded harbour would ram one another. And on other occasions explosions would tear out the guts of boats and do terrible damage.

Meanwhile, during the forties the bay and the Peninsula continued to be a place for recreation. As the town grew, concerned citizens like Jesse Ketchum became increasingly aware of the need

to actively protect public open space and petitioned City Council to preserve part of the waterfront as a "public promenade." Letters, diaries and journals of the day are sprinkled with references to visiting "the Island." Architect/surveyor John George Howard, who perhaps came to know the Peninsula better than any other non-resident because of his numerous surveying expeditions,[22] commented in his characteristically laconic diary style, "May 27, 1843 ... at 3 to the Island shooting" or "May 25, 1846 ... at ½ past 11 on a picnic at the Island home [to Colborne Lodge] with all at 8—they all staid till 11."

The ever-sociable young lawyer Larratt Smith,

who lived in various cottages overlooking the lake, described numerous visits to "the Island"—never the Peninsula—in the early forties. Sometimes he rowed or sailed across the bay with his good friend Sheriff Jarvis's son Bill to do a little shooting:

> Tuesday 13th May [1840]. After the office yesterday I went to the Island with Bill Jarvis in his boat. It was blowing too hard to fish so we did some shooting. Jarvis shot 2 Sand Pipers & I shot a duck and gave it to Henry Draper. Left the office very late & went shooting after dinner, missed a beautiful shot, ducks very shy. Later at home by myself, sat a hen on 7 duck's eggs.[23]

It is not surprising that the ducks were "shy"—it is perhaps surprising that Smith raided their nests in retaliation. In any event, on other occasions he and Jarvis engaged in less violent pursuits: "Thursday 24th [June 1841]. After the office Jarvis & I rowed to the Island where we picked wild strawberries and bathed...."(Wild strawberries still abound on the Island.) Sometimes Smith was flattered to be invited to "fashionable" picnics, held by the likes of Mrs. Widder (whose parties at Lyndhurst overlooking the lake were already famous):

> Saturday 27th [August 1842]. Lovely & hot. I left the office early yesterday & went to Mrs. Widder's pic-nic at the Bend of the Island. Some of the party crossed the Bay in Cull's the *Wave*, & others in Irving's & Stowe's boats. The pic-nic was a very large fashionable affair. Saw Miss Irving there but we did not speak. After a very pleasant party, I drank tea at Mrs. Stowe's & finished off at Culls. Called at Lyndhurst this morning & left 2 cards for Mr. & Mrs. Widder.

Even the chill winds of winter did not keep him away. In fact, sometimes the *lack* of wind was positively disappointing:

> 17 December [1840]. Frightfully cold, the streets all ice, making walking very difficult. Left the office early & skated to the Island where I sailed in Jarvis's ice boat, & finally helped to drag her back, very little wind....

And finally, for Larratt Smith like many other Torontonians "the Island" played a role in his courting activities—even in winter: "Friday 2nd February [1844]. Drove Miss [Eliza] Thom & Mary [his sister] in the cutter with "Jerry" [the horse] to the Island and about the town." By such ventures as this Miss Thom's heart and hand were won.

More organized recreational activity also blossomed on the bay. The officers of the Garrison, with their regimental bands and manly presences, were always lively social assets in a garrison town like Toronto.[24] In 1839 they formed their infamous Tandem Club for the express purpose of racing sporty carioles pell-mell through the snowy forests, down slushy streets and across icy bays. Frequently the sleighs overturned and more frequently their occupants stopped at wayside

Courting by cariole sometimes had its drawbacks, as is evident from J.T. Downman's picture of 1842 or '43, dedicated to his fellow-officers of the 83rd Regiment. While an embarrassed civilian struggles to control his recalcitrant horse, a dashing officer comes to rescue him, and his fair lady.
[Clarkson Gordon]

Fierce competition was not entirely lacking on the bay in winter. As this 1843 drawing by Sir J. E. Alexander indicates, curling was a popular and passionate winter pastime. For many years, "Knights of the broom" gathered along the icefront for grand Bonspiels, the slap of the brooms and the Caledonian shouting of the skips reverberating around the usually quiet wharfs. [PAC (C-98770)]

taverns to warm cooling spirits. Unfortunately there were no convivial watering holes out on the bay—only treacherous ones for ice-fishing.

By 1840 the highlight of summer sporting on the bay was the Toronto Regatta. The 1842 regatta seems to have been particularly splendid. September 5 provided almost exactly the right weather for the occasion: "just breeze enough to send the sail boats gallantly through the water, and not so much as to render the swell an impediment to the rowing boats," according to the *Examiner* of September 7 (though, according to Larratt Smith, it was a bit blowy for the oarsmen). The shore was lined with spectators, the bay was alive with boats of every size and shape, and thanks to Captain Dick the steamer *City of Toronto* was anchored a short distance from the wharfs where it was reportedly "crowded

with the beauty and fashion of Toronto." The competition was keen. Mr. Angus Morrison's *Lapwing* edged out Mr. Irving's *Belle Louise* to take the sailing prize. And the "four-oared match pulled by gentlemen amateurs" was "one of the most beautiful and closely contested matches of the day." Mr. Larratt Smith and three gentlemen friends had gone to the trouble of scrubbing and sprucing up the derelict steamboat *Chief Justice* for the occasion. They also dressed themselves "in blue striped guernseys, white trowsers, blue striped shirts, black belts & black neckerchiefs" and, to complete the sporty picture, on their heads they wore blue-striped nightcaps. Unfortunately, their rowing was not as coordinated as their costumes. But there were compensations. After the events were over Smith and his friends enjoyed a lively moonlight

cruise aboard the *City of Toronto* where they "waltzed & quadrilled to the music of the 83rd Regimental Band."

These regattas, which drew contestants from distant lakeside towns, like Kingston, Oswego, Hamilton and Niagara, were apparently not only fun but also morally uplifting. One of the benefits, the *Examiner* editorialized the next September 13th, was promoting unwonted social contact among "the different ranks." In early Victorian Toronto one must never get too carried away by mere pleasure.

Sometime around 1843 Louis Privat opened his Peninsula Hotel and shortly afterward was joined by his brother Louis Joseph Privat.[25] Between them they expanded and operated their resort until 1853. "But it was one thing to open a hotel," John Ross Robertson commented sagely, "it was another thing to make it pay." So, to attract visitors, the Privats opened the Island's first amusement park, the Peninsula Pleasure Grounds next to the hotel, and to transport the visitors they operated a series of ferries, the first of which was another "horse boat," the *Peninsula Packet*. Going against the tide of technology the Privats had purchased a small steamer, which had operated on the Niagara River, and converted her into a two-horse boat. She was not very large—only sixty feet by twenty-three feet—and had an open deck. The paddle wheel on each side was set in motion by a single horse walking on a treadmill. Invariably the union ensign fluttered gaily from the stern as she moved slowly across the bay. She was undoubtedly a colourful and popular addition to the harbour scene. In 1845, the Privats enlarged the *Peninsula Packet* and added three horsepower— for a total of five horses now walking a circular path at the centre of the boat. Under the heading "Cheap Pleasure" the Privats advertised their

One of several horseboats that crossed the bay during the 1830s and '40s, the five horsepower Peninsula Packet *commuted between Maitland's mainland wharf and Privat's Peninsula wharf.*
[William J. Thomson/MTLB]

boat (which in 1849 left Mr. Maitland's wharf at the foot of Church Street five times daily). They even offered a daycare service in 1849—''Children sent without guardians will be taken care of''—and pasturage for horse and cattle, if the beasts came by the first boat.

The horse boat was used until 1850 when she was replaced by the twenty-five horsepower steam ferry *Victoria*, which also ran from Maitland's Wharf. In an ad dated May 28, 1852, in the *British Colonist*, L. J. Privat promised potential patrons that he would ''run no races with Mr. Tinning's Steamboat'' and assured them that he felt ''much more pleasure in the safety of his passengers than in a won race with ill-attended consequences.''

Once on the Peninsula, visitors could go for a walk and enjoy the fresh air, repair to the hotel and sample its fare or enjoy the numerous attractions of the Privats' amusement park, which included, according to John Ross Robertson, ''a merry-go-round and two large swings ... a bowling alley, known as 'Ten Pin Alley' ... a small zoological collection consisting of a bear, a wolf, a white deer, several racoons and two or three eagles ... [as well as] a good deal of amusement of a somewhat miscellaneous nature....'' This latter entertainment included various cruel pastimes—trap pigeon shooting, turkey shooting and shooting a bear with a candle (the candle, Robertson noted, was preceded by a bullet whose existence remained a secret to the gullible spectators).

The Privats' Peninsula Hotel was primarily a summer resort. But it must also have been popular in winter, for in December of 1845 one of the Privat brothers sent a petition to City Council ''praying for the council to interfere to prevent holes being cut in the ice [presumably for fishing or stocking ice houses] near the road established to the Peninsula Hotel.'' Sleighing parties, cariolers and perhaps the odd skater

This detail from J. D. Browne's 1851 Map of the Township of York labels the mainland wharfs and the Privat brothers' Peninsula Hotel, which is shown in the inset as it may have appeared around 1850. [MTLB]

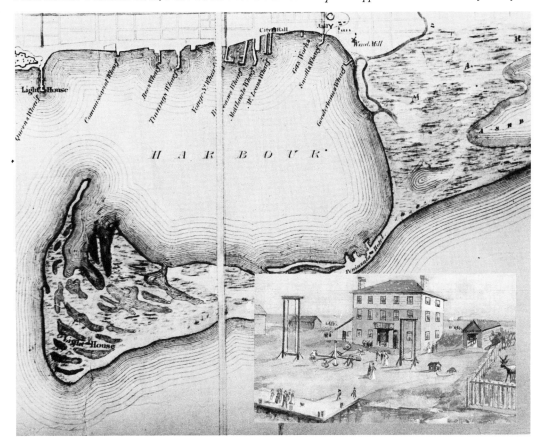

must have welcomed the Privats' fireside and firewater. In fact, by this time the Peninsula Hotel seems to have already developed a reputation as a drinking spot. The righteous Reverend A. W. H. Rose, who visited Toronto in the late forties, observed disapprovingly, "I fear, however, that from its situation, [the hotel] is becoming a sad resort for the drinking part of the community."[26]

Island life, however, was not all fun and games. While many Torontonians were disporting themselves gaily across the bay and about the Island, other poor souls were eking out a grim, mean existence from fishing in the waters off the Peninsula.

Exactly when fishing became commercially important and just when the first fishermen came to live on the Peninsula itself are not known. Back in 1833 a recently arrived immigrant, Henry Evans, petitioned the government for "three acres of waste land on the Peninsula" to use as a base for fishing south and west of the Peninsula. From Evans' petition it is evident that commercial fishing was already well established in the "principal fishing ground" off the Lighthouse, but that no fishermen were yet resident on "the Island." They still returned to the mainland to dry their nets and shelter from storms. "If a House and Sheds were built upon the Island, having a few Acres of land attached to them, for the *very necessary* convenience, and (in part) sustenance, of the Fishermen, when employed in their peculiar avocation," the petitioner argued, "it may be very fairly infered that, they would be enabled to increase considerably the supply of fish, for the York Market; and consequently at a much lower rate than it can now be obtained...."[27] Evans was granted two acres; but, whether he actually followed his "peculiar avocation" or built a place on the Peninsula is unknown.

Just when the City regularized its dealings with the fishermen (if it ever did) is also unknown. As early as 1835 City Council considered raising revenue by renting out the fishing grounds (a scheme which by January 16, 1836, it had to admit, had "wholly failed"). Meanwhile, by the late thirties and early forties fishermen had certainly begun to establish themselves on the Peninsula and build primitive cabins out of the driftwood found along its shores. In 1841 a cluster of shacks was to be found southwest of the Lighthouse, convenient to the richest fishing ground, and somewhat later, according to John George Howard's surveys of 1846 and '47, other "fishermen's shanties" were scattered along "the Narrows" and around "the Tavern" (i.e., Privats Hotel) at the eastern end of the Peninsula.

Although pleasant enough in fine weather, life in these primitive, insubstantial shacks and aboard the small, open fishing boats must have been pretty grim, even terrifying at times—cold, wet and exposed to the ferocious gales that swept across the lake. Periodically the shacks were washed away or both boats and men lost at sea. On one memorable occasion, about the winter of 1840, a fearsome storm swept away a large number of fishermen's huts. The occupants, according to Lightkeeper George Durnan, "only escap[ed] with their lives by running on to the cakes of ice."[28] Nevertheless, life did go on. In 1848, for example, two fishing families, the Wards and the Strowgers, produced babies— each claiming to have produced the first baby born on the Island. And the fishermen, no matter how grim their lives might appear to us, were the first dedicated Islanders—fighting each other and City Hall for the right to continue fishing there.

During the 1840s fishing rights became a matter of great contention, with relations between fishermen and City Hall becoming as tangled

as a fishermen's net caught on a shoal. In the early period fishermen obtained licenses (although some may have skipped this official step) and then simply went out to fish in the general area south of the Peninsula. Some—like David Ward and William Strowger—formed partnerships. Others, presumably, worked independently. Things began to change in 1842 when William and James Wallis asked City Council for permission to clear and have exclusive use of two new fishing grounds off the west coast for a period of four years. Permission was granted and John George Howard laid out new fishing grounds in the spring of 1843. This seems to be the first hint of monopoly.

Then in December 1844 William Geddes, who ultimately became the big kingfisher, began to manoeuvre to create what one group of disgruntled fishermen later called "an unjust monopoly." He spent some £400 to buy out the nets and boats of a dozen or so independent fishermen and obtained their promise not to fish for five years. He also spent money clearing the fishing grounds by removing rubbish and timber and erecting what Council described as "extensive and commodious" buildings to house some thirty to forty men in barrack-like conditions.[29]

In January 1846 Geddes split the fishing community by applying for a seven-year monopoly over all or at least the (profitable) western part of the fishing grounds. One group of independent fishermen, most of whom apparently had had no dealings with Geddes, vehemently opposed his application in order to protect their own freedom of operation. (This group included among others William Warren, James and William Wallace [Wallis?], John and David Ward, John Hanlon and James Durnan.) Another group of twenty-seven loyal employees, who stoutly maintained that Mr. Geddes had had nothing to do with

H. F. Ainslie's 1843 view from the wharf at the New Barracks shows the spray of Niagara Falls across the lake and, closer to home, several neat little fishermen's houses on the Peninsula west of the Lighthouse.
[PAC (C-505)]

their petition, equally vehemently supported Geddes' application.

This latter group painted a very moving picture of the miserable living conditions endured by Peninsula fishermen of that era—especially by the hired hands like themselves—even in the supposedly good times under Mr. Geddes. The "wretchedness and misery [they] suffered" prior to Mr. Geddes' buying out Messrs. Warren & Wallis (among others) seems to have been extreme indeed. When Geddes bought them out that December, both Warren and the Wallises simply turned their hired men out "to the mercy of a severe winter, being filthy, destitute of apparel, and giving [them] only four pence each." Even in better times, when catching plenty of fish, the treatment was "by no means humane"— sometimes receiving "no clothing, no emolument, except now and then" and liable "to

getting your head broke" if they voiced any complaint. When they were turned out "filthy & ragged" in December 1844, Geddes, although having sufficient hands at the time, "took compassion" on them, clothed them and made them feel "comfortable."

What treatment led James Browne and his twenty-seven fellow workers to sing the praises of Mr. Geddes? They explained:

We are now with Mr. Geddes and the treatment we have received from him our appearances will testify, in the first place he procured us long Boots, Pantaloons, Shirts and socks so as to have a change in case of getting Wet, and a luxury never before Known by Fishermen. Every two Men are supplied with a Bed, pillow, 1 Sheet, 2 Blankets and 1 Rug. the fact is by our treatment we greatly resemble Soldiers in a Barrack room, the greatest unanimity and

good will prevails amongst us, no quarrelling, no arbitrary power to domineer over us as formerly by blows and menaces, but Mr. Wm. Strowger who has the management, by his Kindness, and the method by which he orders things to be done commands our good will and Esteem, in regard to sobriety of Conduct there are men here who have for the space of 12 years [since 1834] followed the occupation and they freely assert there never was so much comfort Experienced as at the present time. Even it has been remarked in the City of the uniform good conduct of the fishermen to what it was formerly. On the Sabbath day when formerly we were obliged to work, we observe it as a day of rest and are supplied with Books and Tracts on that day. We must acknowledge Gentlemen that we work far More than we formerly did going out all Winds and weather that we possibly can throw the Seines, but what we used to consider as a toil is a pleasure to us now on account of our being comfortably clad....[30]

*W. H. Bartlett's quaint 1841 print
shows Toronto's outdoor Fish Market,
where the Peninsular fishermen sold
their catch. In May 1848, however, the
City Committee on Wharves and Harbors complained about the "nuisance of
the Present Fish Market" near "a pool
of stagnant water which is so offensive
(sic) that persons are detered from going
to the Market."*   [Clarkson Gordon]

Life for working people anywhere in the 1840s
was harsh. But the hired fishermen on Toronto
Peninsula—who were grateful for a change of
clothes, half a bed, a day off on the Sabbath and
a manager who did not routinely beat them—
seemed to have lived a particularly rude and
rough existence.

City Council agreed that conditions had
improved under Mr. Geddes. Members of the
Committee on Wharves and Harbors paid a
surprise visit to Geddes' establishment on the
Peninsula in January 1846 and they described it as
follows:

Your committee...experianced [sic] an aggreeable

[sic] surprise in finding that Mr. Geddes had
taken the trouble he has in providing for the
comfort of the men employed by him to carry
on the business....

Heretofore it has been remarked that this
particular trade or business has been carried on
in a great measure by Idle and intemperate
Characters. Now your committee can bear
testimony to a very different state of things.

The Buildings erected by Mr. Geddes are
extensive and commodious he has between 30
and 40 men employed there is a degree of
cleanliness observed in the whole management
which does him Great credit and though your
committee visited the place without and (any)
previous notice they found all the men in Mr.

Geddes employ in a perfect state of Sobriety and
presenting a cleanly and respectable appearance.

The committee, therefore, recommended that
Geddes be given an area of the fishing grounds to
the west of the Peninsula for two years at £100
per annum and that the remaining fishing grounds
be divided into two grounds.

The matter, however, did not rest there. The
feuding continued. Over the next few years
various fishermen petitioned for various reasons
until 1849, when exasperated city officials
decided to give Mr. Geddes a seven-year monopoly
on all fishing grounds west of an imaginary
line south from Bay Street (i.e., the western,

most profitable, half of the Peninsula).[31] Geddes was to pay £100 a year, clear one-seventh of his grounds each year and provide a "good and sufficient supply of fish in the Market," whose patrons had earlier complained about lack of fish. With Geddes having a monopoly over the best fishing area, squabbling among the fishermen seems to have subsided.

Throughout the period of the fishing wars City Council's other major obsession regarding the Peninsula was sand. As Toronto continued to grow and to be converted from a town of wood to a city of brick, contractors' carts rumbled over to the sandbar to excavate loads of sand. (One of these contractors was Joseph Bloor, who also ran a brewery in the Rosedale Ravine. On one dramatic occasion in the 1830s, John Ross Robertson related, Bloor's team was dragging a heavy load of sand across thin ice, broke through and was drowned.) Pilfering sand from the Peninsula may have helped hold the city together, but it didn't do much for the source. As a result City Council became concerned about the safety not of contractors like Bloor but of the fragile sandbar. So on March 6, 1843, Council appointed a select committee "to enquire into the present state of the Peninsula ... with a view to restrain the unlimited removal of sand therefrom."

Committee members visited the Peninsula later that month and discovered two places about a quarter mile west of "the Tavern" where "extensive excavations" had been made and such "large quantities of sand" carried away that the ridge of sand separating lake and bay had "almost entirely [been] removed." Should this happen, of course, the result would be "seriously injurious to the Safety and value of the Bay." The committee therefore not only recommended that public notices forbidding such excavations be posted immediately, but also for

the first time recommended that Council apply to the Canadian government for a "license of occupation" so that it could regulate the use of the Peninsula more effectively.

There matters rested for a few years, until the Commissioner of Crown Lands asked City Council early in 1846 if it had any objection to the Crown leasing land on the Peninsula to private individuals. Reporting on March 12, the special committee appointed to investigate the matter concluded that the City did indeed have objections to any "measure, by which the Peninsula or any portion of it should be placed in the hands of any individual or number of individuals for any merely personal purposes." Control should be granted to the City—either by outright grant or by license of occupation—so that the City could control the fisheries and stop the removal of sand. Moreover, the Corporation was the logical authority to make "the improvements which would render the Peninsula a Source of pleasant and healthful recreation and exercise to the Inhabitants of the City generally, for which it is eminently calculated." Negotiations continued and finally, in January 1847, as the bay ice was breaking up, the City was granted not ownership, but a license of occupation for the marsh and Peninsula (for the exorbitant price of £2). The license of occupation may have provided only "feeble tenure," as the *Leader* of July 18, 1853, later suggested, but it was a beginning. From now on City Council would show increasing interest in the development of its Peninsula.

As soon as the City had taken this modest control over the Peninsula, people began applying for leases. The first of these was Reuben Parkinson, a wheelwright by trade, who applied on May 3, 1847. Before dealing with Parkinson and the other applicants, however, City Council

had other more pressing matters to deal with. Toronto was once again attacked by cholera, the worst outbreak in her history, which was brought ashore by the floods of destitute Irish immigrants who were fleeing the potato famine in their native land. Finally, on October 11 the Committee on Wharves and Harbors recommended that the City lease a four-acre lot near what is now Mugg's Island to Parkinson for £1 per annum and subject to such other conditions deemed necessary to protect the "public interest."

Little is known about Parkinson's first hotel. (He and his wife built another better-known hotel some years later on Centre Island.) From John George Howard's surveys and maps we do know that it was built some time during the fall of 1847, that it was a fairly simple, rectangular building overlooking one of the Peninsula's numerous ponds and that it was a "tavern." Parkinson obviously hoped to attract some of the drinking and eating public who frequented the Privats' establishment down near the Narrows of the Peninsula.

We also know that Parkinson at some point built a wharf so that his patrons could row, sail or steam more conveniently to his resort. Beyond this little is known, except that it was listed on the tax rolls for 1848, '49 and '51 and must have been fairly substantial since it was valued at £25 to £30 when fishermen's houses were valued at £3 to £7.10 and the Privats' main building was valued at £25 to £30.

One of the more unusual sights patrons standing on Parkinson's or Privat's Wharf might have seen in the summer of 1849 was Tinning's *Cigar Boat*. This bizarre contraption was a steam-powered paddle-wheeled trimaran, each pontoon being the shape of a cigar. She was "anything but a success," according to John Ross Robertson,

and when severe floods swept away the Don Bridge in the spring of 1850 she was used as a temporary pontoon bridge (much to the annoyance of enterprising local ferrymen who tried to sink her). She never crossed the bay again.

Once City Council had its license of occupation it began casting covetous glances in the direction of the Peninsula and rapidly revised its earlier opposition to leasing land to private individuals. It had John George Howard survey the Peninsula in December 1847 and by the following spring it was hatching some fairly grand schemes. On May 29, 1848, the Committee on Wharves and Harbors reported that it had "inspected the Peninsula, with a view to laying it out in lots for the purpose of leasing to parties," because they had "no doubt that a handsome amount couuld [sic] be realised to the City annually whilst

(Above) *The one and only Tinning's Cigar Boat—"anything but a success."*
[C. H. J. Snider/MTLB]

(Right) *John George Howard, the architect of the Provincial Lunatic Asylum at 999 Queen Street West, was no stranger to grand designs. But this proposal for the Peninsula c. 1850 never got off the ground. The Peninsula, with its Lighthouse, fishermen and two main hotels (Parkinson's in the west and Privat's in the east) remained relatively undeveloped for the next two decades.* [CTA]

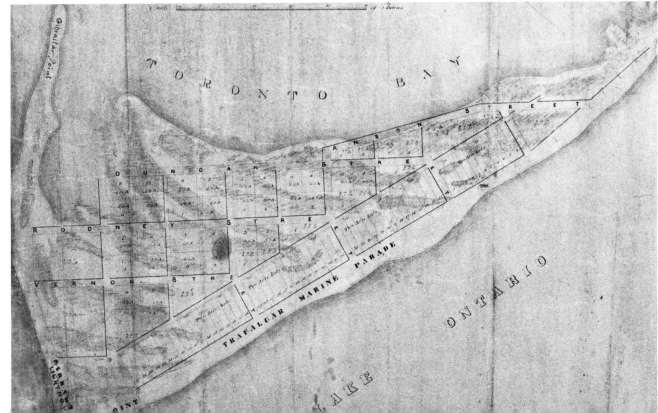

the peninsula would become the most beautiful spot in the vicinity of the City of Toronto.'' (Councils of a hundred years later would adopt precisely the same view.) As a result Howard prepared the first residential plan for the Peninsula (dated c. 1850). Across the south shore (later Lakeshore Avenue, Centre Island) he placed fifty-seven two-acre lots along the patriotically named Trafalgar Marine Parade (reminiscent of English seaside resorts) and elsewhere he placed four- to five-acre lots along streets named after admirals of the Royal Navy—Vernon, Rodney, Duncan and Anson. Nothing came of Howard's grand scheme,[32] but it introduced a theme upon which later Councils would play innumerable variations.

The fishermen, Lighthouse keeper and tavern keepers on the Peninsula were mercifully safe from one of the major events of 1849, which had a profound effect on the physical development of Toronto—the calamitous fire of the night of April 6, which destroyed some ten to fifteen acres of the downtown heart of the city. The lurid orange sky above Toronto as well as the flames themselves were visible all the way across the lake in St. Catharines; so it is more than likely that Peninsula residents, awakened by the fire bells ringing out from atop St. James Cathedral, lined the shore during that "wild night of woe" to watch helplessly but safely as "in a few hours a considerable portion of the city was reduced to a heap of smoking ruins."[33]

In 1850 the Canadian capital returned (temporarily) to Toronto just in time for a period of tremendous growth and prosperity stimulated by "railway fever." On October 15, 1841, Toronto officially entered the Railway Age, with important consequences for her waterfront. A civic holiday was declared and twenty thousand excited spectators (in a city with a total population of roughly thirty thousand) flocked excitedly

to the lakefront to witness the sod-turning ceremony for the Northern Railway, the first to be built in Toronto. They saw Mayor Bowes, "resplendent in a cocked hat, sword, knee breeches, silk stockings and shoes, with silver buckles," make an effusive speech—Mayor Bowes was a great proponent of railways both as public official and private investor. Lord Elgin was equally effusive. Then Lady Elgin placed her dainty foot on the silver shovel and turned the first sod. The cheers of the jubilant crowd resounded across the lake and Lady Elgin retired, too exhausted by her labours to attend the gala ball that evening.[34]

Over the next few years the proposed Esplanade (i.e., the first southward extension of the shoreline built to accommodate the railways) was almost drowned in a sea of political bickering and egregious conflicts of interest as the Northern, the Grand Trunk and the Great Western jockeyed for position and public favours.[35] But by 1859 The Esplanade had been built and the face of the waterfront permanently altered. A barrier had

been created between the city and the lake (a barrier which is only now beginning to be penetrated) and the railroad car was replacing the schooner and the steamboat as the principal form of transportation. Toronto in the latter part of the century would no longer be first and foremost a port city. It would be a railway capital.

Nevertheless, in the 1850s people still came to Toronto by boat. Shortly after the grand sod-turning ceremony Jenny Lind—the world famous Swedish Nightingale—turned Toronto on its ear. Because of the huge crowds, Miss Lind arrived—like a modern-day pop star—by the back door. While a great throng of well-wishers was waiting to greet her at the Yonge Street Wharf, she alighted at Queen's Wharf some distance away and was quietly conducted to her hotel. She gave not one but three concerts in the splendid new St. Lawrence Hall where, with her famous "Bird Song" and "Echo Song"—and most especially with her rendering of "God Save the Queen"—she won the hearts of Toronto. When she left Toronto aboard the *Chief*

Jenny Lind received a warmer welcome than these unfortunates, who had to be deposited on the ice in the winter of 1852 when the Chief Justice Robinson, *portrayed by William Armstrong, could proceed no closer to shore.* [MTLB]

Justice Robinson at 7:30 A.M. the morning of October 24, her departure seemed to be more fitting than her arrival. In spite of the early hour a crowd was present and the band of the 71st was on hand to give a farewell salute as she drifted off around the Peninsula to conquer more hearts in Niagara.

Steamboats like the *Chief Justice Robinson* brought rich and poor alike to Toronto. Ever since the 1820s black American slaves had been following the North Star to freedom in Canada.[36] As early as 1826 the soulful strains of gospel songs were to be heard floating across the waters not of Chesapeake Bay but of Toronto Bay, as a dozen former slaves gathered on its shore for prayer meetings. By the 1850s, especially after the passage of the notorious Fugitive Slave Act in 1850,[37] a continuous stream of fleeing former slaves was pouring into Canada via the famous Underground Railroad. Lake steamers played an important role in some of the these escapes. In one dramatic case a steamer rescued a poor, half-drowned fugitive floating in Lake Ontario on a wooden gate. By the summer of 1852 the Toronto *Colonist* noted that every boat arriving in the harbour from the United States seemed to carry fugitives and lakeside wharfs must have been the scene of great rejoicing and prayerful thanksgiving, although the new arrivals still had to escape the clutches of bounty hunters who stalked the streets of Toronto to kidnap former slaves with guile and bowie knives.

Another visitor to Toronto in the early 1850s was Susanna Moodie, who had spent a decade roughing it in the bush near Lakefield, Ontario, and was then living near Belleville. She was impressed by Toronto, which exceeded her "most sanguine expectations"; but she was most unimpressed by the Peninsula:

The glow of early day was brightening in the

On Emancipation Day, August 1, 1854, Scott's Brass Band led a parade of abolitionists down to Browne's wharf to greet the Arabian *(featured in this detail from Whitefield's 1854 panorama), which had brought a boatload of Hamiltonians down the lake, past the Peninsula, to join in Toronto's lavish celebrations.* [THB/Marine Museum]

east, as the steamer approached Toronto. We rounded the point of the interminable, flat, swampy island that stretches for several miles in front of the city, and which is thinly covered with scrubby-looking trees. The land lies so level with the water that it has the appearance of being half-submerged, and from a distance you only see the tops of trees. I have been informed that the name of Toronto has been derived from this circumstance, which in Indian literally means, "Trees in the water."

If the island rather takes from, than adds to, the beauty of the place, it is not without great practical advantages, as to it the city is mainly indebted for its sheltered and very commodious harbour.[38]

Torontonians, however, continued to flock to

the Peninsula for picnics, boating, bathing and general goodnatured frolicking. As the *Empire* reported on September 1, 1854, "the Island is pretty well thronged with visitors on a warm afternoon." Larratt Smith, by now a family man, left this report of a summer visit in September 1851: "Sunday 7th. Very scorching hot with temperature at 88, the hottest day this year. Yesterday we took the children & all went with [Walter] Cassels to the Island, but returned at 6 in the steamer *Victoria* [from Privat's Wharf]. Eliza suffering from rheumatism in the head and face...."

In the early 1850s, plans were hatched to found what would become for a time the largest yacht club in the world—the Royal Canadian

Yacht Club. The now elegant RCYC, however, had humble beginnings. Around 1850 several keen yachtsmen (like Captain W. H. Fellows; physician, and City Coroner Dr. E. M. Hodder; future City Treasurer H. H. Harmon; and civil engineer cum artist and future Island resident William Armstrong) began meeting to discuss the project. First they sat on flour barrels and sacks of produce in a little warehouse on Melinda Street and then they moved to the relative comfort of a room over John Steel's Saloon on King Street. Thus fortified by flour and malt,

these sailors established the Toronto Boat Club. In 1852 the club was renamed the Toronto Yacht Club, its laws and regulations were first published and its happy activities were well under way. A ''very popular amusement'' in these early days was ''follow the leader'': six, eight, ten or more boats would meet on a Saturday, select one for a leader and fall in line, following him ''wheresoever the winds would carry them'' about the bay and across to the Peninsula. These ''pleasant little trips'' would sometimes last until the following day and were

''often supplemented by a dinner at Privats''' where ''the gentlemen had their little gaieties.''[39]

The yacht club's first clubhouse was serviceable but *not* impressive: a leaky scow moored near the foot of Simcoe Street, west of Rees's wharf. As the muskrats burrowed into the hull beneath them, club officers had visions (some thought delusions) of grandeur: they petitioned the Queen to allow their club to call itself ''Royal.'' And *mirabile dictu* in August 1854 word filtered back to this distant corner of the Empire that Her Majesty had graciously consented. ''We rejoice

A Toronto and Huron locomotive chugs picturesquely along the shoreline while members of Toronto's new yacht club hurtle past Queen's Wharf Lighthouse, toward the safety of the Bay. The members of the club may have been "getting pretty well experienced in this fashionable amusement" according to the Leader *of July 19, 1853, but the yachtsmen portrayed in this dramatic engraving for* Gleason's Pictorial Drawing Room Companion *of October 8, 1853, seem to be hovering on the edge of disaster.*

to hear of the honour conferred on this splendid Club," the *Empire* reported on August 18. "A better or more loyal set of fellows than the members of it are not to be found in her Majesty's Dominions. Success attend them."

Success did attend them, although in 1858 the muskrats precipitated a temporary financial crisis when they sank the clubhouse scow. Club members promptly bought the hull of the old lake steamer *Provincial*, moored it between Tinning's and Rees's Wharfs and refitted it as a new clubhouse. The *Provincial*, however, had her annoying little habits, which club secretary (from 1859-1868) William Armstrong discovered to his cost. "Often was I called up in the middle of the night with the information that she had broken loose," he later told John Ross Robertson, "and then I had to go down and put in the rest of the night getting her fast again." Eventually the *Provincial* solved this particular problem by filling with water and sinking onto the bottom of the bay with her deck above the water. She then served her purpose well until 1868 when some member, with excess zeal, pumped her out and refloated her. She resumed her wandering ways, broke loose, blew out into the middle of the bay, was frozen in the ice and became a wreck. When the City blew her up as a menace to navigation, the club built its first clubhouse proper in 1869-70, a building described by John Ross Robertson as "large and commodious and nearly opposite the Parliament Buildings, on Front Street," on the bayshore west of Simcoe Street. That grand addition to the waterfront, however, was some years in the future.

On the Peninsula in the 1850s changes were under way. In 1853 the Privats sold the Peninsula Hotel to John Quinn. (It later became popularly known as Quinn's Hotel.) Quinn added a second

steamer to the *Victoria's* route, the *Citizen*, which, he advertised, was "built expressly for the trade with every regard for the comfort and safety of her passengers." Furthermore there was "no magazine for gun-powder on board and will not carry powder under any pretense." (Island matters have often been explosive, but seldom literally so.) The return fare was only eight cents and the "accommodating host of the Peninsula Hotel" could now provide a "convenient" half-hourly service for his patrons rather than simply an hourly service. In 1856 the enterprising Quinn initiated a new service for bathers. Early risers could catch a steamer at five-thirty or six and return at six-forty-five "giving ample time for merchants and others to return before business hours."

Competition on the Island route heated up considerably the following year, 1857, when tough old Captain Bob Moodie entered the race for the Island business with his new pleasure steamer, modestly called the *Bob Moodie*. She was, according to the *Leader* of June 2, "furnished in a very superior and handsome manner" and, best of all, she was speedy, able to make as many as four trips an hour. By the end of June, the competition between the steamers to the Island had become very spirited indeed. Moodie had trimmed his trips back to three an hour—still preferable to "the slow and tiresome rate formerly maintained" on the route. But he perhaps let his competitive nature get the best of him when he announced, ungenerously, that "in case a gale should arise, passengers by the other line [Quinn's] need not expect to return in this boat, as Capt. Moodie will in such occasions only carry his own passengers."[40] Quinn soon responded by engaging the equally speedy *Welland*, which made trips every twenty minutes from Maitland's Wharf at the height of the afternoon. Further-

more, in implied contrast to Moodie's gruffness, Quinn's passengers could "expect to receive from him that kindness which he has always shown to passengers to the Island."[41] The slower *Citizen* would transport anyone wishing to travel after three-thirty. By mid-July Moodie and Quinn seem to have come to an accommodation. A season ticket for either line would be applicable on both. And Moodie's (new) *Lady Elgin* would make her trips to Quinn's Wharf itself.

In the early 1850s another innkeeper had established himself on the Peninsula, John Glendinning. Unfortunately, little is known about Glendinning and his establishment. "John Glendinning, Inn Keeper" first appeared on the tax roll for the eastern portion of the Peninsula in 1852 when his establishment was valued at £25. And in 1858 Glendinning's buildings were valued at £100, £20 more than those of his better-known rival Quinn.[42]

The fact that Glendinning's inn was substantial is confirmed by a report of the Toronto Regatta held October 3, 1854. The weather was not ideal—"cloudy and portended squally." Nevertheless a large number of Toronto's citizens congregated at Glendinning's Hotel on the Peninsula to watch the contests, while the steamer *Victoria* chugged festively about the bay with Scott's Brass Band thumping gaily on board. The course centred on Glendinning's. From a boat moored in front of the hotel sportsmen were to make for a crib moored at the eastern end of the bay, then they were to head for a buoy floating west of Glendinning's and then back to the starting point—in all, about three miles. Betting was heavy. Oarsman Thomas Tinning, as usual, won the Championship of the Bay in *Her Majesty*, Michael O'Harra defeated his "very determined [Peninsular] opponent" David Ward in the "most beautifully contested race of the day'' and J. Glendinning seems to have put his own oar in the water, too, but was ''easily'' defeated by John Tinning in his *Sea Pigeon*. Perhaps his mind was on the post-race festivities: ''In the evening about fifty sat down to a splendid supper, got up in Glendinning's best style. After full justice was done to the good things provided, the usual toasts were given, the Company separated at an early hour, well pleased by the amusement which had been afforded them by the members of the Toronto Regatta Club.''[43]

Spirited regattas like this were held throughout the period. Each year large crowds of spectators turned out, colourfully decorated yachts and steamers dotted the bay, splendid bands played rousing tunes and determined oarsmen and sailors tested their skills. (Thomas Tinning became the perennial Champion of the Bay in this pre-Ned Hanlan era.) Sometimes, however, the weather was troublesome, delighting either oarsmen or sailors but rarely both. In September 1856, for example, the *Leader* reported that ''the calmness of the weather'' may have pleased the rowers but it ''proved a great source of mortification to the Yachters.''

On occasion, the weather caused far more serious consequences than mortification or vexation. In the pre-dawn hours of November 29, 1856, for example, Captain Sinclair was trying to bring his new steamer the *Monarch* safely around the Peninsula in a fierce winter storm. There was a heavy sea from the east, it was very dark and it was snowing so heavily that he couldn't make out the Lighthouse beacon. When he judged that he should be clear of the Point, he turned the boat toward the city only to discover that he had misjudged his position. He tried to turn out again toward the lake but a heavy swell drove the boat onto the clay shelving

On December 30, 1856, some of the Peninsula's leading citizens posed for William Armstrong near the wreck of the Monarch, including young William Ward, son of David Ward (#4), rival hotel keepers Emily Parkinson (#8) and John Glendinning (#6); and Armstrong himself (#1).   [MTLB]

of the Peninsula. Her deck cargo was swept away, her hold filled with water and her crew only made it to shore ''with difficulty,'' battling high seas, slippery footing, numbing cold and stinging, wind-driven snow.[44] *The Monarch* was a complete wreck, but she soon became a well-known Island landmark.

Just a few days later another violent snowstorm hit Lake Ontario. Toronto was pelted by sleet,

a number of disasters occurred out on the lake and, closer to home, the schooner *J.C. Beard*, with a cargo of 200 tons of coal, was ''driven ashore at the far side of the Island near Glindinning's [sic] Hotel.'' Happily, the *Leader* of December 4 recorded, ''no lives were lost.'' The crew, presumably, thankfully warmed themselves by Glendinning's fireside and Peninsular fishermen no doubt warmed themselves for the rest of the winter around fires stoked by coal scavenged from the *Beard*'s lost cargo.

Throughout this period lake storms were also drastically altering the shape of the Peninsula, much to the distress of many Torontonians. As early as February 1853 a complete breach was made through the treeless, narrow neck of the Peninsula east of Quinn's Hotel. This breach filled in, but further destruction was an ever-present threat. Meanwhile, the condition of the Peninsula was made worse by the continued removal of sand for building purposes (and perhaps to provide land-fill for the growing Esplanade).[45] In February 1854, therefore, members of the Committee on Wharves and Harbors again went on an inspection tour. Their visit alarmed them enormously: "The whole of that Barrier which has formed and hitherto protected our Noble harbour is in a most insecure and unsatisfactory state," they reported on February 6. The area east of "Privats" (Quinn's) was severely eroded. And the area west of "Privats," although heavily treed, was "by no means secure." Although no breach had been made, there were four places between "Privats" and the Lighthouse where heavy seas had flowed across the low-lying ground into the bay (in a manner not unlike a hundred years later). "It would be unwise," the committee concluded, "to permit sand to be taken from any part of the main ridge of the Peninsula." But because sand was "so necessary for building purposes" they reserved an area northeast of the Lighthouse on the bayside where contractors would be permitted to dig sand for the time being. Clearly, however, "some well-designed plan for the preservation of that narrow belt of sand upon the safety of which the Harbour of Toronto may be said to depend for its very existence" would have to be adopted.

In addition to this erosion at the eastern end,

the entrance to the harbour at the western end was developing into a problem. It was becoming narrower as the Peninsula extended northward from the western point. The concerned Harbour Commission (created in 1850) therefore decided to offer prizes for the best three reports on how to preserve and protect the harbour. The anxious City Council also decided to contribute to the prize money. Some sharp scientific minds were drawn to the problem of the Peninsula. The first "premium" prize was awarded to Henry Houle Hind (a professor of chemistry and geology at the University of Toronto who had a taste for westward exploration), the second premium prize to Sandford Fleming (best known for his invention of a system of standardized time zones and his dream of a transcontinental railroad) and the third premium prize to architect Kivas Tully (whose own plan for The Esplanade, with public open space, seems to have been more in the public interest than the final version then being built on the mainland). A special fourth prize was awarded, diplomatically, to Harbour Master Hugh Richardson. The writers were split on the issue of whether a permanent Eastern Gap should be created or whether the integrity of the Peninsula should be reinforced. But not much came of their efforts. The Western Channel was dredged and a fairly ineffectual thirteen-hundred-foot wooden breakwater was constructed along the southern shore in an effort to hold back the lake.

As the harbour commissioners dithered, public pressure was being exerted to protect and improve "the Island." The *Leader* of July 18, 1856, called the harbour commissioners "a precious set of old women" and condemned their ineffective breakwater as "a very poor scarecrow" vainly trying "to close a channel which the elements have declared shall be open."

Long after the stormy demise of his Peninsula Hotel, an elderly John Quinn, kitted up in full regimental regalia, posed for this portrait in a mainland studio. [Frank Oster]

The editors were heartily in favour of an eastern entrance. They went on to bemoan the current condition of "the Island" (in terms Mrs. Moodie would have applauded) as "a wretched, foresaken-looking place" so changed from the natural beauty known to the Indians years before, and made one of the earliest pleas for the City to take action "to render it an attractive place of public resort":

There are few places so capable of being turned into a delightful summer resort, and yet the only thing that you can find there is a good cool breeze. Nature has done its part, but man nothing; nay less than nothing; for he has not even left all the natural beauties which he found. Of couse nobody expects the Corporation to make tea gardens and summer houses at the Island, while the greater part of the streets are of mere mud; but if any private company could be found who would undertake to effect such improvements as would render the Island an attractive and agreeable resort, they ought to get the opportunity. As no company could improve the whole Island, perhaps the greater half would be sufficient for public purposes. The first thing to be done would be to plant trees, to make gardens, to build light and suitable buildings; and to provide various in and out-door recreations.

The Commission and the Council, however, did little to respond to these suggestions. In December of that year winter storms tore away more beach and battered Quinn's Hotel—"the doors and windows were beaten in, and everything outside swept away" according to Harbour Master Hugh Richardson in January 1857. By September of 1857 the back part of the hotel had been washed away and the bowling alley was about half submerged. During the winter of 1857-58, Quinn renovated the hotel and built a small shed to the west—just in case.

Finally nature herself resolved the long-standing issue of whether or not there was to be an eastern entrance to the harbour. On April 13, 1858, Mrs. Quinn was preparing for a party—a celebration for the workmen who had just finished renovating the hotel. Early in the afternoon, a storm gathered and John Quinn wisely decided to postpone the dinner. Taking his oldest child, seven-year-old Jenny, with him for company, Quinn ferried his workmen back across the bay to the city. While he was still in the city the storm broke with a vengeance. The wind whistled out of the northeast, slamming against the wooden walls of the hotel, threatening to flatten them with its force. Meanwhile, the waves on the lake were breaking higher and nearer until the scrawny cedar post breakwater was submerged in the foam, completely unable to contain the storm's fury. While John Quinn and little Jenny were desperately fighting their way around the eastern end of the Peninsula, the howling hurricane was tearing the hotel apart and the giant waves were carving chunks out of the disappearing beach. When they finally made their way back to the hotel, the scene that met their eyes was a nightmarish one. Years later Jenny still recalled it vividly:

We found mother balancing on a board in the churning water with my baby brother in her arms and my sister Elizabeth clinging precariously to her skirts. She seemed to be standing on the only timber left from the hotel, which was disintegrating and shortly disappeared.

Mother never quite recovered, and they had to send me to Rochester friends for a year.[46]

Quinn was able to rescue his terrified family and move them safely through the swirling, debris-filled water to the little emergency shed further inland.

Finally, in the stormy, pre-dawn darkness of April 14, the last vestiges of Quinn's Hotel were completely washed away. The roaring waves of Lake Ontario sliced their way through the neck of the Peninsula and in a few dramatic hours created a channel four to five feet deep. By May 30 the new Eastern Gap was wide enough and deep enough for two schooners, the *Eliza* and the *Highland Chief*, to sail through.

The Peninsula was, at last, indubitably the Island.

5

Toronto Island in the Age of Ned Hanlan

At five years of age Ned Hanlan was already making news. On September 6, 1860, the sturdy "young navigator" clambered into his skiff on the Island, bent his small torso over battered oars and proceeded to row right across Toronto Bay to the Market Wharf. Later admirers suggested that a boat had been young Ned's baby carriage and pointed out that his favourite toy was a mock rowing shell—a two-inch wooden plank tapered at both ends, with old oars mounted on outriggers. It seems that Ned played on that shell the way other children play on tricycles and, as he grew up, his love of rowing kept him busy, healthy and for the most part out of hot water.[1]

Ned was born on July 12, 1855, and brought to the Island as an infant. While his Irish-immigrant father John Hanlan (or Hanlon) fished in the waters off the Island, Ned played on the sandy beaches, explored the marshy ponds with his playmates, watched the fishermen prepare their boats—and rowed. He rowed everywhere. He rowed for fun. He rowed to visit his friends. He rowed to the mainland to do errands and to go to school. And when the bay or the lake was too rough he skimmed over the glassy surface of the protected lagoons of the Island, which provided a perfect environment for a future world champion sculler.

Meanwhile, the Hanlan family, like all Island families, had to weather the storms that periodically battered their home. As early as June 1858 John Hanlan asked for (and received) permission from the City to move his "shanty" to higher, presumably safer, ground. Apparently the Hanlans first lived at the eastern end of the Island (not far from the David Ward family) and sometime around 1865 moved to the western tip, which later became known as Hanlan's Point. Their westward migration has been colourfully described by John Ross Robertson: "During a terrific gale [their house] was washed away by the raising waters of the lake. As soon as the storm was over the family, nothing daunted, gathered their scattered timbers together, built a raft on which they placed their property, and drifted up the bay, with a fair east wind. They chanced to ground at the present Hanlan's Point, and here they built their home and left a name."[2]

Five years earlier, on September 6, 1860, the day that five-year-old Ned Hanlan was pulling his way across a vast, open bay, Torontonians were working at a fever pitch to put the final touches on the extravagant decorations for the next day's arrival of His Royal Highness the Prince of Wales.

During the afternoon of September 7, several steamers (including Captain Moodie's Island ferry the *Fire Fly*) crammed with "excursionists" set off to meet and escort the prince to Toronto. Thousands of spectators covered the embankment overlooking the bay, while ten thousand more jammed the specially built amphitheatre at the foot of John Street. Behind and above them stretched the magnificent sixty-five-foot-high triple arch, decked with flags and evergreens and flowers and gilded mottoes of welcome. Late in the afternoon a light rain dampened the patriotic crowd, but not its enthusiasm. Thousands of eyes searched the horizon. Finally, at six o'clock, the *Kingston* and her escort were sighted "outside the Island." Thousands craned their necks expectantly as the flotilla puffed past the Point and made its way through a bay crowded with yet more steamers, yachts and darting rowboats. As the *Kingston* landed, an enormous cheer erupted from the "great multitude"— "a vast volume of sound, thrilling, soul-stirring, heart-heaving."

(Above) *William Armstrong painted fellow members of the Royal Canadian Yacht Club shouting loyal huzzahs in the foreground while Torontonians by the thousand crowd the shoreline near the John Street triumphal arch to greet the Prince of Wales' arrival aboard the* Kingston *on September 7, 1860.*
[The National Gallery of Canada]

(Left) *Ned Hanlan "was born on the Island, and a boat was his baby carriage," commented one local journalist of the world champion sculler. "His infant hands went halfway round an oar while other infants of his age were fingering teething rings."* [MTLB]

In the waning light the nineteen-year-old prince stepped quickly ashore to receive and acknowledge the great welcome being offered. The national anthem was sung by the "five thousand little voices" of a colossal children's choir. And, as darkness fell, a great procession filed into the lakeside arena—led, appropriately enough on this eve of the American Civil War, by "the coloured men," followed by the usual assortment of firemen, militia, national societies, officials, bands and school children. The ladies were "waving their handkerchiefs" and the men were "nearly killing themselves with shouting the loyal hurrahs," while several bands played the national anthem.[3]

When the prince and his party drove off along the principal streets they found them elaborately decorated with bunting and flags and evergreens and, after dark, by shining illuminations. Until late at night Toronto was aglow with patriotic fervor, stunning illuminations and splendid fireworks—all especially impressive when seen as a whole shimmering above the bay from the vantage point of the Island. And for the next five days "Toronto gave itself up to the delirium of enthusiasm" inspired by the royal visit.[4]

Royal Canadian Yacht Club members (still using the peripatetic *Provincial* as their clubhouse) were not to be left out in the cold; though they were left out in the rain. They organized a grand regatta for September 11, 1860. When the prince returned that day from his brief train trip to Collingwood, he was serenaded by yet

William Armstrong had a love-hate relationship with the RCYC's second clubhouse, the wilful Provincial, which he had to wrestle back to shore on more than one stormy night. In his painting from around 1869, the Provincial is immobile at last—iced into the middle of the Bay, and near the end of her days. [MTLB]

another children's choir and then escorted from the railroad station to the grand amphitheatre, where he was greeted by the RCYC's commodore, Lieutenant Colonel William Smith Durie. The principals then proceeded to a pier near the RCYC clubhouse to watch the start. As a great crowd elbowed and pushed forward and the fleet of yachts "strained and tugged at their moorings like dogs at the leash," according to John Ross Robertson, the rains descended. The prince, however, refused to scurry to safety, muttering "I must see the start," and even refused the offer of a tattered-looking old umbrella held out by one of his many admirers.

Finally, just before noon, the signal gun was fired and the yachts began to plunge through heavy seas toward the first buoy off the harbour shore of the Island near the Eastern Gap. "Notwithstanding the rain, the scene presented

was very fine," the *Leader* reported the next day. "The yachts standing out to sea with every stitch of canvas set, the smaller boats flitting about in every direction, the enthusiastic crowds lining The Esplanade, the singing of the children in the amphitheatre behind—all contributed to the excitement of the occasion." Unfortunately, the charming prince could not stay; so "amid the thundering cheers of the immense concourse of spectators present" he was whisked away to his waiting carriage.

Meanwhile, drama was high out on the high seas. The racing fleet had run back across the bay and out the Western Gap into the open lake and into trouble. The *Canada*, for example, ran aground, while several other yachts lost stays and halyards and had to limp ingloriously back into port. Through it all that "crack Toronto boat," the *Rivet*, sailed by the distinguished Blake

brothers—Samuel and future Liberal Party leader Edward—captured and kept the lead. Not surprisingly, however, the rowing matches did not come off, the *Leader* also reported, "owing to the unfavourable state of the weather."

To commemorate his visit to Toronto and the RCYC, the prince donated the Prince of Wales Cup (described by the *London Daily News* of August 17, 1861, as "about one of the handsomest things of the kind"), which has sent yachts spinning round and about the Island and lake ever since 1861 when, according to the *Globe*, "a brilliant assemblage of ladies, including many of the youth, beauty and fashion of the City" watched the *Wide Awake* become the first winner.

Young Ned Hanlan, of course, was more interested in rowing than sailing races. In the 1860s, as he grew up, he had before him the inspiring spectacle of annual regattas on the bay.

There, gentlemen amateurs and his father's fishermen friends competed for (separate) prizes. In August 1866, for example, the newly formed Toronto Rowing Club held its second annual regatta. The speedy steamer *Rothesay Castle* carried spectators over the course, while the stylish 17th Regiment Band entertained one and all. In the four-mile ''Fishermen's Race,'' Hanlan's older friends J. Durnan (son of the lighthouse keeper) and Robert Berry (a muscular young black man who fished for the Wards) joined a certain W. Montgomery to propel their ''Silver Arrow'' to victory and a prize of $30. Among the other competitors were P. Gray, another fisherman and resident of the western part of the Island, and mainlander T. Tinning, who again won the silver cup for Championship of the Bay.

But these friendly waters could also be treacherous. On Sunday May 11, 1862, fifteen-year-old William Ward gathered his five younger sisters (Rose, five; Jane, seven; Cecilia, almost nine; Phoebe, eleven; and Mary Ann, twelve-and-a-half) for a cruise on the bay. It was a gusty day and as he was launching the small craft from the beach before his family's house ''on the Marsh shore'' near the mouth of the ''little Don,'' his father, David, tried to dissuade him from embarking. But William was already an experienced sailor and continued on his way. The carefree group sailed up and down the bay for about an hour when William, steering with an oar, decided to come about and return to his home, about a thousand yards away. Young William related the tragic consequences at the coroner's inquest on May 13:

> The wind caught the sail and I slipped off the stern into the water. The boat then filled and capsized, throwing us all into the water. My sisters all rushed toward me in the water. By

This View From Centre Island drawn by D. C. O'Brien in 1862 shows a couple of Island fishermen beside the treacherous bay where that May young William Ward's boat capsized and his five younger sisters drowned. [MTLB]

(Below) *Engraver and long-time summer Islander Joseph T. Rolph painted this rear view of David Ward Sr.'s rustic "homestead" on the edge of Ward's Pond, Centre Island in the 1880's.* [MTLB]

great exertions I righted the boat and got three of the girls out of the water. They all died in the boat. One of the others got into the boat through her own exertions and the remaining one held on by the gunwale. The sail again filled, capsizing the boat a second time. The three dead bodies were washed away. Phoebe hung on by the side of the boat as long as she could and then went down.[5]

Fortunately for William, a man on The Esplanade saw the accident, ran to find a boat and arrived at the scene in time to drag the exhausted youth from the water. The bodies of four of the little girls were found a couple of days later, but the fifth body was not located for ten agonizing days. Naturally, the experience was a traumatic one for William, who subsequently became famous for his lifesaving activities.

Exactly when David Ward moved his family toward the centre of the Island, to the edge of what became Ward's Pond, is not known. One story is that after this tragedy the children's distraught mother paced up and down the shore and her husband decided to move her away from the scene of the tragedy. Whether they moved then or a few years later, the David Wards were certainly established in their new location by the mid-1860s.

Although few changes were made on the Island in the early 1860s, the city was experiencing a boom. The source of this new prosperity was the American Civil War, which had broken out in April 1861. While Americans were busy making widows, Canadians were busy making dollars. Like other Canadian centres Toronto was overrun with commissariat agents purchasing stores for the army and the Toronto waterfront was alive with activity. Commissariat agents were not the only agents in town. Spies—notably Confederate spies—stalked Toronto's streets.

Sometimes they availed themselves of local talent. Even William Armstrong—artist, engineer, prominent member of the decade-old Royal Canadian Yacht Club and later Island cottager—became marginally involved in this shadowy world of espionage. He helped a group of Confederate army officers in Toronto send a vital message to Confederate President Jefferson Davis in Richmond, Virginia: "I suggested the reducing of the message by photography onto mica, which plan was adopted. I printed in large letters on a flat paper the message and reduced it to the size of five buttons. The negatives were then placed under the usual coverings of buttons by Mr. Walker, tailor of King Street. The messenger wore the coat and got through."[6] Jefferson Davis himself was among the Confederate officials who visited Toronto. He stayed on Front Street at the Queen's Hotel, which, with the impartiality of the business place, also

hosted General Sherman, the burner of Atlanta, during a brief postwar visit in July 1866.

During the war American tourists (put off by war-inflated prices, not to mention war-inflicted damage at home) travelled North to vacation. In Toronto, as elsewhere, the Southern visitors seemed to be more genteel and acceptable than their pushy Yankee compatriots.[7] No doubt both sides were represented among the summer visitors who flocked to the Island's shores, some of them bound for the only hotel then operating there, Mrs. Moodie's short-lived establishment.

Although many Canadians benefited from the war and many sympathized with the Union cause, stresses between Canada and the United States increased. There was for several years a very real fear of open conflict, which the building in British ports of Confederate blockade runners like the *Letter A* and the *Letter B* did little to

The Captains of the former Civil War blockade runners the Rothesay *(shown in this drawing by C. H. J. Snider) and the* Chicora *liked to engage in spirited, occasionally dangerous, cross-lake races.* [MTLB]

diminish. Fortunately, nothing came of the antagonism and Toronto later acquired two speedy steamers, the *Rothesay Castle* (formerly the *Letter A* and later known as the *Southern Belle*) and the *Chicora* (formerly the *Letter B*).

When peace returned to the United States, peace of mind did not return to Canada. Quite the reverse. There was an increased fear of retaliation by the victorious, now idle, Union Army. In the late spring of 1866 the fear of invasion turned into a reality, although the perpetrators were not the Union Army, but the Fenian Brotherhood.

The Fenians were a fanatical Irish-American group in favour of uniting all Ireland. They devised the grand scheme of hitting at the hated British by invading the British colony of Canada. The frightened Canadian government called up twenty thousand volunteers, border forts were alerted and Britain again sent regulars to Canada. The British 47th, stationed in the lakeside "new fort" (later Stanley Barracks) tried to brighten the long Toronto winter of 1865-66 by organizing cheerful sleighing parties on the bay and elegant balls at the fort. The City organized a Defence Committee (capitalist William Cawthra headed the list of subscribers with a donation of $1,000). Royal Canadian Yacht Club members and other skilled yachtsmen activated the Naval and Pilot Brigade of Toronto (formed in 1861). Under future commodore, Captain W. F. McMaster, they converted the steamer *Rescue* into a gunboat and proceeded to patrol the lake in the *Rescue* and other armed boats. And throughout the spring of 1866 the Toronto papers bristled with articles about the Fenian threat. Finally, at the end of May, "General" John O'Neill crossed the Niagara River with about fifteen hundred Fenian troops.

Toronto sprang into action and the waterfront was the centre of attention. At 7 A.M. June 1, four hundred men of Toronto's Queen's Own Volunteers marched in the early morning light to the Yonge Street wharf. They embarked on the *City of Toronto*, which carried them swiftly across the lake to Port Dalhousie where they continued by rail toward the expected scene of action. At half-past-two, the *Globe* reported on June 2, a second contingent of eager volunteers embarked on the *City of Toronto*—"carrying with them the best wishes of every loyal and patriotic citizen"—and steamed past the Island toward the Niagara frontier. In their absence the boys and masters of the Upper Canada College Rifles mounted pickets throughout the undefended city.

On June 2 the Canadians engaged the Fenians in a small but spirited skirmish at Ridgeway. The following day word reached Toronto by telegraph that provisions were needed for their Queen's Own Volunteers. A meeting was hastily called and at 2 P.M. the *City of Toronto* set sail again with a great store of free offerings (which included not only such obvious necessities as barrels of sugar, beef, pork, bacon and biscuits, but also tobacco, brandy and rum). For hours after the steamer had disappeared beyond the Island, citizens made their way down the wharf with contributions.

On her return run the steamer carried home seven dead and eleven wounded members of the Queen's Own who had fallen at Ridgeway. Long before the expected arrival of the boat "a continuous stream of people" poured along the city's main streets toward the wharf. "Rich and poor, vigour and infirmity, budding youth and venerable old age" the *Globe* commented on June 4, "were each and all represented in the dense crowd which occupied every available stand-point of the approaches to the wharf on

which the vessel was to deposit our dead and maimed citizen soldiers."

Finally, guided by the steady beacon of the Island Lighthouse, the *City of Toronto* hove into view shortly before 10 P.M. A few days later a mournful pageant wound its way through the streets as the city buried its dead—and shortly thereafter raised a new monument to patriotism in Queen's Park. To prevent further invasions, nine steamers on the lakes were converted into gunboats and border forts were reinforced. The Fenian threat soon evaporated (at least in Upper Canada), but the harrying of the border had the salutary effect of convincing Canadians that Confederation was necessary for defence against the predatory Americans.

In the latter part of the 1860s Toronto was plunged into a post Civil War depression. It was at this point, paradoxically, that the Islanders planted the seeds of modern development. By 1866 Ned's father John Hanlan and his family were well established at the western end of the Island.[8] Hanlan was the Island Constable (a position he held until his death in early 1872) and kept a close eye on potential malefactors and on the general state of the Island. Just when he decided to become a hotel keeper is uncertain. John Ross Robertson suggested that this occurred in 1862, but other evidence indicates that he did not build the first Hanlan's Hotel until a few years later. In any event, sometime in the mid-1860s Hanlan built a wharf (later swept away by a fifteen-foot mountain of lake ice) and a small, one-storey frame hotel overlooking a debris-cluttered beach. A line of recently planted trees marched southward past a small building used as a shooting gallery toward a two-storey gabled house, which was occupied for a long time by Mrs. Durnan, the sister of John Hanlan, and then was later used as a restaurant. Off in the

This photograph of Hanlan's Point c. 1870 shows John Hanlan's one-storey hotel and wharf on the right, Mrs. Durnan's two-storey house in the centre, and the boathouse where Ned Hanlan later stored his racing shells at the extreme left. [MTLB]

distance lay the boathouse where Ned Hanlan was later to keep his famous "needle shells." The reality of running a hotel apparently did not agree with John Hanlan; by 1871 he had reverted to being simply a fisherman and the Island Constable. His family, however, continued to operate the establishment.

Competition for the tourist dollar was keen and Hanlan's Hotel was not the only one built on the eve of Confederation. In May 1866 another fisherman-turned-innkeeper, Patrick Gray, opened "a very substantial and comfortable hotel on the Lake shore of the Island" (immediately south of Hanlan's) "where the pleasure seeker

[would] find everything he may require in the way of edibles and beverages."[9] The "fine steamer *Bouquet*" would "ply regularly between the City and Mr. Gray's wharf nearby."[9] Meanwhile, at Centre Island (then unnamed), Mrs. Emily Parkinson, recent widow of Reuben Parkinson, built a two-storey frame hotel which became a well-known Island landmark. Set at the end of a thousand-foot plank wharf, Mrs. Parkinson's hotel occupied a choice site—facing the rapidly changing skyline of the growing city. In summer the hotel was shaded by tall poplars and spreading willow trees. Patrons could admire the view from the verandahs or stroll out along the pier

or under the leafy pathways. They could also sample the readily available marine amusements, as well as try their hand at bowling in the bowling alley so obligingly constructed by the proprietress. Even in winter the somewhat bleak facade of the hotel was still a welcome focus of attention for ice boats skimming across the frozen bay. At all times of the year the widow Parkinson's sturdy figure—clad in the long, dark, sweeping skirts of the era—was a familiar sight.

During the summer in the sixties a variety of steam ferries were carrying crowds to the Island. One of the most regular of their passengers was the aging artist Paul Kane who "was very fond of the water and during the summer months seldom failed to make a daily visit to the island, returning regularly by the last ferry boat in the evening."[10] In 1865 the Island fleet included "the miniature little steamer the *Ripple*, with her jaunty rig and obliging boy captain," which ran half-hourly between the city and the Island[11] and the *Princess of Wales* where, according to the *Globe* of July 11, 1866, passengers were certain to receive "good accommodation on board and courteous attention on the part of the captain." Accommodation onshore was sometimes a different matter. Shortly before making the above recommendation the *Globe* reported a fight that broke out between a black and a white passenger as the *Princess of Wales* landed at Tinning's Wharf at the foot of York Street. Some of the passengers tried to separate the combatants, but without success. As one drew a razor to put a "speedy termination to the fight," the other "brought his teeth into active operation." The biter seemed to be the more successful—walking away "with a very considerable portion of the nose of his coloured opponent."

Meanwhile, genial Captain William Parkinson

took over the *Bouquet* and advertised in 1868 that "the steamer has been furnished in a tasteful style and in such a manner as to ensure comfort combined with safety to persons wishing to visit this favourite place of resort. The most liberal arrangements will be made with excursions and picnic parties."[12] Perhaps behaviour on the ferry and on the Island was a bit too "liberal" to suit all tastes, for the first complaints about running ferries on the Sabbath were raised.[13] But the 1868 bylaw passed by City Council to regulate the Island ferries did not ban Sunday service. As with Sunday streetcars, it would take another decade for the forces of righteousness to marshall sufficient numbers to halt this sinful practice.

The City continued to exercise only partial control over the Island via its 1847 license of occupation, and murmurs of discontent began to be heard in the Canadian legislature. That body, in fact, had passed a bill authorizing the outright transfer of the Island to the City as early as May 19, 1855, but nothing came of it for over a decade. In the interim, Torontonians' continuing concern for the state of the harbour and the erosion on the Island seemed to ebb and flow with the height of the lake water. Certainly residents were pleased that the 1858 breach in the Peninsula seemed to have had a salutary effect on the city—bringing clear, fresh lake water sweeping into the harbour to wash away the filthy bay water. But the late fifties and early sixties had produced mounting evidence that the same scouring sweep of lake water was also damaging the harbour and threatening to carry away the Island altogether. According to the harbour master's report for 1862, for example, the breach in the Peninsula was nearly half a mile wide and the old line of beach was so eroded that the boiler of the *Monarch* (which had been wrecked

on the south shore of the Island in 1856) was no longer high and dry on the Island, but deep under water about a hundred yards out in the open lake.

The City felt that, since the Canadian government received the revenues from the harbour (via the Harbour Commission), the government (not the City) should also bear the expense of protecting it. But, as Mayor Wilson commented in January 1860, "if the city must bear the charge, let it also have the income and control." Throughout this period, then, public meetings were held, deputations travelled to the capital to present the City's case, petitions were sent and various applications for formal transfer of the land to the City were made.

So, while John A. Macdonald and his allies were busy negotiating for Confederation, the City was busy negotiating for a transfer of the Island. Finally, four days before Confederation, on June 26, 1867, the Canadian government issued a patent which, at long last, transferred owner-ship of the Island (except for a ten-acre reserve around the Lighthouse) from the Crown to the City.

Confederation Day 1867. When the clock

William Armstrong's painting of May 1866 shows the view from Patrick Gray's hotel, past his wharf where the ferry Bouquet *landed (and where the wreck of the schooner* Sophia *lay rotting), toward the Scarborough Bluffs in the distance.* [MTLB]

struck midnight on June 30, 1867, the great bells of St. James Cathedral ushered in a new era. As the carillon chimed out "Hurrah For Canada" and "Rule Britannia," spectators from Spadina Hill to the Island shores could watch great bonfires, rockets and fireworks light up the sky. Not since the 1860 visit of the Prince of Wales had Torontonians seen anything to match these celebrations. At 6 A.M. Captain Woodhouse of the bark *Lord Nelson* made a novel contribution to the festivities—a huge roast ox, which spent the day rotating on an enormous spit over a fire at the foot of Church Street.

To escape the scorching sun, hundreds of Torontonians took to the lake: the *City of Toronto* left the Yonge Street wharf at 7 A.M. with 500 to 600 "pleasure seekers" bound for Niagara Falls and Buffalo; the *Rothesay Castle* "made two trips around the island and through the gap, each time being loaded with excursionists, who were delighted with her sailing qualities"; the little ferry *Bouquet* made half-hourly trips throughout the day, carrying not less than 2,000 holiday-makers to "that popular resort the Island" where they inaugurated the Dominion Day picnic tradition enjoyed by subsequent generations; "innumerable small boats and yachts dotted the bay"; and most of the ships in the harbour were decked out with the flags of many nations.[14] Celebrations continued well into the next night—with more illuminations, fireworks and enthusiastic merry-making, while patrons lounging on Mrs. Parkinson's front verandahs thoroughly enjoyed the spectacle before them.

The following month, on August 10, the Toronto Rowing Club continued the festive mood by presenting a grand regatta which, according to the *Leader*, would "long be remembered as an important epoch in the history of the New Dominion." The band of the 18th Hussars provided entertainment, while such dignitaries as the new prime minister, the Honourable John A. Macdonald, took a prominent place among the cheering spectators.

By this time the City—as the proud new owner of the Island—was being inundated by applications for leases, the first being from Emily Parkinson on July 15, 1867. Because of these "frequent applications," in the summer of 1867 the Committee on Wharves and Harbors hired Charles Unwin to survey the Island and prepare a plan which would lay it out in five-acre lots. Like John G. Howard in 1850, Unwin proposed a wide promenade along the Island's scenic south shore, where Island residents and visitors could stroll, enjoy the splendid view and nip into the lake water for a refreshing dip. He sketched in a number of smaller roads—the most important, he suggested, being "A," from Mrs. Parkinson's hotel southward across the Island to the Promenade. Once this was built—and the required number of bridges erected—visitors would be able to land at Parkinson's Wharf and make their way safely and expeditiously on dry land to the Promenade and beach.

Unwin divided the habitable part of the Island into eighty-three lots of approximately five acres each. He did not bother subdividing either the eastern end (which developed into Ward's Island) or the growing Western Sandbar (which later boasted a long line of summer cottages) because, according to Unwin's report in October, they were at this time "so low, that they are liable to be covered by the waters of the lake in heavy gales." Many of the five-acre lots spanning the narrow, finger-like projections of the Island did in fact also contain large areas of marsh and even water, which lessees eventually could (and, in some cases, did) fill in to extend their portion of dry land. And indeed some lots—like the ones later leased by the Royal Canadian Yacht Club—were entirely under water at this time. Unwin envisioned a major change in the conformation of the Island, moving the northern boundary a considerable distance further into the bay. (This too came to pass as lessees and the City gradually filled in these areas.) Significantly, however, he did not reserve any area for a public park. His was an ambitious plan for a major residential resort—a plan which, after a halting start, did in fact, provide the skeleton for future development.

The leasing of Island lots got off to a spirited start. By September, 1,868 leases for about 20 lots had been approved by Council, each for twenty-one years and most for $25 per year.[15] Moreover, some ambitious schemes for development were proposed. For example, a Mr. Charles Lindsey and company were given permission to erect a "large Family hotel" on lots 6, 7, 8 and 19 (located just west of David Ward's homestead, adjacent to Ward's Pond) so long as the hotel cost "not less than $20,000" and was built within two years. But development itself was not so spirited. Like the hotel developer, many of these early lessees never actually built on their Island lots—a fact which caused concern in the 1870s.

"'The Sixties'," John Ross Robertson reported, were "looked back to by many vesselmen as the Golden Age of lake shipping," a time "when every little lake port owned its own fleet of sailing vessels, and lots of money was being made in the carrying trade." Unfortunately this also meant more maritime mishaps. On the night of December 7, 1868, in a heavy gale and snowstorm, the schooner *Jane Ann Marsh* was wrecked just southeast of the Island. But in the storm no one knew she was there until the following morning when Island fishermen found her cargo of cordwood floating up on the beach. Peering through the clouds of whirling snow they could just make out the loom of her spars.

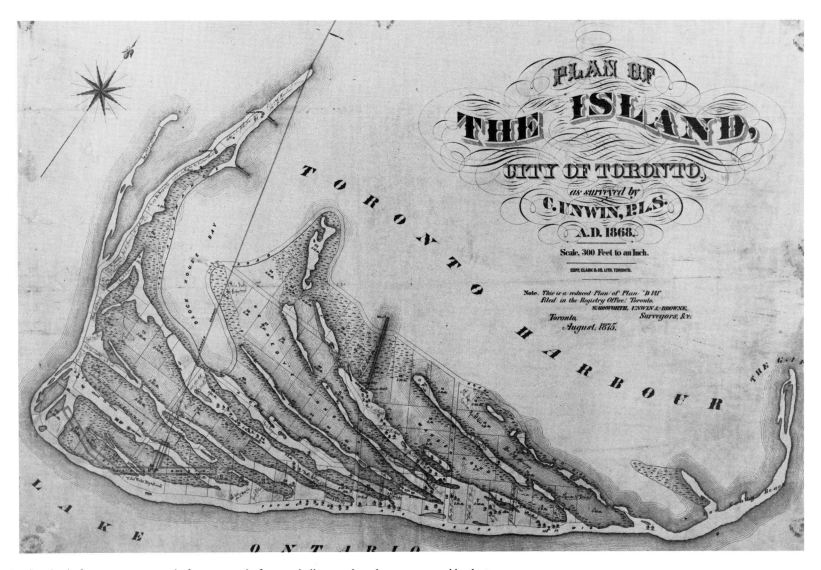

The Island of 1868 was composed of narrow sandy fingers, shallow ponds and extensive marshland. As Unwin's map (in this 1875 copy by Wadsworth, Unwin and Browne) indicates, the main occupants were John Hanlan and his hotel at the western tip (lot #83); Patrick Gray and his hotel on neighbouring lot #82; the Lighthouse where George Durnan had succeeded his father as Keeper; Mrs. Emily Parkinson (succeeded here by Mrs. Mead) and her hotel and bowling alley at the end of a long wharf near the centre of the Island on lot #27; and David Ward, Sr. overlooking Ward's Pond on lots #3 and #4. No one lived at the eastern end which was still just a "low sandy beach." [CTA]

Leasing of Island lots was spirited, but building proceeded at a more leisurely pace. The bucolic atmosphere was captured by Arthur Cox in this view of Hanlan's Point c. 1869. The pace was so leisurely, in fact, that some bovine descendants of these Island residents escaped captivity by swimming the Western Gap and heading for the big city. [ROM]

The crew of ten was hanging desperately to the rigging, giving new meaning to the phrase *frozen with fright*. In the bitter cold, big Robert Berry and twenty-year-old William Ward (who had watched his five younger sisters drown six years earlier) stripped to their underwear and sprang into a skiff. Their fishermen friends waded out waist-deep into the frigid water to push them off. Three times the skiff upset—once end over end—and three times the human life line on the beach dragged them to safety. At one point Berry, who was wearing a thick woolen cap, was struck so hard on the head by the somersaulting boat that the cap was split open and his scalp gashed. His head was tied up somewhat incongruously with a big, red flowered handkerchief and he returned to the rescue work. William Ward continues:

But we did get clear of the beach and reached the vessel. We had to fend off the life boat from the wreck while the other climbed the rigging and with a cordwood stick pounded the ice off the frozen crew. Those lower down were iced up six inches thick. And they were all so numb they could not help themselves. We got them all off but it took seven trips to do it, for we could not take more than two or three at the most in the skiff.

One of the crew was so benumbed and helpless that he slipped between the schooner and the boat as a sea burst over us. The ice on him floated him, and we got him again.

We were seven hours at the work. When we would come ashore with a couple of them, and the men on the beach would get our boat ready for the next trip, we would run up and down in our bare feet in snow half way up to our knees to restore our circulation. We had

to strip to our underclothes to have any chance fighting our way out from the undertow when the boat capsized.[16]

For their heroic efforts William Ward and Robert Berry were each awarded the Royal Humane Society silver medal and Ward was well launched on a lifesaving career that was to stretch over several decades and to save 164 lives.

In 1870 the Royal Canadian Yacht Club moved into a luxurious new clubhouse, which was built on a wharf south of The Esplanade, west of Simcoe Street and nearly opposite the Parliament Buildings. That year's Prince of Wales Cup race provided wonderful entertainment for the spectators at the club, if not for the contestants out on the course. The participants were fighting against a "piping easterly breeze and tumbling sea'' as they headed out through the narrow Western Gap, where one contestant, the good ship *Gorilla*, ran aground on the Western Sandbar and another contestant ran into her. When the *Gorilla* fought free and roared out into the tumultuous waters of the lake her centreboard split, whereupon her inventive, not to say desperate, skipper unscrewed one of the leaves of the cabin table and jammed it down the centreboard box. But in vain; although the *Gorilla* crossed the finish line ahead of her bitter rival *Ida*, after many protests and much chest-thumping, *Gorilla* had to settle for second.[17]

One sportsman who rarely had to settle for second was Ned Hanlan. And the 1870s belonged to him. From the vantage point of the 1980s, when rowing occupies only a small place in the great sporting world, it is hard to appreciate just how popular this world champion sculler was. He was the Wayne Gretzky-cum-Mohammed Ali of his time—combining skill with panache. A superb and dedicated athlete, he was not above toying with, even making fun of, his hapless opponents. He leaped onto the world stage when the Dominion of Canada was still an untried—virtually unknown—nation. Thus when Hanlan became Champion of England in 1879 his one-time backer Colonel Shaw could trumpet, ''Hanlan's victories in England have done more than all the advertizing and emigration agents in the past combined to make known the position and power of the Dominion of Canada.''[18] And according to the Buffalo *Courier* Hanlan had been ''worth more to Canada than their new railroad.''

Although his fouling of an opponent early in his career caused him to be (temporarily) banned in Boston, his public was a generous and adoring one. By the end of his career, ''the Boy in Blue,'' ''the little Kanuck,'' ''the sculling phenomenon'' from Toronto, was hailed as the ''Champion of

Worth,'' who would be remembered ''not only for his skill and exploits, but for a chivalrous bearing suggestive of the knightly days when men contended for honor, and still for honor,'' for ''his example has established a standard of purity that cannot be departed from.''[19] He was Toronto's—and Toronto Island's—most famous citizen.

The decade, however, got off to a quiet start for young Hanlan. The sixteen-year-old fisherman entered his first rowing competition in the summer of 1871. His contribution, however, was relatively unsuccessful and anonymous with newspapers making no mention of his part in

the ''fishermen's race.'' William Ward was among the winners of that race, while fellow Islanders J. Durnan and R. W. Parkinson were among those in the second boat. But future opponents—and victims—were prominent. Tom Loudon claimed that he had been fouled in the Championship of Ontario race (won by Richard Tinning in his sleek shell, *Cigarette*) and proceeded to capture the Championship belt when the race was rowed again two weeks later.

When their shells and skiffs were safely packed away for the winter, Islanders and members of the Toronto Rowing Club organized iceboating regattas. Iceboating could be terrifyingly fast,

Ward's Islander Rowley W. Murphy created this engraving to commemorate William Ward and Bob Berry's dramatic rescue of the crew of the Jane Ann Marsh *in December 1868. This was the first of many lake rescues completed by Ward, who had watched his five sisters drown six years earlier. "Ever since," Ward told a reporter in 1909, "I have tried to help those in distress."* [CI/MTLB]

since the flimsy timber contraptions often reached 60 mph. Courage (or foolhardiness) was thus a prerequisite for the sport. In February 1871 Mrs. Parkinson donated a silver iceboating cup, which appropriately was captured by Captain W. Parkinson in *Fleetwing*. Mr. Robert Mead (who took over Mrs. Parkinson's hotel later in 1873) acted as starter and judge, "giving entire satisfaction to all," the *Leader* reported. Things did not always go off so well. The following winter one race (for a silver cup, a meerschaum pipe and a gentleman's dressing case) had to be called off for lack of wind.

There were stranger sights than iceboats on the bay in winter. Trotting races. On February 21, 1873, for example, two horse races were run on the ice. Mr. Johnston's gallant "Toronto Girl" trotted to victory (and a $150 purse) in the race "for horses that never beat 2.35 mile heats" and Mr. Dunn's "Dusty Miller" steamed and snorted to victory in the (slower) "Butchers' and Drovers'" contest for $120. Slipping and sliding along Toronto's treacherous winter streets was clearly good training for racing on the bay.

In the early 1870s prosperity returned to Toronto and was reflected in another building boom. Between 1872 and 1873 a palatial landmark rose on the waterfront—a grand new Union Station to replace the old wooden shed. Stretching over 400 feet along The Esplanade between York and Simcoe Streets, the red and buff brick building boasted three handsome towers with pointed mansard roofs capped by fanciful little cupolas. The 130-foot central clock tower marked the main entrance which, significantly, open *toward* the bay (not away from it, as it does in the present station).

The great station was erected in just over a year and, on Dominion Day, 1873, it was officially opened. Because of the death of one of

Parkinson's Hotel (shown here c. 1872) was a focus of iceboating activity. On February 26, 1872, for example, six boats started off from Parkinson's wharf and, after a "pretty exciting race," Mr. Parkinson edged out Mr. Noverre. But, in the Toronto Rowing Club regatta a week later, Mr. Noverre had his revenge. After whirling three times around the Bay, Mr. Noverre triumphed in his "Lily," while Mr. Parkinson slumped to a lowly fourth place finish in his not so speedy "Fleetwing." [MTLB]

the railway principals, however, little hoopla attended the opening. In fact the first train passed through at 5 A.M., to be greeted only by the hoarse croak of fog horns set along the line. Large numbers of curious citizens, however, did pass through later in the day. Meanwhile, the average Torontonian was out enjoying the sunny summer holiday. Hundreds of holiday-makers admired the handsome new building—decorated by evergreen trees and a great Dominion flag fluttering above the 130-foot main tower—from the deck of the *City of Toronto* as they steamed off to Niagara Falls. Many "happy family picnic parties" travelled across to the Island. In fact so many Island visitors crowded the ferries and the wharfs

that a near-disaster occurred. Late in the afternoon the heavy business being done by the *Bouquet* proved too much for Parkinson's Wharf. That frail jetty gave way and precipitated a large number of ladies, gentlemen and children into the bay. Fortunately the water was very shallow at that point, so "nothing more serious than an ungraceful drenching of all concerned, and a few slight bruises, resulted from the accident."[20]

The 1870s building boom on the mainland did not extend to the Island, much to the consternation of City Council members. Between 1872 and 1873, however, Mr. James Morris, a prominent barrister, did build the first summer cottage, thereby initiating the great residential resort era of Island life. It was a small (thirty-four by thirty-six feet), squarish, one-and-a-half-storey frame building, located on Unwin's lot 79 near the base of the western point. Morris' little cottage formed the nucleus of what would later become the first Island cottage community. (By September 1879 eight cottages clustered together here on lots 78 and 79.) But his pioneering example was not immediately followed. So,

James H. Morris, Q.C., who built the first summer cottage on the Island in 1872-'73, was called to the bar in 1854 and practised for a few months with another Island enthusiast, Larrett Smith. By 1891, he had a "wealthy and influential clientele" *in his law practice; was a member of the RCYC; and was a Conservative "of the ideal type," according to local historian G. Mercer Adam, from whose book,* Toronto Old and New, *this photograph is taken.*

for a number of years, Morris could paddle in Blockhouse Bay, watch the sun set across Humber Bay and enjoy the pastoral pleasures of Island cottage life in relative isolation.

James H. Morris may have enjoyed the natural or what the 1875 City Council scornfully described as the "wild and dilapidated state" of the Island; but the City was keen to stimulate residential development. It was particularly interested in one grand scheme proposed by future mayor Oliver Aiken Howland and his associates in September 1873. They wanted to develop twenty-two Island lots "into a pleasing place of residence and resort" by landscaping the property and building a "serviceable boardwalk" from about Gray's Wharf in the west, around along the lakeshore, to David Ward's house in the east. Although Council was impressed by the "known standing of the applicants"—and the anticipated yearly revenue of $750—nothing came of the scheme and development puttered along at a much more leisurely pace.

The following year, 1874, was an important one in the development of the Island although it did not start out propitiously. Island Constable George Warin (who had succeeded John Hanlan in 1872) reported in April that the Island was waterlogged and noted a "large breach of about 150 yards in width, connecting the Lake with a large pond known as 'Jim Crow Pond,' which is near Mr. D. Ward's house." This, however, did not deter the city fathers from making the first public improvement to the Island—"a small portion of sidewalk on the west side of the Island," which apparently was a great success.[21] That spring four new leases were signed, which raised the grand total from five, excluding John and David Ward who had no official leases, to nine. To stimulate more interest Council decided to advertise Island lots and, to encourage swift

development, it decided to include a clause requiring the lessee to build within two years "an ornamental summer residence of not less than $500 in value." To protect the bucolic atmosphere, it also included a clause prohibiting manufacturing.

The ad had the required effect. By late September, with visions of the "vast advantages which [would] accrue to the Island itself and the City, in the way of revenue and taxes, by the improvements which will undoubtedly be made," the Committee on Wharves and Harbors was pleased to recommend that nineteen new leases (for lots scattered about the Island) be authorized by Council. In short, by the end of 1874 a quantum leap forward had been made in *leasing* Island lots. And the following year future financier extraordinaire (Sir) Herbert Holt made a great leap forward by immigrating from Dublin and capturing his first job in Canada: surveying some of these lots on the Island.

In the spring of 1875, as the rat-a-tat-tat of hammers rang out across the Island,[22] another milestone in its residential history was passed: on April 26, 1875, James H. Morris and other lessees of Island lots presented the first Island residents' petition to City Council, for various "improvements." This marked the beginning of a long, sometimes stormy, relationship between Islanders and City Hall. Meanwhile, in May 1875, the City decided to become more actively involved in improving the Island. That year the Committee on Wharves and Harbors made a stirring case for public involvement:

> The benefits to be derived by the citizens from the close proximity to a city like Toronto of such a place as the Island, cannot be over-estimated. It is made the resort of thousands, both young and old, rich and poor. The invigorating air which is there to be obtained,

as well as the great advantage the Island affords as a place of healthful exercise, is an inducement to all classes of our citizens to take a trip across our splendid Bay to visit it. This fact is exemplified on almost every day during the summer season, when our merchants and private citizens may be seen escaping for an hour or two from the heat of the City and taking a trip to and a ramble on the Island. Children by the hundreds are also sent over there by their parents, who fully realize the benefits to their health thereby. On a public holiday the Island is completely invaded by the more industrial classes of our citizens, who prefer to enjoy a few hours of the invigorating lake air to a trip into the country.

The committee was also impressed by the private improvements made over the last two or three years—the building of several cottages (four to be exact), each neatly fenced and suitably planted, and the agreement of lessees to plant eight-foot willows and poplars every fifteen feet along their property.[23] The committee, in sum, declared grandly that "Council must consider the Island as one of its most valuable possessions and accordingly [must] take such steps as may be necessary to protect and improve it."

The grandeur of this vision was not, however, matched by Council's boldness of action. It voted to spend $3,500 to extend the plank sidewalk down to Lighthouse Point and then easterly along the southern shore almost to David Ward's house (following Unwin's 1867 plan for the lakeshore Promenade) and to construct a plank sidewalk from Mead's Hotel (until 1873 Parkinson's Hotel) south to connect with the lakeshore walkway (following Unwin's proposed road "A") "so that whether they cross to the [western] Point or to the centre of the Island, visitors may enjoy, without fatigue, the refreshing and invigorating breezes from the Lake, while still at only a few minutes distance from the heat and

bustle of the City." It was a small start, but it pointed the way toward the public park of the 1880s.

All the while the dangerous work of lifesaving went on. Thomas Tinning, who for many years was in charge of a volunteer crew, went down to New York City to buy "one of the latest and most improved boats" available, according to the harbour commissioners' report of July 3, 1872. The new boat—twenty feet long, of metallic construction, with airtight tubes under the seats—finally arrived by schooner from Oswego on October 15, 1872, and Tinning proudly took her to his mainland wharf for future use. Having a new boat was one thing, raising a crew when the need arose was another.

On November 13, 1873, for example, Tinning reported to Council the trouble he had experienced raising volunteers when the schooner *Anne Bell Chambers* was wrecked near Lighthouse Point on the night of October 29. But his suggestion that a paid crew be hired was not acted on and the volunteer system continued for some years more.

Heroic deeds, nevertheless, were performed. During the fierce snow-laden gale of November 14, 1875, both Tinning and William Ward were kept busy. Around ten o'clock that morning the Oswego schooner *Olive Branch* was wrecked about a hundred yards off shore, and half a mile west of the Gap. The breakers were "lashing over her with tremendous force," the *Leader*

John George Howard was on the spot to depict a daring lake rescue typical of the times. Here Thomas Tinning and his gallant crew force their lifeboat through mountainous waves in December 1861 to help the crew of the Pacific, foundering in Humber Bay, just west of the Island and its distinctive Lighthouse. [THB/MTLB]

reported, while Captain Sylvester and his crew of five men and one female cook huddled near the broken foremast, "almost powerless to help themselves." The waves were so high that the fishermen could not launch a boat. One of the schooner's sailors tied a rope around a wooden hatch cover and heaved it toward shore to try to float a line in, but it was no use. Finally, at his father David's suggestion, "the well-known, courageous fisherman" William Ward tied a line around his waist and dove into the breakers to try to grab the hatch. The sea "reared up fourteen feet of solid water," he later told the *Telegram*, but he finally caught hold of the hatch cover and was hauled back to the beach by his own life line. The fishermen then dragged two crew members through the water to shore. Both nearly drowned in the process. Then the line was lost. Finally Ward got another line to the ship. The sailors on board then fastened this line to the top of the mast and slid, one after another, to safety.[24]

Ward's day, however, was far from over. That very afternoon, off the beach at the foot of Carlaw Avenue to the east, the heavily-laden *Fearless* struck bottom and threatened to break up. Captain Ferguson decided to try to make shore in the ship's sixteen-foot yawl, but it was torn loose from the mother ship, oarless and hopeless. The little boat turned over and the captain disappeared forever. As dusk fell both Tinning's and Ward's rival crews came plunging across icy Ashbridge's Bay with the lifeboat. A great bonfire was lit on the beach across from the *Fearless* and a crowd of spectators watched as the lifesavers tried and failed to reach the ship. Tinning was a brave man, but declared that the surf was too high and too dangerous to continue. Ward disagreed and gave Tinning a clout on the head to back up his assertion that he would take the lifeboat. The two men then fought with bare fists in the light of the fire to settle the matter. At last, Ward said, "Let's finish this aboard the *Fearless*!" Tinning and his gallant crew, however, insisted on making the attempt alone but their boat swamped and they were only just able to make it back to shore with their own lives. There really was nothing to do but wait. All night the fire blazed. All night the terrified members of the *Fearless* crew sheltered in the cabin in water up to their waists. And all night the sturdy old *Fearless* held together, after enduring nearly twenty-four hours of merciless pounding. At dawn Ward and Tinning forgot their rivalry, joined hands, fought their way out to the doomed ship and plucked the cook and five sailors to safety. Soon after they landed, the *Fearless* burst asunder.[25] For his part in the *Olive Branch* rescue Ward received a gold watch, a gold medal and, like the other rescuers, new outfits from various clothing firms in Toronto.

The waters of the bay held other dangers. On May 2, 1870, Mayor Samuel B. Harman warned Council about the worrying state of the city's water supply. Noting, in the formal prose of his day, that "the object of this supply is threefold: first, for the extinguishing of fires; secondly, for drinking; and thirdly, for ablutionary and other purposes," the mayor pointed out the obvious: "The proximity of the mouths of certain sewers to the very portion of the Bay from which the Water Company are daily filling the reservoirs" threatened "the health, cleanliness and comfort" of the city. In the less formal prose of our day: the water supply stank. Fortunately, unlike other major lakeside cities such as Cleveland and Chicago, Toronto had a "natural filter"—the Island. So, when the Corporation took over the task of supplying fresh water to its citizens in 1872, it decided to construct a large filtration basin on the Island. It would pump water directly from the lake, rather than from the bay. The water would run through the filtration basin (to clear it of impurities), along a four-foot wide wooden conduit under Blockhouse Bay to Gibraltar Point (the tip of the Western Point) and through a three-foot-wide flexible iron pipe under the Western Gap to the city. It was, to say the least, an ambitious plan, but the new Toronto Water Works let a contract for the work in January 1873 to Messrs. Ginty and Dickey (both of whom soon leased lots on the Island).

While James Morris and his neighbours were building the first summer cottages, Ginty and Dickey were tackling their "novel" project—and, no doubt, providing entertainment for visitors to the Island. Piles of sixteen-foot-long staves of green oak and pine and great iron hoops for the wooden conduit lined the route along Blockhouse Bay. Great lengths of flexible iron pipe— proudly, but slowly, made in Toronto—were amassed along the bayshore. A steam dredge cut its way through the Island to the great marshy area south of the Lighthouse, where it scooped out the enormous filtering basin, which stretched some 2,700 feet parallel to the lake and had a water surface of over five acres. The excavating was impressive; but the landscape created was a bleak one. Meanwhile, the great wooden conduit was assembled and 10,000 feet was laid in a trench cut through the Island and under Blockhouse Bay to the connecting crib at Gibraltar Point. Sand excavated from the filtering basin was loaded on scows and dumped over the newly laid conduit to keep it in place. The conscientious chief engineer even donned "a diver's dress" and descended through the cold, murky waters of the lagoon to inspect the first sections laid in early 1874. All was pronounced airtight.

Workmen at Gibraltar Point faced different problems. Laying the flexible iron pipe under the Western Gap may not have been comparable to laying the trans-Atlantic cable of 1866, but it was still "the largest undertaking of anything of its kind."[26]

Progress on the project was slow and members of the public began to grumble. Some even suggested that the pipes had been laid wrong end first—a charge that the chief engineer

This 1875 photograph shows a work crew laying the flexible iron water pipe "Ward Joint" between the tip of Hanlan's Point and the city.   [CTA]

naturally dismissed. Finally, on November 25, 1875, with ice beginning to form along the Island's lakeshore, the system was ready to be tested. For nearly two glorious weeks over four million gallons of fresh, clear water were successfully pumped to the city. But to the horror of all concerned, on the morning of December 7, a great snakelike creature was to be seen bobbing up and down on Blockhouse Bay—not the Toronto Island monster, but 2,500 feet of the wooden conduit which had floated to the surface. This and various other problems delayed the final opening of the system for two more years.

During the mid-1870s Ned Hanlan was making his reputation, having spent the first part of the decade fishing, helping to run the family hotel and honing his rowing skill. Rowing in this period was a popular, but somewhat irregular, affair. There were no standard boats and no standard courses. Distances ranged widely, depending on tradition and agreement among the competitors, from a short distance like one mile, through intermediate distances like two and three miles, up to five or so miles. Some courses were straightaways, some were curved and some involved turning around a marker. And all were subject to the vagaries of the weather. One constant, however, was the betting. Even gentlemen amateurs (as opposed to "fishermen" or "professionals") placed side bets to ensure that everyone took the matter seriously. And successful scullers like Hanlan could multiply their prize money many times over.

In 1873, Hanlan raced in a shell for the first time and won the Championship of Toronto Bay. The following year, in his first professional race, he astonished local rowing enthusiasts

by defeating his better-known rival, Thomas Loudon, on Burlington Bay, Hamilton. The surprised Loudon immediately challenged the young upstart to a rematch, insisting that the race be held on Toronto Bay and backing up his challenge with a side bet of $100. (At a time when Thomas Tinning was paid only $30 to cover expenses for his trip to New York City to buy the new lifeboat, $100 was clearly a sizeable wager and one that Hanlan could ill afford to lose.) Once again Hanlan defeated Loudon over the short, one-mile course. For good measure the nineteen-year-old Hanlan defeated Loudon—and another good rower, James Douglas—on August 15, 1874, to win the prestigious Lord Dufferin Medal and the Championship of Ontario.

By 1876 Hanlan was famous throughout Ontario, and a group of twenty prominent men in the community formed the "Hanlan Club" to back the potential champion—and win a bit of money. (Among its members were American Consul Colonel Albert D. Shaw and William Ward's older brother David, who travelled with the sculler and was later credited by the *Mail* with being the "discoverer of Ned Hanlan.") The club would look after the details of racing, while Hanlan would concentrate on training and rowing. When Thomas Loudon wisely gave up singles to concentrate on doubles, the club bought his splendid, English-made shell, the *Duke of Beaufort*, for Hanlan. Next, it provided him with a major rowing innovation—the sliding seat. Hanlan was so successful with this that he became known, perhaps indelicately, as "the father of the sliding seat."

On August 12, 1876, Ned solidified his local reputation. At the Toronto Rowing Club's tenth annual regatta—before crowds of spectators on the *Empress of India*, the handsome tug *W. T. Robb*, and the various Island ferry boats—

Hanlan won the two-mile race for the Championship Belt as well as being part of the three-man crew that won the "Fishermen's Race." It was now time for bigger and better things—the Centennial Regatta in Philadelphia, which offered the magnificent prize of $800. But he had not won the money yet. In addition to training for Philadelphia Hanlan continued to help run the family hotel. Unfortunately, he expanded his contribution to include a bit of bootlegging—i.e., selling liquor without a permit to people outside the hotel's licensed area. A warrant was issued for his arrest and Hanlan went into hiding. With policemen patrolling the waters, practice was almost impossible. Just two days before he was scheduled to leave for Philadelphia, his career nearly came to an abrupt end. While he was meeting friends in the Toronto Rowing Club headquarters, lookouts warned him that the police were on the way. As the men in blue entered the front door, the "Boy In Blue" dashed out the back, jumped into a skiff and rowed furiously toward a steamer heading for Lewiston. The astonished police watched helplessly as Hanlan narrowed the distance, pulled even and climbed up a dangling rope ladder. It was a good workout. By the time he returned to Toronto he was the toast of the town and all was forgiven.

In Philadelphia the unprepossessing Hanlan (only 5 feet 8¾ inches tall and about 150 pounds) was a complete unknown. But not for long. After winning his first heat on the three-mile course, he astonished the American rowing world by defeating two well-known Americans, Fred Plaisted and Pat Luther. During this second heat Hanlan stopped rowing and looked around, toying with his opponents. He capped his performance by winning the final, three-mile championship race in record time. Toronto went wild. As Hanlan returned home aboard the

City of Toronto, two huge bonfires on the Island—one near the centre and one on the Western Point—"sent lurid glares towards the sky, lighting up the bay and the esplanade [sic]." He was met at Yonge Street Wharf by a grand torchlight parade. As he made his appearance to be greeted by the mayor, the band struck up a spirited rendition of "See The Conquering Hero Comes." Surrounded by torch bearers and friends waving aloft great rowing oars, Hanlan was hoisted onto a shell balanced on top of a fire wagon. The crowd by this time had swollen to "immense proportions" and "the crush was something terrible." The parade wound its way along the main streets to the Horticultural Gardens, where "the great mass of people" trampled over a ten-yard section of fence to gain admittance to the official reception. After receiving praises—and a $300 watch—from the mayor, Hanlan was

released. He "was again placed on his novel triumphal car and conveyed to the wharf, where boats were in waiting to convey him to the Island."[27] No doubt celebrations in Hanlan's Hotel continued well into the night.

The following year Canadian rowing fans were eagerly looking forward to the $1,000 Canadian Championship race between a strapping young New Brunswicker, Wallace Ross, and the hometown hero. Before the five-mile race the local papers were full of articles about the two young scullers. On the day, the powerfully built Ross complained of the water being too rough; but the race went on. Wearing the blue rowing shirt and red headband that became his trade mark, Hanlan, from the first, "had it all his own way," according to the *Leader*, and "never seemed to exert himself in the least." While Hanlan was "going ahead like a small steam

Wearing the blue rowing shirt and red headband that became his trademark after Philadelphia's Centennial Regatta, Ned Hanlan (right) defeated American Fred Plaisted in a closely fought duel over the waters of Toronto Bay on May 15, 1878. [MTLB]

engine" with a "slow but strong" stroke, Ross was "jerking himself along," the *Globe* scoffed, "with his elbows flying," using short, chopping strokes. It was no contest; Hanlan even stopped to speak to Mr. Tinning and then to some ladies, at other times kissing his hands to various spectators—the consummate showman. Even with all his antics, Hanlan won by thirty lengths. Some sympathy was felt for Ross on account of the roughness of the water—unfortunately only to be expected at this time of year. As for Hanlan, "nothing too extravagant [could] be said"—at least by the hometown press. Ned was now Canadian champion.

The following year, Hanlan again took on the Americans. May 15, 1878, was a memorable day in the history of Toronto. Once again great hoopla preceded the event, with the contestants touring theatres and halls to drum up interest. Special trains disgorged thousands of strangers come to watch the Canadian champion again take on American Fred Plaisted. It was estimated that some forty thousand spectators "saw or tried to see the race"—the largest crowd ever "seen at a boat race on this continent," according to the *Globe*. No fewer than twenty steamers— each "crowded like a beehive"—converged on the two-mile straightaway course in the bay. And "one persevering person counted three hundred and sixty five small boats and then gave up in sheer desperation." Every wharf was "black" with spectators; every grain elevator, warehouse, station or other roof top was occupied. Spectators were even dangling from the rigging of schooners lying in the harbour. At six o'clock the race finally began. This time the hard-pressed Hanlan did not fool around. He pulled his new Spanish cedar shell to a hard-won, but decisive two-length victory over Plaisted— and took another $1,000 purse back to his Island home—and, no doubt, to his backers.

Hanlan was now ready to tackle the United States champion, Ephraim "Evan" Morris. For this, he had to leave Toronto Bay and travel to the Steel City, Pittsburgh. (Some fifty rich Torontonians brought their support and their pocketbooks—anywhere from $60,000 to $300,000—down to Pittsburgh, too.) The rowers' every move was chronicled. Finally, race day, June 20, 1878, "broke over Pittsburgh very much as every morning does, black and murky," the *Globe* reported. Soon after sunrise all roads to the site were jammed, concessionaires hawked their wares and betting stations "were doing a rushing business." As the six o'clock starting time approached, Hanlan received a polite welcome while Morris, naturally, was greeted by a deafening roar. But the American crowd had little more to cheer about that day. Midway through the five-mile race "Hanlan was leading by nearly seven lengths, and taking it easy, while Morris had his teeth set and was pulling as if for his life." Hanlan increased his lead to eight lengths; then, two or three times, the Canadian stopped rowing to allow the American to catch up, before spurting ahead again. Hanlan finally won by three lengths and was Champion of the United States as well as Canada. Torontonians, gathered around newspaper offices and telegraph stations, were jubilant and on his return gave him an even more thrilling reception. Bonfires lit the shore; rockets pierced the night sky; crowds swarmed along The Esplanade; and a band played Hanlan's anthem—"See The Conquering Hero Comes."

Later that year, on October 3, 1878, Hanlan confirmed his supremacy on the North American continent by defeating another American, Charles Courtney, at Lachine, Quebec. After a fierce hailstorm, the race got underway at 5 P.M. as a rainbow arched across the river. Hanlan indulged in no shenanigans this time. The

In this detail from an 1879 lithograph commemorating the Hanlan-Courtney rivalry, the "Boy In Blue" perches in one of his racing shells with the new Union Station looming impressively behind him.   [ROM]

competitors were "prow and prow with each other" for much of the race. Hanlan edged Courtney out by the slim margin of one-and-a-quarter lengths to win the unheard of prize of $11,000. Courtney congratulated him laconically, saying, "You're a good one."

While Hanlan was flourishing, many Torontonians were not. In the second half of the seventies the city was hit by another economic slowdown. One novel Council scheme "to give work to the poor of this City" was the proposal in December 1875 "to have the ponds upon the Island filled up with sand and loam...and so make a foundation or beginning for a public park or pleasure ground, thereby employing a portion of the hard-working and industrious labourers." Whether the depression was the reason or not, most lessees of Island lots failed to live up to the building clause in their leases and many even fell behind in the payment of their rent, to the evident displeasure of the city treasurer in March 1878.

One bright spot on the horizon of Island development was the grand proposal presented by George and Henry Morphy in May 1878 to build "a large summer hotel" on a prime chunk of Island real estate west of the road from Mead's Hotel to the lake, to properly landscape the forty-acre grounds and to purchase a new steamer—all to the tune of $60,000. In spite of Council's obligingly waiving the collection of rents and arrears for the eight lots, nothing came of the scheme. So, in January of 1881, George Morphy trimmed back his expectations and simply took possession of one lot, where he built a summer cottage.

A few relatively minor changes, however, did occur on the Island in the latter part of the decade. In the summer of 1876 twenty-eight-year-old William Ward struck out on his own. He built a small (34 by 26 foot), two-storey frame hotel—one of only two two-storey buildings then on the Island. (The other was Mead's Hotel.) It is impossible to pinpoint Ward's location since, at least initially, it was on a "fishing reservation" (i.e., on an unnumbered part of the Island). By 1881 and through 1883, however, a Ward's Hotel was listed on lot 22, at the corner of what would become Lakeshore Avenue and Manitou Road.[28] Ward's first effort was modest; but it provided useful training for his later, greater one.

Meanwhile, the City was making a few small improvements. In 1876 it built the first "very light" bridge across the lagoon separating the main part of the western point from the sandbar growing to the west. And, rather than erecting a bathing house (desirable—but expensive), the City also fenced off several areas on the Island

Lucius O'Brien's delicate Scarborough Bluffs From the Island, with its lone hunter and his dog walking along the sandy shore, captures the remoteness of the Eastern Point in 1873. [Mrs. J. A. Grant, Shanty Bay, Ontario]

(Below) *Lucius O'Brien's duck hunter crouches quietly among the grasses of the marsh as his unsuspecting quarry approaches. The bay and adjoining marshland were not always as tranquil as this 1873 scene. In mid-September 1878, for example, a vicious rain storm pelted Toronto, sweeping away bridges, trees, carts, even a warehouse, along the Don River and into the white-capped Bay where boats large and small were swept from their moorings and sunk.* [Mrs. J. A. Grant, Shanty Bay, Ontario]

"for the convenience of bathers," who "during the very warm weather" of 1876 flocked to the areas "by the hundreds." In 1877, in spite of Alderman Withrow's interest in examining "the suitability" of improving the Island "for the use of the citizens as a pleasure resort," the City simply voted to spend "not more than $100" to mend Island sidewalks and repair bathing fences. By July 1878 the first Hanlan's Point bridge (of 1876) had been "almost completely washed away" and the bathing place on the Western Sandbar could be reached "only by those having boats." Council, therefore, voted to spend $150 to build "a more substantial one" without delay.

The Island was not the only part of Toronto having bridge problems in 1878. In mid-September (shortly after the spectacular opening of the New Crystal Palace on superb grounds overlooking the lake at Exhibition Park), Toronto and the Island were nearly drowned by a huge rainstorm which dumped over five inches of rain on the city. On the thirteenth of September "the sight of the Harbour was something fearful to look at," Harbour Master John Carr reported, "being covered with all description of timber, also scows, boat-houses, barrels of beer, oil &c., &c., so that it was almost impossible for a steamboat to approach the docks...." Fortunately, however, a change of wind and current carried "the greater portion of material" out through the Eastern Gap, past the Island, into the lake.

In spite of prodding—such as the *Globe's* dismal Dominion Day characterization of the Island in 1879 as being "as barren and unpleasant a waste as one could wish to see"—City Council could not be moved to make major improvements. It did at least vote to spend $80 to repair the plank sidewalk from Mead's Hotel over two large ponds to the lakeshore, which had completely given way and fallen into the water. But clearly a great deal more than this would have to be done to create the "much pleasanter place of public resort" that the *Globe* hoped to see.

In January 1879 Hanlan travelled to England to challenge Britain's best oarsmen. He and his Toronto companions (like William Ward's older brother David) developed an unfavourable view of the English climate (too much rain). But he set about his task with determination. In his first race, against up-and-coming John Hawdon on May 5, Hanlan stunned the relatively unsuspecting British by winning "as he pleased." He was "five lengths ahead at the close," the *Globe* was pleased to report on June 16, "but he might have led by half a mile if he had been so inclined." The stage was set for the big race against William Elliott for the *Sportsman's* Aquatic Championship and Championship of England.

As race day approached, both men were pronounced to be in "capital condition"— Hanlan's muscles being "superbly developed." Betting, as usual, was "brisk" (stimulated no doubt by the large number of Canadians present, who hoped to carry away a great deal of money); all the sporting houses in Newcastle-on-Tyne were crowded; and the foreigner's practices were scrutinized with keen interest. From midnight on "immense parties of pitmen" had already taken up their position along the banks of the sluggish river to cheer on their local hero, while special trains poured in from all directions. The river itself was alive with craft of every sort, including twenty heavily laden steamers. Shortly after noon Hanlan, in his traditional blue shirt and red headband, rowed his shell *Toronto* onto the course, to the great cheers of his Toronto followers. According to the London *Daily Telegraph*,

a fisherman from Toronto, in Canada has made mincemeat of one of the sturdiest and most athletic pitmen who ever went into training upon the Tyne. There is not even the consolation of a difficult defeat, for style beat strength this time in the most emphatic manner, and Edward Hanlan literally played with William Elliott, of Blythe, waiting for him to come on, and then spurting defiantly away and repeating many of the tricks he displayed when he defeated Hawdon last May....Hanlan not only had time to mop out his boat as Elliott laboured along, but he literally rested on his oars, winning with the greatest of ease by eight lengths, and receiving, stranger as he was, an enthusiastic outburst of congratulations from the Tynesiders....[29]

Meanwhile, back in Toronto, a jubilant "Citizen Committee" was formed to welcome him back home in a right royal manner (and to raise enough money in the Homestead Fund to build him a large stone house on Beverley Street, opposite George Brown's mansion).

In mid-July Hanlan and his party landed in New York City. After overcoming his seasickness, the champion sculler went out to Coney Island (where the future hotelier and occupant of "Canada's Coney's Island" was perhaps moved to remark, "I have seen the future and it whirls"). Local journalists were keen to learn if Hanlan would defend his U.S. Championship against his former victim, New Yorker Charles Courtney. Dave Ward told the *New York Herald* that Barkis is willin', but it must be on Barkis' own Toronto Bay. After a large reception at ritzy Madison Square Garden, Hanlan and company boarded an Erie train for the long, hot, dusty ride to Buffalo. En route, much to Ward's delight—and Hanlan's disgust—a restaurateur mistook Ward for Hanlan and fed him lavishly while the others languished hungrily on the sidelines. At the end of the meal, the host revealed to Ward, "I know'd ye the minit I seed ye come in." When Ward asked, "Do you think my pictures do me justice?," the man replied, "Yes, they'se like ye pretty much; at least it's likely they was like ye then, but probably you've improved since you've been across the water,

Rounding Hanlan's Point and crossing the bay, the Chicora, *with Ned Hanlan apparently breaking into a victory dance on top of the pilot house, leads the belching, swaggering triumphal flotilla.* [THB/Marine Museum]

and that makes the difference."[30] Eventually, the returning party made its way to Lewiston, where they boarded the *City of Toronto* for Niagara.

Meanwhile, at about noon of July 15, the *Chicora*, loaded with over three hundred excursionists (each paying a dollar, which went into the Homestead Fund), left the Yonge Street Wharf for Niagara. Just as she was rounding the head of the Island, a great squall "struck her with such force that for a few seconds she was considerably keeled over." She righted almost immediately but went on plunging and pitching about so heavily that many passengers were not only drenched by the torrents of rain, but also seasick. Eventually the sun came out; but the crossing continued to be a rough one.

The trip, however, was well worth it. Around four o'clock, as the band played (yet again) "See The Conquering Hero Comes," the *Chicora* scooped up Hanlan et al and headed homeward. As they passed the *City of Toronto* and *Rothesay* in mid-lake, on their way toward Niagara, each steamer dipped its flag as the passengers cheered

wildly. While they were still several miles out the sleek Gooderham yacht *Oriole I* "came howling along under an immense spread of canvas"—the vanguard of the welcoming home fleet. Soon, the new steamer *Filgate* and a variety of tugs, steamers and yachts began to fall into line in the *Chicora's* wake. By the time she was again "nearing the head of the Island...the fleet of craft, small and large, was so great that the order of their approach could no longer be noted."

Just outside the harbour lay the great *Empress of India* and the *St. Jean Baptiste*. With the sun setting behind them, the *Chicora* turned toward the Western Gap—a three-mile-long flotilla stretching out behind her. As the white sails of the numberless yachts caught the "fiery gleam of the declining sun" and the steamers belched forth dark clouds of smoke that "drifting away down the lake, look[ed] like a great black island floating in mid-air," Hanlan climbed onto the roof of the pilot house to wave his hand "in recognition of the enthusiastic greeting wafted over the water from every craft that came in

sight." Across the "pale, transparent green of the great, heaving, glittering waves," Ned could see the shores—thick with spectators from west of the old fort all the way along to east of the Yonge Street Wharf. Off Queen's Wharf the *Chicora* was brought almost to a standstill for fear of running down one of the countless small boats swarming about. As the steamer headed down the bay, "cheer after cheer went rolling along the shore, passing from wharf to wharf and housetop to housetop"—while "a multitude of steamboat and locomotive whistles sounded a deafening chorus." Occasionally the strains of brass bands came floating across the bay.

It was the greatest reception that had ever been—or ever would be—seen on Toronto Bay. There was only one disappointment for the thousands of Torontonians packing Yonge Street from the wharf to King Street. Rather than landing on the mainland, Hanlan jumped aboard the little tug *Clark* as she ran alongside the *Chicora*, and was spirited directly home, to the Island.

6
The Island of Hiawatha

On Tuesday January 7, 1880, Ned Hanlan pulled on his winter coat, tucked his plans under his arm and set off across the bay toward City Hall. As he walked across the ice perhaps he was envisioning the empire he wished to build on the Island. In any event, the members of the City's Property Committee, meeting in the St. Lawrence Market on Front Street, were undoubtedly exceptionally pleased—even flattered—to have the world-famous oarsman in their midst. And they must surely have been impressed by the ambitious proposal he laid before them.

He wanted to invest between $15,000 and $16,000 of his growing rowing fortune in building a lavish summer hotel on the tip of Hanlan's Point. Being eager to complete the building by May and to take advantage of the winter season when he could haul material over the ice, he had already received tenders for the work and was ready to go. He asked the committee to grant him a lease of the sandy point north of his family's present lot and small home—a request that the committee readily granted, provided he built the new hotel within a year.

City Hall cooperated, but the weather did not. Toward the end of January there was an uncharacteristic thaw and the bay became temporarily open. A foolish youth was even to be seen paddling around on an ice floe. Nevertheless work progressed. During the spring, as he trained for the coming rowing season, which would culminate in his easy victory over Aussie Edward Trickett on the foggy Thames for the World Championship, Hanlan could supervise construction. And that summer the hotel opened for business.

The airy wooden confection became an instant landmark. Hanlan's Hotel, built in the "Stick Style" favoured by contemporary hotels and summer residences across North America (like

the Satterthwaite Cottage of South Hampton, Long Island), had decoratively trimmed verandahs and balconies wrapped around its exterior, and a picturesque Second Empire roof complete with towers from which patrons could admire the view. With flags snapping smartly in the breezes, a fountain gushing gaily on the greensward and a windmill pumping water picturesquely on the bayshore, the hotel immediately attracted ferryloads of visitors. By the turn of the century it was to become so popular that the owners literally raised the roof, to insert an entire extra storey.

The hotel, however, had its problems. The site on the narrow, sandy spit was an exposed one. In fact, during one famous storm in May 1882, spray was blown so viciously against it that glass window panes were shattered; many of the recently planted trees were torn up and blown away, the wharf was damaged and lake water flooded both Ned's and Patrick Gray's hotel further down the Point. Meanwhile, his brother John's ice house was neatly cut in two and his bowling alley was so tipped over that a pin could not have been put up straight in it.

Hanlan had to contend with the wrath not only of nature, but also of man. The Temperance Men were on the warpath and soon to capture City Hall, with reformer (and sometime Island resident) William Howland at their head. Local historian and moralist C. Pelham Mulvany may have applauded loudly when City Council favoured banning the demon rum and all its spirituous companions from the Island, but Hanlan did not share his enthusiasm. When he was refused a license in 1883, a deputation of citizens pleaded the case of the World Champion. But to no avail. Presumably their argument was not strengthened by the antics of some of Hanlan's patrons. In August 1880, for example, one

(Above) *"As [pleasure-seekers] near the landing Hanlan's Hotel looms before them, a large irregular but not unpicturesque pile of wooden buildings," C. Pelham Mulvany wrote in 1884. This detail from William Armstrong's painting dated August 12, 1880, shows Hanlan's newly-opened Second Empire "pile," complete with lush lawns, decorative fountain and ferry disgorging passengers at the wharf.* [THB/Marine Museum]

(Right) *This engraving from* Picturesque Canada *of 1882 shows the landing at Hanlan's Point where, according to Mulvany, a "crowd of holiday-makers [is] waiting to inspect the new arrivals. On the sands are bare-legged lads and lassies digging with wooden spades, building sand castles, and wading in the shallow water. Under the trees and on the hotel porticos are bevies of young ladies, glorious in summer bonnets and holiday costumes. The place is evidently to Toronto what Coney Island is to New York."*

reveller had steered an erratic course back across the bay and fallen into the drink just twenty feet from shore. When he was pulled out, the *Globe* reported mischievously, ''it was evident to his rescuers that he had taken in too much ballast at the Point in the shape of lager.'' The moral, quoth the *Globe* soberly, was: ''Put the ballast in the bottom of the boat.''

Hanlan and his hotel managers seem to have been equal to the challenge of the license denied. Like the Privats before them at the other end of the Island, they began to organize events and provide amusement to attract patrons. In 1880 the *Globe* had complained that the Island offered ''little or no amusement'' apart from the bowling alleys. But by 1884, when Hanlan was off in Australia trying unsuccessfully to defend his world title against William Beach, his manager James Mackie was offering luxurious dining, as well as free concerts by such distinguished groups as the St. Quinten Opera Company of thirty artists, backed by the ever-popular band of the Queen's Own. There were also more exotic attractions such as dog swimming races, and more ill-conceived events, like ''Mackie's Coon Race (coloured boy).'' In this race the poor ''quarry'' was supposed to jump in the water, be given a minute-and-a-half headstart, and then be chased by a group of white men. Thus, before a large crowd, at five o'clock on July 26, black man Charles Smith leaped off the Hanlan's dock and almost immediately three over-eager pursuers dove in after him. After a sharp chase William Rice captured him. But the referee ruled that Smith had not been given an adequate start. So the whole awful business was repeated. T. Kennedy chased Smith into shallow water, grabbed him by the legs and carried away the $10 prize.

During the fall of 1880 down at Centre Island

Around 1882, W. J. Thomson painted this view of Mead's (formerly Parkinson's) Hotel which was, according to Mary Frank, "a large frame structure, white washed and surrounded with very weeping willows [and] stood in what is now the centre of the park." It was demolished in 1887-'88, the first victim of park expansion.   [MTLB]

changes were also in the offing. As Ned Hanlan prepared to do battle with Edward Trickett on the Thames, Mayor James Beaty, Jr., and his bewhiskered companions gathered for their weekly Council meeting in the aging classical farmer's market cum civic hall on Front Street. Here, under the imperious gaze of Queen Victoria, Toronto's city fathers finally decided on November 1, 1880, to establish a public park on the Island.[1]

The politicians had been less than expeditious in making their decision to transform over two hundred acres of marsh, sand and water into a public park. For years, newspapers and members of the public had been prodding them to convert

what the *Globe* had recently described as a ''barren, sandy tract'' into a beautifully landscaped oasis of public resort. So the November 1880 decision to create ''a people's park on the Island''[2] was applauded by such worthies as C. Pelham Mulvany, the fledgling temperance advocate.

As in more recent years, however, not everyone was delighted by the relatively well-manicured park which developed on the Island. To some, the Island in the pre-park era was full of mystery and excitement. Mary Frank, writing in 1916, looked back fondly to the days before the Island Park opened:

Today the Island presents the natural yet finished appearance which is the great achievement in

William Armstrong's duck-shooter hides near the eastern tip of Toronto Island with his gun pointed in the wrong direction. Not far from here, Island Constable William Ward demonstrated his powers of psychic intuition: after a vivid dream, he found the body of a drowned yachtsman "behind a sandy point locally called 'Knock 'Em,' where the duck-shooters used to go." [Glenbow—Alberta Foundation]

park planning. But to those of us who know and loved the Island—well, never mind just how many years ago, it cannot compare with the spot we so loved then. In the days to which I refer, the Island was simply as the Indians knew it, plus the addition of a dock, a few boardwalks, and some cottages built along the lakeshore, very scattered and very primitive.[3]

While Ms. Frank overstated the case, birdwatchers and nature lovers who had explored and crouched in the wonderfully rich expanses of ponds and green marshes, regretted that "the parkifying of the Island...wrought a great change in its flora and fauna."[4] The kingbirds and kingfishers, purple martins and marsh wrens that abounded in pre-park days became increasingly rare. A

small lagoon west of Long Pond, which was later filled in to expand the park, was "the best place at the Island for water lilies...literally carpeted with them," which were appreciated all the more because intrepid adventurers like Mary Frank had to portage their canoes across a narrow strip of sand to reach them.

Even more remote was the eastern tip of the Island. In the days of the Peninsula Hotel later (Quinn's) the Eastern Point had been the most heavily frequented part of the Island; by 1880 it was a deserted, windswept expanse of bullrushes, ponds and vulnerable sandbanks. No fishermen lived there. No hotels stood there. No ferries bothered to stop there. There was not even a

wharf. The only visitors were the ducks, the duck hunters, the more adventurous pedestrians from points west and—occasionally—the odd boatload of stranded holiday-makers. On Victoria Day 1880, for instance, in an accident reminiscent of what befell Leacock's *Mariposa Belle*, the steamer *St. Jean Baptiste* ran aground in the Eastern Gap. Some three hundred hapless passengers returning from Victoria Park in the eastern part of the city had to be rowed in small boats to the Island and ferried from there to the mainland.

But the Eastern Point was about to take on new importance. For years pressure had been mounting to organize a more effective lifesaving system than the existing one which kept the lifeboat at the foot of York Street under the care of Thomas Tinning. The 1873 wreck of the *Ann Belle Chambers* only a few hundred feet off the Island shore had emphasized the problems of having the lifeboat on the mainland. Island fishermen, unable to launch their own boats through the mountainous waves, were forced to stand idly by, helplessly watching two crewmen "drowning by inches" as the weathered old lighthouse keeper George Durnan (James's son) told the *Globe* in April 1880. Not even William Ward could do anything on that occasion. Finally, after the "melancholy death" of two young boys adrift on the lake in late March 1880, the City took action. It held a public meeting in St. Lawrence Hall on King Street to discuss lifesaving, and arranged with the Harbour Commission to take responsibility for the lifeboat and place it on the Island. And who better to take charge of the Island Life Boat Station than the intrepid Captain William Ward?[5]

At the time Ward still lived at Centre Island, but he was evidently willing to move to the shifting sands of the Eastern Point. He built a wooden boathouse on the bay where the narrow neck of land from Centre widened out to form the Point and he was also granted a twenty-one-year lease for two-and-one-half acres nearby where he could build a house. From this spot, the lifeboat could be launched either into the bay or into the lake as the situation warranted. At long last, in October 1880, as the wild ducks were descending on the shore of the Island, the yachts were being put up for the winter and the bay was beginning to take on the deserted appearance of winter, Ward took charge of the lifeboat. In a lull between autumnal storms he spirited his charge to its—and his—new home on the edge of what would soon become known as Ward's Island.

Ward, however, could not live by lifesaving alone, which, beginning in 1883, earned him only $75 per annum in his capacity as captain. He continued to fish. In fact, one of the reasons he moved to the eastern end of the Island was to fish off its shores. His skill was well rewarded—he was known to have taken as much as three tons of whitefish in a single haul from the still rich waters off Ward's Island.

Ward also augmented his income by acting as Island Constable, the same job earlier held by Ned Hanlan's father. He was appointed by Council in July 1880 "to act as general caretaker of the City property on the Island," to protect the property and persons of ratepayers and generally "to assist in preserving good order." Sometimes, however, he fell down in this latter duty. In spite of the 1883 ban on selling liquor, spirits still flowed to the Island. One elderly Ward's Islander, Dad Lowry, for example, later recalled that his first visit to the Island had been in 1885 aboard a tug "carrying barrels of something from the Tom Davies Brewery" to both Hanlan's and Ward's.[6] Hanlan seems to have escaped undetected; but Constable Ward

was caught red-handed, and perhaps red-faced. In 1889 liquor was seized on his premises. Council, of course, disapproved of Ward's "permitting liquor to be kept on his premises and sold thereon," but, in view of his having been "for many years a useful man in saving the lives of a large number of persons from drowning" and of his repentant promise "to make amends by not again breaking the Law," Council simply reprimanded him and kept him on as Island Constable.

Back on the mainland in 1880 the distinguished members of the Royal Canadian Yacht Club decided to change their base of operations from The Esplanade to the Island. Their once-pleasant clubhouse on the waterfront west of Simcoe Street was suffering from "the encroachments made by the Grand Trunk" railway, according to the *Globe* of May 20. Disgruntled members had had enough: railways were fine as investments, but not as neighbours. The relatively wild and remote Island offered a suitable retreat. Club members Lieutenant Colonel H. J. Grasett and S. Bruce Harmon therefore ranged over the Island and selected an appropriate site on the bayside—roughly ten acres of mostly water and marshland, which the club could reclaim and which the City was pleased to lease for twenty-one years at $50 per year. The club sold its Esplanade clubhouse to the ever-hungry Grand Trunk for $9,500 and began to build its new headquarters.

In June 1881 Commodore Arthur R. Boswell presided over a grand garden party that launched the new clubhouse on the Island. Built on a narrow point of land between Jim Crow Pond and Toronto Bay, the RCYC's first Island clubhouse had a rustic charm in tune with its natural surroundings and was quite unlike its more elegant successors built on the same site.

The decoratively trimmed waterside verandahs and the tall viewing tower provided extensive space from which members could watch regattas and other events on the bay. The reading, drawing, billiard and dining rooms—all finished in Canadian pine—provided comfortable corners for gentlemen to discuss recent yachting cruises and races, old military campaigns and even possible business deals. (Like its city-side predecessor, the clubhouse remained a male preserve.) The light, wooden architecture was in distinct and deliberate contrast to the solid brick and stone buildings rising across the bay in the city.

In the early years, most of the boats were moored not at the Island, which was reached by the club's own smart-looking steam yacht with a clipper bow, the *Esperanza*, but at the old moorings on the city side. Convenience, however, sometimes had its price. In 1883, for example, a severe storm wrought havoc in the club's fleet. Many yachts dragged anchors, some were sunk, and two veterans, the *Undine* and the *Ripple*, were driven onto the City Waterworks Wharf at the foot of John Street and beaten into staves.

As the yachtsmen of the RCYC were settling into their new Island home, the resurrection of the Eastern Point as a popular summer resort got underway. In May 1881 former alderman Erastus Wiman offered to build "two Free Floating Swimming Baths" in Toronto at a cost of $10,000. After due consideration, Council decided to accept the generous offer, which would provide free facilities for Toronto's less affluent citizens, and to locate one of the baths "at the extreme eastern point of the Island." This, however, was easier said than done. In early 1882 the sandy point was buffeted by heavy spring storms and the first building was actually destroyed. Another proved to be more free floating than anyone had wanted: it broke loose from its mooring in the terrible blow of May 11-12, but was recaptured and towed to safety. Even the original site was almost washed away. So a new site was chosen and harried men worked speedily throughout the spring to build a wharf and a handsome bathing pavilion in time for the 1882 season.

It was an upstream swim. In fact, by Saturday

June 24, 1882, when the City took formal possession, the Island Baths were still little more than a "skeleton," according to the *Globe* report. Nevertheless, the jaunty *Luella* ferried the "generous donor" and City officials across to the Island, where Wiman recalled those golden days of his youth when he used simply to go down to a wharf, strip off his clothes and take a "header" into the bay. "But now," he went

on, "the proprieties of refinement and the decencies of civilization" prevented this direct approach. So, emulating schemes he had seen in New York City, he was pleased indeed to donate these baths. Former alderman John J. Withrow used all his rhetorical powers to paint a vivid picture of what the baths *would* look like when they were completed. Then, after visits to the RCYC and the other new baths at the foot of Frederick Street, the party returned to City Hall.

One month later, on July 22, 1882, the Island Wiman Baths were finally thrown open to an eager public. About a thousand Torontonians invaded the usually tranquil Eastern Point for the event with its attendant swimming races. They admired Canadian National Exhibition architect Mark Hall's two-storey gray building with its tower and steep mansard roof. They toured the large parlour, the six small rooms upstairs, the gentlemen's and ladies' changing rooms at the back—discreetly separated by a large, open area suitable for meetings—and the bathing grounds in the front, facing the city.

The Wiman Baths were an enormous success—although, according to the *Toronto Island Guide* of 1894, one supercilious English traveller "gave as an instance of the illiteracy of Canadians that on large public female baths at Toronto the sign was displayed as 'Wiman's Baths.'" Instantly they became one of the main attractions of the Island. By 1885 there was even a Sunday ferry to transport eager swimmers to the baths where, the apostle of temperance Mulvany wrote intemperately, "arrayed in blue and red serge bath suits, the athletic youth of Toronto takes his bold 'header' into the depths—there in lovely and close-fitting array, more becoming than any ball dress, the maids of our city disport in the shallows, and under careful guidance venture in

The Royal Canadian Yacht Club's move to the Island was "objected to by a few" members, according to the Globe *of the day, but "many of the most sanguine [thought] that as soon as the members [became] accustomed to the new order of things they [would] readily acknowledge its benefits." In this 1884 photograph, some of the sanguine members and their lady guests stand proudly outside their three year old Island clubhouse.* [MTLB]

the rudiments of swimming. There,'' he continued, ''after the bath these maids may be seen reclining, book in hand, on strand or green sward, or chatting to girl friend or boy comrade as they 'sun their wave-tossed hair.'''

The careful rudiments were taught by another celebrated lifesaver of the era, Captain Andrews, who served as swimming master from 1882 until November 1885, when he was forced by blindness to retire. Andrews had received medals from many countries for his heroic lifesaving efforts, including the Royal Order of Kapiolani from King Kalakaura I of the Hawaiian Islands. Here he taught beginners how to swim by tying a long rope around their waists. He then paced along the boardwalk running down the east side of the baths in front of a grandstand while they splashed in the great pond that flowed over what is now the baseball diamond. He kept a sharp eye on his charges, ready to retrieve them with a long pole should this become necessary. At other times, however, he was positively required *not* to keep a sharp eye on his charges. Modesty, and the law, required young ladies to cover themselves at least ''from the neck to the knees'' with a ''proper bathing dress.'' Captain Andrews would escort each prim mermaid to the edge of the water, avert his gaze while she slipped demurely in to waist level, where she removed the waterlogged heavy woollen overskirt and handed it to the gallant lifesaver. After she had performed a few stately circles of head-up breast stroke, she would retrieve the skirt from the good captain and reemerge, quite unlike Botticelli's Venus.

Young Island men, however, were not similarly encumbered. Even after the baths were opened, men did not have to wear bathing suits over on the lakeshore beach before 9 A.M. and no self-

(Above) *This 1894* Toronto Island Guide *engraving shows swimming master Captain Andrews, his chest bedecked with lifesaving medals from around the world.* [MTLB]

(Right) *Patrons gather for a group photo on the bayside verandahs of Ward's Hotel.* [AC]

respecting young lady would ever venture out onto the boardwalk before that hour. One embarrassed swimmer, however, found it necessary to stay in the water until ten-thirty one morning when a visiting female, ignorant of local custom, sat on the beach to enjoy the early part of the day.

Throughout the decade Wiman and the Wiman Trust continued to make much needed improvements at the Eastern Point. The baths were enlarged by eighty feet in 1883 and a ''Shelter'' was erected at the southern side of the Point; trees were planted, sidewalks were laid, scowloads of earth were transported to fill

stagnant ponds and steps were taken to prevent tacky little refreshment booths or residences from cluttering the area between the baths and the lake. All in all, the Eastern Point was experiencing a recreational Renaissance.

William Ward evidently saw an opportunity to capitalize on this new-found popularity. In 1882-83 he built a hotel near the wharf, facing north across the bay. Although not as magnificent as Ned Hanlan's new edifice at the other end of the Island, Ward's Hotel was nevertheless an impressive structure. Similar in style to the nearby Wiman Baths, the three-storey hotel offered sixty-foot-long verandahs and a four-storey tower from which guests could admire the antics of frolicking bathers in the bay or, turning their backs on "civilization," could search the horizon for lake steamers and workmanlike stonehookers. (And family members could keep an eye out for The Law as they sold illegal alcoholic drinks in the hotel below, until they were caught and forced to entertain some sober second thoughts.) Ward's Hotel was such a success that William soon built a ballroom just west of the main building where dances were held nightly through the summer—except Saturday because of the midnight curfew—and a small shooting gallery just to the east for the additional entertainment of his guests.

Meanwhile, he and his lifeboat crew continued to drill regularly, developing a powerful and even stroke. They were soon called into action. At 6 P.M. on Friday June 27, 1883, clouds suddenly darkened the horizon and in less than half an hour a violent storm broke over the city. A German music teacher named Schlochow and his fiancée Laura Mendon unwisely decided to try to reach town in their boat before the storm broke. They did not succeed. A short time later, when the storm was at its height, a different man in a small boat was spotted struggling to make shore, and Lifeboat Captain Ward, old Captain Andrews of the Wiman Baths and young John Petray of the lifeboat crew dashed behind the hotel to drag out the lifeboat. For some reason it was "found to be worthless for the task,"[7] so they commandeered a Dr. Oldright's skiff and put out to the rescue. As they neared the man he shouted frantically, "Never mind me. For God's sake save the others." He told of a man and woman struggling in the waters beyond. The rescuers "bent to their oars with a will" and soon spotted an upturned boat with a man

clinging to it. Just then the man lost his hold and slipped under. "Faster the crew shot the boat through the foaming waves," the *Globe* reported excitedly. As they came to the spot, Ward dived overboard and brought the drowning man to the surface. Seeing no one else, the crew rowed ashore, carried the unconscious man to the hotel and managed to revive him. As he came to, Schlochow's first words were, "Poor girl, poor girl." Miss Mendon was lost. Andrews and Ward, however, had at least added one more name to their growing list of the saved.

Hanlan's Point boasted one of the best beaches in Toronto. In the 1870s the City had placed a bathing fence to protect swimmers in the area. Now, seeing Wiman's success at Ward's Island, various swimming entrepreneurs began to hatch equally ambitious plans for the western end. In 1883 Ned Hanlan and M.P. and former mayor James Beaty were among those who applied for a lease to the sandbar which was growing up to the west of the hotel. Finally, in the spring of 1884, the City granted to Peter McIntyre a ten-year license of occupation for five hundred feet of lake frontage, provided he build a bathing house worth at least $2,500, sold no "spiritous or malt liquors," and charged not more than 10¢ for bathing box and dress.

McIntyre promptly occupied a nearby house owned by Mayor Boswell and supervised the building of the baths. When they opened on July 28, 1884, his West End Island Baths were highly successful. To keep the crowds coming, McIntyre, like James Mackie at Hanlan's Hotel, used his imagination: in early August, for example, he organized tub races and other novelty competitions for school children. The baths, which soon came under the aegis of Mr. and Mrs. John Turner, were to be a fixture on the Western

Sandbar for over forty years. Generations of Torontonians dressed in the bathing fashions of the era crossed the rickety wooden bridge to "shoot the shoots" down the great water slide and generally cavort in the waters off "Turners Baths"—as they were known long after the demise of Mr. and Mrs. Turner.

Not everyone could enjoy the swimming and other physically active amusements available at Hanlan's Point and elsewhere. But the Island proved to be a boon to even the less hale and hearty, living up to its ancient reputation for curative powers. In February 1883, therefore, Elizabeth Janet McMaster, a summer cottager on Hanlan's Point since 1880, applied to the City for an Island site for a convalescent children's hospital. The City gladly gave the Hospital For Sick Children a twenty-one-year lease, at one dollar per year, for a four-acre site, just southwest of the Lighthouse, on which the hospital planned to build a summer convalescent home for its young patients. The site was a quiet one, overlooking the lake, deliberately distant from any residences and was marred only by some marshy areas in the vicinity and the proximity of the foghorn, whose mournful moan was said to be audible for eighteen miles. John Ross Robertson, founder and publisher of the *Telegram*, contributed the $2,000 necessary to build the home and the only stipulation he laid down was that children of fellow Free Masons be given free treatment.

During the spring of 1883 the first, relatively modest, Lakeside Home For Little Children rose on Hanlan's Point. Also designed by CNE and Wiman Bath architect Mark Hall, the home was constructed of wood in a "light and airy style." It was two storeys high with large windows and deep, shady verandahs on the south and west sides where the young patients could gaze out over the lake during the day and sleep in comfort on hot summer nights. The interior was finished in pine and contained two wards ''for the use of the boys and girls, respectively.''[8]

On July 5, 1883, according to Robertson's *Telegram*, the first group of ''wan and pallid sufferers'' was transferred from ''the heat and turmoil'' of the main hospital to ''the cool breeze and bracing atmosphere of the Island.'' Captain John Turner donated the use of one of his ferries, the *Luella*, to carry the small patients across the bay to land at Justice Featherston Osler's dock not far from the home. To the children the trip must have seemed as exotic as Marco Polo's journey to the Orient. Not surprisingly, they ''gazed in open-mouthed amazement at the new wonders which were disclosed at every turn.'' They were greeted by nurses in long starched white uniforms and a party of Islanders who met them with refreshments of milk, bread and fresh strawberries.[9] The next day those who could walk picked wild flowers (mostly clover, marguerites and sandvines) and decorated their bedridden companions back at the home. For the rest of this summer and many summers to come, the children revelled in the fresh air. Those who were mobile were taken out in boats, allowed to play on the beach and explore their surroundings, while the others were wheeled along plank sidewalks and left to rest on lounge chairs on the lawn.

The tiny invalids, unfortunately, were probably not able to enjoy the extravagant celebrations mounted for the City's Semi-Centennial in 1884, which thrilled so many other residents and visitors to the Island. A full week of festivities was held to celebrate ''fifty years of growth and development,'' as the *Globe* boasted on July 1.

The first Lakeside Home For Little Children is picturesquely mirrored in a nearby pond which, despite its aesthetic appeal, probably constituted a health hazard. [PAC (C-91063)]

Each day had a different theme: Municipal and Historical Day, Military Day, United Empire Loyalists Day and so on. Perhaps the highlight of the week was Thursday night's ''Pyrotechnics on the Bay.'' The mainland was lined with thousands upon thousands of spectators. Some wealthier citizens drove their carriages out onto the docks to watch the spectacle in comfort and privacy. Grand Trunk executives and friends were escorted up the central tower of Union Station, while more plebeian types clustered around its base. Every factory and office window overlooking the bay was darkened by spectators and more adventurous youths clambered up onto roofs. Every skiff, rowboat and steamer was crammed full.

The best vantage point of all was the Island and by 10 P.M. the shores and hotel verandahs and windows were lined by thousands of sightseers.

They were not disappointed by the sights. As clouds obligingly hid the moon and the bay remained a calm mirror, magnificent fireworks exploded and sparkled over the water. The highlight of the evening was a ''bloodless though fiery combat'' waged between a couple of scows rigged up as gunboats and two floating forts made of canvas painted as stonework, glowing blue, red and green. At eleven o'clock, the gunboats attacked, lobbing a heavy fire of rockets, candles, mines and balls of many colours. The fort replied with the ''sullen boom'' of exploding ordnance. The scene provided ''an excellent bit of miniature warfare.'' What all this had to do with Toronto's own history remains unclear; but the ebullient Mayor Boswell's clubmates ranged along the Royal Canadian Yacht Club verandahs and lawns undoubtedly applauded patriotically for the militaristic display. They would soon have the opportunity to do more than applaud.

In early 1885 grumblings of discontent erupted into rebellion in Northern Saskatchewan: Louis Riel had returned. Toronto was stirred to its patriotic roots and an unhealthy whiff of anti-French, anti-Catholic sentiment percolated to the surface. No doubt inspired by fellow club member William Armstrong's exciting accounts of the incredible westward trek with Wolseley in 1870 to put down Riel's first Red River Rebellion, many RCYC members were eager to participate in this new campaign even though the North West Rebellion on the prairies of Northern Saskatchewan was "not an event which

"Steady as she goes." George Gooderham stands at the wheel of the first Oriole *in 1882.*
[RCYC Annals]

afforded much scope for marine activity," as RCYC historian C. J. H. Snider wrote regretfully.

While Riel faced his accusers in Regina, life returned to normal at the RCYC. Vice Commodore George Gooderham liked to cruise and race across the Great Lakes with his son, and keen nautical competitor, William G. At midnight on August 2, 1885 (the day Riel was sentenced to hang), George Gooderham's beloved old *Oriole*, winner of five Prince of Wales Cups in the 1870s, and William G.'s young *Aileen* were moored snugly across Lake Ontario in Niagara, "an inland Newport, famous for its balls and general festivity." But this particular night was, in Snider's phrase, "black as the inside of a wolf's throat," with a gale raving from the east. Just after 1 A.M., a bright spot appeared on the stormy horizon to the north. It grew brighter. Perhaps, God forbid, it was a steamer on fire out in that terrible storm. But no. The light did not move. The compass bearing remained "North-West by North a half North." Toronto was on fire. Spurred by memories of the 1869 fire which had destroyed his distillery and mill, George Gooderham quickly ordered, "All hands make sail!"

Closer to home, Island residents were wakened by the fire, whose light was so bright, according to one old Islander, that he could actually see to read a newspaper on the back balcony. People bundled into clothes and rushed to the RCYC to get a better view. There, across a bay full of whitecaps brightly illumined by the flames, was an unforgettable sight. The entire waterfront west of Sherbourne Street seemed to be on fire: wharfs, coal piles, buildings and sailing schooners were ablaze, though the ferries and most other steamers escaped.

As fire brigades struggled to fight the blaze, the Gooderhams in the *Oriole* and the *Aileen*

struggled to return. It was one of the wildest nights lake sailors could remember, but guided by the pillar of fire rearing higher and higher above the black horizon, the two yachts bounded out across the water. Then, around 3 A.M., the fire seemed to be dying out and the wind dropped. Suddenly, from their stern, the crew of the *Aileen* spotted flares shooting up from the *Oriole*, which had sprung a plank. As the exhausted crews pumped furiously, the two boats limped toward Whitby, which they reached around dawn. The Gooderhams hopped aboard the first train to Toronto to discover that the Esplanade fire had at least spared the Gooderham property at the eastern end of the bay. The bad news was that the *Oriole* could not be resurrected to her old glory. Gooderham would not subject his favourite to the indignities of becoming a stonehooker. "Put the saws to her," he ordered. In a few days, *Oriole I* was just a heap of firewood.[10]

The following year George Gooderham hoisted the Vice Commodore's flag up the mast of his new eighty-eight-foot schooner, *Oriole II*. The mast had been fashioned from two tall pine trees felled out in the country—on the site of the present Casa Loma. Like her predecessor, *Oriole II* was a splendid racer and a centre of hospitality. She won her first (of six) Prince of Wales Cups shortly after she was launched. And every fine summer afternoon when he was not off racing, George Gooderham and a gay party of Toronto's elite would go for a cruise—"junketting" as the spartan captain called it. The visitors' book was sprinkled with the names of distinguished guests, including governors general and prime ministers. (On June 27, 1888, for example, a large party of politicians and businessmen gathered aboard the comfortable yacht moored at the eastern end of the bay. When Prime Minister Sir John A. Macdonald came aboard, he was received by a salute from the gun of the *Oriole II* and presented with a "wideawake hat." With Mr. Gooderham at the wheel, the yacht immediately weighed anchor and set off, propelled by a fresh northwest wind. When the boat cleared the channel, Sir John A. in his new hat and the party of visitors adjourned below to lunch.) For over a decade the handsome black schooner with the golden scrolls was one of the features of harbour life.

Another feature was Hanlan's Point Amusement Park, which by 1888 was humming with a wild variety of attractions—innocent and otherwise. The *Ada Alice*, the *Kathleen*, the *Luella*, the *Canadian* (the first "double-ender") and the other Island ferries brought crowds to enjoy "five minutes of dizziness" on Doty's marvellous

"merry-go-round with its score or more of wooden horses and diminutive elephants, and its wheezy, out-of-time-and-tune organ," to whirl around the switchback railway and to test their skill at the shooting galleries or their brawn at the strength-testing machines. Attracted by the strong-lunged barker, crowds of Torontonians were eager to gawk at the occupants of the "great and only museum of living curiosities." There was no Elephant Man, but there were a fat lady from somewhere in South Africa weighing 510 lbs "without her hairpins," a "wild girl from somewhere in South America" and a "real live Zulu with an Irish accent." The credulous and the cynical alike could then settle down to a luscious saucerful of vanilla ice cream made from real rich Jersey cream bought

from a scow moored nearby. Then it was back to the midway.[11]

Such amusements could on occasion be dangerous. Down at Charles Heber's (formerly Patrick Gray's) Hotel south of Hanlan's Hotel, old Martin Farrell, who operated a modest shooting gallery, was shot dead on June 18, 1888, by one of his customers. At first foul play was suspected; but the coroner's jury ruled that Farrell had been shot by accident and released a shaken William Young.

All was not peaceful lightheartedness down at Centre either in the mid-1880s before the park opened. Around 1886 or '87, as one of the Centre Island ferries was moving off toward the city, a little Italian fiddler, who had been earning a few pennies by playing for the passengers, fell overboard. Hearing the boy's screams for help, Tommy Lightfoot, who worked for Mrs. Mead at her popular clapboard hotel, sprang into the water, although he had a game leg and couldn't swim well. The drowning boy grabbed Tommy in a deadly grasp, while Tommy himself was foundering and screaming, "For God's sake, don't let me drown!" Eventually the ferry stopped, reversed and launched its lifeboat, which proceeded to sink—the rain plug was out. By that time both boy and would-be rescuer had gone down for the last time. Their deaths at least led to a life buoy being placed permanently at the dock.

Other improvements were undertaken at Centre. But the transformation of this part of the Island into an extensive, heavily shaded public park suitable for picnics, lounging and games-playing proved to be a slow one, hampered all the more by the initial lack of a plan and by intermittent lack of funds. Beginning in March 1881 City Council voted to spend $8,600 on improvements and later that spring work crews fanned out

The Doty brothers, whose "hippodrome" is featured in F. W. Micklethwaite's photograph of Hanlan's Point, had a long and varied association with the Island. They operated a ferry company which was taken over by the Toronto Ferry Company in 1890. They ran Hanlan's Hotel in 1887. They operated a carousel, switchback and other amusements at Hanlan's Point from 1886 through 1893. And they operated a merry-go-round at Centre Island Park in the 1890's. [PAC (PA 51894)]

over the Island. During the next several years a solid new City Wharf replaced the rickety old Mead's (formerly Parkinson's) Wharf, the approach to the dock was dredged and a new breakwater/esplanade was stretched along the bayfront, providing both protection and a splendid viewing point; thousands of feet of new plank sidewalks snaked across the landscape; acres of low marshy land and shallow (sometimes stinking, mosquito-breeding) lagoons were filled in (while larger lagoons, like Long Pond, were dredged deeper and banked higher); large expanses of sandy soil were top-dressed and seeded, and thousands of willows, acacias, poplars and other trees and shrubs took root in the newly enriched soil. Work continued year-round. Even in winter great work horses dragging cartfuls of refuse and rich street scrapings threaded their way through skaters and iceboaters, bringing landfill and fertilizer to the Island. In 1885 alone, nine hundred cartfuls were hauled across the bay to fill the swales west of Mead's Hotel.

Still, by the end of 1886 Parks Superintendent John Chambers was forced to admit that, at first glance, "the stretch of sand, marsh and water which compose this so-called park, do not, certainly, appear very promising." With the hearty endorsement of reform Mayor Howland, therefore, Chambers presented an ambitious $120,000 plan for filling, dredging, elevating, planting and generally improving the Island Park so that, eventually, it would "form the City's great park and recreation ground, and take its proper place as the most beautiful natural feature of the neighbourhood—most easy of access, and a conspicuous object from nearly every part of the City."[12]

Chambers's 1887 plan certainly stimulated and guided the development of the park. By October 1887, according to the *Mail*, "a

In winter, City work crews threaded their way through skaters, iceboaters, even ice ploughers (shown in this painting by William Armstrong), to take landfill and fertilizer to the Island Park. [Glenbow—Alberta Foundation]

remarkable change" had already taken place. Where a few months before "there was nothing but marsh and rushes," there was now "smooth level ground for acres." Under the eye of park foreman David Kimmings, a dredge and a gang of men "who otherwise would have been idle"[13] had been working throughout the fall to dredge the area around the new City Wharf and fill the large lagoon nearby. In all, ten new acres of land were created this year and the park was further expanded by the purchase and demolition of the old Mead's Hotel. Not fretting overly long about her loss, Mrs. Mead capitalized on the situation and catered to hungry City employees. She then opened in 1889 another private boarding house on the lakeshore just west of what would become Manitou Road, which in time also became a well-known Island landmark.

In the face of all this progress, a proud Alderman John Irwin led his City Council comrades and a party of friends on a tour of inspection on July 2, 1888. The trees planted the previous year were doing well, the new grass lawns were a lush green and ornamental flower beds and terra cotta vases decorated the landscape. Finally, under the trees where Mead's first hotel used to stand, Alderman Irwin declared the park open to the public.

Work continued. The harsh glow of arc lights first shone on park visitors in July and August of 1888. An Island Park Pavilion, providing shelter and a refreshment stand, was a welcome addition in 1888—but its location near a stagnant, foul-smelling lagoon was less welcome, and caused complaints from the refreshment dealers, residents and Board of Health alike over the next few years. Water for thirsty picnickers and thirsty lawns (but not thirsty cottagers) was finally provided by a windmill, one of many which picturesquely dotted the Island at this time. And the work of filling and reclaiming land continued apace. By the end of the decade, forty new acres had been created and the conformation of the Island had been radically altered. More importantly, Island Park was "daily visited by thousands during the season" since it was, according to Chambers, "now one of the best for pic-nic parties within the City limits, affording ample room for playing lacrosse, baseball and other games, without in any way interfering with the comfort of those who desire to rest quietly."

Another major public work designed to benefit city residents was the ever-troublesome Island waterworks. Although Mayor Boswell crowed in 1883 that an "abundant supply of pure sweet water" was finally available from the Island waterwork system, by the mid-eighties complaints about the foul, inadequate water supply were flooding City Hall (as they would be for years to come). The pumps were old and worn out, the wooden conduit was rotten and leaky, and so on. In 1888 the City voted for a major overhaul of the system, but it was not until May 1891 that water finally flowed through the extended six-foot intake pipe which now stretched out over 2,000 feet into the lake south of the Island, along the 6,000 feet of new steel conduit under Blockhouse Bay and through some 4,600 feet across Toronto Bay in another new steel pipe.

City fathers, however, did not have much time to sip fresh water. On Christmas Day 1892, they received an unwelcome present. The recalcitrant conduit rose from its watery bed and crashed through the ice, "scattering consternation among the skaters," according to the *Mail* of December 27, and stirring wrath among editorial writers. "This is in some points of view an altogether ridiculous thing to have happened," the *Mail* noted sarcastically. A wooden conduit might "disport itself on the surface of the water," but surely not a great steel pipe weighing many tons. And yet there it undoubtedly lay, like some great Antarctic "Thing." At seven-thirty the next morning, Waterworks Superintendent Hamilton, City Engineer E. H. Keating and a

gallant diver crossed glumly over to the Island to survey the situation. The diver found breaks in both conduits. The embarrassed Hamilton tried to lay the blame on Islander, Captain Joseph Goodwin, who was supposed to clear weeds and debris from a screen over the pipe at the Hanlan's Point connecting crib, but Goodwin stoutly maintained that he had performed his duty. In any event, until the breaks were repaired, Torontonians were cautioned to boil their drinking water and were forced to use, once again, polluted bay water which was leaking into the pipes.

During the 1880s the Island, like the rest of Toronto, experienced a building boom. At the western end, earlier summer residents—like engineer and artist William Armstrong, mathematics professor James Loudon and Judge William G. Falconbridge—were joined by others such as businessmen Samuel T. and William J. McMaster, Judge Featherston Osler, merchant and publisher William Gage and City Surveyor Villiers Sankey. Some of these summer places were quite substantial but most, like Professor Loudon's "Sandilands," were suitably—even defiantly—modest.

Over the next decade Torontonians continued building on these desirable Hanlan's Point lots—with their splendid view out over the lake and Humber Bay, their proximity to the best ferry service on the Island and (by Island standards) their relatively high altitude. By September 1894, therefore, the number of assessed buildings in the area had jumped to sixty-four (including hotels and institutions) and the plank walkway south of Heber's Hotel was lined with "dainty cottages with quaint names, fragrant with flowers, and smothered with creepers, and shadowed by pleasant trees," according to the *Toronto Island Guide* of 1894. Here, too, some of

Toronto's most distinguished citizens summered: lawyer Charles Moss in "The Shanty," Colonel Davidson in Colonel George Sweny's "Sahara," photographer F. W. Micklethwaite in "The Breakers," Medical Officer of Health Dr. Charles Sheard in "Tullamore" and music dealer Albert Nordheimer in "Interlaken." A few cottages were even built as investments. For example, in 1888 Ned Hanlan's brother John built and rented six cottages, which came to be known as "Paradise Village" by its enchanted residents. And Wallace Maclean, the flamboyant and political publisher of the *World*, also built a number of small cottages that he rented to sundry individuals and groups, like the members of the Toronto Canoe Club who frolicked at "Fancy Free."

By city standards, of course, Island life in the 1880s was relatively primitive: there was no indoor plumbing, no city-supplied running water and, for a long time, only one store. But perhaps then as now the relatively primitive style of life was one of the Island's attractions. In any event, during this period Hanlan's Hotel also functioned as a sort of community centre for residents on the Point. As early as the summer of 1880 the first church services were held in the dining room, residents' mail was delivered there, the first public telephone was located there, and it was there that residents could dine out, entertain friends or hold meetings.

Hanlan's Point was also the first major tenting area on the Island. It was a group of campers, in fact, who gave Mugg's Island its name. In the 1880s four carefree bachelors—Chester Hughes, Jack Crean, Warring Kennedy and Jack Lye (who later became the Monarch of Mugg's)— pitched their tent near one William Burns' ice house. The lads used to row, paddle or sail to work each day. One time, when rowing back

John Boyd's photograph shows Island campers in the 1890's.   [OA]

would spend their afternoons dressed in the height of fashion "doing King," could wander about the Island beaches and byways without collar or lace ornaments, even without shoes or stockings, "laying up a store of good, robust health."

Campers by this time were numerous enough to form an Island Campers Association and to organize a water carnival at Hanlan's Point on August 21. Owing to the high wind and threatening rain, the carnival had to be postponed. But fortunately, the Citizen Band was at the bandstand and had never played better, thus placating the considerable audience. Two days later the event did come off in spite of the chilly weather and a much smaller turnout. Islanders' boats were festively decorated with bright Chinese lanterns and the Citizen Band once again played splendidly. That night's ferry service, however, was "simply abominable" according to the *Globe*. Indeed, one reason why the crowd was so small was that about two hundred potential spectators aboard the *Sadie* became stranded out in the bay. For nearly four hours these unfortunate souls bobbed up and down helplessly, less than four hundred yards from the mainland wharf. Meanwhile, those who had succeeded in crossing, spent two unpleasant hours being crushed together in the Island waiting "pens" and shouted at by the "stout, loud-spoken ticket collector."

Not only general prosperity and the expansion of the city, but also the development of Island Park and the relocation of the Royal Canadian Yacht Club sparked residential development at Centre Island. In 1879 Centre Island was still a virtual wilderness; but the revival of the park proposal the following summer stimulated a mini "boom" in Island lots and by September 1880, the first five summer cottages had risen at

from the city, they spotted a sign floating on the water, which had been tossed out after a play at the "Royal" had closed. They towed the cast-off sign to their tent site and proudly erected it. The name of the play—and subsequently of their camp and its wild little island—was "Mugg's Landing."

Most campers, however, spread their canvas and their wings on the main part of Hanlan's Point, which was well served by the ferry. The Turners, the Hanlans and Charles Heber all rented out tent sites around their establishments. And the growing Western Sandbar temporarily offered free, if less protected, campsites. By the spring of 1886 the campers were numerous enough to warrant official attention: the Board of Health was investigating "sanitary conditions"— a persistent interest of City authorities over the next century. Conditions seem to have been so bad, at least in the view of City officials,

that the campers were nearly turfed out holus bolus the next year. Only an urgent "numerously signed" petition saved the day.

By 1888 there were "upwards of a hundred tents" on the Island, ranging "from the diminutive eight by six little affair, the primitive home of some camping-out bachelor, to the large marquee, the abode of a whole family." Many of these marquee tents, the *Globe* of July 5 went on to say, were comfortable, even luxurious: "A peep into one of these tents shows that comfort is a chief consideration. Carpeted floors, rocking chairs, plate looking glasses and pictures, heavy rich curtains dividing the sleeping from the day compartments, richly gilded time-pieces, books and bric-a-brac show the taste of the occupants." Rich and poor alike could enjoy the sand, the sun, the fresh breeze and the relative freedom from social constraint. Young "Miss Canada," whose proper mainland contemporaries

Centre Island. Dr. W. T. Aikins, president of the Toronto School of Medicine, and Michael J. Woods, an enterprising live-stock shipper and future alderman, each built a cottage. And druggist Charles E. Hooper built three. He also had good earth brought from the city and dumped at the Island wharf. He then brought it wheelbarrow load by wheelbarrow load to his own cottage, "Clandeboye Place" where he created multicoloured, three-cornered flower beds, edged with white stones collected by the lake. Like their Island neighbours, all members of the Hooper family were to the water born. Little Emilie, for example, was tossed into a nearby lagoon by her two older brothers until she learned to swim at the tender age of three; and her father used to commute by rowboat to the original Hooper Drug Store at 43 King Street West.

As at Hanlan's Point, the first big building boom came the next year, 1881, when over a dozen more cottages were built. By mid-decade about fifty summer residences stretched in a long, straggling line with many gaps from the filtering basin on the west to just beyond the pioneer log cabin of William and David Ward's mother, the widow Ann Ward, in the east. Early life at Centre was attractive to successful businessmen like Frank Cayley, John Catto and Robert Darling and to assorted professionals like Professor Edward B. Shuttleworth, Dr. E. Spragge, accountant E. R. C. Clarkson and barristers Horace Thorne and Robert Smellie. It also attracted ardent sailors like the RCYC's George Gooderham, who in 1881-82 built the first of several Gooderham houses overlooking the lake just down the path from the club, and appreciative artists and photographers like Joseph T. Rolph, who painted a number of Island scenes, John Fraser of the well-known Notman

and Fraser photography firm and Robert F. Gagen.

These builders encountered many problems, however, not the least of which were high water

As a young man, accountant E. R. C. Clarkson (shown here) was not only one of the earliest Centre Island summer cottagers, but also one of the earliest Island subdividers. His eldest son and future business partner, G. T. Clarkson, loved to explore the wilds nearby and was granted a license by the Province of Ontario to collect birds eggs, moths, fish life etc. on the Island "for scientific purposes."
[Clarkson Gordon]

and storms. In May 1882 twelve-foot waves pounded the southern shore. Great sections of beach and new channels were gouged out, every tree planted east of Mead's Hotel was "torn up by the roots and swept away" and "all the houses on the Island [were] damaged to a greater or less extent," according to the *Globe*. Poor John Fraser discovered that his year-old house had been wholly removed; not even a stake remained to show the dimensions of his lot. Charles Hooper's three houses were all flooded and badly damaged, but not moved from their foundations. And other nearby cottages, once safely located nearly a hundred yards from the lake, were now washed by waves, though they held firm. But Torontonians' enthusiasm for the Island was not dampened. By 1884, Mulvany wrote, "neat cottages, bungalow-like Bohemian dwellings of all shapes and dimensions, and comfortable aristocratic villas" dotted the shoreline, while "the gay tinkle of innumerable pianos and the still more musical laughter of Toronto's *belles*" floated out across the Island and the lake on soft summer evenings.

Centre Island life in the early 1880s may have been fashionable but, as at Hanlan's, it was still relatively rustic. "Of modern convenience and modern hygiene we knew very little and probably cared less," wrote Mary Frank in 1916. There was no garbage collection; "an open barrel in the backyard with an occasional burying or bonfire" sufficed. There was no City water; water for all purposes had to be hauled from the lake or pumped by windmill. There was no gas until after 1900 and, of course, no domestic electricity. The only refrigeration was provided by ice cut from the lake, stored in a great ice house and delivered as dripping blocks in the summer by William Burns and later by the handsome Island Constable John Gray with the help of his small son. The only fuel and source of heat to alleviate the chill of an October evening was wood. And, until 1884, there was no store. Unpasteurized milk could be obtained from Mrs. Mead's cow. (The Wards also had cows which ranged across the Island and another cottager kept a cow which ranged ever farther—it once swam from Hanlan's Point to the city.) Everything else had to come by boat.

Then tall, thin, white-aproned William Clark opened his "pioneer store," which was a plain, unpainted shop raised on piles and fronted with a little verandah located on the east side of what became Manitou Road. The spicey scent of ginger, ground coffee, dried apples and prunes attracted all manner of customers, large and small. One day little Emilie Florence Hooper tried to resurrect the barter system. She plunked down on the counter a handful not of coins, but (in her view equally precious) a handful of tiny frogs and toads and declared generously, "I'll give you all these dear little things, if you'll give me a stick of candy!" As the lively creatures started hopping all over the counter, the surprised Mr. Clark cried, "My dear child, if you will gather them all up, and take them out of here, I'll give you a stick of candy!" Puzzled, she nonetheless agreed.[14]

Soon Clark's delivery carts were being pushed around the Island, but Clark's remained the only store for a number of years. So, while small boys and girls with a spare dime revelled in dark ginger ale that made them sneeze, cream soda, sarsaparilla or one of the new-fangled ice cream sodas, mothers—or servants—still had to travel across the bay to do the shopping. Every Saturday morning, therefore, a great gathering of ladies would assemble with assorted baskets, express carts and children to take the still-somewhat-undisciplined ferry over to Church Street. For the children the only penalty was having to wear shoes. Then, purchases made at the bustling St. Lawrence Market, Islanders would struggle back across the dangerous tangle of railway tracks along The Esplanade and pile onto the ferry. As they crossed the bay, Mary Frank recalled, the ladies would be "soundly scolded" by tattooed and mustachioed Captain Andrew Tymon of the *Jessie McEdwards* for the space their overflowing baskets and carts occupied on the floor of the crowded boat. But everyone knew that "his bark was worse than his bite" and certainly Captain Tymon's Island Park Ferry Company, which included five ferries, did a bustling business.

Some services, however, were as good, as if not better than, today's. The *Globe* was plopped on the verandah each morning, while one-cent postage and two deliveries a day brought families on the Island within easy communication with the city.

The Island in these early days was "a paradise for resident boys [and girls] who went barefoot all summer." The odd splinter or patch of poison ivy was unable to slow them down. They caught bass and sunfish and perch in the lagoons, trolled for pike in the deep cuts made by dredges and even speared catfish with forks tied onto sticks. Their scrawny catches, cooked over a driftwood fire, tasted as good as a five-star meal at the Queen's Hotel. On Saturdays lines of city folk had the annoying habit of sitting on the wooden bridges to angle "in our private preserves."[15] Island boys, however, retreated to the old, unused, and dangerous filtering basins where they would swim and sail model boats in peace.

As early as 1882 the growing Island community began to think about building a church. In November Anglican Bishop Arthur Sweatman (later Archbishop of Toronto and Primate of All Canada) first suggested this to the City, but nothing definite was arranged. The following summer a distinguished group of residents met at the lord bishop's Island cottage to lay more precise plans. John Massey acted as secretary, a position he filled off and on for many years. Mr. and Mrs. George Gooderham again generously offered their ample lakeshore house for Sunday services. But clearly this could not be a permanent arrangement. The Honourable Justice Gwynn moved that "without delay" some "suitable building" be erected as a church for Island residents. The motion passed unanimously. The well-organized bishop submitted a tentative plan and various committees were formed. Throughout the summer and winter, funds were raised, a site was located at the corner of what would become Cherokee and Lakeshore Avenues and an architect was found in Arthur Denison—sportsman and future Island residents' leader—who designed and supervised the building of the church and the bishop's cottage.[16]

On Sunday July 27, 1884, Bishop Sweatman conducted the first service in St. Andrew's-by-the-Lake. The neat little Island church—a diminutive Gothic chapel with chocolate brown trim decorating white stucco panels—overlooked the sparkling water and was readily accessible to both Centre Island and Hanlan's Point. The good bishop preached to the crowded pews on the theme, "But it is good for me to draw near to God." He warned that, in retreating to the Island to gain relief from the strains and conventions of city life, Islanders could all too easily forget their religious obligations. The

This photograph taken c. 1884 shows Bishop Sweatman's "Happy-Go-Lucky Cottage" on the left and the newly consecrated St. Andrew's-by-the-Lake on the right. The two buildings cost a modest $3300 and the church remained at this location on the corner of Cherokee and Lakeshore for seventy-five years. [MTLB]

opening of St. Andrew's-by-the-Lake, he was pleased to suggest, "would go far to counteract such a retrograde movement and prevent the breach of the sanctity of the Lord's Day."[17] Afterwards, the bishop retreated down the boardwalk to his own, delightfully whimsical "Happy-Go-Lucky Cottage," which he was to frequent for over twenty years.

By the time the park opened in 1888 the Island had been transformed into a complete village. The summer population, including cottagers and tenters at both Hanlan's Point and Centre Island, had reached about one thousand. George Gooderham had built a second, smaller,

house and Casimir Gzowski, Jr., was among those who had built on fashionable Lake Front (later Lakeshore) Avenue. And Island residents now organized their own amusements, like the "Games" held at the end of August 1888. Sprinkled among conventional contests (like swimming, diving and paddling) were more offbeat events: a hurry-scurry canoe race, a duck hunt, a tub race and even a tilting tournament. Inter-Island rivalry was already blooming and was given an appropriate outlet in a tug of war between the residents east of the Lighthouse and the residents west of the Lighthouse. On this occasion Hanlan's Pointers demonstrated how the

west won. That evening winners and friends knocked the Island sand from their feet and entered Colonel Sweny's appropriately named cottage "Sahara" for the prize-giving.

The Island building boom of the 1880s continued with thirty-seven new buildings rising across the whole Island between September 1888 and September 1889. Residents included barrister W. H. Lockhart Gordon and architect Henry Langley, as well as speculators like Michael J. Woods who built another five houses and accountant E. R. C. Clarkson who built sixteen new houses on what became St. Andrew's Avenue. Clarkson's entire investment, however, was nearly wiped out one languorous Sunday afternoon in 1889 when "Clarkson Village" caught fire. But a bucket brigade from beach to blaze was able to douse the flames and save all but two of the accountant's new cottages.

Despite the building boom, Ward's Island remained relatively undisturbed into the 1890s. So undisturbed, in fact, that when Walter "little Moses" Dodd first arrived there in 1893, it was covered with bullrushes (hence the nickname), sported only about five tents and had a total summer population in houses, tents and Ward's Hotel, of about one hundred. The last boat for the city was at six-forty and the only illumination was "either the moon or the fireflies."[18] City authorities at this time, in fact, were far more interested in protecting Ward's Island shores than in stimulating residential development. Periodic storms washed away beaches, carved new cross-Island channels and generally played havoc with the shifting sands of the Eastern Gap. So the City bombarded Ottawa with motions, telegrams and deputations, which all urged the Dominion government to protect the shores and to create an eastern channel sufficiently deep and stable to accommodate lake traffic. At

(Above) *Michael J. Woods built first his own house and windmill (on the left of this photograph taken by F.W. Micklethwaite around 1890) and then a row of cottages which he rented out.* [CTA]

(Below) *Henry Gray photographed the western end of the Dominion harbour works in 1887. The following summer, on August 1, spectators all along the Island were entertained by the sight of the second "mattress" being towed out the Western Gap and around the Island to be put in place along the Eastern Gap. Hotel guests and the few residents of Ward's Island were perhaps less enthusiastic about their part of the Island being turned into a construction site.* [PAC (C64770)]

last, after lengthy negotiations, their prayers seemed to be answered. In 1882 the two governments had reached an agreement on cost-sharing, contracts were awarded and work on a rudimentary breakwall and a deeper channel began.

In the early 1880s the channel was dredged to a depth of twelve feet, and even that was constantly silting up. The City, therefore, continued to put pressure on the federal government. The two governments, however, became embroiled in a financial dispute and it was not until 1888 that a plan to make the Eastern Gap narrower and deeper, to line it with protective barriers and to toss the dredged sand behind the barriers to keep them in place was adopted. During that summer government engineer Edmund Temple supervised the launching of the first "mattresses" which would line the new channel—enormous basket-like containers, constructed of heavy poles laced together with

wire, filled with brush and sunk by pockets loaded with stones. The system had apparently worked along the Mississippi and was expected to be a less costly substitute for piers here.

The new technique was not entirely successful. On July 29, 1891, for example, the steamer *Steinhoff*, which drew only nine feet of water, ran aground below the Gap. Bad weather, scarcity of timber and changes in plans then all delayed progress. By April 1896, however, major changes had occurred: two great piers lined the newly dredged, 400-foot-wide Eastern Gap for nearly 2,000 feet. Each pier had been constructed of immense hemlock cribs, towed out to the channel and sunk. Then a superstructure, rising six feet above the water, was added and the outermost crib was crowned in 1895 with a lighthouse that would henceforth blink a welcome to all ships wishing to use the channel. Another breakwater stretched along the southern shore almost to the Gooderham property on Centre. But in spite of all the money and effort spent, the channel was apparently not adequately maintained. For the rest of the century sailors continued to complain about the shallowness of the water, and their vessels continued to run aground.

Whatever their defects, the Island breakwaters became popular recreation spots. Cyclists happily roared along the boarded straightaway, while pedestrians enjoyed the cool breezes and the more sadistic chuckled at the schooners and steamboats that still got stuck in the channel.

The federal government did contribute modestly to the residential development of Ward's Island. Its construction company had built a small portable office during the winter of 1881-82. As work progressed the little building could simply be picked up and moved to another location. Then, when it was no longer needed, young **Norman Withrow** (future manager of Massey

Hall) and three skinny companions bought the shack for $40 and inaugurated "Fat Man's Ranch"—the first summer cottage at Ward's Island. Ultimately, Withrow moved the building to the corner of Third and Lakeshore, then surrounded by water, where it became the main part of his house at 8 Lake Shore. Meanwhile, down at the other end of Ward's Island, Mary Blackstock built two little cottages in 1885 and 1889, apparently the first of the Lakeshore cottages that would one day line the narrow band of land south of what would become Sunfish Island. And, down on the main part of Ward's Island, the industrious William Ward had continued to improve his land by dragging

cartloads of brush, cinders and earth from the city across the ice in winter and scowfuls of earth from Ashbridge's Bay in summer. In 1891 he built two houses, rented one out, moved into the homestead himself and gave up operating the hotel. Thereafter he devoted himself to fishing, saving lives when called upon, acting as full-time Island Constable and gardening—the latter so successfully that his strawberries grew to the "size of tomatoes" and were once exhibited in the window of a downtown newspaper office.[19]

Ward's Island's very remoteness, of course, was one of its major virtues in the eyes of some, notably fishermen who angled along its marshy ponds and sandy shores, hunters who, in spite of

According to the Toronto Island Guide *of 1894, an "army of fishermen," like the advance guard shown here at Ward's, regularly invaded the Island to haul out perch, bass, sunfish, pickerel, whitefish—even on occasion the venerable sturgeon.* [MTLB]

city bylaws and Constable Ward's best efforts, still caused "many an unwary duck [to meet] the flying death" and more romantic types, like "the poet whose fervour radiates from him with such intensity as to scorch the vegetation," or simply "the student who wants a quiet nook free from distraction"—all of whom the *Toronto Island Guide* of 1894 assured its readers were to be seen lounging on the breakwater and communing with "the wild waves." Nevertheless, gradually during the nineties increasing numbers of holiday-makers found their way to Ward's Island, whose popularity was no doubt enhanced by the City's "free ferry" that delighted patrons and enraged the rival Toronto Ferry Company, which condemned such "unreasonable and unfair" competition.[20]

The Toronto Ferry Company was not used to competition and had done all in its considerable power to eliminate it. In the late 1880s the ferry business was being consolidated in the hands of a few large operators: notably Captain Andrew Tymon's Island Park Ferry Company and the Doty Ferry Company. Meanwhile, Centre Islander George Gooderham tried to persuade City Council to let him operate an Island ferry monopoly, but withdrew in the face of unseemly publicity. The City, for its part, increased its vigilance by appointing John Robinson as Inspector of Ferries. According to the *Globe* in June 1887, this officer was to ensure that no boat was overloaded, to prevent any "racing or unnecessary whistling," and to look out for any "young men who act in a disorderly manner or molest young ladies."

Finally, in 1890, financier E. B. Osler formed the Toronto Ferry Company, which would dominate transportation to the Island for the next thirty-six years. Osler, like Gooderham, must have known the Island well, having undoubtedly

travelled from his Rosedale home to visit his brother, Judge Featherston Osler, at Hanlan's Point. Not only did Osler acquire the old Doty Company vessels, but he also added two splendid new steamers in the spring of 1890. On Victoria weekend "not the least attractive of the Queen's Birthday sights," the *Globe* reported, was the launching of the $33,000, double-decked, double-ended "palace ferry steamer" the *Mayflower* from the Bathurst Street Wharf. The nine-hundred-passenger *Mayflower* was followed into the water a month later by her sister ship the *Primrose*. John Ross Robertson waxed positively lyrical about these two large paddle-wheelers:

> Their appointments are as nearly as it is possible for them to be perfection and every reasonable convenience is afforded their patrons.... Both these steamers are lighted throughout by electricity, and when loaded with pleasure-seekers at night present a gay and unique appearance. They are universally considered the finest ferry steamers to be found between Hudson's [sic] Bay and the Gulf of Mexico.

In this age before widespread electrification, their twinkling silhouettes must have been an especially memorable sight.

Two years later the Toronto Ferry Company (TFC) acquired Tymon's Island Park Ferry Company to swell its fleet to a dozen vessels. By 1896, according to John Ross Robertson, the company provided a "practically continuous" service from 7 A.M. to 11 P.M. every day (except Sunday) from April to October, as well as a "limited service" on Sundays. The boats ran from Yonge Street and Brock Street Wharfs to both Centre and Hanlan's, as well as from Dufferin and George Street.

The TFC actively set out to drum up business. In 1892 it took over Ned Hanlan's Hotel and the lease for the three-acre northern tip of

Hanlan's Point for the sum of $50,000—not a bad profit for the retired sculler and future alderman, who had spent some $25,000 to build the hotel and paid $15 a year in land rent. There, under the enterprising Amusement Director, J.C. O'Connor, the TFC continued to draw extraordinary crowds of "younger pleasure seekers" to sample "all kinds of attractions, musical, athletic and social." Merry-go-rounds whirled, switchbacks clicked and well-known bands played regularly, while tense spectators gasped at the daring highwire antics of "famous balancers." Just south of Hanlan's was Durnan's Hotel, operated by Ned's sister, where "any number of peanut men, Aunt Sallies, tin-type photographers, shooting booths, pop-corn stalls and all the other nab-nickels that characterize a holiday promenade" were to be enjoyed.[21]

Durnan's Hotel could hardly be described as direct competition, since Emily (Hanlan) Durnan's second marriage in 1893 was to Lawrence "Lol" Solman, the man who later became most responsible for overseeing the TFC's affairs. For both personal and professional reasons the dapper, energetic Lol Solman became heavily involved in developing the Island. His interest only began to flag in the 1920s when his wife died and Sunnyside became increasingly popular. Until then, Torontonians would continue to be amazed and amused by the wizardry of Solman.

While the TFC was working on grand plans to expand its amusement area, the Point continued to be a focus for the rowing and canoeing public. In June 1894 the Toronto Rowing Club hosted its annual spring races at a new clubhouse on Hanlan's Point. Then, on July 2, 1894, a Toronto tradition was inaugurated: the annual Dominion Day regatta, which was then held at the Hanlan's Point Lagoon and now takes place

OUTINGS IN CANADA.

Toronto, Ont.

HOTEL HANLAN,

M. A. THOMAS,
Manager.

Toronto Island.

THE finest and most beautifully situated of any
Summer Resort in Canada. Has accommodation for 150 guests, with all the conveniences to be
found in a modern hotel; with piazza on every
floor, large grounds, billiard rooms, bowling alleys,
lawn tennis and croquet grounds, boating, canoeing
and fishing without limit.

RATES FROM $2 TO $3 PER DAY.

SPECIAL RATES FOR FAMILIES AND PARTIES ON APPLICATION.

F. M. THOMAS, Resident Manager.

(Above) *By the time this ad appeared in the* Wheel
Outings In Canada and C.W.A. Hotel Guide *of
1895, a fourth floor had been added to Hanlan's
Hotel, which is drawn here by another prominent
Islander, architect and sportsman Arthur R.
Denison.* [OA]

(Left) *Ned Hanlan lost his World Championship to
Aussie William Beach in 1884. When he retired,
Hanlan looked after his large family, coached promising scullers like his nephew Eddie Durnan and moved
to the mainland where he represented his Island
Ward 4 constituents for two outspoken terms on City
Council in 1898 and '99. After he died on January
4, 1908, ten thousand Torontonians passed through
St. Andrew's Presbyterian Church where Hanlan lay
in state; and, eighteen years later, the City dedicated
this heroic statue to his memory.* [SDG]

on Centre Island's Long Pond. The Toronto
Rowing Club had another busy afternoon "raking
in the prizes," which were awarded at the
Argonaut Rowing Club's elaborate wood and
stucco fantasy across the bay at the foot of York
Street. These regattas continued at Hanlan's
until 1915.

Canoeists, too, were attracted to the Island's
lagoons. Multitudes of holiday-seekers rented
canoes from Hanlan's, and later Durnan's,
boathouses, to paddle, some more and some less
skilfully, through Island waterways. Members
of the Toronto Canoe Club, established in 1880
by "9 men with the love of the slender craft
in their hearts,"[22] had their main clubhouse on
The Esplanade; but they used "Fancy Free"
cottage on Hanlan's Point as an Island base for
their activities—canoeing and otherwise. Then,
in 1889 and '90, these sporting gentlemen
caused a sensation on the bay with their thirty-
foot, twenty-five-man war canoe, the *Unk-ta-
hee*, or God of the Waters. Whether they caused
a sensation on the Island goes unrecorded.

In the summer of 1894 the TFC began in
earnest to expand its Island empire. Great noisy
sand pumps spewed out sand sucked from the
lake bottom to create new land north and west of
the existing point. By December one hundred
and fifty men were working on the Hanlan's
Point improvements and by 1898 the TFC had
increased its land area from 3 to 12.9 acres and the
assessed value of its property from $18,500 to
$67,750.

Most of the TFC's attention was focused on
expanding the amusement area, but it did not
ignore Hanlan's Hotel. In fact, it shifted it to face
the lagoon regatta course rather than the bay
and also tried, unsuccessfully, in 1895 to break
through the temperance barrier. More successful
was the decision to appeal to the cycling craze
of the gay nineties. Torontonians, like people

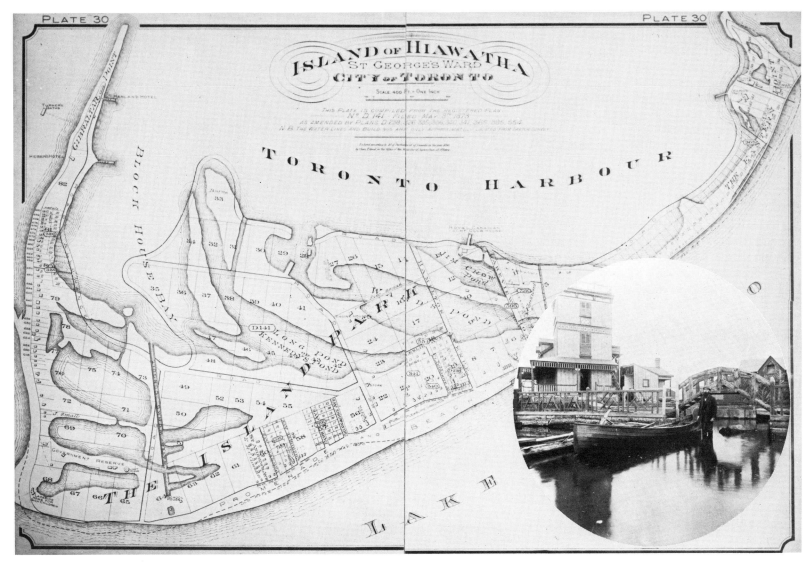

PLATE 30

PLATE 30

By the time Charles E. Goad (inset at his new Island home) produced this 1890 map of what he called the "Island of Hiawatha" after Longfellow's popular narrative poem, he knew the Island at first hand. Its contours had changed markedly since Unwin's 1868 mapping, as a result of strenuous work by City work crews and individual residents bringing over fill and fertilizer. The main residential areas were Hanlan's and Centre, while Ward's Island was left to the Wards and the Wiman Baths. William Clark's store was the only store on what the 1894 Toronto Island Guide *called Middle Road and great areas were still relatively wild and unoccupied.*   [Thomas Fisher Rare Book Library (map) CTA (Goad photograph)] across North America, had fallen in love with the bicycle. Ever-pessimistic publishers prophesied the end of the book: people would simply be too busy bicycling here and there to read. And dour Presbyterian ministers regarded the wobbly contraptions as nearly as sinful as Sunday streetcars—likely to spirit the multitudes away from church and off to seek pleasure. Whatever its moral or intellectual effect, the bicycle was indeed popular and the Island was obviously a perfect place for a spin. Island pathways, in fact, were becoming so crowded that they were positively dangerous and as early as 1894 there was a suggestion to ban bicycling on Island sidewalks. Even after a special bicycle path was built at the urging of Alderman Ned Hanlan and others, complaints still made their way to City Hall. But the more the merrier as far as the ferry company was concerned, as it advertised in the 1895 *Wheel Outings in Canada.*

In 1897 professional baseball came to Hanlan's Point. On the cold Friday afternoon of May 21, some two thousand hardy Toronto fans turned out to cheer the hometown Maple Leafs of the International League. For the first time, the cry of "play ball" rang out across the newly built Hanlan's Point playing field. It was a "seesaw game all along," according to the *World* report. And while everyone seemed pleased with the new diamond, undoubtedly the shivering spectators were disappointed to lose the opener to Rochester, 11-10 in extra innings.

Fans soon had another view of the Nine, when they played a double-header against the Syracuse Stars on the Queen's Birthday. As Toronto teams know only too well, Toronto fans have little patience and what little they had was severely tested on this occasion. Even with the threat of rain, twenty-five hundred fans crossed over for the morning game. By the time

A month after opening day, depicted in this cartoon from the Toronto World, Toronto fans finally had something to cheer about. The "monster crowd" in the Hanlan's Point stadium cheered wildly as the hometown nine caught fire and practically knocked the Rochester invaders into the bay, winning 20 to 12. [MTLB]

the Leafs had lost by an embarrassing 7-0, some youngsters were debating "whether the Torontos could beat a carpet, or not"—and finally decided they could not. Jack-of-all-trades Lush was a "good sticker and outfielder," according to the *Globe,* but "could not play the position" he was assigned. Neither could Casey. (Any team with players called Lush and Casey could not be all bad.) As for short-stop Wagner, he was "like a sieve" and "nearly everything went through him." Undeterred, an enormous crowd pushed into the stadium for the afternoon game (even the fences were hedged with howling rooters), only to see their Leafs throw the game away by "deplorable fielding." The fans may have been disappointed, but the Toronto Ferry Company manifestly was not. It enjoyed a record day.

Reporter Augustus Brindle later recalled the hodge-podge of attractions at the Point of the late 1890s: the Hanlan's Hotel "that seemed to be just about to topple into that part of the Bay'';

Mrs. Hanlan's crowded "old eating house under the willows"; Dave Godfrey's band which drew fifteen thousand people to one Sunday concert; Jim the ice cream man who made his creamy confections from lake ice stored in the old ice house; popcorn, lemonade and ginger-beer vendors who beguiled hungry youths "before there was ever a yard of cement walk on the island"; actors who gave "thrilling performances when the old red, green and blue lights blinked over the Bay and when the canoes and dinghies swarmed in around"; and the "old fortune teller who had her Sybilline cave under the wall of the baseball diamond." Moreover, just to stay on the right side of the religious community, the ferry company obligingly placed its Roof Garden over the ferry shelter at the disposal of the Church of England and Reverend (later Canon) H. C. Dixon conducted the opening service in June 1897. During the rest of the week, of course, the Roof Garden presented less serious offerings— like the sweet sounds of the Cosmopolitan

Trio and the singing and mimicry of Mary E. Cunard.

Not everyone, however, was enamoured of the ferry or the ferry service provided by the Toronto Ferry Company. Throughout the nineties (indeed, right through the nineteen-sixties) many schemes were proposed to bridge the Western (and/or Eastern) Gap and provide public transit directly to the Island. In October 1891, for example, the *Globe* argued in favour of a proposal from "local capitalists" to build a swing bridge over the Western Gap and provide

a street railway which would transform the "Island of Hiawatha", now "as completely abandoned as the coast of Labrador" in winter, into an all-year suburban resort. Then in 1893 City Engineer Keating proposed a "high level" bridge to carry both water and people across the Western Gap.

Not surprisingly, most Island residents were not at all enthusiastic about any proposal to bring clanging streetcars over to disturb the tranquillity of their pastoral retreat. So, in May 1895, the Island Residents Association (formed

the previous year) fired off a protest to City Hall. They wanted assurance, in the form of a new clause in their leases, that no railway would be allowed on the Island. When that had no effect, they turned to Ottawa and on June 15 the minister of the interior even travelled to Toronto to make a personal inspection of the Island. The results were equivocal: no trolley line was built, but Ottawa did not intervene and the City certainly did not give up the idea.

In 1897 the Island bridge and streetcar proposal even became entangled in the horse-trading surrounding the Sunday streetcar controversy that had obsessed Torontonians since the beginning of the decade.[23] After having lost two plebiscites about allowing Sunday streetcars to break the Sabbath, the Toronto Railway Company reached an agreement with Mayor Robert Fleming and City Council to hold a third plebiscite on the condition that the TRC agree to extend its service to the Island over a City-financed bridge. The company had no intention of actually building an unprofitable line to the Island. But since it seemed unlikely that the City would ever put up the $100,000 or more necessary to build a bridge across the Gap at Bathurst Street, the company was willing to gamble. Anything to get another referendum. In the weeks leading up to the May 15 vote, Toronto was awash with rhetoric. The "Saints" thundered from the pulpits, editorialists on both sides lectured endlessly from their papers and the public poured into halls across the city to give vent to its opinions. In the end the pro-Sunday-service forces triumphed by a mere 321 votes. But in all the hoopla, the Island service was ignored—a policy that the Toronto Railway Company would continue to follow for years to come.

For its part, the Toronto Ferry Company could breathe a sigh of relief. No bridge would

The Lakeside Home For Little Children was a great success, so benefactor John Ross Robertson paid to rebuild and expand it in 1891. It took this new, shingled, curvilinear form which was popular in American summer hotels and cottages of the day. [PAC (C-90996)]

THE LAKESIDE HOME FOR LITTLE CHILDREN. TORONTO ISLAND. SUMMER HOME OF HOSPITAL FOR SICK CHILDREN TORONTO. COST $40,000. 125 BEDS be built to cut into its business. But competition might come from another quarter. Throughout the summer of 1897 one of the strangest vessels ever to be built anywhere was taking its weird shape down at Polson's shipyard at the foot of Frederick Street: Knapp's Roller Boat, a giant cylinder, 110 feet long and 22 feet wide, with open tapered ends and two large engines, which was designed to roll over the water like a log rather than plough through like a normal boat. The passenger cabin would remain still, while the outer cylinder revolved. Large numbers of sightseers gathered daily to watch the construction of the boat. Finally on September 8, "in the presence of an immense gathering and amid considerable excitement," according to the *Globe*, the boat slipped, or perhaps rolled, into the bay. It did not sink. But before long, it became painfully clear that rather than attaining the hoped for 25 to 35 mph, the boat would be lucky to reach 5 mph, on a glassy smooth surface. On rough water it was completely unmanageable. So the Roller Boat did not prove to be a transportation revolution.

In the early 1890s City Council experienced its first serious, but temporary, qualms about developing the Island as a residential resort. In January 1891, Council passed a bylaw prohibiting the renewal of Island leases in cases where Council had the option not to renew them. This action was applauded in some quarters—for example by the Toronto Trades and Labour Council and the *Mail*, which was irate about Council's past administration of the Island. Charging various aldermen with being "only too ready to give away to their friends not only the public money but the public land," the *Mail* maintained in October 1893 that the park "belongs to the people" and "should not be reduced but on the contrary ... it should be extended."

But opposition to leasing Island property was short-lived. By August 1894 the *Mail* had made a nimble about-face and was arguing, "It is a great advantage to have a good class of residents on the Island; it keeps money in the City; and it gives busy people, who would find it difficult to go away, the opportunity of summer relaxation." And on September 24, 1894, Council repealed the lease ban and proceeded to

renew Island leases, at higher rates. (Island residents, a notoriously disputatious lot, vigorously opposed what they considered to be unreasonable rent hikes.)

These hemmings and hawings of City Council had little effect on Island development. During the 1890s nearly sixty more buildings sprang up; by 1900 the overall summer population was about three thousand, and many distinguished

When Knapp's Roller Boat rolled out of the Eastern Gap on April 22, 1898, after undergoing some unsuccessful modifications, "so much steam and smoke was thrown out that the vessel was soon hidden away, and seemed like a war vessel under fire," according to the front page of the Star. *[CTA:JC]*

names had been added to the list of Centre Island residents. For example, Alderman John Irwin, who had done so much to promote Island Park (some suggested that it should be named ''Irwin Park''), found his way across the bay to 306 Lake Front in 1890. He retired from municipal politics the following year and by 1894 was simply but elegantly listing his occupation as ''gentleman.''

Surveyor/cartographer Charles E. Goad, whose first map of the Island in 1884 had been horribly inaccurate since it was not based on any actual surveys of the Island, obviously got to know the place better. He established his estate ''Floreat'' on the northern edge of Ward's Pond around 1890 and modestly commemorated the event in large letters on his new 1890 map of the Island. For over twenty years Goad lavished attention on his property: filling and improving the marshy surroundings, carving out islands and waterways, operating his own little steam ferry, supervising a large vegetable garden, laying out a lawn tennis court, building several additional houses and, most of all, expanding and decorating ''Floreat'' itself. Dominated by a square observation tower—showing the Stick Style at its height—and encircled by vine-covered verandahs, ''Floreat'' grew gradually and lovingly. Rustic bridges arched over curving lagoons, a primitive kraal squatted on the lawn and each spring a newly designed section of fence was added to the surrounding wooden fantasy.

In 1894 coal merchant and ex-municipal politician Elias Rogers retreated to ''Belvedere'' on Lake Front Avenue and budding stationery magnate Samuel M. Toy (of Grand and Toy fame) summered less grandly in ''Karaitta,'' one of E. R. C. Clarkson's cottages on St. Andrew's Avenue. A few years later young Arthur L.

Charles E. Goad, father of the Canadian fire atlas, whose company had mapped over 1300 towns by the time of his death in 1910, sits on the steps of his beloved ''Floreat'' in this 1897 photograph by another Islander, F. W. Micklethwaite. [CTA]

Massey landed on the Island for the first time. He was followed by architect E. J. Lennox, who was recovering from the arduous task of building his grand, pink Romanesque City Hall on Queen Street. Massey and Lennox, like their other Lake Front Avenue neighbours, undoubtedly enjoyed the ''sweep of sky and lake before them,'' the ''never ceasing rush and wash of waters on the sand and shingle'' below, and the ''glamour of stars'' and occasional streaming Northern Lights in the heavens above.[24]

Financier Aemilius Jarvis, later hailed by Commodore George H. Gooderham as ''the greatest yachtsman'' in the history of the Royal

Elias Rogers, who had unsuccessfully tried to tarnish Ned Clarke's image in the mayoral battle of 1888 by intemperately accusing teetotaler Clarke of issuing liquor licenses to Island establishments, retreated to "Belvedere" on the right of this 1890 watercolour. His neighbour, lawyer W. H. Lockhart Gordon, who occupied "The Breakers" for many years, dabbled in Island, not municipal, politics by becoming President of the Island Association in 1894. [MTLB]

(Below) *Aemilius Jarvis (centre) is surrounded by the crew of the* Canada, *winner of the first Canada's Cup in 1896.* [RCYC Annals]

Canadian Yacht Club, also found his way to the Island, first to one of the houses built by Charles E. Goad on what would become Chippewa Avenue and later to a house on Bayfront Avenue, where he lived for many years within easy reach of the RCYC. Jarvis was involved in many of the most dramatic sailing events of this and several succeeding decades. On Dominion Day 1891, for example, he participated in what the *Globe* called the "closest and most exciting race ever sailed on the lakes." This was the first contest for the Queen's Cup, a magnificent silver trophy presented to the club by Governor General Lord Stanley (who also donated the famous NHL trophy). The event attracted the "elite of the lake" and the "cream of the cream." Among the entries were Commodore A. R. Boswell's new steel-hulled Scottish cutter, *Vreda*, and Jarvis's five-year-old veteran *White Wings*. At first the breeze was light, but as they neared the finish line off Exhibition Wharf, the wind picked up dramatically. With every stitch of canvas up, *White Wings* appeared headed for victory. Jarvis had a big balloon jib set, which was pulling until the top mast bent like a bow. Meanwhile, aboard the *Vreda*, George Evans was up to his neck in water in the lee scuppers.

"Desperate measures were necessary," he later told RCYC historian Snider, "and I therefore got down on my knees on the deck of the *Vreda* and put forth a moving prayer to the great god Boreas that he would smite us both with his blasts in the hope that something would carry away on the *White Wings*." His prayer was answered. After twenty-eight-and-one-half miles of hard sailing, within sight of the finish line, the *White Wings'* topmast snapped. With the wreck hanging in confusion over her decks and the balloon sail dragging in the lake, she limped across the finish line. Boswell's *Vreda* won by two seconds.

Boreas looked with favour upon Jarvis, however, and the RCYC cutter *Canada* on another important occasion—the first international contest in 1896 for what became known as Canada's Cup. A thrill of pride ran through Canada when Jarvis won this trophy in the United States. Upon his return from Toledo, he was carried in triumph to the great Horticultural Pavilion (where Allan Gardens now stands) to be greeted by a large crowd of admirers, including His Worship Mayor Robert Fleming. Out of his depth in this nautical crowd, the somewhat flustered "People's Bob" did not know how to address Jarvis and coined a new rank, "Skippadore."

Meanwhile, another famous sailing family, the Gooderhams, was busy expanding its Island empire and raising yet more sailors. The first Gooderham place at 244 Lake Front (Lakeshore) was improved and a second mansion was built next door in the late nineties by William G. At a time when the RCYC clubhouse was valued at $4,000, this second summer estate was valued at $8,000, and, more importantly perhaps, provided an excellent view of RCYC races out on the open lake.

As early as 1894 this whole area east of Hamilton Avenue (later Hooper) was regarded by the *Toronto Island Guide* as "one of the pleasantest in the Island." Under an umbrella of giant pines, the cottages in this vicinity were of a more substantial character than elsewhere and "the lucky well-to-do folks here enjoy[ed] country benefits within hail of their city engagements." Rather than the bathtubs and old bedsteads full of flowers found elsewhere on the Island, residents here cultivated real flower gardens. The decorative and luxuriant "flowers and creepers that bloom in the dooryards," as well as the "better choice" in paint colours, definitely "show[ed] what taste may effect."

The Gooderham children, like other children, were probably oblivious to the swank surroundings and more concerned with the important business of playing. Young Norman Gooderham, who was destined to become famous in the annals of international sailing by winning more international contests than any previous RCYC member, began to find his sea legs in this period. He used to accompany his grandfather George on his daily cruises in the *Oriole II*, dreading the outings more than a thrashing at school because of the seasickness that often accompanied them. But Gooderhams sailed; so Norman conquered the waves, as well as his seasickness, in the era's popular little Wilton Morse dinghy.

Island residents in the 1890s, as always, were subjected to a number of hazards and nuisances. Besides the periodic violent storms there were the mosquitoes which infested the still numerous stagnant ponds and lagoons and also the masses of stinking fish which from time to time were washed up onto Island beaches. There was also City Hall, which as owner of the Island was a perpetual and sometimes unwelcome presence.

It was mostly to deal with this latter problem that the growing Island community banded together to form the Island Association in 1893, with Centre Islander W. H. Lockhart Gordon as its first, industrious president. Drawing its membership and executive from the three main residential areas, the association's purpose was simple: "to protect and advance the Island's interests." Naturally it became involved in a wide range of issues: e.g., sanitary (or unsanitary) conditions, ferry services, provision of utilities, fire and police protection and improvements to Island Park as well as the residential areas.[25]

On August 20, 1894, the Island Association became involved with a higher level of government when Prime Minister Sir John Thompson visited the Island to be fêted and, incidentally, to inspect the Dominion harbour works at the eastern end. After appropriate ceremonies at City Hall, the P.M. and the civic party were ferried across the bay for a "sumptuous luncheon" at Centre Island. The Park Pavilion had been transformed into a "bower of beauty" festooned with brilliant flags and bunting and banked around with fragrant flowers and luxuriant foliage. The band of the Queen's Own played "sweet music on the lawn," while the visitors munched, drank and talked their way through lunch. After appropriate toasts were exchanged, and after a photographic session, the party wended its way toward the breakwater. On the way toward the Eastern Gap the association's president Gordon and several of the members intercepted the official group and escorted them to Gordon's nearby home, "The Breakers." Complimenting Thompson on his recent success as one of the arbitrators of the Bering Sea dispute with the Americans, Gordon went on to discuss more local concerns—such as finishing the breakwater and creating a "safe and pleasant walk" along it as "a very gratifying memento to Toronto citizens of the visit to the Island of their distinguished Premier.'' After making appropriately noncommittal noises, the prime minister moved on to inspect the Island works, and ended the visit with more refreshments and an informal reception at the RCYC clubhouse. From a social point of view, at least, the visit had been ''an unqualified success,'' but when the party disembarked from the *Luella* at the RCYC's mainland wharf and Alderman John Hallam baldly told the prime minister that they expected a grant of at least $100,000, Sir John ''only smiled and said nothing.''[26]

Another major Island organization was formed at about this time, the Island Amateur Aquatic Association (IAAA). In the early days the Gooderhams kindly let the association hold dances at their house, but members soon built the first Aquatic Hall overlooking Long Pond. Although the IAAA undoubtedly performed a useful political function—by inviting members of City Council to its entertaining and keenly contested regattas—its main purpose was recreational. In 1894, for example, it organized a series of regattas on Long Pond, which culminated on Saturday, August 25. Both sides of Long Pond (including the grandstand on the north side) were thronged with spectators. Many residents were comfortably ensconced in hundreds of canoes and boats ranged along a boom protecting the south side of the course. Some of the residents were dressed in ''Boarding House'' colours— the ''Calithumpians'' wore ''the non-sectarian colors of their organization, orange and green,'' while the ''Myobs,'' clustered around a yacht gaily trimmed with flags, bunting and bullrushes, wore large knitted saucer-shaped hats in brown and blue. The Toronto Canoe Club and the Argonauts each sent a fully-manned war canoe to cheer the participants on. The entertainment

itself was ''excellent,'' though occasionally bizarre. A tilting tournament eventually saw all the participants dumped into the lagoon and in the ladies' and gents' tandem ''great amusement was caused by the upset of the two Wade brothers, one of whom was dressed as a lady,'' whose disguise proceeded to come fetchingly apart in the water.[27]

As the residential community grew, little St. Andrew's-by-the-Lake began to bulge at the seams; so in 1895 the church was enlarged by moving the chancel farther back and adding a transept, thereby nearly doubling the seating capacity. Island church services, like other aspects of Island life, were distinctive and almost defiantly unconventional. One Sunday afternoon *Telegram* publisher John Ross Robertson journeyed over from the city to attend church. The little *Arlington* was crowded, mostly with people ''of the working classes'' and, as he strolled along the narrow wooden walk across Island Park, he passed parents pushing prams and picnic parties ''spread out on the grass in reckless confusion.'' Rowers glided about the lagoons, barefoot children dashed along the beach, a magnificent surf beat against the shore and far out on the lake ''white wings glistened clearly against the dark blue of the waters.'' Robertson slipped into the last pew of the crowded church for the 4 P.M. service, where he soaked up the atmosphere and was pleasantly struck by ''the unconventional style of dress'' of the worshippers. The latest fashions were not to be seen. Young ladies avoided ''those villainous high hats'' which were the height of fashion but distasteful to Robertson. Instead they wore low-crowned straw bonnets and simple white dresses that complimented their tanned complexions. Many young men wore yachting costumes and many little boys were attired in sailor's suits. All in all

this ''variety of dress, taken with the plainly furnished chapel, the open windows through which the breezes came laden with vigour and health, the sound of the surf on the shore and the gay laughter of little children playing on the sand made the room pleasant, cool, airy and bright.''

The Island community, of course, was primarily a summer one, with a couple of thousand summer residents by 1888. Nevertheless, a few hardy souls—like the Wards at the far distant Eastern Point, Park Superintendent David Kimmings at Centre, George Durnan and his family at the Lighthouse and various Hanlans at the western end—weathered the storms and the various other hardships of winter life. Legend has it that these year-round residents knew spring was coming when the bear from the Hanlan's Point Amusement Park zoo dug himself out from under the bicycle track.

In the early 1880s Katherine Durnan, wife of Lighthouse Keeper George Durnan, had begun teaching the three Rs to Island children at her home during the winter. Finally, in 1887, thirteen residents petitioned the Public School Board to establish a school for the children of permanent residents. The board agreed; the City provided a treeless, windswept site near the Lighthouse and in November 1888 the little one-room schoolhouse opened with seventeen students. The early years were precarious; in fact, sometimes the school was closed for lack of sufficient students. But in 1896 the Island Public School was made permanent. The teacher, Miss Helyer, was paid the fulsome salary of $350 because she acted as *de facto* principal, and Lighthouse Keeper Durnan received $100 per year to be the caretaker.

Because no stores remained open on the Island during the winter, the main problem faced by residents was travelling to the city for supplies.

Not a windswept Prairie schoolhouse, but the windswept Island schoolhouse of the 1890's. [Island Public School]

Sometimes they even went on short rations because they could not cross the bay. Generally speaking they were better off in the dead of winter when the ice was frozen solid, though problems sometimes arose even when they could walk across the bay. One winter in the late 1870s John Ward, an uncle of David and William Ward, lost his way in a snowstorm while crossing the ice toward the Island, and walked out onto the lake and was drowned. On another occasion Ned Hanlan began walking across what appeared to be good ice; when he was some distance out he came on a stretch of thin ''leathery'' ice which he crossed by the ingenious method of rolling for two hundred yards. Experienced Islanders, therefore, learned to travel with a knife or an awl which they could dig into the ice if they happened to plunge through.

One of the most dramatic—and tragic—crossings occurred in the Western Gap on January 27, 1894. At about three-thirty that Saturday afternoon five Islanders who had all been in the city for the day met at Queen's Wharf to return home. Because the bay was not frozen solid, they had come over in a rowboat. As the winter sun sank Miss Sarah Forrest (the current Island schoolteacher who boarded at the Durnans), Island Constable John Gray and his wife, Island Park Superintendent David Kimmings and George Ham (the caretaker at the Lakeside Home For Little Children) pushed off from the wharf and easily broke through the scum of ice covering the channel. To their east the bay was frozen, while to their west beyond the mouth of the Gap immense cakes of ice bobbed in the restless water. Suddenly the swift current of the channel caught the ice floes and swept them toward the boat, crushing it against the wall of ice to the east. While Ham emptied his recently filled milk pail and desperately tried to bail, the small craft was crushed like an eggshell, dumping the hapless travellers into the numbing water. Kimmings picks up the tale:

[T]he ice closed in over our heads. I was close to Miss Forrest when we went down, and as I rose again I managed to seize her by the shoulder and bring her up with me. With the other hand I broke through some thin ice overhead and got hold of Miss Forrest with the other hand. Suddenly the ice came together again and we both were crowded under. I managed to retain my hold on the ice, though my head was forced under the water, but Miss Forrest slipped from my grasp and went down, and I never saw her again. I succeeded in forcing another hole through the ice, and once more got my head above water.

Meanwhile Gray had come to the surface and grabbed his wife, holding on until the ice crushed in on them, and drove them under. He was more fortunate than I was, though, and when he came to the surface again had still a hold on Mrs. Gray. Once more the ice came together and we all went under for a third time, this time being carried under the solid ice. Gray lost his wife in the struggle which followed, but in a moment he got her again and brought her up.[28]

This time the two Grays and Kimmings were able to hold onto the edge of the ice, while their legs were being bashed and lacerated by ice floes under the surface. Ham was eventually able to claw his way up onto the shelf of ice and lie face down, not daring to move for fear of being plunged under once more. Fortunately, some crewmen on the *Chippewa*, which was moored nearby, saw the accident and began to lob bits of lumber unsuccessfully toward them. Finally, they tied a line around a brick and hurled it within a few feet of Ham. By crawling carefully across the ice, Ham was able to reach the line and pass it to the others. With the greatest of difficulty the four survivors were drawn to shore. The body of the less fortunate Miss Forrest was later dragged out of the bay and sent home for burial.

During the summer, the bay was far more hospitable and the Royal Canadian Yacht Club

The RCYC was well-established on the Island by the time this photograph was taken in the 1890's. [RCYC]

continued to flourish. By 1894 the club's membership of 750 was reportedly the largest in the world and there were over sixty yachts flying the club colours. The Island clubhouse, opened in 1881, was by now comfortably overgrown with vines, while the lawns, bowling greens and tennis courts were properly manicured. Moreover, it was no longer a strictly male preserve and the Wednesday Ladies' Days were eagerly awaited by guests and members alike.

In the same year, the club built a new mainland pier and clubhouse at the foot of Simcoe Street. Appropriately, it was designed by an active RCYC member, Norman B. Dick, and his partner. The new clubhouse was "a spirited piece of Classical architecture," according to architectural historian William Dendy—very much in the mode of the Southern Plantation/Colonial

Revival style becoming popular in North America at the time. (The Gooderham's Island mansion was another example.) It was quite blatantly a piece of facade architecture, designed more to be seen and admired "mirrored white and shining, in the lake as a proud expression of the Club's importance" than to be used, except as a shelter while awaiting the club steamer *Hiawatha* or as a grandstand for watching regattas on the bay. For all its appearance of solidity and grandeur, the wood and stucco building was not designed to withstand the rigours of the Toronto climate.

It did not have to withstand these rigours for very long, however. In January 1896, when club members were tucked safely in bed dreaming of the coming summer's sailing, disaster struck. At 3 A.M. fire broke out and quickly enveloped the "handsome airy structure." A stiff north wind drove the flames directly toward the lake "casting fantastic fairy-like shadows, and shapes over the frozen surface of the Bay." So brilliant was the light, in fact, that "the outlines of the Island loomed up clear, and bold, adding to the strangeness of the picture."[29] Pyjama-clad caretaker Thomas Lilly and his wife, who lived on the top floor, had a narrow escape, but many of the club's prized possessions did not. The new RCYC mainland clubhouse that soon rose on the same site proved to be longer-lived, but poorer in club memorabilia.

Fire was not the only threat to yachting (let alone life and limb). "The bicycle," snorted RCYC chronicler C. J. H. Snider, "was the first of many menaces which have threatened yachting as a sport, golf and motoring being its immediate successors." But in the late 1890s everybody rode a bicycle, so the RCYC attempted to harness this pedal power (and keep its members) by forming a bicycle club in 1896. As a result, Snider

lamented, "Club spins of an afternoon or evening replaced the pastime of sailing with many." Some members were able to combine the two activities: Commodore Aemilius Jarvis, for example, regularly cycled from his office down to the mainland clubhouse, en route to a sail. And no matter what crusty old salts like Snider felt, "One of the common sights of the time was a yacht's dinghy towing astern, loaded to the gunwales almost with the bicycles of her knickerbockered crew."

By the 1890s Island Park was already clearly "the playground of the people," according to the *Toronto Island Guide*. But the leisurely life at Centre Island was in marked contrast to the sometimes frenetic pace at Hanlan's Point, with its lady sharpshooters, daring high divers, cuddly dog and pony circuses and the ever-changing midway attractions. By 1894 the heart of the park already had a settled look, with pleasant shady walks and lush green lawns, although it was still relatively wild around the edges.

The City worked in fits and starts to improve the park. In 1890 it built a new Island Park Wharf to accommodate the Toronto Ferry Company's new boats the *Primrose* and the *Mayflower*, which sparked an immediate increase in the number of visitors. The Toronto Ferry Company, for its part, built a bandstand in the park in 1893 and sponsored free afternoon concerts to attract more ferry patrons. Other concessionaires were also attracted. The Doty family (whose ferry operations had been bought out by the TFC) offered to build a "handsome" merry-go-round in 1891, which it then operated for most of the decade. Another new-fangled swirling contraption, which had only recently found its way to the amusement mecca of Atlantic City, was added in 1895: a ferris wheel which lifted adventurous patrons above the trees for a look at the water. Then, with the Doty merry-go-round pumping and hooting in the background, enthusiastic aquabats could don their elaborate swimming costumes in the new Centre Island Baths on the southern edge of Long Pond and wade into the (relatively) warm lagoon water. More intrepid swimmers, of course, crowded the beach and plunged into the colder, less placid lake.

Meanwhile, amateur boaters splashed and zig-zagged across Island lagoons, inspiring amusement, if not outright laughter, from the more skilful:

> As a rule those who go "boat riding" know little of rowing, and while the connoisseur is to be found at the boat clubs on the city side or at the western ferry wharves, the plain citizen disports himself around the lagoons in the Park with great satisfaction to himself and his

company. The finger of technical scorn may be directed towards the crab-catching amateur, but much enjoyment is to be had for 25 cents an hour by the unskillful waterman, who is dextrous in his jollity though clumsy beyond pardon in his feathering.[30]

As a reward, the "overheated and perspiring swains and fathers" could retreat to a nearby refreshment stand for a large ice-cream soda. Naturally, Island businessmen were keen to tap this water-borne trade. Ned's brother John Hanlan and Joseph Goodwin (the captain of the *Ada Alice*, which provided off-season ferry service for workmen and residents) competed for the attention of the amateur Centre Island argonauts of the nineties. As early as June 1890 Hanlan had sought permission to erect a tent and rent out boats in the park, but the City's Executive Committee turned him down. Hanlan

solved the problem by building a boathouse around 1891 outside the park boundaries on the south side of Long Pond east of the bridge, not far from where the present boat-rental operation is. Around 1900, when John Hanlan died, Emily and Lol Solman took over his boathouse and then around 1907, Edward English took it over. With its broad ramp, distinctive red-roofed yellow tower and convenient refreshment stand, "English's Boathouse" became a landmark on the lagoon. Meanwhile, Joseph Goodwin was concentrating on the park. By 1892 he seems to have established a boat business and in 1893 even offered to pay the City $50 for the privilege of renting boats in the park. By the end of the decade Goodwin was well established and continued until 1913, when his Island Park "boating privilege" was transferred to English.

This photograph taken around 1895 shows three of the elaborate boathouses which lined the mainland waterfront: the RCYC boathouse which burned down in January 1896 (left), the Toronto Canoe Club (centre, with flag) and the Argonaut Rowing Club (right). Both the RCYC and the Toronto Canoe Club had Island bases, and the Argonauts nearly saw the error of their ways by leasing land for a time on Mugg's Island where they hoped to build a new clubhouse. [MTLB]

The increasing crowds put increasing pressure on existing facilities. New waterclosets, for example, were needed and, fortunately, built. And the old refreshment pavilion had become "entirely inadequate" for the large number of visitors, especially on rainy days when drenched picnickers tried to huddle under its limited shelter. So in 1892 an extension was added. The enlarged pavilion was enjoyed not only by the hoi polloi, but also by such luminaries as the principal of Upper Canada College for a benefit concert, the Independent Order of Good Templars for their annual church service and Prime Minister Sir John Thompson for the famous civic luncheon in August 1894. Hughes & Company, the long-time operators of the Island Park Pavilion, also sought permission to sponsor a series of Sunday "sacred concerts"— not only to praise God, but to attract customers.

Just as the number of individual park visitors increased, so did the number of group picnics and sponsored events. On Dominion Day 1893, for example, holiday-makers were no doubt astonished to hear the distinctive strains of the Salvation Army band "Glory Hallelujahing" across the park. The Salvation Army was out in force, having a picnic.

Then, on Monday September 3, 1894, another group turned out in force: "labour" went on holiday, not on strike. For the first time in the Dominion, Labour Day was a legal holiday and Torontonians celebrated in suitable style. Labour badges of red, white and blue were seen everywhere in the streets, outgoing steamers were crowded, in spite of the threatening weather and, above all, thousands flocked to the Island for Toronto's first official Labour Day picnic. A "good many family picnic parties" spread out on the grass and early arrivals were entertained by not one, but two bands, who "made the willow

leaves quiver with their rivalling airs." The 48th Highlanders "blew bold Highland strains" from the bandstand in the centre of the park; while the Queen's Own band, "confident of its charms," withdrew to a clump of trees at the farthest edge of the park and played to a "small audience of connoisseurs." Initiating a Labour Day tradition, politicians were numerous and the clichés plentiful. After speeches by the likes of Lieutenant Governor George Kirkpatrick and the "mellifluous" businessman Mayor Warring Kennedy about the "dignity of labor" and feisty rebuttals by the likes of that "old war-horse of labor" Alfred Jury, the crowd of working people was undoubtedly relieved to return to the sports events, which included a "time of wild excitement" on the baseball ground. Finally, a number of youthful celebrants ended the day by dancing under the stars at the Park Pavilion.[31]

In spite of these celebrations, 1894 was not a good year for labour or business. Toronto was sinking into a depression. Parks Superintendent John Chambers did what he could to provide

Island Park of the 1890's (reproduced in this Edwardian postcard) looks not unlike the Island Park of the 1980's—apart from the top hats. [AC]

some relief—and some stimulus to the now lagging Island Park development. Parks Department workers had created a "very pretty little island" for waterfowl (partially stocked, as an appropriate political swan-song, by former Alderman John Irwin). They also had razed one of the "greatest eyesores" on the Island, William Ward's "old fishing hut on the lake front," which had obstructed the view of the lake from the park. But now, in October 1894, Chambers, spurred on by the call for a "comprehensive and efficient plan" for the park and the obvious need to "furnish work for those out of employment" began an ambitious work programme, which led, among other things, to the development of Manitou Road.[32]

While the TFC was working feverishly to expand Hanlan's Point at the western tip of the Island, hundreds of City workers converged on Centre Island. During 1894 and '95 sturdy steamers towed scowloads of earth and street sweepings from various points on the mainland to the park. Steaming horses dragged sand

On Victoria's Diamond Jubilee, June 22, 1897, the Island was alive with happy summer scenes like this one. [AC]

dredged from Long Pond and other lagoons over to be dumped in the two hitherto noxious ponds east and west of the pavilion, to create another fourteen acres of parkland. And large gangs of workmen braved the cold to work on the park and take home a pay packet. The old, low wooden bridge across Long Pond was demolished and replaced by a substantial iron one with an aesthetically arched silhouette; and the road south of the bridge leading toward the lake (formerly known simply as "Middle Road" now known more euphoniously as Manitou Road) was filled, graded and lined with trees. The work was cold; in an excess of sympathy and generosity which they later regretted, Council members voted to give the men hot coffee—a perk which they later rescinded. And the work was ill-paid; at fifteen cents an hour it was hardly a get-rich-quick scheme. But, given the alternative, it was welcome.[33]

Few businesses lined Manitou Road at this time. The Island Supply Company was using William Clark's old place to sell "high class groceries, fancy fruits, nuts, bread, and other necessities" as advertised in the *Mail & Empire*, but "the building presented a shabby appearance" and needed planting, painting and repairing according to City officials.

Ironically, in the latter part of the decade as the economic climate improved work on the park continued, but at a more modest pace. Meanwhile, pressure was beginning to mount on civil servants to prepare a comprehensive plan for the development of *all* the Island. Chambers, however, was not to be hurried and did not respond until after the turn of the century.

Eighteen-ninety-seven was Queen Victoria's Diamond Jubilee and "Toronto the Loyal" was determined to demonstrate that its "corner of the Empire was not backward in its demonstration of affection and gladness." Indeed, two years later, many of its sons would eagerly volunteer for the war against the Boers. For the time being the downtown was awash in a sea

of red, white and blue bunting. All major buildings were "richly and appropriately ornamented" with flags, bunting and electric lights. The five-year-old Parliament Buildings in Queen's Park were particularly stunning—ablaze with thousands of incandescent globes forming a gigantic crown and other appropriate designs, whose "rays could be seen far out over the lake."

Throughout the afternoon and evening the City "gave itself up to pleasure with a zest seldom seen in this somewhat stolid Anglo-Saxon community." A gigantic procession, some twelve thousand strong and five miles long, wound its way to Exhibition Park. The bay was "white with the sails of yachts," the RCYC was the sponsor of a race won by Aemilius Jarvis and the Island itself was packed with pleasure-seekers throughout the day and long into the night.

By 9 P.M. hundreds of people had gathered in Island Park and hundreds more bobbed in boats out on the bay. Toronto sparkled "like a distant fairyland," with electric lights gleaming and fireworks scattering in showers over the water. Just east of Island Park Wharf an enormous bonfire of three cords of wood, brush, tar and coal oil, stood ready to be lighted. (Street Commissioner Jones had built it two days earlier and, struck by the "horrid thought" that someone might set it off prematurely, he had assigned men to sit on it—and the two mainland woodpiles—for two successive evenings. In this case, sitting down on the job was positively admirable.) All went well. At nine o'clock, three rockets announced that the pile was about to be fired and, an instant later, amid the cheers of the crowd, it was a mass of flames. All in all, satisfied Torontonians could bask in the pleasure of a "perfect holiday" and a grand display.[34]

7
Edwardian Heyday

The turn of the century ushered in the Edwardian heyday of Toronto Island. In January 1901 fun-loving (some would say dissolute) Edward at last inherited the throne from his aged mother, Victoria; and nowhere in Toronto were the high spirits of the age more evident than on the Island. Torontonians had celebrated the final Victorian Dominion Day in suitably quiet style. "The sobriety of Toronto at holiday seasons is turning into a proverb," the *Globe* noted with satisfaction, "and yesterday was in this respect no exception to the rule." Nevertheless, July 1, 1900, was a "red letter day" in the annals of Island history, with the largest crowd on record visiting Hanlan's Point. Large audiences gathered for open-air performances of the maudlin but instructive *Uncle Tom's Cabin*, which remained popular in Canada far longer than in the United States. Meanwhile, on the lighter side, Harry D'Esta and his "wonderful and amusing marionettes" were packing them into the Roof Garden. On the previous afternoon, the Tecumsehs and the Torontos had put on a splendid show of lacrosse that was "not far from downright brutality" and raised mighty cheers from the thirty-five hundred spectators in the stadium. The ferry company, however, "seems to have been the only company that lost money at all"; a team of runaway horses knocked over their ticket stand and sent a "shower of silver" into the Yonge Street slip. The ticket seller was recovered, but the money was not.

Aptly symbolized by the grand new King Edward Hotel—conceived, designed, financed and opened by Islanders[1]—which supplanted the aging Queen's Hotel as Toronto's most luxurious watering spot, Edwardian Toronto was buoyant and self-satisfied. It was a time of prosperity, when fortunes were made—and lost—with astonishing rapidity, as Casa Loma's Sir Henry Pellatt learned to his cost. It was a time of explosive growth, when Toronto's population grew from about 200,000 in 1900 to about 470,000 in 1914, and Toronto's new electrified streetcars stretched out to bring distant suburbs like Deer Park and North Rosedale under City control. And it was a time of seemingly unbounded optimism, when publisher, Board of Trade president, and one-time Islander, W. J. Gage could look to the future and see "the greatest city of all Canada—a city of over a million people...expressive of all that uplifts and is beneficent."[2] To be sure, Toronto had her poor; entire families could be seen scavenging in garbage dumps along the waterfront. But leaders of society did not dwell overlong on such economic (indeed, moral) misfits.

Nor did Lol Solman, who became manager of the Toronto Ferry Company in 1901 and promptly allied himself with that other great entertainment entrepreneur of the age, the mysterious Ambrose Small. Small was the slight, unpretentious millionaire who was to disappear in 1919 more magically than his illusionist friend Harry Blackstone. For the time being, however, Small was firmly in sight and had agreed that Solman would look after the steamers, the hotel and the restaurants, while he would take charge of the attractions at the Point. According to the *Mail & Empire* of March 26, 1901, Small and Solman intended to "strike out on new lines" in their management of the Island—notably to bring vaudeville and big bands, as well as "first class" sporting events to the amusement area.

All went swimmingly until the evening of September 8, 1903. About 8 P.M. Eddie Durnan, Ned Hanlan's nephew and another champion

The Toronto Ferry Company's flagship, the Bluebell, *lands Edwardian pleasure-seekers at Hanlan's Point c. 1906.* [AC]

oarsman, discovered a fire in the wooden grandstand, about half an hour after the Tecumsehs had finished a practice. He immediately telephoned in an alarm to the Lombard Street Station. But, within two hours, the old wooden stadium (which had been expanded to hold ten thousand spectators) was no more. The great blaze drew hundreds of city-dwellers to the downtown wharfs—and thousands more to the Canadian National Exhibition grounds. Meanwhile, city firemen were rushing across the bay on the *Primrose* and the volunteer Island Firemen (organized only three years earlier) were cycling furiously to the blazing Point. But they were hopelessly underequipped so that "it was like fighting the fire with a garden hose," according to the *World* report. Only shrewd, courageous

work prevented the fire from "sweeping away the pavilion, the dining pavilion, the theatre stage, the swings shed, and dear knows what all." As it was, by morning only "a ring of smouldering debris mark[ed] the spot where previously stood the grand-stand and bleachers of the athletic field and the barroom." The ever-inventive Solman, who estimated the loss to the ferry company at about $15,000 to $20,000, made the best of a bad situation: he ordered ferries to take large crowds over to see the blaze at close quarters. Not surprisingly, he and others were soon calling for better fire protection at the Island.

Meanwhile, Island Park was becoming ever more popular and crowded. In 1902 alone, for example, 192 group picnics were spread and 174 games of baseball, 68 cricket matches, 38

football matches and 5 lacrosse matches were played there. So, prodded by the newly formed Island Committee,[3] Parks Superintendent John Chambers finally unveiled his Island plan in December 1903. Chambers had spent an interesting fall dashing around the countryside visiting parks from Philadelphia to Montreal and from Coney Island, New York to Belle Isle, Detroit. He was impressed by the "colossal expenditure" on the various American parks; but the City, apparently, was not, though it is too bad that Council consistently refused to hire the world-famous landscape architect Frederick Law Olmsted of New York's Central Park and Montreal's Mount Royal Park to help Chambers. The park superintendent also spent time becoming more familiar with the idiosyncracies of Toronto's own Island under the guidance of city surveyor, and Hanlan's Pointer, Villiers Sankey. Without the help of an expert, Chambers was forced to admit, the Island "closely resembles a maze, where one goes in at one place and comes out at the same point."

The fruits of his labour were workmanlike, if not exciting. Like all early Island plans, Chambers' plan assumed that the Island would continue to have both parkland and residential areas, and was intended to improve both. But unlike other plans before and after, Chambers did *not* recommend bridging over or tunneling under either Gap to provide access for street cars or automobiles. Probably the major results of Chambers' plan were the eventual creation of the thirty-six-acre Athletic Ground called

Goad's 1903 map shows the expanded Hanlan's Point Amusement Park area, with the hotel looking across the regatta course lagoon toward the Western Sandbar (not shown here). The growing cottage communities are prominent at Hanlan's and Centre (but the tenting areas along the Western Sandbar and on Ward's Island are not included), and "Manitou Road" still only has one store. [Thomas Fisher Rare Book Library]

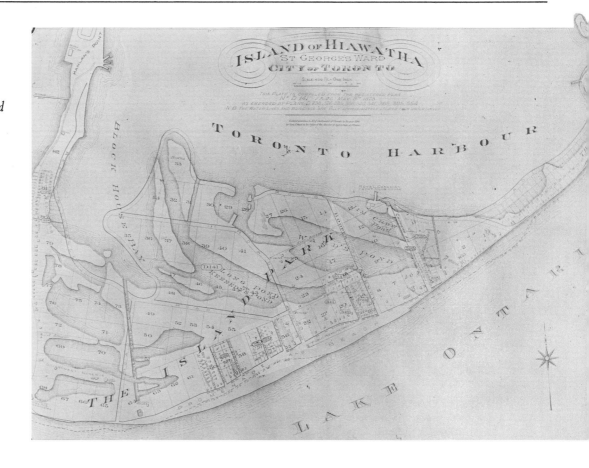

"Toothpick Island" (now Olympic Island) from "the island and swampy ground" between Centre Island and the Royal Canadian Yacht Club, and the cutting of major channels north and east of Chippewa Avenue.

By 1903 "Drake's game" of bowling on the green was "in full swing" at the RCYC according to Snider, and the sailors began "that excellent custom" of taking the bowlers along with them on the final cruising race of the season. Sportsmen and non-sportsmen alike could sip tea on the club's ivy-covered verandahs and admire the view across the bay toward the city. Before a year was out, however, the view would be radically altered, the bowling green marred and the verandahs destroyed altogether. For 1904 was the year of the great fires.

On the night of April 19-20 the commercial heart of Toronto was devastated by a great fire that "swept through the wholesale centre of the city, leaving in its track acres of smoking ruins, where a few hours before there had been huge warehouses and factories." Beginning at 8 P.M. near Bay and Wellington, the fire swept rapidly toward the lake, pushed by a 30 mph wind blowing, fortunately, from the north. "Thousands upon thousands" of sensation seekers were "drawn from every corner of the city" and some of them began pillaging. Guided by the sickeningly orange sky, special trains of firemen arrived from Niagara Falls and other points, while steamers passed the Island with reinforcements from Brantford, Peterborough and elsewhere.

(Left) *The City's new weed cutter pauses, weeds dripping, on an Island lagoon to pose for a City photographer in November 1905. The machine was imported from England where it had been "most effective in English rivers," according to City records; it was hoped that it would "put an end to the intolerable nuisance of weeds" in this tangled corner of the Empire as well.* [CTA]

(Below) *No bellyflops for Gorman's famous diving horses, as crowds watch from the Hanlan's Point Amusement Park c. 1907 and the aging bridge to the Western Sandbar marches across the lagoon in the distance.* [CTA:JC]

Several of these boats were "stationed along the waterfront and did splendid service," pouring water on the advancing flames. The Volunteer Fire Brigade of the Island did not shirk its duty. It crossed the bay and was among those later commended by City Council for its "generous and prompt response."[4]

After a busy winter of repairing damage from its own fire the previous September, the Toronto Ferry Company reopened the refurbished Hanlan's Point Amusement Park with much hoopla on May 24, 1904. It was another record-breaking day, complete with a festive balloon ascension, from which the charred remains of the devastated downtown were still clearly visible. Not resting on his laurels, Lol Solman set new records the following Victoria Day when the *Telegram* estimated that fifty thousand had crossed over. But there was a fly in the ointment: the ferries seemed unable to handle the crowds and there was "much swearing and gnashing of teeth" at the overcrowded wharf. Large numbers of people, of course, circumvented the ferry system by taking their own boats across the bay. In September 1905 one idiot attracted a large crowd onto the deck of the *Primrose* by demonstrating how closely he could follow the swells of the

boat in his canoe. About halfway across the bay, he lost control of his craft, which was sucked into the paddle wheel and crushed. Fortunately, the witless and nearly exhausted individual was plucked to safety. But most people relied on the ferries—and on patience.

Fortunately, other boaters were more skilful and less foolish, since the Toronto of 1904 had ''over 1,200 boats of one description or another, stately yachts, grimy coal schooners, pudgy ferry boats, and tiny butterfly-like sailing dinghies, the nondescript sailing craft of a score of rigs and graceful curves, palace steamers and the useful rowboat.'' While the most graceful and breathtaking were the great yachts, undoubtedly the most popular boat in the first decade or so of the century was the lowly dinghy—''the chubby little varnished fellow with a yellow sail like a butterfly wing''[5]—which was safe, easily handled by one person and roomy enough for three or four. The most famous of the sixteen-footers was *White Cap*, whose skipper was A. J. ''Plug'' Phillips of the RCYC. Phillips, RCYC historian Snider commented, could ''do anything'' with the *White Cap*. Meanwhile, young Norman Gooderham made his own snub-nosed fourteen-footer famous on the bay, snapping up virtually every prize in sight.

Although this very bay had acted as a protective shield against the April fire downtown, it became a hazardous barrier later that summer when fire struck directly at the Island itself. About ten o'clock Monday August 15, 1904, RCYC steward Robert McCheyne left the weekly dance in the ballroom of the old Island clubhouse and went upstairs to his family's flat. To his horror, immediately over the bed where his ten-year-old son Robbie was peacefully sleeping, a fire had broken out. Pieces of burnt

shingles were dropping down on the sleeping child and the bedclothes were beginning to smoulder. Snatching up the child in his arms, McCheyne dashed downstairs and, on his way out, warned orchestra leader Glionna and club members, who were in the middle of a waltz. As the music died out the cry of fire was passed around the room. Without any unnecessary bustle or excitement, the ladies were escorted out to safety on the bowling green and the gentlemen then returned to save whatever they could. Although many valuables were rescued and stored temporarily in the ''annex,'' many invaluable records, pictures and models were destroyed. Perhaps aroused by the sight of the great tower burning, Vice Commodore George H. Gooderham was on the scene shortly after the outbreak of fire. Unfortunately, the city firemen did not arrive as promptly. By the time the *Island Queen* had made her way back from Centre Island and the firemen and Island residents at the city docks had sorted out who should go over first (the firemen, at last, were given precedence), it was after 11 P.M. and the fire had practically consumed

RCYC members and their guests gather for one of the many splendid garden parties held at their second clubhouse on the Island. [AC]

the whole clubhouse. The ''scene of many a brilliant social event…and the landmark of the Island'' was no more, the *Star* reported the next day.

Even while the embers were still smouldering, Commodore Stephen Haas told the *Globe* that ''rebuilding operations would be commenced immediately on a larger and more extensive scale.'' Club members applied themselves to the task with characteristic energy. By 1905 the cool, elegant classicism of Sproat & Rolph had replaced the rustic informality of the old clubhouse. The second clubhouse, like its predecessor, was to welcome many prestigious guests, like Rear Admiral H. S. R. Prince Louis of Battenberg, who was entertained at a dinner and garden party that first summer.

RCYC members were not the only Torontonians to feel satisfied this year. Regular visitors to the Island, all too used to the pushing and cursing aboard overcrowded Island ferries, must have cheered lustily when the Toronto Ferry Company expanded its fleet. On Easter Monday 1906 a large number of steamboat men, civic

officials and other citizens gathered at Polson's Iron Works to applaud the launching of the TFC's newest "Queen of the Bay," the magnificent *Bluebell,* capable of transporting thirteen hundred holiday-makers at a time in style and comfort. On opening day, May 24, 1906, the *Bluebell* and her two smaller sisters, the *Mayflower* and the *Primrose* ran continuously from the old Yonge Street Wharf, enabling the TFC to handle "the record crowd in a record manner." All day the various amusements "reaped a rich harvest," according to the *Telegram.* Apart from long line-ups at the ever popular Figure 8 roller coaster and elsewhere, the only probem encountered by most people was "a difficulty in spending their money fast enough." And the new attractions—like the vaudeville shows in the new theatre, the Tour of the World, the roller rink and the towering "Hurgle Gurgle"—were inspiring screams of delight from the holiday crowd.

The ferry fleet may have prospered, but 1906 proved to be a bad year for ships and barges and a busy year for that experienced lifesaver William Ward, now aged sixty. By the turn of the century old William had taken "a sort of general charge" of the eastern tip of the Island, according to John Ross Robertson. During the long cold winters, of course, the Wards were the only

people living on that exposed part of the Island, giving Captain Ward the right to be properly scornful of what he called "Fair Weather Islanders" who came for July and August and "hurriedly departed when the first cool evenings came."[6] Certainly the Wards were no effete city types. By 1901 five sturdy little Ward grandchildren plodded two miles each day to the one-room school, which that winter had an enrolment of only twelve. And grandfather William continued on with his traditional activities of policing, fishing, lifesaving and expanding his Island empire.

By 1906 Special Constable Ward had been patrolling the Island for over a quarter of a century in fair weather and foul. But, by now, the City Police Department had a staff of constables on duty at the Island throughout the year and

some City politicians favoured dispensing with his services. Ward protested, as did his solicitor and fellow-Islander W. H. Lockhart Gordon, and found friends on the powerful City Board of Control. The board duly recommended that "in view of Mr. Ward's knowledge, experience and courage in saving life," he should be kept on by the property commissioner in some undefined capacity.

That summer Ward was able to display his famous lifesaving skills yet again. Early on the morning of August 24, 1906, with the seas running eight feet high and a fierce east wind whipping the sails of the Ward windmill into a fury, one of William's sons went out to hose off some of the moss-covered fishing nets stretched out on the beach in front of the breakwater. In the distance, "her spars looming in the early

Toronto's biggest sandbox: four young tenters enjoy a Ward's Island backyard c. 1908. [CTA:JC]

dawn,'' he saw the black, three-masted schooner *Reuben Dowd*—''with rudder gone, bulwarks stove in, and her squatted foresail and loosely brailed head canvas slatting wildly in the strong east breeze.'' During the previous night the heavily laden schooner had fetched up at the Gap, her crew desperately shouting for help. Within minutes of sighting, Captain Ward (obviously still fit and nimble), his three sons and five other Island residents got the lifeboat out of the boathouse, launched her and pulled out to the schooner. After four hours of hard work, the lifesavers managed to take seven frightened people— three men, three boys and a woman—off the old coal boat. Lumps of coal continued to wash up on shore for several weeks and rats that had deserted the sinking ship temporarily infested the Island.[7]

Then in September the old steam barge *Gordon Jarry* was burned to the water line, apparently by hoodlums. Constable Ward gave the alarm as flames lit the sky over nearby tents and shanties, and he raced to the fire station for a hose, but could not get in. Meanwhile, Captain Joseph Goodwin chugged onto the scene in the fire tug *Nellie Bly*. Goodwin organized a bucket brigade and after a hard fight managed to bring the flames under control. This was not the last heard of the *Gordon Jarry*, however. She sank off ''Haney's Point'' on the bayside of Ward's Island and for several years formed a nasty obstacle to shipping.

In November the lifesavers were called out once more, but not until one vessel had already sunk and six men had drowned off Hanlan's Point. On November 21, 1906, the steam barge

Resolute approached Toronto in the grip of a furious fall storm. With the seas running high, she tried in vain to enter the harbour through the Eastern Gap, then made her way around the Island to shelter off the Western Sandbar. Captain Sullivan rowed ashore to discover that the Western Gap was only eleven feet deep—too shallow for the *Resolute*. They would have to lie in the ice off the Sandbar until the storm abated and they could enter the Eastern Gap.

This plan was fine until midnight when the wind shifted from èast to west, turning the protective Island shore into a potential death trap. With only one hope left, the weary sailors weighed anchor, fought their way back around the Island toward the Eastern Gap, hoping to now be able to pass through. No luck. The lake was still too stirred up. They returned to the western side of the Island.

By now, however, the *Resolute* was leaking and her cargo of slack coal was shifting. Lifebelts were hurriedly distributed and two lifeboats launched as the ship foundered. One boat immediately capsized, sending five of the crew to their deaths. Meanwhile, Captain Sullivan and Second Engineer Topping grabbed hold of the canvas-covered cabin top which had ripped loose. The cabin top broke up, sending Topping to the bottom. Miraculously Sullivan, holding on ''like grim death,'' was caught by the current and swept to safety through the Western Gap. When morning finally came, the beach of the Western Sandbar was littered with wreckage— trunks, mattresses, cabin doors, deck fixtures and broken windows. And about a mile up the lake opposite Dufferin Street, the spars and wheelhouse of the foundered steam barge were just visible above the top of the waves. Six men drowned and a ship was wrecked ''all because there was not enough water in the channel.''

The drama was not yet over. As the *Resolute* was breaking up, her consort, the barge *Locke* "swayed, and lurched, and rolled and pitched, and tossed on the breakers," her anchors still holding, but a white flag snapping in the gale from the mizzen masthead. Further south, "dangerously close to the Island shore," the three-masted schooner *St. Louis* "dived and pitched among the combers, her anchors holding her head to the wind, but letting her slip back, inch by inch, in the surging of the wild seas." Word reached Captain Ward and the lifesaving crew at the opposite end of the Island. Their sturdy craft was towed through the Western Gap by the tug *Maggie R. Mitchell* from the safety of the harbour into the maelstrom beyond. There the seas were so enormous the tug was often lost from sight in the great watery hollows, but the two boats battled their way through the billows to the *Locke*, where the lifeboat was cast off. As the tug made for shelter, Ward and his crew got alongside the wallowing barge and managed to drag six men and two women over the rails into the lifeboat. Then it was "Pull All!" for safety as the little craft was swept before the wind on into Queen's Wharf. Once again the tug towed the lifeboat out, this time toward the *St. Louis*. In due course that schooner's captain, mate, four sailors and cook were all safely brought aboard. As the lifeboat came home "with the precious freight," the crowd lining the piers gave her well-deserved cheers.[8] The one positive result of the wreck of the *Resolute* was the creation of a new, deeper Western Channel in the summer of 1908.

In this prewar era the Island residential community grew by leaps and bounds, with over a hundred new buildings rising across the Island (excluding the Western Sandbar). Much of this activity was concentrated at Centre Island, where almost fifty new cottages were built in the decade between 1904 and 1914.

While increasing numbers of Torontonians were heading north to sample the wilder summer pleasures of Muskoka's blue lakes and rocky shores, many Torontonians were still attracted by Toronto Island's more "civilized living," according to Mary Mallon who arrived on Centre Island as a babe-in-arms at the turn of the century and spent more than sixty summers in three different family cottages. "The advantage of the Island," she observed, "was that you had your husband and your menfolk with you all week and there wasn't any of this motoring [or railroading] up and back." Not only that, you had mail twice a day, gas and, later, electricity and telephones (although on a somewhat delayed basis), and you had fresh food, rather than camping rations, and a variety of stores to choose from.

By 1905 Manitou Road, which ran from the bridge over Long Pond to Lakeshore Avenue, was already known as "the business street of Centre Island"—complete with a new freight wharf near the bridge. On very busy days like Saturdays and holidays the broad boardwalk down the centre was still too narrow to accommodate the shuffling, bumping crowds. Pedestrians even spilled over onto the planked bicycle path, to the great danger of both bicycle rider and pedestrian.

By August 1914, Manitou Road (also known as the Main Drag) boasted a wide range of services. Frederick Ginn now operated a grocery store as well as an ice-cream parlour. Ginn's brother-in-law, Thomas Clayton, had opened a meat market next door. The Forsythe Laundry had (temporarily) joined the New Method Laundry in an attempt to keep Islanders clean. (In later years the Swiss Laundry and the Parisian Laundry joined in.) Oliver Spanner had created his grand restaurant. The Farmer's Dairy had joined the old City Dairy. But the City Dairy, which had started out as a small refreshment stand near Long Pond at the beginning of the century, was *the* dairy, attracting thirsty dancers from the Island Amateur Aquatic Association dances and greedy small boys, who bypassed the friendly soda jerks to build their own triple-scooped skyscraper sundaes. And, of course, both English's rambling old boathouse on Long Pond and Pierson's (formerly Mead's) handsome

Looking south from the bridge over Long Pond, past English's (né Hanlan's, then Solman's) Boathouse, down along Manitou Road around 1913. [AC]

clapboard hotel just around the corner from Manitou Road on Lakeshore Avenue, continued to do a thriving summer business.

Most of the Centre Island cottages built during this era were located west of Manitou Road just in from Lakeshore, along such sandy new streets as Shiawassie, Ongiara, Mohawk and Iroquois. After Lakeshore, the best address on the Island was probably Iroquois, which was opened for development around 1906. To ensure that a better class of Island residences appeared on this very important thoroughfare, the City had taken the extra precaution of requiring each Iroquois lessee to build a house worth at least $2,000. Potential Islanders were undeterred, and by 1916 only four lots remained unleased.

The City took other steps to "heighten the residential tone of the Island"[9] and prevent shabby little subdivisions from pockmarking the landscape. It began setting higher minimum values for Island cottages and to prevent speculation (a hitherto respected Island tradition) it began to require new lessees to build within a year, and prohibited any person from holding more than one property. Finally, in a crusade against boarding houses, Council tried a variety of measures, such as stipulating that new houses were to be for "private residence" only or could be occupied by only one family or could contain no more than ten rooms. But trying to prevent boarding houses from flooding the Island was like trying to hold back the waves of Lake Ontario. Ultimately, boarding houses were put up and large houses were subdivided to meet a lively demand for cheap accommodation.

In spite of all this building activity, acres of wild land cut by bays and lagoons remained to be explored by children who were "practically amphibious from the age of two," according to one nostalgic old Centre Islander, Alex Day

"Winters were mere interludes," wrote former Centre Islander Alex Day, recalling the years when he, like these barefoot explorers of 1905-10, spent his summer days roaming the mysterious wilds of the Island. [OA]

who grew up on St. Andrew's Avenue. Regarding winters as "merely interludes," these young Island residents could hardly wait to return each summer to explore the wild outback behind their houses, "the scene of innumerable forays and battles." A heady of mixture of Boers, Pathans, Zulus, Robin Hoods, Indians and Captain Morgans lay in wait behind every bush or tree to test the mettle of these young adventurers. Back at home, as adults tried to scratch a garden out of the sandy soil, their offspring busily scratched about beneath the houses, building elaborate tunnel systems "with all kinds of pitfalls and shuddery effects to scare the younger ones." Future mariners "spent a lot of time and ingenuity making model sailboats" and young fishermen lined the lagoons casting for perch

and catfish. On one glorious occasion one group's patience was rewarded handsomely—"the gang took out about 200 catfish from one pool" where the hapless fish had been trapped by the building of the filtration plant in 1911. Saturday nights, of course, were a highlight for young and old, when towering bonfires were lit on the beach and everyone on the street joined in the fun—toasting marshmallows, gobbling potatoes cooked in their jackets, munching succulent fall corn and harmonizing (more or less) to tunes such as "Seeing Nellie Home," "Santa Lucia" and any Stephen Foster song.

Communal activities of another sort continued to be organized by the growing Island Amateur Aquatic Association, which celebrated the new century by holding the "most successful, most enjoyable and most largely attended'' annual regatta in its history. Island residents and hundreds of visitors lined up along the grassy banks and floated in canoes, punts and rowboats out on the smooth surface of Long Pond. Those present were reminded, somewhat grandly perhaps, of ''the pictures of the Henley regatta.'' An orchestra entertained the spectators between races, the contests were lively, and the money raised for the Lakeside Home For Little Children reached $17.[10] The association also held dances every Friday night at Aquatic Hall on Long Pond, where dancing couples embraced to the music of Glionna's Orchestra, under the watchful eye of ''Patronesses'' like Mrs. Robert Smellie, Mrs. Arthur R. Denison, Mrs. Lionel Goldman, Mrs. James D. Trees, Mrs. E. J. Lennox and Mrs. A. L. Massey.

The IAAA's well-nurtured political connections soon came in handy. By 1905 the old Aquatic Hall was bursting at the seams; so architect and sportsman Arthur Denison and saddle merchant Samuel Trees approached City Council about a

new site for a larger clubhouse. In the end the City agreed to lease a new site on Long Pond west of Manitou Bridge for twenty-one years at a nominal rate. And to encourage IAAA activities to be sober as well as healthful, the City stipulated that ''no intoxicating liquors shall be permitted to be sold on the premises.'' By the summer of 1907 the IAAA was firmly entrenched in its new waterside villa, whose broad verandahs and flag-bedecked silhouette dominated this section of Long Pond and continued to attract large crowds to its regattas for many years to come.

In the first decade of the century the Hanlan's Point residential community also continued to grow and took on a more established look. Toronto's legal establishment, for example, was represented by the arrival of Robert Cassels and Judge Frank Anglin. By this time, a long, straggling line of cottages—all facing westward— stretched south of the old Heber's Hotel (now operated for the City by Thomas Clegg). Many had a baby carriage at the front door and a

bicycle or two at the side. The trees were taller, the gardens were more luxuriant and a concrete path even replaced the old wooden sidewalk. By 1905, in fact, the Hanlan's Point community was large enough to put an end to the peripatetic church services conducted since 1895 by the Brotherhood of St. Andrew at various locations, like the hotel parlour, the Open Air Theatre and the Roof Garden over the old ferry shelter. The burghers of the Point decided to build their own Anglican church. They obtained a lease from the City in 1906 and opened their neat little white church, St. Emmanuel, in 1907, on the southwest corner of what became Hanlan Memorial Park.

Undoubtedly the major residential development at Hanlan's Point during this period was the transformation of the Western Sandbar from a tenting community into a cottage community. On the old Heber property, around the aging Turner's Baths, on the Solman/Hanlan property and all along the Western Sandbar, tents and shacks were scattered higgledy-piggledy over the sandy landscape, sheltering several hundred hardy and enthusiastic campers.[11]

By June 1902 the campers were attracting unfavourable notice from City officials who, in the light of the reportedly ''unsanitary conditions'' of the camping areas, began to try to regularize and control camping privileges. Even some campers were less than enthusiastic about the scruffy appearance of their precincts. In March 1903, for example, an anonymous ''Poor Camper's Wife'' complained to the assessment commissioner that the ''old shacks and fences'' on Thomas Clegg's place were ''a disgrace to the Island.'' But most campers were enthusiastic and by June 1903 were ''clamoring for permits,'' which the City granted.

The assessment commissioner persisted in his

"We had the time of our lives" during last Friday night's dance at the new Aquatic Hall, commented the correspondent on the back of this postcard showing the IAAA's other main activity: regattas. [AC]

campaign to clean up Heber's and the Sandbar and before the 1903 season opened, the City adopted his plan. Regular lots were laid out in the area north of Turner's Baths, small cottages once placed near Heber's Hotel and Turner's Baths were relocated in this area and the camping area was regulated much more stringently.[12] As a result of these actions, the "camping area" north of the baths soon became, in fact, a cottage community. Tents were replaced by neat little 18-by-22-foot cottages, with verandahs at the front and back. In 1904 a tiny plank sidewalk was laid north of the baths for the convenience of campers, though, as Sandbar residents pointed out, it was not all that convenient: mothers pushing prams regularly slipped off and got stuck in the sand, while two pedestrians could not conveniently pass without one stepping aside. Eventually, a grander, four-foot-wide path was laid. Meanwhile, wells were sunk, boathouses were built and W.C.'s were dug. Ultimately, thirty-seven little four-room, one-storey cottages stretched along the sandy northern reaches of the Sandbar. By June 1905 the assessment commissioner could report proudly that "tents are a thing of the past."

Life on the exposed Western Sandbar was sometimes precarious. While tenters had been particularly vulnerable (a violent storm in September 1894, for example, had blown the tents "down as flat as postage stamps" and scattered lighter articles of furniture over the landscape[13]) cottages were still vulnerable to storm and flood. A "stiff southwester" on May 9, 1904, for example, "gobbled up a generous slice of the Western Sandbar," making it "very uncomfortable for several of the cottagers" who had already taken up summer residence there. The storm carried away the central spans of the bathers' wharfs at Turner's Baths, undermined the veran-

dahs of several cottages and dashed right up against the fronts of houses which two years before had been a full thirty feet from the water's edge. Beside two southerly cottages homemade breakwaters of heavy timbers were "ripped to pieces," as two women occupants worked waist-deep in water to rescue the timbers in order to repair the barrier. Both cottages were also standing in the water.[14]

A storm of a different sort, however, was about to break over the Bar south of the baths. In this area, an irregular, relatively unregulated mixture of tenters and cottagers continued to squat on the sand. They built breakwaters, dug drinking wells, laid sidewalks, constructed W.C.'s, cleared weeds from the lagoon, transported soil, planted trees, laid out gardens and generally did their best to transform a sandy wasteland into a pleasant summer resort where they lived in places affectionately named "Lobsters," "Maple Leaf," "Bachelors' Hall" and so on. Although officialdom frequently looked askance at their efforts, some tenters were extremely proud of their summer homes, so when the City decided in June 1905 to lay out only twelve 50-foot lots in an area where nineteen cottages and tents were located, an unholy Bar brawl erupted. Who would be allocated the coveted cottage sites? The main guiding principle was to be length of residence. For months City Hall was deluged with claims and counter claims and residents who had lived for years in apparent harmony were suddenly at each others' throats— verbally at least.

Most seemed to agree that old George Thompson in "Paardelburg Cottage" (an eighteen- to twenty-year resident), Thomas Stiff (a sixteen-year resident) and Harry Webster in "Poplars" (a seventeen-year resident) deserved lots. But after that consensus vanished. Eventually

the City was reduced to requiring competitors to file sworn affadavits about length of residence and to sorting through the mounting pile of evidence. Ultimately, the lots were assigned and, by the end of 1906, the weary assessment commissioner was able to report proudly that "the Western Sandbar [has been] greatly improved by the complete removal of 17 unsightly shacks, which were scattered all over the beach south of Turner's Baths. These have now been replaced by twelve one-story buildings, of neat design, which front the lake…leaving a wide stretch of beach open to the public. Sidewalk laid and trees planted."

Meanwhile, down at Ward's Island, William Ward was gaining more tenants and neighbours—and almost saw a rival hotel built in 1904 when a group of Toronto investors (including hardware magnate Thomas E. Aikenhead) approached the City with a proposal to lease land along the Eastern Gap and southern lakefront to build a $300,000 "high class summer hotel and resort" on "what many call an eyesore." Unlike Hanlan's Point, however, the scheme was to be no honky-tonk parade. (One condition of their proposal was that "no Merry-go-round or other noisy appliance be placed on the land near to our site.") This was to be a high-toned resort "to compare favorably with the best on the continent" and to attract "the first class tourist travel and the better class of customers from the United States and elsewhere." In April 1905 the City condoned the idea and approved lease terms. But, if William Ward and the operators of Ward's Hotel worried about future competition, they needn't have. This grandiose scheme— like so many others—evaporated without leaving a trace on Island shores.[15]

A more indelible mark, however, was left by less affluent individual Torontonians who

(Above) *F. G. Alexander began summering on the Heber property in 1889. By 1902, when this snap shot of "Harmony Cottage" and its dour occupants was taken, a primitive wooden shelter had replaced the canvas one.* [CTA]

(Right) *Wash day, Ward's Island style.* [TIA]

voted with their plimsoled feet. To them Ward's Island was not an "eyesore," but a veritable— if somewhat sandy—summer paradise. Around the turn of the century, the Wiman Baths were converted into summer apartments—six in the main Wiman Building and five in the Wiman Terrace. Campers, like the Reverend Wilkinson who conducted Sunday services at the Wiman Shelter for many years and regarded himself as one of the "aborigines of this reclaimed desert,"[16] were also allowed to pitch tents on the Wiman lots.

Eventually, in 1902-03, the City took control over the Wiman property, continuing to employ James B. Marshall as caretaker, rent collector and general Ward's Island factotum. Among his neighbours in the Wiman buildings during these early years were plumbing contractor Fred Armstrong, Sam McBride, the boisterous lumber merchant who entered municipal politics in 1905 and eventually became mayor, Nathan Mills of the T. Eaton Company and Mrs. Jacobs who ran a small grocery business for the handful of tenters until 1907. Still, in 1903 fewer than a dozen tents dotted the Ward's Island landscape. At the end of that season, Marshall was delighted to report to his new City employers, in typically ungrammatical fashion, that "not withstanding we had a large number staying here and a large number of visitors we have had no accidents of any kind, and everything went on nicely *no friction.*"

During this early period, the City paid relatively little attention to Ward's Island. Park Superintendent John Chambers, in fact, made only a passing reference to the area in his 1903 plan where he recommended that most of Ward's Island "be set apart for park purposes." For the time being, however, apart from laying the

In this 1908 Ward's Island photograph, the lady of the tent approaches the kitchen shed holding an umbrella—just in case the skies open up before dinner is safely transported to the canvas dining room. [CTA:JC]

odd walkway, filling in the odd unsightly lagoon and tucking the odd public W.C. in amongst the bushes, the City pretty much left residents to fend for themselves.

Life on Ward's Island at this time was necessarily informal and fairly primitive. There was no City water until about 1906. Residents had to build windmills to pump up water (like the Wards) or sink wells four or five feet into the sandy soil (like most tenters). One of the hazards of these wells was toads. These wide-eyed little creatures (whose descendants still hop about Ward's Island each spring) used to leap into the holes and contaminate the contents. "Daddy Frank" Staneland, who first tented at Ward's as a small boy in 1899 and summered there until his death in 1981, recalled that when this happened, "We'd walk way down to the end of the pier, where the Gap is and get two pails of water and bring it home and boil it" for drinking water. Eventually, the City put in running water to communal cold water taps dotted around the campground. At washing time, campers had to fill pails of water and slap dirty clothes against slatted washboards. Sometimes, however, more inventive measures were adopted by Daddy Frank and his friends. "When our pants would get dirty, we'd take a cake of soap down, wash our pants in the Lake and swim around and then we'd come up and hang them to dry."

Naturally there was no electricity or inside or outside lighting. The arc lights which now illuminated Island Park did not advance down the boardwalk to Ward's Island. Late-night revellers making their way home from the last

Centre Island ferry around midnight had to make their way across the pitch-black terrain by instinct. Sometimes even stalwarts like Daddy Frank found this late-night walk "scary." Meanwhile, on the campground itself, the tents were lit by coal-oil lamps (some burning jewel-like through shades of multicoloured leaded glass) and tenters visiting friends or checking their stays on a stormy night stumbled around after dark holding kerosene lanterns before them, yet still cutting their legs on tent pegs and tripping over guy wires. Eventually, three lonely lights signalled the coming of the electrical age: one on the pier at the Eastern Gap, one at the wharf and one over Withrow Avenue which led to the lake.

In summer, without electricity or refrigeration, Islanders adopted the old-fashioned root-cellar approach to preserving food. They dug holes in the ground and lowered their goods down in a tin box. Daddy Frank Staneland, for one, got tired of lying down to scramble for his eggs, so he arranged an ingenious "dumb waiter" pulley system to raise and lower his goods.

Naturally, tenters were careful to keep cooking fires away from canvas tents. In the era before they were allowed to build small cooking sheds, Ward's Island chefs had to simply cook over an open-air fire or stove. Cooking over an open fire may be very romantic but it had its drawbacks, like rain. On rainy days Island cooks could be seen hunched under umbrellas cooking over a

off the lake. An east gale could literally rip guy wires anchored by stakes driven five feet into the ground "right clean out," according to Daddy Frank. As the wind rose, the more intrepid among the tenters would don their slickers and rubbers and go outside to hold their tent ropes in an effort to keep their homes from blowing away. Others would simply sit inside and hope. Sometimes the wind would creep in between the outer "fly" and the main tent, ballooning the tent up so that campers had to spend unpleasant hours trying to wrestle inflation to the ground. Daddy Frank finally solved this problem by inserting large springs between the main tent and the "fly" so that the wind could blow "right through" his tent without ballooning it. Soon other tenters followed suit.

At other times, however, the wind would flatten tents altogether. On one famous occasion, some years later, every single one of the 165 tents then on Ward's Island was blown down. "And you know what that meant," Daddy Frank grimaced. "People had dishes land up against the tent and smashed and, oh what a mess. And your bedding was all wet and, oh dear." Eventually the effects of the wind were mitigated by the poplars that Daddy Frank planted. Unfortunately, while reducing one hazard, he created another one which still plagues Ward's Islanders today: poplar fluff. "I never knew there was a male and a female tree," Daddy Frank admitted. "The female tree is the one with all the fluff on it." It was like a midsummer snowfall, with tents (and later cottages) blanketed by cottony white seeds.

A less predictable hazard was the Ward family's docile old white farm horse. On one occasion,

hissing fire and then dashing back to the tent. The innovative Daddy Frank erected a canvas runway to protect his mother between cooking area and tent. Eventually he and others were allowed to build the kitchen and enclose the runway which, in the fullness of time, were all incorporated into the Ward's Island cottage architecture.

Laying in provisions posed other problems. After Mrs. Jacobs of the Wiman Building was felled by illness in 1907, contractor Thomas Stiff, Jr., whose family had tented on the Western Sandbar since 1890, was given permission to operate a grocery and refreshment tent. But then, as now, Ward's Islanders had to bring the bulk of their groceries over from the mainland. Each Saturday, Ward's Island mothers would impress reluctant sons into helping with the shopping at the St. Lawrence Market which, at that time, was located near the water's edge though north of the railway tracks. Young Daddy Frank Staneland, dressed as always in his bathing suit and reluctant to set foot on city soil, would row his mother across the bay and wait for her in the boat, bobbing up and down as coal boats, lake steamers, ferries, pleasure yachts and stonehookers passed by. "When I'd see her coming," he laughed, "I'd go and get the parcels and put them in the boat. But you couldn't get me over to the city!"

One perennial hazard of tent life was wind, especially the vicious east wind sweeping down he broke loose and charged into the tent community, with the Wards' aged black retainer, Old Ned, in hot pursuit. Ultimately, with guy wires and a lady's pantaletted swimsuit streaming from his head, Old Dobbin plunged into the lake and cooled off.

In spite of all the hazards, in these early days before any organized activities Ward's Islanders still had lots of fun. Sometimes they used to sail down to Hanlan's Point for a night's amusement; but unless they got over there by 7:30 P.M. they couldn't find a place to tie their boat up. Usually, however, there was ample entertainment at home. Informal baseball games were played among rival "boys camps" with names like "Wacousta," "Chatanooga," "GymSix," "Otazel" and "Osoeze." (The latter two bequeathed their names to two of the baseball teams that still do battle annually.) Corn roasts on the beach were always popular. And the French Canadian *chivaree* was adapted to Island life. Virtually the entire crew of campers would turn out to bang pots and pans outside the tent of newlyweds—or, if there wasn't a newlywed couple around to chivaree, some unfortunate older couple was chosen instead. As if that wasn't enough commotion, early each day Art Gay and the "dozen lusty boys" at "Wacousta Camp" roared their morning serenade:

> The bears are on the hills,
> The bears are on the hills.
> Get up you lazy lubber
> The bears are on the hills.

Unfortunately for neighbouring campers, the City's watchdog, caretaker James B. Marshall, was by this time going deaf.

Having sorted out the confusion on the Western Sandbar, the City turned its attention to the eastern end of the Island. At the urging of

chauvinistic Ward's Islander Alderman Sam McBride, City Council adopted a plan in November 1906 to fill in and develop the long neck of land leading to Ward's Island from Centre, construct a roadway, dredge a two-hundred-foot channel north of the improved lots and create a small island of about twenty acres in extent north of the channel. With the "wastelands" along the breakwater banished to memory and forty-nine newly improved lots properly developed with summer cottages, the City eventually expected to reap over $4,000 in rents, not to mention taxes. So, the following spring, the *Daniel Lamb* and the other City sand pumps promptly turned their nozzles toward the marshland north of the breakwater to create the proposed cottage lots. They also chugged through the shallow waters along the northern shore, "sucked up the old bullrushes and everything," as William Ward's grandson Fram later recalled, and began to spew forth the sandy

wasteland that later became Sunfish Island. The transformation of the eastern end of the Island took longer than expected[17] (there was the unfortunate interruption of a world war); but the 1906 plan did ultimately lead to the residential development of the Lakeshore strip and to the creation of Algonquin (*né* Sunfish) Island.

In the meantime, with camping having been prohibited elsewhere on the Island, tenters dragged their tent poles to Ward's in ever-increasing numbers. In 1904 there were only ten tent sites. In 1905 there were seventeen. In 1906 there were twenty-eight and aging Mr. Marshall heaved a sigh of relief in August as he reported, "I take great pleasure in saying that everything past of [sic] pleasantly."[18]

This was more than Parks Commissioner John Chambers could report, for all was not well in Island Park, or at City Hall. By 1907 rumours and charges of misconduct had become so insistent that on November 11, Council appointed Judge

These members of "Kamp Kanibuls" look somewhat more menacing than the high-spirited lads of "Wacousta" and the other Ward's Island "boys camps." [AC]

The T.C. Robinettes were among the Toronto families who summered at Centre Island around 1910. Here, surrounded by family and help, is one of Canada's most distinguished lawyers, John J. Robinette, on his tricycle. [Joyce and George Robinette]

Winchester to conduct an inquiry into Chambers's administration of the Parks Department. Even with the able assistance of lawyer (and future Islander) Thomas Cowper Robinette, K.C.—a "consummate actor" with "unusual gifts for the exposition and enforcement of his opinions"[19]— Chambers was unable to halt the investigation. And even after Chambers's resignation on January 20, 1908, the Winchester inquiry went on. During the spring, a parade of 151 witnesses marched down to City Hall to testify about Chambers's slack (some would say corrupt) administration. Animals had disappeared (for profit?) from Riverdale Zoo. Old City lumber from Exhibition Park had been sold and the profits apparently pocketed. City-grown flowers had been (perhaps endearingly) delivered to Chambers's friends on Council, and so on.

In his own defence, the harried Chambers claimed that he had been overworked and understaffed and that his periodic pleas for administrative help had been consistently rejected by Council. "I want to point out," he stated, "that while there were mistakes and irregularities in the office, I had no more assistance in an executive way when I left the Department than I had when I was only spending $25,000 a year." Judge Winchester certainly had to agree that Chambers "lacked" that administrative ability which was necessary for the successful operation of the department under him.

Many of the witnesses who trooped down to

City Hall were Islanders or knowledgeable about the Island and included such formidable figures as Lol Solman of the Toronto Ferry Company; City Surveyor Villiers Sankey and Medical Officer of Health Dr. Charles Sheard of Hanlan's Point; and City Engineer C. H. Rust and Island Amateur Aquatic Association president Arthur Denison of Centre Island.

Poor David Kimmings and the Island Park he supervised came in for a beating. Kimmings, it seems, had a drinking problem: "On frequent occasions Kimings [sic] was under the influence of liquor," the judge wrote, and "at such times he had not proper control of his men." They quarrelled, *they* drank and they showed "no respect" for their pie-eyed supervisor. At a time when no liquor was sold on the Island, Kimmings's (informal) tenant Robert Ringham imported "considerable liquor" from the mainland. The obliging Kimmings would even deliver it from the dock to the little cottage behind his. There, on Saturdays and Sundays, Ringham and his nameless "companions" would have a high old time carousing and generally turning the supervisor's island into another "Tight Little Island."

Kimmings transgressed in other ways. He kept cows on the Island, whose hay was cut and gathered by City employees. He assigned Parks employees to look after his garden. He received money from Island residents for manure and good earth to improve their sandy lots. He and his men grew potatoes and delivered bagfuls to Chambers. He apparently fished illegally, kept poultry at City expense and allowed some Island residents to use City wood. In spite of all his transgressions, however, witnesses testified that "his work was done very faithfully," that he "kept the Island very well" and that he was "most obliging and worked at all hours, day and evening and assisted people in every way possible." Judge Winchester concluded, generously, that "while Mr. Kimings [sic] keeps away from liquor, he is a faithful servant to the City."[20] Whether or not he could keep away from liquor in the future became a moot point. James Hutchinson moved into the supervisor's residence and took over his job.

Meanwhile, James Wilson (who had been in charge of parks at Niagara Falls) took over Chambers's job as parks commissioner. Perhaps it was not Chambers who said "Après moi le déluge," but it should have been. Throughout 1908, the Island from Hanlan's to Ward's was awash and Wilson's staff was valiantly splashing in place trying to keep up. Hanlan's Point ballgrounds looked "more like a swimming tank than anything else," Eddie Durnan told a *Telegram* reporter on May 7, 1908. And Ward's Island was no better off, according to caretaker Marshall's hastily scrawled note of May 15: "this end of the Island is complete[ly] flooded, water all over." The Wiman Bath roof was leaking, the Wiman Shelter was "completely surrounded by water" and much of the tenting area was waterlogged.

Not only was the water exceptionally high throughout the season, completely covering large residential areas and parkland, but the entire Toronto lakefront was blasted by exceptionally fierce eastern gales. The waters of Lake Ontario rolled "like mountains decked with snow," according to the *Telegram* of May 7, sending spray shooting more than thirty feet in the air. On the Island sidewalks, trees, telephone poles and fences were ripped up and carried away. Gas and water mains lay exposed along the shore. Lawns were flooded and, when the waters retreated, were left covered by a residue of sand. Even the granite breakwater afforded little protection. Rivers flowed down not only Clandeboye and Hooper Avenues east of the breakwater, but also down Oriole and Chippewa. Repairs made after one storm were ripped out by the next, and workmen trying to repair damage done to the Royal Canadian Yacht Club breakwater were driven away by later tempests. At the height of the watery attacks, even hip-booted Islanders could not walk safely along the exposed lakefront.

The City tried to cope. It erected temporary sidewalks to replace impassable flooded ones. It prohibited residents and workmen from taking sand and gravel from the vulnerable southern beach to fill low areas around houses, but it did send City sand pumps around to afford relief to Island leaseholders willing to pay for the work. The City's powers, however, were limited and any relief afforded was, at best, modest.

Islanders were discouraged, frustrated and in some cases, irate. In June, the Wiman Building tenants complained vociferously to City Hall that there was *not a space of ten square feet of dry grass on this part of the Island.* There was, as a consequence, "absolutely no place for children to play." Furthermore, "garbage and other waste matter (liable to breed disease)" was "floating about indiscriminately" because it couldn't be gathered up. The area where tennis and baseball were played was "practically under water" and the Shelter, which was *the only place to hold social gatherings, &c.,* could only be reached with the "aid of boats or rubber boots." And former Wiman tenant Fred Armstrong was regretting his decision of 1907 to jump the sand pump and lease the easternmost of the (still un-improved) Lakeshore lots. In spite of the City's warning that the land was really not in a habitable state, Armstrong went ahead and built his house. By 1908 he was hiring men to dump wheelbarrows of fill around it so he could get in and applying, unsuccessfully, to the City for a rent rebate. He had made his waterbed; now he would have to lie in it.

The assessment commissioner was equally hardhearted where Centre Island widow Mary O'Dea was concerned. She fired off this catalogue of grievances to City Hall:

> I got no revenue from the house in 1907 [because of supposed bureaucratic bungling]. I hoped for better things in 1908.
>
> Then the lake rose in its might, and threw me as a broken reed upon its wave washed shores. I could not get into my house. I could not put it in order for renting. I could not ask prospective tenants to wade to their knees in water to see a summer residence, and when finally the sand pump left it possible to effect an entrance, people were disgusted with the Island, they would not even come to see the house. I advertised, I placed it in the hands of real estate men, but not one applicant came during the whole summer. Re. the sand pumps. I hailed with joy its possible advantage by converting a water lot to a dry one. I didn't lease a *water lot....* My dismay at receiving a bill for $29.60 was extreme. Many gentlemen on the island advised me not to pay it. The advice was unnecessary, for I couldn't, I haven't the money. All the running expenses of ground rent, taxes, insurance, water, has to come out of an income of $142. per annum. A very small balance is left for room rent in the City, food, etc.

In view of the sodden condition of her property, Mrs. O'Dea might have found the assessment commissioner's judgment that she had "no ground" for complaint somewhat ironic.[21]

Visitors that summer, understandably, were few. The noisy old hurdy-gurdy in James E. Cronkwright's merry-go-round was uncharacteristically silent, as Island Park patrons stayed away in droves and the unhappy concessionaire

tried, but failed, to get a $100 rent rebate. The ducks and the weeds, however, flourished. The little wildfowl pond near Long Pond was improved, while water plants speedily choked up all the still water channels and lagoons. Fortunately, Commissioner Wilson reported to Council, a new English steam weed-cutter "proved to be quite efficient for combatting weeds in the channel, and managed to keep these open." It chugged through the wider channels at about 7 mph, with stern paddle wheel splashing and Y-shaped blades snipping. The old weed-cutter machinery was fitted up in a scow and ignominiously made to do duty in collecting the cut weeds.

Surface water was not the only problem troubling Torontonians. Providing safe drinking water presented a perennial challenge and it was only in 1908 that the City completed improvements first suggested by City Engineer E. H. Keating in 1895. The main change was the construction of a five-thousand-foot-long tunnel under the bay, which, it was hoped, would prevent sewage—which lay three- to four-feet deep on the bottom of the bay—from contaminating the water, and would eliminate the inconvenience of pesky pipes bobbing to the surface. Contractors Haney & Miller began active operations in 1906—and established an unsightly shipyard and storage area that fall

Grim and grimy members of the "Blasting Gang" pause long enough in their tunneling under the bay in 1908 to pose for the City photographer. [CTA]

at Ward's Island. After the usual range of setbacks, the contractors set gangs of workers to the grim and grimy task of scooping out the tunnel from both sides of the bay simultaneously. Their aim was true and the headings met on July 14, 1908. On December 30 water was admitted to the tunnel and on January 1, 1909, pumps began taking their supply.[22]

One unfortunate byproduct of the construction was "Haney's Point" northeast of the Wiman Building. For several years Haney's "dilapidated frame store-house" balanced precariously on the water's edge. Bits of "old iron and parts of broken machines" were strewn about. And in spite of repeated attempts to nail the place up, it was always broken open again and used as a resort for "questionable characters" and as a privy by lazy "parties who [would] not take the trouble to walk the distances to use the conveniences provided by the City." It was only in September 1911 that the old storehouse was removed and the point was properly incorporated into the campground.[23]

In 1909 the new commissioner, James Wilson, having kept his head above water the previous year, presented his grandiose $100,000 plan for the Island, which featured a tunnel and cross-Island boulevard for autos and other vehicles, a major athletic ground at Hanlan's Point, large botanical gardens and sports grounds at Centre and, apart from the Western Sandbar cottages, the continuance of the residential community. The necessary $100,000, fortunately, was never appropriated, so Wilson plodded along at a more mundane pace with the usual clearing, filling and planting, though by the end of 1910, only a quarter of Island Park's 240 acres had been properly sodded and made usable. The old drinking troughs with large, shiny, thick-lipped brass cups chained to the top were replaced by sanitary cupless drinking fountains. Spacious concrete

walks were laid which, supposedly, would at all times be above the level of highest water. A new cement bridge of neat design (in Wilson's view a great improvement on the wooden structures hitherto in vogue) was built over a newly built channel at Chippewa, opening that area for greater residential development. New Centre Island baths were built at the end of Manitou Road and Olympic Island was opened up.

The year 1909 brought disasters as well as grandiose plans. Early on the morning of April 20 William Ward's one-storey frame Lifeboat Station and its contents went up in flames. Captain Goodwin once again steamed to the

rescue aboard the *Nellie Bly* and Island firemen gathered on shore. All to no avail. The station was a complete loss and its charred remains were pushed down to prevent accidents. The first lifeboat, which had proudly participated in the City's Semi-Centennial Parade of 1884, was half buried and became a flower bed. In June a fire alarm system was finally installed which linked the east end of the Island with the Pumping Station at the Filtration Plant so that water pressure could be adjusted and firemen dispatched when necessary. And in September a new lifeboat arrived and was put into service.

In May of 1909 the Island Public School also met a fiery fate, though Island parents were

"All Going to Centre Island," by any available means in 1907: old-fashioned sleigh, new-fangled motor car, and perennial perambulator. [CTA:JC]
(Right) Rumpled John Ross Robertson and dapper Lol Solman pose on the steps of the Lakeside Home For Little Children on opening day, 1909—two days after the disastrous school fire next door. [PAC (C-91305)]

perhaps not as distressed about this as they might have been. Ever since the Board of Education had voted in 1905 to keep the school open from May to October, attendance had been somewhat uncertain. While the summer community was burgeoning, the winter community remained

quite small, probably less than a hundred hardy souls. No wonder—there was still no running water, no electricity and only infrequent ferry service when the bay was unfrozen. At least, after freeze-up the bay barrier was turned into a link and people could walk, iceboat, even drive

back and forth across the ice. One reason for the poor attendance at the school was undoubtedly its location in the distant, desolate area near the Lighthouse; so in July 1908 Island parents unanimously recommended that the school be moved to a site near Hanlan's Point.

Whether the Board of Education would have agreed is uncertain. But nature, or perhaps an arsonist, took a hand. At 11 P.M. on the evening of May 24, 1909, only hours after Victoria Day fireworks had evaporated over the city and firemen had doused half a dozen small fires ignited by fire-crackers and incautious celebrants, flames were discovered bursting from the windows of the school. Lighthouse Keeper Captain Patrick J. McSherry (who had succeeded George Durnan in 1905) sounded the alarm, as did firemen at Ossington and Bloor who also spotted the blaze. Captain Goodwin and the *Nellie Bly* made a daring run along unlit lagoons guided only by the fierce light of the blaze. To no avail. The school was lost and Miss Regan and her pupils had an unexpected holiday. The Board of Education moved quickly to approve a new building on a site slightly further to the west. The new school that opened in September with fifty-two children formed the nucleus of the present school.

While debris was being cleared from the scene of the school fire, Toronto Ferry Company manager Lol Solman was catering to ever-increasing crowds of thrill-seekers at "Canada's Coney Island." By now Solman had already identified "the fickleness of public taste" as his major enemy—and ally. "A little bit of everything in the line of recreation devices," he once explained, "is the first law of a successful amusement area." And since the public always wants something different, something new must always be provided.[24] So, in 1908, the House of Fun and the Royal Gorge had joined the merry-go-round, the Figure-8 and the other popular older amusements to enable the Point to compete successfully with the newly opened Scarboro Beach. And this year, there was keen curiosity about Solman's new sensations and general agreement that the Human Whirl, the Big Scream and the Crystal Maze fully justified the promoters' descriptions. On opening day the new Gem Theatre presented an excellent series of new-fangled ''cinematograph pictures,'' as well as a clever slack-wire act. Meanwhile, over at the great wooden stadium, the Leafs split a double-header with Newark and, in the evening, Tom Longboat, the famous Onondaga runner who had won the 1907 Boston Marathon, impressed two thousand spectators by loping to an easy victory over Tom Coley in the twenty-mile race.

At the height of the season, however, tragedy struck. At mid-afternoon of August 10, 1909, a tiny spark of flame from red fire powder ignited a dressing tent outside the flimsily constructed Gem Theatre. Clara Andres, the ticket-taker at the nearby switchback, left her box to watch the blaze. Then, in an unwise gesture of loyalty to her employers, she dashed back to retrieve the money and tickets from her booth—only to be caught by the flames, which by then were enveloping the great Figure-8. A police constable valiantly tried to save her, but, after uttering one scream, she fell among the flames and was lost. The fire, propelled by a strong southwest wind, swept ''with cyclonic rapidity'' through the Figure-8, the Scenic Railway, and the Old Mill, whose tar-covered waterways turned into tunnels of fire. It then leapt the fence and ate its way around the big baseball stand, the open bleachers, the dressing rooms and the Toronto Rowing Club. While an alarm was sent to the city for the fire tug *Nellie Bly* and city firemen, brigades of volunteer firemen tried, ineffectually,

Squabbling boys paddle in the water while competitors paddle on the regatta course overlooked by the old Hanlan's Hotel of 1907. [CTA:JC]

to stay the progress of the fire. Even members of ''the fair sex'' were conspicuous, carrying buckets of water and manipulating garden hoses. But their efforts were, as usual, handicapped by the lack of water pressure and small size of the hoses. The *Nellie Bly* soon arrived and threw a stream of water on the grandstand. But the fire had too firm a grip and the stadium was, once again, reduced to ashes.

Meanwhile, Hanlan's Hotel was the scene of feverish activity. Hotel guests, some still in bedclothes from afternoon naps, were pitching trunks and belongings out of windows. A group of policemen was rolling the grand piano down

the sidewalk out of danger. The manager's wife, Mrs. Little, directed evacuation operations ''with military precision'': waiters, porters, bellboys and guests all carried silverware, trunks, gramophones, bird cages—even a black and tan dog—down to Green's motor launch, which spirited them to safety over on the Western Sandbar. (Some silver and trunks were, unfortunately, dumped in the lagoon.) An army of workers fought desperately to save the hotel itself. Employees dashed buckets of water on the roof. The *Nellie Bly* was dispatched to give aid, but could not make her way through the lagoon's shallow water. Inevitably the cornice of one of the towers caught fire. Quickly, Chief Thompson and his men joined several lengths of hose together and dragged it up through the building and out onto the roof. When the signal was given to turn on the water, the firemen pointed the nozzle and braced themselves. Not a single drop emerged. "If we had got a stream of water to go six feet we would have been able to save Hanlan's Hotel," the chief said later. "As it was, we had to turn around and drag our hose out again and let the place burn." The whole roof on the north side soon was ablaze; the balcony encircling the building became a wreath of fire; and, within a half an hour, the hotel was reduced to a heap of smouldering ruins.

The direction of the wind suddenly changed and carried the flames toward another group of buildings: the Japanese Amusement Parlors,

the House of Fun and the Penny Arcade all fell victim. One of the few buildings not destroyed was an ice-cream booth, although the intense heat soon began melting the confection. Thankful firefighters, with eyes smarting from the smoke and cheeks stinging from the heat, slathered their faces with the rapidly dissolving chocolate- and strawberry-flavoured cold cream.

The fire only briefly threatened the little houses south of the amusement area, but caused hundreds of scared patrons to flee the amusement park. More than seventy years after the event, Mary Mallon, nine years old at the time, remembered seeing the smoke and flames rising above the trees from her Centre Island home. And most of all she recalled the long line of weary people trudging past her house on the way to the ferry docks: "It was like a refugee scene," she mused. By six o'clock that night, Hanlan's

Point was "a charred waste, strewn with the ashes of a world of amusement."[25]

The ruins were still smouldering when the irrepressible Lol Solman announced that a bigger and better pleasure resort would rise from the ashes of the old one. "We have the whole place clear to start upon," he announced to the *Globe*. "A complete plan, free from any hampering considerations, will mean a good deal." For the time being, however, the Point became "the Mecca of the curious and the morbid-minded." A twenty-minute ferry service ran to the ruins, curiosity seekers picked over the rubble for souvenirs, the Italian Boys Band played merrily away on an improvised bandstand and thousands of surprised visitors were delighted to find "the glitter of many lights and a round of entertainment." The merry-go-round had miraculously survived and was whirling as gaily as ever; the

Hanlan's Hotel shortly before it was completely consumed by the fire of August 10, 1909.   [CTA]

Big Scream was still screaming; and the surviving shooting galleries were still attracting amateur marksmen.

Solman set to work immediately after the great fire—cleaning up the debris, drawing up plans, negotiating with the City and, finally rebuilding the Point in steel and concrete. While some of his dreams were not realized (no hotel was built to replace Hanlan's and little filling was done to expand the area), the Point was ready for opening day 1910. The smell of popcorn, gunsmoke and candy floss once again filled the air. Some, like *Globe* reporter Augustus Brindle, might have grumbled that the rag-tag amusement area had become "overcivilized," but not many. The fine old merry-go-round was joined by new attractions, such as a stomach-churning roller coaster called The Dips. As before, a multitude of special events attracted immense crowds. Darling's Dog and Pony Circus, the prickly "comic mule" (that bucked even the "most daring adventurer" off his unruly back) and a great variety of bands all performed to the cheers of the crowds. But perhaps the greatest cheers of 1910 were reserved for "the Marvel of the Age," the "Great Holden." This "most

daring Man on Earth," according to the *World* of June 19, sped down a long narrow chute on a bicycle and leaped into a giant wheel where he flew around at such speed that he became nearly invisible. Then "this same daring chap" climbed up to a platform more that one hundred feet above the amusement park and dove backwards, turning a somersault in mid-air, into a small tank of water. Nightly the crowds roared their approval for these death-defying feats.

The baseball Maple Leafs settled into their rebuilt stadium. On Victoria Day, the *Globe* was happy to report, they "grabbed both games" from the Jersey City Skeeters—their "snappy and aggressive" play delighting over twelve thousand "wildly enthusiastic fans and fanettes." For another fifteen years the Leafs would cause normally sober men to dash frantically for the ferry and inspire normally obedient youths (like Morley Callaghan and his schoolmates) to play hookey in order to visit what Brindle called "the most breeze-blown baseball diamond and grand stand in all America." There they could even enjoy, for a time, a draught of Star Beer and cheer the dashing exploits of players like Babe Ruth, the "Sultan of Swat," who, on one

memorable August day in 1923, sent a Maple Leaf pitch soaring right over the bleachers plunk into the bay "with a mighty splash." In spite of the Babe's "titanic tap," the Yankees "burlesqued the affair" and dropped the exhibition game 8-2 to the hometown heroes.[26]

June 18, 1910, must have been a proud day for Lol Solman and the TFC, the day they launched a grand new ferry—the *Trillium*, which would delight generations of Torontonians. Shortly after noon, little Phyllis Osler, granddaughter of Toronto Ferry Company president E. B. Osler, christened the $75,000 new ferry at Polson's Iron Works, and watched the *Trillium* slip, sideways, into the bay. Workmen worked feverishly to make her ready for service by July 1. Despite her unfinished state—with little paint or accoutrements—she was nevertheless *the* popular boat on that hot, hazy Dominion Day. All the children wanted to wait for her, though wise mothers rushed for the first available boat, realizing that with the temperature hovering at 93 degrees and crowds pushing eagerly forward, it was no day to be waiting for special boats. The TFC carried some forty-nine thousand picnickers, swimmers and amusement-seekers to the Island that one day, a record that was not equalled until the war years.

The launching of the *Trillium* was marred only by the fact that while dignitaries and spectators were gathered at Polson's for the gala event, crews were dragging the bay for the bodies of two women drowned the previous night, when the ferry steamer *John Hanlan* had ploughed into an eighteen-foot gasoline launch, the *Cecilia*, about halfway across the bay. The two men from the *Cecilia* were able to stay afloat, but the two women, presumably weighted down by the elaborate fashions of the era, sank. The less than contrite captain of the *John Hanlan* accused the *Cecilia* of peculiar behaviour and commented

One Globe *reporter waxed enthusiastic about a 1910 outing to the twinkling, rebuilt Point with its "rim of coloured lights approaching" and the "far drone of the merry-go-round" discernible as she ferried across the bay.* [AC]

to the *Telegram*, "My only wonder is that we have not had more collisions in the bay.... Those sailing the small crafts and launches are usually making their way to the city side after an evening at the Island, and they purposely cross our bows to make us stop.... many of them have no lights, which of course is contrary to marine law. The *Cecilia*, however, had proper lights." Whether her marine behaviour was also proper remains a mystery.

Less controversial but equally spirited boating activity took place on the Hanlan's Point regatta course where the annual Dominion Day regattas continued to be held right up to the war. On July 1, 1904, for example, when the Toronto Rowing Club's Lou Scholes was off in England about to capture the Diamond Sculls at Henley, water enthusiasts in Toronto were enjoying the keenly contested rowing, paddling and swimming events at the 11th annual Dominion Day regatta near the old hotel. Not everyone, however, was enchanted by the Hanlan's Point regatta course, which was only a half-mile long (necessitating turns for longer races), a scarce three feet deep on average, and periodically clogged with slimy weeds. From time to time, therefore, proposals for new courses were made, but Council was not quick to approve them.

Finally, in 1911, aquatic interests, led by the Argonaut Rowing Club, came out of the boathouse to put pressure on Council. The rowers wanted the City to tear down the ancient, crumbling bridge across the lagoon between Hanlan's Point and the Western Sandbar where Turner's (now Atkinson's) Baths still slouched at the water's edge, and to improve the regatta course. On October 31 City Council agreed to spend over $22,000 to construct a three-quarter-mile course, which involved demolishing the old bridge, filling the "low, marshy portions" of the eastern bank, straightening the western

bank and dredging the lagoon to a depth of eight feet. Thereafter, Western Sandbar commuters would begin their daily journeys to the city by rowing across the regatta course or cycling around it to catch the ferry at the Hanlan's dock.

Down near the Lighthouse and new school, dredges and gangs of workers were busy tearing up another part of the Island in order to create a new filtration plant. Approved in May 1909 and

City Council became bogged down in a dispute over whether or not to replace this ancient but unsafe bridge across the Hanlan's Point lagoon to Turner's Baths. In the year this photo was taken, 1909, the bridge made a contribution to the debate by collapsing at various points. [CTA:JC]

(Below) Arthur Goss captured this view of building the Filtration Plant on October 10, 1911. [CTA]

opened in 1911, the Filtration Plant was undoubtedly much needed, but Parks Commissioner Wilson still found it "somewhat unjust" of Council to "take this large area for filtration purposes, without compensating in kind for the land so occupied."[27] But take it Council did. And the construction caused a fair (or unfair) degree of disruption. Construction crews removed sand and gravel from the shore west of Manitou Road, further endangering an already vulnerable area. Long Pond was temporarily closed and used as a settling basin, so merchants had to lug supplies overland from the main docks: English, of English's Boathouse, had to set up business elsewhere in a tent and sportsmen eager to row and paddle competitively had to find other avenues. Clean water had its price.

But in spite of all the disruptions, pleasure-seekers continued to flock to the park. Increasing numbers came by motor boat. In fact, just as the car was beginning to overrun mainland roads, so the gasoline launch was beginning to overrun Island lagoons: because of the "excessive speed maintained by motor boats in the Island Channels, thereby damaging the sand banks and endangering the lives of those using small craft," Council in 1912 slapped a 5 mph speed limit on all motor boats using Island waterways. But, as always, the people came mostly by ferry. Families crowded somewhat anxiously along the railings, young couples strolled lazily down the decks and "youngsters loved to crowd into the sterns of the old high ferries," according to future mayor Nathan Phillips, "and start swaying in unison back and forth, to see if they could get the boats to rock and roll."

At the end of the trip to Centre Island, youngsters would race down the gangplanks and over to pump up and down on Cronkwright's more magnificent merry-go-round with its new

The spirit that built an empire shows up in the grannies' tug of war at Centre Island c. 1908. [CTA:JC]

hurdy-gurdy. There, the easily-pleased Sunday School picnickers of 1912—dressed smartly but uncomfortably in Buster Brown suits or starched white middy blouses over stiffly pleated skirts—got their money's worth. "We whirled and dipped and screamed on the prancing horses, wild-eyed and with flaming nostrils," the "fat rocking dolphins" and the "ferocious striped tigers" as the calliope ground out "Meet Me Tonight in Dreamland," according to one reminiscing picnicker.[28] Comely maidens in long skirts scurried earnestly along the beach in egg-and-spoon races or, throwing caution (and reserve) to the wind, dashed fiercely along in running races. Portly matrons proudly displayed

their charges in beautiful baby contests. Even grim-faced grannies in flowered hats rolled up their sleeves and joined tugs of war. And, after the sun went down, young lovers danced to the tinkling music of an old tambourine piano at the dancing pavilion or under the stars out on the fresh green grass because the pavilion was crammed full.

As the Point and the park were enjoying heady Edwardian success, extensive alterations were about to be undertaken along the entire Toronto waterfront. For years, effective, coordinated development had been stymied by fragmented land-ownership and by the inadequate powers of the original Harbour Trust. In 1911 the powerful

Board of Trade became so frustrated by the situation that it spearheaded the drive for more effective harbour management. Its efforts were rewarded in May 1911 when the federal government passed legislation creating a new, five-person Harbour Commission, with much greater authority than its predecessor to develop the entire Toronto waterfront from Woodbine on the east, through Ashbridge's Bay and the central harbour to the Humber River on the west.

The Toronto Harbour Commission's first job was to design a $20 million plan for the development of the waterfront, which it unveiled in November 1912 to thunderous applause.[29]

Most of the activity was to be concentrated elsewhere (in transforming Ashbridge's Bay into a major port and industrial quarter, dredging the harbour to a depth of thirty feet and extending the mainland central waterfront over a thousand feet southward), but the plan did anticipate some major changes to the Island. On the positive side, it contemplated creating some three hundred and fifty new acres of parkland. This suggestion, however, was more than offset by the proposal to bridge the Eastern and Western Gaps and build a meandering boulevard across the Island. For years, local politicans (even park planners like Commissioner Wilson in 1909) had been trying to bridge these gaps. Here, finally, seemed to be their golden opportunity. The federal government even agreed in June 1913 to spend some $800,000 to build the movable bridges as part of their contribution to implementing the plan. From then on, Toronto politicians would pester Ottawa—on an almost yearly basis in the 1920s—to live up to this

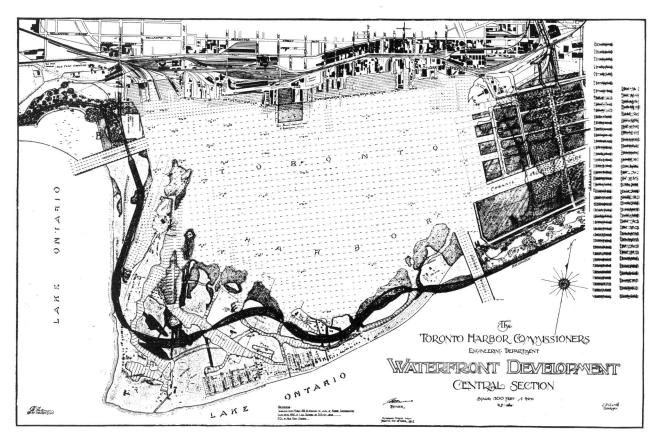

The Harbour Commission's dramatic 1912 plan to transform the Island (in this detail) and the rest of the waterfront. The Commissioners envisaged large chunks of new Island parkland, two bridges over the Gaps connected by an automobile boulevard snaking along the length of the Island, and the continuation of most, but not all, residential uses. [City of Toronto]

commitment. Such bridges and boulevard, of course, would have paved the way (literally) to the destruction of the Island as a pastoral retreat from the city across the bay. Fortunately, from this perspective, a war and a depression intervened, preventing the government from spending large sums of money on such non-essential projects. Nevertheless, the City lived in hope and actually began acquiring Island properties (mostly at Hanlan's Point) for the future Island Boulevard.[30]

The Toronto Harbour Commission was not the only threat to residential life at Hanlan's Point. The City posed constant problems. Parks Commissioner Wilson, for example, proposed to demolish the forty-nine cottages on the Western Sandbar in his 1909 plan. The cottages weren't destroyed, but the City's determination to replace creative chaos with civic order continued, plunging residents and City officials into repeated battles over a multitude of stringent, nitpicking regulations about size, materials and design of the cottages.[31] Some of the rulings became laughable. For example, a Mrs. Thompson was allowed to erect a model house "upon the clear and mutual understanding that the structure is to be used only as a child's playhouse and for no other purpose whatsoever" (like sleeping). Nothing seemed to spook City Hall as much as the thought of an unauthorized sleeping body. Except, perhaps, an illegal tent, which set both City officials' and sometimes other cottagers' blood aboil. No, Mr. Lindsay could *not* erect a tent as sleeping quarters for the cook: this might have been an era of domestic bliss for employers, but the servants would have to live in the cottage, not in a tent. Exceptions to the no-tenting rule were made only in "extreme cases," as a mayor was later informed by the assessment commissioner; so, Mr. Frank Everist was permitted to erect a 10-by-12-foot tent next to his cottage

for his "delicate" son. Mr. Everist's neighbour Mrs. Munro was not happy. Perhaps making a mountain out of Everist's marquee, she complained bitterly to City Hall: "It is 10 feet from our door and windows and you can imagine what it is to have a crying child for the most part of the night so close to one's sleeping quarters. Our view is entirely shut out and our dining room in darkness." But the tent remained for the season.

Fire, as always, was an ever-present threat to Island cottages, but fortunately a relatively infrequent reality. Nevertheless, fire did occasionally take its toll in the residential areas. On Sunday afternoon April 20, 1913, a fire started in John Wedd's vacant cottage at 620 Lakeshore. While a neighbour headed for the public phone across the lagoon to sound the alarm, Lol Solman and his chauffeur spotted the fire from the Bay Street Terminal. Perhaps fearing a repetition of the 1909 devastation at the amusement park, they jumped into a boat and steamed over to the scene. Sparks flew across Hanlan's Point—all the way to the Lakeside Home. And the fire itself spread rapidly to six other nearby houses which were so dry that they fell easy prey to the flames. Boarding-house operator Mrs. Horwood, contractor Arthur Dinnis and Alderman Alfred Burgess were among the losers. But quick work by Captain Goodwin of the *Nellie Bly*, Lol Solman, Eddie Durnan and about twenty-five other residents (who saved one house by wrapping it in wet blankets) at least prevented the fire from spreading further. So, although Alderman Burgess lost two of his three Island houses, he did not lose 618 Lake Shore rear, which he rented out that season to an impecunious young artist, Frederick Varley. Varley, it seems, discovered Island Park more than a year before discovering Algonquin Park with his painting companions

Tom Thomson, A. Y. Jackson and Arthur Lismer.

From 1910 on, Ward's Island was attracting more and more Torontonians looking for a cheap but pleasant summer holiday.[32] Among the applicants for a tent site in 1910 was one Mrs. Crew, who wrote that she was "anxious to get over to the Island this Summer on account of the children's health." The poor woman had nine youngsters between the ages of twenty-one months and fourteen years, four of whom were

Artist Frederick Varley appears to be using a piece of drift wood to paddle his boat near his Hanlan's Point home in the summer of 1913.   [Maud Varley/ National Gallery of Canada]

"very delicate in health." Her husband, she assured Mr. Taylor of the Assessment Department, was sober, hardworking and reliable, but the eleven members of the family (not surprisingly) could "barely live" on the $11 he brought home faithfully each week. She asked for a free camping permit, but the City was not in a charitable mood. A great number of other campers, however, were able to scare up the necessary $15 to $20 and passed a very successful season on Ward's Island, where they "all vied with one another, in making life worth living," as campground caretaker James Marshall happily phrased it at the end of the 1910 season.

Marshall, of course, was always pleased when he could report that residents were like "one happy family" and that there had been "no friction." But sometimes conflict did arise, even in this summer Eden, and sometimes the ugly prejudice which festered beneath the placid surface of WASP Toronto erupted. In the summer of 1911, for example, a large family of "foreigners" crowded ten-strong into a small tent on Haney's Point and aroused the ire of nearby residents of good British stock. Not only did these so-called Swedes allow their children to run about naked; but their male elders drank to excess, their English consisted mostly of oaths and, according to neighbours' reports, they failed to use the W.C.'s provided. The *coup de grâce* came in the form of a personal rebuke: "They [had] even gone so far as to effect an entrance into an immediate neighbour's tent during his absence and deposited therein that which was decidely objectionable and obnoxious, and very aggravating upon his return." (Whether the insult was unprovoked or even how the offended neighbour discovered who left the calling card went unreported.) In any event, as a result of neighbours' complaints, Marshall

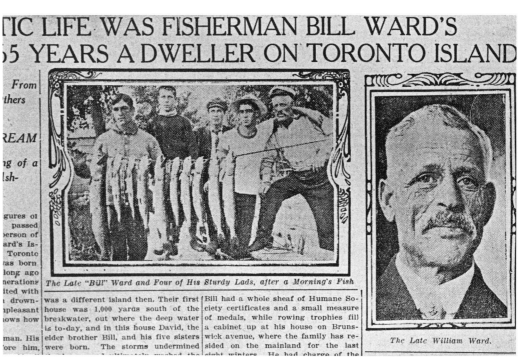

The late Bill Ward (right) and four of his sturdy sons after a successful morning's fishing in the waters off Ward's Island. [Star/MTLB]

received instruction from City Hall "to keep a close watch on all that goes on at this tent." The "Finlanders," as they were also called, were not ejected; but they certainly did not return the following season.[33]

Elsewhere on the expanding campsite, life went on as usual. One pleasant change in 1911 was the arrival of dozens of Eaton's girls who had formed a swimming club. Each weekday evening and on holidays, these keen aquatic shop girls swarmed across Ward's Island, changed in the two large tents (properly supervised by a responsible grown woman) and splashed in the foam.

Another delightful attraction was Daddy Frank Staneland's gangling and mischievous cousin, who disported herself not on the beach but on the stage—Beatrice Lillie. The future Lady Peel's hilarious Cockney routines rolled them in the aisles at the Shelter on many occasions before she left Toronto in 1914 to seek her fortune in Britain and to become, according to Noel Coward, "the funniest woman of our civilization."

On the more sober side, the tiny Queen's Own Rifle Signal Corps was given permission in 1911 to pitch three bell tents on the Island shore. Finding a site, however, presented certain problems. "Steady" and "respectable" the lads may have been, but not entirely beyond influence or temptation. Captain Mason suggested a spot beyond the breakwater on the lakeshore. But, with the pretty young things from Eaton's frolicking around their tents on this beach, the Island Committee was reluctant to place the QOR camp nearby. In the end, the military youths were placed at Haney's Point, which was hardly an isolated location and had developed a far from savoury reputation. Little did these summer soldiers suspect that in a few years time they would be testing their wireless and semaphore skills not on the fringes of a holiday resort but in the middle of a war.

Nineteen-twelve and the old order changeth. Early in the year, both "the Laird of Ward's Island" sixty-six-year-old William Ward and his older brother David who had once backed Ned Hanlan, died.[34] So, as the Royal Canadian Yacht Club was celebrating its Diamond Jubilee that summer with a grand and glorious garden party in honour of the club and their Royal Highnesses the Duke of Connaught and Princess Patricia, a new generation of Wards was taking over the family domain—a domain that was becoming somewhat seedy in the eyes of City Hall. Ward may have nurtured a luscious orchard that tempted small boys like Frank Staneland to a life of crime, but his sons were left in charge of property that left City officials dismayed. By July 1913 the Wards had fourteen cottages, four tents and one hotel crammed onto their 3½-acre site. Outdoor water closets were provided for the 175 people living there, but "conditions surrounding the hotel" were reportedly "not such to encourage the use of the accommodation provided." The ice house near the hotel kept the ground "continually in a moist condition" and, worst of all, when the wind blew from

The Ward's Island lifesaving station in 1915 with the motor launches that later sparked so much trouble.
[Star]

the southwest "the closet odor wafted all over the place."[35]

On the more positive side, William's eldest son Frank became coxswain of the lifesaving crew, which was taken over from the Dominion Government by the newly created Toronto Harbour Commission in that same year of 1912. In 1913 a new boathouse and observation tower were built at the Eastern Gap. This "splendidly equipped station" soon became "one of the show places of the Island with its beautiful buildings, high steel look-out tower, and fast launches."[36] Here too, however, William's offspring ran into trouble. At the end of 1913

friction mysteriously developed among the members of the lifeboat crew. After an investigation, all twelve members including Captain Ward were dismissed and W. E. Chapman took over.

Frank and his brothers turned to other work. Frank moved into the cartage business—a real need in a summer community with annual migrations—as well as into sundry other activities like renting cottages, building verandahs and even selling refreshments at the CNE. And Fred, with $1,400 sunk in equipment, continued as the only professionally licensed fisherman still operating from the Island in 1912. In addition to providing an income, Ward's fishing activity also seems to have provided picturesque entertainment for the summer emigrés from the city. The more romantic early-risers could enjoy a "plunge in a fresh-water sea, with the sun rising out of its unbroken eastern horizon, and watch the honest fishermen hauling up the whitefish." The hungrier members of the community, awakened by the pungent scent of fish frying over open fires, could breakfast on fresh salmon trout or whitefish bought directly from the fisherman. "It is not a hard way to make a living," Fred told the *Star Weekly* of August 3, 1912, "as long as you have other resources when the fish don't come around." The fisherman no longer had to knit or mend his own nets because he could buy ready-made ones by the pound and, with modern power boats, he no longer risked being becalmed in the winter "six miles from shore in ten below zero, with

the seat of his oilskin overalls frozen to the deck." Fred, in fact, no longer bothered with winter fishing. He and his brothers ran iceboats on the bay and gave "confiding tourists from abroad a Canadian experience at the rate of sixty miles an hour for fifty cents a trip."

In 1912 the City also made a major change in Island administration. Ward's Island caretaker James B. Marshall was becoming aged, infirm and unable to keep a proper watch over the campground. Moreover, he was accused of a variety of minor transgressions, which he naturally denied. But City Hall decided that it was high time to replace the eighty-four-year-old caretaker who, if he wasn't actually dishonest, was at the very least "taken advantage of by campers in many ways," according to a City report.

In short order, the City hired Marshall's assistant of five years, dapper Walter F. Dodd. Dodd had been a resident of Ward's Island

for nineteen years and knew "every resident and lot" on it. He was also well acquainted with prevailing attitudes. For example, in his letter applying for the job, not only did he recommend that he should have "authority to stop all ball playing and other games on the City property, and dancing in the pavilion on Sunday," but also that "certain Finlanders (whose names I shall submit to you) shall not be permitted to locate at Ward's Island." The City was agreeable to his suggestions.[37] Dodd's reign was to be vigorous and restrictive but, as he was a friend of many campers, it was also probably reflective of majority wishes and prejudices. Over the years, King Walter, as he became affectionately known, "ran the place with an iron hand," according to Fram Ward.

By the summer of 1912, the campground itself was becoming very crowded. The previous season, two lavatory buildings with six W.C.'s

(Right) *Ward's Island's "tent city," 1911, with the Wiman Baths (now apartments) behind and the Ward's Hotel beyond.* [CTA:JC]

(Below)*According to the* Star Weekly *of August 3, 1912, campers and hotel guests at Ward's Island could "lie upon the broad sand beach of a coast resort" only twenty minutes from the heart of "modern sky-scraping Toronto" and lazily "watch the fishermen dry their nets."* [Star/MTLB]

Arthur Coulson (right rear) and friends pose uneasily outside the Ward's Island tents of 1913-14, with the new wooden street and the spindly trees stretching behind them. [Eleanor Sinclair]

more regular pattern. Not only did McBride's voice boom out across the bowling green and baseball field, it also reverberated across the Council Chamber. Some idea of Sam's political style can be gained from Nathan Phillips who wrote succinctly in his autobiography that "McBride had a terrible temper." One time he actually got into a fist fight with one of his fellow aldermen and received a black eye. On another famous occasion, "during a discussion of food prices in the Council Chamber, McBride threw a can of beans at Alderman Joe Beamish. It missed him but made a large dent in the panelling." McBride certainly made his mark at City Hall. No matter, McBride remained the darling of Ward's Islanders and always looked after their interests.

It was a busy spring for City workmen. They surveyed the campground, hammered great cedar posts at the corners of the five main camp areas, graded the site, removed unsightly brush, strung lighting, laid water pipes and put down six-foot-wide plank sidewalks, thus transforming the previous "casual location of the tents" into an attractively "systematic concentration" which accommodated more campers.[39] The basic pattern for the future Ward's Island cottage community was established by this 1913 layout and its eastward extension in 1915.

When campers arrived in May 1913, moving was easy. They looked over their changed addresses and simply picked up the kitchens and carried them to their new locations. Some of the old and dilapidated looking tarpaper kitchens were a source of annoyance to City officials, so caretaker Dodd was instructed to have them

each had had to suffice for the 685 campers and the hundreds of visitors who had found their way to this once-remote corner of the Island. These bathrooms were reportedly efficient as far as they went but, clearly, they did not go far enough. To relieve the immediate pressure, the City expanded lavatory facilities for the 1912 season and hatched more grandiose plans to lay the campground out in streets which would "improve the appearance of the camp," expand its capacity and, like Baron Haussmann's plan for Paris, give the City authorities "better control" over the occupants.[38] In the meantime, disappointed individuals and worthy groups, including even a troop of Baden-Powell Canadian Boy Scouts, continued to be turned away.

Urged on by that pugnacious Ward's Islander Alderman Sam "How he hollered! How he roared!" McBride, the City spent $1,500 in the spring of 1913 to lay the campground out in a

Arthur Coulson and another bachelor friend relax outside "Kichikiwanna" (or plain old number 25). It wasn't "Floreat," but it was just as imaginatively decorated. [Eleanor Sinclair]

replaced with properly constructed ones which, according to strict City regulations, were to be of dressed lumber and stained dark green. Campers got on with the job of decorating their new nests (with elaborate driftwood lattice-work, fanciful signs and even the occasional little rock garden) and, most of all, with having fun.

They lounged out front in camp chairs. They fixed up boats and sailed, paddled and drifted around coves and lagoons. They visited back and forth, day and night. They picnicked. On Sundays, they prayed in the Shelter and on week-nights they waltzed and two-stepped to the merry music of an old upright piano. When the racy foxtrot first came in, astonished elders requested couples to dance properly. The dancers, in fact, waltzed right up against officialdom. Their dances, it seems, had been held without permits and attracted hordes of admission-paying visitors from the city. The City was determined to put an end to this misbehaviour. It was aided by residents themselves who banded together to form the Ward's Island Association (WIA), which sponsored weekly dances for residents only, and used the admission money for the benefit of the community.

The WIA became the social and organizational heart of the community for the tenting era. Beyond dancing, it also organized a multitude of other activities and events, like the grand annual Sports Day. The athletic Daddy Frank Staneland was asked by James Merrick (a prominent Toronto lawyer and Ward's Island resident) to run the first Sports Day. One of his tasks was to raise money for prizes, a task he approached with some trepidation. He made up a list of possible contributors, beginning with the "big names" like Sam McBride, Nat Mills and Fred Armstrong (the first president of the WIA). He tentatively marked them down for $2 each

and then worked his way down to people he thought would give 50¢. Screwing up his courage, he approached McBride, who was "kind of a gruff fellow." "Mr. Mac...," he began. "What do you want, sparrow?" McBride shot back. Nervous young Frank explained his list. "Let me see that list!" McBride exclaimed. "Two dollars! What do you mean two dollars?" Staneland gulped. "What can you do with two dollars?" McBride continued. "Here's ten dollars." Then he went over to collar his friend: "Nat Mills, give me ten dollars." And so it went. In the end they had so much money that they bought gold clocks to present to the winners of the usual run of Sports Day events like twenty-five-yard dashes, and of less conventional contests like the needle and thread competition and the boot race, in which competitors had to find their

shoes which were all jumbled up together in a huge pile.

Fun was fun. But it mustn't be allowed to get out of hand. The City, and Dodd, were always eager to keep a tight rein on the community. In this summer of 1913, although it did not "anticipate any trouble," the City took measures to forestall any problems. To cast a "beneficial moral effect" over the newly laid-out tent city, the City policeman on duty at Centre Island was instructed "to visit Ward's Island at irregular intervals during the night."[40] Some lads nevertheless seem to have escaped the constable's wary eyes by hopping into rowboats and venturing across to the wilds of uninhabited Sunfish Island for long-remembered midnight stag parties. But world events would soon cast a pall over such youthful highjinks.

Centre Island, May 30, 1914, and these war canoeists are not off to war, yet. [PAC (PA-61056)]

8
For King and Island

August 4, 1914. The summer season was at its height. Every Wednesday night Island Amateur Aquatic Association dancers gathered merrily in their brightly lit Aquatic Hall overlooking Long Pond and every Saturday IAAA members splashed up and down the lagoon in anticipation of the grand annual regatta to be held later that month. Over at the Royal Canadian Yacht Club, sailors discussed the *Nirwana*'s third successive victory in the international George Cup (this time under Aemilius Jarvis's son, W. P. D. Jarvis) and anxiously awaited the arrival of *Valiant* from Chicago to challenge the newly built *Ahmeek* for the prestigious Richardson Cup. Meanwhile, Torontonians had just spent a tense Civic Holiday weekend. As usual, city-dwellers had flocked to the Island, but their minds were elsewhere. Even the Maple Leafs seemed to be distracted by "the war news" and dropped two games to the invading Providence Grays. Finally, on Tuesday evening, any lingering uncertainty was banished.

Thousands of loyal citizens gathered outside downtown newspaper offices in Toronto to await official word. When the notice was finally posted at 7 P.M. (midnight British time), the crowd was silent for a moment and then burst into a cheer—"not for war, but for the King, Britain, and—peace gone—victory." Heads were bared, the anthem was sung and then great processions fanned out through downtown streets, lustily chanting "Rule Britannia" and other patriotic songs. Union Jacks floated proudly aloft, while a fife-and-drum band and part of a brass band joined the main procession.[1] Not since the Boer War of 1899-1902 had Toronto experienced the thrill of such patriotic fervour.

Ironically, 1914 was to have been "Peace Year" at "the Ex." But before the close of this year's Canadian National Exhibition, trainloads of Toronto volunteers had already set off for training at Valcartier, the Germans were smashing their way toward Paris and thousands of troops already lay dead on foreign battlefields. By the time of the next Exhibition, its site had been transformed into a military camp with bell tents, heavy armament and khakied troops cluttering the lakeside grounds.

The war had an immediate effect on the Island and Island residents, as it did on all Canadians. Needless to say, the IAAA's last dance of the season on August 5 was "rather sad" according to former Centre Islander Mary Mallon. The IAAA's final regatta was never held. And the planned Richardson Cup challenge was postponed indefinitely. "With Britain's ultimatum," commented RCYC chronicler C. H. J. Snider, "sports activities faded like breath on the pane."

Feeling the call of Empire, men rushed to sign up. Sportsman, Boer War veteran and future Ward's Island Association president Alec Sinclair was reportedly the first Canadian to enlist.[2] The crews of the *Ahmeek* and the *Nirwana* and virtually every other yacht in the RCYC "were thronging recruiting stations and scrambling into khaki or blue serge like men pulling on oilskins for a heavy squall."[3] The "boys" from the "Chattanooga" camp on Ward's Island, who had become a familiar sight waddling across the tent ground with their tame pet duck (won at the Ex) volunteered to a man. And soon the volunteers began to march off to war—the Layton boys from Mohawk, the Jarvises and the Trees and the Gordons from Lake Shore, and on and on and on. Islanders, like mainlanders, flocked to University Avenue to cheer them along as they marched from the Armories down to Union Station. The bands played. The crowds waved flags and cheered "loudly and incessantly."[4] Officials gave speeches and old soldiers

like Honorary Colonel Albert E. Gooderham of the Royal Grenadiers stood proudly aside as their boys passed by. "I guess to me it was rather thrilling," remembered Mary Mallon who watched the first contingent go out at the tender age of fourteen. "We didn't realize what was going to happen."

Those left behind threw themselves into war work. William K. McNaught of Centre Island, for example, helped raise $100,000 for a battery of armoured cars, supervised the recruiting, organization and equipment of the 109th Regiment of Canadian Militia (for which he was made honorary colonel) and the 84th and 169th Overseas battalions. Aemilius Jarvis immediately vacated his Island house and became a veritable dynamo. While his two sons of military age

(Above) *The war comes to Toronto Island: a student pilot and his instructor navigate their Curtiss Flying Boat by the Hanlan's Point Amusement Park (right) in the summer of 1915, while intrepid boaters watch.* [Smithsonian (A 344C)]
(Right) *The homefront: what the lads were fighting for.* [TIA]

went overseas, he ran an impressive recruiting campaign for the British Admiralty in the Province of Ontario and also acted as a "confidential agent" of the British government to secure "mystery ships" for patrol purposes. And many of Jarvis's neighbours also packed up their summer belongings and returned to their homes in the city where they remained during the war years, leaving their Island homes in darkness as silent testimony to the death and destruction abroad.[5]

The city hummed with war-related activity. Militia men, fuelled by wild rumours of possible invasion by Germans living in the neutral United States, drilled several evenings each week in specially lit schoolyards and down on the lakefront in Harbour Square, and participated in a test mobilization, which Minister of Militia and Defence Sam Hughes later denounced as absurd and needlessly alarmist. Fears about sabotage and small-scale infiltration were perhaps not so wildly absurd. To counter these, troops guarded the Welland Canal, special immigration officers were assigned to Canada Steamship Lines boats like the *Cayuga* and the *Chippewa* to scrutinize passengers boarding at U.S. ports (their chances of actually spotting a real spy, however, seem remote) and steamship sailings were not listed in local papers. Regular troops camped at Exhibition Park, Queen's Park and elsewhere and drilled in parks throughout the city: infantry assaults were mounted up the slopes of High Park and armoured vehicles rumbled through Riverdale Park. Recruitment meetings were held in theatres, even on the steps of City Hall. And when recruiting slowed down, recruiting officers like Captain Gooderham of the Highlanders fanned out across downtown streets taking more aggressive action, such as collaring likely-looking prospects. Civilians flocked to munitions, airplane and shipbuilding factories to feed the war machine. Polson Iron Works down on Toronto Bay, for example, turned from building decorative ferries and lake steamers to forging grim warships. And groups across the city raised money for all manner of war materiel, from ambulances to machine guns.

City Council, of course, threw its support behind the war effort. Its first action, on August 24, 1914, was to contribute a hundred horses from civic and police departments. By 1920 the City had spent some $13.5 million on war-related matters, like insuring soldiers, sending Christmas gifts, giving recruiting grants and so on. Mayor Tommy Church—elected for the first of seven terms in January 1915—was everywhere. Wearing his familiar straw boater, he sent the troops off. (There were those who claimed he knew every one of the thousands of Toronto soldiers overseas.) When the wounded were invalided home, he met the trains. When the casualty lists were posted, he checked them and went off to comfort bereaved families. When the victorious troops finally returned, he was there smiling and shaking hands. And throughout the conflict he voiced the well-worn clichés that Torontonians wanted to hear. In August 1915, for example, his worship assured his City Council colleagues that "the heart of our Empire is sound and will weather the storm in this world's fight for the battle of the Lord and of civilization against the forces of reaction and barbarism."

Long-time Island resident, Robert F. Gagen, portrays wartime shipbuilders hard at work in Ashbridges Bay. [CWM/NMM/NMC]

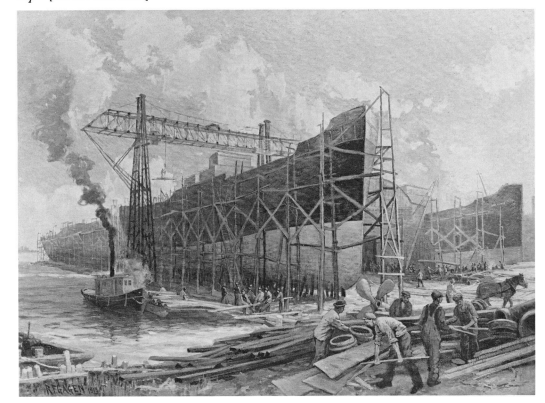

The City even posted guards on the Island— for example, at the Filtration Plant to protect the city's water supply from possible sabotage. Private Stoddart of the 48th Highlanders was on duty at the wireless station at the Lighthouse when he spotted a fire at the Lakeside Home For Little Children early in the morning of April 22, 1915. (At the same hour, his compatriots overseas were about to become engaged in Canada's first major test of the war, the second battle of Ypres, where Canadian troops held fast as clouds of deadly chlorine gas floated towards them—the first time the terrible gas was used during this war.) The City Fire Department was immediately alerted, but sent its firefighters off to the mainland Hospital for Sick Children. By the time the firemen did arrive at the Lakeside Home, it was too late to save the great wooden landmark which had graced the Island landscape for so many years. Only a small section survived the fire. Fortunately, at least none of the little patients was in residence at the time. By July John Ross Robertson was already approaching City Council with designs for a new, more fire-resistant, "cottage plan" Lakeside Home, comprising a two-storey central administration building flanked by one-hundred-foot-long, one-storey patient pavilions facing the lake. His request for additional land from the Dominion Lighthouse Reserve was readily granted and the new Lakeside Home was used as a children's hospital until 1928.

As early as spring 1915, innocent enthusiasm for the war changed to grim resolve as the casualty lists grew. Aemilius's son, young Lieutenant W. D. P. Jarvis, winner of the last Prince of Wales Cup in 1913 and his last international race aboard the *Nirwana* in July 1914, was killed at St. Julien on April 24, 1915. Thereafter, "every Canadian list of killed or wounded contained the name of one or more members of the Royal Canadian Yacht Club," club historian Snider recorded patriotically. Men who had been "hauling in the mainsheet or hiking out over the weather gunwale" only a few short years earlier, now lay in Flanders fields forever— including Jarvis's crewman on the winning *Nirwana*, Captain Leslie Gordon. The Gordon family, like other Island families, was hard hit. Captain Maitland Lockhart Gordon also died of wounds. And the eldest son, Major (later Colonel) H. D. L. Gordon was wounded, but fortunately survived and returned to Toronto in 1918 to continue his accounting career with two other Island associates, E. R. C. Clarkson's son G. T. Clarkson and keen sailor R. J. Dilworth. Before that happy time, however, Major Gordon underlined the horrifying reality of the war in a letter to his father W. H. Lockhart Gordon. The text was reprinted in the *Globe* of July 5, 1916. Of the more than 1,000 men in the battalion, he reported, only 76 remained unwounded and of the 32 officers, only one was then on duty.

Not even civilians were immune. In May 1915 the sinking of the great Cunard liner *Lusitania* stunned all Canadians, including Islanders, whose longtime neighbours Mr. and Mrs. George Copping perished with over 2,000 others.

That same month the sandy northern tip of the Western Sandbar was transformed into Canada's first air school. Regarded earlier as more of a curiosity than anything else, the airplane came into prominence during the First War, and Canada's first military "Birdmen" trained off the Island's shores during this summer of 1915. On May 10, 1915, Toronto's Curtiss School opened with eleven students. These candidates were young, "British, well-off, and cocky."[6] But, because of the high wind, only four of them were actually able to savour their first taste of flying. After this unsatisfactory start, the school changed its schedule: instruction would be given early in the morning and late in the afternoon when the wind tended to be light and the water calm. So, beginning the next day, bleary-eyed candidates who lived on the mainland gathered at 5 A.M. at the foot of Spadina and were ferried over to the Western Sandbar. Wakening the mechanic George, who slept near the three planes, they were ready for their training flights in the strange, whale-like Curtiss F-type Flying-Boat. The Flying-Boat was a hundred-horse-power biplane with room for two men—a pilot and an observer. It took off from and landed in the water on its belly. Instructor Pierce, clad in blue coat, with a balaclava on his head and rubber boots on his feet, would clamber into the cockpit with one of his students. They would head out across the bay and when they reached the awesome speed of 60 mph, would lift off the water into the wild blue yonder. Up there, Pierce might tease a young recruit out of his nervousness, teach him how to manoeuvre the beast and, pointing to the rising sun, remind him, as the poster did, to "Beware the Hun in the Sun." Those dwarfed on the ground below would exclaim in awe: "She's going up by bounds" and "My, that's the highest flight yet. He must be 300 feet up."[7] For perhaps six minutes the plane would dip and rise over the bay and the lake, entertaining early risers on the Island, as well as crowds of spectators on weekends.

Student pilots—like young Jack Keens of Mohawk Avenue (who was later shot down but survived) Grant Gooderham of Lakeshore Avenue and Fred Armstrong, Jr., of Ward's Island—could pick out their cottages far below.

The pleasant side of flying: student pilots and their friends pose in front of a Flying Boat at Hanlan's Point in the summer of 1915.
[Canadian Forces Photo Unit (PMR-71-17)]

And young Bert S. Wemp—future air ace and Mayor of Toronto—could dream of the day when airplanes would be an everyday sight in the peacetime city and a permanent airport might spread over the Western Sandbar. After the brief flight, instructor and student would head back, past The Dips and the stadium on Hanlan's Point, to set their craft gently down on the water and float to rest on the broad beach of the Western Sandbar near the hangars. Sometimes, however, the landing was not so gentle. On Victoria Day 1915, after instructor W. A. "Billy" Dean and one of his five pupils had landed on the water, they sprang a leak and ran out of gas. As the lake grew rougher and the water mounted in the plane the airmen dismantled the wings and managed to manoeuvre it to shore. The incident was regarded as somewhat of a learning

experience (at least by the warm and dry *Globe* reporter), having brought the flier "into actual contact with the difficulties of aviation."

By the time the Toronto Curtiss School produced its first two graduates on July 11, forty young aviators had already begun practising figure-eights and motor cut-offs and landings, making it "the biggest aviation school in existence" according to the *Mail & Empire*. By the end of that month, eleven pilots were on their way overseas and by the end of the flying season, the school had certified sixty-seven pilots without a single fatality or serious injury—no small feat in those unpredictable early days of aviation.

Throughout the war the Flying Corps had an all-too-often-fatal attraction for Island boys. Fred Armstrong, Jr., trained at Hanlan's Point

in the summer of 1915 and even flew over the regatta at Ward's. By August 1917 he was a commander of an air squadron. "At a boy, Freddie!" cheered the month-old *Ward's Island Weekly*. "Drop a bomb for us on the Kaiser's pate." All members of the athletic "Gym Six" camp also went to the front, and all but one were in the aviation corps. Not all returned. Thirty-year-old Lieutenant George Pierce was killed in action only two months after arriving in France, while his brother, Lieutenant Albert Pierce, also a flier, was wounded, but not killed, at Zellebeke. Younger Island boys had to wait their turn to be killed, like eighteen-year-old Lieutenant Frederick William O'Shaunessy Douglas, who left school, joined the Royal Flying Corps in September 1917, was commissioned in February and by August 1918 was lying dead in France. The list went on.

Throughout the war, Hanlan's Point attracted large crowds of soldiers and civilians eager to forget for a few precious hours "unpleasant thoughts of a mighty struggle on the battlefields of Europe," as the *Globe* commented on July 2, 1915, and more personal fears that at any moment a messenger would knock at the door with a telegram. Worry could be kept at bay by swaying to the thirty-five-piece sound of Liberati and His Wonderful Band, by laughing at the flickering antics of Charlie Chaplin and the Keystone Kops at the Free Outdoor Moving Pictures, or by rollicking up and down over the mighty Racer Dips.

So on July 1, 1915, "war or no war, Toronto celebrated Dominion Day in good old fashioned style," the *Globe* reported. The city "was in holiday dress," with flags of the allied forces fluttering from every pole. As recruiting sergeants fanned out across downtown, tacking up posters and tackling likely—but increasingly reluctant—prospects, some 45,000 people were ferried to the Island (an astonishing 12,000 more than the previous year). There the holiday-makers spent a glorious, sunny day sampling Island treats: the twenty-second (and last wartime) Dominion Day regatta on the new three-quarter-mile Hanlan's Point course; two baseball games at the stadium; and the usual potpourri of picnics, amusements and general merry-making.

The following Dominion Day, Torontonians were cheered by the *Globe*'s "splendid war news" and some 56,000 ebullient patriots crossed the bay under bright, sunny skies. (The euphoria soon evaporated as the British "advance," which had taken 9,500 prisoners on its first day, stalled and both sides became mired in the infamous killing ground of the Somme Valley.)

Meanwhile, the Royal Canadian Yacht Club "carried on," according to historian Snider. Indeed, members felt it was a patriotic duty to do so, for "it meant much to the men overseas and on the seas and under the seas in the submarines, to know that back in Canada, among the willow-trees billowing in their silver-green, the old blue ensign was flying at the yacht club." But the rhythm of club life was much altered. The fleet was laid up from the first week of the war and for four years club topsails disappeared from Toronto Harbour. All races, except dinghy races, were cancelled and the dismantled fleet, swinging idly at moorings or hauled out into the marine yard, rapidly disintegrated. Some of the best yachts, like the proud new *Ahmeek*, were sold to prosperous Americans who were still unentangled in the deadly web of war. Many

others, like Jarvis's *Zahra* and Gooderham's *Clorita*, were stripped of their lead ballast and lead keels to make bullets, "broken up at a time when lead keels were of more use in stopping the Hun invasion than in winning cups."

By August 1915 wounded men were already coming back from overseas. The club lawns, "an oasis at all times, and particularly amid wartime conditions which were turning city parks into drill-grounds and war gardens," were dotted with convalescents from the hospitals every morning. Twice a week the club steamer *Hiawatha* took patients out for a sail on the lake, served refreshments and returned its charges to a fleet of automobiles provided by club members at the foot of Yonge Street. Those who remained on land enjoyed watching the dinghy racing and, beginning in 1917, cheered the dinghy skippers competing for a new cup donated

Two Ward's Islanders who went off to war: Arthur Coulson (left) who returned, and George Pierce (right) who did not. [Eleanor Sinclair (Coulson picture) WIW/MTLB (Pierce picture)]

by Mrs. A. P. Townsend in memory of her son Lieutenant Alan Jarvis Townsend who had been killed in September 1916 during the Battle of the Somme.

For its part, the Parks Department, like other civic departments, was certainly affected by labour shortages and high prices. Many of the "best men" were on active service, Mayor Tommy Church reported in January 1917, and many other good workers had been attracted elsewhere by "the high wage-rate offered by munitions and other manufacturers." Those who were working were older, less agile and more accident-prone than their predecessors.[8] In addition, there was no City money for major capital improvements in Island Park or anywhere else, so development and maintenance suffered. Park concessionaires, too, were affected by war-inflated prices. When the Island Park refreshment privilege came up for renewal in late 1916, the City agreed to food concessionaire Bulmer's request for a 10 percent rent reduction to cover higher costs.

By this time not all Island volunteers were "boys." Ward's Islanders Mabel Swain and her sister were among the first contingent of VAD nurses enlisted in Canada, who sailed for Britain from Montreal on September 16, 1916. Located only a ferryboat ride across the Mersey from Liverpool, the Swain sisters were "constantly reminded of Toronto bay and so of Ward's." In spite of the "great deal of hard work"— including looking after a fellow Ward's Islander who was later invalided home to "the Canvas City" on Ward's Island—the nursing sisters were cheered by the "sure feeling that we *are* 'doing our bit.'"[9]

Those left behind also wanted to "do their bit." In 1917 the Ward's Island Association got permission from the City to cultivate a Red Cross Garden behind Ward's Hotel, so on July 1, 1917, the *Ward's Island Weekly* reported, a large crew turned out to celebrate Canada's fiftieth birthday by digging a patriotic potato patch. Politician Sam McBride "tackled the job with his usual energy" and almost completed an entire furrow by himself. At the last sod he gave the spade a "vicious push into the earth and severed a large fat worm." "I wish that wriggling twister was the Kaiser," scowled Sam. "It's that old bird who is responsible for me working in this potato patch."

"Blackface" was featured in masquerades and minstrel shows both on and off the Island in this era. This weird creature was a popular figure of fun around Ward's Island and even got his picture in the Weekly *of September 1918.* [David Amer]

Elsewhere on the Island that day, a record 65,000 Torontonians celebrated the Dominion's fiftieth anniversary in a less taxing—though equally sober—fashion. Having survived the crossing (between 2 and 5 P.M. the efficient Toronto Ferry Company transported an astonishing 30,000 celebrants, who never had to wait in the "pens" for more than a few minutes), holiday-makers were treated not to an old-fashioned regatta (which was cancelled for the war's duration), but to a new form of entertainment: an airshow. A dozen planes from Camp Borden flew down from Barrie in battle formation. All along the route people rushed out of their houses to gaze up at the "very small specks in the heavens" on what was "probably

This 1915 view of Ward's Island from the lifesaving tower shows the thriving tent community, the Wiman Shelter (middle left), the low Wiman Terrace leading to the towered Wiman Building (centre) and the new Alexandra Yacht Club at the end of the pier (middle right). The lagoon in the foreground would soon disappear. [THC]

the longest sustained'' flight yet made in Canada. Undoubtedly the best place from which to admire their antics was the Hanlan's Point Stadium, where fans were watching the Leafs slog their way to two holiday victories over the Rochester Hustlers. The attention of these spectators was temporarily diverted by the squadron of army airplanes which sported and gambolled in the sky overhead, darting in and out of fleecy white clouds set against an azure background and piloted by ''the gallant birdmen who [were] preparing to make their contribution toward maintaining the supremacy of the allies in the air.''[10]

By 1918, in spite of the record crowds, even the TFC was feeling the pinch of war-inflated prices. As a result, ferry fares were increased (from 5¢ to 8¢ for one single adult fare and from 10¢ to 15¢ for a round trip).[11] And war-weary Torontonians spent a miserable, overcast Dominion Day on July 1, 1918. Only 25,000 people ventured across the bay and the cold, windswept waterfront was almost deserted.

Warmth and joy only seemed to return with the end of the war (and the lowering of the ferry fares).

Ward's Islanders, however, kept warm by slaving away over their victory cabbages and cucumbers, which they sold at a weekly Red Cross Market at the Shelter to raise funds for the war effort and, incidentally, help war-inflated household budgets. Some Islanders, however, were not so gung-ho. ''It Makes Us Sick!'' fumed the *Ward's Island Weekly* on August 25, 1917, as the nation was plunging ever more deeply into the disastrously divisive conscription debate. On the ferry recently, a certain Ward's Islander was ''brightening the corner where he was, by saying what a fine lot of people the Germans were, etc. ad nauseum.'' If it were not for the fact that the *Weekly* was read mostly on Sunday, ''we would use some good, plain old English words to describe the Germans as they have been revealed to the world since the war, right down from his satanic majesty the Kaiser to the more ordinary grade of German devils,

who are daily murdering women and babes, and placing men on top of 'U' boats—and then submerging. Our energies today should rather be directed to shooting the brutes than making excuses for them.''

The war, in fact, provided a convenient excuse for anti-foreign attitudes to resurface. The ''temper of Council'' was indicated by its directive in May 1915 to all civic departments to ''dismiss forthwith from the Service of the City, all persons of German, Austrian or Turkish birth, who are aliens or not naturalized British Subjects.'' In order ''to preserve peace and quietness among the residents at Ward's Island'' and generally to avoid ''trouble later on,'' campground caretaker Walter Dodd was instructed not to grant any camping sites to ''persons who may not be desirable'' and ''particularly...alien enemies.'' Mrs. Rose Tate, a Scottish immigrant, fell afoul of this directive, because she had a German boarder, Mr. Eric Gaedé, living under her roof in the city and in her tent at 17 Second Street on Ward's. The needy widow relied on his $7.50 per week payment. In spite of the fact that Gaedé, like other enemy aliens, reported to the authorities each week and gave assurances that he was both ''in sympathy with [the] British Cause'' and even ''ashamed he [was] German,'' City officials would not relent. Gaedé had to go.[12]

Few Islanders were troubled by philosophical questions about the enemy; they simply devoted themselves to helping their side. The whimsical baseball players hit on a novel approach to fundraising. At their final game in 1918 between the "Neverwuzzers" and the "Hazzbins," oldtimers arrived in even less orthodox uniforms than usual: as Aunt Jemima, as the polka-dot clown, as a modish bathing beauty, as a red-headed cop, and as a warring rooster constantly crowing "fowl," and so on. The "merry burlesquers" passed the hat and raised a respectable $40.

Meanwhile, more conventional methods were adopted by the good ladies of Ward's Island, Centre Island and Hanlan's Point, who got together for fundraising, bandage-rolling and "knitting, endless knitting," as Mary Mallon sighed. "Women who knit socks in public may have been a curiosity in Toronto in 1915," wrote historian Jesse Edgar Middleton, "but not in 1916. Every woman who could knit was hard at it all the time, and bridge parties and dances had given way to knitting parties and bandage socials." So, no doubt, knitting on the ferries and in the park and on the verandah and at the Shelter were also common sights. The Shelter, in fact, became the centre of Ward's Islanders' war work. There they held concerts and euchre parties, and "package nights" and bazaars to raise funds for the Red Cross and to inspire donations for the care packages sent to each Ward's Island soldier. These packages (containing such rare delights as Chiclets gum, cigarettes, plug tobacco, chocolate bars and copies of the *Ward's Island Weekly*) inspired many thank you letters from "over there." Walter Kellog who had gone missing on July 31, 1917, wrote from a prison camp in a suburb of Berlin, where he shared news and good things with a fellow POW named Conn. Smythe. H. W. Slater, living in a bell tent heated by a stove

retrieved from an old German dugout, was delighted to substitute cake for regulation hard tack. Harold Wilkinson apologized for not having written sooner: "At the time [the parcel] reached me, I was a little too busy to write anything but a 'whizbang,' but the parcel certainly was appreciated."

The letters, naturally, were studded with references to the Island and Island friends. Frank Wilkinson wrote at the end of October 1917, "Through the pages of your W. I. Weekly I have followed with interest the good times you have had during the past summer, and you may be sure I have often wished I could just drop

over there and have one of our good old games of ball again....The old war is running along in about the same old way. Lots of mud and rain....we are all working our best to finish off old Fritzie so that we can before very long, join the good old crowd at Ward's Island."

Such thoughts of home, of course, sustained the lonely soldier at the front. In fact, perhaps the most important role played by the Island during the war was a psychological one. While crouched in his dugout on the line, the weary khaki-clad "Islander" could let his mind escape from the rats and the mud and the ceaseless artillery of Flanders back to the dream-world of his "Island youth."

During the war, Harbour Commission dredges, sandpumps and pile drivers converged on the Island. In 1914 the area near the RCYC received attention (left) and in the fall of 1915, the Ward's Island campground was nearly doubled (right). [THC]

In contrast to the rest of the Island, where the prewar building boom had nearly ground to a halt and increasing numbers of houses were left dark and vacant, the wartime Ward's Island campground was full of life and crowded to the breaking point. In spite of the damper placed on larger capital projects during the war, the City and the Toronto Harbour Commission decided to nearly double the camping area at Ward's Island by filling in the pocket of water between the campground and the pier along the Eastern Gap, which was "nothing but a collecting place for floating rubbish of all kinds."[13] (The Toronto Harbour Commission, in fact, forged ahead with its 1912 plan to reshape the waterfront; so that, by 1919, it had reclaimed 826 acres, including 110 acres at the Island.[14]) In the fall of 1915, therefore, the Harbour Commission's great hydraulic dredges converged on the eastern end

of the Island and by November the THC reported "the greater portion of this area is ready for occupation." In the summer of 1916, the campground was laid out much as the cottages are today and the camping population jumped by over 300—to about 875—in the first year alone.

Ward's Islanders carried on their "old time gaiety despite the war."[15] Like each Island community, they were fiercely chauvinistic. "Over at Centre the prevailing idea is comfort and luxury....We at Ward's Island are content with four walls of canvas, happy in health, and bubbling over with vitality in our enthusiasm." Far from wanting luxurious cottages and a luxurious lifestyle, Ward's Islanders did not even want cottages at all. "Keep it simple" was the *Weekly*'s watchword. Their self-proclaimed little "Bit of Heaven" was simply a "city of

tents, each having a slight individuality of its own, and yet standing out as one homogeneous scheme." Few wished to alter this arrangement.

There were, however, drawbacks to life in the increasingly populous tent city, some more obvious than others. The weather remained a potential adversary. (At one point, for example, the *Weekly* observed lightly, "it's a mild winter we're having this summer.") And noise was another predictable nuisance—snoring, laughing, arguing, ukuleles and gramophones. "Sojourners at Ward's live so close to each other that it is important that all should have consideration for those who occupy the adjacent tents," the *Weekly* advised. "Let no one be thoughtless enough to chop wood at six a.m., and thus disturb the sleep of the neighbours; and when having a hilarious time or a musical soiree remember that the frenzy of those happy moments should ooze away at 11 p.m. so everyone may gain a well-earned repose." The gramophone was an especial curse. In 1917 the paper suggested mildly a "record exchange" so a tent on First could exchange records with "a certain tent on 4th Street." Instead of hearing "The Sunshine of Your Smile" until "you longed for a storm," you might "get a bit of Harry Lauder, or 'The Long, Long Trail.'" By 1918, the *Weekly* was fed up: "we trust lots of people will break their last year's records."

Rats, however, were a less expected nuisance. Nevertheless, Ward's Islanders seemed to take even these pests in stride. Daddy Frank Staneland recalled one time that he had been bitten on the toe while asleep. This toe was a little "sore" when he went off to work. It was only when his wife called to report that she had discovered blood at the bottom of the bed, that he investigated further. "I looked at it and here was the teeth marks on my foot." The *Ward's Island*

Weekly took the rat problem as calmly as Daddy Frank did. Reporting an increase in the rat population, the *Weekly* cautioned residents on August 25, 1917, "Now, it is up to you this fall to get rid of them....leave the poison around the floor. If everybody will unite in this we are sure of a clean out of rats." Well, even Eden had its serpent.

Ward's Island Association activities proliferated and prospered. The "Dingbats," "Iron Dukes," "Osoezes" and other baseball teams on Ward's competed fiercely nearly every night. Inter-Island baseball swung into high gear and Ward's Island fairly consistently ran off with the championship.

The bowlers contended with their "steeplechase" of a green. The course had a sort of "switchback," so a skilled bowler could send the bowl around the root of a tree and back to the kitty if he hit the groove. They hoped for better things in the future.

Quoits were also "all the rage." City-bound Islanders were warned "to use the sidewalks and not rush across the quoit beds" to catch the ferry, otherwise they risked being injured by a high-flying quoit. And the battle for the championship often came down to a titanic struggle between bellowing Sam McBride and cigar-smoking Nat Mills, who was one of the few Islanders to build a cottage on the improved Lakeshore lots during the war.

Tennis players were finally well served when two courts were laid out at a picturesque spot in front of the hotel, convenient to the Bulmer's Ice-Cream Parlour. When a young fellow finished a set with a young lady, he could escort her right into Bulmer's and order a Banana Split. "It will then be her advantage and the young man will feel the deuce," the *Weekly* punned along.

Marathon swim 1918-style: Marilyn Bell's precursors splash across Toronto Bay. [WIW/MTLB]

Sailors regularly cluttered the bay with their jaunty little dinghies, with competition undoubtedly being heightened by the relocation to Ward's Island of the Alexandra Yacht Club around 1915, even if the club's membership was severely depleted by the war.[16] And long-distance swimming began to attract "Island mermaids." In the Cross-Bay race of 1917, for example, Miss Pickard defeated all comers, splashing home in fifty-seven minutes. Meanwhile, the annual WIA regattas and Field Days continued to draw large crowds, with the "Tilting contest" in canoes being especially popular among the two thousand spectators.

The Shelter was the focus of many WIA activities. Over a hundred card players "battled away in a jovial fashion" at the opening monthly euchre evening in 1918. The weekly dance on Tuesday, August 14, 1917, set "the record for the season" and "the shelter looked like old times" with rousing oldtime dances like the "Paul Jones" catapulting toe-tapping Islanders into action. The annual Senior Masquerade of 1917 "eclipsed all others" with 114 adult Islanders appearing "in every costume from a tramp to royalty." As an extra treat, the piano was augmented by Jim Filby's Orchestra at the post-Masquerade dance. To everyone's delight, a "dandy new floor" was laid and waxed in time for the opening night dance of 1918—an old-fashioned "barn dance." Ely's four-piece orchestra was so popular that "everybody was sorry to stop when the last number had been played."

The Shelter was also used for more serious occasions. The Reverend J. W. Wilkinson conducted Sunday services, whose attendance had reached almost three hundred by 1916; the war no doubt accounting in part for the increase. At a special service held in July 1918, Reverend Wilkinson, with several sons at the front, asked "God that He will guide Great Britain and her Allies and bring them victory in this great world struggle for freedom, liberty and national integrity" and besought "God's help and blessing at this time, and His protection for our boys at the Front."

Ward's Island may have been crowded during the war, but Sunfish Island across the lagoon remained barren and uninhabited except for Billy Dean's hangar. Sometime during this period Dean, who had taught hopeful aviators to fly earlier in the war, decided to move his Curtiss Flying-Boat, the *Sunfish*, from Hanlan's Point down to the western end of Sunfish Island. He hired Frank Ward to move his drums of oil and other equipment down and offered Frank's young son Fram a free trip down the bay. They roared along the water down to Sunfish, where Dean nosed the plane up on the beach, jumped out and clumped up on shore in his great big rubber boots. "You press your foot on that thing," he instructed his young assistant. "My God, it won't go up in the air with me, will it?" asked a nervous Fram. "No, no," Dean assured him. So Ward pressed the pedal and the rear pusher engine shoved the boat up on the beach to safety. Fram Ward fetchingly suggested that Sunfish Island got its name from Dean's flying-boat which "had a big mouth on it and looked something like a sunfish"; but a 1913 map of the harbour indicates that it was named after the fish, not the plane, which only came to Canada in 1914.

As the Royal Canadian Yacht Club approached the season of 1918, the war was in its fourth year, the Germans were mounting their last great offensive, four hundred club members were "with the colours" and "few were left to carry on save old men and boys and women in black," according to the annals of the RCYC. To add to their misery, early on the morning of May 9, 1918, fire broke out in the grand Island clubhouse. The lookout at the Ward's Island Life-Saving Station spotted the flames and immediately summoned Lifeboat Captain Chapman. Island firemen stationed at Hanlan's Point bicycled to the scene, while City firemen crossed the bay and fought the flames until 8 A.M. The steward, A. R. Baiden and his wife and the chef made a miraculous escape as fire swept down the hallways. Meanwhile, club members who had moved to the Island early in the season helped the firemen and Islanders "were particularly valiant" in rescuing valuable objects. But the water pressure was poor and the main portion of the handsome club building was destroyed. With so many members overseas, rebuilding would have to wait.

Overseas, the killing and maiming continued right to the end. By spring 1918, for example, the Ward's Island lads of the old Chattanooga Camp had seen their numbers sorely reduced. "There have been some changes amongst those boys," wrote Lieutenant "Davie" Sykes in a shaky hand from a Red Cross hospital in France. "Esten, Davis and Moat dead, and Sonmer a prisoner. I guess Sonmer doesn't realize how

This hazy snapshot, taken by young Fram Ward, shows Billy Dean's famous Flying Boat, the Sunfish, *resting on the shore of Sunfish (now Algonquin) Island. Early in 1914, Dean purchased the* Sunfish *from the American Curtiss Company, hired pilot Theodore C. Macaulay (who later trained pilots at the Hanlan's Point school in 1915), and brought the craft to Canada—the first Flying Boat to be owned or flown in Canada. Piloted by Macaulay, the* Sunfish *was involved in another dramatic first: flying 1200 feet above Toronto, Norman Pearce snapped the first photographs ever taken in Canada from an airplane.* [David Amer]

lucky he is being interned, as it is a lot better than front line stuff, take it from me.'' Sykes went on: ''About the first time I was in the line I got two pieces of *minnenwerfen* in the knee, and then a machine gun bullet burned a streak down my face, and then gas, but I am lucky (horse shoes all over).'' With no voice and a bad cough from the gassing two months earlier, Sykes thought he might at least ''get over to blighty.'' But other Islanders were not even this ''lucky.'' Captain Brian Melville Loudon, for example, was killed September 1, 1918; Lieutenant Christopher F. Trees was killed in the Battle of Cambrai on September 29, 1918 (his brother Lieutenant Alexander George Trees had been badly wounded August 9, 1918); and the ''very gallant gentleman,'' according to the St. Andrew's-by-the-Lake plaque, Lieutenant Richard Henry Hacker was also killed at Cambrai on October 10, 1918. Even Armistice Day held little joy for some; pilot George W. Duggan, son of the second oldest member of the RCYC, was killed November 11, 1918.

Back home on November 11, joyful, ''peace mad'' Torontonians danced in the streets, tossed tickertape out of office windows, dragged bells and pots and pans and other noise-makers behind them, burned the Kaiser in effigy and dusted policemen with talcum powder. Over 100,000 people celebrated a solemn service of thanksgiving in Queen's Park.[17] The rejoicing was heartfelt, but tempered by the thought that 10,000 out of the 70,000 Torontonians who had joined up would never return.

The initial euphoria was tempered for other reasons as well. The troops were slow to return home. Tom Longboat, for example, the marathon runner who had ''done his bit'' as a dispatch bearer at the front, only returned in May 1919. Others were even more delayed, having been sent off to Russia in a futile attempt

to help White Russians chase ''Bolshies'' across Siberia. And the crippled survivors of a war in which over 60,000 Canadians had perished were a powerful, lingering reminder of the past— and required attention long into the future.

Deadly influenza, which had earlier swept Western Europe and Britain, returned with the troops to Canada where it soon enveloped cities, towns and countryside: public gatherings were forbidden, schools were closed and churches were holding only one service on Sunday. By the time the initial epidemic was over, 150,000 Torontonians had fallen ill and 1,750 had died.[18]

Then the country was plunged into a severe postwar depression. Polson Iron Works on the bay, for example, closed in 1919 when the war contracts ran out. To forestall the problems of soldiers' reentering civilian life, the City had agreed in April 1919 to organize various vocational programs such as placing veterans with professional gardeners, bowling-green keepers and foresters. By summer 1919, therefore, men who had been smashing through the Hindenberg Line only months before, were to be seen tamely mowing, raking and pruning on the Island and in parks across the city. Thankful to be no longer dodging bullets, they nevertheless had perhaps expected more from life upon their return.

The growing legions of unemployed and underemployed vets certainly expected more. Perhaps stirred by such demonstrations as the Winnipeg General Strike in May-June 1919 (and a sympathy strike closer to home in Queen's Park), the City was moved to provide some relief. On December 20, 1920, for example, ''in view of the large number of unemployed citizens at present in the City,'' Council allocated $100,000 for various parks improvements, including $16,400 to raise five acres of low-lying lands on the Island. The impact of the pro-

gramme, at best, was minor. Men were given only part-time work (on three-day shifts) and ''only bona fide residents'' of the city for the previous year were eligible. Recent immigrants from elsewhere in Canada or from overseas were not.

Moreover, in spite of heavy non-English immigration in the prewar years, anti-''foreign'' (now especially anti-German) feeling ran high, particularly in the face of this depression. City Council's Island Committee, for example, initially refused to authorize the subletting of a Western Sandbar cottage to Mr. M. C. Reimer in 1919 because ''Reimer was an alien name.'' (All was well, however, when the committee discovered that Reimer was Sir William Mulock's chauffeur, an Englishman by birth and had served two years in the Canadian Expeditionary Force overseas.)[19]

The high postwar prices, of course, hit the poor and unemployed more severely than anyone else. But Island cottage builders and even yacht

Harbour police patrol the waterfront of February 1920 on an iceboat. [THC]

Ward's Islanders gathered on the Pier for this group photograph in August 1919. It was at this regatta that champion sculler Jack Guest humbly began his winning career. He and his small partner won the boys' rowboat race—with a log in the bottom of the boat to provide the necessary extra ballast. [MTLB]

club members also felt the pinch. In 1920, for example, Mary's father, James T. Mallon, was astonished by the cost of lumber and labour when he built his new house on Oriole Avenue, looking out over the bullrush-lined lagoon toward the Royal Canadian Yacht Club. Over there, plans to rebuild the RCYC clubhouse had been drawn up in 1919, but the scarcity of skilled labour, the postwar reduction in output and the very high cost of materials placed the price tag for a new building at $500,000. So members decided to wait, "inconvenient though it may be."[20]

Meanwhile, early 1919 proved to be a time of fire and ice down at the eastern end of the Island. The Alexandra Yacht Club's brief sojourn was brought to a violent end in January. On January 10 the clubhouse was battered by an "ice shove" and totally demolished by a 60 mph gale, resulting in a loss of over $5,000. The club soon retreated to a safer mainland site on the new "Aquatic Reservation" west of Bathurst Street where it built a new clubhouse, while Ward's Island scavengers gathered up the tattered remains of the old club to knock together kitchen "shacks" to adorn their campsites.[21]

Then, on the morning of May 9 as engineer Ernest Delaney was tinkering with one of the motorboats at the Life-Saving Station, the machine backfired, set off an explosion which blew him into the air and sparked a fire which soon enveloped the building. Fram Ward, who was later a fireman on the Island, was working on a sailboat outside his father's place when he heard "this heck of a roar" and saw flames shooting up. He ran down to the corner of Withrow and Lakeshore and pulled the fire alarm. Soon Davy Maxwell appeared and they ran toward the fire, dragging the hose to the end of its line. Too short. "Well, you might as well have had a garden hose," Ward commented fifty-five years later. Meanwhile, Captain Chapman, trying to save what he could from the flames, was badly burned and sent off to St. Michael's Hospital along with Delaney, who was also seriously burned. The light wind blowing at the time spread the flames, but fire fighters who arrived in boats at least managed to prevent the blaze from spreading to nearby houses. The fire had completely destroyed the boathouse, the two power launches and all the lifesaving paraphernalia. For many years thereafter, the

Observation Tower stood lonely vigilance over the campground and the lakefront.

On the lighter side, the return of peace brought a return of carefree pleasure-seeking at the Island. For Torontonians at large, July 1, 1919, was the "first Dominion Day in five years that the monster of war did not cast its shadow over the nation."[22] Even with a streetcar strike, some sixty thousand people journeyed over to the Island (leaving one thousand bicycles at the docks). The bathing beaches were crowded, as was the regatta course, where "North America's greatest annual aquatic carnival, the Dominion Day Regatta was resumed." Young Johnny Durnan (son of Ned Hanlan's nephew, sculling champ Eddie Durnan) made a fine debut by winning the junior sculling event. However, it would not be a Hanlan's Pointer but a Ward's Islander—Jack Guest—who would set the rowing world afire in the twenties and thirties.

While young Jack and his boyhood companions were practising fiercely for their first Island competition later that summer, President Wilson (of the Ward's Island Association, that is) welcomed almost 1,500 summer residents whose "hearts and homes have been made glad by the return of loved ones after years of absence and the splendid victory.'' With the return of the veterans, the Ward's league grew to eight teams, and "baseball [was] king." The players launched themselves into an expanded schedule, while enthusiastic spectators lined the field to happily and loudly bullyrag the stickmen and chaff the umpire. Sailing, too, benefitted from the return of the troops, as sailing on the bay "gained a new life." Then on July 30 the entire Ward's Island community celebrated the end of the war with a grand "Welcome Home Night" at the Shelter. That pavilion was "filled with tables...overflowing with eatables, flowers, cigars, cigarettes, candies, etc." The patriotic decorations were large flags tastefully draped around pictures of the king, Lloyd George and Sir Douglas Haig. The banquet, lovingly prepared by Island cooks, would have been "a credit to Delmonicos" and the concert went "with a swing from start to finish."

Over on barren Sunfish Island, the YMCA set up its first Sunfish Camp for working boys who were unable to take an out-of-town vacation. A total of sixty-five youngsters camped in tents and enjoyed even more primitive conditions than their Ward's Island neighbours. There were no City lavatory buildings or City water. There wasn't even a bridge connecting the sandy little island with the major island. Nevertheless, the camp was a howling success and continued to grow during the next decade.

This first postwar season was brought to a suitable climax by the grand annual Ward's Island Sports and Regatta days. On August 16, Island children and adults ran, jumped and cavorted their way through thirty-five "land sports" events, which included, among other novelties, a "balloon race," a "wheelbarrow race," a "veterans peanut rolling race" and a grand tug of war in which the general

Two postwar visitors to Toronto outside the Harbour Commissioners' two year old bayside building: a captured German U-boat (above) and a captivating Prince of Wales (below).   [PAC (PA-30314)/THC]

"Islanders" team (ungenerously) dragged the "Veterans" to dusty defeat. A week later, aquatic Islanders gathered on the pier for the regatta in which they splashed and paddled their way through seventeen events, including a "tub race," which provided a fine way to get back into the swim of Island life.

Meanwhile across the bay, on August 25, 1919, Edward Prince of Wales descended on Toronto and set off demonstrations of unrestrained joy and adoration. "Toronto fell head over heels in love with the Prince of Wales," the *Globe* proudly announced. And it was true. From the moment he stepped off his special train at Standish Avenue, near the lieutenant governor's baronial mansion Chorley Park in Rosedale, the handsome, khaki-clad "Smiling Prince" was greeted by scenes of unparalleled patriotic pandemonium. Three thousand "devoted subjects" shook his hand at City Hall. Over 100,000 enthusiasts jammed Exhibition Park and braved a downpour to hail his opening of the first peacetime Canadian National Exhibition. And "the elite of Toronto" steamed over to the Royal Canadian Yacht Club for a garden party in his honour.

The large public ferries were pressed into service to help club launches bring elegantly turned-out guests across the choppy bay. Service uniforms of blue serge double-breasted jackets, white trousers and white yachting caps were the order of the day for members, though black morning coats and striped trousers formed an acceptable alternative. Ladies were resplendent in their broad-brimmed hats and rainbow-coloured afternoon dresses. Finally, wearing only serviceable khaki, the youthful prince boarded the club launch *Hiawatha*, which swiftly crossed the white-capped water, its Royal Standard snapping in the stiff breeze. As he passed the Admiralty training schooner, *Pinta*, "middies" hanging

from the rigging shouted full-throated hurrahs and the club fleet, dressed in colours, made a brilliant picture riding at anchor in the strong wind. As he landed at the specially built wharf (known thereafter as the Prince of Wales Landing and kept inviolate for years to come), the prince was greeted by Commodore George H. Gooderham, former Commodore Aemilius Jarvis and other officers of the club, who escorted him aboard Gooderham's flagship, the four-masted *Oriole III*. He then strolled along the flag-lined wharf to inspect the grounds and the clubhouse (the one-storey ruins had now been roofed over and made presentable) and to meet the brilliant assembly pressing across the lawn.

The prince laid the cornerstone for the new clubhouse, presented the Prince of Wales Cup to Norman R. Gooderham, had a snack and another smoke under the large marquee on the lawn and departed after less than an hour, only to return again that evening for a dinner and ball. During these later festivities, the prince excused himself and retired, the dancers supposed, to catch a few moments of well-deserved relaxation. When

Scenes from the Prince of Wales' triumphant visit to the RCYC on August 25, 1919: a very public arrival and a private search for illumination. [RCYC]

he did not return, his anxious hosts began a search for him. They discovered him on Commodore Gooderham's *Oriole*, which was now moored in the lagoon and decorated with electric lights in place of the pennants she had sported by day. He was surrounded by hundreds of canoes and was "relaxing," historian Snider noted, by strolling along the decks and leaning over to shake hands with "the thousand boys and girls who swarmed around the *Oriole*'s manganese sides!" Prince Charming to the last and, as the *Globe* reported, "always so very human."

Gradually the postwar economic fog lifted. The twenties brought flappers and cars and aeroplanes and radios and movie stars—and prosperity. The Island roared with the best of them. But changes were brewing. In April 1920 Lol Solman managed, with difficulty, to persuade City Council to reinstate the wartime fare raises—the first of a number of financial wrangles with City Hall in the early twenties. On April 1, 1922, the Toronto Ferry Company lease for Hanlan's Point expired, plunging the TFC and the City into protracted negotiations for a renewal. Meanwhile, City politicians contributed to the cloud of uncertainty hanging over the ferry company by resurrecting their interest in bridging the Western Gap. With boring regularity throughout the twenties, Council "urged" the Dominion government to proceed with the work. Consequently, as early as March 1923, the TFC was reluctant to make capital expenditures on wharfs and the like "owing to the uncertain future of the Company." Arrangements for the ferry service continued to be in such a "nebulous state" that on November 30, 1925, Council finally decided to seek permissive legislation authorizing the City to operate a ferry service to the Island.

Meanwhile, the immensely practical Mr. Solman himself was perhaps frustrated, but not altogether displeased by the City's action. His own interests had been turning from the Island to the mainland. The car, not the ferry, seemed to be the vehicle of the future. And in 1922 the first automobile-age amusement park opened on Humber Bay at Sunnyside, with Solman as its experienced manager. Not long afterwards he decided to transfer his Maple Leafs from Hanlan's Park to a new cityside stadium. On April 29, 1926, amidst great hoopla, fourteen thousand cold but enthusiastic fans motored and trammed to the opening of Maple Leaf Stadium on the water's edge at the foot of Bathurst Street. "No more ferryboats" for the fans, the newspapers promised (and, perhaps, no more profit-making crowds for future operators of ferryboats).

Whether the City was serious in its desire to take over the ferry service, or was simply trying to pressure the TFC's Solman into paying higher rates, is unknown. In any event, Solman himself became keen to be bought out by the City, at a hefty price. He was so keen, in fact, that at least one person, Alderman Alfred E. Burgess (a fellow Island property owner), accused him of attempted bribery. According to Burgess, Solman had boasted that any price above $300,000 would enable him to "buy up members of Council" and land the City with what Burgess told Council was "a bunch of junk." When confronted with the charges, Solman, naturally, denied them in full. But, he went on to relate that Burgess had asked him for a job and he had said he would give him one if he helped in the sale of the ferries to the City. "Later he came in and I loaned him some money," he told the *Globe*. A curious defence against a charge of bribery. In any event, whether acting from conviction or financial incentive, City Council

members finally voted on April 21, 1926, to buy out the TFC for $337,500. As of November 1, 1926, the City became the proud owner of eight ferry boats, as well as a decaying stadium (with no big league tenant), a merry-go-round building (with no merry-go-round), a bandstand, a swimming club and sundry other Hanlan's Point structures. The City's new Toronto Transportation Commission (TTC), which had taken over the old private Toronto Street Railway Company in 1921, would soon be in the ferry business.

The year 1920 ushered in what many regarded as the Golden Age of tent life on Ward's Island. Certainly, the community experienced a population explosion, which peaked in mid-decade.[23] Each spring brought with it the communal ritual of "putting up." As Daddy Frank Staneland recalled, "all the men would come and help you to put up your tent and then you'd go to the next one and help them" raise the heavy ridge poles—twelve or fourteen feet high—and rig the tent over them.

In 1920 tenters were struck by an apparently highly contagious "verandah germ," as one after another built "palatial verandahs" of wood across the front of their tents. By 1921 Frank Ward was in the verandah business and by 1923 was helping his son Fram (who leased one of the last available tent sites that year) put on an extra-large verandah. Caretaker Dodd, whom Ward had known all his life, was "over more than once, at my Dad hollering, 'You can't put a big verandah like that on there, Frank.'" But Ward replied contemptuously, "Run away, Walter. Run away. Jesus. After all, ain't we the Wards?" So Fram got away with building a large verandah, which was later incorporated into his Lenore Avenue cottage.

Another welcome addition to the Ward's

While the Toronto Ferry Company's Lol Solman wrangled with City officials over the future of the ferry service, TTC employees' families, like these young racers on July 30, 1926, continued to enjoy the pleasures of Hanlan's Point. [TTC]

Commission, and a complete collapse of the current mainland clubhouse in July 1920, forced the QCYC to search for yet another site. Under the steady hand of Commodore Aemilius Jarvis among others, the QCYC building rose on its two-acre site during 1921 and ever since that time, QCYC sailors have been based on Sunfish (later Algonquin) Island.

Like many volunteer organizations, the Ward's Island Association experienced financial problems. To wipe out the deficit, Ward's Islanders organized "a monster garden fête and gala week-end" from July 30 to August 1, 1921, complete with a "monster midway." On this first Gala Day, everyone got into the act, "fussing up" old Ward's Island so that the expected three to five thousand visitors would go home feeling that they had seen "something worth while." Attractions included baseball games, tennis tournaments, bowling competitions and numerous booths like the Music Shop "featuring all the latest popular songs 'a la Jolson,'" like "Mammy's Little Sunny Honey Boy." Other booths included Touch & Take, Ice Cream, Fish

Island landscape was the tiny Ward's Island Association clubhouse office of 1920. The colour scheme was "quite snappy"—"a sort of maple walnut shade trimmed with a violent green, which makes the grass fade away into second place," all capped by "pretty shingles...of a red tile color." The whole building was raised on posts, "so that no matter how deep the water gets after a rain storm the executive will have dry feet."

Meanwhile, across the blue lagoon changes were also finally taking place at the eastern tip of Sunfish Island. In February 1920 the City opened the completed forty-five-acre island to any "aquatic club" wishing to locate on the Island. By May, the already-well-established Queen City Yacht Club again approached the City for a lease. Organized in 1889, the QCYC had first occupied a floating boathouse moored on the east side of Queen's Wharf at the foot of Bathurst Street. In 1901 it leased land from the Argonaut Boathouse Company where it built a clubhouse. By September 1904, the club had thirty-five sailing skiffs and yachts, exclusive of

dinghies in its fleet, and by 1909 QCYC skipper George Cornell dominated the sixteen-footer competition on the bay. After failing to get a lease in 1908 on the still unfinished Sunfish Island, which was then being created by the City according to its 1906 plan, the QCYC built a clubhouse on the mainland. Now, the redevelopment of the waterfront by the Toronto Harbour

The reason for the Queen City Yacht Club's move to Sunfish Island is obvious from this view of its mainland clubhouse on July 12, 1920. [THC]

Pond and, of course, Home Cooking stocked with goodies baked early that morning in kitchen shacks across the campground. The following week, the *Weekly* trumpeted modestly: "Gala Days—Huge Success. July 30 and August 1st Make History." The deficit was wiped out and the surplus used to buy a WIA wagon and a new Nordheimer piano for the Shelter. At the time, however, no one seemed eager to repeat the highly public exercise. But, propelled first by financial necessity and then by tradition, Ward's Islanders have organized Gala Days ever since.

Community growth, coupled with a postwar baby boom in Toronto's self-proclaimed premier "infantarium," had their inevitable results: scads of youngsters roaming around Ward's Island having fun and, if the truth be known, getting under foot and even into mischief. By 1924 the move was on to provide "a well organized all around programme for our boys and girls [which] would work wonders." Thus was born in 1925 another great Ward's Island tradition, and one of Toronto's earliest forms of daycare: Supervision. It was highly competitive and (not surprisingly) somewhat sexist. The boys, divided into tribes, got off to a quick start on June 29. Their programme was designed "to meet the contingencies of days to come in business, sport and social life," and included lots of sports, the odd field trip to Fisherman's Island across the Eastern Gap, and even knot-tying. Meanwhile, forty-six girls were on hand July 6 to begin their equally competitive, but less strenuous programme (mothers were assured that their little girls would not "over tax" themselves). Like the boys, the girls were divided into tribes which competed in activities like tennis, swimming, and volleyball, as well as nature study, sewing and story telling. Points were assigned to nearly everything. (Ward's

Islander Jack Bradley's earliest memory was "being thrown in the lagoon and learning how to swim" at age five in 1929. "We used to do that to all the kids. The team captains got an extra point if you learned to swim." The system was harsh, but effective: "Every kid could swim like a duck.") At the end of each week the winning boys and girls tribe could run its banner up the new flagpole in front of the new improved, but still small, clubhouse. Supervision was an immediate success from both the children's and the parents' standpoint. "The benefits are so obvious that it could hardly be otherwise," the *Weekly* commented. And this early success continued on down the years.

In 1925 the YMCA Camp gained a firmer foothold on Sunfish Island when the City allowed it to replace its tents with more permanent wooden frames with canvas sides; and by 1928, the number of boys attending the camp had grown to 261, of whom 116 were "working boys." By this time, the campers were welcome, contributing members of the greater Ward's Island community. One way they ingratiated themselves to their neighbours was by organizing "Ward's Island Night At Sunfish," always a great hit. On August 13, 1928, for example, the boys put on "spectacular" swimming and diving exhibitions, whipped the Ward's boys at water polo, lost two volleyball games and

The lagoon between Ward's and Sunfish Islands on September 6, 1928. Here QCYC members moored their boats, Sunfish YMCA campers challenged Ward's Island boys to water polo, and Supervision children learned to swim, quickly. [TTC]

provided entertainment (like boxing contests and skits) on a specially constructed stage. Then "the evening wound up with a bonfire, a little sing-song and big EATS," provided, fortunately, by the more experienced cooks on Ward's Island.

Camp life on Ward's thrived throughout the decade. The baseball players continued to rouse and entertain, though their uniforms (if they could be called that) also aroused some controversy in this era of more formal tenting. One anonymous lady wrote a scathing letter to the *Weekly* on June 30, 1927, and touched off a correspondence almost worthy of the *Times*. "It is just like a masquerade every night. The boys are to be complimented on their grotesque get-ups" in every colour of the rainbow and sporting advertisements for everything from left-handed doorknobs to cigar stores. Finally, one poor but unrepentant ballplayer replied, "I think the people who are writing about our costumes are ridiculous....Do they want us to play ball in evening clothes?" (To this, the *Weekly* editor interjected, "Evening clothes! We should say not. Even we would hesitate to go out there and play ball in our pyjamas.") The harassed player continued, "We turn out every night to amuse the crowd, and put up the best brand of ball we know, and it is not intended to be a fashion show."

A blow (or bowl) for women's liberation was struck by the good ladies of Ward's Island who finally invaded the former male preserve of the bowling greens. The men seem to have reacted to the charge with good grace: "The bowling green is increasing in popularity and it is a pretty sight to see the Ladies bowling, dressed in variegated colored sweaters wearing, of course, the most charming smiles," reported the *Weekly* on August 7, 1920.

The traditional round of Ward's Island entertainments was augmented in the twenties by minstrel shows and vaudeville. In August 1920, the "ebony Minstrels" took Toronto and the Island by storm. They wowed Ward's Islanders with a special concert on August 20 and then took the show on the road. Accompanied by a Jazz Orchestra of some twenty-five Ward's Islanders, the Ebony Minstrels journeyed to the mainland and "up to [Euclid Hall] hospital, where many maimed veterans lie." There, "the Ebony Minstrels certainly gave the boys at Euclid Hall an interesting evening, while the niggers themselves had a pretty good time," the *Weekly* reported with the unconscious but prevalent racism of the day.

In 1925 Islander Tom McClure and his friends launched the Red Pepper Revue with "Burlesque Extraordinary" and "Minstrels Supreme." Drawing on stunning local talent (like Lou Coleman on the ukulele, Percy Miller as a song and dance man, Earl Ludlow as the "Caruso" of the Island, and McClure himself as a ventriloquist complete with "Fat" Miller, a local Babe Ruth, as his dummy), McClure was able to put together shows that were sure-fire hits for years with the local audiences. Even Island children got into the act for the last show of 1928. Budding young entertainer Eddie Dillon acted as director and "interlocutor," four buddies proved to be competent "end men" with their calculatedly local jokes and the chorus belted out such standbys as "Sleep Kentucky Babe" and "In the Good Old Summertime."

Ward's Island residents enjoyed an increasingly luxurious lifestyle. The ferry service was vastly improved over the old days when the last ferry to Ward's was at 6:30 P.M. Now the last boat was around 11 P.M. and extra ferries were laid on to carry hordes of cheering spectators from one island to another for the fearsomely competitive Inter-Island Baseball games. Islanders still had to navigate across the "death trap" railway crossing at the foot of Yonge and Bay Streets in order to catch their boats. But campers didn't have to travel as frequently to the city, or even to the stores of Centre Island, as they used to, because Simpson's began to send one and then several "representatives" on daily rounds to drum up business. They took orders for fresh groceries, pots, pans and picnic supplies, natty striped blazers, "books for leisure hours" like *Gentlemen Prefer Blondes* or *The Silver Spoon* offered in July 1926, even "Rice Lake Canoes" for $49.50 and up-to-the-minute "refrigerators" (i.e., ice-boxes) at $14.25. "If you desire," one Simpson's ad of 1920 suggested, "you need not leave your cottage verandah all day long." Eaton's, on the other hand, was a bit slower off the mark and did not even start advertising in the *Weekly* until 1926, when it started to push "cool summer frocks for the younger set," radios, ukuleles, phonographs and even books.

A sometimes too "merry milkman" clattered in and out amongst the tents and the Lamantia Brothers pushed their heavily laden fruit carts across the Island. At Centre, according to Mary Mallon, one handsome brother was known as "Rudolph," after the matinee idol Rudolph Valentino. But at Ward's the welcome was sometimes less generous. "The Dago's prices were high/And the Islanders would not buy," a dreadful *Weekly* ditty went. "When his waggon got stuck/He cried, Tougha da Luck,/ I fell jus' lika could cry."

Bulmer's dining room at the old Ward's Hotel offered a "full course Dinner" for only seventy-five cents and also offered a delicious range of creamy confections at its old ice-cream parlour. But, even here, there were some

Santa in sleigh with reindeer

December Morn
"—where once a garden smiled."

drawbacks. "It is simply awful the way the young sheiks hang around the ice cream parlor," one self-proclaimed "Flapper" complained. "Every time any of us go in for a soda or cone or anything, we have to pass a line of boys who seem to have nothing better to do than to hang around and 'gawk' at us." Meanwhile, an older member of the community was equally offended by the behaviour of the young people, perhaps of both "Flappers" and "Sheiks": "I enjoy a walk down to the end of the pier in the evening," she huffed, "but lately since the warm weather arrived it has been most embarrassing. When

(Left) *Only verandahs and kitchen sheds greet the forlorn Santa in this September 1928* Ward's Island Weekly *cartoon by Greg Clark's old sidekick Jimmy Frise.* [MTLB]
(Below) *Centre Island, July 1, 1920—the perfect time and place for a picnic.* [CTA]

I was younger we did not gather in couples on the ends of piers until all hours of the night." Another Islander helpfully suggested that she "take a stroll down the beach" because "she ain't seen nothin' yet."

New-fangled forms of entertainment also soon found their way to Ward's Island. The first "talkies" flickered across the screen at the Queen City Yacht Club "novelty night" on Sunfish Island in 1929. And, above all, radio invaded the airwaves. The first harbinger of the Island radio age was the "inventive genius" who appeared as "Radio," the most "up-to-the-minute-costume" of the 1922 Masquerade. Islanders, of course, had to simply put up with some loud pests, like the periodic moanings of the fog horn at the Eastern Gap. But in the case of radios, weary residents could at least fight back. They could cite the "rule of the Island" that "at eleven o'clock all instruments of torture must be extinguished." They could point to the hallowed tradition that "the last boat whistle is a kind of curfew bell." They could prevail upon caretaker Walter Dodd, the Ward's Island Enforcer, to make a personal call on the offenders. Or they could buy their own radio and fight wireless with wireless.

While Ward's Island flourished as a residential resort, Torontonians flocked to Centre Island. On August 1, 1921, for example, as Ward's Islanders celebrated their first Gala Day, many of Toronto's citizens spent a refreshingly cool Civic Holiday at Island Park. The Toronto Postal Workers Association lugged lunch baskets instead of mailbags across the bay for perhaps the largest group picnic on the grounds. Another large party of "some of Toronto's colored citizens" spread out under the willows to celebrate Emancipation Day as well as the Civic Holiday. "Innumerable family groups" lunched on the grass. Everywhere an "easy-going game of ball" was in progress. "Troops of pretty girls" wandered about in lovely frocks. Children and adults alike converged on Osborne and Naylor's splendidly renovated merry-go-round, now playing jazz. Young lovers lingered in the shadows away from the crowds and, from time to time, the "occasional khaki-clad figure" strolled across the green, reminding everyone that "this whole scene typified a freedom which had been dearly bought." Over at the YWCA "Holiday House" at 302 Lake Front (Lakeshore) "many young women who help along the work of the city during the hot summer months" gathered for healthful recreation under the care of Miss M. S. Ramsbottom, Sport Officer. After a "delicious tea" on the verandah and under the trees, the girls adjourned to the park for an evening's program of sport, including a baseball game, a potato race, a wheelbarrow race, a seventy-five-yard dash and a tug of war.[24]

Other evening "sports" became increasingly popular—like the tango, the bunny hop and the black bottom. In 1921 W. J. Reed laid a new dance floor at the Park Pavilion, and attracted legions of enthusiastic dancers every night (except Sunday, of course). Elsewhere the competition was heating up. Not only did the Island Amateur Aquatic Association continue to hold dances at Aquatic Hall on Long Pond, but merchant Fred Ginn expanded his empire on Manitou Road— or the Main Drag as it became known. He built his palace—or, more properly, his "Casino"— across from Pierson's Hotel (formerly Mead's), with "the best dance floor in the city." It was "beautifully built" and "springy," Mary Mallon recalled, remembering evenings spent dancing to the music of first-class bands like Al Linton's orchestra. People came from the city to dance there, but after the last ferry swept them away,

Islanders kept on dancing until 1 A.M. or so. The Park Pavilion was off limits to some young Islanders, being considered a bit daring, even "rather tough," laughed Miss Mallon. But curious dancers could sneak over to peek at the more "far-out dances." Ginn's Casino, by contrast, was more "staid" and proper. "Mr. Ginn was very, very particular about his clientele," confirmed Alan Howard, the former curator of the Marine Museum and former Centre Islander of forty-one years standing. "The ladies had to be in summer frocks and the gentlemen had to be in jackets, ties, trousers." Despite the roaring twenties, thirsty patrons couldn't quaff spirits at Ginn's, but they could indulge in all

manner of soft-drink and ice-cream fantasies. They had a delicious choice of locales—Ginn's own lofty restaurant overlooking the dance floor with its slowly turning Casablanca-style fan, the Farmer's Dairy up the street, or, the *pièce de resistance*, the City Dairy's "truly old-fashioned ice cream parlour," as Mr. Howard described it, with the marble tables and the wire chairs and the great long counter.

For Royal Canadian Yacht Club members, the outstanding event of 1922 was the opening of their new Island clubhouse. Their postwar patience had paid off and their new building cost only $115,911, rather than the inflated estimate of $500,000 in 1919. On June 10, 1922, delighted

Farmer's Dairy under construction on Manitou Road, May 14, 1919. Island dairymen were so eager for business that as soon as summer residents arrived around May 24, there would be "almost a scrap on the back porch," according to Centre Islander Mary Mallon. [CTA]

members and their ladies toured the classical recreation—oohing and ahhing at the upper verandah with its sliding glass panels and, most especially, at the architect's *chef d'oeuvre*, the immense ballroom done in the style of a fine ship's grand saloon whose polished floor thousands of slippered feet would test that summer. To complete the picture, former Commodore Aemilius Jarvis donated two murals by Owen Staples to fill the large lunettes at either end of the ballroom.

The end of the war had sparked a mini building boom on the Island, with over forty cottages rising between August 1919 and August 1924. Among the new residents were art dealer Percy Roberts, publisher John McClelland, architect C. P. Band, businessmen Fred McLaughlin and Leonard J. Wookey, and journalist/alderman William Plewman. Some of the postwar Islanders were determined to shake off the horrors of the war by concentrating on having a good time. The self-named Hounds of Cherokee became a local legend between 1915 and 1920. These young bachelors indulged in riotous parties, engaged in wild boat races around the lagoons, which often deteriorated into hand-to-hand combat, played endless practical jokes, frequently swam to work when they missed the early morning ferry after late-night partying, held full-scale wakes when one of their number abandoned bachelorhood for matrimony and presumably gave that "holy terror" of law enforcement, Sergeant Miles, a run for his money.[25] Other, tamer residents were happy to reinstate their annual pilgrimage to the Island and to carry on with such traditional Island activities as regattas, tennis, bridge parties, evening musicales, ladies' teas on the RCYC balcony, and so on. And, beginning in 1925, they added visits to entertain the ailing war veterans who stayed at the new Soldiers Summer (later the Red Cross)

In this 1924 painting by H. S. Palmer, young Jack McClelland (centre) hatches future publishing plans while his sister Betty (left) pours tea and Margaret (right) admires the view from the bayside lawn of 37 Chippewa Avenue. [Betty Stark]

Outpost at 570 Lakeshore, just north of the Lakeside Home For Little Children. In 1925 there were seventy-five "incurable patients" at the Christie Street Hospital, twenty-five of whom would be brought over at a time for two-week visits to enjoy the Island's well-known salubrious breezes and generally "vary the monotony of hospital life."[26]

The postwar growth of the summer community was reflected in Island institutions. The popular Island Amateur Aquatic Association expanded its operations several times during the decade because its bowling greens, tennis and badminton courts and other facilities were continually outgrown. Little St. Andrew's-by-the-Lake called on Canon Dixon (of Little Trinity and the Orange Order) to assist the energetic

but overtaxed Bishop Reeve. Later in the decade, after the deaths of Bishop Reeve and Canon Dixon, Professor Mercer-Wilson took charge of St. Andrew's for three years. Among the familiar Island sights during his tenure were the popular weekday children's services on the beach: the children would march along the lakeshore and down the Main Drag, carrying a banner, ringing a bell and singing along to the sighs of Mrs. Carr-Harris's portable harmonium. By 1922, the Island's Catholic community was finally large enough to build St. Rita's at the corner of Iroquois and Mohawk. And on Sunday July 16, 1922, Archbishop McNeil solemnly dedicated the tiny brown church, before a large congregation that filled the aisles. No longer would the faithful have to gather at the ferry dock each

Sunday and steam to the city for High Mass, because the Sunday boat left too late for the shorter early Mass.

Other services improved as well, notably fire protection. At the instigation of Alderman (and long-time Island resident) Charles A. Reed, a fireboat capable of navigating Island lagoons was put into service in 1923 and appropriately enough was called the *Charles A. Reed*. In January 1925 two firemen were assigned to the Island for the winter and a little gas-driven,

but hand-drawn, pumping engine was purchased. And around 1926 the Fire Hall was improved on Manitou Road.

Nineteen twenty-seven was an experimental year for the Toronto Transportation Commission. While certain civic officials were "strongly and unalterably of the opinion that all public services should pay their own way," after the November 1926 purchase of the TFC ferries they agreed to continue the existing fare structure for a year, and to absorb any deficit.[27] In addition

the TTC took over the operation of the amusement park at Hanlan's Point. They were helped in their search for solvency when Canada celebrated its Diamond Jubilee on July 1, 1927, with a "prolonged paean of rejoicing." At midnight of June 30 hundreds of canoeists dotted the placid waters of the bay to admire the "gigantic bonfire" lighted on the Island at precisely 12:01 A.M. The "lurid, oil-fed flames" soared a hundred feet upward, casting a reflection seen for miles and sending spectators home to bed in a festive mood. (TTC executives must have been in a festive mood, too, having reaped the profits from the evening's special "Jubilee Bonfire" service to the Island.) The July 1 activities were suitably extravagant and the war veterans over at the Island Outpost were not forgotten in the rush of celebrating. Charitable ladies met the 9 A.M. ferry from the Island, drove the boys about the main streets and watched the great parade of elaborate historical floats which provided a condensed review of great incidents in Canada's past. Of all the enormous crowds that lined the parade route along Bloor Street from Withrow to Dufferin Parks, the *Globe* reported, there was "no group that derived more pleasure from the display of floats than those returned men." After lunch they took the one-fifteen ferry back to their Island home where their comrades awaited a detailed account of the spectacle.

During the day, out on the bay sailors and scullers were celebrating in a grand Jubilee Regatta. The sculling discovery of the day was now-twenty-one-year-old John "Jack" Guest of Ward's Island, who took both the junior singles and the quarter-mile dash. "Finely proportioned and developed," young Guest was expected to "come on" in the future. (Indeed, he did.) Then the holiday was brought to a glorious climax with massed bands and fireworks in Riverdale

Patients old and young journey to the Island aboard the John Hanlan: *on June 6, 1927, World War I veterans from the Christie Street Hospital make the trip; and on May 22, 1928, ailing youngsters set out for their final season at the Lakeside Home For Little Children.* [TTC]

and Willowvale Parks. With only the silvery crescent of a new moon and a few bright stars dotting the sky, the grand pyrotechnic display stood out with a "kaleidoscopic effect." A fiery Maple Leaf, Union Jack and even Sir John A.'s puckish visage twinkled over the city sky, enthralling more than 200,000 spectators along the waterfront.[28]

Then in August, Islanders, like all Torontonians, had another opportunity to demonstrate their patriotism. Edward Prince of Wales and his brother Prince George came to dedicate the "Princes Gate" at the CNE and open the new Union Station (which was *finally* ready). At the suggestion of Art Gay, Ward's Islanders dragged nine wagonloads of boxes and crates laboriously to the beach where they built an enormous bonfire to welcome the princes as they steamed toward Toronto. They topped it all off with a fireworks display that projected a shimmering "W.I.A. Welcomes Their Royal Highnesses" over the lake. According to newspapermen on the princes' boat, "our little stunt was considered by the party on board as the most spontaneous and spectacular of any occurrence during the Princes' tour." Whether this was true or not, Islanders could at least bask in the warm glow of royal approval for the rest of the summer.

After a relatively successful first year, when 160,000 people visited Hanlan's Point, the TTC was determined to do better. If the rundown condition of the area were fixed and new attractions added, the commission was convinced that it could at least double the number of visitors.[29]

By Dominion Day 1929 the TTC had become almost too successful for its ability to cope. But the 40,000 who crossed over were well rewarded for their efforts. The annual regatta over at the Hanlan's Memorial Course, for example, was "one of the most brilliant" in several years, according to the *Globe*. There were some problems, however. Food, for example. Late in the evening, supplies were still being sent over from the city to feed the hungry multitudes. The 9 P.M. boat to Hanlan's brought, not loaves and fishes, but twenty tubs of ice cream. For the most part, the "orderliness and good humour" of the crowd was admirable. But with startling suddenness, a furious downpour lashed the

"What the Sam Hill (right) is going on here," Sam Cohen (left) might have asked during this 1928 TTC picnic pillow fight championship at Hanlan's Point.
[TTC]

After World War I, flying aces Billy Bishop and Billy Barker formed Bishop-Barker Airways to fly from Toronto Bay (shown here) to Lake Muskoka. But few vacationing Torontonians were willing to trust the flimsy-looking contraptions, and the company soon failed. Barker later chaired the committee that recommended building airports at the Island and at Malton.
[Canadian Forces Photo Unit (RE 22069-1)]

unsheltered crowds waiting to return home and caused near panic. Instead of retreating to the pavilion, as instructed by the police, the crowd surged forward toward the already full "pen." Children were separated from parents, and three or four women fainted. One dignified young clergyman was seen piloting a pram to safety, and order was rapidly restored.

That master of bread and circuses Lol Solman was not one to take such competition lightly. The unsentimental manager of Sunnyside hit on a bittersweet ploy to attract thousands of jaded Torontonians to his mainland amusement area. At midnight of July 19, 1929, an airplane swooped across the bay and dumped fire bombs on the retired "veteran ferry boat" *John Hanlan*, which was set ablaze as promised in an ad "to make a Roman holiday for the people whom she has carried across Toronto Bay for fifty years." Surrounded by clowns and pretty dancing girls spreading confetti, some old Island patriots watched the spectacle with more than a little sadness. "For these old-timers," the *Globe* reporter noted, "there was more than a shell filled with barrels going up in smoke and fire at midnight. As flames licked from hull to deck they watched the destruction of a visible link with the past."

As for the future, some major changes were in store for Hanlan's Point. In June 1929 the Toronto Harbour Commission approached the City with a proposal for a combined airplane and seaplane base on the northwest section of Toronto Island comprising the Western Sandbar and the end of Hanlan's Point:

> Since the first airplane flight in 1903, commercial aviation has made exceptionally rapid strides and a new commercial and industrial era is beginning with the airplane just as surely as new eras began with steamships, railroads and automobiles....Toronto should grasp the full

significance that air service is a fast-coming industry and provide facilities now that will assure it becoming an integral part of the airways of the future on this continent.

The best place to do this, apparently, was on the Island. The THC was asking for approval of stage one of a four-stage plan. Stages one and two would provide an "air harbour" for seaplanes and amphibians off the Western Sandbar, while stages three and four would require filling the regatta course lagoon between the sandbar and Hanlan's Point to provide land for a full-scale airport.

While City Parks Commissioner C. E. Chambers was amenable to the building of the "air harbour," he was strongly opposed to using any of the land on the Island for an airport:

> The Island is essentially a playground of the people, and as a recreation area will grow in demand and value with the growth of the City. The lake front on the west shore of the Island— a considerable portion of which would be utilized in the airport as planned—boasts one of the finest beaches on our waterfront, and should be preserved and developed for park purposes.

City Council, therefore, consented only to stage one of the scheme and asserted that this approval "in no way—either by implication or suggestion— implies approval of the ultimate development of a combined air harbor and airport."[30] But such grand projects often have a momentum of their own. Hanlan's Point would soon be turning its back on its past and winging its way into the future—with major consequences for Torontonians and Islanders alike.

In the meantime, Ward's Islanders' favourite son Sam McBride finally battled his way into the mayor's office and Ward's Islanders were proud to call him "Our Mayor." "Over in Toronto Sam McBride is 'His Worship, the

Mayor.' Here on Ward's he is your neighbor," the *Weekly* said proudly on July 14, 1928. "Sam is a good neighbor, and his friends at Ward's took the opportunity last Friday evening to let him know they think so." A bagpiper in full regalia and Ward's Island Association bigwigs escorted Mayor Sam from his five-year-old home at 84 Lakeshore to a Shelter overflowing with well-wishers. Former WIA president Jim Wilson made an appropriately congratulatory speech and then handed the mayor a large, golden key "emblematic of the freedom of Ward's Island."

Sam was reelected mayor in 1929 (and in his Inaugural Address to Council declared in typically bold—but, in this case, unwise—prose that "Prosperity is Dominion-wide"). Naturally, he enjoyed his "freedom of the Island" and one evening came upon a puzzled couple of visitors from New York City who were wandering aimlessly about. He engaged them in friendly conversation and introduced himself as the Mayor of Toronto. The incredulous visitors barely resisted introducing themselves as Herbert Hoover and General Pershing. When they later discovered that they really had been talking to Toronto's mayor they were, naturally, "delighted." "Sam is sure of at least two votes," the *Weekly* chortled on August 3, 1929, "if he ever decided to run against Mayor Jimmy Walker in New York."

Toward the end of the decade hints of changes were also just barely evident in the Ward's Island tent community. Back in 1922 WIA president Bert Adams and eighty tenters had approached the City for permission to place wooden roofs over their tents, with no luck. But before the end of the decade, the first cottage was allowed to replace a tent, although, according to Fram Ward, it was only allowed as a special favour to a man whose son was handicapped and terrified of wind and thunderstorms. "The

Future historian William Kilbourn (left) digs in the sands of time at Centre Island in 1929, while (above) *his future wife, the Reverend Elizabeth Kilbourn (née Sawyer, centre) sees the world in a grain of sand on the Ward's Island beach in 1928.* [William and Elizabeth Kilbourn]

Ward's Island, September 16, 1929: wooden veran-dahs and kitchen sheds, but, for the most part, canvas walls and roofs. [CTA]

kid used to get all upset,'' Fram recalled, ''so he went over to the City Hall and said, 'Lookit. My boy almost goes into hysterics.' So they gave him a permit to build.'' Meanwhile, other Islanders, less enamoured of the rustic life under canvas that they used to extol, also began dreaming not only of a wooden roof over their heads, but of wooden walls around their sides. In the face of City opposition to permanent cottages, Daddy Frank Staneland revealed, Ward's Islanders began cunningly, and with amused satisfaction, to circumvent the rules: ''You weren't allowed to close [the tent] in. This was canvas. But a lot of us fooled them. We put the canvas outside and then had wood inside at each end.'' To continue the charade, he explained, ''In the winter time we'd take it down.'' In the not-too-distant future, Ward's Islanders would be able to come out of the canvas into the open as cottagers. For the time being, however, they would have to remain closet cottagers.

Throughout the decade, the Island's winter population remained quite small, though some welcome changes were made. When the days shortened and the park lights were cut off, the Island was a black and dangerous place, not only for the scattered residents, but also for Works Department employees (at the Filtration Plant, for example) and constables on patrol. Bundled up against the cold, pedestrians stumbled along dark pathways, which were especially hazardous on dark and stormy nights. Petitions were sent to City Hall and finally, in 1922, fourteen winter lights were lit at Centre along Lakeshore and Iroquois. The system was apparently a success but needed expansion. The following winter eighteen additional lights were kept shining, thus linking Centre and Hanlan's by a necklace of bright lights. Residents, however, had to wait some years for electricity in their homes, just as they had to rest content with having no winter water supply. The works commissioner doused any hopes for that by reporting in early 1922 that it would cost a whopping $221,415 to provide filtered water and fire protection to Island residents during the winter.

During this decade, the City also began to debate whether or not to build a larger, two-room schoolhouse.[31] Eventually, a second room was added to the existing school. In the meantime, young Islanders continued with their one-room-school education. For example, Alan Howard, son of Dr. Norman J. Howard who was in charge of the City's water purification system, entered the Island School at the ripe old age of seven-and-a-half in 1921. Young Alan only had to walk some five minutes to school, but many of his schoolmates had to come from the far reaches of Hanlan's Point and Ward's Island. Sometimes they were unable to make it. Mr. Howard remembered well the time when a "terrible blizzard" hit the Island. "For two days the teacher and I sat by the stove and had our lessons alone. I was the only student in the place." On most days, however, twenty or so students would appear. Warmed by a "great pot-bellied station agents' stove" burning coal at the back of the school and a horizontal boiler stove burning wood (usually stoked by senior boys) near the teacher's desk, the nine classes bent obediently over their lessons. The girls and boys "facilities" were located in sheds at the foot of the schoolyard (necessitating a quick dash in cold weather) and the strap was "apparent and applied on suitable occasions," but the teachers, Mr. Howard believed, were "very good"

and the education was "first rate." It was certainly memorable.

In spite of improved winter services, the Island continued to be primarily a summer resort for the Masseys and the masses. The poor, especially, relied on inexpensive outings to the Island. "We went to the Island every Sunday," one immigrant recalled fifty years later. "We took over pots and pans at the start of the summer so we could cook out. We left them under the bushes and picked them up every week."[32] But Torontonians of all stations and degrees trekked back and forth across the bay. Even as the decade drew to a close and increasing numbers of city-dwellers were hopping into trains, buses and even their own automobiles to explore the surrounding countryside, legions of afficionados were still attracted by the Island's many charms. On July 1, 1929, for example, the largest crowd since 1921 "fled from the heat and noise of the city to the green swards and cool lagoons" of Island Park. Picnics were "so numerous that one party seemed to drift into another" and the crowd of picnicking humanity was so dense that "there were few patches of green visible here and there in the mass of color provided by summer attire of men, women and children."[33] A short time later, on July 25, 1929, on lawns ablaze with bunting and flowers, hundreds of well-heeled guests arrived for the Royal Canadian Yacht Club midsummer garden party. Scarlet-coated bandsmen of the 48th Highlanders serenaded the party-goers, while Commodore George H. Gooderham recalled "proud memories" of the club's prewar past and looked forward to a "still greater future."[34] The only discordant note of the day was sounded by business headlines like "Western Provinces Greatly Need Rain" and "Stocks Are Erratic."

The end of an era: the forty year old Island ferry, John Hanlan, *meets a sad, fiery death at midnight of July 19, 1929.* [TTC]

9
The Sandy Thirties

At the final stroke of midnight, March 5, 1934, Toronto "blasted and blazed its way into its second century as a city." Governor General Lord Bessborough set off a lone rocket which shot up from the waterfront and burst "far over the sullen waters of Lake Ontario." In response, a hundred rockets were launched at fifteen-second intervals from the exposed tip of the Toronto Island and exploded into great cascades of stars high above Hanlan's Point. Even in the depths of the Great Depression, precipitated by the Crash of October 1929, Toronto had managed to scrape together $150,000 for Centennial celebrations; and this was the opening salvo of the six-month outburst.

The governor general joined Mayor William J. Stewart, Prime Minister R. B. Bennett, Leader of the Opposition William Lyon Mackenzie King and twelve thousand civic patriots in the comparative comfort of the Coliseum at Exhibition Park to ring in Toronto's second century. Meanwhile, an intrepid band of harbour commissioners, churchmen and assorted civic officials ventured across the ice-clogged bay to the lonely Western Sandbar aboard a Harbour Commission tug bearing the appropriately historic name of *Rouille*. While the multitudes on the mainland prayed and sang their way through a lavish nightwatch service, this small group gathered for a simple ceremony in a temporary shed on what the *Telegram* called an "historic spot" of Toronto. No doubt inspired by Reverend John Gibson's unexpected disquisition on the symbolism of fire, complete with allusions to the ancient Druids, they marched out "into the windswept dark of the sand bar" to ignite a great cone-shaped bonfire. Fanned by a stiff west wind, the flames soon soared fifty feet into the air, lighting the "serried faces of the thousands of citizens who lined the waterfront for two miles" and triggering a cacophony of shrill tug whistles and automobile horns across the water.[1] Torontonians in 1934, as in 1884 and on other grand occasions, had once again turned to the waterfront to celebrate.

As the blanket of the Depression had settled over the city, the Island continued to draw large crowds. Even on Dominion Day 1930, when the weather was "as inconsistent as the stock market," the *Bluebell* and her sister ferries were taxed to the limit, slapping back and forth across the bay with regatta fans, picnickers and "frantic mothers" desperately trying to keep track of their offspring who, more often than not, seemed to be dangling precariously from upper deck railings and whooping fiercely like "a troop of wild savages."[2] And the following year, on the hottest Dominion Day thus far, the Toronto Transportation Commission also set a record. As city pavements buckled and candles melted in their holders, fifty thousand Torontonians gasped "Breezes! Give us breezes!" and staggered on board Island-bound ferries. Even some who made it over to the Island proceeded to collapse and had to be whisked home by harried lifesavers.[3]

During the 1930s, of course, the Island was only one of several waterfront attractions. Sunnyside continued to pack them in with its midway and special events. Exhibition Park attracted patrons to its waterside greensward, although attendance at the CNE itself sagged with the economy. And the Eastern Beaches park, opened on Victoria Day 1932, attracted upward of 100,000 on various occasions, turning the normally balmy beach area into a "seething mass of humanity."[4] Even the Palais Royale, which was thronged by crowds of up to a thousand a night—all eager to swing to the likes of Eddie Duchin, Cab Calloway and Artie Shaw—posed an effective threat to the more remote Dance Pavilion at Hanlan's Point.

(Above) *Toronto's Centennial bonfire at Hanlan's Point, 1934.* [THC]
(Top right) *Waiting for the nightly invasion: Hanlan's Point Dance Pavilion, 1928.* [TTC]
(Right) *Free entertainment at the Point: swing your partner...1931 style.* [TTC]

Nevertheless, the Island held its own. "The Island was a Godsend during the Depression," according to former Centre Islander Alan Howard, "because it didn't cost very much to go there and you could have a wonderful day for an absolute minimum of expenditure." Moreover, people who could no longer afford to travel to distant summer resorts could compromise by staying several days in one of the Island hotels or proliferating boarding houses. So, in spite of competition from the mainland, crowds still made their way to Hanlan's Point to lounge on the wonderful beach, sample the free amusement park attractions (ranging from dancing elephants and whippet races to concerts by regimental bands) and attend assorted grand events.

Toronto policemen, for example, left their beats to sweat and strain at the Annual Police Games which were frequently held at the Hanlan's Point Stadium now abandoned by the baseball Maple Leafs. The "brogue of old Erin" was the dominant accent on Victoria Day 1932 when three to four thousand enthusiasts attended the Irish football game and other sporting events sponsored by the Gaelic Athletic Association. Not to be outdone, the Scots—including the usually dour Mayor Stewart—invaded the stadium in May 1934 for a day of highland dancing and highjinks. Meanwhile, the Toronto Liberals gathered at Hanlan's for a day-long picnic in

August 1933 (the Toronto Tories had earlier gathered in Island Park where sack races replaced riding races for the day). Even several thousand "old Cabbagetowners" (including Mayors Stewart, Wemp and Church) thronged to Hanlan's Point during the 1933 Civic Holiday to reminisce, eat foods of every description, with the exception of cabbage, and stomp enthusiastically during the oldtime fiddlers contest. Dancers were regularly attracted by "Harold Rich and His Versatile Canadians." And the more highbrow culturati were attracted by *Faust* al fresco: some five thousand opera lovers applauded the triumphant première of open-air opera at Hanlan's Point Stadium in July 1936.

The amusement park—with its whip, honeymoon special, old-fashioned merry-go-round, roller rink, bumper cars, fortune teller and other attractions—may not have been as popular as during Lol Solman's reign, but it still drew respectable crowds. Young Jimmy Jones, whose family moved to Hanlan's Point in 1932, must have been the envy of his friends. Because both his parents worked at the amusement park, Jimmy got to hop on the rides for free—and collect stray change. "They had a loop-de-loop. It was a sort of basket on one end and a basket on the other. You'd stop it at the top and people's loose change would come down," he recalled gleefully. Meanwhile, Jimmy's father, who was paid to clown around, used to leap from car to car on the speeding "Whip." "He was pretty good on his feet," Jimmy, Jr. recalled. "If there was a girl and a fella in the car that he was jumping between, he'd go out of his way to kiss the girl and jump out again. And they just loved it. They'd line up to ride this Whip and see all his antics."

Centre Island was also jumping. While some of the old families, like the Gooderhams and

the Masseys, returned year after year, many less affluent newcomers—bank clerks and secretaries and sales clerks—made their way across the bay for a few weeks of relatively inexpensive summer fun. The Main Drag, of course, was in full swing and many young people rented rooms or apartments nearby. Toronto writer Robert Thomas Allen and his wife Helen took an apartment at Centre Island when they were newly married in the mid-thirties. A smile crossed Mr. Allen's face and a faraway look came into his eyes as he recalled those halcyon days—listening to the big bands at the Casino, or sitting on a rickety stool, lazily kicking sand on the floor while sipping a tall ice-cream soda at the still-popular City Dairy.

Centre was a mecca for sociable, unattached young Torontonians, who would share rooms to save money. But, as the landlady would invariably say, "You're only in your rooms to sleep."[5] And this seemed to be almost true. After work hours Centre Island hummed with activity. At five o'clock, the beaches became crowded, even when the water was too cold for a dip. Then the restaurants filled up. And after dinner a steady stream of humanity eddied up and down the Main Drag—dancing, gossiping, lounging and generally enjoying life.

Popularity had its drawbacks, among them bicycles. Cycling was known by all Island residents to be a "basic condition of life," as novelist Hugh Hood has written. As a result, the Main Drag became thick with cyclists. By June 1938 the situation was so hazardous that the City passed a bylaw prohibiting bicycle riding on Manitou Road between the bridge and the lakeshore (as well as on any Island bridge or along the new boardwalk between Ward's and Centre). Cyclists were supposed to dismount and walk their wheels in these areas. But in spite

Jimmy Jones, Sr. clowning around on the Whip at Hanlan's Point in the 1930s. [TIA]

of PC Weller's best efforts to inspire the fear of the law, this proved to be an unenforceable rule: there were simply far too many freewheeling cyclists for the two-man Island police force to supervise.

The Main Drag, of course, was more than a social centre. It was the commercial lifeline of the Island. Hanlan's Point and Ward's Island each now had a small grocery store, but all Islanders depended on Manitou Road, as well as the delivery services of both Eaton's and Simpson's for supplies. Clayton's Meat Market and Dominion provided groceries. Mr. Marshall, who also operated a year-round drugstore in North Rosedale, provided pharmaceuticals. The Dominion Bank opened a branch. The Farmer's Dairy and the City Dairy still vied for customers, while several laundries struggled to keep men's white flannels white and ladies' dancing frocks pressed. And several restaurants catered to the needs of hungry Islanders—from fine dining at the old Pierson's Hotel overlooking the lake to more mundane fare at the newly opened Honey Dew. There was really little reason for

Islanders to go to the city—except, perhaps, to earn a living.

Family life at Centre went on with little change along the shady side streets. And the Island Amateur Aquatic Association—with its tennis and badminton courts, bowling greens, boating facilities and grand old clubhouse hovering on the edge of Long Pond—provided another social centre for less transient Centre Islanders. But even the stately old IAAA was not immune to internal bickering and external economic pressure. It fell on bad times in the mid-thirties when rival groups were set up, and its clubhouse

was finally taken over by the City in the summer of 1938 for unpaid taxes.

Fortunately, young Aubrey Ireland, Jr., whose father had been a champion canoeist, caused some more welcome excitement for the IAAA during the thirties. He started modestly at the foggy Dominion Day regatta of 1930 where he paddled to victory in the Juvenile Tandem. By 1936 he impressed oldtimers like Jack Guest of Ward's Island as he starred at the forty-first Dominion Day regatta, which was held under sunny skies and on smooth waters along the Hanlan's Point course. According to the *Telegram's* Sporting Editor and long-time Hanlan's Pointer James P. Fitzgerald, the 1936 regatta was "like old times." Both paddlers and spectators, who lined the banks in their thousands, had a marvellous time, there being "no more clannish spirit anywhere than in aquatics." Ireland continued his winning ways and in August 1939 reached the pinnacle of his success. Wearing the colours of the newly formed Toronto Island Canoe Club, he won the Canadian Canoe Association singles championship in record time as well as the tandem championship with teammate Terry Evans. He and Evans were even recommended for the team to represent Canada at the forthcoming 1940 Olympics in Finland. But Hitler and his Russian allies had other ideas. By 1940 Finland had been overrun and Aubrey Ireland was joining up.

In contrast to the hustle and bustle of life along the Main Drag, life at the Royal Canadian Yacht Club continued at such a sedate and gracious pace that nary a whiff of Depression has seeped into club historian C. H. J. Snider's official history of the club. Mother Nature, however, stirred up some excitement in the windy season of 1931. On June 20 the entire RCYC fleet was caught in a severe squall off Port

In the depth of the Depression, the Bluenose *raised flagging spirits when she made a triumphant visit to Toronto on May 22, 1933. Rounding a bend off the Island, the world famous Lunenburg schooner presented a stirring sight to the multitudes—sails full set and glinting in the setting sun. As she moved regally through the Western Gap, she was a "symphony of motion and grace"—no doubt able to turn on a dime.* [TTC]

Dalhousie, which set it tossing about like corks in the lake. Giant masts were snapped like matches and great sails carried away. The fleet limped home the next day, only to be severely tested once again during the club's final course race on September 19. This last great blow of the season sent shingles from Island residences whirling clear across the lake to Grimsby, but did no serious damage to the yachts or yachtsmen. For the most part, in fact, RCYC members enjoyed smooth sailing through the decade—turning out for evening sailing parties, games of lawn bowling, tennis and croquet, which proved popular with the tea and dinner dance guests who, Snider reported, "as always were enraptured with the club's lawns."

For many Canadians, however, life in the thirties was less gracious. Even the Centre Island ferry—one of the joys of an outing to the Island—played a part in at least one suicide. As early as January 1930 Mayor Bert Wemp was alerting City Council to its responsibility to provide work in the "unemployment situation" faced by the City. By fall, flat-capped, coveralled workmen were filling and grading areas of Island Park as part of the City's Unemployment Relief Programme. Over the next few years, a variety of Island works were undertaken as part of the effort to give work to the growing legions of unemployed: the wharf at Hanlan's Point was repaired, new bathing stations at Hanlan's Point and on Centre Island at the lakeside end of Manitou Road, were built, channels were dredged, cottonwood trees were removed, concrete sidewalks were laid, shorelines were protected, areas at both Centre and Hanlan's were raised and graded and City-owned Island houses were painted and repaired. The wages may not have been princely, but they certainly beat the twenty cents a day doled out to men in relief camps. And the work may not have been exciting, but it was certainly more socially useful than acting as a life guard when you could not swim or digging holes and filling them in—both tasks that were assigned to men on relief in the Toronto area.

The new Centre Island Police Station near Manitou Bridge was another make-work project ("for men unemployed for some time but not destitute or on relief because of help received from friends, relatives or elsewhere") and provided an opportunity for local officials to take credit. On Saturday July 7, 1934, Mayor Stewart (fresh from a whole battery of Centennial events) journeyed to Centre Island to open the new police station. Chief Constable Draper (the notorious dispatcher of "Draper's Dragoons," the mounted police who swept through Queen's Park to bang heads and clear away supposedly radical unemployed men) took charge of the station and, like the mayor, "stressed the absolute dearth of actual crime on the islands." Similarly, Ward's Island Association president Art Saywell took advantage of the occasion to boost his own end of the Island and to stress that there was certainly "no need for a police station at Ward's."

Ward's Islanders, for their part, opened the decade in fine style, with a hero's welcome for champion rower Jack Guest, who had won the Henley Diamond Sculls on July 5, 1930. On Monday evening July 21 the City of Toronto celebrated Jack's victory with an official reception, helped by a hundred and fifty Ward's Islanders. But the *real* reception for "our own Ward's Island Jack" was held the following night. A huge crowd packed the Shelter and spilled out onto the surrounding park. The "Guests of the evening" were piped along the boardwalk

A quiet game of croquet in 1937 on the lawn outside the RCYC's third (and current) Island clubhouse.
[RCYC Annals]

from 92 Lakeshore with father Guest's stunning blue delphiniums to the Shelter, where "Good old Sam McBride" made an uncharacteristically short speech and presented a silver tea service from the WIA to the tongue-tied rower. (Sam had more time for such leisure activities that summer, since he had lost the 1930 mayoralty to World War I air ace Bert Wemp, whom McBride had unwisely called a "coward.") Immediately after the presentation, a huge bonfire was lit on the beach; a fireworks display was launched over the lake and "the crowd, well supplied with paper hats and noisemakers milled around in the sand and had a great time," according to the *Weekly*.

Life in the Ward's Island tent community continued on much as it had in the twenties. "Fat" Miller and his Otazels won the opening game of the decade, and baseball was still king. Ward's scruffy players invaded Hanlan's and Centre with hundreds of camp-followers in tow and fairly regularly captured the Inter-Island Championship. Somewhat more genteel bowlers and tennis players also enjoyed a fair degree of success against Hanlan's Point and Island Aquatic Association teams. And the usual round of dances, euchres, Union Church services (like "Baseball Sunday," "Bowling Sunday" and "Girls Supervision Sunday") and special events filled the breezy Shelter.

Happy YMCA lads enjoyed the "sand and sunshine at Sunfish Camp again!" while a greater number of "Cenymca" boys camped along the lakeshore than ever before. The sixty "Cenymca" boys played host to a contingent from the Broadview "Y" camp at Hanlan's Point and ingratiated themselves to the wider Ward's Island community by helping at the Church services, putting on "Demonstration Nights" (complete with boxing and wrestling matches

(Above) *April 1932, Hanlan's Point Depression project: "spring cleaning" on Hiawatha Avenue.*
[Sun: Telegram *Collection*]

(Right) *On July 12, 1930 the* Ward's Island Weekly *saluted another home-grown sports hero, sculler Jack Guest.* [MTLB]

that were greatly enjoyed by visitors like veteran sports writer and *Star* editor Lou Marsh) and organizing "Moonlight Cruises" on steamers that conveniently stopped at the Gap to take on revellers.

Ward's youngsters continued to amass Supervision points for all manner of activities— first time swimming the lagoon, first time shooting the chute, first time diving off the springboard and so on—under the watchful eyes of leaders like Aussie Ernest Saunders and Helen Patterson who, fresh from a spell in Beverley

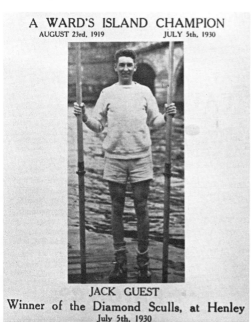

A WARD'S ISLAND CHAMPION
AUGUST 23rd, 1919   JULY 5th, 1930

JACK GUEST
Winner of the Diamond Sculls, at Henley
July 5th, 1930

The R-100 slips between the largest hotel in the British empire (the Royal York, centre) and the tallest building in the empire (the 34-storey Canadian Bank of Commerce, right) on August 11, 1930. "British blood surely ran faster as the greatest achievement of the century passed over our heads," the Ward's Island Weekly *proudly commented.*   [YUA:TC]

Hills, diplomatically declared that "99 per cent of our girls are just as smart and quite as beautiful as the movie queens." (There was a brief reaction against grasping competitiveness under Howard Conquergood, who sought to make the activities "so interesting that the boys will WANT to be out." Gentle Howard, however, only lasted one season.)

Radios had replaced gramophones as a perpetual source of complaint. Rats, cats, dogs, the "good ole" Wards Island Association constitution, the cost of Supervision and the need for a big clubhouse were all hot topics that inspired feverish letter-writing and dominated the annual year-end complainers' or "Kickers' Meeting" in the Shelter. And at least one WASPish "Old Timer" was becoming annoyed with Ward's popularity. "Every bench and every corner on Sunday is occupied by all sorts of people," he complained in the *Weekly.* "Some of the sights to be seen are far from refreshing. Sunday afternoons around here are getting to resemble an international holiday." But welcome or not, crowds of "pic-nickers" (as Islanders called the invaders) continued to flock to Ward's where they used the "Houses of Parliament" (i.e., the public lavatories) to change into their bathing suits and headed for the beach.

The literal highpoint of the 1930 season was the August 11 flight over Toronto and the Island of the great British airship R-100. Awakened by the hum of her motors and the welcoming sirens of ships in the harbour, pyjama-clad Islanders stumbled out of their tents at about 4:30 A.M. to gaze in awe at the moonlit ship sliding by overhead. One barefoot enthusiast wanted to ring the bell on the Ward's Island Shelter, but mercifully, the rope was locked away. By the time the ship made her second pass over the city at the more respectable hour of 9 A.M. and the rest of Toronto gave her a glorious welcome, many of these early-rising Islanders were probably snoozing back in their tents.

The other highlight of the 1930 season was the annual Ward's Island Gala Day on the Civic Holiday weekend when the mercury soared to 95 degrees and Torontonians headed for the water and the Island. As the good ship *Trillium,* which had been crossing the bay since 1910, approached Centre Island, there were so many swimmers off Olympic Island beach that "you might have walked dryshod on bathing caps, only that they bobbed about so."[6] At the full tide of heat in mid-afternoon a melody lifted above the hot exasperation of a crowded ferry deck: "Happy Days Are Here Again." Toes began to tap and voices began to join in as cool relief spread over the port side of the ferry. While the year's largest crowds headed for Centre Island, Ward's Islanders primped and preened for their annual fundraising party: delicious homemade cakes and cookies were displayed and devoured, raffle tickets were sold, ever popular "Housie Housie" and other games were set up and residents turned out to have some fun. Unfortunately, however, receipts were not up to the previous year's total, "owing no doubt to the depression and hard times," according to the *Weekly.*

Ward's Islanders tried to ignore the Depression as much as possible. "Depression has hit us all more or less," 1932 bowling chairman Al Randall commented, "and it's time to forget our troubles and worries." But when tiny tots appeared at the 1932 Junior Masquerade as "Happy Days" and "Depression," it was undoubtedly a summer sign of the times. "Happy Days" won a prize, while "Depression" lost out to the likes of "Bo Peep" and "Rooster" and even that exotic Thirties favourite "Gandhi." The *Weekly* did not dwell on the hard side of life. Apart from the odd serious note—like the 1934 call for an old tent for a "native of the North who is trying to get off relief by camping near a lake and acting as guide during the summer months"—most of the references were lighthearted, but pointed—like the prophetic joke published on August 22, 1931, "Next year they will refer to 1931 as the good, ol' days."

Times did worsen. Relief lines lengthened. Panhandlers wandered downtown streets. People

lost their homes for unpaid taxes. Men rode the rails and camped in hobo "jungles" on the edge of cities across Canada—like the "Don Valley Campers" who dropped from freight trains entering Toronto and gathered in "huts and hovels" (and even in the warm kilns of the local brickworks) on the nearby river flats.

By comparison, Ward's Island campers were living in the lap of luxury, and were even looking forward to having "permanent roofs" over their heads. In 1931 the WIA under President Frank Staneland swung into action. After the usual toing-and-froing and dithering about, it persuaded City Council to allow Ward's Islanders to raise the roof—i.e., to build permanent cottages on their campsites.[7] Each "permanent"— as the cottages were called—had to contain no more than 840 square feet and had to be approved by the city architect and parks commissioner, had to have electricity and had to be "maintained in a state satisfactory" to civic officials. The rest of the traditional rules incorporated in the "Notice to Campers and Tenants" and the seasonal "License of Occupation" were to continue to apply (e.g., no dogs, no boisterous or unseemly behaviour, and so on).

Even before the final regulations were passed in December, Ward's Islanders pulled out their hammers and saws and got to work on

(Above) *On August 22, 1931, Ward's Islanders posed for this sports day photograph with new cottages rising around them. Cottages replaced canvas so quickly that by August 1934, the* Ward's Island Weekly *was lamenting, "Ye modern girls with shorts and curls/Be sad, weep and lament/For romance is disappearing/With the passing of the* TENT." [CTA:TIA]

(Right) *As cottage-building took off, Simpson's published this ad in the 1933* Ward's Island Weekly. [MTLB]

their permanents, as they fondly referred to them. A thriving cottage industry soon sprang up: Sheppard & Gill Lumber Co. (Sheppard of Third Street) immediately advertised "Permanent Roofs—Built for Eternity" (which sounded more like a mausoleum than a summer cottage); Fred A. Dixon, "the big shot builder," complained to the *Weekly* that "folks are ordering their permanents so fast that he hasn't been able to finish his own 'permanent'"; and architect Bob Maginnis "made a nice job of the new Lye cottage." Simpson's, naturally, got into the act. In 1932 it advertised awnings to keep the sun off builders' shoulders and in 1933 it was offering to build the whole thing—nice "Simco Cottages for Comfort and Economy," at the low, low price of about $450.

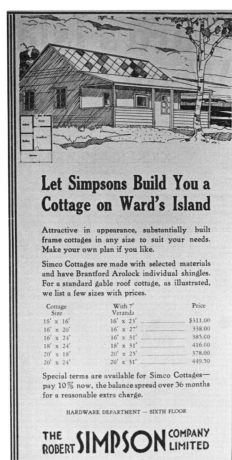

All "campers" wrestled with the great question: to build or not to build. Comfort, convenience, permanence—even snobbery—were all reasons to go ahead. ("If we don't build," the fictitious "Mae" wrote to her equally fictitious cousin "Ethyl" in the May 1932 *Ward's Island Weekly*, "I guess I will have to put up with the high hat from both my neighbors.") And build Ward's Islanders most certainly did. So many, in fact, that as early as July 30, 1932, correspondent "A. Modern" suggested to the editor that a cottage should replace the tent in the *Ward's Island Weekly* logo. The editor loyally responded, "Why abandon the tent? No matter what we live in, let us hope the old camping spirit remains around here." Two years later some residents were already looking back nostalgically to the good old tenting days, when storms threw people together and life was more informal. Small consolation though it might have been, cottage life at Ward's could never be *too* formal in this era before indoor plumbing when residents were to be seen "Tramping down the lonesome trail/Each morning with that awful pail" on the way to the "House of Parliament." For good or ill, Ward's Islanders continued the building spree that transformed the eastern tip of the Island. (In spite of a general Depression slowdown, by 1937, 130 cottages had sprung up and only 32 campsites remained.)

The cottage brought with it social as well as physical change—and planted the seeds of divisions that would grow more evident in later years. Cottage-owners began renting their "permanents" for all or part of the season and creating a class of so-called "transients." By the end of the 1935 season *Ward's Island Weekly* editor (and minstrel show trouper) Eddie Dillon was suggesting that a "Site-owners Association" be formed to protect the interests of the more permanent residents. While welcoming temporary residents

into the community, Dillon and others worked themselves into a dither over whether these renters should be allowed to vote on WIA constitutional amendments or the expenditure of surplus WIA funds or—the burning question of 1935—whether fences should be put up. Neighbours did battle publicly at the Kickers' Meeting and elsewhere, disproving Robert Frost's ironic dictum, "Good fences make good neighbours."

In 1937, the year when Ward's Islanders finally got yearly leases instead of seasonal licenses of occupation,[8] the Ward's Island Leaseholders Association was formed to deal with such issues and with any problems arising between leaseholders and renters. Eddie Dillon, not surprisingly, served as president. Nearly all the 190 leaseholders loyally turned out to the first few annual meetings and the WILA dealt with the usual matters of dogs (prohibit them), cyclists (curtail them), rats (eliminate them) and sanitation (improve it). But, after the heat of creation, the WILA lapsed into relative inaction: "It is not very active all will admit," Dillon was forced to report in July 1939. Nevertheless, the group was against renting becoming a way of life or livelihood, and went on record at the 1939 annual meeting as being "against the use of leases in this community for money-making purposes"—a sentiment that has carried on down through the years and colours actions and attitudes today.

The other major change at Ward's Island in the late thirties concerned the clubhouse. For years residents had engaged in the "time honored discussion about building a big clubhouse" to replace the little "dog kennel we have now," as "Mae" wrote in her column of September 4, 1937. Wouldn't it be dandy, Ward's Islanders dreamed, to have a spacious hall where meetings, dances and other entertainments could take place in comfort and style. A place which,

according to one writer in 1936, would lend a desirable air of "exclusiveness" to the summer community.

Dreams were cheap; but a clubhouse was not. How could they afford something that would cost $2,000 to $3,000? (Hanlan's Pointers, it was reported, had spent a whopping $5,000 on their clubhouse.) And could a clubhouse be erected without abandoning the Supervision programme for kids? Debate raged fiercely until, on August 26, 1937, Ward's Islanders finally decided to have their club and Supervision too: WIA members voted to build a clubhouse for $2,600 and to "leave Supervision alone." Passions subsided and the clubhouse was raised. Everything went relatively smoothly, although some blackguards made off with a pile of lumber that was supposed to be used for the floor. So when Islanders arrived in the spring of 1938 they were delighted to "find a building bright and new/the Island's social rendezvous" standing proudly at the northern edge of the bowling green. On June 11 the clubhouse was formally opened before a sea of blue blazers and white flannels. Two minutes of silence and the "Last Post" honoured WIA members, like old Walter Dodd the long-serving caretaker, who had died the previous winter. Then on to happier business. Wally Randall handed over the keys and the WIA clubhouse was thrown open to community use.

Islanders were not slow to follow the poet's advice: "Now that we have the doggone thing/ Let's use it 'til the rafters ring." Tommy McClure's annual review ("Harold Rich and the Hollywood Kiddies," which was headed for Sunnyside) was the first reserved-seat concert in the building. Churchgoers like "Mae" enjoyed going to Union services "in a building with walls and windows instead of that drafty old Shelter," although dancers and "Kickers"

Two of Ward's Island's most prominent citizens: (left) *once and future mayor, Sam McBride in July 1936 and* (above) *one-time Ward's Island Association President Frank ("Daddy Frank") Staneland in August 1980.* [WIW/MTLB; David Hawkins/*Maclean's*]

sometimes longed for the drafty old days when lake breezes swept away the steamy summer heat. Clare McConnell and his orchestra "dispensed swing to the 'jitterbugs' or what have you in the new Willow Grove dance hall." And Eddie Dillon and his piano-playing partner Dorothy Wright put a new face on the Grand Annual Minstrel Show. Girls (named the "Coal Black Mammies") joined the boys (equally regrettably entitled the "Black Trash") on stage for the first time. Nevertheless, the audience was thoroughly delighted by Wilma Stein's "snake hips" and laughed heartily at new "endmen" like Jack Bradley. All in all, it was "fun with comfort" and the hall itself immediately became the centre of Ward's Island social life.

Ward's Islanders in those days prided themselves on being not only a busy but also an open and welcoming community. Not everyone, however, found them so. One disgruntled "Newcomer" did not mince words: "Of all the self-centred, clannish, small-town places you certainly head the list." Needless to say, "Newcomer's" fighting words sparked an avalanche of protest. The *Ward's Island Weekly* editorialized sanctimoniously that "if his complaint [of being snubbed] is justified—he is the one to blame." Another suggested he jump in the Gap with a stone tied around his neck. Sometimes that vaunted "Ward's Island spirit" had a darker side.

Others perhaps had even more reason to complain than "Newcomer." In the mid-thirties Hitler had loosed on the world a flood of anti-Semitic propaganda that was eagerly lapped up and regurgitated by the likes of Quebec fascist Adrien Arcand. Torontonians, for their part, were far from impervious to racist tirades. Overt discrimination in housing and recreation was blatant. Whole residential areas were protected by so-called Gentlemen's Agreements or covenants not to sell to Jews. Visitors entering Toronto passed a large "Gentiles Only" sign at a private beach. Summer resorts displayed signs stating "No Jews or Dogs Allowed." Yacht clubs and other recreational clubs were restricted. "It was quite overt," one commentator has said. "It was the normal viewpoint to say, 'Well, of course we don't allow any Jews in here. We're a good institution.'"

In the summer of 1933, not many months after Hitler had bullied and plotted his way to the chancellorship, Torontonians got their first real taste of his tactics. "Swastika Clubs"

Hanlan's Point, August 9, 1933. On the very day that Toronto policemen sweated and strained at their annual games, Mayor Stewart called Swastika Club members and Jewish leaders down to a meeting at City Hall where he declared to both sides that the police would "keep order." [CTA:GM]

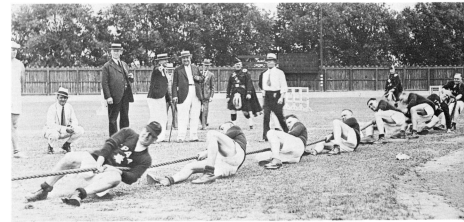

sprang up in the solidly British Beaches area of the city, with the avowed aims of excluding from their area "all obnoxious and undesirable elements who tend to destroy the natural beauty and the property value." Gangs of enforcers with swastikas stencilled on their sweatshirts and bathing suits patrolled Kew Gardens and the boardwalk, harassing Jewish picnickers and bathers. Then, as things cooled down in the east end, trouble erupted in the west end, with a six-hour pitched battle in Willowvale Park on August 16 between pipe-wielding members of the infamous "Christie Pits" gang and local Jewish boys.

There may have been no Swastika Clubs or riots on the Island, but there was open anti-Semitism. Ward's Island—that self-proclaimed happy, tolerant, welcoming little community, where newcomers were counselled to join the WIA in order to participate in community life and preserve their "self-respect"—Ward's Island was "restrictive." "Jewish people couldn't get on," one former tenter commented with a mixture of astonishment and embarrassment. "I don't know how they got away with that. But if they did get over here," she continued, "there was no way they could join the [Ward's Island] Association....It was pretty bad."

It was pretty bad over at Centre, too. As early as 1929, Jewish Alderman Nathan Phillips had protested against a sign on an Island hotel which advertised that it catered to "Gentiles of refinement only." With little effect. By the mid-thirties, signs saying "Restricted" or "Gentiles Only" were popping up in front of rooming houses and big hotels like the Manitou on Manitou Road. J. J. Glass, a Jewish alderman and chairman of the Parks and Exhibitions Committee, managed to have a clause inserted into Island leases that no sign could be erected

without City approval. But signs were like weeds and kept springing up.

In spite of the signs, there was "quite a little Jewish community" at Centre, according to the daughter of one Jewish family there. "For my parents' generation—my parents were not well off—it represented a chance to be part of the middle class, to have a summer place with trees and fresh air and an outdoor feel. They didn't have enough dough to go away to a summer house. But to rent on the Island was affordable. And it had that feel of Edwardian leisure and space and goldenness." They, like all Island residents, enjoyed bobbing along the lagoons in tiny, gaff-rigged dinghies, lounging on long gracious verandahs, picnicking under ancient willow trees and strolling home along a moonlit boardwalk.

But sometimes their "golden place" became tarnished. One summer a number of Jewish women were attacked. One day a friend of this same woman's mother "came down the walk in front of her rented house and a man jumped out from behind a hedge and beat her up." There was also a "fair amount of vocal anti-Semitism." "One day, for example, my father—who was very athletic and very strong and impulsive—was coming over to work on the ferry in the morning. And a man brushed up against him and said, 'You kikes ought to go back where you came from.' And my father tried to restrain himself from getting into a fight. But he couldn't help it when the man kept making a lot of comments and as the ferry docked, my father grabbed the guy, punched him out and I think threw his bicycle in the harbour." Not surprisingly, the Jewish community "just kept themselves to themselves" as much as possible. But, at least, "if they toughened their skins a bit, they did get to enjoy the Island."

Winter Islanders continued to be a "breed apart," as frequent visitor and future co-founder of the Island Yacht Club, Ben Dunkelman observed. So they were. From the time the last ferry was put up for the winter at the end of November until the time the first ferry started running again in April, the sandy outcropping guarding Toronto's harbour belonged to the "dyed-in-the-wool Islanders," who numbered only a hundred families, or about three hundred hardy souls in 1933.[9] Through the thirties Ward's Island was virtually deserted. But winter residents were dotted about Centre Island and along Hanlan's Point. Life out on the exposed Western Sandbar must have been particularly rigorous, with the insubstantial little summer cottages at the mercy of the vicious north wind. Sometimes the motivation for occupying these places was simply an economic one. Mrs. Cecilia Constable, for example, rented her 105 West Island Drive cottage "mostly as an act of charity" to a Mr. Oldershaw who, she assured City Council, was "a very respectable man, with a large family and out of work." The long, cold winter of Depression continued.

Whatever the reason, by mid-decade about ten families were wintering on the Bar. Among these was the Jones family, whose parents worked at the amusement park during the summer. Jimmy, Jr., remembered that the "winters were always rough." The first winter on the Bar, his family (like families all over the Island) trudged over a mile down to the Filtration Plant to get drinking water, which they put in a big milk tin and laboriously dragged home on a sleigh. Toward the end of that winter they found out that neighbours about ten houses away had a pump in their front yard. Great! "And then in the spring, somebody came into the house we were living in and said, 'What have you been

going to Bains' for to get water? You have a pump in your own house, right beneath this trap door.' And we lifted the trap door and there was a pump.''

Most winters, of course, the bay froze and provided an icy avenue back and forth to the city. And every winter the Western Gap froze solid. Fireman Fram Ward, who spent one winter during the thirties at Centre Island (and other winters in the city), recalled one unrewarding journey via the Gap. One night when it was ''cold blasted weather,'' he was off to ''blow a saxophone in an orchestra'' at the King Edward Hotel. Hearing that the Gap was frozen, he decided to return late that night rather than stay with his mother in the city. Still ''dolled up'' in his tuxedo, he got a ride to the Maple Leaf Stadium around midnight and headed across. ''Here I am with a blasted big saxophone and a lot of music under my arm and all the rest of it. Not a soul around. So I started off and the ice was splintered.'' Despite this he got across the Gap, headed down the frozen regatta course, and then right on down Long Pond. Finally, home to an anticlimax. A triumphant rat-a-tat-tat on the locked door. No answer. ''So, to cut a long story short, I had to sleep in a [porch] room that was below zero!''

(Above) *This battered old 1939 photo shows some of the Island's winter residents enjoying a convivial evening at the Manitou Hotel. The bearded eccentric is the hotel's operator, William Sutherland, and next to him is Jimmy Jones Sr., without clown costume.* [TIA]

(Left) *The timeless* Ned Hanlan *on a frosty January morning in 1962. From 1932 to 1965 this steel-hulled steam tug brought workers to the Filtration Plant; teachers to the school; and provisions and transportation services to winter residents.* [YUA:TC]

Sometimes the crossing, if not the final result, was more harrowing. One couple left their cottage in an iceboat to attend a ball in the city. They whizzed across the icy bay, in all their finery, with no trouble. But by 2 A.M., when they were ready to head home, a blizzard had come up. Nevertheless, they gamely started out. Within a few hundred feet, the whirling snow had blotted out the city lights. Their boat swung around in the terrific wind until they lost all direction. Scudding along the ice at dizzy speed, they struck a snowdrift and capsized. Before they could right their craft, it was blown away into the blizzard. They were left wandering for what seemed to be hours until they hit shore. At first they couldn't even tell if it was the city or the Island. When they finally got their bearings, they realized that they were, miraculously, only about a mile from home.

During the thirties the winter community experienced modest growth and became "quite a little metropolis," according to Alan Howard who lived on Lakeshore Avenue just east of the Filtration Plant. "We got mail delivery, first of all a central post office where you picked up the mail and latterly an actual postman coming around. And we got delivery of bread and delivery of milk. Simpson's and Eaton's had delivery all the year round." But without reliable winter water and reliable transportation it was bound to remain small, and "confined," according to Mrs. Alice Aitken, who spent her first winter there in 1939. Nevertheless, "it was a lovely existence. Everyone knew everyone else. We all took our children for walks. Carol singing. And there were lots of parties and we all went together."

Not surprisingly, during the Depression years relatively few new cottages were built except on Ward's. In fact, some people on the Island,

as elsewhere, lost their houses for non-payment of taxes. A few clusters of new houses were, however, built on large lots that were subdivided. One cluster of six was built on the Western Sandbar across from the dilapidated old bathing station; so it came as quite a shock when only a few months later, residents at the Bar were faced with a grave threat to their very existence. Not cold north winds. Not floods. Not storms. But an airport and a tunnel.

For years City Council had been pressing Ottawa to build a bridge to the Island. In spite of repeated approaches, the City made little headway.[10] Until 1935, that is, when, faced with an election later that year, Prime Minister R. B. Bennett proposed his "Canadian New Deal."

Included on the multimillion-dollar list of public works was a million dollars for a two-thousand-foot tunnel to run from the foot of Bathurst Street, under the Western Gap, to the Island. It was commonly believed that once vehicular access to the Island was assured, the "natural sequence" would be to build an airport south of the Western Gap. Toronto Tory M.P.'s, like former mayor Tommy Church, were delighted. Toronto's CCF mayor, that charming elder statesman of Toronto labour, Jimmy Simpson was delighted. And soon the Board of Trade, the Toronto Harbour Commission and, less easily, the City Board of Control fell in line behind the proposal.

On the other hand, Liberal M.P.'s were *not*

To the joy of 1935's mayor Jimmy Simpson and the unmitigated wrath of 1936's mayor Sam McBride, work actually began on a tunnel under the Western Gap in the fall of 1935. Here a surveyor peeps through the bush on the Hanlan's Point side. [THC]

delighted. ''It looks as though...the real reason why the Liberals opposed the island tunnel was because it was for Tory Toronto,'' scoffed an ebullient Mayor Simpson when the bill passed committee stage.[11] Only too true, it seems, as Toronto would learn in the not-too-distant future.

In the meantime, West Island Drive residents, twenty-five of whose cottages along the Western Sandbar would be demolished if the post-tunnel airport were constructed, were *not* delighted. In a rare show of resolve, the West Island Drive Association passed a motion at the end of May against the construction of an airport. This was the only time that the WIDA ever flatly attacked the very idea of building an airport. Later, their aims became more modest, and successful. Even now, however, West Island Drive residents did not press their case vigorously. They sent their resolution off to City Hall, watched events unfold and, when the tide turned against them, began to retreat.

Fortunately for them, the ''two-fisted, red blooded, go-getter''[12]—''Mr. Islands'' himself—City Controller Sam McBride was most certainly *not* delighted. He was outraged and fighting mad. Not one to retreat, McBride charged straight ahead and threw every roadblock he could think of in the path of the tunnel. For example, on July 3, McBride moved that the million dollars not be spent on the tunnel, but on ''something more worthwhile.'' The motion was voted down, 1-4, by the rest of the City Board of Control. Finally, after a mammoth debate on August 8, 1935, City Council approved both the tunnel and the airport projects by a vote of 15-7.

Work soon got underway on the tunnel, but not the airport. Sites were surveyed, pavement on Bathurst Street south of Fleet Street was torn

Men and machines scoop out the mainland approach. [THC]

up, sand was scooped out, sewers and public utilities were moved, all in preparation for driving the tunnel under the Western Gap.

Meanwhile, at the end of August the WIDA again appeared before the Board of Control with a gentle request. ''If the proposal to remove their cottages is carried out,'' they wondered, would the City consider giving them other ''appropriate and desirable land on the Island'' where they could place their homes, and paying for the cost of removal. No decision was made at this time and the board advised them to ''await developments.''

For his part, the ungentle but persistent McBride did not sit back to await developments. He continued his opposition and sought to shape events. He carried his verbal campaign to the radio airwaves and he made his own privately financed trek to Ottawa to lobby against the projects, suggesting that the government might spend the money on something more worthwhile, like a new seawall to protect the south shore of the Island.

The fall of 1935 brought a federal election, just in the nick of time for Island residents. Campaigning on the catchy slogan ''King or Chaos,'' wily William Lyon Mackenzie King swept back into power (where he remained until 1948). By the end of October, the tunnel project was halted and then, in spite of frantic efforts by McBride's Council opponents, scuppered altogether. Whether this resulted from McBride's efforts or from a natural Liberal disinclination to give a million dollars to Tory Toronto was a moot point. The project was dead.

McBride nevertheless carried his opposition to

the tunnel right on into his newest mayoralty campaign, and was not shy about taking credit. "If there's anything I'm proud of in my 30 years of public service," he told Monarch Park ratepayers, "it is stopping the tunnel."[13] McBride was elected to his third term as mayor and by August 1936 the large hole that had been cut into the north wall of the Western Gap, was being refilled by Public Works Department employees. During the summer, however, McBride's battles—and age—caught up with him. He spent long weeks in hospital and, although he was well enough to return to his beloved Island cottage in mid-July, he never recovered his health. In November Toronto lost one of its most colourful personalities. His body lay in state at City Hall, the funeral was broadcast by radio and as a fitting tribute, Island ferries (as well as city buses and streetcars) came to a standstill for two minutes. As a further memorial, the doughty new ferry launched in 1939, which still plies across the bay, was named the *Sam McBride*.

In the summer of 1936, West Island Drive residents settled back to enjoy the pleasures of Island life. A new ferry, the *William Inglis*, joined the fleet (and is still in service in 1984). On Dominion Day, topcoated picnickers boarded the *Inglis* and the other ferries in order to spend a cool but pleasant day on the Island. Paddlers splashed energetically through the traditional regatta. Over four thousand jubilant Sons of Scotland literally packed Hanlan's Point for their jubilee celebrations. And ailing veterans made their annual pilgrimage to the Red Cross Outpost with its wide, screened-in balconies and airy wards with their uninterrupted view of the lake. The burning issue of the day, in fact, seemed to be whether men could appear in topless bathing suits on Toronto's beaches.

Topless bathing paled into insignificance in

"Aida" al fresco at Hanlan's Point in the overheated summer of 1936. The stage was set up near second base, the stadium reportedly had good acoustics, and the natural setting was "attractively picturesque with the encircling trees, glints of water, stars overhead, and twinkling lights of Toronto in the distance," according to the Globe and Mail's *critic.*   [TTC]

mid-July when Toronto was hit with one of the worst, if not *the* worst, heat wave in its history. On July 8 the mercury shot up to a record-breaking 104.5 degrees and stayed in the upper registers for a week. People tried everything to escape the heat. Thousands spent the night in mainland parks and at mainland beaches. Thousands more headed for the Island and stayed till the last moment, when they crammed the ferries and became overheated all over again. Hundreds more simply stayed on the Island, making the rounds of hotels and rooming houses in an often unsuccessful search for accommodation. The Manitou Hotel turned away more than sixty people on one night alone. Fred Ginn's

Casino, Pierson's and private residences could have rented their rooms several times over. Those who were lucky enough to find a room, had to fend for themselves, as hotel workers were rushed off their feet. "We gave them their blankets and sheets," William Sutherland of the Manitou Hotel said, "and they went off to make their own beds; we were so busy we couldn't do it for them."[14] Many of those earlier turned away from the hotels found their way to the park and beach, where they slept out under the stars. Whether any were doused when the fire tug sprayed the parched lawns in Island Park one midnight goes unrecorded, though the spray might well have been welcome.

The Island may not have been as hot as the city, but "for the first time in twenty-seven years," one old resident had to admit, "the Island *was* hot." Heat had "conquered the last outpost," as one *Globe* reporter observed. Even Island residents' activities were curtailed and everyone prayed for relief. Finally, cooling breezes swept down over the province and the mercury plunged 29 degrees in one night. By the end of the seven days of blistering sun and record heat, however, some 227 people in Ontario, including 91 in Toronto, had died, mostly the very young and the very old.

The City may not have been able to stop the heat waves, but it did take some action to stop the lake's waves. For years, the City and the federal government had been squabbling over who should pay what. Finally, spring storms in 1936 emphatically underlined the fact that the old breakwater along the lakeshore between the Eastern Gap and Oriole Avenue was "almost completely disintegrated" and would not "withstand a period of high water and storm."[15] By September the City and the federal government had finally reached an agreement concerning a new concrete breakwater to be capped by a new boardwalk. Islanders, for their part, formed a new, *political* organization, the Island Ratepayers Association (or IRA, though the acronym was not deliberately provocative) to represent Islanders "from gap to gap." High on their list of priorities were improved fire protection; alterations to the design of the new breakwater which, they felt, would not "do all that is expected of it" (they were later proved right when storm waves washed over the top, became trapped and created rather than prevented flooding); stopping work on the breakwater during the coming summer of 1937 so that "construction noises will not interfere with island residents or the renting of properties next year" (this most certainly was not done); and for the first time in Island history sponsoring an all-candidates meeting for the purpose of trying to "mould opinions of island voters in favor of the [city-wide] candidates who will pledge themselves to be in favor of general island development."[16] Nevertheless, in spite of its avowedly political intent, the IRA remained in the background when Islanders faced their next major threat—a resurrected Island airport.

Despite its earlier tunnel setback in 1935, the City did not abandon the airport idea. The most outspoken opponent was gone and times were changing. A trans-Atlantic service and a trans-Canada airway were both expected to come into being in 1937. So, on November 18, 1936, the City created an Advisory Airport Committee under the titular leadership of Air Vice Marshal and World War I air ace Billy Bishop, who knew Toronto Bay well from the days of his short-lived Bishop-Barker Airways. Predictably, this committee really investigated not whether, but *where* to build a Toronto municipal airport.

As the City quietly continued planning for an airport, West Island Drive residents—by now some 260 strong—settled back to enjoy another

Construction of the new lakefront breakwater between Ward's and Centre began in the spring of 1937 and continued right through the height of the July heat wave (here), causing a great deal of unwanted disruption to residents along the route who, according to the Island Ratepayers Association, had to put up with "plant and equipment and piles of material" in front of their cottages during the entire season. [THC]

Residents of these threatened Western Sandbar cottages formed the West Island Drive Association in the summer of 1937. Their plan was not to oppose an airport, but to negotiate with the City for compensation and new Island lots. [CTA]

Island summer blissfully unaware of the storm that was about to break over them. They had been lulled into a false sense of security not only by the halting of the tunnel/airport in 1935, but also by the City's own actions over the past several years. It had allowed six new houses to be built in the area. It had encouraged, and in many cases demanded, costly improvements to existing buildings. And it had spent $12,000 to build a new bath house at the southern end of the Bar to replace the now-demolished Turner's Baths and to lay a new, three-quarter-mile concrete sidewalk.

On June 21, 1937, however, City Council voted to terminate the West Island Drive licenses. If, as Council expected, the Island airport project was to get off the ground, these houses would have to go, the lagoon (or regatta course) between the Bar and Hanlan's Point would have to be filled in, and part of the amusement park would have to be demolished. Even before Council approved the airport, notices to vacate the fifty-four threatened houses by December 31 were sent to West Island Drive residents. This thunderbolt from an apparently clear blue sky

shocked the residents into rapid action. On Sunday June 27 they crowded into the Hanlan's Island Association clubhouse, which was safely located in parkland across the regatta course. Politics, not lawn bowling, was the order of the day. They appointed a special committee to present the views of the residents, to negotiate for compensation to cover costs and losses, to procure a "favourable location" where their houses could be moved, to act as "mediator and negotiator" between residents and any City, provincial or federal agent or body and to keep residents informed about any development affecting them.[17]

From the outset it was clear that the residents accepted the decision to construct an Island airport as a *fait accompli*. They never tried to overturn the basic decision. They did not even register the mild opposition that they had tendered in 1935. They had more modest, and perhaps more realistic, goals: first, to find a new site for their homes and second to gain financial compensation and/or assistance for moving them. They did not consider *fighting* City Hall in the way of Islanders since the late 1960s, but they

most certainly did try *influencing* City Hall. They used many of the traditional means: they lobbied, especially politicians like their own alderman, Nathan Phillips, and Controller (soon to be Mayor) Ralph Day; they negotiated (with a fair degree of success); and they appeared in "large delegations" to state their case before City committees. Occasionally they became piqued, but they did not confront or demand. Perhaps their acceptance of authority and their generally (but not universally) deferential attitude toward City officials is best summed up by the phrase "we waited upon" the Board of Control or some other committee, a phrase that is sprinkled throughout the minutes of the West Island Drive Association.

As the City pondered the fate of the Island and the fifty-four families involved, Torontonians celebrated, or endured, an unusually cool Dominion Day 1937. Perhaps it was only fitting that overcast skies and a cold wind cast a pall over Island celebrants. Far fewer holiday-makers ventured across the bay than usual and even a military band stationed near the regatta course lagoon apparently failed to adequately stir the blood of the crowd huddled together for warmth along its banks. Nevertheless, the competition at this 1937 Dominion Day regatta, "possibly...the last on the Hanlan's course," which would be filled in if the proposed airport went ahead, was as stiff as the breeze that ruffled the waters of the course.

The following day four controllers and eight aldermen (including Nathan Phillips, Adelaide Plumptre, who was the first woman on Council, and Stewart Smith, who was the only declared Communist on Council) toured the proposed airport site and tramped through the wilds of nearby Mugg's Island where, several councillors felt, West Island Drive residents might be allowed to move. (Only three days later one unfortunate swimmer was to drown a few feet from this shore in the tangled weeds of the lagoon, a sadly appropriate metaphor for the fate of plans to develop Mugg's Island as either a residential area or as accessible parkland.) In any event, when they returned to City Hall, the members of the Board of Control struggled to come to terms with the report submitted by Bishop's Airport Committee on May 31.

Finally, on July 9, 1937, after some political manoeuvring, the fate of West Island Drive residents was sealed. At the end of a mammoth two-day debate, enlivened by the entry of a colourful new member named Allan Lamport (who supported the Island airport), City Council voted to construct the main airport (and a new seaplane base) at the Island, and an auxiliary airport at Malton. Joining Mayor Robbins in the 14-7 vote to proceed with the Island airport were both of the Islanders' aldermen, Nathan Phillips and R. H. Saunders. As a result, not only the fifty-four West Island Drive houses, but the hallowed Hanlan's Memorial Regatta Course, the old baseball stadium and assorted other amusement park attractions would "vanish in the path of progress," as the *Telegram* put it on July 21.

Now, haunted by the spectre of their December 31 deadline, West Island Drive residents began meeting endlessly with City politicians and staff in order to push along the search for a new site and for financial assistance. Members of the Board of Control were sufficiently moved by their presentations that they again journeyed across the bay to inspect possible lots on the main part of Hanlan's Point and the remote fastness of the Monarch of Mugg's Island.

Nevertheless, as July turned into August, little visible progress had been made. To be fair,

July 30, 1937: (left to right) Controller Hamilton, Mayor Robbins, the "Monarch of Muggs" John Lye, City Clerk Somers, and Controller Wadsworth meet to discuss the possibility of moving the Western Sandbar cottages to Mugg's Island to clear the way for the proposed Island Airport.   [Star]

the City had other matters to worry about, notably the appalling polio epidemic then sweeping across Toronto and Ontario. As the epidemic gathered strength in August, civic authorities closed supervised playgrounds, delayed the opening of public schools and worried about the approaching Exhibition which was bound to draw great crowds of children. Should they ban children from the Ex? In a scenario reminiscent of Ibsen's *An Enemy of the People*, some members of the local Board of Health were reluctant to use the word "epidemic" or to prohibit children from the fair. Bad for business. (Mayor Robbins angrily asked the board's acting chairman if he wanted to "kill the Exhibition." "Of course not," Alderman Saunders shot back. "But neither do I want to kill children.")[18] Meanwhile families coped as best as they could. A number of Island summer residents, like the Mallons and the Kilbourns, remained on the Island much later than usual, in order to inhale the well-known

healthful breezes and avoid contamination. Even if their parents lived in terror, Island children enjoyed more than an extra month's vacation that summer.

On October 4, 1937, West Island Drive residents finally attained their first goal—a new site for their cottages—when City Council approved Parks Commissioner C. E. Chambers's plan to develop Mugg's as a park and Sunfish as a summer residential community. Mayor Robbins, for one, was pleased, especially with the thought that, when fully developed, the new Sunfish community would reduce the annual ferry deficit by nearly $3,000. West Island Drive residents themselves would have preferred nearby Mugg's rather than distant Sunfish. Still, they were satisfied. Sunfish (soon to be called Algonquin) was undoubtedly better than oblivion.

Parks Commissioner Chambers, for his part, was very enthusiastic and saw this decision as the first step toward developing the entire Island into a great City park. "Our plans call for no Coney Island development," he explained to the *Star* on October 2. On the contrary, these plans, if implemented, would transform the Island "along the lines of the present Island park between the ferry landing and the cottages at Centre Island," which, significantly, would remain. "But all this will take time," he admitted. "For the moment we will concentrate our efforts on Mugg's Island and Sunfish Island."

Although Chambers did not plan to release any more land for cottage development after Sunfish Island was developed into 103 fifty-by-one-hundred-foot lots, he was obviously pleased with the project. He told the WIDA that "every encouragement would be given by the Parks department to home-owners to develop their homes and grounds to a point where though not pretentious or expensive the very neatness & well kept appearance would make it a showplace of the city." It would become "the first 'town-planned' summer cottage site near Toronto."[19]

That fall, as the Parks Department geared up to prepare Sunfish Island, work got underway on the airport. Here progress was rapid. "At the western end of the Island," the *Star* reported on October 2, "two great sandsuckers, powerful graders and nearly 100 men are already creating new land and revamping the old where gleaming concrete runways, 3,000 feet long, will soon cushion the wheels of huge transport aeroplanes....When this work is finished Toronto will have a modern airport on her front doorstep." Just off Mugg's Island the two huge sandsuckers were slurping up a muddy mixture of sand and water from the bottom of the bay and driving it through long black pipes carried on pontoons toward the Western Sandbar. One pipeline crossed the corner of Mugg's, plunged under Blockhouse Bay and emerged again at Hanlan's

Point near the upper end of the regatta course, which was disappearing daily into a swampy quagmire that would one day be a solid runway. The other pipline bridged this lagoon on giant stilts, crept across the Western Sandbar in a great Y-formation and poured its double flow directly into the lake. A round-helmeted diver spent his days underwater strengthening the seawall, while a great yellow tractor chugged along the top of the Bar, gouging out whole sand dunes and flattening every sand hump and bump. Work continued into December, although several days of snow "materially hampered operations"[20] (not to mention the health of workers, some of whom had been on Relief). By the end of January, work had practically ground to a halt and the dredges were laid up for the winter, after having spewed out over 1.2 million cubic yards of fill. The wheels of bureaucracy may have ground slow, but the wheels of "progress" did not.

As work on the airport continued apace, West Island Drive residents concentrated their efforts on pressing the City for financial aid and on moving house, literally. They negotiated with contractor Arthur Sagar to move their cottages on a barge down the regatta course, before it was filled in, and then across to the new locations, all for approximately $350 per house. On top of this, residents would have other

October 12, 1938: the Island Airport after a year of construction.   [THC]

expenses: repairs would have to be made to houses damaged in transit, septic tanks would have to be installed, new gardens and walks would have to be laid, new chimneys would have to be built, and so on. At the same time as they were negotiating with Sagar, therefore, they also negotiated with the City to help defray some of these moving costs. In the end the City agreed to exempt West Island Drive residents who moved their cottages to Sunfish from three years (or $225 worth) of ground rent for their new lots. But it did not agree to their request to halt the filling of the lagoon—that watery escape route which was disappearing daily. West Island Drive residents, therefore, after a great deal of effort, had reached their second goal of receiving some financial aid. It was not a complete victory, but it was, they agreed, "acceptable."[21]

All eyes now turned toward Sunfish Island, Work on the airport may have been buzzing along, but it was a different story down at Sunfish. When the Parks Department got the go-ahead from Council on October 4, Sunfish Island was mostly sand and trees. The Queen City Yacht Club occupied the eastern tip and the Sunfish Camp occupied a cluster of log and canvas sheds elsewhere. For years, young boys like Jack Bradley had swum across the lagoon to use the camp's diving board and to build their forts and play their Cowboys and Indians in the surrounding forest. And young girls like Daddy Frank Staneland's daughter Mardi Webster had journeyed across to a sandy spot in the middle for their "overnights" (which were always raided by the boys). All of this was about to change as the Parks Department transformed Sunfish into Algonquin Island.[22]

The transformation, however, was maddeningly slow. With the sandsuckers at their backs and the December 31 deadline before them,

Bar residents again trooped down to City Hall on November 3 to urge the City to speed up its work on Sunfish. Surely, since the "need for haste is so obvious" the work crew composed of sixteen men, four teams of horses and one tractor could be increased, they suggested.[23] To circumvent the problem, Parks Commissioner Chambers suggested that the houses could be moved in two stages: first, further along Hanlan's Point to a temporary site for the winter, so that work on the airport could proceed unimpeded and then to sites on Sunfish when they were ready. Although the residents naturally objected to this more costly, less convenient scheme, this is precisely what was ultimately done.

In the meantime, the search for alternative sites on Hanlan's Point itself intensified. Perhaps some residents were unimpressed by the prospect of living on barren Algonquin, which by now was almost treeless. And perhaps, faced with an unattractive choice, some Hanlan's Pointers decided that they were, after all, Hanlan's Pointers first and foremost. To accommodate these

loyalists, the City decided to lease a number of the sites that it had carefully been acquiring since 1913 for the Harbour Commission's proposed scenic boulevard across the Island. (Although these particular lots were now taken off the reserve list, the boulevard itself was far from dead.) The following spring Hiawatha Avenue was extended southward and more lots were opened up. As a result, various residents who had planned to move over to Algonquin thought better of the idea and chose to move their houses, their lilac bushes and their loyalty just down the Point.[24] It would turn out to be a fateful decision.

Finally, the bizarre two-stage procedure of moving the little cottages got underway. Ex-Hanlan's Pointer Jimmy Jones, who was a boy at the time, remembers watching this extraordinary process with fascination:

> I can remember seeing them. They floated them. There was a lagoon, that's all filled in now, that ran from the bay almost up to the Hanlan's Island Association.

After being floated down the disappearing regatta course, West Island Drive cottages huddle on the edge of Blockhouse Bay for the winter of 1937-38. [THC]

They moved the houses on rollers. Horses would walk in a circle and a cable was on the house and the house was on rollers, so that the horses would walk on this turnstile. And they would stop and they would move the houses and the turnstile way ahead and rearrange the wires on another house and start again and as a roller would drop out the back end, they would move it around to the front end and they kept it going this way. They put them on barges and floated them down the first part of the lagoon, put them in the park [at Hanlan's Point] and they sat there [all winter]. And then [in the spring of 1938] they put them in another barge on the other side of the lagoon, which is Blockhouse Bay, and took them on down here to Algonquin.

Nothing went smoothly for residents or their mover, contractor Arthur Sagar. The dredging companies working on the airport refused to cooperate by burying their twelve-foot-high pipelines at strategic points, so Sagar had to build runways over them. Even sandstorms of unusual severity swirled around them because the old undergrowth which used to anchor the beach had by now been stripped away. Nevertheless, by mid-December 1937 the first stage of floating them down the regatta course lagoon was well underway. Then some of these cottages were moved to their final resting places elsewhere on Hanlan's Point, but most clustered forlornly in the park waiting for the ice to thaw and Algonquin to be made ready.

Through the late fall and on into the spring, workers prepared Algonquin. The work force included relief labour chosen from "former employees of [the Parks] Department familiar with this type of work" who had been laid off because of the Depression.[25] They stripped the area where houses were to be placed of all trees and levelled it as "flat as a billiard table," according to the *Globe* of July 18, 1938. They

May 10, 1938: workmen at Hanlan's Point prepare to move one former West Island Drive cottage on rollers toward a barge, while workmen down at sandy Algonquin Island lay pipes and work on recently deposited cottages. [Sun: Telegram *Collection*]

built a picturesque wooden bridge to Ward's, laid ten-foot-wide concrete sidewalks and sank water mains. Finally, the second stage, watched by wide-eyed Ward's Island campers like Mardi Webster, got underway. All went swimmingly, relatively speaking; so that by mid-June 1938 about thirty old West Island Drive cottages, with their distinctive battered skirts and miniature mansard windows, had arrived by barge and been deposited on their choice new sites around the perimeter of the island. Soon the first residents arrived—Earl and Anna Norton moved in to 3 Wyandot. They had no gas, no electricity and no deliveries. But they were home at last.

The new Algonquinites may have been pleased and relieved. But Parks Commissioner Chambers (who had visions of a neatly laid-out summer resort) was not delighted by the tacky appearance of many of the houses, which needed paint and "proper" chimneys. So the new residents of Algonquin spent the summer of 1938 painting, hammering and planting.

Former Bar residents may have been undismayed by their admittedly bleak surroundings, confident that in time Algonquin Island would become the "pick of the Islands."[26] But other Torontonians were definitely less optimistic. Even sand-toughened Ward's Islanders were scornful: "Everyone said, 'I wouldn't live there if you paid me,'" tenter Mardi Webster recalled. "It looked like a desert." Torontonians at large were also unimpressed by Algonquin, which was described by the *Globe* of July 19, 1938, as "sand just sand"—hardly the sort of advertising that a real estate agent would welcome.

Not only was the physical environment bleak, so was the economic climate. The Depression ground on, and at least one prospective Algonquin cottage builder was forced to give up his lease because he had been out of work for several months. As a result the expected Algonquin Island rush did not materialize. City fathers, who had been inspired by dreams of avarice to plunk $75,000 into developing Algonquin in order to attract builders, were disappointed by the lacklustre response. Less than a dozen additional leases had been signed for new cottage sites and only a few buildings were actually under construction.[27] Mayor Ralph Day commented to the *Globe*, ''I am very disappointed that this land has been developed and made available for a considerable number of people and yet so very few have come forward to take advantage of it.'' As it happened, not only was Mugg's Island not developed for cottage use, as businessman Mayor Day had hoped, but it was not even developed for park use, as Commissioner Chambers had hoped and planned.

Residents on the Western Sandbar were not the only victims of ''progress.'' The great Hanlan's Point Stadium—one time home of the Maple Leafs and the Tecumsehs, sometime host to sporting heroes like Tom Longboat and Babe Ruth, more recent venue for outdoor opera, TTC picnics and Toronto Police Games—fell before the wreckers' ball. But other amusement park favourites, like the merry-go-round, the whip, and the roller rink, survived on the edge of the new airport to enchant one last generation of Torontonians as planes flew by.

July 1, 1938, while Algonquinites were puttering around their new community and Ward's Islanders were welcoming that other group of refugees from the Western Sandbar, the Broadview ''Y'' Camp, the aquatic fraternity gathered at Centre Island for the first Dominion Day regatta on the new Long Pond course. In spite of rain dripping from leaden skies from early morning until late afternoon, the show went on, producing one of the best regattas in years. And 1938's stand-out proved to be young Jake Gaudaur, Jr., who swept to victory in the high school singles event in a style reminiscent of his illustrious father.

Unfortunately, the 1938 Dominion Day regatta was to be the first and only one to be held in the lee of the grand old Island Amateur Aquatic Association clubhouse. For over thirty years the club had stood guard over happenings on Long Pond. But on the evening of January 29, 1939, the building went up in flames. Hundreds of motorists on the mainland stopped their cars along the waterfront to watch the spectacle across the bay. Meanwhile, four Island firemen from the nearby fire station on Manitou Road and several volunteer residents battled the blaze, dashed bravely into the burning building to save nine canoes and a dinghy and worked hard to prevent the blaze from spreading to nearby houses and St. Rita's Church. One eighty-year-old gentleman who had been in bed suffering from broken ribs was forced to evacuate his house and stand miserably in the cold because sparks were landing on his roof; fortunately, his house did not ignite. It took more than half an hour to drag the little Model-T pumper to the scene. ''The pumper, even when it gets into action,'' William Sutherland of the Manitou Hotel complained, ''pumps enough water to nicely fill a garden hose,'' the perennial complaint of Island firefighters since early in the century. Furthermore, no fireboat was able to come to the rescue. The *Charles A. Reed* was in drydock; but even if it had been afloat, the wooden-hulled fighter could not have made it through the icy lagoon.

(Left) *January 29, 1939: the spectacular fire that destroyed the old IAAA Aquatic Hall on Long Pond and underlined the need for improved fire fighting services on the Island in wintertime.* [Sun: Telegram *Collection*]

The burning of the old clubhouse underlined the always serious fire hazard faced by Islanders, especially during the winter when summer water pipes were turned off and lagoons were frozen. It also highlighted the City's stony response to their predicament. "In 15 years, I have been trying to get decent fire-fighting equipment placed here, but have got nowhere," William Sutherland complained. "Possibly the fact that there are only about 70 votes cast from the island in municipal elections has something to do with the lack of decent fire-fighting equipment there." As recently as the previous week, Sutherland, representing the Island Ratepayers Association, had ventured down to City Hall to try again, aided by Alderman Nathan Phillips who argued that no matter what the cost "the municipality owes all its citizens, wherever they may be, adequate fire and public protection." But Mayor Ralph Day remained unmoved. Sutherland commented sourly, "Perhaps the city will wake-up to the terrible fire hazard on the Island when about half the cottages are 'wiped out.'"[28] Although the next month four houses at Ward's Island were burnt down, fortunately this never happened. For the time being, these small losses were certainly not enough to shake more money loose from a tight-fisted City Council.

The year of 1939 began with one patriotic display and ended with another. On the eve of World War II, Torontonians went wild with excitement as King George VI and his good queen made their historic visit. Local newspapers carried reams of reports on every detail of the royal progress through Quebec, Ottawa and finally to Toronto for their glorious—but short—one-day visit. On May 22 nearly two million loyal subjects lined the royal route, including the world famous Dionne Quintuplets then aged

almost five who had travelled down from Callander, Ontario, and donned their frilliest frocks to greet the royal couple. Over on the Island, as elsewhere across the city, patriotic flags festooned houses and, as a permanent commemoration of the royal visit, the nearly-completed island airport was named Port George VI, Toronto Island Airport.

Throughout the summer, news from abroad was grim; but, by and large, Torontonians were able to enjoy what was to be their last peacetime summer for almost six years. Large crowds crossed the bay to luxuriate in the unusually fine weather over the Dominion Day weekend and again on the August Civic Holiday weekend. Island residents continued to enjoy their usual summer fun. Down at Ward's, for example, at least a hundred children in costume turned out for the annual Junior Masquerade, where the likes of David Dillon as "Mr. Chamberlain," Barry Barnett as "Mammy Yokum," and Fram's son Bill Ward and his friends as the "Slap Happy Gang" carried off prizes. Many of the contestants there, as well as in the Gala Day sports, would be in uniform before too long. And some, like Ralph Naylor, who won second prize in the Running Broad Jump, and Ralph Sturgeon, who captured a first prize as "Simple Simon," and Blatchford Dodd, who had taken over his father Walter's old job as overseer, would never return. But for that summer, the minstrel show went on; the inter-Island contests went on; and the Annual Corn Roast, followed by an animated Serenade, went on, and on, until 2:30 A.M., Saturday, September 1.

That same day, Hitler marched into Poland. And on September 2 the Second World War began "unspectacularly, not unexpectedly."[29] Canada officially entered the war a week later. By that time she had already suffered her first

casualties: the hapless refugees and tourists aboard the Montreal-bound Cunard liner *Athenia*, which was torpedoed and sunk in the icy blackness of the North Atlantic on September 3.

Unlike August 1914, there were no bonfires, no effigies and no parades. Canadians accepted the news of war with grimness and determination, but no elation. The German display at the CNE was unceremoniously torn down. "Trade unionism in martial mood" turned out for its annual Labour Day parade.[30] And a magnificent air show of Hawker Hurricanes (soon to become famous in the Battle of Britain) stunned thousands of spectators at the Exhibition grounds as the fighters skimmed barely six feet above the choppy lake waters and "flirted with death" in the skies overhead. The crowd was given a chance to see "one good reason why enemy air-raiders are steering clear of England," an enthusiastic *Globe* reporter marvelled on September 8. The following day, another CNE attraction, the "Sentimental Gentleman of Swing," Tommy Dorsey, captured public attention when he landed at the Island Airport. He was immediately pelted with questions about American opinion on the war. "Some people think we should get in the war and go over there and help knock that guy's block off. While others feel we should stay out and give the Allies what help we can," he stated diplomatically.[31]

Meanwhile, Canadians were revving up the old war machine. After the Exhibition closed, the CNE grounds were again turned into a military camp. The militia was called up. Veterans of the First War, too old for active service, volunteered to guard civic property deemed vulnerable to enemy sabotage. Over on the Island, as a brilliant searchlight flashed across the nearby wilderness, a great-coated, iron-helmeted, Balaclavaed sentinel with an ancient firearm was posted at the

(Left) *The present day ferry veteran* Sam McBride, *under construction in May 1939, and* (Right) *on a trial run in November 1939. City fathers originally feared that the machinery for their new ferry had been lost with the* Athenia, *but this, fortunately, was not the case.* [TTC]

Filtration Plant to protect the purity of Toronto's water.

As before, crowds of young men lined up to enlist—some for purely patriotic reasons and some for more economic ones. Novelist Hugh Hood's fictional, but accurately drawn, year-round Islander, Mr. Cawhill, was among the economic volunteers. Cawhill boarded the *Bluebell*, walked the two miles from the docks to the Fort York Armouries, enlisted and, as a token of his enlistment, received a thick warm khaki overcoat with brass buttons and a wide collar, which was much admired by his neighbours back on the Island. He had signed up "not so much from patriotic motives as because the army offered him the first steady job he'd ever had, plus the possibility of some training in a trade." Inspired by similar inducements, men on relief flocked to sign up. By January 1940 Mayor Day was able to tell the new Council, "Largely as a result of the war the number of persons on public relief is diminishing." Ever the businessman at heart, the mayor looked forward to improving tourism: "With Europe and many other parts of the world practically closed to American tourists," he suggested brightly, "the possibilities of still further developing the business in Canada are tremendous, and it is but good business to prepare to take advantage of this source of new wealth to the Country." At least Mayor Day could see a silver lining. The Island would help provide more glimmers of light in the dark years to come.

10

War, Winter and Waffling

November 1, 1940, was a typical, miserable November day. But, as the winds of war swept across the Island and the nation, Mayor Ralph Day joined a band of civic and military officials at the Island Airport. Under the cold fall drizzle, the topcoated mayor, accompanied by Air Commodore George E. Brookes, inspected the RCAF guard of honour and stepped forward to present an appropriately bellicose gift purchased by the Mayor of Toronto Fund. "I now have a great deal of pleasure in formally presenting these two Grumman aircraft, produced in Canada, for the use of the Royal Canadian Air Force in our crusade against a ruthless enemy, knowing full well that the pilots who fly these machines will continue to display that indomitable spirit that will ensure the successful conclusion of the war," the mayor concluded patriotically. Commodore Brookes replied in kind, the RCAF band struck up "Roll Out the Barrel" and the two new fighters roared down the runway and off into the wild gray yonder. After an exhibition flight around the Island and over the city, the planes headed east on the first leg of their journey overseas.[1]

Meanwhile, back on the tarmac another ceremony was underway. Mayor Day presented two red, white and blue Norwegian flags to Captain Larsen and Major Oen, commanders of the Royal Norwegian Air Force contingent who were billeted at the old Lakeside Home For Little Children and were training pilots and support personnel at the Island Airport. That very day, the RNAF had increased its own air strength when three Douglas attack bombers arrived from California. And every month the RNAF was also increasing its manpower. Ever since the fall of Norway the previous June, in the early stages of the Nazi blitzkrieg across Europe, young men had been making their way

by foot, by ski, by boat or by stolen plane out of occupied Norway, and ultimately, to the somewhat unlikely destination of Toronto. "It is the dream of every young Norwegian to join us," according to commanding officer Major Ole Reistad, "and they are coming in every day."[2] Sometimes they came alone. Sometimes with friends. And sometimes with families. (Toddler Liv Ullmann uttered some of her first cries and whispers at Toronto's "Little Norway" while her father Viggo trained mechanics at the Island Airport.) Sometimes the journey to the training station was an easy one, as in the case of Oleg Sorenson who had been teaching at Upper Canada College and who simply hopped on a southbound streetcar. Sometimes the journey was enough to make Ulysses blanch, as in the case of young fishermen who broke through the Nazi patrol and *rowed* 450 miles to Britain en route to Toronto; and the even more extraordinary case of "Willy" Skrede, who travelled 37,000 miles in 373 days by ship, train, donkey and camel to finally land on the Island, only to be rejected for pilot training because of the still unhealed broken back he had suffered en route. Still, he worked for two years as a ground mechanic spurred on by the hope that one day he would be accepted into the pilot-training programme.

However they got there, by August 1942 seven hundred Norwegian pilots who had trained at "Little Norway" in Toronto were overseas on active service. Airmen who only a few months earlier had been flying in slow, unspectacular circles over Toronto's harbour were now in hot pursuit of German aircraft over France and Holland. Now-Lieutenant-Colonel Ole Reistad beamed and spoke enthusiastically about his graduates. "They have been used extensively in the English channel and take great delight in

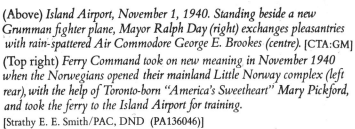

(Above) *Island Airport, November 1, 1940. Standing beside a new Grumman fighter plane, Mayor Ralph Day (right) exchanges pleasantries with rain-spattered Air Commodore George E. Brookes (centre).* [CTA:GM]

(Top right) *Ferry Command took on new meaning in November 1940 when the Norwegians opened their mainland Little Norway complex (left rear), with the help of Toronto-born "America's Sweetheart" Mary Pickford, and took the ferry to the Island Airport for training.*
[Strathy E. E. Smith/PAC, DND (PA136046)]

(Right) *Some of the two thousand Norwegians who trained at the Island Airport between 1940 and 1943 head for their P-36 trainers in April 1941.* [National Film Board/PAC, DND (PA136047)]

swooping down on railway trains along the coast."[3]

Back in Canada the Norwegians slipped right into Toronto's wartime life. Apart from some unpleasant rumour-mongering about these foreigners, which Lieutenant-Colonel Reistad dismissed as "fifth columnist" calumny, the welcome extended seems to have been warm. They worshipped at Hanlan's Point's Emmanuel Church. They attended fundraising bazaars. They went out sailing with Island residents, and sometimes shared an unexpected dunking in the lake. And they courted and married local girls who, Reistad cautioned, "must be prepared to stand many trials" because "our boys are at war and will have to go" to serve their country.[4]

Most of their time, however, was spent in training and nearby Island residents became almost inured to the incessant buzzing of "those darn Norwegians roaring 'cross the Park."[5] Occasionally mishaps did occur—like the time Pilot Officer

Sandorg and a student made an unscheduled, but perfect, "pancake" landing in the bay after their engine conked out at two hundred feet. Another Norwegian pilot gave the alarm by circling over the lifesaving station and waving until the lifeboats were launched.

Sometimes tragedy struck. On March 26, 1941, for example, Corporal Rasmussen was killed when his Fairchild training machine narrowly missed crashing into the Island and came down in the Eastern Gap with explosive force not far from Gap Lightkeeper Alf Winslow's place. That summer the Gap again became a graveyard. Sunday, July 27, 1941—the first fuelless Sunday of the war—was a scorcher, sending thousands of Torontonians to seek relief on the Island and at beaches all across the waterfront. But it was just another working day at "Little Norway" for student pilots like Kaara Moe, who had escaped from Oslo and arrived in Toronto the previous November. This particular Sunday he and his companions were flying their blue Fairchild EM 62 planes in a routine V-formation about three thousand feet over the crowded beaches, when Moe's plane started into a dive. "I thought he was just stunting," a *Globe* reporter commented later. Moe tried to use his parachute, but his feet became stuck and he went down with his plane about four hundred yards off the Lighthouse on the pier. There was a terrific explosion, which shuddered and reverberated for miles across the waterfront, bringing bathers to their feet and lifesavers dashing immediately to the scene of the crash.

At six that same evening, while a dredge, a diver and a lifesaving team were still trying to recover the wrecked plane and the pilot's body, a freak storm struck out of a clear blue sky "in blitz-like manner" according to the jargon of the day. In only five or six minutes, the storm

On June 20, 1941, ferry Captain Straker was astonished when a high-powered Northrop bomber slammed into the top deck of the Sam McBride (shown here after the crash) before plunging into the bay, carrying two Norwegians to their deaths. [CTA:GM]

uprooted trees, toppled concrete lampposts, blew in windows, tore down hydro wires and capsized a dozen boats. (Lifesavers had to temporarily suspend dragging operations in order to rescue overturned boaters). Ward's Island bore the brunt of the storm which, according to the *Ward's Island Weekly*, "caused more havoc than any storm that can be recalled by any of our Islanders." Further tragedy was only narrowly avoided as massive trees sliced through two Ward's Island residences. "It was like an earthquake," reported a shaken George Goulding (walking champion at the 1912 Stockholm

Olympics and twenty-five-year resident of Ward's Island). Over at 2 Fourth Street, Bill Sceviour was sitting on his front verandah while the rest of his family was gathered together in the back kitchen. Suddenly a large tree toppled right onto the canvas tent in the middle, smashing through a steel bed in the living room. "When this terrible crash came," Mrs. Sceviour recalled, "I ran out to the front. I was sure my husband was killed. I guess I got a little hysterical."[6]

The first summer of the war, 1940, began with a record fog when the blaaaah of the fog horn and the clanking of the fog bells sounded for almost eighty hours. In spite of this inauspicious beginning—coupled with the constant stream of disastrous headlines about Dunkirk, the fall of France and Britain's lonely vigil—residents and visitors alike discovered that, as the *Ward's Island Weekly* commented on June 29, the Island provided a welcome "peaceful corner in a war-torn world."

As in the previous war, the Royal Canadian Yacht Club cancelled all international racing and competition for club trophies. Younger members enlisted in droves (by 1941, 224 were on active service and by 1945, 501); while older members shuttled back and forth to Ottawa or to some war project. The annual Dominion Day regatta was cancelled for the duration of the hostilities and Inter-Island Baseball—that mainstay of Island competitive life—had to be cancelled for lack of time and manpower. Most traditional Island activities were nevertheless able to carry on. Ward's Island was able to field its usual four house teams for one last year. Dancers were still flitting around like Ginger Rogers and Fred Astaire at the WIA clubhouse to the live music of Jim Bottomly and his band. The real British and Allied navies may have been taking a drubbing out on the North Atlantic, but Frank Hanger and his "British Navy Rink" (of ancient and venerable Island lineage) were sweeping all opposition before them out on the bowling green. Even traditional activities took on a military cast. Little Peggy Cooper, for example, won a prize at the 1940 Ward's Island Junior Masquerade for her rendition of "There Will Always Be an England."

Islanders large and small, old and young threw themselves into war work. Major Alec Sinclair of the 48th Highlanders went off to Camp Borden to serve in his third war (he had served as a young man in South Africa and then in the First War), while his wife Kate became the moving force behind the Ward's Island women's "War Effort Group," which sewed, knitted, quilted, baked and raffled in order to send clothes to British bomb victims, dollars and goods to the Red Cross, and socks, cigs and other goodies to Ward's Islanders serving overseas. By mid-July the Ward's Island Association clubhouse was transformed into a busy workroom each Monday, with ladies bending over patterns and sewing machines stuttering away. Sometimes, unfortunately, the turnout was less than hoped for: "You know the war is being fought on Monday even if it is washday," the *Weekly* cautioned on July 27, "and the refugees have to be clothed that day as well as others." Even tiny tots hardly able to hold a needle earnestly sewed and pricked their fingers for the boys overseas.

The good ladies of Centre Island not only stitched and knitted their way toward victory three days a week at the Manitou Hotel, but also operated a supervised bicycle parking lot at the Centre Island docks to raise money for the Red Cross. Group of Seven luminary Franz Johnston donated a painting to be raffled in aid of the Red Cross Outpost. Individual Victory Gardens were planted in backyards across the Island; Victory and twenty-five-cent War Stamps were patriotically purchased (Mrs. Eddie Dillon of Ward's Island sold $130 in the course of this first summer); and young "War Guests" began arriving from overseas. The first children from Britain arrived over the Civic Holiday weekend in early August 1940 and some, in the course of their stay in Canada, visited the Island. Mary Mallon, for example, brought a group over for a day's visit to her Centre Island cottage and the RCYC. "I remember one little boy

looking around. You know, they have a cannon either side of the mast at the Yacht Club and they have cannon pointing out at the lagoon. He said, 'My, this place is awfully well defended!'"

Above all, Islanders enlisted and a few were already overseas. Centre Island's John Rutlege joined the 48th Highlanders in September 1939, arrived in England in December and participated in that "hair-breadth escape" from Dunkirk in June 1940. And Ward's Island's Frank Hillock, called up on the day war was declared, reached England in February 1940 as part of the first Canadian air unit to go into action—the 110th (A.C.) Squadron. According to the *Weekly*, he had already seen "considerable action"—including dodging bombs dropped in his path as he was taking off—when the Battle of Britain began in earnest in August 1940. The rate of enlistment was slower than in the last war; by August 17, 1940, for example, only thirteen Ward's Islanders had signed up for active service. (By the end 135—compared with 150 in the First War—had served.) The attrition rate, fortunately, was not as great; but sacrifices were made. Of the first group of thirteen Ward's Islanders, one became a POW, one was badly injured but recovered and one was killed. On the brighter side, one steadily advanced to the rank of wing commander, and one earned the Distinguished Flying Cross.

Whatever the future might hold, Islanders did their best to give their friends a proper send-off. In late August, for example, Ralph Naylor and Ross Dunfield left on the seven-fifty boat en route to Brandon, Manitoba and the RCAF. A group of friends escorted them down to the dock and the captain of the *William Inglis* hooted a special salute on the whistle as the ferry pulled away. It was a scene that would be repeated many times over the next several years.

The number of people visiting the Island during the Second War did not reach the peaks of the First War, when there was a baseball stadium at Hanlan's Point, not yet an amusement park at Sunnyside and more ferry boats paddling across the bay. But large numbers did cross over for a day or a few hours of amusement. Throughout the war Toronto teemed with soldiers who had all heard of the Island. Many went dancing at the Point or along the Main Drag, sunbathing and swimming off the beaches and picnicking in the park or in more secluded spots dotted around the fringes. The first Dominion Day of the war, July 1, 1940, however, was a disappointment, when intermittent showers made dodging raindrops the favourite sport of the day and made life difficult for the First World War veterans who defied the elements to attend a picnic at Hanlan's Point. The sun did shine, however, over the Civic Holiday in early August. Although wartime production schedules kept thousands of workers on the job, thousands more headed off to Muskoka and Haliburton, and a summer record of sixty-six thousand headed across the bay.

Not every visit to the Island ended happily. On Sunday September 29, 1940, a pretty twenty-two-year-old Finnish-Canadian named Aune "Spooky" Newell disappeared. One week later, old Harry Lemon, a Parks Department employee and Island resident, was making his usual Sunday circuit of the Island. As he stepped carefully along a seldom-used path about four hundred yards northeast of the Filtration Plant, a woman's black shoe caught his eye—and a trail of women's clothing led him to the gruesome discovery of a woman's body. Aune Newell had been strangled by one of her own silk stockings and buried in this remote, overgrown spot under her own black coat and a pile of dogwood and sweet clover.

"If it hadn't been for this shoe catching my eye I'd never have found the body," Lemon told reporters.[7] He refrained from touching the pile, because "I knew I mustn't touch it for fear of disturbing evidence," and he hurried back to the normally quiet little police station on Manitou Road. It would be quiet no longer. As the alarm was sent to the mainland, Lemon and Island Constable Agnew returned to the scene of the murder—the advance guard of an army of investigators who would comb the area and question Island residents in their search for evidence. Constable Agnew later told police he had seen the victim and an airman at the city docks board the two-fifty ferry for Centre Island on September 29. Then on October 15 Agnew identified Aune's estranged husband, Aircraftman Hugh "Bill" Newell, in a line-up (a line-up which Newell's defence later claimed was "a farce and a sham"[8]). And on October 31 Newell was charged with murder.

The sensational "Silk Stocking Murder" occupied Torontonians for months. A parade of technical experts made their way to the Island and then to the witness box. A soils expert made at least four visits to try to match soil along the lagoon to soil on boots found in Newell's basement. A botanist tested seeds and rotting vegetable matter. An acoustics expert ascertained whether residents along Iroquois Avenue could have heard the victim's screams. Since the case against Newell hung on a thread—small blue fibres allegedly discovered on a twig near Aune's body which purportedly came from Newell's uniform—textiles experts were called by both sides. Even a cloth-cutter from a fashionable King Street tailoring firm testified.

Newell himself was alternately quiet and composed and hot-headed and belligerent. At one point, the former pole vaulter nimbly leapt

The first of an increasingly gruesome series of police photos taken at the scene of Aune Newell's murder in a remote corner of Toronto Island. [Metropolitan Toronto Police]

(Below) *"I knew at once it was a body,"* Harry Lemon told Star *reporters on October 6, 1940.* [CTA:GM]

out of the dock and was reprimanded sharply by Mr. Justice W. D. Roach. At another point he complained to the jury that he was not being given a "fighting chance" to prove his innocence.[9] His reading material ranged from reports of a similar, but unsolved, Philadelphia silk-stocking murder to the Scriptures. Ominously, the first two trials ended with a hung jury. But, after months of investigation and months of courtroom battles, the Crown won its case. On February 12, 1942, Bill Newell went to the gallows at the Don Jail, still protesting his innocence. Meanwhile, children over at the Island dubbed the lonely, deserted spot where poor Aune Newell's body had been found "Murderer's Island." For years afterwards brave youngsters would venture across and, convinced that the murderer had thrown money in the lagoon, would look in the water for this treasure.

Since the outbreak of the war, local authorities had posted guards at important municipal works and generally kept a vigilant eye out for any suspicious activity along the vulnerable waterfront. Sometimes the vigilance had its comical side. One beautiful autumn day Mary Mallon's brother Albert, who taught art, went down to the Eastern Gap with an electrician friend to do some sketching. Before long, according to Mary, "two big men were standing by them and one of them says, 'Hum, not bad. Why are you here?' And then showed their badges." Unable to show any identification, the two artists were taken off to the mainland police station, where their paintings were confiscated while they returned home to collect identification. It all got sorted out in the end—and the police at headquarters even admired the pictures. Another artist, David Milne, also liked to paint down along the waterfront at this time, but he was never troubled by the long arm of the law.

In any event, by the end of 1940 Civilian Defence preparations, notably Air Raid Prevention (ARP), were being put in place. Warden posts were established throughout the city and an army of middle-aged to elderly civil defence workers were issued steel helmets, arm bands, gas masks, first-aid kits and instructions. By the end of 1941, in fact, an astonishing fifteen thousand active volunteers were involved and ready to "render efficient service in the event of a bombing or acts of sabotage," as Mayor Conboy told City Council at the beginning of 1942. Sabotage perhaps. But bombers? Just how enemy planes with a range of about four hundred miles might attack Toronto is not at all clear. Still, at a time when U-boats were sinking ships in the St. Lawrence, the danger seemed real enough.

The Toronto Island was designated District E of Division I of the City ARP system. Centre Islander Alf Whisken was appointed as district warden, several "posts" were located in cottages on each of the main islands, and dozens of wardens were designated. Every few weeks, wardens and ordinary residents dutifully marched off to lectures and movies at one of the Island halls. On June 18, 1942, for example, they attended a lecture at Hanlan's Point clubhouse on gases "which can be expected to be used by the enemy whenever a raid comes to us." Then on July 2, 1942, representatives from across the Island met at the WIA clubhouse. After Ward's warden Ernie Hewitt, who also organized several minstrel shows, had tickled the ivories, the earnest lecturer discussed "High Explosives" and showed several dramatic British movies, including "It Can Happen Here," which of course was the guiding spirit behind ARP.[10]

The highest moments for Toronto's ARP system were the great Blackouts—the first being on June 18, 1941. Immediately before the alarm was sounded at ten-thirty, the Island, as seen from the top of the highest building in the Empire, the Canadian Imperial Bank of Commerce, was "a particularly bright patch and its lights fingered in reflection across the bay." There was a festive atmosphere throughout the downtown: some seventy-five thousand people swarmed to Sunnyside, and thousands more milled around City Hall with its giant Victory Loan thermometer still aglow. When the sirens and whistles wailed the alert, a "black curtain" swept across the city. Gaudy Sunnyside was plunged into darkness, as was Hanlan's Point across the bay. Yonge Street went black, as did the Main Drag. Over at Ward's Island, some of the girls enjoyed watching the show from the pier—with their mothers, or perhaps other friends. And overhead an ARP official reported a total blackout from Gap to Gap. Through it all, the Norwegian planes zoomed about, lending an air of reality to the exercise. When the powerful anti-aircraft searchlight in front of City Hall picked out the planes passing overhead, cheers rose from thousands of throats, although when an "enemy" plane scored a direct hit, causing smoke, flares and explosions to erupt in the area, the cheers turned to startled gasps. When the lights came on again all over Toronto, everyone had a shared sense of excitement and achievement. Toronto would be prepared if the Germans attacked. Moreover, it was a great public-relations exercise guaranteed to bump the Victory Loan thermometer a few degrees higher.[11]

The war and wartime regulations touched every facet of Island life. All too soon Ward's Islanders learned of their first casualty, Flight Sergeant Allan Bye, who went missing off the English coast on May 26, 1941. Early in 1942 Centre Island's Betty McGill (whose summer

A wartime family picnic at Centre Island. Even during such happy events, the war was ever present. On July 1, 1941, for example, when the largest crowd since 1931 swarmed over the Island "in full merry-making mood" to celebrate a sunny Dominion Day, yachters, bathers and picnickers could spot "a corvette steaming majestically across the horizon—a grim reminder that Canada and the Empire is fighting for the retention of the democratic freedom they were enjoying," according to the Globe and Mail.   [Val Fiedler]

romance of 1940 led to marriage and the birth of a son the following year) learned that her husband George had gone down in January during his first operational flight and had been made prisoner. (He was later one of the officers shot by the Gestapo in March 1944 when the famous "Great Escape" from Stalagluft III failed.) In May 1942 Duggan Roddy, also of Centre Island, who had married his wife Margaret a mere eight days before heading overseas, plunged into the North Sea when his Wellington bomber ran out of fuel returning from a raid. As soon as she learned of his death, Margaret joined the Red Cross and insisted on being sent overseas, where she remained to the end of the war.

Despite such personal tragedies, Island life went on. Every purchaser of an Island house now had to sign a declaration that he or she was neither an "enemy" within the meaning of the law, nor "acting as an agent or otherwise on behalf of any such agent." (Why this might have deterred any real enemy agent remains a mystery.) Rent control regulations slapped on by C. D. Howe's powerful Wartime Prices and Trade Board meant that the City could not raise ground rents when leases came up for renewal, a regulation that was no doubt warmly embraced by Island residents and the Royal Canadian Yacht Club when their leases came due.

The boys in Supervision, Ward's Island's version of summer day camp, like boys across the Island and the city, started collecting salvage to sell for the Red Cross—first just papers and later rubber, metal and rags as well. Ward's Island

was able—barely—to field four baseball teams in 1941 (ably assisted by new Islanders like Bill "Big Boy" Sewell, father of a future mayor). Some of those who had enlisted, like "Nifty" Ralph Naylor, were still able to get home on leave and work in a game of ball. But by 1942 resources were so depleted that only three teams could be mustered. Of the servicemen suggested for the *Ward's Island Weekly*'s dream "fourth" team, one (pitcher Allan Bye) was already dead, another (first baseman Colin Blaver) was a Japanese POW after the fall of Hong Kong, and several more would never play peacetime baseball again.

There was a constant coming and going of servicemen. Islanders with a homing instinct returned for weekend leaves and embarkation leaves, while hot city-trapped soldiers were invited over for dinner and an evening swim. Weary war workers, unable to get away for a longer holiday, also found their way to the Island to stay at places like the YWCA Holiday House at Centre for a weekend or a fortnight while they commuted back to their munitions plants in the city.

Traditional Island events all showed the signs of war. Music for the Ward's Island weekly dances was provided by records when Jim Bottomley was "urgently requested to do his tootling exclusively for the army." Ward's Island's Gala Day, much reduced in scope from prewar days, added a popular new attraction, "Hit Hitler"; unexpected guests graced the Senior Masquerades—like "Winston Churchill," "The Bulwark of Democracy" and "The Parachutist," who dropped in (not literally) in August 1941; and funds raised by the annual Minstrel Show were sent to war causes like the Red Cross British Bomb Victims' Fund.

In the summer of 'forty-two, as tire and gas rationing became more severe, Torontonians became "bicycle-minded." Many rusty cyclists dusted off ancient relics and wobbled off to join the two-wheeled traffic. Islanders, of course, had always been bicycle-minded, so residents and visitors alike provided ample business for the mushrooming "bicycle livery" and repair shops.

Stricter rationing also kept many Torontonians home on holiday weekends. Often they visited the Island. But on Dominion Day 1942 only a relatively small crowd ferried to the Island; more exciting entertainment was provided elsewhere. In the afternoon tanks rolled impressively across Riverdale Park to simulate an armoured attack. Then, in the evening thousands of spectators along a mile of waterfront witnessed a mock invasion of Sunnyside, which was taken "by a quick-descending force of invaders from ships well out from shore" in a lively illustration of the tactics expected to be used when the Second Front was opened in Europe. The attackers closed in on the defenders, opening up with bursts of their Bren and Tommy guns and finish-

Not far from where American troops had actually landed in April 1813 to capture York, on Dominion Day 1942 mock invaders approached Sunnyside Amusement Park in ships sweeping in from the lake off the western side of the Island. One group of attackers (including these grim-faced lads) jumped into waist-deep water and waded ashore in the face of simulated rifle and mortar fire. [CTA:GM]

The Centre Islander *of August 18, 1944 celebrates the hard-working juvenile salvage crew, their express wagons piled high with newspapers.* [MTLB]

SALVAGE DRIVE BY THE JUNIOR RED CROSS

SAVE YOUR PAPER AND BOTTLES

Phone Mrs. Del. Earle, WA. 0077 and these Busy Little Workers will pick them up.

ing off "the enemy" with bayonets and spirited hand-to-hand combat. If only Dieppe could have been captured as successfully as this position near Sunnyside's bandshell. But alas it was not to be so.[12]

For months Canadian troops had been languishing restlessly in Britain. Finally and disastrously the Long Wait was over. On August 19, 1942, an Allied force, including nearly five thousand Canadians, stormed the port of Dieppe at dawn. By the time picnickers were crossing to Toronto Island that day (including a group of immigrants from the war port of Greenock, Scotland), the Canadians were making a desperate and bloody retreat back to England, leaving nearly three thousand of their number dead, dying or captured.

In the spring of 'forty-three, General Montgomery and his "Desert Rats" may have been in hot pursuit of the Afrika Korps across the parched sands of North Africa, but back on Toronto Island there was plenty of water. Too much water, in fact, as the lake rose and the rains fell. By Victoria Day weekend in May (which was unusually quiet because every ounce of powder was now being used to make real explosives, not festive firecrackers) Island horticulturalists were thwarted from planting Victory or any other kind of gardens. Bowling greens were so soggy that balls nearly disappeared and skips were becoming skippers, and water was literally washing against the sides of some cottages. Members of the Centre Island Community Tennis Club daily checked their sodden courts, gloomily paddled their soggy way home and finally abandoned all hope of opening the club that season. By mid-June when a new lake level record was set, the Island was aptly described as a "water babies haven." Parts of the Main Drag were inundated, with narrow wooden

duckboard bridges providing the only crossings. Normally high-and-dry park benches could now be reached quite easily—by canoe. All water faucets at Pierson's Hotel were removed to prevent more water flowing into septic tanks and the kitchen of the Wayside Inn was flooded out. But as usual, according to the *Globe* of June 16, "Centre Island carried on."

So did Ward's Island. A *Casablanca* enthusiast chimed "You must remember this/The Island sure is bliss,/With water up so high./Our cottage soon will float away/As fog rolls by." Another local wag suggested as "the sidewalks turn into canals,/Why don't some enterprising pals/Get busy on a set of locks,/With gondola service to the docks." Shoppers might have welcomed a gondola service to the Main Drag, when stores halted home delivery service because of the flooding. And Controller Fred Hamilton joked that mosquitoes were so large on the Island this year that they were knocking bicycles off the sidewalks. "We're lucky," the *Weekly* cracked patriotically on July 31. "They are knocking factory buildings down in Germany." Ward's Islander Wing Commander Frank Hillock, in fact, was appreciating the "wooden wonder's" abilities. On patrol over Holland he crashed through some wireless cable which wrapped itself around the Mosquito's wing and fuselage. No matter. He still got home—and the copper wire was confiscated as valuable war salvage.[13]

Some Islanders became unnecessarily alarmed about the possibility of an epidemic. But, in contrast to the early 1950s and 1970s when unfriendly politicians eager to throw Islanders off the Island raised the spectre of a health menace, there was no move to close cottages. In fact, Island residents, not politicians, raised the alarm in 1943. In any event, Medical Officer of Health

Dr. Gordon Jackson pooh-poohed the possibility of an outbreak of typhoid fever.

Even when the Ward's Island baseball diamond was dry enough to play on, the community could not field two teams; so Ward's Islanders were reduced to following the far-flung careers of former baseball players like Ross Vaughn in Cairo and Bruce Randall in Malta and playing the occasional exhibition game against such city teams as the "very sporty" University of Toronto Air Force nine. Rationing was now so strict that the talented cooks of the Ward's War Effort group had to cancel their annual homebaking sale and hold a raffle for a quilt instead. Supervision children worked feverishly to raise enough money to buy the first of two special bicycle wheelchairs for the Red Cross Outpost at Hanlan's Point. The gift was named "Winnie" in honour of the British prime minister; so from then on "Winnie" sans cigar was often to be seen along the Main Drag and at various Island events.

The casualty lists grew and Island hearts particularly went out to people like Mr. and Mrs. Thompson of 612 Lakeshore who suffered a double shock on May 28. Just as they were recoiling from the horror of learning that their younger son, twenty-one-year-old Flight Officer Ivan, was missing, they received news that their older son Flight Sergeant Gordon had been shot down on an air ferry trip to North Africa and was in hospital recovering from "slight injuries." Gordon returned; Ivan did not.

Good news made its way to the Island as well. Ward's Islander George Shiels, for example, was on board the corvette *Oakville* (one of those uncomfortable but effective buckets-of-bolts that were doing so much to protect the North Atlantic convoys) when it sank a German U-boat and took on a number of prisoners. Then, on

Islanders after church outside St. Andrew's-by-the-Lake in the summer of 1944. [CI/MTLB]

August 30 Ward's Island gave a real hero's welcome to Wing Commander Frank Hillock— "one of the 500 fighter pilots of the first line who saved Britain in 1940," trumpeted the *Weekly* when he came home for a well-deserved extended leave. As he made his way slowly to the flag-bedecked Hillock residence from the docks, Frank said with becoming modesty, "It was all routine, you know." Hillock's leave, however, was not all rest and relaxation. He was one of the dashing fliers sent around for a Victory Loan Drive and he managed to pay a visit to the busy de Havilland Mosquito plant at Downsview where he shared a few front-line flying tales and bolstered war workers' morale.

In the fall of 1943, as Montgomery and his boys (including many Islanders) were slogging their way toward Cassino en route to Rome,

a large group of Islanders gathered in the Casino on the Main Drag to witness the birth of a new social—and political—organization, the Centre Island Association. There was nothing undercover about the new CIA. Unlike the Island Ratepayers Association founded in 1936, the CIA was to include renters as well as homeowners. It was to promote the interests of the Island and to include representatives of all the main Centre Island associations. With the permission of the powerful Wartime Prices and Trade Board, it was authorized to use scarce newsprint to publish the weekly *Centre Islander* to gather and voice opinions.

By 1944, as battle-hardened Allied forces pushed relentlessly up through Italy and Allied Command laid meticulous plans for the Invasion, some families had sent all their children off to

war—two, three and more sons and daughters were now at risk. Hanlan's Pointers and Centre Islanders, for example, were equally proud of the four paddling, battling Oldershaw boys and their brother-in-law who were spread through the three services—including Dick and Charlie who were in England awaiting D-Day and Tom, who was convalescing in Italy after catching some shrapnel in his knee early in 'forty-four. Tom could see from his hospital window the Isle of Capri, Italian fishing boats and lots of fellows swimming and lying on the beach—"a similar scene to what you would see at the Island on a busy day," as he wrote to his mother and the *Centre Islander*.

Then, June 6, 1944. D-Day. As then-Lieutenant Ben Dunkelman of the Queen's Own Rifles wrote in *Dual Allegiance*, the sky over the Channel was "black with skeins of aircraft droning their way towards France" to pound German positions; and the Channel was reassuringly "alive with vessels of every conceivable type and size." Many Islanders were aboard these vessels and were among the troops that hit the Normandy beaches shortly after dawn. Lieutenant Jack Choate of Ward's Island, for example, was in charge of one of the numerous landing craft which transported Canadian troops to France that day. Centre Islander Gordon Murray of the QOR had an uncomfortably narrow escape. The Bren-gun carrier he was in hit a mine as they approached shore and two buddies were killed instantly. Gordon was knocked out, but the shock of hitting the water quickly brought him to again. He climbed on another carrier, collected another rifle, and continued on into the fray. Engineer Captain George Smith of Ward's Island's Wiman Terrace hit the beach during the first hour and moved out successfully with the Royal Canadian Engineers.

The race to the Rhine was on. There was little time to rest or write or even think about anything but survival. So it was only on July 5 that Charlie Oldershaw crouched in his slit trench "with shells and mortar fire going on over head" to pen the first letter to reach the *Centre Islander* from Normandy. He had just finished reading an old *Centre Islander*, inconveniently interrupted by a mortar landing not six feet away. "I got covered in mud," he wrote calmly, "also the Islander got ripped but I read what was left." After relaying some colourful front line tales, Oldershaw concluded in his you-are-there style, "Well, the jerries are taking pot shots at us across a field, so I'd better sign off and get down to brass tacks."

As the Allied forces were fighting their way across Normandy, Lady Astor's "D-Day Dodgers" were slugging it out in "sunny Italy." Centre Islander (and former milkman) Fen Callaway certainly was taking in the sights, as he revealed in a letter in the *Centre Islander* of August 25. "Have travelled quite a bit since I wrote last. Have seen Ortona, Naples, Pompeii, Cassino, Monastery Hill, Hitler lines, etc. Naples is very picturesque, balconies, palm trees overlooking the blue water." The ancient ruins of Pompeii were memorable; but so were the modern ruins of Cassino which was by now "just so much rubble." All in all, in fact, the Grand Tour had its drawbacks in 1943-44. "The last battle was some battle," Callaway concluded. "The trees looked like fall with no leaves on and not one tree escaped having a few bullets or shrapnel holes in it. Saw quite a few of dead Germans and pools of...." Some of Callaway's Island acquaintances were also taking in the sights—and sometimes a bullet or a piece of shrapnel.

Back on the home front in 1944 record numbers of Torontonians crossed to the Island: 1.3 million, a peak for the TTC years. On Dominion Day the wharfs were so crowded that "compared to the ferry docks, a bargain basement was a morgue," reported the *Globe*. And a hot Sunday could attract so many picnickers that the congestion aboard the sturdy *Bluebell* and *Trillium*, according to another oppressed *Globe* reporter on August 14, was "something to frighten a sardine." Having miraculously survived the crush on board the ferries, the harried, overheated escapees from city life lined up for food, lined up for a changing room and lined up for the beach. In contrast to these overburdened, overworked, white-skinned city-dwellers, the tanned residents of the Island "stalked around barefooted and burdenless."

Centre Islanders hold a martial Mardi Gras on the Main Drag to raise money for the Island Red Cross Outpost and the new Centre Island Association. [Sun: Telegram Collection]

The familiar wartime routine continued. Centre, like Ward's, was unable to operate its usual baseball league and could only scare up enough players to participate in a modified Inter-Island series. The popular Centre Island "Cherokee" ball team was by now scattered to the four winds and the fabled 1942 Ward's Island "fourth team" was still taking casualties: Flight Officer Gordon Besley of Fourth Street, Ward's Island went missing June 13 while on anti-submarine patrol off Iceland and, at the other side of the world, Pilot Officer Ross Vaughan went missing in August while flying a Beaufighter over the Burma Jungle.

The Centre Island Association joined forces with the Red Cross unit to raise funds by organizing bingo, euchre, dancing, movies and

benefit concerts at the Casino to suit all tastes from "swing" to "nostalgia." Down at Ward's a record two thousand enthusiasts (including a row of invalids in a place of honour along the clubhouse verandah) attended a "Stupendous, Gigantic, Colossal" Senior Masquerade with the likes of "Susie the Welder." The war by now had taken most of their minstrel show endmen into the services (like former interlocutor POW Colin Blaver, whose weight had dropped to 125 lbs, but who kept up his morale by putting on a minstrel show in his Japanese camp). But a show had to go on: The Gay Nineties Review, which even featured servicemen home on leave singing "Roll Along Wavy Navy," "This Is the Army" and "Captains of the Clouds"— not exactly gay nineties material, but show-stoppers nonetheless.

Through it all, Island associations sent the local newspapers to Islanders far away who appreciated this contact with "home." Able Seaman George Shiels, for example, wrote in August 1944 from the dank confines of the HMCS *Lanark*, "Although I feel a tinge of nostalgia when I read them, I am more than glad that mother keeps sending them to me. They bring back pleasant memories of past summers, in the same way a certain melody may bring back the flavour of a past incident.... The 'Weekly,'" he concluded, "is the next best thing to being on the Island."

Soldiers' families anxiously followed the great march to victory. Mary Mallon, for example, had two brothers overseas, one in Italy and the other in Holland. She posted a large map of the European theatre and another of Italy on the shingled verandah wall of her Oriole Avenue cottage. Each day she read "The War Reviewed" by Hanlan's Pointer W. R. Plewman of the *Star* and moved pins across the maps. "You could

just see the trap closing on the Germans" until, eventually, her brothers met.

But the road to peace was a rough one. Flight Lieutenant Ralph "Nifty" Naylor, for example, was killed on March 26, 1945 when his Mosquito bomber crashed near Eindhoven, Holland. (His parents were undoubtedly deeply touched when they learned after the war that the pupils of a nearby primary school had "adopted" the grave of their son, keeping it well tended and supplied with fresh flowers.) Bruce Randall came down into a German farmyard and "from then on [did] not have any pleasant experience to relate" about his treatment in a German prison camp, according to the *Weekly*. Rifleman Tommy Swallwell of the Regina Rifles was badly wounded in action in Germany in March, but, he wrote his mother philosophically, I "am more than lucky to be alive."

The end of the war in Europe triggered wild celebrations from London to Toronto. In Halifax, which unwisely closed its liquor stores and tried to impose a curfew, celebrants turned into rioters; but in Toronto the celebrating remained enthusiastic and goodnatured, with revellers decorating their policemen as maypoles, rather than scuffling with them. May 8 was the official VE Day, but Torontonians, like Londoners, got the jump on officialdom, with street parades, pipers, ticker tape, bunting and fireworks spreading through the city. May 8 itself was more subdued, beginning with a sunrise service at Sunnyside and culminating in a thanksgiving service at midday in front of City Hall. Out on the bay, the somewhat diminished RCYC fleet dressed ship with everything in the flag locker and, over on the Island, in the bright early spring weather, visitors mingled with residents for the holiday. Then, the following Sunday, as Canadians across the country gathered

in local churches, sixty Islanders gathered in the Island Public School to celebrate a national Day of Thanksgiving for Victory.

Soldiers overseas were happy but relatively subdued. "We didn't do much celebrating, as most of us were just happy that we got through it O.K.," wrote Dick Oldershaw from Holland. In spite of the local dances and the movies shown every night, he was eager to get back to the Island: "I'd just love to get back in time to have a swim in the lake or go paddling down the lagoon in a shell. It seems funny but those are the things we dreamed about when we were in the slit trenches."

As the months of occupation dragged on, soldiers' eagerness to return home was palpable. Writing to "Hodgson Hacienda" on Centre Island, Ric Base commented, "At present I would very gladly trade with Tommy [Hodgson] the whole town of Neuenburg together with its Hitlerite handmaidens for the use of his backyard palace and a case of blackhorse ale." The non-fraternization policy, he commented, was working out pretty well, more especially because "the only German words I know are Nix and Nay and you can't even fraternize on Centre Island with a vocabulary of such limited proportions."

Back on the Island, hearts were lighter, but war work continued throughout the summer. Bob Saunders, that super popular, "atomic bundle" of a newsboy become mayor,[14] opened the annual Mardi Gras celebration at Centre Island. A Highland piper led the children's parade along the Main Drag; the ladies of the Red Cross operated a variety of booths, including home cooking (in spite of the ever-present rationing), white elephant and raffle tables; and everyone crowded "the deck" in the evening to enjoy dancing and open-air movies. Ladies from

When Ward's Island Supervision boys camped overnight at Snake Island, "it was obvious that sleep was a second thought for many of them," a tired Supervisor reported to the Ward's Island Weekly *of July 20, 1945.* [WIW/MTLB]

each of the main islands took turns entertaining casualties of both wars at the Island Red Cross Outpost. Supervision children raised enough money to buy a second wheelchair for the Outpost, but had plenty of energy left over for their usual round of recreational activities, like the ever-popular "overnight" to Snake Island, which had replaced Sunfish Island as a suitably wild and exotic destination when Sunfish was transformed into Algonquin Island.

The final end of the war came swiftly. As Ward's Islanders were enjoying a festive, but rainy, Gala Day, Japan "rocked … under the most devastating destructive force ever known to man."[15] On August 6, 1945, Hiroshima disappeared in a mushroom cloud that would irrevocably alter all life on earth. On August 14, after Nagasaki had also been blown up into atomic dust, Japan surrendered. "Toronto went noisily mad last night. Feelings pent-up by 5½ years of war suddenly burst like an atomic bomb," the *Globe and Mail* reported on August 15, with an unfortunate turn of phrase. Whatever the implications of the nuclear age might be,

the world war was over, and that was all that mattered.

Wednesday August 15 was officially V Day, but, as before, Torontonians began celebrating early and, for some reason, "ultra-Conservative Toronto went to Chinatown" to cavort happily along Elizabeth Street[16] while Ward's Islanders snaked noisily among their cottages in a Victory parade. Bonfires burst into flames on the beaches (only to be doused by the local constabulary). And "teenagers" (that new breed of humankind) boarded the Tuesday night ferry "dressed in their usual disreputable Island garb" the *Weekly* laughed, in order to parade "merrily up Bay Street, with the City joy-makers." Everyone recovered sufficiently to celebrate the official holiday. A great ballgame—with one team of servicemen—was thoroughly enjoyed by all. Doc Bruce Vale, back from a long campaign in Italy and Holland and still in uniform, umpired at first base and gave the servicemen all the breaks—to no-one's particular annoyance. Gala Day sports events, held over in anticipation of this *real* Gala Day, went off splendidly. Then, as

darkness fell, a grand display of fireworks poured their splendour out over the lake. Finally, a grand Victory Dance in the clubhouse brought the day to an exuberant close.

The war was over. The barbed wire around the Filtration Plant came down. City Council passed an $8.5 million postwar public works (and job creation) scheme, which included about $360,000 for Island improvements, mostly shore protection schemes. And the boys came home.

By summer 1946 the Island was more or less back to normal. On a rainy July 1 the Dominion Day regatta returned to Long Pond after a five-year, war-enforced blackout. Life also returned to normal out on the open waters of the lake. While Royal Canadian Yacht Club sailors with spinnakers flying competed once again for club trophies, a new breed of sailor emerged down at Ward's Island—the members of the Cove Fleet. Night after night during the winter of 1945, ardent yachtsman Jack Clapp had pored over a series of bewildering sketches with fellow sailors Ted Lye and Bob Torrence to create the remarkable little eight-foot Sabot Pram. Contemptuously dubbed a mere "bath tub toy" by old salts used to grander vessels, the tiny one-hundred-dollar yacht was designed to be cheap and safe, the ideal first boat for young mariners. So it proved to be. Clapp and Lye supervised the building of the dinky toy fleet and in May 1946 the first six prams got their bottoms wet—successfully crossing from the city on a day when a dirty squall whipped up the waters of the bay and kept larger boats cowering at their moorings. Thereafter the little pug-nosed vessels with the colourful sails and the wooden-shoe insignia were a common sight on the bay. The fleet grew. By August 1948, when Cove Fleet sailors sailed away with top honours at the Junior International Yacht Regatta to win the coveted Aphrodite Cup, bathtub yachting had come of age and Cove Fleet graduates would go on to make their mark in other boats and other waters. With the return of the servicemen, the baseball leagues were back in full swing. At Centre Island the formerly dispersed Cherokees were so far out in front that the other teams seemed to be lost in comparison. But down at Ward's the league race was the closest on record and former POW Colin Blaver was sufficiently recovered to hit .400, second only to batting champion Jack Bradley's .471.

For Ward's Islanders the symbolic return to civilian life came on July 31, 1946 with the grand "Farewell To Arms" banquet honouring the 135 men and women of Ward's who had gone to war and the nine who would never return. The clubhouse was resplendent with silk flags decorating the walls, red, white and blue bunting criss-crossing the ceiling, welcome-home pennants hanging along the balcony, two large Union Jacks draped from ceiling to railing and lavishly appointed tables arranged in a giant V. Veterans, friends and neighbours filled the clubhouse, and themselves, to bursting.

The end of the war also brought physical changes to the Island. Because the need for a summer convalescent home was expected to be greater than ever, the Red Cross spent $20,000 to renovate the twenty-two-year-old lodge in 1946. The piano was overhauled for the periodic concerts and sing-alongs conducted by Islanders and other entertainers, and a new library, radio and record player were added to the recreational facilities. For all the renovations, however, veterans of the Second War were not as eager to visit the Island Outpost as the older men. Times had changed and the younger men seemed to prefer life in the city, where even those in walking casts could get to a movie on their hospital leaves. But the ''old warriors'' were quite content with things as they were; so for the next five or six years, veterans of the First War continued to be brought by car and ambulance across the Airport to their shady, sprawling old summer home by the lake and Island men and women continued to donate fruit, cigarettes, boats and time to their cause.

(Above) *"Chubby" Henderson (left) and the other 1948 Aphrodite Cup winners pose for the* Ward's Island Weekly. [MTLB]

(Left) *Island Canoe Club members prepare for the 1946 regatta season in this* Centre Islander *photograph by Sir Ellsworth Flavelle. The Dominion Day regatta featured the younger generation, but paddling and war veterans Bert Oldershaw and Bill Stevenson showed the crowds what the oldsters could do by paddling away with the senior tandem, en route to the 1948 London Olympics.* [MTLB]

In 1946 the Centre Island Association finally got its clubhouse. After being denied a building permit during the war on the grounds that more essential construction was required, the CIA circumvented postwar shortages by buying an RCAF equipment depot at the foot of Yonge Street, dismantling it and transporting the precious sections of the finest seasoned lumber across the bay to its shady new site near Long Pond, just south of where the old Island Amateur Aquatic Association clubhouse used to stand. By early August the foundations were ready and by the end of August the race was on to raise both the building and the funds by winter. While most Torontonians were cheering Viscount Montgomery during his fleeting visit on August 31, Centre Islanders were loyally patrolling the Main Drag instead of Bay Street for yet another ''Big Street Jamboree'' to raise funds for their building. And before long, Centre Islanders' dream of having a place for holding community events under their own roof was a reality.

The major development of the 1940s was the growth of the winter and year-round community, from a few hundred to a couple of thousand souls. This had a profound effect not only on the physical and social fabric of the Island, but also on its political future. During the late forties and early fifties, most City politicians still regarded the Island as a summer resort (or, at most, as a temporary year-round community), whereas this new breed of Islander regarded the Island as *home* and was prepared to fight to keep and improve it.

During the war and just after it, however, City politicians had temporarily looked to the Island as an antidote to the acute housing shortage created when soldiers, war workers, and their families poured into Toronto. Strict regulations, therefore, were enacted to ensure that only

Former infantryman John Singer finds his old uniform warm and comfortable while he delivers bread by sled in February 1945. Behind him is Perc. Hughes, the only store open during the winter.   [Sun: Telegram Collection]

''essential war workers'' were allowed to move to the city. Even summer residents were affected when the Island was included in the ''Toronto Congested Area'': people wishing to rent a couple of housekeeping rooms at Ward's Island for the summer, for example, were required to obtain a permit as a safeguard against non-essential outsiders entering the Toronto congested area and ferrying to work.

The housing situation had become so tight that even in a wet summer like that of 1943, with water up to the front doors and rumours of

typhoid in the air, accommodation on the Island was often better than anything available in the city. ''We rented for that summer and we took the twins over there when they were five weeks old,'' Mrs. Tony Hopp of Algonquin Island recalled thirty years later. ''I had to take the washing out on the wagon and wear rubber boots to hang up the diapers in the backyard.... But I didn't have any choice. We either had to sit beside a railroad or come over here.'' And other summer residents who had been accustomed to renting an apartment in the city for the winter, had to make a choice: the mainland or the Island. Increasing numbers chose the latter.

Faced with this housing crisis, the City began casting covetous glances toward the Island. In 1942, for example, it had conducted a survey of how many Island houses could be used in the winter and ordered the Toronto Transportation Commission to extend its regular ferry service from October 16 to November 30 ''to encourage people to remain in residence at the Island,'' though for the time being, the City remained somewhat ambivalent about the degree of *encouragement* it would give to people to move to the Island for year-round residence.[17]

With or without official help, during the war more and more residents began braving the rigours of an Island winter and rediscovering ''the satisfaction of small-town life.'' There were euchre parties to raise money for smokes for the Island boys on active service; the teenage dances every Saturday night at the Manitou Hotel under the name of the ''Barefoot Bums'''; the Island hockey teams practising slapshots on the lagoons; Ladies Guild meetings to sew thousands of slings and perform other Red Cross work; village shopping at PC Hughes, the only store open anywhere on the Island; and so on. ''I've made more friends since I've been over here than I did in all my life in Toronto,'' boasted one refugee from the housing crisis in February 1945, who now snuggled happily into an upstairs apartment heated by a Quebec heater. Meanwhile, about sixty-five members of the younger generation trudged through the snowdrifts to the little two-room country school that doubled as a church on Sundays. The police and firemen, for their part, found life pretty dull: the biggest excitement of the day being the morning pilgrimage of an old gentleman dubbed ''Arthur Mometer'' up to the station to check the temperature.[18]

Primary schoolers show the flag outside the two-room Island school in February 1945.
[Sun: Telegram *Collection*]

In the off-season, voyagers to the city clambered aboard the sturdy steel-hulled *Ned Hanlan*—christened ''Headache Hall'' by occupants of its inky depths as it crunched noisily through ice floes to the city. Inventive Islanders found other ways to cross the bay. When it was frozen solid, many Islanders walked, aided by a guiding line of Christmas trees planted in the ice at the end of the festive season. And some well-balanced Islanders even rode bicycles across the slippery highway, though ''sudden turns would result in nasty bumps,'' according to Harold Aitken.

When the bay was open, some Island residents had their own boats, which was usually a good way to beat the limited tug and ferry services. But even this form of travel was sometimes treacherous. Fram Ward recalled one tragic St. Patrick's Day accident during the war when it was ''blowing a howling hurricane'' from the east. One man with an outboard offered to give three or four other Islanders a ride home after their evening's celebrating. About five got in the boat and made it as far as the ferry dock at Hanlan's where the waves swamped them. ''You could even see all their fingernails were torn where they were trying to grab hold of the icy pier,'' he reflected grimly. None succeeded.

Winter Islanders still had no resident doctor during the war. ''But we're healthy,'' they chirped. ''We don't need one.''[19] And there was always generous Dr. Norman ''Joe'' Howard, Alan Howard's father, who was a bacteriologist and Toronto's Director of Water Purification. He provided free emergency care for more than thirty years and saved many lives.

The recently formed Centre Island Association was also pleased to report a number of modest gains for the winter community—winter postal delivery, improved garbage collection and better snow removal thanks to the airport bulldozer

The family of war veteran W. H. Lewin move into their new Island winter home on September 28, 1945. [Sun: Telegram *Collection*]

which cleaned the two feet of snow dumped by the Great Blizzard of December 12, 1944. The ten-foot drifts were simply too much for the Island's one lonely horse behind an old-fashioned wooden snow plough to cope with. Such gains may have been small, but they were significant in terms of recognition by City Hall.

While increased numbers of woolly denizens of the drifts were digging in for the winter at Centre and Hanlan's, Ward's Island was still almost deserted. Only Fram Ward and his family had returned in 1945 to winter in the former family fiefdom after an absence of some years.

(Far left) *Petty Officer B. M. Tomkins and his wife unload lumber in September 1945 to make their new Island quarters suitable for winter occupancy.* [Sun: Telegram *Collection*]

Describing his fellow-Islanders of the early 1950s as "some of the zaniest citizens allowed to run around without a leash," author Hugh Garner went on to describe the Manitou Hotel lounge as "the only beer parlour in Ontario where patrons have to watch out for kids on tricycles riding around the tables." Here some older, teenaged patrons of the hotel listen to the beat of the jukebox in January 1947.
[Sun: Telegram *Collection*]

The soon-to-be renovated and decapitated Ward's Hotel was still shut tight,[20] the Wiman Buildings and the little cottages were dark and shuttered and mounds of fairy-white snow were piled high.

But here and across the Island, the winter population grew by leaps and bounds during the continuing postwar housing crisis.[21] Some of the recent winter immigrants hunkered down contentedly in well-insulated rooms, while others simply had to make do with drafty places, complete with nail holes and ill-hung doors, because they had "nowhere else to go." They taped up the windows, bought electric and coal heaters, left the water running so pipes wouldn't freeze (or tapped the nearest fire hydrant) and bought lots of woollies. "It's amazing what a few sweaters will do, and heavy socks," those who had braved previous winters counselled the newcomers.[22] To those just back from overseas, however, these were not great hardships, as former Centre and Algonquin Islander Mary Madrick pointed out. "Even if we were only in one room with two kids, we were home."

Moreover, "we were young, most of us, and we rather enjoyed being different. Because we *were* different." They were another generation of the enduring non-conformists who have always populated the Island.

The bustling, tremendously tightly-knit community indulged in all sorts of communal activities, like the great Christmas festival along a snowy Main Drag decked out with coloured lights, complete with carols, bitter cold and jolly old Saint Nick dispensing presents to each child. More stores began to stay open along the Main Drag, while more and more trucks rumbled and skidded around Island streets during the off-season delivering coal, milk, bread, groceries and goodies from Eaton's and Simpsons to the thirteen hundred or so winter residents. And the Manitou Hotel continued to be a gathering place for everybody on Centre—for card-playing and

beer-drinking adults and for be-bopping teenagers who warmed their toes and their souls around the shiny, loud-mouthed Wurlitzer jukebox in the main lounge.

New organizations and forms of entertainment attracted winter residents from across the Island to Centre. Island veterans, for example, decided to form a branch of the Canadian Legion there in the late forties. By June 1950 it had a hundred members who gathered for darts, cards and conversation at places like Fran's Wayside Inn until they built their own clubhouse on Iroquois at the north end of Mohawk Avenue. Six "very fine alleys" which were "on a par with any city bowling alleys" according to the *Ward's Island Weekly*, replaced the well-worn but distinguished old dance floor at Ginn's Casino in 1950. And the seven-hundred-seat, gray-stone, "art moderne" style Island Theatre opened on Iroquois just west of the Main Drag in the fall of 1950. At last, the *Weekly* boasted, Islanders could see the "latest pictures from Hollywood" without making the long, cold, sometimes unpredictable trek to the city.

Old Island institutions, like the school and St. Andrew's-by-the-Lake, also grew and changed with the community. By June 1948, when a Home and School Association was formed, with representatives from each of the communities, the school facilities were taxed to the utmost with overcrowding. Parents of over-energetic four- and five-year-olds were clamouring for a kindergarten. But no luck. Regular classes were already spilling over into temporary quarters. The school was growing at a phenomenal rate: from only 68 in December 1946 to 256 in December 1950, and to a winter peak of 534 in December 1954. Even before the first two-room addition was authorized in 1947, the Toronto director of education was recommending that another four-room addition be built. And when *this* addition was opened, pressure had already mounted for another.

Changes were also made at St. Andrew's-by-the-Lake. The church was first heated and opened for winter services in 1945. The following year, the Rectory was winterized and on December 1, 1947, the energetic Reverend Trevor Jones moved in to become the first full-time pastor on the Island. Reverend Jones threw himself into community life, including political life. But the most visible product of his pastorship was the Parish Hall, built in 1952-53 to provide a year-round, central location not only for church activities, but also for girl guides, boy scouts, and other Island groups. It was "a real community project," according to former Centre Islander Mrs. Alice Aitken. "The minister even mixed the cement." The whole Island, from Gap to Gap, became involved, although Lake Ontario almost vetoed the whole project by rising so high in 1952 as to flood much of the Island. But ingenious schemes were devised to outwit the lake and proceed with the work.

Appropriately enough, a gang of sturdy lads laid the floor in one Labour Day and everyone was so jubilant that lights were strung up with extension chords and an impromptu square dance thumped and swirled to celebrate the occasion. Church members were kept busy all fall and on into the new year. At last, on January 30, 1953, the job was finished. The permanent lights were turned on and the hall was ready for use.

The winter community grew not only at Centre but all over the Island. The barracks-like Lakeside Home was converted into small housing units and renamed Chetwood Terrace. By the time the Schoenborn family arrived in 1951, over a hundred people, with relatively little money but lots of children, lived in this new Island settlement. As German emigrés, the Schoenborns were surprised, and delighted, by the warm welcome they received. "We were in

Before moving to barrack-like Chetwood Terrace, the Schoenborn family lived for the summer at "romantic" 11 Clandeboye Avenue, with ten wooden pillars and a lagoon at the front. [Al Schoenborn]

our new apartment in Chetwood Terrace,'' Al Schoenborn recalled, ''when someone knocked on the door and said, 'I'm your new neighbour. Tomorrow's a dance. We hope you will come.''' Some Canadian customs, however, were puzzling. Their three little boys were scared when some strange-looking creatures also knocked on the door, but they were soon soothed when the significance of October 31 was made clear. ''It was Halloween,'' Luise Schoenborn laughed, ''and we had no idea what Halloween was!''

The main Hanlan's community was also growing. Their pretty little white church, Emmanuel, was closed, so churchgoers converged on St. Andrews, but in 1948 the local grocery store at last stayed open—no more long treks hauling wagons and toboggans down to the Main Drag and back. In 1947, the Hanlan's clubhouse was heated and remodelled as a year-round community centre that hosted everything from concerts and meetings to amateur theatricals. And, in order to alleviate some of the pressure from their juvenile members, Hanlan's Point residents started a nursery school at the renovated clubhouse in 1948.

At the other end of the Island, Algonquin was undergoing a radical transformation: a building boom, accompanied by conversion to year-round living. At the end of the war there were still only about fifty cottages, most of which had been moved down from the Western Sandbar in 1938 and plunked on the periphery. Only a handful of these owners were winter residents. By May 1949, however, there were eighty-nine cottages and a substantial winter community. Many of these new cottages lining the interior streets were built by returned veterans with their veterans' grants and, in many cases, the sweat of their brows. They built their tidy little postwar bungalows in spite of the fact that they, like other Algonquinites, had leases with

Postwar bungalow building on Algonquin Island: by May 1951, all 107 Algonquin lots had been built on. [CTA:TIA]

non-compensation clauses: if the City terminated the leases in 1968 (the termination date established for all Algonquin leases) they would receive no money for their houses. One of these vets was fireman Fred Mazza. He and his wife and their infant twins had all been living with his parents until 1948 when he applied to the City for a lot on Algonquin. ''I was glad to get the place, so I wasn't worried about the terms of the lease,'' he commented later to the *Globe and Mail* when a number of dire plans were floating around. ''But Controller Innes said no political body would ever throw a veteran out of his home,'' he observed bitterly some years later, on the eve of possible eviction.

Compensation or not, security or not, the winter community on Algonquin grew apace after the war and developed into the usual active and tightly knit Island community, holding

bridge parties, skating on the lagoon and working toward a common goal, in this case, the Algonquin Island Association (AIA) clubhouse, which was built around 1951. This winterized, brown-stained barn of a building immediately became the focus of Algonquin community life, sheltering everything from Sunday School, bridge club, drama society, badminton and square dancing to special events like the Christmas Party and the travelling ''Tug Boat Follies'' from Centre Island.

Across the frozen lagoon, where miniature Barbara Ann Scotts practised their own versions of a sitz-spin, Fram Ward began to have winter company: in 1946 four families stayed, in 1947 twelve, in 1948 about thirty-seven and, from then on, it just ''pyramided,'' according to Ward. In those early years, winter life at Ward's was not exactly luxurious, even by Island standards. "I had babies. I had no water in the house and no toilet," Mardi Webster said of her first winter in an unwinterized summer cottage. She went down to the nearest fire hydrant for water and to the public washrooms warmed by space heaters for other amenities. Somewhat less rugged souls made sure that their cottages were properly insulated, with all the cracks sealed up and the sides banked up, and stoutly maintained that they were "as comfortable as in a city home."[23] Insulated or not, Ward's was beautiful in winter. And it was fun. "There was always a party going on," the sociable Mrs. Webster emphasized. Then in 1948, with the Ward's Island Association clubhouse closed up tight for the winter, Tony Hopp's store in the remodelled former hotel became a kind of social club, where Ward's Islanders gathered to play euchre or cribbage or, when TV came in, to watch Ed Sullivan or bet on the fights. At Christmas, an Island-hopping Santa visited Tony's and handed presents out to the forty excited children gathered there. And Island cottages were so brightly decorated and the open house hospitality so festive that "even the occupants glowed" according to the *Weekly* of June 1950.

Transportation, however, remained the bugaboo of winter life and a perennial flash point in relations with the City. Anyone left shivering in the cold for over an hour while full boats passed by without stopping was bound to get hot under the collar. The City, of course, was well aware that reliable, relatively convenient service was essential to allow—or even *persuade*— Islanders to stay on the Island in winter. But rather than improving the service in order to encourage people to stay, the City only *reacted* to periodic prodding from disgruntled Islanders. In the fall of 1946, for example, it was only after a deputation of Islanders went down to City Hall to speak in public before the Parks Com-

(Below) *The* Centre Islander *celebrates the newest in Island winterwear.* [MTLB]

mittee and in private with Mayor Saunders and a group of civic officials that the City made several necessary improvements. These included hiring a third icebreaking tug, the *J. C. Stewart*, to join the *G. R. Geary* and the *Ned Hanlan* on the winter route to Hanlan's Point and the Filtration Plant docks, and providing the first bus to carry passengers from the east end to the Filtration Plant. Most Ward's and Algonquin residents were appreciative but not all. One old Islander growled when he saw the new bus, "Humph. The Island's getting to be too soft. Just like the city." The ultimate insult.

He needn't have worried. At best, the rigours of winter travel were still substantial. In the "freezing blackness of the predawn hour," the trio of "snub-nosed, stout-hearted, thick-skinned tugs" ground and crashed their way across the bay "come blizzard, or sleet or hail or foot thick ice." Anyone "allergic to the roll of a ship is hereby advised to avoid the first Island trip each day," cautioned *Globe* reporter Arthur Cole

His name's Crusoe. Says his family have always been Islanders.

in January 1947. The lucky ones could clamber down the steel stairs into the hull, but the others had to remain on deck despite the fact that "an outside voyage across Toronto Bay in mid-winter can result in severe frostbite to exposed portions." So Islanders adopted the multilayered mode of dress that has always distinguished them from their elegant but effete city cousins.

The new Island bus service from "Tony's" to the Filtration Plant was not exactly like the Rosedale bus. The "Black Maria" panel truck was dark, dank and perpetually crowded. Of necessity there was method to the madness within. "The boys got in first. The wives were on their lap. The kids on top. All the dogs and sleighs underneath the seats," Mary Madrick explained. Then this mass of teeming humanity bumped and joggled its way down to the dock, while the overflow was left in its frosty wake, still walking. In spite of such difficulties and the constant tug of war with the City, most Islanders would never have considered moving to the mainland. "I don't mind working there," said one incredulous, wide-eyed young lady

the next January after another foul-up. "But I'd never want to live there."[24] Instead the Islanders began to flex their political muscles. They would rather fight than switch.

The other major issue that periodically pitted Islander against City Hall officials was high water and flooding. In spring 1947, when the waters of Lake Ontario reached and then surpassed the record of 1943, Islanders went on the warpath. Ward's and Centre Islands were the hardest hit, although Hanlan's Point was by no means spared. Fierce gales swept the high lake waters right over the patently inadequate southern breakwater, bay waters ate away at northern shores and lagoon banks at both Hanlan's and Ward's and unusually heavy rains continued

to pelt the already sodden ground. Water swirled down the Main Drag, inundated lawns and invaded basements. Only the hundred or so ducks paddling across the flooded picnic grounds were happy. By contrast, merchants at Centre Island were "up in arms" at what they considered to be "the continued negligence of City Council to protect them from flood damage and resultant loss of business because of heavy rains and lack of drainage."[25] They dug a ditch to drain the twenty-foot pavement along Manitou Road and lambasted City Hall—to little effect. After prodding by both man and nature, City Council was still only willing to lay temporary sidewalks and construct small breakwaters along Hanlan's Hiawatha Avenue and Ward's Bayview Avenue. It was not yet willing to raise the long southern breakwater, a much more substantial and expensive improvement.

Islanders, as usual, soldiered on. Many summer cottagers were delayed, but still packed their rain gear and ventured across the bay, somewhat unsure where the bay stopped and the Island began. There may have been no toilets, no tennis, no bowling and no badminton, but there was lots of spirit. "There is nothing impossible on Ward's Island, Toilets or no Toilets, come Hell or High Water," chanted the *Weekly* encouragingly on August 15. The dismal downpours played havoc with Supervision schedules, but a new, somewhat waterlogged, generation of Islanders began their athletic careers, like future mayor John Sewell who jumped and raced to third place finishes in the Gala Day events for six-to-eight-year-old boys, while his father built a sturdy stone breakwater to fend off flooding near 94 Lakeshore Avenue. Inter-Island Baseball was washed out, but determined Ward's ballplayers rode out the storms and dashed onto their own diamond whenever the centrefield was not "a

Manitou Road merchants try to keep flood waters at bay, June 8, 1947. [CTA:GM]

combination of deep mud and water among the tall grass.'' Then, hallelujah, in early August, the weather broke, baseball was immediately back in full swing and the Island was happy again.

It was during this soggy summer of 1947 that a new Island ship of state was launched: the Inter-Island Council (IIC). The four existing residents' associations now banded together to deal with matters that concerned them all and to present a united front to City Hall. The creation of the IIC marked a turning point in the evolution of Islanders' political behaviour. From then on, Islanders went on the offensive. For example, in its first ''Brief on Transportation,'' presented in April 1948, the IIC fiercely attacked both the Toronto Transportation Commission and the City. ''What has the TTC or the City done to decrease deficits by attracting summer visitors to the Island?'' it asked rhetorically. ''Even if the TTC had campaigned to stimulate ferry-travel, what has there been to offer additional people they might have brought across the bay? How many people would make a second trip after seeing the deplorable state of the Island? How many would wade barefoot a second time along walks that should have been raised?'' And so on. The gloves were off. Ferry deficits were not the fault of Island residents (as some politicians were charging). They were the fault of the TTC and the City. Transportation was a mess. And the Island was a mess. By the end of the forties, therefore, it was clear that Islanders had found a political voice. Whether it would be strong enough would soon be tested.

In December 1947 the Toronto City Planning Board (TCPB) set the Island planning merry-go-round pumping and whirling. For the next seven or eight years a mind-numbing assortment of Island plans were splashed across the front pages of the Toronto dailies, calling for everything

August 16, 1947: floods may come and go, but life carries on.   [CTA:GM]

from wildlife sanctuaries to warehouses and commercial dockyards. In December 1947 the TCPB was careful to emphasize that it did not endorse its preliminary Island plan, but was merely presenting it to stimulate interest. Nevertheless, the 1947 proposal closely resembled plans later endorsed by the board in 1949 and 1953 and provided the context for all future discussions. It was therefore much more than a mere curiosity along the Island's tortuous route to becoming a Metro park.

What did the TCPB propose? For the first time, a civic body suggested eliminating all existing housing (though not all residents) and

replacing it with more ''permanent'' buildings (including apartments and hotels) along Manitou Road and the Lakeshore. And for the umpteenth time, a civic body recommended building a tunnel under the Western Gap, along with a cross-Island highway and parking for five thousand cars.

Islanders were not amused. Although the TCPB plan did not pose an immediate threat to all residents (work would have begun on uninhabited Mugg's Island, cottages would be eliminated only when deemed ''obsolete'' and new permanent housing would replace the frame houses), adoption of the report would

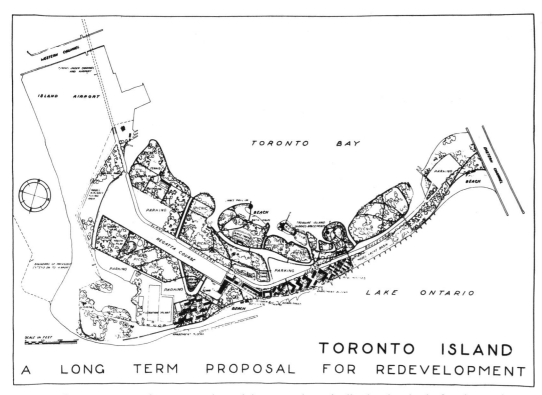

TORONTO ISLAND
A LONG TERM PROPOSAL FOR REDEVELOPMENT

In 1947, the Toronto City Planning Board issued this proposal to radically alter the Island. If implemented, Ward's Island would have been turned into a parking lot, Algonquin Island into picnic grounds, and Manitou Road into a shopping centre for new apartment dwellers and hotel guests. [City of Toronto]

sound the death knell of the Island community as it then existed.

The TCPB proposal was designed to stimulate debate. And stimulate debate it did. Public meetings were held across the city, IIC members sharpened their pencils and their tongues as they prepared an appropriate response and City politicians struggled vainly through the spring to come to terms with the Island's future. But Islanders and politicians could agree only on the need for a long-range plan.[26]

While Inter-Island Council members spent the summer of 1948 contemplating the Island's future (including a proposal to call in all leases by 1968 and a $3 million tunnel-highway-sand plan to raise and develop the Island), Island residents and visitors frolicked as usual. On a wonderfully sunny Dominion Day, the Centre Island Association created a miniature midway along Manitou Road, while swimmers, paddlers and rowers created a "three-ring aquatic circus" out on Long Pond.[27] Island Canoe Club stars

Bert Oldershaw and William Stevenson, who were just about to leave for the London Olympics, gave the hometown crowd something to cheer about as they narrowly won the Senior Tandem. And that political ringmaster Alderman Allan Lamport announced to general applause that the City would spend $65,000 to improve the regatta course. Happy officials heaped praise on the alderman and even suggested renaming Long Pond, "Lamport Pond." (Before long, however, other Island officials would be heaping abuse, not praise, on the alderman, who would reply in kind.[28])

Then, in mid-August, Centre Islanders put on the second edition of the "Ferryboat Follies" at the CIA clubhouse. The Follies engaged the talents of all manner of Islanders from salesgirls and office boys to football players and mechanics—the common element being "a defiant, collective nose-thumbing across the bay at the big, bad city." The 1950 edition even got political: the son of "a villainous Bay Street big-shot who planned to lease the Islands, evict all residents and turn the Islands into a rich man's pleasure resort" fell in love with a comely Island girl and threw "a monkey-wrench into the old man's vicious scheme."[29] If only real life could have been so easy.

The IIC tried to fashion its own monkey wrench and, on August 12, 1948, issued a strongly-worded proposal to enhance the *status quo*. Stoutly rejecting all grandiose schemes to build tunnels or apartments or hotels, it, not surprisingly, suggested that the existing assets of the Island—its parkland, its beaches, its lagoons and, of course, its existing residential communities—should all be improved—not radically altered or eliminated. For the first time, Islanders argued that the residential areas could be a positive

An Eaton's delivery man prepares for his Island rounds on April 18, 1949. [Sun: Telegram *Collection*]

attraction—a "decoration" to the park as they put it. This was an idea whose time would come not in the 1950s or even in the 1960s, but in the seventies and eighties.

The City failed to come to grips with the future of the Island in the fall of 1948, but it did manage to scare residents by reviewing its lease policy. For once civic inaction worked to the Islanders' benefit. Council deferred any decision on whether or not to terminate leases in 1968 or to change lease conditions until the Island's future was decided. But the climate of uncertainty remained. At the very least, the City still contemplated removing all present residents in 1968, possibly before. From this time on, the sword of Damocles dangled over Islanders' heads.

During the late 1940s and early 1950s, zoot-suited "gangs" roamed Toronto's streets looking for action—taking over a soda fountain here, a dance hall there—and generally shocking (even thrilling) the conservative local populace. In early 1949 "well ordered, law abiding" Ward's Islanders were most distressed to learn that city "hooligans" had even crossed the bay to invade the Island. Down at Hanlan's Point, the Dovercourt Beanery Boys and the Junction Gang had already shouldered their way into the Teen Terrace where they created such a disturbance that "the police had thrown up their hands" and padlocked both Hanlan's Point dance halls to clear out the miscreants.[30] And early in that same year "Ward's was subjected to a visit of young Toronto hooligans of both sexes," the *Weekly* reported. "In the short space of hours they turned our little Island paradise into a little hell on earth." No details were given.

Anxious to prevent any repetition, the Ward's Island Association vowed to screen all visitors "carefully," to patrol the beaches "vigilantly" and to report to the executive the name of any young person who played "host to visiting hooligans." "We intend preserving that wholesome, well-ordered community life which has nurtured three generations of Ward's Island youngsters into honourable maturity and clean citizenship," the *Weekly* trumpeted. And indeed no further incidents seem to have marred that summer's fun.

Meanwhile, Centre, "the hoyden of the 1930's and 1940's," according to *Globe* reporter Cameron Smith, was doing roaring business, with its "beer hall in the Manitou Hotel that turned out free-wheeling revellers almost every night of the week," its "garish stores on Manitou Road that crushed between them shoppers,

oglers and visitors who pushed and shouted and sweated and loved every minute of it" and its "riotous Saturday night dances that made tongues cluck on other parts of the Island." According to former Hanlan's Pointer Jimmy Jones, "Centre Island was the playground and you'd go there to whoop it up. Whatever you wanted to do," he commented wisely, "you went to Centre Island to do it. You didn't do it in your own backyard."

As Islanders prepared for a busy fall of planning confrontations, Toronto was rocked by the worst waterfront tragedy in its history. On the evening of September 16, 1949, the white luxury liner *Noronic* rounded the Island, passed Island ferries and nosed in to tie up at Canada Steamship Line Pier 9 beside the *Cayuga* and *Kingston*. Around 2:30 A.M., when most of her American tourists were all snug in their beds, all hell broke loose. Within half an hour the ship was "a blazing inferno" and the first explosions were tearing her apart. Panicked pyjama-clad passengers jumped into the bay, whether they could swim or not. Fire engines screamed from across the city bringing a thousand firemen to battle the "holocaust" on the waterfront. The following day, fifty thousand curious onlookers poured into the area, creating the worst traffic jam in recent years—all to gaze on the twisted, blackened hull that had become a deathtrap for over a hundred people. "Holocausts and catastrophes are something you read about," an obviously stunned Lotta Dempsey reported in the *Globe and Mail*. "They don't happen in Toronto harbor." But on September 17, 1949, tragedy did strike[31] and until November when the hull of the *Noronic* was towed out the Western Gap en route to the Hamilton scrap furnaces, Island residents passed the grim, silent remains

When the Noronic *burst into flames "which cast a glow in the sky like a battery of blast furnaces," the fire tug* Charles Reed *(right) steamed from its berth at Centre Island, and across the bay to play all its hoses on the burning luxury liner. As over a thousand firemen fought the exploding blaze, "burned, battered, bleeding and shocked people" wandered the dockside, and ambulances and taxicabs rushed the injured off to hospitals and emergency Red Cross posts set up at the elegant King Edward and Royal York Hotels.*   [YUA:TC]

every time they ferried back and forth to the mainland.

Inter-Island Council members—and other Islanders—made many trips to City Hall that fall to respond to the relevant sections of the Toronto City Planning Board's Official Plan for the whole city. The approval process was lengthy and tortuous, made all the more complex by Islanders' stout rejection of the Planning Board's recommendations to raise the level of the Island, to replace existing housing with apartments and hotels and to build a cross-Island motor

highway.[32] Finally, on November 21, 1949, City Council dealt with its first Official Plan. Six hours of debate swirled around the plan, most of it dealing with the Island section. Mayor Hiram E. McCallum—a rabid anti-communist—could barely control his contempt for Islanders' communist alderman Norman Freed. Islanders' other alderman, Nathan Phillips, gamely put forward a motion to substitute the Inter-Island Council plan for the Toronto City Planning Board proposals in the Official Plan. The motion lost 9-10. And a compromise motion (to raise

the level of the Island, to build a highway, but *not* to demolish existing housing) was passed instead. As a result of hard work, numerous appearances at City Hall and the issuing of toughly worded statements, Islanders won a partial victory; there would be no references in the Official Plan to terminating the leases or demolishing existing housing on the Island. The future of the residential areas was left open. Islanders, however, came within a whisker of winning a *total* victory at this 1949 meeting. If they had, the whole future of the Island might have been very different. The continued existence of the residential community would have been a more or less settled fact, not an open issue.

The Island may have been included in the City's 1949 Official Plan, but nothing concrete (or otherwise) came of it, as 1950 provided Islanders with a breathing spell. Lawn bowlers could concentrate on bowling, baseball players on baseball and paddlers on paddling. The Island Canoe Club reached peak form at the annual Dominion Day regatta, mopping up the opposition as effectively as the North Koreans who had roared across the border a week earlier in a headlong dash toward Seoul. Soon more young Canadians would be off to war.

The decade, however, started off with an agreeable bang for future mayor Allan Lamport. On January 2, 1950, Toronto voters supported Lampy's pet project, Sunday Sports, and sent him hurtling along the political track toward the mayor's chair in 1952. Sunday visitors, for all their sins, would now be able to bowl down the six outdoor alleys of the "Centre Island Bowla-way" on the Main Drag.

Spring 1950 saw the end of the tenting era on Ward's Island: the final two tents were folded up and replaced by cottages. And fall brought the retirement of little Minnie Rorke who had run the grocery store since the mid-1930s. She was suitably fêted by all her Ward's Island neighbours, who threw a surprise candlelight dinner at "Tony's" refreshment parlour. Tony Hopp then took over the operation of both stores in the old Ward's Hotel.

Down at wild and deserted Mugg's Island that spring, the Island Yacht Club was born. As war hero Ben Dunkelman explained in *Dual Allegiance*, "I discovered that the existing yacht clubs were closed to Jewish applicants—which I dealt with by helping to found a Jewish yacht club." Dunkelman and his yachting friends obtained a lease for several acres of what was mostly swamp and scrub land and set about developing the club. By February 1953 they had eighty-five members and a toehold on what Islanders still referred to as "ghost island," where, according to another founder, Dr. B. Willinsky, there were still "all kinds of pheasants and other game." Much labour and expense were to be involved before the enterprise became the major yacht club it is today.

In March 1951 the next round of planning for the Island opened. Flush with victory in ridding Council of all communists, Mayor McCallum was keen to clear up uncertainty about the Island's future. On his motion the Board of Control asked the Toronto Harbour Commission to cooperate with the Toronto City Planning Board to prepare "definite plans for the development of the Island" and to report to Council within six months if possible. As usual, the issue of the tunnel came up. While various civic officials again may have harboured great hopes of federal assistance for this project, Islanders had a very useful ally in C. D. Howe who, like his Liberal predecessors in 1935, was "not interested in making any financial contributions." With the Korean War raging, no steel could be

At the June 1950 annual yachtsmen's church service on Long Pond, Ken Butler and future federal deputy minister of finance Ian Stewart take up the collection. [Sun: Telegram Collection]

(Right) *The Island Yacht Club rises from humble beginnings on Mugg's Island, June 1952.* [YUA:TC]

allotted. "We are having enough trouble building the Toronto subway," he told the *Star* of March 3. "I certainly wouldn't encourage this thing in wartime."

In the spring of 1951 lake waters once again were on the rise and plagued Islanders from early spring right through to fall. By May the water was almost as high as the 1947 record. A storm sent wind-whipped Lake Ontario crashing over boardwalks and breakwaters; many homes were marooned in the middle of great ponds; the school bus, which could normally negotiate up to a foot of water, was halted; foot-travel was virtually impossible without hip-boots; and many of the duckwalks put down a week earlier by City workmen and Islanders had impertinently floated away. By mid-July the 1947 high-water record had been swamped: Islanders were tired of living "amid muck and mud"[33] and a large delegation waded over to City Hall to demand a higher seawall. No luck.

Islanders returned to their soggy isle to cope as best they could. But for the first time in Ward's Island history, it dared to rain on the children's parade. The exotically attired youngsters beat a hasty retreat to the clubhouse where young Marion and John Sewell took first prize in the "Fancy" class for their rendition of "The Rose and the Bee." And the ground remained so saturated that any heavy rainstorm could cause havoc. "Today I am amphibious," a woebegone *Telegram* reporter wrote on September 1. "My entire apartment on Centre Island is under five inches of water." Soft-drink bottles and slippers were floating around his living room, the phone was out of order, but at least the socks left scattered about the bedroom floor "in careless bachelor fashion" would not have to be washed. Mother Nature even dared to cause havoc on the eve of the royal visit of Princess Elizabeth and the Duke of Edinburgh in early October, when gale force winds tore away festive bunting lining downtown streets and again turned Island streets into swirling eddies of water.

In September 1951 the Toronto City Planning Board and the Toronto Harbour Commission unveiled their colossal Joint Proposal "to obtain the maximum use of this natural asset for the largest number of the citizens, to serve the 'many' not the 'few.'"[34] "To serve the many not the few" soon became a catch phrase. In 1951, it meant building a tunnel and allowing cars—not eliminating residents. Later, however, after the tunnel idea was permanently laid to rest, the seductive phrase came to mean turfing out Island residents.

If this plan were implemented, the Island would be straightened out, tarted up and overbuilt. Winding lagoons were dangerous and hard to maintain—straighten them or fill them in. Unkempt cottages with no indoor plumbing were an affront to postwar suburban man—tear them down. Narrow, carless streets were antiquated and outrageous—widen and pave them or obliterate them altogether. Big cars, big developments and big, but significantly unspecified costs were all signs of progress.

"They might better burn down the clubhouse than fill the lagoons," complained James Hyland of the RCYC.[35] Most Island residents were also vehemently opposed to the scheme which, if anything, was worse than the 1947 plan. "This is incubator island," said Mrs. Tony Anthony. "Kiddies are welcome here. If they tear down our old houses and build big new apartments, where will we go?" Where indeed? As for the tunnel, it would be a disaster. "The charm of Toronto Islands," Alan Howard told a meeting of Women Electors, "is that for the price of a street car ticket people without cars can get away from the traffic and tension of the city to completely different surroundings." Everyone agreed the Island needed improvement, but not this kind of devastation. "Fix it up, sure," commented Bruce Robinson of Cherokee Avenue. "But the plan? It stinks."[36] This was a theme that Islanders pushed—perhaps more eloquently and less succinctly—over the next little while.

The proposers of the plan defended it, saying that in the face of constant ferry deficits the Island should be "a self-sustaining recreation centre for the metropolitan area of Toronto." But they also retreated as a result of the barrage of criticism. The sixty-thousand-seat stadium? Not a serious intention. Moving Sunnyside? A mere possibility. The politicians were also backing off; so the Joint Proposal was shunted to a back burner. Islanders, supported by the *Globe* and a growing body of opinion "in favor of keeping the island as a natural park," this time staved off disaster at the hands of civic planners.[37] But the language of the plan, with its emphasis on deficits and on "serving the many not the few" coloured all future discussions.

In spring 1952 the forces of nature again began to undermine the Islanders, both physically and politically. The lake, which had never receded completely from its 1951 levels, was on the rise. And City Hall was being as unhelpful as ever. When a proposal to raise the seawall was shelved by the Board of Control on February 20 because Mayor Lamport was away, Islanders struck, almost literally. Banner headlines screamed the news across Island and city: TAX STRIKE IS ISLANDERS' THREAT UNLESS CITY BUILDS UP SEAWALL. "If we don't get our seawall," said housewife Mrs. J. W. Barnes of Chippewa Avenue, "we don't pay our taxes." The Islanders' new senior alderman, Allan Grossman, was supportive, "We can't justify the threat to

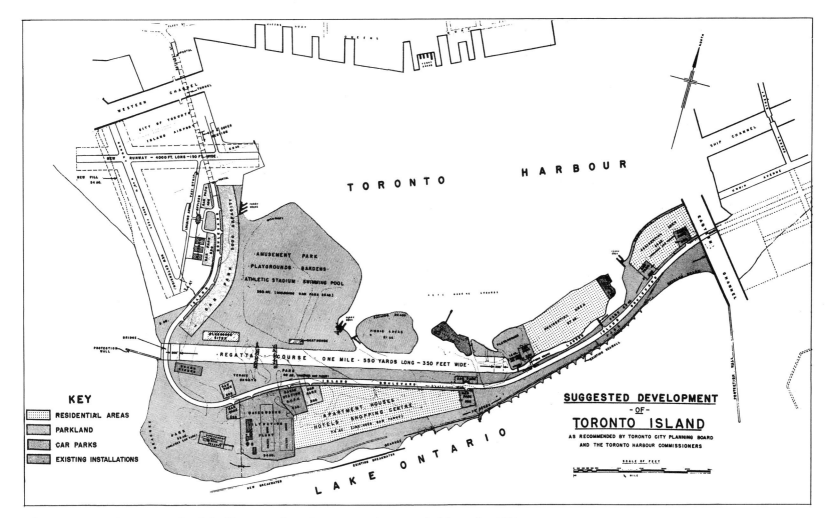

The Toronto City Planning Board and the Toronto Harbour Commission joint proposal of September 1951. The single "most important feature" of the plan was the four lane tunnel under the Western Gap which would provide automobile access to a cross-Island boulevard. "Broadly, the Island is now a century behind. It's in the Victorian stage," THC Chairman Bosley commented. "We want to bring it up to 1952." To do this, the plan also envisioned a swing bridge over the Eastern Gap and parking for 1100 cars. [City of Toronto]

On March 13, 1952, the Island was pounded by what Fire Captain Duncan Florence described as the highest waves he had ever seen. The seawall was clearly no match for them. [Star]

Lamport temporarily backed away. Trucks soon rumbled across the airport in the evenings carrying material to raise the seawall. And on June 16, residents cheered as a small section of heightened seawall proved its worth during a major storm.

Undeterred by the watery disaster around them, Royal Canadian Yacht Club members celebrated their grand centennial. In mid-July 1952, just as the City agreed to complete the seawall, eight hundred members and guests turned out in their best attire for a gala Centennial Garden Party. Celebrants sipped tea to the stirring strains of the 48th Highlanders Band, RCYC bowlers took on the Granite Club, the Dolphinettes put on a display of ornamental

withhold taxes, but we can sympathize with them. The suggestion of a three-foot addition to the seawall is practical and the city should not hesitate any longer."[38]

The tax strike itself never received much support, and it was ill-timed from a political standpoint. The atmosphere at City Hall was changing, as Alderman Grossman discovered when he raised the seawall issue the next day. He argued that the City had an obligation to help Island residents. And, unless the City did something, there might be a health menace. Unlike 1943 and 1947, however, the argument backfired. Rather than mobilizing support, it inspired Parks Commissioner Love to reply that because of this possible health menace, all residents might have to be removed.

This theme was adopted and elaborated on

with characteristic enthusiasm by Mayor Lamport. About two weeks later on March 19 he sparked banner headlines when he told the Board of Control that the Island was "no place for human habitation in the winter time."[39] Lamport's remarks reflected his image of the Island as a summer resort, rather than a permanent community, and his desire not to spend more money on it. And, a cynic might add, the "health menace" threat provided a convenient excuse to get rid of noisy, demanding Islanders.

The Medical Officer of Health Dr. Pequegnat soon took the sting out of Mayor Lamport's argument by declaring that, in fact, there was *no* health menace on the Island from the flooding. The *Globe and Mail* advised the mayor to "stop the terrorizing which has been going on for so many years, and get the protective works started."

swimming and the ladies were resplendent in their silk, lace and organdy gowns.

The new seawall, however, could not perform miracles. The lake rose to new heights, the rains poured down in astonishing profusion and Islanders endured the soggiest summer in living memory. Manitou Road became a veritable canal and business took a plunge. The dedicated Victorian Order of Nurses visiting nurse pulled on her gum boots and cycled through puddle and pond to give liver injections and otherwise tend the chronically ill marooned in waterbound houses. The Centre Island Community Tennis Club was washed out and washed up. Normally luxuriant gardens became suitable only for

The Island Theatre was no ordinary cinema. During the spring floods of 1952, for example, manager "Hobby" Hobson hired Durnan's water taxi to slosh around picking up movie patrons. [OA]

Pedestrians shuffle carefully along duckboards in front of the Manitou Hotel facing the Island's Grand Canal of 1952. [Al Schoenborn]

water lilies. (Wendi Hanger recalled that her father's magnificent roses at 45 Shiawassie Avenue were all killed and the septic tank under the rose bed gave new meaning to the phrase "smelling like a rose.") Hanlan's Point Amusement Park, which had been declining for years, suffered further depredations: the buildings were left in such a mess that even university boys refused to work in them the next summer. Paddlers at least were in their element: the Island Canoe Club sent three of its members—Tommy Hodgson, Art Johnson and Bert Oldershaw—to

the Zatopek Olympics in Helsinki at the end of July. Most other sportsmen had to make do as best they could.

One of the interesting new sporting events turned out to be "cat-walking": performing a balancing act on the ten-inch-wide catwalks criss-crossing the Island. Of course, some were better walkers than others. Ward's Islander Peggy Jackson, the *Weekly* reported, was navigating very successfully one day, starting to feel proud of herself, "when suddenly she slipped off and went in up to her shoulders, sitting down." And Wilf Menzies failed to make a new turn, stepped straight ahead as usual, and fell forward, flat, into the water. Catwalk stories began to take on the legendary character of fish stories.

In spite of the hazards and delayed arrivals, by

early August all but fifteen Ward's Island houses were occupied. Making a virtue of necessity, summer residents held a ''Ward's Island High Water Talent Show'' and the ''High Water Four'' warbled with the best of them on Barbershop Night. The season, however, ended up on a high-and-dry note with a rejuvenated Minstrel Show, which featured a new generation of talent, like Liz Coleman who stunned the audiences with her dancing to ''Ballin' the Jack'' and her heartfelt rendition of ''Angry.''

''Even when Toronto Islands were half submerged by Lake Ontario,'' the *Globe* reported November 11, 1952, ''the stork apparently has no trouble finding them.'' As a result the Island School, now with about 450 pupils, was again bursting at the seams. Two classes were using the Red Cross Outpost and the Board of Education, supported by Island parents, was about to launch a campaign to almost double the size of the school, to seventeen rooms. In the course of their campaign for a school addition, Islanders were about to run headlong into Mayor Lamport and the collision would have far-reaching consequences.

Not since Sam McBride had Toronto seen a mayor as colourful as Allan Lamport. He could make headlines at the drop of a hat—or a metaphor. (''It's like pushing a car up a hill with a rope,'' he said, or ''If I'm going to be stabbed in the back I want to be there'' or, of Henry Moore's controversial sculpture, The Archer, in Nathan Phillips Square, ''It has the earmark of an eyesore.'') Like old Sam, Lampy was a tough, bluff fighter, given to reacting hastily and not always thoughtfully. But his views on the Island were very different from McBride's ardent, unvarying advocacy.

Apart from not wanting to waste taxpayers' money on such potentially unprofitable fripperies as the Island, Lamport was as unpredictable as the proverbial serpent on a rock. Sometimes he favoured residential development; sometimes he did not. Sometimes he favoured major commercial and industrial development; sometimes he did not. Sometimes he adopted mutually contradictory positions at the same time (e.g., favouring both recreational and major industrial

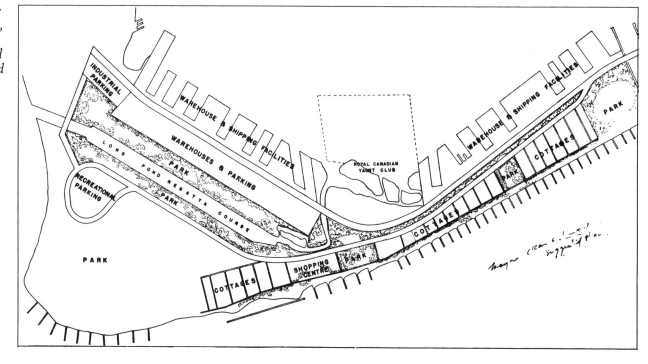

In April 1953, shortly before the official creation of Metro Toronto, Toronto Mayor Allan Lamport issued his extraordinary dockyard plan for the Island. He envisioned roads, parking lots, deep sea docks, warehouses—and more warehouses—cottages and parkland all coexisting happily, and profitably, on Toronto's beleaguered island. [City of Toronto]

uses simultaneously). And sometimes he did a complete about-face within a matter of weeks.

In December, on the eve of the 1952 election, Lamport extended cheery "Greetings to Islanders" in the *Centre Islander*. Commiserating about the floods, he wrote regretfully that "life on the Islands has not been the same care-free existence so many of you formerly experienced," and promised that as mayor he was "determined to do everything possible to restore our Islands to their original beauty and usefulness." But somehow, once safely back in the mayor's chair, Lamport saw the future differently. In his inaugural address to Council on January 6, 1953, he dropped a bombshell that exploded once and for all the Islanders' carefree existence. Not only did he promise to take quick action on the Island (polite applause), but he presented a totally new proposal: docks and warehouses along the northern bayshore and elimination of all residences (gasps of outrage).

The *Globe and Mail* jumped to the defence of the Island in an editorial labelled "They Will Ruin the Island": "This shameful plan to destroy the Island park must be stopped for good. They must not take the Island away from us."[40] In the face of such hostile reaction, the mayor stuffed his plan temporarily back in a drawer.

As another winter waned, Islanders pressed forward with their demand that the City spend $205,000 to nearly double the size of the school. On April 1, the City Board of Control agreed, over the vehement protests of the mayor. That same day, Lamport resurrected a somewhat modified industrial plan for the Island. This was no April Fool's joke; it was a monstrosity. Bridge. Roads. Warehouses. Dockyards. The mayor said it was "an opportunity for turning a civic deficit into an asset" and, amazingly, that "the beauty of the plan is that there is a minimum of interference with things already on the Island"—a claim that was patently ridiculous.[41]

Reaction was swift and damning. Ultimately, perhaps the most important effect of this extreme plan was to so polarize opinion that there were increasing calls from inside and outside City Hall to develop the Island as a natural, pure park.

All of his Board of Control colleagues opposed the mayor's scheme. The *Globe and Mail* attacked this "vandal proposal."[42] The mayor's dream was the Islanders' nightmare and they woke up screaming against it. "This appears to be a plan to withdraw the Island from the metropolitan administration as a park," Inter-Island Council spokesman Alan Howard said, referring to the federation of Toronto and twelve surrounding municipalities into Metropolitan Toronto that was about to come into being. "The only ones who would benefit are big business interests who see the Island merely as a money-making opportunity rather than as a public park for the benefit of all citizens."[43] Islanders would prefer to trust their future to Metro than to the mayor.

Not one to take criticism lightly, Lamport lashed back, suggesting that the (vexatious) permanent residents might have to go. Toronto "cannot be governed by a few who want privileges which have to be paid for by the rest of the citizens," he declared. And, warming to his theme on the eve of the creation of Metro Toronto, Lamport asserted that "as long as we have permanent residents on the Island, we will have permanent headaches and permanent deficits."[44]

The future of the Island was far from settled. But by creating an atmosphere of tension and internal bickering and by demonstrating the extremes to which the City might take planning for the Island, Lamport paved the way for the transfer to Metro. Into this imbroglio walked the newly appointed first Metro chairman, Frederick G. Gardiner.

11

The Metro Bulldozer

On April 15, 1953, Metropolitan Toronto Council held its inaugural meeting in the Romanesque splendour of the Provincial Legislative Chamber at Queen's Park and changed the course of Island—as well as Toronto—history. Conservative Premier Leslie "Old Man Ontario" Frost benevolently watched over the proceedings and encouraged his Metropolitan protégés, saying, "This is a trust and challenge to make Toronto a model for all large cities." Then, cutting through the pomp and circumstance, Metro Chairman Frederick Goldwin Gardiner (or "Metro Goldwin Mayor" as he later laughingly called himself) moved to centre stage. "Mr. Prime Minister," he declared, "we accept that challenge." In a characteristically brief address he hailed the "new era" and introduced his Metro colleagues. Appropriately enough, Toronto Mayor Allan Lamport—the other political heavyweight of the day, whose support was essential to the success of the Metro experiment—was seated next to Gardiner. When his turn to speak arrived, the garrulous Lamport gave a lengthy address and promised that City members would not "gang up" in the new Council. "We know you have a difficult task," he commented, "we know you need help, and we are prepared to give it." The chairman then called on a suburban member to make some "brief" remarks and Etobicoke Reeve Beverley Lewis obligingly spoke for less than a minute, promising suburbia's "whole-hearted support" as well. So amid much fellowship and *bonhomie* was Metro Council born on that bright, brisk spring day.[1]

No one, of course, was deceived by all this sweetness and light, least of all Fred Gardiner. Gardiner was a "tough, truculent, corporate lawyer,"[2] who had been reeve of wealthy Forest Hill (one of the thirteen constituent municipali-ties of the new federation) for eleven years and a Conservative Pooh-Bah for much of his adult life. When Premier Frost was looking for a suitable chairman to nurture his Metro baby, he turned to his long-time friend and confidant. Gardiner was inspired by this friendship, and by the challenge. Frost had given him only one piece of advice: "He just told me not to get run over by a streetcar before April 15." Before long, as Gardiner's biographer Timothy J. Colton observed sardonically, "Toronto politicians were taking counsel on how to avoid being run over by Frederick Gardiner."[3]

Dubbed by one of his later Metro colleagues, Phil Givens, as "Big Daddy," after the domineering patriarch in Tennessee Williams's play *Cat On a Hot Tin Roof*, burly Fred Gardiner dominated Metro Council during his years at its helm, from April 1953 to December 1961. As Metro chairman, Gardiner could only vote in the case of a tie, but he was, as Colton put it, "fully engaged in every collective choice made by Council." He was fearsomely well informed and determined to persuade, cajole and even bully Council members into supporting him. Whatever the method used, Metro Council followed his lead with astonishing regularity; on the Island issue, therefore, as on other issues, what Gardiner said and did was important. His figure moves like a bulky *éminence grise* behind the pages of the public record.[4]

By the end of his eight-year term in 1961, Gardiner may have been considered the most powerful appointed official in Canadian municipal history; but at the beginning of his term he was faced with the considerable task of welding together into a working unit a potentially explosive Council composed of frequently warring factions—notably the City (with half the votes) and the suburbs (with the other half).

A Metro bulldozer at work, January 20, 1966. [YUA:TC]

On May 12, 1953, the Inter-Island Council released the Islanders' own plan to improve the status quo. It advocated keeping and improving the existing residential areas, and improving existing parkland in order to attract more visitors and reduce the nefarious ferry deficits. It did not advocate building a tunnel or a bridge to allow an invasion of mainland autos. It did not envision highrise apartments or docks or Olympic stadia. And it definitely did not recommend destroying or otherwise harming existing residential areas.
[Elizabeth Amer]

Early on Gardiner won Lamport over to seeing himself as the chairman's right-hand man on issues affecting the City's interests. As a result, Lampy used his own forceful personality to swing a frequently reluctant City Council behind Gardiner and the Metro idea. On a personal level, Gardiner and Lamport initially shared a healthy respect for each other and worked well, if not always quietly, together. This relationship helps explain Lamport's radical about-face on the Island issue during the summer of 1953.

Also critical to Metro's early success was Gardiner's bulldozer approach, an approach which he felt was vital to pushing Council and the public behind the Metro idea. Metro's early years, Gardiner once said, represented "a time when imagination had to be translated into physical accomplishment to prove that the first metropolitan government on the North American continent would work."[5] Or, as he said on more than one occasion, "Plans, plans, we've got a million plans. Let's get the godamn shovels into the ground."[6] So Gardiner (like his contemporary, Robert Moses, the "powerbroker" of New York) emphasized large-scale, highly visible public works, such as expressways, water treatment plants and housing projects. The Toronto Island—a big, potentially flashy and impressive project—fitted neatly into this approach. Even in 1953, before Metro Council had officially begun doing business and before there was a Metro Parks Department or a parks commissioner, or a parks system, Chairman Gardiner was eyeing the Island and preparing the way for its eventual transfer from the City to Metro.

The City proved to be an effective, if not always conscious, accomplice. For months before making up their minds to transfer the Island to Metro, City politicians wallowed about in a mire of plans and suggestions for the Island's

future. They discussed the old Toronto City Planning Board/Toronto Harbour Commission Joint Proposal of 1951, Mayor Lamport's wild-eyed dockyard plan of 1953, the old Inter-Island Council proposals of 1948 and plan of 1949—all of which involved endless debates about tunnels, boulevards, increased recreational use, different recreational use, more residential development, less residential development and so on. In the midst of this confusion, they artlessly invited Big Daddy into the debate, at a special meeting to be held on May 14, 1953. Gardiner was only too happy to oblige.

If he was planning at this stage to demolish Island houses, however, he certainly didn't let on. Quite the reverse. The week before the special meeting, Gardiner declared that "the Island is now a Metropolitan area problem and the Metropolitan Board must study it carefully before any decisions can be made," thus earning the plaudits of the local press and forever altering the issue.[7] At the same time he emphasized that he favoured combined recreation-residential development for the Island, saying, "There's plenty of room for both."[8] Island residents were further encouraged by a tour he made not long after becoming Metro chairman. Gardiner pedalled from one end of the Island to the other, his ample form spilling over his bicycle seat, talking to residents and reassuring them that he saw no reason why the community should be eliminated. Intentionally or unintentionally, Gardiner lulled Islanders into a false sense of security that if Metro took over the Island, residential use would continue and they could stay. Islanders, therefore, never protested the transfer to Metro. In fact, they encouraged it. And then Gardiner "turned around, within four months," a former Islander recalled with understandable bitterness, "and proposed that the

Island community be eliminated. I don't know what caused him to change. But...it all changed." This unwelcome surprise, however, still lay in the future.

Two days before the first special meeting to discuss the Island's future on May 14, 1953, the Inter-Island Council released its own Mark II plan for the Island, which displayed an uncanny, though not surprising, resemblance to its earlier schemes to enhance the *status quo*. "We see no reason why this small oasis in a desert of smog and traffic congestion should not be retained," IIC Vice-Chairman Alan Howard emphasized.[9]

On May 14, when Howard, Gardiner, Lamport and a variety of Islandophiles met with the City Parks and Exhibition Committee, talk was easy but decision-making was not. Significantly, Mayor Lamport retreated from his dockyard plan and suggested simply that the City should discuss this plan with Metro because it might "prove easier to develop the Island on a Metropolitan basis."[10] Gardiner seemed more than amenable to Lamport's suggestion. Moving into an apparent vacuum at the City level, Gardiner made a strong pitch for Metro's role: "I don't see for the life of me how you can divorce the development of the Island from Metropolitan planning."[11] All plans, he suggested, should be submitted to Metro Council for its consideration.

No decisions were taken. The City Parks Committee decided to meet again (and again) to discuss the matter. Meanwhile, Mayor Lamport flew off to London to visit the Queen, or at least to attend Elizabeth's coronation on June 2.

There was to be no coronation amnesty for Islanders, however. Mayor Lamport returned to Toronto with renewed determination that dock facilities should be built on Toronto Island. Within hours of landing, Lamport lashed out at his opponents—the Inter-Island Council foremost among them—whom he described as "pressure groups which think in terms of centimeters instead of miles" (adding metric insult to imperial injury). "Would their minor needs bow to the greater needs of the City?" he asked rhetorically. He was spurred on in his quest for docks by the possibility that when the St. Lawrence Seaway was finished, Hamilton—God forbid—might take away some of Toronto's industrial development. "I don't dare let Toronto harbor get behind Hamilton harbor," the mayor worried to the *Globe* reporter. Babbitt was alive and well and living in Toronto. Islanders didn't have to respond to this latest outburst. The press jumped all over the mayor's scheme and by the next Parks and Exhibition Committee meeting, Lampy was again in almost full retreat.

On June 25 the committee held another special meeting to discuss the Island's future. Once again Metro Chairman Gardiner threw his weight around and radically altered the whole debate. After the committee had ineffectually discussed the TCPB/THC plan and come to no conclusion, Gardiner announced that if the Island were to come under Metro's control, it would have to remain "essentially a park." It could not be further developed residentially or commercially. "Unless the Toronto Islands become established as a Metropolitan park, our Council will have nothing to do with it," Gardiner growled. "The uses envisioned here today do not make it seem likely that it will become a Metropolitan park."[12] So much for the TCPB/THC plan. While Gardiner was clearly opposed to *additional* residential or commercial development, he remained unclear about the future of *existing* houses. All he said here was that the Island would have to remain "essentially"—but not necessarily "exclusively"—parkland. Mixed signals from Gardiner continued

J. V. Salmon captured this view looking toward Lake Ontario along the Main Drag on September 15, 1954, after the summer visitors had left the street to winter residents, parks department workers and the odd delivery truck. [MTLB]

to beep across the bay through the prolonged transition period.

When they weren't stewing over Lamport's latest proposal, Islanders were busy with their usual summer pursuits. The "Ferry Boat Follies" hit the boards, and Islanders' funny bones, for the seventh year punning at the Centre Island Association clubhouse. Masqueraders reached new imaginative heights by depicting the "Conquerors of Mount Everest." Ward's baseball players won "the most hair-raising, spine-tingling, screaming, jump-for-joy climax in many a year" when Ken "the rifle" Lye blasted a Hanlan's Point pitch over the sidewalk and between the cottages on Withrow Avenue. Politics, however, were not entirely absent. A federal election was being fought; so Spadina Riding Liberal M.P. David Croll braved the

Dominion Day rains to do a little Main Dragging among his Island constituents. While water-logged spectators lined the lagoon and the Manitou Bridge to watch the annual regatta, Croll cheered on the paddlers and cheered up the residents by promising "to do his best to keep the island free of cars."[13] He said nothing about bulldozers, however. And on August 10 avuncular Louis St. Laurent's Liberals romped to victory.

On October 8, 1953, the City Parks and Exhibition Committee finally voted to transfer the Island to Metro for park and non-commercial purposes. Only Islanders' alderman, Frank Chambers, spoke against the mayor's suggestion that Islanders should only remain until their leases expired. Mayor Lamport told him he was "hanging on nobly to a lost cause," but as far as he and committee members were concerned, the Islanders would have to go.[14] The committee's recommendations, however, did not enjoy a swift and easy passage to City Council. They stalled at the committee level until after the New Year and the next civic election.

On January 12, 1954, Metro Council held its first working meeting "in a mood of marked disharmony and functional antagonism," according to the *Telegram*. The City-Suburban split, which was to exercise such a strong influence on the fate of the Island in the seventies and eighties was clearly present from the outset. As a result, Gardiner had to play his political cards shrewdly. Immediately before the first meeting, he announced that Metro had no authority to assume control of the Island without the City making formal application. Despite motions from City Alderman Roy Belyea, Big Daddy continued to insist that Metro could not take over the Island except at the City's express request. Gardiner's motivation was clearly political, not legal, and his assessment of the political situation was probably accurate. It would *not* have been a good idea for Metro, especially in 1954, to seem to be too eager to gobble up bits and pieces of local municipalities; Metro Council, always potentially explosive, might fly apart at the seams. If the City could be persuaded to *ask* Metro to take over the Island, that would undoubtedly be the best solution.

The City was only too happy to oblige. After years of indecision, wrangling and, at times, acrimonious debate, City Council finally voted on February 22, 1954, to offer Toronto Island to Metro Council for development as a park and recreation area. To hurry the process along, the City asked Metro to make up its mind within six months—not that it would hold Metro to any such deadline, as it turned out. For those who genuinely believed that the Island should be a park but did not want the City to pick

up the tab, for those who simply wanted to unload a costly headache and for those who were hostile to Island residents and wished to see them removed, the City vote to transfer the Island to Metro was a logical one. And the lopsided nature of that vote, 20-0, was a reflection of this final coalescence of opinion among City politicians.

No motions to save Island homes were proposed. No eloquent speeches to save the little community were made. Former supporters either did not realize what their decision might mean or politicians had come to accept the idea that it was time for Island residents to leave and for the Island to be just a summer playground. After years of unsatisfactory relations with the City, Islanders did not push their supporters at the City level to oppose the transfer. They preferred instead to deal in the future with Metro, and the friendly big man on the bicycle.

With the City's request firmly in hand, Gardiner and Metro could now move toward taking over the Island and deciding what to do with it. (The latter problem, in fact, created a year-long delay.) On March 16, 1954, Metro Council voted to approve the transfer *in principle*, pending a report on the Island's future from the far from independently minded Metro Planning Board. The Island was on its way to Metro, but wasn't there yet.[15]

In spite of prognostications of doom and gloom by some politicians and press about their future, Island residents themselves were pleased by events, hoping, as Inter-Island Council officer Harold Aitken wrote in the May *Centre Islander*, "that Metro [would] realize the potentialities of the Island and [would] proceed to rehabilitate and develop it as should have been done years ago" and that Islanders would be relieved of "that feeling of insecurity and uncertainty which

Houses such as this inspired young journalist William French in August 1954 to write fondly about Island architecture which then ranged "from a Southern-style mansion through Victorian rococo, ranch-style to Oriental, neo-neo to neo-antique, hodge-podge to the Pavilion at Brighton."
[*Globe and Mail*]

has resulted from the frequent and contradictory but invariably unfavourable outbursts from the City Hall.''

For the time being, however, the City was still in charge and soon struck fear into the hearts of Island residents. In the spring of 1954 the City considered terminating eight Lakeshore Avenue leases that came due that year. After several appearances at City Hall, Islanders and their eloquent spokesman, former Islander and Commodore of the old Island Amateur Aquatic Association, M.P. Donald Fleming, persuaded the City to renew until 1968 *all* leases as they came due. It was, however, only a partial victory. The City also included a (possibly worrying) provision that any leases could be terminated upon one year's notice if that was required for the implementation of a City, or Metro, redevelopment plan.

For parents of young children, 1968 was still a long way away and their children still had to go to school. On June 2 over 600 smiling Islanders and their honoured guests from the City crammed into the new auditorium to celebrate the official opening of the nine-room addition to the Island School. The school's Rhythm Band thumped earnestly under the direction of Miss Elizabeth Cook, Kindergarten directress; the school choir chirped sweetly; and the Superintendent of Toronto Public Schools, Mr. Z. S. Phimister, looked over-optimistically to the future, asserting that ''Islanders will not stop until they have a collegiate institute and technical college right here.'' As it turned out, the school never exceeded the peak enrolment of 587 reached that September.

Not surprisingly, Mayor Lamport, who had so vehemently opposed the school addition, did not show up for the ceremony. Perhaps he had other things on his mind, for at the end

of the month he resigned as mayor and, with Gardiner's backing, went on to his great reward at the Toronto Transit Commission. He was succeeded on June 28 by Controller Leslie Saunders, an overly enthusiastic Orangeman whose anti-Catholic rhetoric stirred up a storm of protest and led to the election of Nathan Phillips in a closely contested three-way race. Islanders' former alderman, the sociable Nate Phillips, thus became the first Jewish, in fact the first non-Protestant, mayor in Toronto's history.

Two events took Torontonians' minds off the local election in the fall of 1954. Just before midnight on September 9, a virtually unknown Toronto teenager slipped into the dark lake waters off Youngstown, New York. When she emerged nearly twenty-one hours later at Sunny-side, before some 100,000 delirious spectators, she was a national heroine. Gutsy little Marilyn Bell had battled cold, heavy swells, exhaustion and even interference from a growing flotilla of admirers, including the smokey old *Ned Hanlan*, to succeed where three others had just failed. She alone had crossed Lake Ontario; moreover, she had done it, as she told the *Globe and Mail* in her winning way, ''for the honour of Canada.''

Then, a little more than a month later, Toronto was again taken by storm by an equally unheralded but far more dangerous female: Hazel. When Hurricane Hazel slammed into Toronto Island on October 15, ''it was black and terribly forceful,'' according to Algonquinite Mrs. Lillian Hopp, who had spent the day in the

October 16, 1954: on the windswept expanse of the Island Airport, even cement blocks and thick ropes were no match for the force of Hurricane Hazel.   [THC]

city. By the time she made it back to the Island, the rain, which caused far more damage than the wind, was coming down "in sheets." The scene was so wild that she did not dare let her four little children make their way home alone from the babysitter's house nearby. Meanwhile, her husband Tony, who ran the Ward's Island stores, had a narrow escape: returning to the Island from Detroit, he was "on the last bus that got across the Humber Bridge before they closed it" and it was washed out. Down at Centre Island the situation was even worse than at the eastern end. Hazel whipped wind and water right over the new breakwall and across the Island. "Porches, fences, pets, sheds, windows, assorted bits of our house were blown or washed away," journalist William Burrill later wrote.[16] A frantic Mrs. Burrill lashed five-month-old William to an unhinged door, just in case she had to try to throw him to safety. The house teetered uneasily on eroding foundations, but withstood the onslaught. And young William avoided a dunking, or worse.

Ironically, although Toronto Island was less severely affected by Hazel than other areas were and less severely pounded than it was by other storms, the hurricane provided yet another reason—or excuse—for Metro to take it over and convert it into pure parkland. "When Hurricane Hazel descended upon us in late October 1954 it proved that a tragedy can leave something good behind," retired Metro Chairman Fred Gardiner wrote in the *Globe and Mail* of October 30, 1969. "It left us the idea that turned the Toronto Islands into parkland."

In the interim, winter descended on the Island and with it came thoughts of the "Cinderella run of the TTC": the four coal-burning, cinder-spewing tugs that bashed and crashed their way from one chilly side of the bay to the other. Even

December 15, 1954 at the Island Theatre: "All those against the tripling of the ferry fare to the Island raise your hands"...and up they go. [Sun: Telegram *Collection*]

in the best of times, the service was far from ideal. But when the TTC decided to triple the fares from ten cents to thirty cents in December 1954, Islanders saw red. A special edition of the *Centre Islander* shouted WAKE UP ISLANDERS! And a large crowd of wide-awake, indeed very angry, residents jammed the new movie theatre at Centre Island.

Given the uncertainty surrounding their very existence, Islanders couldn't have picked a worse time to clash with public officials. But clash they did. They held more meetings. They organized deputations. Some, like Mrs. Rosamond, a quiet, bespectacled Algonquin Island housewife, even refused to pay the increase. Over the protests of the TTC collector, she dropped the old fare into the box en route to the city with her two small children. But for the time being most Islanders only grumbled as they resignedly paid their thirty cents and shuffled on board. Uneasy peace temporarily returned to the bay.

Finally, on January 7, 1955, tempers again reached the boiling point, and Islanders staged what came to be known as the Great Tugboat Mutiny. On that fateful below-zero morning, one tug broke down and the other three were

At the end of their Tugboat Mutiny on January 7, 1955, Island mutineers walked the plank at the mainland docks, where many stalked past the ticket window without paying. [Sun: Telegram Collection]

sharp blasts on the whistle. Island police rushed to the dock by car and the Harbour Police roared over from John Street by boat. Eventually other boats came to the rescue and carried the top-coated, fedoraed mutineers to the city. Order was almost restored, although scores of still-angry passengers rushed through the turnstiles without paying.[17]

Political reaction was quick. Newly elected Mayor Phillips, usually a friend of Islanders, called for reports on the incident. "I can understand the feeling of people," he said, "but it is no justification to take the law into their own hands." Island leaders tried to calm their troops, cautioning them to "behave like adults," and pleaded for "sweet reason" on both sides. But TTC vice chairman, Allan Lamport, characteristically, stole the publicity limelight. "If that sort of thing goes on," he growled, "we will ask Metropolitan Council to relieve us of the obligation of providing this service." What were Islanders complaining about, anyway? They were receiving "arm-chair service" according to Lamport, who rode to work in a limousine. Perhaps, he suggested yet again, residents might have to move off the Island altogether.[18]

The TTC's threat to suspend service annoyed just about everyone from the Islanders to the Metro chairman and sparked a major political clash. In the end, a two-hour "peace conference" involving the TTC, the City Board of Control and Island residents[19] led to City Council's agreeing on February 1, 1955, to subsidize a return to the ten-cent fare for the rest of that winter. The controversy fizzled out and life returned to what passed for normal on the Island.

But the political fallout from the Great Tugboat Mutiny was lasting. At that same February 1 meeting, City Council also voted to ask Metro to make up its mind, once and for all, about

running hopelessly behind schedule. At Hanlan's Point a rapidly-growing crowd stood shivering with cold and rage as several fully loaded tugs passed by without stopping. When the partly full *H.J. Dixon* finally docked at Hanlan's after having taken on passengers at the Filtration Plant, it had room for only ten or twenty more passengers before reaching its legal limit. No daggers flashed between bared teeth as the 125 "happy pirates" of Toronto Island swarmed aboard the *Dixon.* No scum of the seven seas

tried to capture a treasure of used TTC tickets or stormed the wheelhouse to wrest control of the ship from mild-mannered Captain Lahey. But no one would budge when the captain tried to clear the overloaded decks. "We just refused to get off again," Hanlan's Pointer Al Schoenborn commented later. "There was a lot of arguing but nobody hit anyone." As these things go, it was a fairly mild mutiny. It was, in fact, more of a sit-down strike than a mutiny. In any event, the captain blew a distress signal—five the proposed Island transfer. In the politically charged atmosphere of January 1955, neither City nor Metro politicians could possibly have been unaware of the row and of the link between Islanders and political headaches. Metro Council might well have been even less inclined to advocate continued residential use of the Island after this headline-grabbing spectacle.

The temporarily high ferry fare and the uncertainty about the future had begun to have an effect on the Island community. "I love the Island," explained Ralph Fleming who decided to move from Cherokee Avenue to North York, "but I just can't afford the fares and my nerves won't stand the uncertainty any more. We have no security of tenure in our Island homes and I might as well beat the stampede off." Other Islanders, both tenants and homeowners, began to pack their bags and leave; so many, in fact, that by January 1955 one classroom at the newly expanded school was about to be closed. And many others began to contemplate a move.

Business all over the Island was way down. William Sutherland, owner of the Manitou Hotel, reported that fourteen rooms he usually rented during the winter were empty. All sorts of services were affected. Milkman Percy Emslie reported that seventeen of his customers had left while the TTC fares were up, but Percy himself was a survivor. As Islanders disappeared over the next few years and his territory shrank, he nevertheless continued delivering milk to Ward's and Algonquin Islands, right up to September 1982. One grocery store that used to remain open all winter stayed closed this winter. The other three groceries were sharing the remaining business: "People must eat," Mr. Lamantia commented optimistically. But people cut back on more obvious luxuries. "Since the fares went up, people who normally had their

trousers cleaned every week, now only get them pressed or make them last two weeks," said dry cleaner Charles Singer. And theatre manager Gren Hobson was anxiously waiting to see if his new "family plans" and first-run attractions would pull in enough movie-goers to keep his business going. Perhaps hardest hit of all was the hardware store. "This morning," explained Joan Folley, "a lady came in to buy a doorknob. When I told her the price she said, 'Oh, I might be moving if things stay the same. I'll hammer the old knob on with a nail.' That's the way it's going lately."[20]

Meanwhile, Metro was gearing up to make a decision about the Island. Boards and committees met, reports and plans were drawn up (including a proposal to provide parking space for an astonishing 11,810 cars on the Island) and costs were estimated (including the dramatic news that the long-sought tunnel would cost between $5 million and $8 million). Chairman Gardiner now came out in favour of a tunnel. "Neither a bridge over the Eastern Gap nor an improved ferry boat service would be able to handle the potential traffic if Metro develops the Island as a natural playground," he told the *Globe* in February 1955. Moreover, he boasted, "a road on the Island will do it no more harm than the road placed on Belle Isle in Detroit"— thus providing Toronto with an interesting new model of civic grandeur based on the car capital of the Western world. As for the residents, most of whom opposed cars on the Island, Gardiner began attacking them and began projecting the negative image that lasted: "We cannot take [the Island] over to preserve it as a place of undisturbed living for a few thousand residents who think it is their private property and should be preserved at public expense," he wrote the *Globe* on March 5.

Despite these ominous portents, Island residents did almost nothing by way of organized political action. They did not appear before any Metro committees, directing all their complaints and suggestions for the Island's future at the City instead. Had they wanted to scuttle the transfer at the Metro level, they might well have succeeded by exploiting the City-Suburban split. But they never tried this, in the mistaken belief that Metro would be a better landlord than the City.

Finally, on March 22, 1955, after years of debate and indecision, Metro Council met to decide the Island's future. Mother Nature herself demonstrated a wonderful sense of occasion, sending "the worst blow since Hurricane Hazel" howling across Lake Ontario. Islanders stayed at home to "batten down the hatches," while Metro Council unanimously voted to take over the Island as part of the Metro Parks System, to continue the ferry service and to have the Metro Planning Board prepare a comprehensive plan. Whether some or all residents would be allowed to stay remained an open question a little while longer.

No motions against the transfer were proposed. In fact Islanders' own alderman and long-time supporter, Allan Grossman, seemed positively elated. This was "the first really constructive step in relation to the Islands in 20 years," he said. "All Ontario should be proud of the Islands. They should be the show-place of the nation." Grossman had by now accepted the idea that all Island residents would have to go eventually, and told reporters that "Island residents know they have to leave by 1968," though the final recommendations left some doubt.[21] But in any event, neither Alderman Grossman nor his Island constituents were aware of the fact that many of them would have to leave long

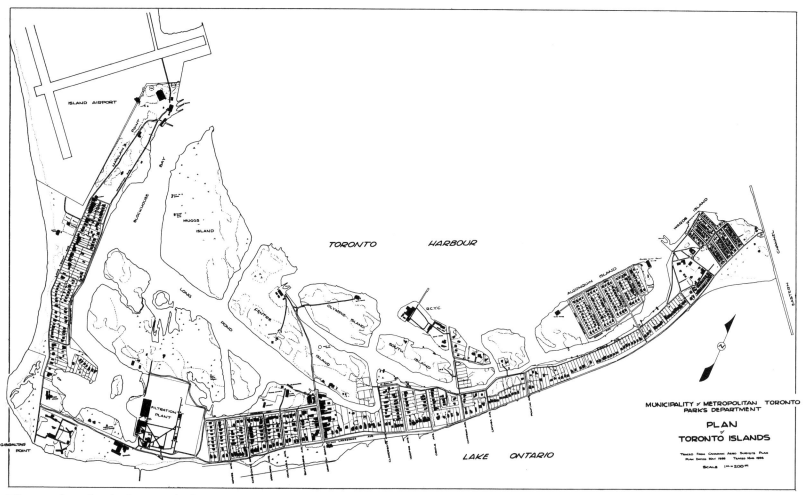

This map shows the Island at its peak of residential development, in 1955. [City of Toronto]

before 1968. The handwriting may have been on the wall, but Islanders were not ready for the bulldozers that would roar in and remove the writing and the wall.

Uncertainty lasted for a little while longer. On April 13, the ninety-seventh anniversary of the creation of the "Island," the Metro Executive established a sub-committee to hammer out details of the forthcoming transfer with City representatives. Its chairman was none other than Fred Gardiner, who moved swiftly and boldly. On May 25 Metro and City negotiators announced that City Council would be asked to dedicate *all* its Island property, residential and recreational alike, as parkland and to transfer the whole lot to Metro. Gardiner's committee had thus engineered a major policy shift. "Until today," the *Star* commented, "Metro had indicated it would only take over parks and recreational portions of the Island. Under the new arrangement it will also take over [residential] leases.'' Moreover, Gardiner announced that ''when leases came due, buildings on the Island should be demolished, rather than rented until the longer leases expired in 1968.''[22] For the time being, Metro was not proposing to terminate leases *before* they came due; it was only picking off the ones that came up or were handed in. But even before Metro officially took over on January 1, 1956, bulldozers would begin scraping across the Island landscape, tearing down homes vacated by the first to leave.

How did Islanders react to these Metro decisions to transfer the entire Island to Metro and to eliminate all housing? Once the decision was made, as in the airport issue of 1937, they did not try to overturn it. Occasionally they tried to hasten or delay the inevitable, but they did not try to avoid it. Some people stuck their heads in the Island sand and hoped that the whole thing would blow over. A couple of dozen homeowners at various spots on the Island actually jumped the gun and handed their leases into the City before they were up. (Among these were the owners of the grand old former Gooderham estate at 254 Lakeshore.) And more continued to do so after Metro officially took over on January 1, 1956. In contrast to the current situation at Ward's and Algonquin where residents would not receive compensation, the people who turned in their leases at this time received compensation, which probably made them less obstinate and no doubt took the fire out of any opposition. They directed their energies not toward collective action or opposing the plan, but toward negotiating individual compensation settlements. In fact, Islanders were so fragmented and demoralized that they did not even try to influence the first Metro plan of February 1956, which in fact actually proposed to hasten the pace of lease terminations.

Hard on the heels of its decision to take over the Island, Metro voted to establish a parks department and to hire a parks commissioner. The link is significant, for as Metro's first major park, the Island was to assume an emotional and symbolic importance that it might not otherwise have had. In July Thomas W. Thompson became its first parks commissioner. Like most senior Metro administrators of the era, Thompson was young (forty-two), energetic and virtually handpicked by Gardiner, who scrutinized all candidates for senior appointments and interviewed people on the short list. Not surprisingly, he and Gardiner saw eye to eye on the Island's future. Thompson—like Gardiner—grew with Metro. When he was hired, he had no staff, no furniture and no parks. A decade later, he supervised a staff of 450, oversaw a park system of five thousand acres and was better known than most Metro politicians. He was Tommy ''Please-Walk-On-the-Grass'' Thompson, a man who could be ''extremely gracious,'' according to one Islander, but who could also be ''just like an immovable rock,'' against which many Islanders would come to grief.

The pier at the Eastern Gap during a storm in 1946. Nine years later at this same spot, 25 year old Centre Islander Douglas Beall was swept to his death by Hurricane Connie. [CI/MTLB]

In the summer of 1955 all this uncertainty combined with a doubling of the ferry fare to diminish the Island's popularity with the general public. The Main Drag was attracting fewer and fewer visitors. The Casino, which once housed name bands and did a thriving business, was now a bowling alley closed in summer. The ''aristocratic Pierson Hotel'' on the Lakeshore, formerly packed with summer guests, was sparsely populated and its elegant lawn ''an empty expanse of rich green devoid of bowlers.'' An open-air dance floor up the street, once the scene of riotous good fun, was now ''a neglected patch of cement.'' And the colonial Wayside Inn was just ''another empty building,'' with its back rooms ''a graveyard for rusty bicycles'' once rented to clamouring crowds of weekend visitors.[23]

To add insult to injury, the Island was badly hit by the dying blows of Hurricane Connie on August 13. With their fears feeding on the ten-month-old memory of Hazel, Torontonians expected the worst of Connie. Ground crews lashed planes down at the Island Airport and residents cast worried eyes toward a lake whipped

to fury. Fortunately, the destruction was not nearly as severe this time, but the Island took the brunt of the storm and suffered more damage than at the hands of Hazel. Toronto's only victim of the storm was swept off the pier and drowned in the Eastern Gap, hundreds of feet of boardwalk were ripped away, trees were blown down all over the Island and so much water roared across Island streets between lake and lagoons that Islanders were canoeing down the Main Drag the following day.

That fall the Metro Planning Board—unaided by briefs from Islanders—discussed the Island's future. On the table before it lay a plan by the internationally respected planner, Hans Blumenfeld, who was then Assistant Director of Metro Planning. It was a plan to warm the cockles of Islanders' hearts, and raise the hackles on Gardiner's neck. Blumenfeld, more than a decade ahead of his time, recommended that the Island should contain *both* houses *and* parkland, because "without the residences, the island would be a less interesting place." Metro, therefore, should take over only the park and unused areas and leave the rest with the City. He also made a strong plea for keeping the Island free of cars as a "pedestrian Island." This was to be the view adopted by Islanders' supporters many years later, but in 1955 Blumenfeld's arguments fell on deaf ears. New Metro Parks Commissioner Thompson was silent on the subject of ferries versus cars, but argued strongly against the idea of having both park and houses. In contrast to Blumenfeld's romantic vision of life on the Island, Thompson believed "that existing housing on the Island [was] of little value and should be removed." In short, he said, "the Island should be developed simply, with plenty of open space." Not surprisingly, the Gardiner-dominated Planning Board agreed and sent its staff

away to prepare another plan. In December the board adopted a general plan that gave the parks commissioner considerable scope "for the development of a large park in a simple and relatively inexpensive way."[24]

This left Commissioner Thompson free to prepare his first of many detailed plans for the Island. It would be neither simple nor inexpensive, but it would reflect Gardiner's own views on the subject. While Thompson was busy drawing up his vision of the Island's future, Gardiner, along with TTC Chairman Lamport, was busy drumming up support for automobile access. Predictably, Mayor Phillips took a very dim view of any bridge or tunnel proposal, as did the *Globe and Mail*, which called it "Still a Stupid Idea." But, equally predictably, both the *Telegram* and the *Star* gave strong support to auto enthusiasts, pumping out editorials as freely as motorists pumped in gas during these halcyon days of low-cost fuel.[25]

On February 10, 1956, Parks Commissioner Thompson revealed his grand, $14.5 million, ten-year plan. Prominent among his recommendations was a "tunnel [or bridge] to paradise," as the *Telegram* poetically put it. "This is an age when the majority of people expect to be able to drive an automobile to within a relatively short distance of the picnic table and beach," Thompson argued, "and to deny this privilege is to purposely restrict the use of any park area." He also recommended raising the level of parts of the Island, dredging a mile-long regatta course, laying out three major picnic areas and building a children's wonderland—and, incidentally, demolishing all the houses and buildings in an orderly fashion, sweeping from Hanlan's Point eastward. No mention was made of Ward's Islanders' one-year non-compensation leases (presumably they could be picked up quickly whenever the

land was needed for a parking lot or a picnic area), but Algonquinites would be evicted as their leases came due, or at the latest by 1968. The pace of acquisition elsewhere was to be quickened. All compensation leases on Centre and along Ward's Lakeshore area were to be acquired by 1962.

Metro Chairman Gardiner jumped to support the plan, and Metro politicians swiftly fell in line. Only Mayor Phillips and four City colleagues protested, not against terminating Island leases, but against allowing cars on the Island. So far, so good, for Gardiner. But here matters ground to a halt. When Metro politicians, gripped by a severe case of "tunnelophilia," approached the federal government to pay for their habit, they received a cold shoulder from Works Minister Robert Winters. Despite lamentations by the likes of Alderman William Dennison, who sniffed, "This means the Island will remain in the horse and buggy stage of development forever,"[26] Metro Council was forced, in May 1956, to cut back its Island plan to about $4 million. But it still retained money to acquire and demolish houses.

Chairman Gardiner, ever the political realist, took a car tour of the Island with Commissioner Thompson in July and promptly announced that many years would pass before the playground was invaded by automobiles. He now concluded that over the next ten years, the Island without cars could be developed as one of the finest recreational centres in North America. The *Globe and Mail* applauded this conversion on the bay to Toronto Island; the *Star* and the *Telegram* fumed; and the tunnel was temporarily shelved.

Ironically, just as Gardiner was rediscovering the virtues of the ferry service, the last great sidewheeler, the *Trillium*, was retired and sold to the Metro Works Department, which planned to hack off her superstructure and convert her into a garbage scow, like her ill-treated sister ship the *Bluebell*. Fortunately, the powers that be had a change of heart. On September 17, 1957, she was ignominiously towed to a lonely lagoon near the Lighthouse where she languished for sixteen years, a sad reminder of past glories, until she rose again from the marshes in 1973.

Meanwhile, elsewhere on the Island, tunnel or no tunnel, Metro's plans had already caused a mass migration of year-round Island residents back to the city. By May 1956 the school population had dropped to about 350, and ten of the school's seventeen classrooms had closed. The first demolition permits were issued to Metro for houses on Hiawatha, Lakeshore and St. Andrew's, and sales to Metro ran at the rate of five and six a week. By July Metro had acquired 120 houses and had hired a contractor to demolish fifty-nine.

Nevertheless, Islanders tried to carry on bravely. Harold and Alice Aitkin's daughter Catherine was married at St. Andrews-by-the-Lake and enjoyed a garden reception at the family's Lakeshore home. Sailors Mary and Paul McLaughlin proudly announced the birth of Terry, the future skipper of the 1983 challenger for the America's Cup, the *Canada I*. And the usual round of activities continued, at least down at Ward's. "It looked a long way from 'The Last Days of the Island' down at the park last Saturday evening," commented the *Ward's Island Weekly* about the annual Senior Masquerade in August. "Whatever is missing at Hanlan's or Centre this year," it went on somewhat unfeelingly, "Ward's Island is still going strong, and we hope to be very much alive for a long time to come."

Ward's lived on, but the rest of the Island

now rapidly became "a giant graveyard of houses." The demolition programme picked up speed in the fall and winter of 1956-57, as the Parks Department prepared to raze and raise a large part of Centre. Great steel-clawed backhoe machines rumbled across lawns and backyards, tearing and ripping their way through fragile wooden reminders of a bygone era. Smoke curled upward into the gray winter sky, as the piles of splintered wood were set on fire. Then the bulldozers pushed earth over the dying embers of a dying community, leaving "only mounds of earth where homes once stood." And the Metro workmen moved on to the next target, and the next, and the next.[27]

Few Islanders watched the demolitions. "It's almost like seeing a friend being buried," commented a bus driver sadly. By January 1957, 125 buildings were already gone. Such Island landmarks as the old Casino, the Gooderham mansion, the Carousel at Hanlan's and the Wiman buildings at Ward's were no more than memories. There were few streets that had not lost at least one building; while others had almost completely disappeared. Even the Centre Island Park—scene of picnics and rallies and good fun since 1888—had the appearance of a "winter battleground," scraped of topsoil and littered with the trunks of more than a hundred uprooted trees. Indeed, as the *Globe* reported on January 10, 1957, "the Island, as it is known by Torontonians who proudly call themselves Islanders, is vanishing quickly."

In spite of the devastation, Torontonians did continue to visit the Island, but they came in

Winter 1959: a snow-suited child watches the debris of a neighbour's house burning across the street from 4 Shiawassie Avenue. [TIA]

declining numbers and Island businesses were soon in deep trouble. In contrast to residents who wanted to stay as *long* as possible, businessmen wanted their long-term leases to be expropriated as *soon* as possible, so a system of arbitration was worked out with Metro in the fall of 1957.[28] The system may have been an improvement, but it was less than ideal. A year later, while

Balmy Beach pulls ahead of the Island Canoe Club at the ICC's regatta of June 23, 1957. Behind the canoeists, Centre Island is in the process of being raised and suffering "from a deluge of earth, burying streetlight poles up to their shoulders," according to one surprised visitor that July. [YUA:TC]

two-month proposition. The place would be a graveyard for 10 months of the year." And others certainly objected to the low compensation being offered, like Bill Roddy, a resident on the Lakeshore since 1931 who was busy selling off his furniture at "scrap prices," and were so depressed by the turn of events that they were willing to leave. But others wanted to stay on

Demolitions along the Main Drag: at the north end of the street, the police station (below) awaits its fate; and (right) at the south end, the venerable old Pierson Hotel meets it. [CTA:TIA]

sanding furniture in his hardware store, Percy Miller described his experience to the *Star* of October 2. "This place cost me $22,000 to build eight years ago, and I asked $35,000 for it from Metro because of the great business I have built here. Do you know what they offered me?—and I guess I'll have to take it—$17,000. I can't start a new business again. I don't know where to turn."

Residential property acquisition and demolition proceeded smoothly from Metro's point of view until the spring of 1958 when Commissioner Thompson recommended that fifty-one houses between Hooper Avenue and the Filtration Plant be cleared. The Inter-Island Council now, for the first time, entered the fray and managed to persuade Metro to extend the expiry date until March 31, 1959.[29]

But the destruction and the desolation spread. "People lived on the edge of a precipice,"

according to Alan Howard, who was among the last to leave Centre Island in the spring of 1959. "You never knew when the axe was going to fall." As it happened, Metro, by and large, terminated the leases as they came due. So initially demolitions were dotted around and "you got gaps, like a mouth full of bad teeth." But the gaps widened as more teeth were pulled.

Islanders by this time were becoming both bitter and confused. Some families had been told to leave, while others on the same streets had never been approached at all by Metro. While not necessarily objecting to the park in principle, some certainly objected to the park in practice, like old Bill Durnan, whose ancestors had first settled on the Island in the 1830s. "It's a shame when there is so much vacant land on the Island that could be turned into parks," to knock down homes. "Sure it's nice to have a big park," Durnan went on. "But here it would only be a

as long as possible, either from sheer necessity or from love of the place.[30]

Nineteen fifty-nine was not greeted happily by the forty families who were sticking it out in the controversial part of Centre Island between Hooper and the Filtration Plant. On January 2 they voted to ask for another delay until at least the end of the school year and on May 5, Metro Council agreed to allow those who were not actually in the way of park development to stay on, some to May 15 and others to June 25, 1959. As a result of what the *Globe* called "vigorous opposition," most of the area's residents had gained a temporary reprieve. But their protest was over; and the last of the houses and the last store, the Lamantia Brothers' grocery store, were soon turned over to Metro.

After the temporary slowdown of 1958-59, property acquisition and demolition continued unimpeded. By September 1960, hotels, some 20 stores, and 261 houses (or over a third of all Island buildings) had gone down before the

A few buildings survived the Metro onslaught: here the Manitou Road fire station floats toward its new (and current) Ward's Island location on May 12, 1960.   [YUA:TC]

bulldozers. Only 45 of the original 285 houses at Hanlan's and Centre remained. (By contrast, only 20 buildings at Ward's Island had fallen and Ward's, as the *Weekly* later proclaimed, was "very much alive.") The Hanlan's Island Association clubhouse and Emmanuel Church were gone. The ancient and honourable Pierson's Hotel was gone. The postwar modern Island cinema was gone. The Centre Island Association clubhouse, the rectory and the six-year-old parish hall were gone. The tiny trim Manitou Road police station was gone, though its companion, the squat little firehall, had been laboriously floated eastward to its new home at Ward's Island. And both the picturesque Centre Island churches—St. Rita's and St. Andrew's-by-the-Lake—had been carefully moved from west of the old Main Drag to new locations midway toward Ward's.

Meanwhile, the winter population had become so small—about 800—that the TTC, in its wisdom, stopped the winter tug service. Winter residents, most of whom lived at the eastern tip of the Island on Ward's and Algonquin, now had to travel in their packed bus along bumpy roads all the way across the Island to use the little airport cable ferry—in all a journey of *at least* an hour to cover perhaps two miles as the seagull flew. When the "last pocket of colonists on Ward's Island" protested against the substitution of the notoriously unreliable airport ferry for the tugboat, they found an unexpected ally in the Metro chairman, whose friendship with TTC Commissioner Lamport had turned sour. Using the airport cable ferry was a dumb idea, pronounced Gardiner. "It's time the TTC returned to the sensible system of using tugs to cross the harbour," he said, prompting surprised cheers from the Island—and backpedalling from the other three TTC commissioners, who

fell in line behind the Metro chairman. The *Ned Hanlan* was soon back on the Island route, and the ferry service was on its way to eventual takeover by Metro on January 1, 1962.[31]

Meanwhile, park development proceeded apace. Tons of earth raised the level of the park, and buried almost all traces of the former occupants. Some walls and walkways that led nowhere remain to this day along the boardwalk. Lush green sod was laid over acre upon acre of picnic grounds. And new park attractions began to appear. Perhaps the most successful was also the first: the Farm, which opened on May 15, 1959. The fences were deliberately low ("I want the children to be able to go over the fences and rub noses with the cows," Parks Commissioner Thompson told the *Telegram* on opening day, and the arrangement was deliberately untidy. "We're aiming for the tidy untidyness of the average well-kept place," the commissioner added. Among the more unusual occupants was a pink-eyed Angora rabbit, donated by a red-eyed ten-year-old Rod MacKenzie because "my parents were leaving the Island and they wouldn't let me take Harvey." At least one member of the family was able to stay on the Island.

In stark contrast to the new farm and to the scruffy excitement of the old Main Drag was the coolly elegant new Avenue of the Islands which replaced it in 1961: a broad cement mall with fountains, geometrically sculpted trees and formal flower beds stretching from the renovated old Manitou Bridge to the lake. To some people Metro's Island Park development represented "official sterilization," while to others it was a "project worthy of a great city." The difference of opinion remains to this day.

When Fred Gardiner stepped down as chairman at the end of 1961, Metro's Island Park

A novel form of winter transportation takes off on Algonquin Island in January 1962. [YUA:TC]

development was well in hand. It had been, according to architectural historian Eric Arthur, no mean achievement; Arthur, for one, would have liked to have seen Gardiner's name "associated in some way with the 'new' Island," for it had been, he wrote the *Star* on October 20, 1961, "his creation." Certainly, when Gardiner had started his term, there had been no Metro Parks Department, no Metro parks commissioner and no Metro Parks system. Now all were functioning strongly. And the Toronto Island was the first major Metro park. It became the jewel of the system and a symbol of the success of Metro itself. Perhaps that is why in later years, despite the change in public opinion, the parks commis-

(Left) *Children rub noses, not with cows, but with a donkey at Far Enough Farm on July 21, 1964.* [YUA:TC]

(Below) *Two of the main protagonists of the 1960s stand glumly near a new amusement at Centre Island in May 1967: Alderman David Rotenberg (in profile near the Model T) and Parks Commissioner Tommy Thompson (in the stetson hat).* [Sun: Telegram Collection]

sioner and a majority of Metro politicians were so grimly determined to develop the Island as originally planned.

As William Allen moved into the Metro chairman's office, with the blessing of the outgoing boss, the Island's political landscape was changing. During the rest of the decade, opposition to the acquisition and demolition of Island houses grew in intensity and bitterness until residents and their champion, the razor-sharp, fast-talking Alderman David Rotenberg, challenged Metro at every possible point. This era of growing opposition was characterized by periodic mammoth Council debates, shrewd political and technical manoeuvring, earnest individual efforts and limited group endeavours. Through most of the period, the political manoeuvring was orchestrated by Alderman Rotenberg, with Islanders following his lead. By and large they did not challenge the idea of the park, only its timing. And their success was reflected in the slower pace of demolitions. During the Gardiner years, Metro bulldozers had rolled lickety-split over close to 300 buildings; whereas during the Allen years, the pace slackened to 90,[32] leaving about 260 houses still standing defiantly on Ward's and Algonquin at the end of his term.

In the spring of 1962, as Metro prepared to demolish the deteriorating old dance hall at Hanlan's Point, C. Ross Anderson, an architect and a third-generation Islander who canoed to work in the summer, launched the first—and in this period, the only—direct frontal assault on the Metro plan to convert *all* the Island into parkland and to demolish *all* the houses. He asked Metro to restudy the Island plan ''with the aim of combining park expansion with rehabilitation of the Island community.''[33] Anderson managed to stir up some interest. Even Metro Chairman Allen did not reject the proposal

On June 6, 1963, Hamilton Cassels, Q.C. appeared for the second time before the Metro Parks Committee to oppose Commissioner Thompson's $12 million Island plan. He was assisted by Dr. E. G. Faludi who argued that: "Far from being incompatible, residential use enhances the attractiveness of the Island for recreation. Without them, the Island will be a silent tundra in the winter and during the summer weekdays, a lonely and quiet park with a reduced number of visitors." [Sun: Telegram *Collection*]

out of hand. After a sunny tour of the Island, on May 30, which included a long climb to the top of the newly renovated Lighthouse and a house-burning ceremony, courtesy of the Parks Department, Allen told the *Globe*, ''If the turn-out [of park visitors] is lower than expected, we are not going to allow valuable land to sit idle. Apartments on the east end would not be a hindrance to the park's use and it would mean tax revenues,'' he continued, thus feeding both Islanders' hopes of continued residence and their fears of a real estate conspiracy to drive them off.

Any rekindled hopes were doused in March 1963 when Tommy Thompson unveiled his $12 million, twenty-year scheme for the Island that rejected further consideration of any type of housing on the Island and recommended that all 362 remaining houses be removed in stages by 1968. He also proposed a potpourri of park projects: a puppet theatre, a marina, swimming pools, a sportland on Algonquin and a funland amusement area on Ward's. Politicians were impressed, but Islanders were not amused. Richard Barrett of Algonquin, for example, didn't like the prospect of exchanging his house for a golf course, or some such sports project. ''Grimm's wildest fairy tales,'' he grimaced to the *Telegram*, of March 15, ''were never so fantastic as this plan.'' Islanders prepared to do battle.

On April 11, 1963, Islanders appeared en masse before the Metro Parks Committee, of which Alderman David Rotenberg was a member, to oppose the $12 million plan and the demolition of more homes. Prior to the meeting they had garnered support from a variety of prominent groups and individuals. Here their spokesman was Hamilton Cassels, Q.C., a well-known Toronto lawyer whose family had summered at Hanlan's Point in the Edwardian era. He attacked the Thompson plan with verve as too expensive and too destructive of the natural character of the Island, asking that Island leases be extended and that the current natural type of development be continued. The politi-cians seemed to be impressed; so on a motion by City Controller Phil Givens, the committee voted to defer a decision on the plan until they had a chance to tour the Island, guided by Island residents as well as Commissioner Thompson.

The protagonists survived the tour and reassembled before the Parks Committee on June 6, 1963, to take another kick at the plan. About a hundred Islanders crowded into the Council Chamber. Mr. Cassels again carried the IIC colours into battle, while reinforcement was provided by the diminutive city planner Dr. E. G. Faludi, whom Islanders had hired to prepare an alternative plan which, not surprisingly, pushed for a continuation of a residential com-

Mrs. Velma Grieg sits on the boardwalk in front of her threatened Lakeshore home and garden on November 14, 1964. Mrs. Grieg was among those who stayed until the bitter end. By September 1968, the Griegs and Commissioner Thompson were even feuding over the flowers in this garden. "Your flowers? They aren't yours. They are ours. Don't you touch them," Mrs. Greig said Mr. Thompson had told her.   [Sun: Telegram *Collection*]

munity. Faludi won the headlines, but not the day.

The committee's discussions were heated and, from Islanders' perspective, unsuccessful. In the end the committee rejected both of Alderman Rotenberg's motions to extend leases, but did vote to defer dealing with the $12 million plan. As far as this committee was concerned, Metro's acquisition policy would stand—and Islanders' houses would fall, by 1968. Islanders left the meeting angry and disappointed, with their leaders muttering darkly about Tommy Thompson being "strung up by his toes."[34] This was the last time for the next four years that Islanders took a prominent public role in their own defence.

On June 18 Rotenberg next took the battle to full Metro Council where the debate droned on for nearly three hours before an overflow audience of Islanders. Some Metro councillors, in fact, took exception to the large number of Islanders present. The imperious East York Reeve True Davidson, for example, said that it was "disgraceful" that such a mass of people appeared in order to "intimidate" Council. But Metro Council was not easily intimidated and resoundingly defeated motions by both Rotenberg and Controller Givens to delay the acquisition and destruction of Island homes. Undeterred, Rotenberg orchestrated another lengthy but still losing battle at Metro Council in September.[35] Notices to vacate by September 15, 1964, would go out to another twenty-one Lakeshore homeowners.

By the end of 1963, therefore, the Islanders' record of opposing acquisitions and demolitions was not very impressive. Houses continued to tumble, and Islanders continued to perform "every quirk of island life like a defiant ritual," as sometime Islander and full-time writer Harry

Bruce wrote in the *Star* of September 16, 1963. While Commissioner Thompson was observing astutely that "today, it is politically possible to turn the Island into a dynamic park" but "give these people another 10 years and it will be politically impossible,"[36] Alderman Rotenberg was busily devising new ways to accomplish that delay. He adopted a different approach over the next few years, relying on his own sharp presentation of facts in the public arenas, buttressed by behind-the-scenes political manoeuvring. The Islanders' role was reduced to supplying him with facts and quietly lobbying politicians. Rotenberg frequently appeared to lose (most of his motions were in fact voted down), but somehow compromises were made, technicalities were used and extensions squeezed out.

The Lakeshore battle for the final eighty houses between Hooper on Centre and Lenore on Ward's got underway in earnest. While Islanders like Paul and Mary McLaughlin courted politicians with boat rides and homey tours of the Island, Rotenberg kept sniping from behind every technical tree and bush at City Hall. In the spring of 1964, after a great deal of political toing-and-froing, Islanders had a taste of success. Commissioner Thompson wanted to expropriate eighteen houses between Hooper and Chippewa. In a surprise move, the Metro Executive voted 4-2 to delay the expropriations to September 1965. Ironically, their saviour this day was their old arch foe, Allan Lamport, who was back on Metro Council. Controller Lamport was fed up with spending money on the Island and argued that Metro could not afford to build the campsite for underprivileged children that Commissioner Thompson, tugging at the heartstrings, was proposing.

On May 21, 1964, when the expropriation issue came before Metro Council for the *third* time, Council finally agreed to the delay, but reaffirmed its intention to ultimately acquire the houses. Metro Chairman Allen was outraged by the defeat. "I have never heard of a more persistent and strong, self-centred lobby," he spat out to the *Star* afterward. Others agreed that they had been subjected to pressure. But it must have been a pretty pleasant form of pressure, since it seemed to consist mostly of boat tours

In October 1963, as he strolled by one "proud old dowager of a deserted house," boarded up and waiting for the end, third generation Islander C. Ross Anderson told columnist Bruce West, "It's like seeing an old friend die, a little bit at a time." This "friend" died in September 1964.   [YUA:TC]

"I would if I could," thinks one of Commissioner Thompson's juvenile supporters in July 1964. [YUA:TC]

through meandering lagoons, cocktail parties and dinner invitations. So much for canapé canvassing.

While Islanders returned home to savour the sweet taste of partial success, tend their gardens, enjoy the summer and advertise their cause by painting SAVE OUR HOMES on the Algonquin Island retaining wall, Commissioner Thompson went back to his drawing board. If Alderman Rotenberg and his cohorts wanted a plan, he'd give them a plan—and more ammunition, as it turned out.

In October 1964 Commissioner Thompson unveiled yet another multimillion-dollar plan for the Island. (By this time, Metro had spent about $8.6 million developing the park, including more than $3 million for property acquisition, and had completely cleared the western half, from Hooper to Hanlan's.) Now Thompson proposed spending another $4.4 million to finish both the park and the Island clearances by 1971. In addition to the picnic areas and improved beaches, the commissioner had some flashier suggestions—like a mini-monorail, an underwa-

William Ronald retouches his mural at the Ward's Island Rectory in June 1968.   [Sun: Telegram *Collection*]

ter aquarium, an amusement park at Ward's, a par-3 golf course at Algonquin complete with floating balls and, yes, a children's camp on Snake Island.

Before a newly elected Metro Council dealt with Thompson's Master Plan in March 1965, the tunnel fetishists were again up to their old tricks. The driving force behind this new campaign was none other than Metro Chairman Allen, who raised the issue in his 1965 inaugural speech to Council. While opponents fumed and spun their wheels, the campaign for a buses-only tunnel under the Western Gap picked up speed until it slammed into the same roadblock as its predecessors: money. When a price tag of about $10 million was placed on the project and no help was forthcoming from Ottawa, interest in the tunnel went underground. Allen, a political realist like his predecessor Fred Gardiner, finally commented, "the ferry service is here to stay."[37]

Meanwhile, Metro pressed on with Thompson's Master Plan, which sought to acquire the final twelve houses still left between Hooper and Chippewa. During a "heated but orderly" three-and-a-half-hour debate at Metro Council on March 23, 1965, Chairman Allen marshalled enough support to smash Alderman Rotenberg's opposition efforts and to endorse *part* of the Master Plan: the children's camp recommendation (which would come back to haunt Allen and Thompson) and the new property acquisition schedule. In the *Telegram* Ron Haggart wrote what he must have thought was the Islanders' epitaph: "Last night, the political power of the Island Residents was destroyed. We shall hear no more of them. The vote against them was humiliating, 17-5." It was undoubtedly a setback; but it was far from Haggart's "final and decisive battle."

Islanders and their supporters went away to lick their wounds and invent new ways to slow the bulldozers. Over at Ward's Island, for example, the Reverend Paul Hopkins, the hip rector of St. Andrew's-by-the-Lake (who had initially startled Islanders by whisking around his parish on a motorcycle wearing a black leather suit), prevailed on his flamboyant friend, William Ronald, to paint a mural in the Rectory. The theory went that Metro would never demolish a building containing an important—and *valuable*—work of art. So Ronald (a member of

Toronto's abstract-expressionist group Painters Eleven in the 1950s) splashed a great galloping mural across the walls and ceiling of the Rectory. The ploy generated a lot of favourable publicity in the summer of 1965, which heartened Islanders, even if it accomplished little else.

Rotenberg and his few new converts to the cause, like Aldermen Charles Caccia and Hugh Bruce, went back to City Hall and to more traditional obstructionist tactics. In May, when Thompson sought approval for $600,000 to finance the children's camp, Rotenberg *et al.*

The Trillium *settles (literally) into her new home near the Filtration Plant in August 1963. Two years later, Robert Thomas Allen wrote, "It now rests tired and worn out amid the bullrushes of Lighthouse Pond, like the ghost of an old love barge, silent and peeling and sagging in the middle like a lot of the people who still remember the days when it was as 'in' as Beatle wigs."* [Sun: Telegram *Collection*]

opened fire on the camp—and on the associated property acquisitions. Initially unsuccessful, they gathered some useful temporary allies, like Scarborough Reeve Ab Campbell, who was appalled by the high cost. "When children go to a campsite they don't expect to live in a palace," he told Council on May 14.[38] Finally, on August 5, success. A bill to expropriate the eleven properties in question failed to receive the two-thirds majority required for third reading that day. The bill would have to be reintroduced another day, when a simple majority would suffice.

What appeared to be just a temporary technical delay, however, turned out to be much more. It was the key to as much as a four-year reprieve for some Island residents. More important, it also had an immediate, symbolic effect on Islanders who were "tingling with new hope." And, as the *Globe* suggested on August 26, 1965, a "new breed" of Islander began digging in—encouraged not only by this small success but, increasingly, also by the new spirit of dissent sweeping the continent in the sixties. It was a time of anti-war, anti-establishment feeling, symbolized by the massive Teach-In at the University of Toronto in October, which captured international headlines and galvanized Canada's own New Left. People who would never have thought of fighting City Hall—let alone of winning—began to think again. And they even had a glorious new City Hall to fight against. On September 13, 1965, exuberant Torontonians celebrated the opening of Viljo Rewell's unusual structure by dancing in the outdoor pool and getting lost in the building's unfamiliar curving corridors.

But, like it or not, Metro just kept rolling along. Alderman Rotenberg and his allies might be winning the delaying battles, but they were losing the war. In spite of their outraged protests, more houses continued to fall in 1966 until there were only forty-four homeowners with compensation leases left on the narrow neck of land leading to Ward's Island, the final Lakeshore homes scheduled to be acquired in stages by 1968. And another 260 plus with non-compensation leases on Algonquin and Ward's were scheduled to be acquired in 1968. At this time, Metro park devotées added a new tactic to their strategy: they began trying to create the impression that Islanders, especially Ward's Islanders, were living in some sort of slum, with no toilets, no proper heating, defective wiring, and so on. It was undoubtedly easier in this heyday of "slum clearance" and "urban renewal" to rationalize demolishing bad houses than good ones.[39]

During the summer of 1966, while City inspectors were combing Island residences eagerly looking for defective wiring and other flaws, Torontonians began returning to the Island in numbers reminiscent of the pre-Metro era. For the first time since 1953, over a million visitors ferried across the bay. Some were literally bowled over by the experience, like the de Havilland Company merrymakers, who were thrown to the deck when the *William Inglis* crashed into the Hanlan's Point dock, sending eleven people to hospital with minor injuries. Several times, unfortunately, real tragedy did strike. For example, a young plastics worker, eighteen-year-old Mario Liscio—one of the tide of Italian immigrants that had found its way to Toronto, and Toronto Island—drowned in "Gasoline Alley Lagoon," the third canoeist to drown that summer.

The fall of 1966 brought more reports and more dissension when Allen and Thompson tried to get the old 1965 summer camp Expropriation Bill back on the tracks. Sparks once again flew and Chairman Allen even threatened, not for the first or last time, to "wrap [the residential area] in a red ribbon and give it back" to the City.[40]

The spectre of the Expropriation Bill, naturally, struck fear into the hearts of the eight Lakeshore households still remaining in the threatened locations. Mrs. Ethel Huard, a seventy-two-year-old widow, had moved with her prospector husband from a mining town in Northern Ontario in 1944. They built their home and slaved over their property. "I was only fifty years old when we started here. I was young and I worked like a dog. But I can't do it now. I'm crippled up. I got asthma," she told the *Globe and Mail* on October 4. "It was our first real home. We came here thinking we'd die here. It was like paradise."

It was not quite yet paradise lost. In spite of Allen's best efforts, Metro dallied and dithered, causing the chairman to depart from his usually smooth, urbane demeanour. Rotenberg *et al.* managed to stave off third and final reading of the bill and Mrs. Huard and her neighbours could relax until after the December municipal election that would produce a new restructured Metro Council with representatives drawn from the city and five (not twelve) boroughs.

As Canadians moved into Centennial Year, Islanders and Metro moved toward another showdown. Metro Chairman Allen was tired of being portrayed as the "big bad wolf" for expropriating homes on the Island and declared that Metro Council would have to decide soon whether to go ahead with clearing the remaining houses, or turn them back to the City.[41] He found a willing ally in Toronto's newly elected mayor, William Dennison, who denounced Islanders' attempts to link the housing crisis with preserving their homes as simply a ploy for cottagers to keep their summer cottages at the expense of other Metro taxpayers, conveniently ignoring the presence of year-round Islanders.

Before a crucial meeting on May 18, Tommy Thompson combined politics with pleasure: he took Parks Committee members to the Island for some fun and games at the new children's amusement park that was about to open. There, Metro politicians were to be seen going around in circles, on the new, old carousel that concessionaire Warren Beasley had imported from the Catskill Mountains. (Ironically, one of the Island's own magnificent merry-go-rounds had been dismantled and carted off to the U.S. to swirl at Disney World.) To the patriotic oompah-pah of ''God Bless America,'' Alderman Mary Temple and her confrères pumped up and down on hand-carved wooden horses, ostriches, lions and tigers. Controller Margaret Campbell blew the whistle of a model Iron Horse of the 1890s. And ''engineer'' Tommy Thompson, eager to get his Island plan back on the track, hopped on board and led a trainful of politicians smoothly around this 1800 foot railroad. Equally determined to prevent him, Alderman David Rotenberg, sans duster, squired the still-undecided Alderman Temple out for a ride in a shiny Model T.

Meanwhile, down at the eastern end of the Island, residents were also preparing for the May 18 meeting. And some major changes were in the making. Now that the 1968 deadline for the 265 homeowners with non-compensation leases on Ward's and Algonquin was coming uncomfortably close, a small group from this area got together and decided that they should not simply rely on Alderman Rotenberg but should become active and press their own case at Metro. For the first time since 1963, Islanders decided to go as a deputation to Metro Parks Committee.

May 1967 and politics can be fun—at least at the new Centre Island amusement park. [YUA:TC]

But they still shied away from acting as their own spokesmen and decided instead to hire lawyer and NDP M.P. Andrew Brewin to present their case for a five-year extension.

On May 18 Brewin gave a polished performance on behalf of the 310 homeowners covered by the new Island Home Owners Association, making a moral appeal to Metro not to throw people out of their homes during a housing crisis. Chairman Allen remained unmoved, but the rest of the committee was badly split and

at least one member, Mary Temple, was leaning toward granting a five-year extension. To head off any possible defectors, Chairman Allen proposed what became the Great Allen Compromise: take the forty-four remaining Lakeshore homes with compensation leases now (i.e., December 31, 1967) and give the other leases, which would expire at the end of 1968, an extension of only twenty months, to August 31, 1970. The committee finally adopted Allen's compromise by the narrowest of margins, 4-3.

The Allen Compromise moved unchanged through to Metro Council, where it ran up against Rotenberg and his well-coached troops. On May 30-31, 1967, the two sides went at each other hammer and tongues for seven hours. As they broke for dinner, Rotenberg made a fatal tactical error: he persuaded his old friend Alderman Tony O'Donohue to return after dinner. ''Well, somewhere in the middle, Bill Allen who was a great lobbyist, one of the greatest, got at Tony and convinced him to change his vote,'' Rotenberg later commented. After dinner, the reinvigorated, reindoctrinated councillors continued the debate on into the small hours of Wednesday morning. When the votes were taken, all motions to extend the leases or delay the decision were rejected and the Allen Compromise ended up with a 14-14 tie. ''If Tony hadn't come back,'' Rotenberg later laughed ruefully, ''I would have won by one vote.'' As it was, Chairman Allen broke the tie in favour of his own solution. The forty-four Lakeshore houses would go at the end of 1967; and the other Island houses would stay for twenty months, until the last day of August 1970.[42]

The Islanders' first foray back into the political limelight had been partly successful: they had gained a twenty-month reprieve (not a five-year

View of some of the condemned Lakeshore houses from the Algonquin Bridge.
[Al Schoenborn]

Torontonians turned their backs on the lake and rushed at midnight to City Hall Square, for a "Splash In" at the pool. Throughout the day and on into the following night, the celebrating continued with parades, free birthday cakes, street dancing and fireworks. Over at the Island, the Centennial Marina was under construction at Centre Island and the annual Dominion Day regatta was under way on Long Pond. The old Island Canoe Club may have been gone, but it certainly wasn't forgotten, as the Oldershaw name was still prominent among the list of winners, helping the Mississauga Canoe Club splash to an easy victory. Down at the eastern end of the Island, the piper piped, the champagne corks popped and 200 Queen City Yacht Club sailors cheered as Algonquin Islander Frank Madrick finally launched his forty-foot yacht. "No, it's not a Centennial project," the thirty-eight-year-old boat-builder quipped. "But it feels like it took 100 years."[43]

The celebrating continued on past the July 1 weekend. Toronto's West Indian community sprouted blazing costumes and "jumped up" Trinidad-style to steel band music on Toronto's own Island in the sun. It was the first Caribana, which was to become an annual event. And Toronto's Italian community elevated its annual Italian Day Picnic at Centre Island to the first of the mammoth International Picnics, complete with smiling politicians, bountiful Miss Bikini hopefuls, sauce-spattered spaghetti-eating contestants, red-white-and-green flag-bedecked ferries and Valpollicella hidden in thermos bottles. From now on it was CHIN up and anchors away for the reportedly largest annual picnic in the world.

While most Canadians were enjoying the warm good feelings and *bonhomie* of Centennial summer, a cold war descended on the eastern

one) for some (but not all) of the remaining houses. So Islanders came away with mixed emotions. Some Lakeshore residents felt that they had been sold down the river by their neighbours and were undoubtedly bitter. But many other residents, covered by the twenty-month reprieve, got a whole new lease not only on Island life, but on political life as well. "I think about 1967 I was kind of prepared in my mind to go in 1968," reflected Wendi Hanger of Ward's

Island. "But as soon as we got a chance to stay, the whole viewpoint changed. Wow! You can fight City Hall, honestly, really? It could actually happen? Isn't this something!" So it was. But it wasn't everything, yet.

"This day is Canada's," declared Prime Minister Lester Pearson on July 1, 1967, as Canadians across the country and around the world engaged in a frenzy of patriotic celebrating. In contrast to earlier anniversaries, tip of the Island. Sniping and accusations issued forth from both camps. Islanders accused Metro of deliberately harassing residents, making them so uncomfortable that they would leave. Take, for example, the War of the Weeds. The grass in some places was at least thigh-high, covering picnic tables and benches, and the weeds were having a wonderful summer. Residents saw Metro's refusal to cut the grass and weeds as part of a plot. But Commissioner Thompson denied this. His budget had been cut, so the grass and the weeds weren't.

Metro had its own complaints about Island grass, as Metro police were sent to investigate accusations that the Island was becoming a haven for beer and pot parties. Then, in September, Chairman Allen stirred things up some more. He accused Islanders of profiteering from the twenty-month extension granted in May. Commissioner Thompson elaborated later to the press: a man, he believed, had taken over two Island properties and was renting space out by the night to York-ville hippies. The impression created by these reports was not only that the Island was becoming some sort of hippy haven, but that Islanders themselves were engaged in a plot to exploit poor Metro and make a financial killing. The war of words and images marched onward.

Commissioner Thompson marched on as well, issuing a report in late September that recommended demolishing (rather than renting) most of the thirty-seven remaining houses in the controversial Lakeshore area (the others would be used for such purposes as housing the Island Park superintendent). Despite valiant resistance by Alderman Rotenberg and such allies as City Controller Margaret Campbell (who commented at one point, "I can't support putting people out of their homes so we can put in picnic tables"),[44] Council voted on Halloween

1967 to acquire the (now) thirty-three remaining houses. As a concession to the tightening housing situation, Chairman Allen moved, and Council agreed, to allow year-round residents in nineteen houses to stay on as monthly tenants until August 31, 1968. The others would have to leave their Island homes by the end of 1967.[45]

Residents of the unprotected houses delayed moving until the last possible moment, hoping for one more last-minute miracle. But none came. And as they left, Metro ripped out the plumbing (to prevent "hippies" or anyone else from moving back in) and demolished the houses where compensation settlements had been reached. Meanwhile, the year-round residents who remained endured one of the worst winters in many years. "One morning it took us 4½ hours to get through the ice, and that's only a mile," drawled Harold McDermid, captain of the sturdy little ice-breaking *Ongiara*, which had been on the route since 1963.[46] Sometimes she couldn't make it across at all without help, as on the frigid January morning when one hundred passengers were trapped for an hour by ice near the Ward's dock until a tug pulled them free.

Then as spring returned and more settlements had been reached, more houses were swiftly demolished. Work crews, understandably, took a certain amount of professional pride in their efficiency: on a "good day," the five-man crew could obliterate two houses. According to Thomas Wray, a veteran of scores of house wreckings, "The buildings were tinder dry. They crumble[d] at the first push of the machine. And the debris burn[ed] easily." If the Metro Parks Department was "on its toes," the *Globe* reported, it could rush in, lay sod, deposit a picnic table and create "instant parkland," all in one day.

Island children, who passed the wreckers and

the bulldozers and the fires on their way to and from the school, naturally found the whole thing puzzling but pretty exciting. "Watching a steam-shovel ripping a house down for a kid was just mind-boggling. You just stand there with your mouth open and watch," recalled Ron Mazza of Seneca Avenue and a future Island activist. "Not fully understanding what was happening, you just sort of treated it as enter-tainment." But underneath the children's excitement was a genuine feeling of unease, even fear. "Our kids came home," one concerned father recalled, "and said, rather anxiously, 'We

Spaghetti-eating multi-culturalism at the July 1967 International Picnic at Centre Island. [YUA:TC]

will get a warning, won't we before they come and burn the house down?''

Island adults were devastated. Many couldn't bear to watch the destruction or even pass by the empty places where homes had once stood. And those who did watch, like Algonquinite Ruth Putt, never forgot the experience:

> I'll never forget the sound. [The wrecker] seemed like something prehistoric, you know, like a big animal—that you see in those science fiction movies—that go into a city and just wreck everything. I'll never forget it. It's just one of those things that's like a nightmare. If [the wrecker] couldn't knock something down, they would take the head—something like this—and crash it into [the house]. It was a battering ram. It was just as if it was going right through me. It had big teeth on it and it was jointed like an elbow and wrist and it could reach out, with these claws, and it would just go into a roof and *crash*. It's an awful crashing, crunching sound. All the wood splintering and if it came down on the way and ripped out glass, there'd be all the panes of storm windows and windows, all crashing. And I'd see all this *destruction*. Wanton destruction. Absolutely. Thousands of dollars. And the people who had lived there and had to get out, they'd stand there. You could just tell that this was the end of it. They didn't know what they were going to do.

> Well, as soon as they'd get them wrecked, they'd run the bulldozer over [the debris] and crush it all down, and scoop it all up in a pile and they'd set fire to it. And it would never be erased from your mind, ever. Because, that was *the end*. You just felt so terrible. There was just nothing there anymore.

By the end of May only twelve repossessed houses stood ''in broken dignity'' along the Lakeshore—vacant and vandalized. Doors hung ajar, windows were broken, screens flapped in the wind and Island youngsters cycled in and out

through open doors and around litter-strewn living rooms. Mary Walsh, whose grandfather had built the big old Lakeshore house that nourished five generations of her family from 1885 on, commented sadly to *Globe and Mail* reporter Cameron Smith, ''We were so careful in leaving everything nice and tidy in case Metro wanted to move somebody else in. And then they let this happen. It's absolutely disgraceful.''

Spirits were higher down at Centre Island Park, where politicians, once again, sampled concessionaire Warren Beasley's newest offerings. While other Council members floated, tooted and munched their way through various amusement park delights, Metro Chairman William Allen spent ten minutes up in the air waving to friends from the new Sky Ride.

Allen, of course, was not the only politician who was riding high in the spring of 1968. As Toronto Islanders made one final attempt to save the seventeen remaining occupied Lakeshore houses, Trudeaumania swept the land and the bachelor prime minister kissed, danced and swan-dived his way toward victory on June 25. At a more mundane pace, Alderman Rotenberg and his cohorts went through all the familiar motions to try to wheedle one last reprieve for the doomed Lakeshore residents. No luck. On June 11, 1968—the eve of one of Trudeau's frenzied campaign visits to Toronto—Metro Council put the lid on any more extensions, no matter how temporary. These Islanders would have to leave by August 31.

A pleasant interlude in the final Lakeshore battle was provided by the Mariposa Folk Festival, which landed on Toronto Island over the weekend of August 9-11. Commissioner Thompson opened the festival with a speech and a bawdy song, prompting one long-haired, bare-footed youth to sigh, ''He's too beautiful.

Mariposa '68 moves to Olympic Island. [YUA:TC]

That Metro cat is out of sight, right out of sight.'' For three days and nights, Joni Mitchell, Murray McLaughlin, Gilles Vigneault and scores of other performers enchanted thousands of visitors lounging under the leafy greenery of Olympic Island and even inspired informal hootenannies in the all-too-long ferry lines.[47]

Joni Mitchell's ''Clouds,'' however, were not

Mary McLaughlin (shown here on September 11, 1968) raised Commissioner Thompson's ire once again when she objected to Metro's burning the debris of her neighbours' former houses. "Let them charge us," snapped the Commissioner. "They watched us burn 400 houses over there up to now. What did they think we were doing? Heating and bending them?" [YUA:TC]

the only disturbance on the horizon. Islanders' traditional Gala Day weekend was brought to a thunderous close as the wildest storm of the season swept across the Island. And most disturbing of all: the August 31 deadline was approaching, all too rapidly. Many Lakeshore residents packed their belongings and left sadly, though quietly. But not all. After the August 31 deadline passed, eleven residents remained in the doomed houses and continued to fight a rearguard action. Davie Maxwell vowed that he

would not leave until he was offered proper compensation. "A settlement must be made. If Mr. Thompson is able to cut off the utilities, it will be inconvenient, but we will stay." Thompson, for his part, felt unjustly criticized about the compensation issue. "I am not a dictator. I don't set the prices for the houses, the property commissioner does that." But on September 3, he took the initiative. "I will have to ascertain if we are legally entitled to bulldoze those homes this afternoon," Thompson told

reporters. "When we act, we will act, not talk." By the next day, however, no action had been taken against the eleven defiant holdouts and Thompson had reduced his response to reporters' questions to a terse "no comment."[48]

A few days later, Islanders began sniping from another direction, charging that Metro was breaking a bylaw against burning debris at a demolition site. "It's not just the danger to my house and others near-by," said Mary McLaughlin, as a debris fire raged beside her house. "It's the principle of the thing."[49] But all this last-ditch opposition was to no avail. By November Metro had gained warrants of possession. Finally, all of the Lakeshore houses were vacated and demolished, and a number of veterans from the Lakeshore battles had moved to other houses on Ward's and Algonquin, where they could continue to live on the Island, and live to fight Metro again.

At the end of the decade, with the last of the Lakeshore houses demolished and with the August 31, 1970, Allen Compromise deadline fast approaching, the residents on Ward's and Algonquin would finally come directly under the Metro gun. The battles of the sixties were over. It was now time to prepare for the battles of the seventies. The style would change, many more people would become directly involved and Islanders would begin to attack the park plan itself. But many of the arguments and many of the tactics would remain the same. The struggles of the sixties had left a legacy of bitterness on both sides that would provide the context for more recent political events.

We Shall Fight Them on the Beaches...

Even the baseball players were there. So were the assorted dogs, the small children, the sandalled shock troops and the blazered battalions. In all, about two hundred Islanders—old and new alike—crowded into the great wooden Ward's Island Association clubhouse to witness the birth of a defiantly political organization, the Toronto Island Residents Association—or TIRA, as it soon became known. That gathering on Wednesday July 30, 1969, was "the biggest public meeting that had been held in a very, very long time," according to Ward's Islander Maureen Smith, one of the spark plugs behind the formation of the new organization. Island residents were sufficiently worried about their looming deadline to put aside more pleasant summer pursuits in order to find out what the meeting's co-chairmen, Ward's Island Association President Peter Gzowski and Algonquin Island Association President Mark Harrison, had to say.

The idea of protesting and fighting City Hall was as foreign to some Islanders (especially older ones) as the pictures of Mars and of the men walking on the moon that were coming over their TV sets that summer. But a new spirit was sweeping across the city and beginning to touch the Island. Just that afternoon, in fact, the *Star* carried a report of city ratepayer groups rallying together "to form a city-wide organization to protect homeowners from 'ill-considered' City Council decisions"—a reform group that would become the Confederation of Residents and Ratepayers Associations, or CORRA for short. Closer to home, Gzowski and Harrison had prepared the way for the new organization by publishing a rousing "Open Letter to the Islanders" in the July 11 issue of the fifty-three-year-old *Ward's Island Weekly*. Amid the notices for Bingo and Gala Day, they sounded the call to arms:

Anyone who's really looking forward to the bulldozers crunching through his house next fall [when the extension ends in August 1970] needn't bother reading much further. The bulldozers will come all right, and you won't have to worry about them; just relax and enjoy the time our two communities on Ward's and Algonquin have left.

But if you haven't given in yet, read on. If you believe, as we do, that there is a clear and logical case for commuting the death sentence on Island living, stay with us. If you believe, as we do, that if the case is put forward in clear and logical terms the inevitable will at least be postponed, then we have something to tell you.

This is an open letter to announce the beginning of a new political body, the Island Residents' Association. For short: the IRA—and you can make of that what you will.

Mark Harrison called the meeting to order. The nearby baseball diamond may have been empty, but the brightly lit bowling green boasted assorted white-haired, white-ducked competitors and occasionally the clinking of the bowls and muffled epithets floated into the clubhouse on the gentle summer breeze. Harrison welcomed everyone to the meeting, "particularly the new residents of the Islands," and outlined the brief history of the IRA (not to be confused with the extinct Island Ratepayers Association). Then rumpled media man and co-chairman, Peter Gzowski, read the agenda in his mellow "Radio Free Friday" voice and proceeded to conduct the business of the meeting. At the end, he opened the floor to questions and comments. Most were supportive and helpful enough; but one irate lady from Belfast turned the air Orange with her protest against calling the organization the IRA. To Mike Harrison's great relief, however, this meeting confirmed the name and he was able to distribute the "I support the IRA" buttons that he had had already made up for the occasion. The protest over the name, however, did not disappear. By August "the Troubles" in Northern Ireland were once again making headlines and on August 28 the Executive voted to change their name to the *Toronto Island Residents Association, or TIRA.*[1]

Apart from this controversy, the meeting was a resounding success. Seven committees were formed, more than 150 members volunteered their services and Islanders were the proud owners of a brand-new organization constituted for the "single purpose of preserving the Toronto Islands community." Before this meeting Harrison and Gzowski had called it "one of the most important in the Islands' history." And so it was, for it established the residents' association which has survived to this day and has been instrumental in prolonging the life of the remaining Island community.

While Island politicos were hard at work, Islanders and off-Islanders enjoyed the usual

Showdown at Algonquin Bridge: Islanders young and old wait for the arrival of the sheriff on July 29, 1980—and appeal to Ontario Premier William Davis to save their community. [Star]

round of Island festivities. On the same day that Prince Charles was being invested as Prince of Wales, over six hundred competitors splashed and strained at the annual Dominion Day regatta, now hailed by organizers as the world's largest combined rowing and paddling competition. Later in the month geese scattered as war canoes again swooped down Long Pond for the Canadian Canoe Association southern Ontario trials. Island ferries proved inadequate to their task on several occasions. On the Sunday of the great International Picnic, over 36,000 people descended on the Island. After the day's fun, many weary, hamper-hugging, homeward-bound picnickers had to wait three hours to cross the bay, while harried policemen had to form a human chain, holding each other's nightsticks to control the crush of passengers waiting at the Centre Island dock. Some even had their ties torn off. A couple of weeks later, Mariposa folkies were caught in hour-long line-ups as they were making their annual pilgrimage to hear the likes of Bruce Cockburn, Ian and Sylvia and Joni Mitchell. Joan Baez may have arrived effortlessly via the shoreline, walking barefoot in the water, patting kids on the head and saying hello to some big dogs, but she came by launch, not ferry. Her fans would either have to walk *on* the water, or wait in lines, singing "Michael Row the Boat Ashore." Then the Civic Holiday weekend in early August brought Gala Day to Ward's Island, complete with games, sports and dinner-in-the-park, and Caribana with a thousand rhinestone-bespeckled Masqueraders and ten jubilant steel bands to Centre Island.

One visitor to the Island who had no problem with the ferries was Prime Minister Pierre Elliott Trudeau. But he encountered other problems. On what became known world-wide as Wood-stock weekend, the prime minister came to

An enthusiastic member of the crowd joins Miss Caribana '83 and her attendants on Olympic Island. [SDG]

"old Tory Toronto," ignored pickets at the Princes' Gate, opened the Exhibition and sped across the bay in a police launch to attend a Metro Liberal Party picnic at Centre Island. Shortly after he had landed, three well-groomed and neatly tailored young men surprised the police guards, who had been on the lookout for any "bearded, beaded hippy-type." The three youths dashed madly toward the prime minister, waved Mao's little red book as well as anti-Trudeau posters and shouted a variety of anti-Trudeau, pro-Marxist slogans. Burly policemen soon wrestled the attackers to the ground, hand-cuffed their wrists and hustled them off—still shouting—to a nearby police boat. Excited members of the Liberal crowd shouted "Kill the bastards" and "Long live Trudeau." Meanwhile, Trudeau—the veteran of the St. Jean Baptiste Day fracas—coolly side-stepped the melée and continued nonchalantly on to the picnic, where he shook hands with the faithful, danced with Miss Toronto, planted kisses on willing cheeks

and was adorned with two leis. Trudeau then disappeared across the bay in a police launch and returned to Ottawa to his House full of "nobodies."[2]

The summer of 1969 also provided drama of a different sort out on the lake. It was one of the biggest years in sailing that Toronto had ever seen. And undoubtedly, the highlight was the RCYC's defence of the seventy-three-year-old Canada's Cup, known as the America's Cup of the Great Lakes. After months of preparation the defence itself proved remarkably easy, if not disappointing. The scarlet-hulled *Manitou* carried RCYC colours into the contest against Cleveland's chunkier *Niagara*. She sailed away with the first two races, though the final mam-moth 204-mile test provided some exciting moments for both crew and supporters back on the club verandah. For thirty-seven hours the two yachts did battle with spars and spinnakers out on the blustery great lake, until Skipper Connolly radioed RCYC general manager

(Above) *Centre Island, August 15, 1969: still waving their little red books, the assailants are quickly surrounded...and the smiling Prime Minister moves on through the Liberal crowd.*   [*Globe and Mail*/ PAC (PA-136134 and PA-136137)]

Colonel Frank Ovens. "You might put a little something on ice, if you could, Colonel," Connolly's voice crackled over the air. "Does this mean that *Manitou* has won?" asked the cautious colonel. "What do you think?" chuckled Connolly. Champagne corks popped and about 150 yachting enthusiasts who had been keeping a night watch gathered in the darkness on the Island shoreline to welcome the *Manitou* and her weary but successful crew home around 2:30 A.M.[3]

It may have been smooth sailing for RCYC yachtsmen, but clearly there was rough weather ahead for Island residents. Some changes worked to their advantage: notably the fact that in September 1969 the avuncular, snow-haired Ab Campbell was elected Metro chairman. With him in the chairman's office, prospects for a lease extension seemed to improve. Whereas former Chairman William Allen had "carried out what amounted to a vendetta," according to one Island activist, Campbell was at least not vehemently anti-Islander and was less inclined than

his predecessors to use all the powers of his office to crush Islanders' resistance. As for the composition of City and Metro Councils, the December 1969 elections provided both pluses and minuses. Arch-foe William Dennison was re-elected mayor. David Rotenberg switched wards and topped the polls in Ward 11. June Marks was elected senior alderman in Ward 6, thereby becoming Islanders' Metro Council representative. And several new "reform" aldermen were elected who would have a profound effect on both Island and mainland political developments over the next several years—notably, John Sewell, Karl Jaffary, David Crombie and William Kilbourn.

During the winter, kids skated on the lagoons, iceboats skittered across the bay, pied piper Tommy Thompson led a hundred happy hikers across the Island and the TIRA Executive decided after endless debates to hire Andrew

Brewin to present another brief at Metro Parks Committee. As Executive member Peter Cridland later commented, "We had to develop our own tactics. And we did, in fact, begin to take the initiative away from the politicians [like Rotenberg] that supported us at the time."

The Parks Committee set April 9 as the day on which Mr. Brewin should appear and decided to tour the Island before that meeting. The Executive concentrated on polishing its brief and Maureen Smith concentrated on polishing the community. "Maureen's Mobs," as they were fondly called, swept, raked, shovelled, tidied and painted their way through the early spring. "The Island was in a dreadful mess and I just about killed myself getting it cleaned up," Ms. Smith later recalled. "For years afterwards," she continued laughingly, "when anybody saw me walking down the street, they'd go and grab their rake."

All to little avail, however. When Thompson and his political charges descended on the Island, he again won the battle of tours and the war of images. On Ward's, for example, "they walked lickety-split down Channel, up Third Street, across Lakeshore and in *behind* the houses along Willow," complained a thoroughly disgusted Maureen Smith. "They were literally walking through people's backyards. And they didn't go *in* any of the houses or meet any of the residents." As he whizzed by nice houses and lingered over scruffy ones, Thompson, of course, was trying to create an impression of tacky, unhealthy, little shacks, probably containing equally tacky and unsavoury, but selfish, characters. Wouldn't it really be better for all concerned to sweep these eyesores off the Island and replace them by a beautiful green park usable by millions of ordinary Torontonians? Rival tour guide David Rotenberg, meanwhile, unsuc-

(Right) *Parks Commissioner Tommy Thompson points out an item of interest to Toronto Mayor William Dennison (third from left) and other members of the Metro Parks Committee who stomped across parkland and through Islanders' backyards on April 9, 1970.* [YUA:TC]

cessfully tried to reroute the tour past sturdier houses to create a positive image of homey, picturesque little cottages occupied by just ordinary folks, who were doing nobody any harm, especially when there was no immediate need for more parkland.

Thompson and the politicians returned to City Hall to decide the Islanders' future. Brewin, followed by Marks and Rotenberg, spoke in favour of an indefinite extension. But with visions of paint peelings and dirty backyards still dancing in their heads, a majority of the committee, led by Metro Chairman Ab Campbell, could not be budged beyond a one-year extension (to August 31, 1971), and this only so long as the houses met housing, fire and health standards (all acceptable to Islanders) and so long as there was no assignment of leases or subletting of the houses. This latter condition was completely unacceptable to Islanders, who not only would lose money if they could no longer sell their houses, but, more importantly, would see their numbers gradually and inexorably reduced and their community destroyed, as leases were turned over to Metro and houses were bulldozed.

Acceptable or not to Islanders, the chairman's approach was acceptable to Metro Council, which adopted it on April 21 with only minor amendment. Islanders left the "great mushroom" Council Chamber with an extension— and a warning from North York Controller Paul Hunt that this would be the last extension. Islanders, however, were neither moved, nor moving. And they were secure for at least one more year.

While Island residents wielded tennis rackets and paint brushes that summer of 1970, mainlanders continued to trek across the bay. Snow-haired senior citizens began to feed the ducks and play shuffleboard at the former Anglican Rectory on Ward's Island. And gate-crashing youths disrupted the gentle Mariposa Folk Festival by swimming the lagoon to Olympic Island. "It was the most incredible scene I've ever seen," festival organizer Buzz Cherkoff recalled. "We were fending them off as best as we could."[4] Mariposa magic triumphed despite this invasion—and despite the ferry line-ups and what the Harbour Police called "a madhouse" atmosphere created when eighty-five

thousand people inundated the park during the weekend.

Fall 1970 brought the election of a new TIRA Executive and preparations for the 1971 lease extension fight. Although many options were discussed, in the end, as Maureen Smith put it succinctly, the Executive decided to "leave everything to Rotenberg"—and worry as the countdown to June began.

Islanders had plenty to worry about. In November 1970 the Metro Parks Committee approved a $5 million park development programme that included money to demolish Island homes. Then in early 1971, on his first attempt, Rotenberg failed to get the demolition money deleted and Metro Chairman Campbell reiterated Metro Council's determination to remove the houses. So far, so bad. But things soon began to look up when Rotenberg began chipping away at the demolition dollars.[5] And Islanders calmed their nerves by preparing a statement of "Why Residents Believe Their Leases Should Be Extended," which was sent not to the Parks Committee but to Island residents via the new Island newspaper, the weird and wonderful *Goose and Duck*.[6] (The *Goose and Duck*—with its melange of politics, information and irreverent humour—did much to raise Island spirits during the few years of its existence.) Then on April 6 eighty loyal TIRA members shuffled into the AIA clubhouse to discuss the TIRA statement and, perhaps with more enthusiasm, to watch a TV film about the Island that had originally been shown on CBC's "Gzowski Journal." Shortly after this Islanders indulged in another time-honoured method of fighting fear: eating. The smelt were running and Island fishermen were high. Not to be selfish about it, they donated their catch to feed one hundred and fifty diners at the AIA smelt-fry-cum-dance on April 30.

As Islanders followed the *Goose and Duck*'s advice "renew your tranquilizer prescription" because of delays at Metro, conflict erupted within the community over how to deal with the demolition of houses. In late April the Metro Parks Department demolished two houses whose owners had followed the letter of Metro's "no sale—no rental" law and handed in their leases when they moved from the Island. To demonstrate or not to demonstrate, that was the question. In the end, after much debate and many letters to the *Goose and Duck*, both sides agreed with TIRA Executive members John Woodburn and Freya Godard that "the most effective way to prevent more houses from being torn down is not to hand in leases to Metro."[7] The conflict between low-key, non-confrontation tactics and high-profile, aggressive action was not resolved here.

As April turned into May Metro politicians may have been stuggling with the thorny Island issue, but Premier William Davis and his colleagues had more pleasant waterfront duties to attend to. On Saturday May 22, 1971, the premier and his friends gathered by the waters of Humber Bay to admire architect Eb Zeidler's $23 million, 96-acre futuristic playground, Ontario Place, and to throw its pods and twinkling sphere open to tourists and voters alike. It was a grand occasion—even if the crowds were disappointingly small. Balloons, clowns, redcoats, roving troubadours, fireworks and, of course, speeches. "There are no politics here today," the premier intoned unconvincingly from centre Forum. "There are only people finding and enjoying themselves." Mercifully for provincial accountants, more people pushed through the turnstiles on Sunday; while out on the lagoon, the two Island clergymen from St. Andrew's-by-the-Lake and St. Rita's bobbed among eighty-five assorted boats, leading an

ecumenical yachtsmen's service, which had been "a tradition long associated with the neighboring but naturally formed Centre Island."[8]

On June 25, the Metro Parks and Recreation Committee rejected Alderman Rotenberg's motion that the leases be extended for another year (until August 31, 1972) and narrowly adopted Etobicoke's John Carroll's "compromise" motion (which Islanders regarded as no compromise at all): extend Ward's leases one month, to September 30, 1971, and Algonquin leases one year, to August 31, 1972. As he rather

callously told his colleagues, "clean-up" Ward's Island this year and deal with Algonquin Island next year. So much for the low-key approach at the Metro Parks and Recreation Committee. The next Metro Council meeting would be Islanders' last chance.

Islanders were stunned, but not beaten. "The community just went ZINK!" according to Maureen Smith. "We're not going to be divided." In the brownish light of the WIA clubhouse that night, somebody asked, "Are we prepared to accept it?" and the rest of the crowd

THINGS THAT GO SPLASH IN THE NIGHT

The wind was a torrent of darkness, among the Island trees,
The moon was a ghostly ferry-boat, tossed on cloudy seas,
The road was a ribbon of moonlight, over the vacant park,
And an Islander came smelting—smelting—smelting—
An Islander came smelting, and cursed as he tripped in the dark.

Anonymous Goose and Duck *poet*   *[Goose and Duck]*

replied, "No! All or nothing!" It was, Ms. Smith continued, "the first time in years that the two Islands [Ward's and Algonquin] had said, 'We're in it together, through thick or thin.'" They were "up against a solid truth, that one Islander can't exist without another, because there aren't enough of them." First store deliveries would go, then perhaps the school, then the ferry and so on. It was true in 1971 and it would be true later.

TIRA now roared into action. It prepared a strongly worded brief to Metro Executive and Metro Council which declared that Islanders were "a single, united community" and were totally opposed to the Metro Parks Committee proposal to destroy half the houses. "To destroy needlessly a century-old community," they declared, "would be irresponsible and immoral."

June 29, 1971, the day of decision. As the Metro Council meeting started that afternoon, the Council Chamber was packed with about four hundred Islanders and their supporters, including small children romping on the carpeted floor behind the public gallery and mothers pacing back and forth pacifying infants (and themselves). Islanders, in spite of their numbers, had been carefully cautioned not to make any outbursts that would have disrupted Council. And, mostly, they followed their orders.

June Marks opened the debate with an emotional, tub-thumping speech in favour of Islanders. She even dared to suggest that the community should be made permanent. But on this occasion she only proposed a motion drafted by Rotenberg to extend the leases for a year, with an automatic renewal clause. "June Marks gave such a rousing speech," Maureen Smith recalled, that Islanders broke their self-imposed oath of silence.

The debate, of course, was not all to Islanders' liking. Mayor Dennison once again led the

A BRIEF from the TORONTO ISLAND RESIDENTS' ASSOCIATION to the MEMBERS of the EXECUTIVE COMMITTEE and COUNCIL of the MUNICIPALITY of METROPOLITAN TORONTO
June 29 1971

The Toronto Island Residents' Association, comprising the entire population of Toronto Island, requests that the Executive Committee and Council of the Municipality of Metropolitan Toronto grant a renewal of the ground leases on both Ward's and Algonquin Islands, with periodic reviews and adequate notice of termination, and without unreasonable restrictive clauses that treat Island residents more harshly than other tenants of Metro.

The proposal of the Metro Parks Committee, which was the product of a tie vote, is not acceptable to the Islanders, who consider themselves a single, united community. To destroy half the houses would be to kill the community.

Neither the Parks Commissioner not the Parks Committee has ever tried to prove a need for the 5 percent of the total Island acreage that our houses occupy, and with good reason, for such a need does not exist and cannot be proved to exist.

The 250 single family houses, which are owned by the Islanders, although standing on leased land, provide 800 people with low cost housing. Evicting the residents at this time would aggravate the present shortage of such housing.

If the houses on Ward's Island are destroyed, the taxpayer will be paying for 15 acres of land for which there is neither plan nor money for development. The ferry deficit will also increase since at present some 20 percent of the total fares come from the Islanders.

Nor is the Island community a burden to the taxpayer; without subsidy, we support two churches, two community centres and a comprehensive programme of social and recreational activities. The car-free environment; the combination of residential and park uses of land; and the variety of ages, incomes, interests and occupations of the residents make the Island the kind of community that many modern planners are trying to create.

For 125 years the presence of this residential community has provided mainland visitors with variety, contrast and human interest. Countless mainlanders have been rescued from drowning by Island residents. The absence of these residents will result in an increased and needless loss of life.

Until the access problem to the Island is solved, thereby establishing the need for more parkland, our ground leases should be renewed. To destroy needlessly a century old community would be irresponsible and immoral.

After Metro Parks Committee voted on June 25, 1971 to take over Ward's that year and Algonquin the next year, Islanders fired off this toughly worded brief to preserve their "single, united community." [AC]

attack, and he was, in Smith's immortal phrase, "like a walking Michael Best column," attacking Islanders with the same enthusiasm as the *Star* columnist. At the end of his speech, Islanders gave him a cool—not to say arctic—reaction. "When he'd finished," Smith continued, "there wasn't a sound. Nobody booed. Nobody hissed. Nobody did anything. There was just stone, dead silence when he'd finished. It was just amazing."

But David Rotenberg had obviously done his homework, and his lobbying, well. North York Controller and future Metro Chairman Paul Godfrey, for example, was a new boy on Council and relatively unversed in the ways of the Island. "I hadn't been on long and I didn't know all the facts. I was lobbied quite heavily by David Rotenberg and June Marks, who were able to convince me to give them an extension." Godfrey certainly was not alone in falling under the influence of Rotenberg, for the final vote proved to be, as Smith would say, "a runaway victory for Islanders": 16-8 in favour of the Marks-Rotenberg motion. Islanders were safe for another year, and possibly longer.

Victory was celebrated in fine Island style, with a huge party to which friend and foe alike were invited. Rotenberg was met with cheers, a bicycle with which to lead the happy parade and a formal roll of honour declaring him Island ambassador to Metro Toronto.

During the summer, Islanders worked hard to improve their houses—"If It Doesn't Move— Paint It!" the *Goose and Duck* recommended—in hopes that they would be on the Island not just for one year, but for many. And the summer of 1971 also saw the resurrection of the Cove Fleet sabot prams which had bobbed on Island waters during the later forties and early fifties. Commodore George Stein rounded up the likes of Paul Henderson (1953 Cove Fleet Champ and world class sailor), Barclay Livingston (1960 Olympic sailing competitor) and Peter Gzowski (reputed "Polish Indoor Champ").

Politics, however, was never far beneath the surface. While even the Junior Masquerade turned to political satire with a rendition of "Privileged Islanders" (tiny tots sitting in an appropriately primitive shack built on an express wagon), disgruntled Metro politicians continued taking potshots at Island residents. And a frustrated Tommy Thompson complained, "They tell me I can't have any money [for the development of the Island] because I haven't got the land. Then the next year I'm told that if I get the land, I won't have any money to develop it."[9]

That fall the parks commissioner began to fight back, raising the issue of "illegal" subletting (i.e., renting or selling houses rather than turning their ground leases over to Metro, which would then be able to demolish the houses). The provincial election on October 19, which landed Brampton's own Bill Davis back in the Premier's Office with a solid Tory majority, provided anti-Islanders with new ammunition, since Metro officials and *Star* reporters were able to check the voters' lists against Metro records of "bona fide tenants." Moreover, occupation information revealed by the voters' lists converted Scarborough Controller Gus Harris—a long time CCF/NDPer—from a relatively mild, soft-spoken opponent into a very outspoken, even bitter opponent. "We had been giving them a year's extension from '68 on," Harris said in 1975. "And then I discovered the type of people who were over there"—architects, law-

yers, accountants, educators, and so on. So, after Mayor William Dennison retired at the end of his term in 1972, Gus Harris was ready, willing and able to take over his role as arch anti-Islander.

Meanwhile, the Toronto waterfront was changing. The new year brought the opening of the long-awaited, half-million-dollar ferry terminal located at the toe of what would become the high-rising Harbour Square hotel-cum-condominium complex. Great was the excitement of Islanders, though great was their disappointment when no waiting room—let alone a heated one—was located. Some disconsolate Islanders even began to look back wistfully to the good old days in what the *Goose and Duck* nostalgically referred to as the "evil yellow waiting room" at York Street. And greater yet was their disappointment when the snows vanished and the mud came. Islanders pushing prams and dragging bundle buggies became hopelessly mired along the then pathless approach to the terminal.

On the Island, at least, winter came skidding to an exuberant halt. "Well, if we had to have winter, that was a great way to end it," the *Goose and Duck* chirped. Ice covered the Island from one end to the other; so kids and adults laced up their skates and headed for the hills. "Packs of 10 or 15 people swirling between the houses like roller-derby all-stars, careening off across the park, between the bushes and trees all the way to Hanlan's, then back to the amusement park at Centre to slide down the hills like so many giggling penguins. Eat your hearts out, you city people!" crowed the *Goose and Duck.*

Moreover, in the spring of 1972 Islanders, for once, were not skating on thin ice politically. Neither Metro politicians nor Parks Commissioner Thompson bothered to raise the issue of Island leases, so they were automatically

extended for another year. Islanders heaved a collective sigh of relief and, in mid-June, were able to raise a stein to their future success at the newly opened Brau Haus on Centre Island.

July 1972 brought the Mariposa to (almost) end all Mariposas. While Mick Jagger and the Rolling Stones were swaggering and jumping at Maple Leaf Gardens on the mainland, folk music's superstars were inundating the Island. So were the rains, which turned part of the area into a swamp. It wasn't the weather that threw the festival into a uproar but the Coming of folk music's Messiah, the reclusive Bob Dylan. Unannounced and unrecognized he had visited the site with Gordon Lightfoot. For some reason he decided to return. As the slight, bandannaed music man came back over the little arched bridge to Olympic Island, people finally recognized him and pandemonium was

Bandannaed Bob Dylan and Canadian folk hero Gordon Lightfoot at Mariposa '72 when Dylan's unexpected visit created a near-riot. "They stumbled over trees and they stumbled over tables and chairs and picnic baskets following this...Messiah!" commented festival advisor Ray Woodley, who stumbled to safety with Dylan's son on his shoulders. [Star]

loosed on Centre Island. With difficulty, Dylan was shepherded into the performers' area and the crowd was kept at bay beyond a flimsy snow fence while the Harbour Police was summoned. Immediately two boats whooshed over to Olympic and whisked Dylan safely away. All Mariposa organizers hoped for the next year's festival was no rain—and no Dylan.

Out on the lake that summer, RCYC yachtsmen lost the Canada's Cup in a hard-fought and close contest to the Detroit Bayview Yacht Club sailors, but pram skipper Chris Barry showed his mettle by winning the coveted John R. Clapp Memorial Trophy, symbolic of victory over the Cove. Celebrations of his triumph were enthusiastic. "There was almost as much wine inside the WIA clubhouse as there was rainwater outside, as the Cove Fleet held its first annual Presentation Dinner and Orgy September 29," the red-eyed *Goose and Duck* reported in October. Admiral P. George Stein ("Swiss Navy, retired") presented the prizes. Canadian Olympic sailing coach Paul Henderson "entertained the distinguished assembly with anecdotes of his progress from Cove Fleet duffer to international competition among the crowned heads of Europe and back to the Cove Fleet." And a staggeringly good time was had by mariners one and all.

As summer faded into fall, the spotlight was turned on politics. The country-at-large was most concerned about the federal election on October 30. At a time of rising inflation and high unemployment, Trudeau and his troops crisscrossed Canada with a slogan of "memorable absurdity": "The Land Is Strong."[10] Even pre-election handouts like Toronto's Harbourfront "Park"[11] failed to persuade the voters to give the Liberals another majority government. So on October 31 the Liberals went into the toils of a minority government and Trudeau, reportedly, went into a state of shock.

Islanders, for their part, loyally helped Liberal M.P. Donald Macdonald sail back to Ottawa as their Lord of the Isles (and Rosedale). But they were far more concerned about the approaching civic election, in which two strong Island supporters were battling to succeed William Dennison as mayor. On the one side was David Rotenberg and on the other the tiny, perfect reform candidate, Alderman David Crombie, who had lived briefly on the Island, had close friends there and had made very strong pro-community statements. (The third candidate, Alderman Tony O'Donohue, was discounted after he abandoned his pro-community stance of 1971.)

Although the TIRA Executive apparently succeeded relatively well in sublimating election hostilities, Islanders at large did not. Political

Winter 1973 and the changing Toronto skyline provides a new backdrop for an old sport.
[Doug Ganton/CTA:TIA]

passions were running at an all-time high. The Rotenberg forces ran a fairly aggressive, high-profile campaign appealing to Islanders' loyalty.

The Crombie forces were in a difficult bind and decided to run a low-key campaign. No ads. No canvassing. Just literature drops and a strong statement by Crombie in the election issue of the *Goose and Duck*. It worked. And when Crombie rode the crest of the wave of reform into the Mayor's Office on that cold, miserable, snowy December 4, many Islanders (even some who had loyally voted for Rotenberg) were delighted and looked forward to working with the new mayor.

There was also a spirited race on the Island for the two aldermanic seats. Incumbent June Marks took aim at Islanders' loyalty for services rendered. Reformer Dan Heap took aim at "old guard" Marks. And former Islander-opponent, William Archer, canvassed Island homes, leaving the impression that he now would support an extension.[12] In the election, Islanders voted overwhelmingly for Marks. Heap came in a distant second. And Archer trailed behind. But Ward Six at large made Archer the new senior alderman (and Islanders' Metro Council representative) and Heap the junior alderman.

David Crombie's election was accompanied by major changes on both City and Metro Councils. At the City level, Torontonians elected Crombie, but also elected eleven "reform" aldermanic candidates. Of these, seven would also sit on Metro Council where they would help decide the Island's future. The magnitude of the reform victory was totally unexpected; and there were scenes of wild joy aboard the trusty old *Ongiara*, as well as down at City Hall.

In sum, although they had lost Rotenberg, Islanders had gained a mayor who apparently wholeheartedly supported them, a City Council

The romantic side of Island flooding in the spring of 1973.   [Doug Ganton/CTA:TIA]

that included a large group of people who believed in the preservation of established neighbourhoods, and a Metro Council with several promising new faces. According to Maureen Smith, "after the election, there was a great wave of optimism on the Island" and prospects for 1973 were exciting. Buoyed by this excitement and Alderman Karl Jaffary's enthusiasm, the TIRA Executive decided to try to gain a five-year extension on their leases.

Before the winter lifted, Islanders took not to the streets but to the ice for their soon-to-be-annual Winter Carnival. Babies were bundled all snug in their sleds, while older Islanders gobbled goodies and chased one another in races across the lagoon. But politics, of course, were not

entirely absent. Politicians were invited over and squired around by proper Islanders to give them a more positive view of Island life than they got on "Tommy's tours."

That spring Commissioner Thompson quietly launched a new campaign to terminate Island leases, suggesting that Metro should either proceed with the park (and demolitions) or return the residential areas to the City.[13] While the Islanders and their supporters scurried to marshall their arguments for a five-year extension, Mother Nature took the parks commissioner's side: 1973 was another high-water year and, as in 1952 (but not in 1943 or 1947), high water became a political weapon in the hands of Islanders' foes. As Islanders were pumping out their yards, the press was pumping out stories about the rising water and linking the high water with a fear of typhoid from flooded septic tanks. And Commissioner Thompson did not feel able to allay Mayor Flynn of Etobicoke's fears when Flynn asked anxiously, "Are we in danger of a possible typhoid outbreak?"[14] It was water music to the ears of Islanders' opponents. But before they could press home their advantage, the City's Medical Officer of Health Dr. G.W.O. Moss jumped into the debate to announce that the rising lake level posed no direct threat to public health on the Island. Nevertheless, it was the non-existent typhoid menace that caught the headlines.

Commissioner Thompson, taking advantage of Mother Nature's offerings, led the Metro Parks Committee on a two-hour "puddle jumping tour" of the Island. To preserve their community from the encroaching lake, Islanders had piled nearly four thousand sandbags around the perimeter and had rented electric pumps to drain the water from their front lawns. And to impress the committee, they had also "staged an orgy of home improvement" according to the sympathetic *Star* columnist Alexander Ross. One man even swept his roof and one woman washed her dog. "The place fairly sparkled" on April 19. Of course, as Ross also pointed out, whether you evaluated Island homes as "charming" or "squalid" depended "on your value system"—and on what you saw. What the politicians and their press retinue saw on this particular tour was designed to emphasize the "squalid," not the picturesque. Commissioner Thompson seemed to go out of his way to show "mud not flowers" and to delight in the devastation caused by the lake.

When Parks Committee members returned to the dry corridors of City Hall, visions of muddy puddles still swam before their eyes as they

Under the paternal gaze of tour guide Tommy Thompson, Metro Parks Committee Chairman Fred Beavis leaps onto a sandbag dike during the "puddle jumping tour" of April 18, 1973. [Star]

convened to deal with the Island. Former TIRA chairman, John Woodburn, sans galoshes, presented the carefully worded TIRA brief in favour of a five-year extension and eliminating the no-transfer clause, but his suggestion sank without a trace. After fierce speeches, committee members voted to end all leases as of August 31, with Chairman (and City Alderman) Fred Beavis casting the unfriendly tie-breaking vote.

When Metro Executive met on April 26, 1975, Mayor Flynn, following up Thompson's report earlier in the spring, set the proverbial cat among the pigeons. He proposed what he called his "put up or shut up motion." Metro Council should ask the City to take back Ward's and Algonquin Islands, but if the City did not agree to do so by May 23, Metro would terminate all residential leases as of August 31, 1973. No return, no extension. It was time for the City to put its money where its mouth seemed to be. If it wanted to preserve the Island com-

munity, it would have to administer and pay for it. If it was not willing to do so, fine. Metro would tear down the houses and create a park.

For completely contradictory reasons, both those who wanted to get rid of Islanders (like Mayor Flynn) and those who wanted to help Islanders (like Mayor Crombie) ended up voting in favour of the Flynn motion. As Islanders left the Metro Executive meeting, they still hoped to wrest a five-year extension from Metro Council; but the bubble of post-election euphoria had definitely burst.

On May 1, 1973, several hundred anxious but well-behaved Islanders packed the yellow-carpeted gallery of the Council Chamber to watch their fate be decided by the men and women of Metro Council. For five and a half hours, Metro Councillors debated, sometimes eloquently and often passionately, the future of this tiny—but undeniably special—part of Toronto. As the debate unfolded, Islanders could be forgiven if they had wondered if the two sides were even discussing the same people and the same place. Proponents of more park talked about "housing" and "housing conditions" (not to mention "disgraceful" or potentially "catastrophic" conditions). They tended to regard Islanders as selfish, or transient or greedy. On the other hand, Islanders' supporters placed a higher value on preserving "communities," regarded the Island as an "historic," a "colourful," even a "unique" community and saw Islanders as likeable and interesting, even intrepid and admirable.

The dialogue of the deaf continued on into the night and the procedural wrangling became intense, a sure sign that patience was running short and tempers were running high. At the end of the long debate Metro Council rejected Scarborough Controller Gus Harris's motion to terminate Island leases immediately and adopted a slightly revised version of a compromise motion proposed by Ward Six Alderman William Archer. Islanders' leases would be extended for a year until August 31, 1974, while the City and Metro Parks Commissioner Thompson made their proposals.[15] Significantly, however, Metro Council gave no promise or indication that it would, in fact, accede to any request by the City to return the land or preserve the community. Islanders, for their part, were discouraged, but not despondent. They had not got the five years that they had hoped for, but they had got another one-year extension and, as Maureen Smith said, "There was always that ray of hope that the City [report] would win."

The City wasted no time in getting down to work on its proposals. On May 2, the day after the Metro Council decision, it established a Toronto Island Committee, which worked full-steam-ahead to produce a large report in a short time.[16] As City staff with clipboards and tape

measures fanned out across Ward's and Algonquin Islands (often with an overworked TIRA member like Maureen Smith in tow), Islanders could have been forgiven for occasionally resurrecting an ancient dream of forming a republic. But independent or no, Island life followed its age-old rhythms. Sailors bowed their heads for the annual Blessing of the Fleet on the lagoon near the churches. Sunday worshippers, like Alice Aitken, enjoyed the "country church" atmosphere at St. Andrew's-by-the-Lake and the decidedly informal approach to worship displayed by Islanders since the time of John Ross Robertson. Mariposa Festival followers moved west from soggy Olympic Island to imbibe their folk music "with chicken and wine," as *Globe* critic Jack Batten put it, without the fuss and disruptions of the previous years.

Even theatre-lovers were able to stay home to enjoy one of the highlights of Toronto's summer theatre season: Open Circle Theatre's critically acclaimed *"I'm Hanlan, I'm Durnan, He's Ward"* at the WIA clubhouse. Company members had spent several weeks in the spring slogging through the mud—trusty tape recorders slung over their shoulders—in order to create this inventive "rambling history"—complete with Mrs. Simcoe, Tommy Thompson, Fingers-the-Wonder-Dog and actor Ray Whelan's wonderful waddling goose and duck imitations. For city-dwellers like *Star* theatre critic Urjo Kareda "the ride out, with stripes of sun still in the sky...a ride back at night, toward bright lights, and the soft dogs-and-kids sounds of the place itself—all were part of a lovely experience."

As the summer wound down, the City planning staff wound up work on what the September *Goose and Duck* billed "the report to end all reports." It wasn't, but it was big—170 pages of facts, figures, opinions and analy-

"170 Lakeshore Avenue": while Metro pushed for more parkland, visitors and former residents could still stroll by overgrown areas like this, where houses used to stand, still showing former addresses and paths to nowhere. [SDG]

sis—the product of a frantic summer of activity designed to leave no grain of Island sand unturned. The conclusion? That the Island community should stay. Not just for a little while until the park was needed. But as a permanent, possibly expanded, City neighbourhood.[17]

Most Islanders were delighted. TIRA Executive members had a few qualms, but after a meeting with planners and politicians in the lounge behind the Council Chamber where City Council was embroiled in a debate over Mayor Crombie's controversial forty-five-foot downtown building height limit, TIRA decided to follow Alderman Jaffary's advice to "present a united front." TIRA would concentrate on promoting the City report, both on and off the Island. On September 19, therefore, Islanders crowded into the WIA clubhouse to give overwhelming support to the report, including the recommendations for controls to prevent Island house prices from rising.[18]

Off-Island, the report was greeted by the predictable paeans of praise and howls of outrage when it was publicly released on September 21. Then, after the report entered the political forum six days later, it swirled through the City approval process with a satisfactory outpouring of pro-Island community sentiment.[19] And the City Council debate on November 21, 1973, proved to be, in Ward Six Junior Alderman Dan Heap's words, a "happy and agreeable occasion." With relatively few Islanders in the audience, the City Council debate was a low-key, pleasantly lopsided affair that lasted less than an hour. The only speaker who found it less than agreeable was Alderman Archer who rose to give what he later described as "the loneliest speech that I have ever made" before "the chilliest audience that I could ever have"—his Island constituents, whom he was about to vote against. The overwhelming majority of City Council, however,

disagreed with Alderman Archer and voted 17-2 in favour of preserving the community, transferring the residential areas back to the City and following the other recommendations of the report.

Although, as recent convert Alderman Reid Scott had said at City Executive, "we will need all the help we can get at the Metro level" there was "a general sense of extreme optimism," according to Algonquin Islander Ron Mazza, who later became heavily involved in Island politics. "The City's endorsement was the first time we'd ever had official political support." It was no longer "a tiny group against the whole world." The forces of community preservation were marching onward and upward to Metro.

At the Metro level, however, events had been unfolding differently. During the summer, ailing Metro Chairman Campbell had been succeeded by Paul Godfrey, the young, energetic engineer from North York whom journalist Jon Caufield described as "among the suburban politicians most disliked by the City new guard."[20] He was elected, according to Mayor Crombie, "on an anti-City vote" and made the Spadina Expressway and the Island issues "part of his political difference with the City." Within hours of his election Godfrey was telling reporters about Metro's need for the Spadina Expressway. As for the Island, no one yet could tell what he would do. He had voted both ways on the issue in the past. But he was already on bad terms with the large block of City representatives who were well known to be strongly in favour of preserving the Island community. Godfrey could, of course, choose to stay neutral but that seemed an unlikely approach for a Metro wunderkind eager to establish himself as Council's natural leader.

Meanwhile, Tommy Thompson and the powerful Metro bureaucracy were preparing to

do battle. Metro commissioners in general occupied an exalted position at Metro, and suburban members in particular tended to defer to them. Commissioner Thompson, moreover, had come to occupy a special place in that bureaucracy and to exercise special influence over Metro politicians. By 1973 he was one of the most senior Metro civil servants and one of the best known, not only inside City Hall but outside as well. "Tommy Thompson," Etobicoke Controller Bruce Sinclair commented admiringly in 1975, "is one of the few living legends we've got." What Tommy said and did mattered—and mattered a lot.

Commissioner Thompson waited until mid-October to go public. Then he released two reports dealing with the future of the Island. His own plans for the eastern end of the Island took up fewer than three pages. Much of the now occupied area, he said, would be "simple grass and trees," with group picnic facilities. For Ward's Island he envisioned an artificial speed-skating rink to increase winter use, a swimming pool, tennis courts and various support facilities. For Algonquin Island, he dropped the par-3 golf course proposal and resurrected his old ace up the sleeve: a campsite for under-privileged children. This flimsy plan, which lay in stark contrast to the weighty City tome, disappointed even some of his staunchest supporters.[21]

Thompson's second report, his direct response to the City's proposals, confirmed *Sun* journalist Ron Haggart's judgment on October 21 that he was a "skilfull political in-fighter from way back [who had] mastered the civil service art of writing reports and commentaries that are non-political, yet deliver the needed ammunition to the right politicians." Here he tried to undercut the credibility of the City report and to reinforce various negative images of the Island and Islanders. Thompson's report may have been inaccurate, as the City planners pointed out in a point by point rebuttal dated November 13, 1973. But it was effective. Many of his arguments—and inaccurate statistics—were to be repeated by politicians and journalists in the weeks to come as they sought, once and for all, to rid the Island of its pesky residents.[22]

Islanders did not hold out great hopes for their first test at Metro, the Parks and Recreation Committee meeting of November 29. They were right to be pessimistic. In spite of impassioned speeches by TIRA Chairman Maureen Smith and City Alderman Elizabeth Eayrs not to destroy "a living community," the committee (including Metro Chairman Godfrey) voted 6-1 in favour of Controller Harris's motion to terminate the leases in August 1974.

Islanders had suffered a resounding defeat in the opening round of the Metro decision-making process. But prospects for the next round—at the Metro Executive level—looked much brighter. City Hall was abuzz as both sides redoubled their efforts to win support. But as December 4 approached, neither side was confident of having tied down its votes. Before the Metro Executive meeting Mayor Crombie and Chairman Godfrey agreed not to debate the issue but to let it go forward to Metro Council without a recommendation from the Executive. Round two—Metro Executive Committee— was therefore a draw. The third and final round, the next Metro Council meeting, was coming up on December 11, 1973. There the vote was expected to be very close. The *Sun*'s John Downing thought it might even come down to a 16-16 tie, with Godfrey casting the decisive vote against Islanders.

Islanders' old supporter, David Rotenberg, continued his own quiet lobbying campaign, canvassing most of Metro Council and even escorting Etobicoke Controller Bill Stockwell on a personal tour of the Island. And his advice to City politicians like Mayor Crombie and Alderman Jaffary was to let a suburban politician "carry the ball" and "the rest of you [City] people shut up!" Because, even as they went into the December 11 meeting, it was clear that the traditional City-Suburban split was rapidly becoming a yawning chasm on this and other issues. By December 11 "they were so polarized," David Rotenberg later commented, "that...if the other guy said 'black,' they said 'white'; if they said 'red,' the other guy said 'green' automatically. If the City wanted something, [the others] would vote against it." The only hope for the Islanders was to avoid a City-Suburban confrontation over the Island.

City politicians were dashing around trying to nail down support. One of the prime targets, of course, was Metro Chairman Paul Godfrey who, like his predecessors, exercised tremendous influence over Council members. "Support the Chairman and support the Administration. That's the way Metro has always run," Alderman Elizabeth Eayrs later commented cynically, but accurately. In cases where councillors had no strong personal opinion (and most suburban politicians were "profoundly indifferent" to the facts of the Island issue, according to North York Controller Barbara Greene), the natural tendency was to follow the Leader. Someday he might toss a political tidbit your way. Crombie, Eayrs and Jaffary were among those who tackled the Metro chairman, but with no noticeable successs. Godfrey may not have cared much one way or another at the beginning; but once he made up his mind to push the park position, he did not sit idly back. On the Island issue, Alderman Jaffary later observed, "it was pretty clear" that Godfrey was "putting on the muscle."

As Islanders and their supporters came down

In a quiet moment two weeks before the Island issue exploded at Metro Council, Toronto Mayor David Crombie (left) confers with Metro Chairman Paul Godfrey (right). [*Star*]

Metro Council was not interested in 1973, or in 1981 when this photograph was taken. [SDG]

to the wire at the all-important December 11 meeting, they got the feeling that the City position as laid out in the City report was "dead." Not enough borough members would support creating a permanent community or returning the land to the City. But hopes were still alive for some reasonable compromise.

The emotional four-and-a-half-hour debate began with a compromise motion for a very modest extension and continued with Scarborough Controller Harris's impassioned anti-Islander speech. If the people on the Island had been in the lower income bracket, he suggested,

"they would have been off years ago." Pro-community forces countered with anecdotes and statistics that painted a picture of the Island community as being mostly year-round, socially diverse, egalitarian and deeply rooted. But neither side made much headway with the other. Controller Stockwell, after three hours, attempted a compromise motion, noting that since May the two sides "had only dug the trenches deeper." And now "we almost find today that we are facing a war, not a debate."

After hours of negotiating and arm-twisting, Mayor Crombie and his allies may well have

realized that all compromise motions were doomed to failure. When Crombie rose near the end of the debate, he gave a rousing, impassioned defence of the Island community. It may not have won any votes, but at least it made him and Islanders feel better. Crombie concluded, "Obviously, I think the Island should be preserved, the Island community. It has adorned this City and this Metropolitan area for a long, long time." Then he presented his own compromise motion to renew Island leases to 1980 (to put residents "on a par with the yacht clubs" whose leases ran until then) and to attach various conditions to the ground leases, such as year-round residence.

Finally, Metro Chairman Paul Godfrey rose to give his first speech about the Island and to slam the door shut on any form of compromise. If you believe that housing should continue on the Island, he argued, "then vote for something that is permanent." But if you, like me "believe that it should be a park, don't leave a cloud over people's heads. Remove [the houses]. Make it a park and make it the best park we can for all the citizens of Metro." Make a "decisive decision" today.

And they did. At long last the vote was taken. When all of the compromise motions failed (and compromisers even voted against each others' compromises), Controller Harris's motion to terminate the leases as of August 31, 1974, passed by a stunning margin of 20-12.[23]

Opponents of Islanders reacted with jubilation. A group rushed over to Commissioner Thompson, resplendent in his green (parks commissioner) suit, to clap him on the back, pump his hand and generally congratulate him. The opposition press, like Michael Best of the *Star* and John Downing of the *Sun*, eagerly printed paeans of praise to Metro Chairman Godfrey and credited him with the "big win."

But most City Council members were bitter. Some tried to comfort Island friends. Others sat fuming. In the end most agreed with one City politico's assessment that "it was a shockingly vindictive vote" and that most suburban members were voting not on the facts of the case, but on the basis of "any old wounds they could dredge up in terms of the City versus the Suburbs."

Islanders themselves sat in shocked disbelief— some in tears, some with anger rising—and then moved quietly out of the Council Chamber. More than the usual winter gloom descended on the Island as defeated residents filtered back across the bay. "It was as though half the Island had died," Maureen Smith reflected. And yet, a spark of defiance still burned underneath. "We're not going to lie down and play dead," asserted Ward's Islander Kay Walker, who had survived the German Blitz and planned to survive the Metro Blitz.

The day after the Metro Council decision, North York Mayor Mel "Bad Boy" Lastman, who had voted against Islanders, sparked a glimmer of hope when he recanted. If he changed his mind, perhaps others would, too. That same evening, December 12, Islanders jammed into the AIA clubhouse for a meeting that was expected to be just "for crying on each other's shoulders," but ended up as a pep rally and morale booster, "an affirmation 'to fight to the end.'" Fighting Bill Metcalfe of the TIRA Executive laced into the Metro enemy, sketched skeleton plans to fight on, promised to exhaust the political and legal avenues before adopting "guerilla warfare." But, if need be, he promised "to chain myself to my front door."[24] Of necessity, Islanders were beginning to adopt a significantly different tone, and were already on their way into the next phase of their fight to remain Islanders.

That year the festive season was not very joyous. As Christmas lights twinkled from the two hundred and fifty beleaguered little houses, some Islanders sank into despair, some were defiantly optimistic, some took refuge in an "eat, drink and be merry" approach to the season. But all performed each Christmas ritual with special care, only to find that even the comfortable old traditions sometimes laid traps for the unsuspecting. As he read the lesson during the Christmas service at St. Andrew's-by-the-Lake, one old Islander's voice cracked and he broke down in tears. Soon, half the congregation was weeping, too, overcome by the thought that this might be their last Christmas on the Island. All in all Christmas 1973 had none of the buoyant optimism of the previous year.

Ward's and Algonquin Islanders were facing an entirely new situation. They were no longer protected by the security of even a short lease extension. Never before had they been faced with having to *reverse* a Metro Council decision to terminate their leases. Now, however, unless they took quick action to reverse the decision—or found a way around it by legal action or provincial intervention on their behalf—the end was in sight.

Islanders faced three basic tasks as the August 31, 1974, deadline approached. First to hold the community together, preventing Islanders from turning in their leases and abandoning the Island. Second, to reverse the Metro Council decision, if they could.[25] And third, to develop other strategies for continuing the fight in case

Skiers leave the church service at St. Andrew's-by-the-Lake. [Al Schoenborn]

they failed at Metro. To accomplish all of this Islanders organized a massive "Spring Campaign."

Plans for the campaign, of course, did not spring forth full-blown from the collective brow of the TIRA Executive. Far from it. But while TIRA was still agonizing over how to approach the problem (whether to drum up mass public support *or* to rely on quiet backroom lobbying *or* to build alliances with residents' and special interest groups across Metro or, as happened, to use all three approaches), Metro struck. It sent each household a formal, soon to be infamous, notice of termination.[26] It also sent a letter suggesting that Islanders book the ferry early "in order to avoid full booking in August, 1974," offering to aid "those residents who may require assisted housing" and, to sweeten the pie, offering financial inducement to leave early in the form of an adjustment of prepaid rent and taxes. TIRA, however, was ready and waiting. The Executive sent every Island house notice both of the Metro letter and of a TIRA meeting:

DON'T PANIC

You will notice that the letter is a direct appeal to you personally to book and leave early. If you believe the community should stay, as the TIRA executive does, and as the vast majority of the residents of the City and Boroughs do, you will want the community to act as a whole and not on an individual basis. Metro of course wants to divide and conquer and will probably be doing other things in the future to try and get people on an individual basis. This is war, they are dead serious, and they mean to kill us, picking us off one by one. In times of war every single person gives all he's got. Come to a public meeting—join the resistance movement.

On January 28, 1974, hundreds of Islanders bundled up and crunched along snowy paths to attend the Spring Campaign kickoff meeting at the AIA clubhouse. They eagerly lapped up a healthy serving of fiery rhetoric directed against Metro in general and the Metro chairman in particular. They expressed their solidarity and commitment to staying on the Island by voting *not* to book the ferry as Metro had asked and *not* to contact Metro about housing, but to set up their own self-help Housing Task Force. They voted to hire Dale Perkins, an affable, corduroy-jacketed United Church minister-cum-community organizer to co-ordinate the campaign. And they were so enthused by the lanky WIA president and TIRA spokesman David Harris's energetic explanation of the Save Our Community Campaign Plan, complete with charts and rhetorical flourishes, that they adopted the plan, approved a $25,000 budget, agreed to hire a lawyer and, most importantly, volunteered by the hundreds for the myriad of tasks that needed doing. Islanders now had a plan and that fact alone kept people together.

The Public Support Committee chaired by David Harris was off and running. Invitations were sent out to politicians for the upcoming Winter Carnival; posters invited mainlanders to "Come Across to the 1974 Toronto Island Winter Carnival: Celebrate 150 Years of Homes,

(Above) *Still smiling after all these years: 1974 spring campaign organizer Dale Perkins ploughs down a Ward's Island street in January 1981.* [SDG]

(Right) *About five thousand visitors crossed the bay for Islanders' 1974 Winter Carnival. MPP Allan Grossman may not have warmed anyone's toes, but he certainly warmed Islanders' hearts when he said, "It doesn't take much imagination to see the kind of waste wilderness this would be without people." And many mainlanders were glad to sign petitions to save the Island community.* [Sun]

Families and Friends Living in Toronto Harbour''; and Islanders were exhorted to dress in ''period costume,'' which would be both appropriate and photogenic. The carnival on February 16-17 was a now typical ''Island'' way of mixing politics with fun. Everywhere Breughelesque winter scenes caught the eye and political messages tugged at the ear. All in all, it was great entertainment, it sparked lavish press coverage and it made about $1,750 for the campaign coffers. But it probably had little, if any, effect on Metro politicians.

Nor, sadly, was the campaign to gain support in the suburbs having discernible success with the suburban politicians. This campaign was, in the dispirited words of its leader, Ward's Islander and man about the CBC music world, David Amer, ''ill-founded but well-organized.'' Working four and five nights a week, he and his tireless troops donned their best suburban uniforms (no granny dresses or gum boots) and fanned out across Metro to drum up support. They won endorsements from literally dozens of groups and caused a veritable flood of letters to pour into Metro Council during the next few months. But it soon became clear that Metro politicians were not going to be turned around by letters and resolutions from citizens groups or even meetings with constituents; and the borough groups themselves were not going to care enough to ''put it on the line'' for Islanders. They would listen politely, pass a pro-Islander resolution and that would be about it. There was the case of intransigent North York politician John Williams. When asked ''What if we got every ratepayers' group in North York to pass a resolution, is that going to help?,'' he replied bluntly, ''No.'' Like T. S. Eliot's perverse Rum Tum Tugger, ''he will do/As he do do/And there's no doing anything about it!''

Post Metro Social Services Committee Press Conference, May 23, 1974: Islanders stand while TIRA Co-Chairman Elizabeth Amer (not shown) reads their biographies in an effort to present the "human side" of the effects of Metro's continuing determination to demolish Island homes. [CTA:TIA]

There were some gains, but not many. Most notable was Scarborough Mayor Paul Cosgrove who announced that he had been convinced by the housing crisis argument and by the fact that more parkland was not needed at that time. As a result, he would sponsor motions to reopen the issue and to extend Island leases.[27]

Elsewhere, however, things fell apart. ''Mass'' rallies in the boroughs failed to mass, pro-Island motions appeared prematurely at local councils in Etobicoke and York and were voted down, and relations with City politicians temporarily became strained almost to the breaking point as no one made the desired political breakthrough. Even Mother Nature seemed to be conspiring against the Islanders: an Island Spring Festival, complete with an historical pageant of *voyageurs* portaging across a modern approximation of the ancient Carrying Place (now covered by the lake) and an emotion-packed ''Bulldozerama'' designed to graphically display what would happen if the Spring Campaign failed, was washed-out and washed-up, not once but twice. And festival organizer David Harris was left holding not the bag, but several hundred pounds of uncooked hot dogs.

But time and Metro Council would wait for no Islander. Now was the moment to decide whether or not to press on with Cosgrove's motion. With many misgivings, they decided to go ahead, via the Metro Social Services Committee. ''We have nothing to lose by reopening the issue now and everything to lose by *not* doing so,'' City lawyer and respected ''old'' Islander Bill Ward told his neighbours gathered at the AIA. ''I don't know how we'll fare at Metro Social Services Committee,'' he added. ''But it's worth a try.''

They did not fare well. The next morning, on May 23, 1974, fifty Islanders of all sizes, shapes and descriptions, from babes in arms to eighty-

year-old widows, struggled into Committee
Room 3 only to watch their motion be tossed
out on a technicality. They didn't even have
a chance to present their brief.

From now until May 31, events happened
thick, fast and, for the most part, disastrously.
Just days before the next Metro Council meeting,
North York Council voted against a pro-Islanders
motion (framed and pushed by an optimistic
John Sewell, but not by pessimistic Islanders) and
killed any lingering chance of capturing North
York Mayor Lastman's wayward vote. Then
Mayor Cosgrove couldn't even find a seconder
for his motion. And, worst of all, when he
did (wavering Mayor Lastman, the Friday before
his Council voted), he didn't even bother to
tell Islanders that the motion would come before
Metro Council on May 31. That news only
reached the Island on Wednesday, May 29, by
radio. And now they were faced with the impossible task of cramming two weeks' worth of
lobbying into less than two days. The grand
finale to their grand Spring Campaign. "What
could you do with only two days left?" campaign organizer Dale Perkins later asked.

Islanders, nevertheless, were catapulted into
action. TIRA Executive members dispersed
across Metro to lobby their most likely converts.
The Island bush telegraph buzzed into action,
alerting people to the Metro Council meeting
and to a hastily organized Island meeting that
very evening, May 30. So Islanders once again
gathered nervously at the WIA clubhouse. After
much discussion, Islanders decided to demonstrate
outside Queen's Park the next day while Housing
Minister Sidney Handleman met with Metro
politicians to discuss the housing crisis in Metro.
Typically, there was some debate over just how
polite the picket signs should be and one frustrated newer Islander finally said, "It's time to

*Picketers past and present. At least one Tory, John A. Macdonald, seems to support the Islanders'
cause...meanwhile, the "Bird Lady" Ruth Putt temporarily puts down her wounded mallards and picks up a
placard to picket outside Queen's Park on May 30, 1974.*   [CTA:TIA]

stop being polite. Otherwise, they're just going
to politely push us off the Island." The Queen's
Park junket was a useful warm-up for the main
event (and "Sir John A. Macdonald" proved to
be a photogenic, if temporary, ally).

On Friday May 31, 1974, Islanders piled onto
the 8:30 A.M. ferry and invaded the mainland.
When they marshalled in the field behind Harbour Square, half of the Island seemed to be
there. Even seven-year-old Chris Jones, who had
scarlet fever, ignored her doctor's instructions
to go home to bed, saying, "No. I have to
go and picket City Hall to save my house!" She
gained a half-hour reprieve from her doctor—
but not from Metro Council. The pram-pushing,

placard-carrying, traffic-stopping troops moved
out and marched up Bay Street to City Hall,
escorted by a team of cyclists riding their sturdy,
balloon-tired "Save Island Homes" bicycles.
Since their issue was not due for debate until after
lunch, Islanders planned to picket in the square
during the morning rather than fill the Council
Chamber immediately.

Metro Council, however, had a surprise in
store: it varied the order of business and immediately stamped out Islanders' hopes of success.
With virtually no debate, it voted 17-15 against
Cosgrove's motion to reopen the issue. As
Islanders were still filing into the Chamber they
realized that they had lost, without Council's

At Nathan Phillips Square on May 31, 1974, Islanders and their supporters form a large circle under the window of Metro Chairman Paul Godfrey's office.   [CTA:TIA]

even having discussed the merits of the case. Controlled pandemonium broke out. In contrast to December 11, 1973, when Islanders had left silently and dejectedly, this time they leaped to their feet, as planned, to sing "O Canada!" Their political supporters immediately jumped up to join them, while their opponents rose somewhat grudgingly to sing the national anthem. Islanders kept this up for several minutes, then started chanting slogans like "Save Island Homes" and "We Won't Go." Some began shouting angrily at individual Council members. Opponents like Mayor Blair of East York turned red, while supporters like City Alderman Karl Jaffary were more than sympathetic. Whether

politically good, bad or indifferent, Islanders continued their chanting, forced a brief adjournment and retreated to the square and then the ferry, knowing that their massive effort during the Spring Campaign had failed. They were defeated, but strangely elated by the cathartic effect of their demonstration at City Hall. One elderly lady gleefully reported that it had taken her sixty years to get politically involved and she had loved it!

As furious City politicians immediately began plotting another offensive at Metro Council, one that would not actively involve Islanders, Island residents licked their wounds, calmed their nerves and faced the future. On June 4

lawyer Peter Atkinson announced that the Island legal team had found good, but still necessarily secret, grounds for challenging Metro in the courts. This meant that Islanders could stay in their houses beyond the August 31 deadline pending the outcome of legal challenges. From now on an all-important legal security blanket was expertly and comfortably spread over the Island. And organizer Dale Perkins, whose contract was now up, added his own reassurances, "I have no doubt there will be a political solution at some point." Just when that point would be, however, remained an open question.

Mayor Crombie inventively worked out another approach, which threw Islanders into a temporary tizzy (under his proposal, some 10 percent to 20 percent of the existing residents would have had to leave) but was still shot down in flames at the next Metro Council meeting on June 18. Crombie was furious. He stormed out of the meeting and gave an impromptu press conference. "Meridian [a private development company] in its worst day never destroyed seven million dollars worth of housing," he exclaimed. "What bothers me most," he went on, "was they simply didn't want to talk about the houses, let alone the community. Council just had a lust to get the current residents off the islands."[28]

While Islanders settled back to heed Peter Atkinson's advice to "take the summer off," mainlanders swarmed across to the Island in their thousands to attend Mariposa, Caribana and the CHIN International Picnic. CHIN picnickers, in fact, were treated not only to the traditional spaghetti and bikinis, but to the federal political roadshow. On the last weekend before the federal election, all three leaders visited the picnic in search of fun and ethnic votes: David Lewis joyously, Robert Stanfield awkwardly and Pierre

(Left) *Prime Minister Trudeau, with his crowd-pleasing wife on his arm, made an informal but triumphal tour of the International Picnic on July 7, 1974. Margaret gave a little speech about love and accepted a "Save Island Homes" button from Island residents, while her debonair husband exhorted the friendly crowd to "make it a great day tomorrow" by voting him back into power.* [Peter Holt/CTA:TIA]

(Right) *Islanders up to their old tricks—cycling and politicking.* [Peter Holt]

Trudeau triumphantly. As for the ordinary picnic-goer who didn't have private transportation, the expedition sometimes proved to be horrendous. Ferry line-ups were nasty, brutish and long. "Forget everything I told you about human nature, honey," one harassed mama told her offspring. "Start shoving and shove that way."[29]

Residents, for the most part, stayed down at their end of the Island, basking in the sun, watching the Ward's beach grow (by about ten acres, as the Toronto Harbour Commission dredged the harbour entrance and also created the protective outer Leslie Street "spit"). In early July, they launched the first of their legal actions

and braced themselves for what would become a real legal roller-coaster ride, right up to the Supreme Court of Canada. This legal action confirmed that August 31, 1974, was "no longer a date to fear," as lawyer Peter Atkinson again assured his fellow-Islanders in mid-August. And so, on August 31, no one moved. In fact, in a characteristically humorous and defiant manner, Islanders held a big beach party to celebrate their "New (Island) Year" and to effectively publicize their determination to stay.

On the broader political front, Islanders also cast their eyes toward the December municipal elections, which would elect the new (expanded) Metro Council. In contrast to 1969 and 1972, TIRA decided to take an active role this year and the election produced mixed results. Their Senior Alderman William Archer went down to defeat; but some unwelcome old faces were back on Metro Council, notably Tony O'Dono-hue and William Boytchuk. Early in the life of this new Council, Islanders pressed forward with another initiative. Hoping to ride down the (imaginary) centre, they adopted the moderate, hardworking accountant Alderman Art Eggleton as their new champion. But this Metro Council was even more split along City and Suburban lines than the previous one. There was,

in fact, no middle ground left to capture. And so on April 8, 1975, Eggleton's motion was hammered to death by a 22-13 vote. It was a decisive defeat that made abundantly clear the futility of trying to win concessions from the new Council. Islanders would have to continue to rely on legal actions to buy time, meanwhile working out a new political strategy. The first step would be to forget about Metro Council for the time being and concentrate on the Province.

A few weeks later, Islanders won their first, partial legal victory.[30] With the possibility of total victory on the horizon, they threw themselves into an orgy of home improvement. On the communal side, Island life was hopping.

The WIA scaled new heights, repainting and re-roofing the clubhouse in confident anticipation of a long future. It organized the usual range of summer activities, and held a bang-up Gala Weekend (complete with mini-midway, white elephants, sporting events, dinner-in-the-park and, to appeal to the gambling types—which surely included every Islander—a Monte Carlo Night). Parents of small Islanders met throughout the summer to organize a new Montessori-style daycare programme, which opened in a renovated AIA clubhouse in September and by 1980 had attracted some forty-five little participants, including a contingent of tiny commuters from the mainland. And TIRA, taking its commitment to maintaining morale and mocking Metro seriously, held another Island New Year celebration on August 31. Year II on the revised Island calendar.

Before the next legal battle was joined, the voters of Ontario unwittingly assisted Island residents. On September 18, 1975, they reduced the Davis government to the status of a minority government. Both the New Democratic Party (now elevated to the ''Official Opposition'') and the Liberals (now dropped to third place) were on record as supporting an Island community. Their combined strength would, ultimately, prove to be a most useful prod to the Tories. Another useful prod would be Islanders' energetic new Conservative M.P.P., Larry Grossman (son of their former alderman and M.P.P. Allan Grossman). Now Islanders began to push Grossman the Younger to make good his campaign promises of support: they wanted him to persuade the Conservative government to *transfer* the residential portions of Ward's and Algonquin Islands from Metro to the City, which would maintain them as a *permanent* community.[31]

In January 1976 the Island's newly formed ''Orange Carte Opera Company'' presented

Gilbert and Sullivan's *Trial by Jury*. This turned out to be a good omen when on St. Patrick's Day the Ontario Court of Appeal ruled that the Metro eviction notices sent out in 1974 (for August 31, 1974) were null and void because of their wording. Metro Council's subsequent appeal of this decision to the Supreme Court of Canada meant Islanders were safe for yet another year.

Meanwhile, out on the bay everything old was new again. On May 19, 1976, the 1910 paddlewheeler *Trillium*, refurbished at a cost of over a million dollars, made her matron voyage on the choppy waters of the lake. In an excess of enthusiasm, the fireboat *Wm. Lyon Mackenzie* turned on all her jets, showering not only the *Trillium*, but also all on board her. ''I have never seen a fireboat in operation before,'' commented one drenched passenger in evening dress, ''and I never want to see one again.''[32] After the

members of the York Lions Steel Band had dumped the water out of their steel drums, the show went on and three hundred passengers danced the cruise away.

The following May, just before Premier Davis's over-anxious and unsuccessful attempt to regain a majority Tory Government at Queen's Park, the Supreme Court of Canada heard Metro's appeal. On June 23 the Court brought down its decision in favour of Metro: the eviction notices were valid. The *first* stage of the legal fight was at an end. But Metro still had to obtain writs of possession for the houses.

Islanders were downhearted, but not despondent. ''Our best tactic,'' Algonquin Islander Pam Mazza commented when she heard about the Supreme Court ruling, ''is just not moving—just staying here.''[33] So, as Metro backhoes dug up the park to lay a sewer line, Island residents dug in their heels. They continued to

Security of tenure or no, Islanders kept on renovating, with the aid of their building cooperative—WARAL— formed in 1976. That summer alone, Islanders brought about $20,000 worth of materials over to the Island. [SDG]

renovate their houses and even resurrected the Island Canoe Club which, according to the *Island News*, had been "destroyed along with everything else in the great Metro Parks purge of 1957." Then, to celebrate another Island New Year, Island thespians performed Penny Kemp's Island fantasy, *The Epic of Toad and Heron*, in the Island's own Toad Hall, the WIA clubhouse. When the time came, Islanders would don their toad-stencilled "Save Island Homes" T-shirts, link arms and squat fast.

At the end of July Metro opened the next round of the legal battle. As a test, the residents of six (of the 252) Island houses were served with applications for writs of possession. The six test targets were carefully chosen. They were all relatively well off and/or summer residents, who would inspire the least amount of public sympathy if an appeal to public sentiment were made. But Islanders weren't about to be picked off one by one, so TIRA went to bat for the Island Six just as vigorously as it would go to bat for the Island 252. But on October 19, 1977, Islanders lost in the opening round of the second legal fight: Metro won writs of possession for the six houses from the York County Court, and swiftly won writs for the remaining 246. Island lawyers, however, were unabashed and hired John J. Robinette (the legendary Toronto lawyer and ex-Centre Islander) to handle their appeal.

In the interim Islanders fought back with wit and resourcefulness. In mid-December, Islanders' citizen band DEW line went into operation. If the sheriff and his men landed, the Toronto Island Radio Network (or TIRN) would beam the information to receivers across the Island. For the time being, "Big Kay" Walker and Co. broadcast daily ferry reports, Island School sports results and wounded-wildlife health bulletins from "Bird Lady" Ruth Putt, who

The Toronto Island Residents Association Yacht Club was inaugurated on February 5, 1978 with suitable pomp and circumstance: a one gun salute, a ribbon cutting ceremony, and a sailpast—on the ice. Here "Admiral" Bob Kotyk salutes his sailors, while "Tommy Thompson," a papier mâché veteran of earlier Island "New Year's" parties, strokes his chin thoughtfully. [Sun]

ministered to the sick at her Algonquin Island home. But Radio Free Island was in place. At their Winter Carnival in February 1978, Islanders declared themselves to be a yacht club, the Toronto Island Residents Association Yacht Club, because the yacht clubs were better treated than the residents. Finally, as if TIRN and TIRAYC weren't protection enough, Islanders organized their ultimate weapon: the "Home Guard." This well-named force consisted of plucky Islanders who were prepared to don yellow hard hats at the first sign of trouble and race to surround or occupy any houses about to be taken over by the sheriff. Their main offensive weapon was rumoured to be a remarkable ability to go limp at the drop of a sheriff's hat.

As a revivified Island Canoe Club splashed around the regatta circuit and the Island legal war canoe prepared for another voyage to the Ontario Supreme Court, Islanders relished their annual village fête, Gala Day, over the August Simcoe holiday weekend. But even as they rummaged through old clothes, admired old photos of tent life and tucked into juicy steaks at the Gala barbecue-in-the-park, residents couldn't help wondering, "Will this be the last time?" And they couldn't help speculating on just how they might react should Eviction Day ever arrive. Insisting that she was "as militant as a pussycat," TIRN anchorwoman Kay Walker nevertheless

also insisted to a *Star* reporter that she wasn't about to move quietly. "If they bring Curly Hair over here," she said in a pointed reference to Paul Godfrey's newly permed hairstyle, "I'll punch him in the nose. If I have to go to jail for something it might as well be that.... I don't like being told where I can live." Things could become, as the defiant Walker suggested, "very nasty" very quickly.[34]

Against this background John J. Robinette and Island lawyers went before the Supreme Court of Ontario. But on October 20 the court rejected their arguments and ruled that Metro's writs of possession were valid. Islanders had fifteen days in which to decide whether or not to seek leave to appeal this decision.

Four days later, therefore, Islanders gathered at the AIA clubhouse and on the advice of Peter Atkinson voted overwhelmingly *not* to appeal.

July 1, 1982: the resurrected Island Canoe Club sends its ladies' war canoe out to do battle on Long Pond. [SDG]

report on what was happening; and a somewhat frantic "Home Guard" chased after the intruders and practised wily acts of passive resistance. "I almost turned around and walked away," said one softhearted actor/sheriff of his encounter with a mother holding a baby.[36] In addition to testing defences and reinforcing Islanders' solidarity, the "war games" received extensive publicity and firmly planted in the minds of many a graphic image of just what unpleasantness would follow any decision to try to enforce the writs of possession.

While Provincial opposition parties kept up the pressure on the minority government in the Legislature (including adopting a non-binding Liberal resolution to transfer the residential

"Basically your legal advisors are not telling you that it's got to go back to the public forum," Atkinson told his neighbours. Rather than being downcast, Islanders seemed positively to relish the prospect. Toronto City Council had just reaffirmed its request to the Province that the land be transferred back to the City, on a 18-1 vote, with only mayoral candidate Tony O'Donohue dissenting. There was another municipal election under way. And, more important, with the threat of the imminent destruction of over 250 homes and an entire community, the reluctant provincial minority government might *at last* be forced to act. So, Islanders voted to ask their MPP (now Minister of Industry and Tourism) Larry Grossman "to present a Government Bill transferring the ownership of the land now occupied by the houses on Toronto Island from the jurisdiction of Metro Toronto to the City

of Toronto." Mr. Grossman, who appeared later in the evening, promised to try to persuade his Cabinet colleagues to introduce such legislation and to "fight like hell" for his Island constituents. "I quite understand," he concluded, "that all hell will break loose if the discussions aren't successful."[35]

Islanders did their best to reinforce this impression. The next weekend they held "war games." Actors pretending to be the sheriff and his men staged an invasion and the Island defence system was tested: roving hard-hatted spotters sighted the landing; the new fire siren atop the WIA clubhouse screamed out its warning; the CB network beamed out a running

October 1978, Islanders hold war games to test their defences against this acting Sheriff. [Sun]

areas back to the City) and Metro Chairman Paul Godfrey railed against any such interference in "local matters," Grossman *et al.* scurried to find a resolution to the conflict. No luck. So on December 14, 1978, Minister of Intergovernmental Affairs Tom Wells announced not a final resolution but a reprieve for about six months while he acted as a "mediator" between the City and Metro. This Provincial reprieve initiated a period of behind-the-scenes negotiating between Metro Chairman Godfrey and newly elected Mayor of Toronto John Sewell. But though Sewell made at least three proposals for the City to take (or buy) back part, even all, of the Island, it seemed that there was no offer that the Metro chairman could *not* refuse.

By October 1979 it was clear that mediation had failed. It was also clear that the Province was still not willing to transfer the land to the City. The most it was willing to do (and only because it was a minority government faced with a united opposition) was allow Islanders to remain as long as they wished; but when individuals left or died, their houses and leases would be turned over to Metro. Gradually, but inevitably, the Island community would disappear. In his response, TIRA Chairman Ron Mazza summarized Islanders' long-standing opposition to any form of attrition: "They [the Province] seem to have missed the point that it's the *community* that we are trying to preserve, not our own individual rights to live here."[37]

Islanders and their supporters tried to prevent the "attrition" bill from even being introduced. NDP member Richard Johnston led the charge both inside and outside the House. And Mayor Sewell, in a last ditch effort to stall Wells's "so called 'solution,'" emphasized that as of October 17 his offers to Metro were "still on the table."[38] But the minister was not for turning.

On October 19, "Foggy Friday," as a heavy mist enveloped Queen's Park, Mr. Wells introduced Bill 153. Wells called it a "compromise"; but opposition parties called it a "slow death Bill" and rejected it out of hand. In the end, because of the sustained outcry, the Government did not press forward, but let the bill simply die at the end of the session in December. Island supporters were confident that in the face of such strong resistance, the Government would introduce new, amending legislation in the spring session.

In the meantime, Islanders, voting with their feet, so to speak, gave clear evidence of their own determination to stay: by December the *TIRA News'* "Post-Eviction-Baby-Boom" total had reached nine new Islanders expected in 1980. And early in the new year one resident, at least, again proved the value of having a community on the Island. On January 15 Ward's Islander Jamie Smith hauled a nearly exhausted mainlander, Max Sarty, out of the frigid waters of the Eastern Gap. The Harbour Police raced him to St. Michael's Hospital, where he recovered nicely. The grateful Mrs. Sarty was an instant convert to the Islanders' cause. "These people are beautiful people," she wrote to Mayor Sewell, in February, "and I want them to stay." Mayor Sewell may have agreed; but other Metro and Provincial politicians remained to be convinced.

Sewell decided to take the initiative. He worked out his own "compromise" proposal for the City to buy back part of the Island and began lobbying Metro politicians. He even had some initial success: notably, Gus Harris, now Mayor of Scarborough, who, *mirabile dictu,* agreed to second the motion, and Mr. Wells, who called the Sewell proposal "ideal."[39] But the pieces did not fall into place before the Metro

Council meeting. And the Sewell campaign stalled as the Short Take Off and Landing port took off. Only a week before Mayor Sewell had optimistically filed his Island motion, Metro Council exploded over the perennially controversial STOL facility proposed for the Island Airport site. For years the City had resisted efforts to allow jets in the heart of downtown Toronto. After an incredibly bitter, four-hour debate, Metro Council voted 21-8 in favour of Etobicoke Controller Winfield Stockwell's motion to send Metro Chairman Paul Godfrey to the Canadian Transport Commission hearing to support STOL. Sewell was incensed, accusing Metro of steamrolling over the City. City politicians were incensed. And suburban politicians were incensed. It was hardly a propitious time to bring up the Island issue.

Mayor Sewell, however, doggedly persisted. At the next Metro Council meeting on February 26, 1980, he made a low-key, unemotional speech in favour of what he called his "compromise." He was baited by a few opponents, but did not allow himself to fire off any hot retorts. It soon became clear, nevertheless, that a number of Metro councillors were still smarting after the acrimonious STOL debate and opponents reportedly fell only one vote short of voting to evict Islanders immediately. In the end, after six hours of heated debate, Metro Council voted 18-15 to proceed to evict Islanders if the Province failed to pass its compromise (attrition) bill by June 30, 1980.

Unfortunately for Islanders, this Metro Council decision paved the way for a Provincial pincer movement: Wells asserted that, in view of Metro Council's decision, Islanders' only hope was to accept his bill, which was reintroduced on March 13, 1980. Islanders, it seemed, were to be caught, perhaps crushed, between writ-

Toronto Mayor John Sewell, dressed in his comfortable jeans and leather jacket of old, brings people to their feet at the gigantic rally on July 1, 1980, by declaring that "the Toronto Island community is here to stay." [SDG]

weather. As supporters continued pouring in, folk singers wailed protest songs on various subjects. Morris dancers jingled the bells on their legs "to ward off evil spirits." And the Island's own Home Guard Choir, in yellow hard hats, led the growing crowd in a variety of Island resistance songs, like "We Don't Plan to Go" and "Metro Blues." While Canadians from sea to sea raised their voices to sing "O Canada ... We stand on guard for thee," Islanders and their supporters sang a newly penned anthem, "O Island Homes on Trawnna's fair Island ... We stand on guard for thee." Finally, the air raid siren on top of the WIA clubhouse screeched its announcement of the beginning of the formal part of the rally.

Ward's Islander and school principal Les Birmingham was the master of ceremonies at the rally. He opened the official proceedings by declaring, "First of all, we are a community and that's why we're here." The politicians and mainland speakers, gathered near the flag-draped stage, were more than eager to lend their support. Mayor Sewell, dressed in his blue jeans and leather jacket of old, brought the partisan crowd to its feet by declaring:

> The Toronto Island community is here to stay. ... This is a fight that we're all in. It's not just people who live on the Islands. It's not just people who live downtown. It's not just people who live in the City of Toronto. It's everyone in Metro. It's a fight that we all have to pay attention to because we know that you can't go around destroying communities. If they destroy this one, they'll destroy others.

And world-renowned urbanologist Jane Jacobs, competing with the ferry whistle, struck an equally responsive chord when she commented:

> But, really, you don't need to invoke practical reasons as to why this community shouldn't be

waving Metro councillors and attrition-offering Provincial Tories. But they stuck to their guns and on June 19, 1980, the last day of the Provincial session, they came away from Queen's Park with more than they expected, but less than they needed. During the morning, Tories (including now-M.P.P. David Rotenberg) tried to persuade Islanders to accept Bill 5 (including attrition) in return for a summer-long investigation of the issue and a promise of no evictions while the inquiry was under way. No deal. So, in the afternoon, Wells withdrew his bill and set up a Commission of Inquiry into the Toronto Islands under lawyer Barry Swadron.[40] Wells would ask Metro to delay evicting Islanders until after the commission reported, but he couldn't promise Metro would listen.

It didn't. After the last Metro Council meeting before the June 30 deadline, Chairman Godfrey told the *Star,* "As far as Metro Council is concerned, it's over."

But not as far as Islanders and their supporters were concerned. While Island lawyers searched, yet again, for legal means to delay the evictions, Island residents declared their defiance and prepared for a massive show of support on July 1, a Dominion Day like no other in the history of Toronto Island.

Islanders put on a brave face and a grand show. As lunchtime approached, the normally uncrowded Ward's Island ferry began unloading hundreds of mainlanders, who surged onto the open field where the rally was to be held, spread out their picnics and began to enjoy the sunny destroyed. It shouldn't be destroyed because it's lovable. It's unique. It's a lovely thing. It's wicked to destroy lovable, unique and lovely things.... When people defend a place the way you Islanders are defending this, that's the greatest argument of all. It says: it's worth saving.

Finally, invoking all possible means of support, Islanders ended the rally by gathering around a sacred drum brought over by members of Toronto's native community, who dedicated an honour song to Island residents.

July 2, 1980, brought not the sheriff but a brief legal delay: Islanders' resourceful lawyer, Peter Atkinson, challenged the validity of the writs and the Province wanted the legal situation to be clarified before the sheriff went hurtling in.

While the press kept up a media blitz and thousands of CHIN international picnickers suffered yet another year of interminable ferry line-ups, Commissioner Barry Swadron was cooling his heels, waiting to get his inquiry started. Metro, however, was proving perverse. Not only did it refuse to participate in the Swadron Commission, but, irony of ironies, it was in the process of approving new twenty-five-year leases for the three private Island yacht clubs. The yacht clubs would be safe for a quarter century; the residents, perhaps for only a matter of days.

On July 24, 1980, Islanders lost another legal round when Ontario Supreme Court Justice John O'Driscoll ruled that Metro's writs were valid. That night, with reporters swarming among them, tense Islanders immediately voted to seek leave to appeal the decision and went on "Red Alert," in case the sheriff decided to swoop down on them before the appeal was granted. While Peter Atkinson prepared to go to court midweek, his neighbours prepared to repel the sheriff.

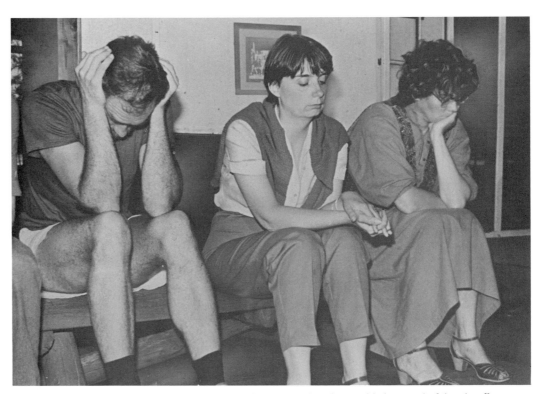

July 24, 1980: a bleak moment as these three Islanders contemplate the now-likely arrival of the Sheriff. [*Star*]

Monday morning, July 28, 1980, dawned dark and drizzly. Fog horns moaned on the lake. Commuters to cityside jobs caught the early morning ferries and disappeared into the mist. Just about the time they arrived at work, the siren atop the WIA clubhouse wailed out its warning: *the Sheriff is coming!* The phone chain immediately contacted Islanders at work and mainland supporters who had promised to help on Eviction Day. "From all points of the city we headed home," Islander Linda Rosenbaum later wrote in *This Magazine*. Down to the docks where the "Island Navy" (water taxis and Islanders' own assorted small craft) waited to shuttle residents, press and supporters across the

bay. Meanwhile, the Island was a beehive of activity. Kay Walker, resplendent in her yellow slicker, sat under a huge lawn umbrella at the Ward's dock, radio in hand, scouring the bay for any signs of unusual activity. Other raincoated spotters cycled along the Island's perimeter, looking for the first signs of invasion. Street signs and house numbers disappeared. And Jack Bradley's house overlooking the baseball diamond was turned into communications HQ.

It was a long wait. Shortly before three-thirty, the siren again wailed and the slickered Island lobby massed at the Algonquin Bridge in the rain. Rank upon rank of ponchoed protesters gathered behind banners like "Save Us Bill

Davis'' and a grim-faced line of TIRA Executive members, arms linked. Media hordes circulated on the perimeter. A worried two-and-a-half-year-old told her mother, ''I don't want to move.'' Her mother calmed her saying, with more certainty than she perhaps felt, ''We're not moving. That's why we're here.'' Then two sleek gray sheriff's cars (numbers 12 and, of course, 13) motored slowly toward the crowd from Centre Island, en route from the Airport ferry. The crowd broke into song: ''like a tree standing by the water, we shall not be moved''

and other unusually appropriate chants. Acting Sheriff Joseph Bremner and his Deputy Boris Kashuba wanted to meet representatives quietly, in their car—away from the madding crowd. No deal. So, surrounded by a mob of media people poking microphones and cameras at them, TIRA co-chairmen Elizabeth Amer and Ron Mazza negotiated quietly, but firmly, with the sheriff. Ms. Amer suggested that the sheriff and his men were jumping the gun and asked for a twenty-four-hour delay while the matter of the writs was settled. In the end, the sheriff

agreed to the delay. As the officials retreated, to the wild cheers of Islanders and their friends, the sun came out. They had stood together—and had won. Not the war. But a real moral victory. And, if need be, they would do it all again.

This showdown at the Algonquin Bridge was the emotional high point of the long war to save the Island community and brought national attention to the Island issue, but the legal and political manoeuvring continued. On July 31 the Ontario Court of Appeal granted Islanders the right to appeal the O'Driscoll decision that

"We have seven hundred people, two hundred children, with no place to go," TIRA Co-Chairman Elizabeth Amer tells the Sheriff in this photograph by Boris Spremo. "We're getting no compensation. We're in a desperate situation. We're simply asking you to wait twenty-four hours." [Star]

Metro's writs were "timeless" and valid. Since the appeal wouldn't be heard until the fall, the way was cleared for Islanders to enjoy their summer and for Barry Swadron to go ahead with his inquiry, with or without the formal co-operation of Metro.

Confident that he could find a solution that would make no one "violently unhappy," Swadron climbed on a rented bicycle in early August and toured the controversial area "to get the lay of the land" before opening hearings on August 14.[41] Between then and November 5 Islanders and mainlanders, experts and laypeople, City officials and Metro officials, politicians and politicians-in-waiting paraded before the commission. As at the City's own, more limited, hearings in November 1973, public sentiment was very much in favour of retaining the community: "No matter which way you slice them [the two-hundred-plus informal oral and written submissions]," Swadron wrote later, "the marked majority of submissions showed support for the retention of the residential community on the Toronto Islands: speakers very much more so than writers."[42] And throughout the fall, a great mass of material on all manner of Island matters—from firefighting to frogs, Indian land claims to yacht club leases, septic tanks to social surveys—was collected, tabulated, discussed and, ultimately, assessed.

By the time Islanders went into court on September 24 to appeal the O'Driscoll writ decision, Swadron was snowed under and undecided but, according to the *Globe*, still confident that his report would offer "logic, reason and justice." Meanwhile, the 1980 municipal election campaign was swinging into high gear. Mayor Sewell received a warm welcome when he took his campaign to the Island for a Sunday walk on September 28, but the controversial mayor

was more coolly received elsewhere in the city; and the newly-curled, well-financed Art Eggleton was making visible in-roads. In the midst of the campaign, the Ontario Appeal Court ruled that Metro's writs were indeed valid. The Province forestalled evictions, but only after the sheriff had delivered (by mail this time) new notices to vacate Island homes by November 17 and after Eggleton had defeated Sewell on November 10. The Conservative government at Queen's Park, it was reported, wanted to make sure that Radical John received no credit for pressuring it to save Islanders. On November 13, therefore, the Province introduced a bill to stay the execution of the writs (and save the Island community) until July 1, 1981.

Swadron could finish his report in relative peace and Islanders could enjoy the Christmas season and the second annual New Year's Day volleyball game, played on the beach in eight inches of snow.

Amid rumours that he would recommend preserving the Island community, Commissioner Swadron submitted his report, aptly titled *Pressure Island*, to Tom Wells on January 12, 1981. Wells, however, did not see fit to make public the long-awaited document until March, in the middle of a Provincial election campaign and only after Islanders' long-time supporter, NDPer Richard Johnston, had received and leaked the recommendations. Commenting that "it would be unhealthy for the dispute to arise again this generation," Swadron recommended that the present houses and community be allowed to remain, but not allowed to expand, for twenty-five years, until July 31, 2005. He also recommended that Metro retain ownership of the land, but lease it at "fair market value" to the City which, in turn, would administer the residential areas and grant leases to Island resi-

dents. And then days before the election, Wells held a press conference to announce the Province's response: "...the essence of the report is that a community on the Toronto Island should be continued and those who are resident in the community should pay their way. The principle is acceptable to the Government of Ontario and we will take appropriate steps to put this into effect." Then, after Premier Davis and his Tories won their longed-for majority government on March 19, Islanders began to work hard to hold them to their election promise, even though they had lost the leverage of a minority government. Whether they would be successful remained to be seen.

Metro, meanwhile, was livid, both with the Swadron report and with the Province's hasty response. Calling the Province's support "a crass, political move on the eve of an election," Metro Chairman Godfrey vowed from under the hot Florida sun that "Metro won't give it up that easily."[43] And Metro Council duly voted, 25-12 on March 17, to spend up to $250,000 to fight the Province by hiring Tory lawyer and hockey impresario Alan Eagleson to lobby his friends at Queen's Park and engaging an ad agency to design a campaign to convince the public at large that Metro was right and the Province and Islanders were wrong. It was all a "waste of money," commented Wells to the *Star* on June 18.

On December 9, 1981, the Provincial government finally introduced its complex legislation to preserve the Island community until 2005.[44] Metro Chairman Godfrey still promised that Metro would wage "all-out war to block the legislation";[45] but Metro's war was doomed to failure in the face of Provincial determination to press on. In spite of Metro's crassly distorted "On No Mr. Bill" ads, which annoyed the

Not a political, but a literal, tug-of-war at Gala Day 1982. [SDG]

usually reticent Swadron so much that he held a press conference, the Island bill became law on December 18. Islanders had finally won the war, by preventing demolition of the houses. Could they also win the peace, by negotiating acceptable terms for remaining on the Island?

Hardly had the New Year arrived and Arctic conditions descended on the bay than Metro and the City were squabbling over the Island. Metro childishly stopped ploughing snow from the residential streets until Chairman Godfrey over-turned the "departmental decision" by Commissioner Robert Bundy. More serious conflicts loomed on the horizon: who owned the houses and how much rent would the City (and therefore Islanders) have to pay Metro.

In mid-February Metro's negotiator, the same Robert Bundy, shocked Island forces when he proposed that the City should pay Metro $1.8 million per year to rent the land *and* the houses. "The figure is just laughable," said TIRA Co-Chairman Peter Dewdney, although neither he nor his neighbours were laughing.[46] Islanders' new alderman, John Sewell, who had won a by-election and now served as the chairman of the City's Toronto Island Working Committee, agreed; so the City formally rejected the proposal and prepared to go to arbitration to settle the dispute.

Spring brought the warm weather and the big ships back to the Toronto Harbour: far fewer than in the golden, olden, pre-container days, but the captain of the first cargo-bearing ship to leave or enter the port still donned the ceremonial top hat. The season also brought new plans to revitalize the central waterfront, what Mayor Eggleton called "this last frontier" of the city.[47] On the Island frontier the City agreed that the residents did indeed own the houses and emphasized this by again asking the Province to transfer ownership of Ward's and Algonquin back to the City from Metro. This would "end the misery" of these protracted conflicts, Mayor Eggleton commented to the City Executive on May 7. But in the absence of any such resolution, all parties continued doggedly on toward arbitration.

In the meantime, life on the bay and Island continued. The renovated *Trillium* was still trying to recover from the previous June's humiliating reverse when she unexpectedly sailed astern and rammed and sank Captain John's Restaurant moored at Queen's Quay. Renovating Islanders, forced by a Metro Parks ban on transporting building materials via Metro ferries, adopted a "Smugglers' Cove" approach to home improvement. Harbour policemen, faced with being merged with the Metro police, reminisced about exciting events along the lakefront (like the unnerving time the lonely lookout at the tip of the Leslie Street Spit stepped outside his hut to get a better look at the stormy lake and his hut blew away). Naked sunbathers at Hanlan's Point Beach, confronted by plainclothes policemen, were forced to turn tail and retreat to less accessible spots. And residents of the eastern end of the Island not only enjoyed the traditional attractions of their 61st Annual Gala Day, but also declared their faith in the future by holding a communal "Island Christening" of all the recent juvenile additions to the community.

While Island lawyer Eldon Bennett looks anxiously on, Arbitrator Gordon Atlin checks the foundations of one Island house in order to determine if it is a "fixture" or a "chattel." [*Globe and Mail*]

After one unfortunate false start in the fall of 1982 when Arbitrator Robert Robinson died before rendering a complete decision, arbitration hearings got under way a second time in May 1983, more than two years after the initial rent dispute. The new arbitrator, Gordon Atlin, toured the Island and agreed with his predecessor's partial ruling: Metro owned the houses.[48] As he prepared to move on to the next stage of determining the rent to be paid, Islanders declared their outrage. TIRA Co-Chairman Linda Rosenbaum said bluntly, "Metro's continuing quest for ownership of the houses we built, bought or maintained is nothing more than attempted theft." "We're not going to pay rent on houses we own," echoed her co-chairman, Peter Dewdney.[49] Islanders would take every legal action possible. But they would also continue to pressure the Province to change the legislation and they would prepare themselves in any other way necessary to defend "their" homes. On June 20, 1983, they took their protest to Nathan Phillips Square for the first time in several years, with balloons, babies and posters. That same day, inside City Hall, Mayor Eggleton offered his own, and the City's, unqualified support: "We agree that the Island residents own their own houses and the way this can be achieved would be to have the Province turn over Ward's and Algonquin Islands to the City."[50] Metro's own Thirty Years War was by no means over.

While the main contestants continue to squabble, Toronto Island's six hundred political veterans—survivors of countless trips to council

chambers, legislative chambers and judges' chambers—remain poised in their eccentric and much-loved little Island homes, ready to launch themselves across the bay to do battle, yet again, to preserve their community and remain "Islanders."

In the distant past a cavalcade of characters from Canada's history had brought life to the Island's shores. Summering Indians, buckskinned explorers, black-robed Jesuits and intrepid fur traders like Mackenzie and McGillivray all passed this way. Redcoated English soldiers and invading

Americans, horseback-riding ladies and duck-shooting gentlemen, wretched commercial fishermen and pioneering hotel keepers all left their footprints on the Island's sands; long before the Island became a popular resort for millions and a well-loved home to thousands down through the years. As the city celebrates its 1984 Sesquicentennial, citizens with a sense of history can only hope, at a time when Toronto is finally reclaiming its own downtown waterfront and when people are once again living as well as playing along the edge of the bay, that Toronto's oldest waterfront community will also be allowed to live and prosper and make its own distinctive contribution to the city's future.

Window on another world. [SDG]

Notes

Chapter 1

Unless otherwise noted in the text or footnotes, all quotations in this chapter are found in: Percy J. Robinson, *Toronto During the French Regime*. Toronto: University of Toronto Press, 2nd edition, 1965.

[1] Mohawk historian William Smith quoted by Al Chandler, "Island Made in Hurricane," *Globe and Mail*, December 19, 1954.

[2] E. J. Pratt, "Brébeuf and His Brethren."

[3] A minority of scholars have argued that Toronto means "trees in water." Whether or not the name derived from this source, the image of the Island or Peninsula as it would have appeared across the lake is an apt one. See Percy J. Robinson, "Appendix I—The Etymology of 'Toronto,'" pp. 221-25.

[4] Father Louis Hennepin, *New Discovery of a Vast Country in America* (Toronto: Coles Publishing Company Limited, originally published 1698), p. 54.

[5] Henry Scadding, D. D., *Toronto of Old* (Toronto: Adam, Stevenson & Co., 1873), p. 32.

[6] Duncan Campbell Scott, "Night Hymns on Lake Nippigon."

[7] J. C. Bonnefons, quoted by Robinson, p. 127.

[8] Henry Scadding, D. D., *Brief Memoir of the Old French Fort at Toronto* (paper read at the dedication of the foundation stone of an Obelisk to mark the site, laid in 1884), p. 7.

[9] "Journal of Walter Butler. 1779," *The Canadian Historical Review* (December 1920), p. 388.

[10] Ibid., p. 387. Just before Butler's voyage past Toronto and across the Peninsula in March 1779, Brant, too, had travelled along the north shore of the lake, carrying a letter from Lt. Col. Bolton at Niagara to General Haldimand at Quebec.

Chapter 2

Unless otherwise noted in the text or footnotes, the quotations from Mrs. Simcoe are taken from: Mary Quayle Innis, ed., *Mrs. Simcoe's Diary*. Toronto: Macmillan of Canada, 1965; and the other quotations from early visitors or settlers are taken from either Edith G. Firth, ed., *The Town of York 1793-1815, A Collection of Documents of Early Toronto*. Toronto: University of Toronto Press for The Champlain Society, 1962; or from Edith G. Firth, ed., *The Town of York 1815-1834, A Further Collection of Documents of Early Toronto*. Toronto: University of Toronto Press for The Champlain Society, 1966.

[1] Simcoe had served with distinction in the American War of Independence and had led his Queen's Rangers (the regimental descendants of Rogers' Rangers) in a number of successful engagements. They were disbanded at the end of that war, but Simcoe was given permission to reorganize them and bring them with him to the new province of Upper Canada which was created along with Lower Canada by the Canada Act of 1791.

[2] Joseph Bouchette, *The British Dominions in North America* (London, 1831), p. 89, footnote.

[3] Both Simcoe and Governor General Lord Dorchester agreed that Niagara (or Newark), which would soon be under the guns of an American fort, would not be a suitable capital for a British province. But beyond this they could not agree. Dorchester wanted Kingston to be named capital and Simcoe wanted a new town, London, to be built on the Thames River. York almost by default became the capital of Upper Canada and remained so until 1841.

[4] Quoted by Edwin Guillet, *Toronto From Trading Post to Great City* (Toronto: The Ontario Publishing Co. Ltd., 1934), p. 21.

[5] Quoted by Eric Arthur, *Toronto No Mean City* (Toronto: University of Toronto Press, 1964), p. 23.

[6] George Landmann, quoted in Frank Norman Walker, *Sketches Of Old Toronto* (Toronto: Longmans Canada, Ltd., 1975), p. 47.

[7] Quoted in Austin Seton Thompson, *Spadina: A Story of Old Toronto* (Toronto: Pagurian Press Ltd., 1975), p. 47.

[8] John Ross Robertson, who published six volumes of *Landmarks of Toronto* between 1894 and 1914, declared that the first bridge over the Don at Queen Street was built earlier, in 1803.

[9] *Upper Canada Gazette*, June 18, 1806.

[10] Dr. William Warren Baldwin to Firth, April 22, 1812. Baldwin Papers, Ontario Archives.

Chapter 3

Unless otherwise noted in the text or footnotes, the quotations from visitors or residents are taken from either Edith G. Firth, ed., *The Town of York 1793-1815, A Collection of Documents of Early Toronto.* Toronto: University of Toronto Press for The Champlain Society, 1962; or from Edith G. Firth, ed. *The Town of York 1815-1834, A Further Collection of Documents of Early Toronto.* Toronto: University of Toronto Press for The Champlain Society, 1966.

[1] Roger Hall and Gordon Dodds, *A Picture History of Ontario* (Edmonton: Hurtig Publishers, 1978), p. 11.

[2] Quoted in Austin Seton Thompson, *Spadina: A Story of Old Toronto* (Toronto: Pagurian Press Limited, 1975), p. 71.

[3] Quoted in Ibid., p. 71.

[4] Colonel C. P. Stacey, *The Battle of Little York* (Toronto: Toronto Historical Board, 1963), p. 3.

[5] Charles W. Humphries, ''The Capture of York'' in Morris Zaslow (ed.), *The Defended Border: Upper Canada and the War of 1812* (Toronto: Macmillan Company of Canada, 1964), p. 260.

[6] Edith G. Firth (ed.), *The Town of York: 1815-1834, A Further Collection of Documents of Early Toronto* (Toronto: University of Toronto Press for The Champlain Society, 1966), p. xviii.

[7] Marjorie Wilkins Campbell, *The North West Company* (Toronto: The Macmillan Company of Canada Limited, 1957; revised paperback edition 1973), p. 114.

[8] Some use was made of it. For example, on August 22, 1809, Ely Playter noted in his diary: ''Joel B[eman] call'd [at Playter's farm near the Don] & took breakfast on his way to town with a load of Goods from North West—a large canoe and a Number of Men....''

[9] Sources differ over how many bridges there were before the war and how they were destroyed. According to this petition, there were two—not one as Dr. Scadding and others indicated—and they had been destroyed by order of the Royal Engineer in the spring of 1813 as a preventive defensive measure, rather than by Sheaffe as he retreated.

[10] E. A. Talbot, *Five Years' Residence in the Canadas,* 1824, vol. 1, p. 100.

[11] Dr. Walter Henry, *Trifles From My Port-folio, or*

Recollections of Scenes and Small Adventures during Twenty-Nine Years' Military Service (Quebec: William Neilson, 1839), p. 112.

[12] *York Gazette*, January 14, 1815.

[13] Ibid.

[14] *Canadian Freeman*, April 5, 1832.

[15] *Canadian Freeman*, May 17, 1832.

[16] The town of York was run not by elected representatives, but by appointed Magistrates—usually prominent merchants with strong Tory links. The system not only offended the democratic sensibilities of people like William Lyon Mackenzie—a matter of little importance perhaps—but also gave rise to a number of practical problems: lack of sufficient attention by part-time Magistrates; lack of money; and lack of adequate authority to deal with such emergencies as the cholera. When it was decided to elevate the town to the status of city, there was great debate over the name of Toronto. To Chief Justice Powell the name was appallingly ''wild and Terrific''; but to others, the old Indian name was sonorous and unique.

[17] Quoted by John Ross Robertson, *Landmarks of Toronto*, vol. 5, p. 388.

Chapter 4

[1] The advertisement was dated September 5, 1833, and was placed in local newspapers as well as papers in Montreal, Kingston, Gore and Niagara. See *Courier of Upper Canada*, October 4, 1833 and *Canadian Freeman*, October 3, 1833.

[2] Benjamin Knott, letter dated 28 August 1832, acknowledging receipt of a letter informing him that Lt. Gov. Sir John Colborne had agreed to his petition for land on the Peninsula. (Public Archives of Canada.) According to the *York Directory*, Knott's factory was still on the Peninsula in 1837, but he later moved back to the mainland.

[3] ''Extracts From Memorandums of William Helliwell'' in Edith G. Firth (ed.), *The Town of York 1815-1834, A Further Collection of Documents of Early Toronto* (Toronto: University of Toronto Press for The Champlain Society, 1966), p. 339.

[4] The history of the early Peninsula/Island hotels is shrouded in the mists of time. It is impossible to

trace a continuous story from the scattered records that do remain. In fact, it is often impossible to tell where a particular hotel was located, when it was built, who built it, who later owned it, what it looked like, or, in some cases, whether it ever existed at all. This is equally true of other early buildings, like fishermen's houses.

[5] Charles Wolfe, ''The Burial of Sir John Moore.''

[6] Letter from George Heathcote to Mayor Sullivan, 30 March 1835, City Council Papers, City of Toronto Archives. Heathcote, who was seeking financing for a steamboat he was building, emphasized that his new boat would expedite ''visiting the Peninsula...to which many families resorted during the Sickness of the past Summer to enjoy the salubrity and freshness of Air, that cannot be found in our City, particularly in our summer Months.''

[7] *Upper Canada Land, Mercantile, and General Advertiser*, Toronto (late York), February 21, 1834.

[8] Henry Scadding, D. D., *Toronto of Old* (Toronto: Adam, Stevenson & Co., 1873), p. 85.

[9] On April 3, 1835, William Gooderham, whose mill stood at the elbow of the bay, and several other businessmen petitioned the City to improve the road from King Street to the Windmill, which in the muddy seasons of spring and fall was ''almost impassable.'' Messrs. Knott, Palin and Anderton also signed this petition since, they shrewdly perceived, the road to the Windmill was also the first section of the road to the Peninsula and their Peninsula Hotel. City Council Papers, City of Toronto Archives.

[10] Quoted in ''New Bridges At the Peninsula,'' *The Recorder*, Brockville, August 28, 1835 and *Patriot*, August 28, 1835.

[11] Palin advertisement, September 4, 1835.

[12] By-law enacted May 23, 1836. City of Toronto Archives. The by-law also forbade people from taking sand or gravel from the neck of land leading to the Peninsula, a practice that soon became a major problem. Some form of toll apparently had been instituted earlier, because the toll keeper, old Peter Redmond, complained in a letter to the mayor dated April 21, 1836, ''that since the weakness of the Ice has rendered it dangerous to cross the Bay, a large number of Waggons, cattle etc. are daily crossing the Peninsula Bridges and their object is constantly to avoid the Toll. The same practice was pursued last

fall, and will no doubt be continued during the coming season.'' City Council Papers, City of Toronto Archives.

13 William Kilbourn, *The Firebrand: William Lyon Mackenzie & the Rebellion In Upper Canada* (Toronto: Clarke, Irwin & Company, 1956), p. 123.

14 *The City of Toronto and the Home District Commercial Directory and Register with Almanack and Calendar for 1837.*

15 Anna Jameson was a well-known author in her day, as well as a protofeminist and shrewd observer of life around her. Her domestic life was unhappy; but she decided to join her husband, Robert Jameson, in Toronto for a brief period in 1836-37. She was warmly welcomed by the local literati in New York City—including Washington Irving. She then set off (unwisely) for Toronto very late in 1836 and, after a harsh journey, just managed to catch the last steamer out of Niagara before the lake was frozen closed for the winter. Her arrival in Toronto—which contrasted so sharply with her welcome in New York—set the tone for her next few months in captivity: the wharf was cold and deserted. In the summer of 1837 she made a remarkable journey through Indian country to the northern shores of Lake Huron before returning to England on the eve of Toronto's 1837 Rebellion. Anna Jameson, *Winter Studies and Summer Rambles In Canada*, vol. 1 (London: Saunders and Otley, 1838; Coles Canadiana Collection, 1972). All Jameson quotations come from this source.

16 Quoted by Kilbourn, *The Firebrand*, p. 191.

17 Quoted by A. G. Meredith, *Mary's Rosedale & Gossip of Little York* (Ottawa: The Graphic Publishers Limited, 1928), p. 141.

18 Quoted by Kilbourn, *The Firebrand*, p. 207.

19 Quoted by J. M. Careless, *Brown of the Globe*, vol. 1 (Toronto: The Macmillan Company of Canada Limited, 1959; reprinted 1966), p. 26.

20 Quoted by E. C. Kyte (ed.), *Old Toronto: A Selection of Excerpts From Landmarks of Toronto by John Ross Robertson* (Toronto: The Macmillan Company of Canada Limited, 1954), p. 119.

21 Sir Richard H. Bonnycastle, *The Canadas in 1841* (London: Henry Colburn, Publisher, 1841), p. 135.

22 Howard's distinctive, black-caped figure was frequently to be seen striding over virtually every inch of the Peninsula—in virtually every kind of weather. On May 9, 1843 and again on May 11, 1846, he laid out fishing grounds. And in chill December 1847, he drew a survey of the Island from Privat's Tavern westward. He even rowed his Upper Canada College students around the bay to practice taking soundings and may well have led them over to the Island (or Peninsula) for additional practice. Howard's sturdy assistants, like Fred Passmore and William Smith, also spent long hours bobbing up and down in the bay taking soundings, as well as braving icy lake winds while clumping about over the rock-hard ground of the Peninsula in February (1847). Howard Papers, Baldwin Room, Metropolitan Toronto Public Library.

23 Quoted by Mary Larratt Smith, *Young Mr. Smith In Upper Canada* (Toronto: University of Toronto Press, 1980), p. 38. The other quotes from Larratt Smith are from this source.

24 Larratt Smith frequently described the arrival and departure of the various regiments. The wharfs, in fact, played a role similar to Union Station several generations later.

25 According to John Ross Robertson, the Privats opened the Peninsula Hotel in 1843, although Louis Privat does not appear on the Assessment Rolls until 1845.

26 Quoted by Edwin C. Guillet, *Pioneer Inns and Taverns*, vol. 3 (Toronto: by the author, 1954), p. 152.

27 Quoted by Firth, *The Town of York 1815-1834*, pp. 79-80.

28 *Globe*, April 28, 1880.

29 ''Petition of William Waring [Warren] and other Fishermen,'' January 5, 1846 and ''Petition of William Geddes,'' January 19, 1846. City Council Papers, City of Toronto Archives. Also Report of the Committee On Wharves and Harbors &c., *City Council Minutes*, January 26, 1846.

30 James Browne et al, ''Petition of Several Fishermen in Support of William Geddes,'' January 31, 1846. City Council Papers, City of Toronto Archives.

31 ''Petition of Alexander Stewart and others of the said City, Fishermen,'' July 31, 1846; ''Petition of James Wallis of said city, Fisherman,'' July 31, 1846; ''Petition of Alexander Stewart, John Charlton, William Warin and Henry Wallis... Fishermen,'' September 21, 1846; and ''Letter from Mr. Keele on behalf of John Charlton,'' September 4, 1848. City Council Papers, City of Toronto Archives.

32 Over the next few years few people applied for leases and those who did apply generally wanted to build hotels, not houses. Howard apparently designed a hotel for a Mr. Cameron, but this was never built.

33 Firemen's petition, quoted by F. H. Armstrong, ''The First Great Fire of Toronto, 1849,'' *Ontario History*, vol. 53 (September 1961), p. 220; and *Examiner*, April 11, 1849.

34 *Globe*, October 16, 1851 and John Ross Robertson, quoted by Kyte, *Old Toronto*, p. 296.

35 Most politicians, businessmen and railway officials—sometimes in the same person—seemed to take the view that what was good for the railways was good for Toronto. See Frances Mellen, *The Development of the Toronto Waterfront During the Railway Expansion Era* (Toronto: University of Toronto, Dept. of Geography, unpublished Ph.D. thesis, 1974) for an account of waterfront politics in this era.

36 In 1819 Chief Justice John Beverly Robinson ruled that ''the negroes [are] entitled to personal freedom through residence in Canada.'' Quoted by Daniel Hill, *The Freedom Seekers* (Toronto: The Book Society of Canada, 1981), p. 93. In Simcoe's time slavery had existed in York and a number of his advisors, like Peter Russell and William Jarvis, were slaveowners. Although personally opposed to slavery, Simcoe adopted a typically Canadian compromise—he outlawed the importation of new slaves. Gradually—and literally—the practice died out. By 1833, slavery was officially abolished in the British Empire, which stimulated many American slaves to head northward, to the Niagara Peninsula and elsewhere in Canada.

37 This Act authorized slaveowners or their agents to track down fugitive slaves living in free northern states and to take them back into slavery. As a result, fugitives no longer stopped in these northern states, but continued their flight to Canada.

38 Susanna Moodie, *Life In the Clearings*, edited by Robert L. McDougall (Toronto: Macmillan of Canada, Laurentian Library #39, 1976; originally published in 1853), pp. 205-6.

[39] *Globe*, May 20, 1880.

[40] *Leader*, June 29, 1857.

[41] *Leader*, July 1, 1857.

[42] Surprisingly, just where Glendinning's substantial establishment was located remains a mystery. According to the Assessment Rolls, it was located on the eastern portion of the Peninsula and since it was not mentioned in the later reports of the 1858 storm that swept away Quinn's Peninsula Hotel, it must have been west of that unfortunate building. But it is impossible to be more precise. The Assessment Rolls also indicate changes in the fishing community. By 1852, fishing magnate William Geddes was the only person listed on the western portion of the Peninsula and by 1858, only two fishermen were listed on the eastern portion: David Ward, with property valued at £40 and John Ward with property valued at £20. How complete these records were remains unknown, though it was in the City's interest to at least list the major property owners.

[43] *United Empire*, October 10, 1854.

[44] *Globe*, December 1, 1856.

[45] On February 6, 1854, both John Glendinning and Joseph Lang petitioned Council for the position of Watcher or Protector of the Peninsula. Lang, who had grown up in the area and was "fully acquainted with almost every yard" of it, pledged that "the Trees on the said peninsula will not be cut or injured, nor the Sand removed therefrom without your worshipful body being early apprised of the depredators." City Council Papers, City of Toronto Archives. Another applicant, however, John Roddy, was appointed "to remain in charge of the Peninsula," to prevent the illegal removal of sand. *City Council Minutes*, February 13, 1854.

[46] "Death of Mrs. Jennie Oster Removes Last Survivor of Famed Island Storm," *Telegram*, February 7, 1939.

Chapter 5

[1] *Toronto Colonist* quoted in *Evening Telegram*, October 12, 1878; the TPL Scrapbook, vol. 4, p. 685 (Metropolitan Toronto Reference Library); and Frank Cosentino, *Ned Hanlan* (Toronto: Fitzhenry & Whiteside, Ltd., 1978), which gives a good account of Hanlan's life and career.

[2] John Ross Robertson places this event in 1862. The Assessment Rolls, however, indicate that Hanlan was living somewhere on the eastern half of the Island between 1862 and 1865. Thereafter he was listed on the western half. His petition to City Council in June 1858 indicates that he was established somewhere on the Island before 1862.

[3] *Globe*, September 8, 1890; and C. C. Taylor, *"Toronto Called Back" From 1887 to 1847* (Toronto: William Briggs, 1887), p. 157.

[4] G. Mercer Adam, *Toronto Old and New* (Toronto: The Mail Printing Company, 1891; facsimile edition by Coles Publishing Company, 1974), p. 38.

[5] *Globe*, May 12, 1866, which described the event but gave the wrong names, and *Globe*, May 14, 1866. A few years earlier, the Wards had lost three other children to smallpox, which periodically ravaged Toronto.

[6] Quoted by Henry C. Campbell, *Early Days on the Great Lakes: The Art of William Armstrong* (Toronto: McClelland and Stewart Limited, 1971), p. 9.

[7] Robin Winks, *Canada and the United States: The Civil War Years* (Montreal: Harvest House, 1970), p. 231.

[8] On June 25, 1866, City Council granted John Hanlan a lease for two acres at the western end of the Island and in the same year the Assessment Roll listed him in the western part of the Island for the first time.

[9] *Leader*, May 19, 1866.

[10] Obituary, February 1871, quoted by Russell Harper, *Paul Kane's Frontier* (Toronto: University of Toronto Press, 1971), p. 45.

[11] *Globe*, July 27, 1865.

[12] Quoted by Edwin C. Guillet, *Toronto From Trading Post to Great City* (Toronto: The Ontario Publishing Company Limited, 1934), p. 82.

[13] For example, on July 16, 1866, the Young Men's Christian Association as well as the Rev. John C. Manly and friends petitioned City Council to prevent steamers and other pleasure boats from running to the Island; and on May 18, 1868, Rev. Dr. Willis et al similarly petitioned Council to "prevent the desecration of the Sabbath" by steam ferryboats running to the Island. City Council Papers, City of Toronto Archives.

[14] *Globe*, July 2, 1867.

[15] These were not all new leases, since Gray's, Hanlan's and Parkinson's hotels were included. Furthermore, many of the leases were never signed. To make matters even more complicated, neither David nor John Ward had leases for the lots they were occupying.

[16] *Evening Telegram*, May 15, 1909.

[17] C. H. J. Snider, *Annals of the Royal Canadian Yacht Club, 1852-1937* (Toronto: Rous & Mann Limited, 1937), pp. 44-45.

[18] Quoted by Cosentino, *Ned Hanlan*, p. 29.

[19] *Toronto Island Guide*, 1894.

[20] *Globe*, July 2, 1873.

[21] *City Council Minutes*, May 3, 1875.

[22] By the end of April 1875 four summer cottages stood on the Island: Mrs. Baines' and John Duggan's on parts of lot 78; and Mrs. William Armstrong's and Mr. Morris's on parts of lot 79. By the end of April 1876, one more was added on lot 78. Assessment Rolls for 1875 and 1876.

[23] Residential development met with general approval in the mid-1870s. The *Globe*, for example, advanced an early version of the mixed-use arguments in vogue a hundred years later:

> Those portions of the Island available for the purpose, without interfering with the convenience and enjoyment of the public, have been leased to persons who contemplate erecting summer residences. During the open [summer] months, the Island will, therefore, have a population of its own, who will have an interest in all measures calculated to promote public improvements or to preserve order.

Globe, April 30, 1875.

[24] Compiled from *Leader*, November 15, 1875; *Evening Telegram*, May 15, 1909; and C. H. J. Snider, *Telegram*, June 8, 1940.

[25] C. H. J. Snider, *Telegram*, June 8, 1940.

[26] Thos. O. Keefer, December 29, 1875, Appendix to *City Council Minutes*, March 31, 1876, p. 70.

27 *Globe*, September 15, 1876.

28 Ward's first hotel was listed in the Assessment Rolls of 1877 through 1883. From 1877-1880, it was on the unnumbered "fishing reservation." In 1880, Ward was also listed as the lessee of lot 22, which, according to the Roll, had no building on it. Whether the Assessment Roll is inaccurate, or whether Ward moved his hotel from another location, cannot be determined. In any event, from 1881-1883, the 34-by-26-foot hotel was definitely listed on lot 22 and was shown on a contemporary map.

29 London *Daily Telegraph* reprinted in *Globe*, July 1, 1879.

30 *Globe*, July 16, 1879. The rest of the homecoming is based on this *Globe* account.

Chapter 6

1 Bill 1028 originally set aside 46 lots (#28-75, excluding part of #33 which included an ice house and #69 and #72 which contained a number of cottages) and the Western Sandbar which was inching its way northward beyond Hanlan's Point. Campers and then cottagers took over the Western Sandbar, while sizeable chunks of land near the Lighthouse reserve were later dedicated to the Lakeside Home (#68), the Island Public School (first part of #64 and then part of #65) and various waterworks schemes like the present Filtration Plant (#61-64, 48-52). Manitou Road and large residential areas were also encouraged to grow along the lakefront on lots #56-60. On the other hand, the City later passed bills to expand the Island Park east of Manitou Road, north of Long Pond. For example, Bill 1824 (May 23, 1887) dedicated the Mead Hotel property on lots #27 and part #25 and Bill 1925 (November 21, 1887) dedicated the rest of lots 25 and 33 and lots #14, 15, 16, 17, 24 and 26 to parks purposes. In order to help finance the venture, all revenue derived from Island residents was originally to be placed in an "Island Park Fund" and used to maintain and improve the park. From the outset, therefore, the City had a vested interest in expanding the residential community. By 1888, the City was deriving about a $1,000 a year from Island rents. Since this was hardly enough to mow and rake the area, let alone improve it, other funds obviously had to be found.

2 C. Pelham Mulvany, *Toronto Past and Present*, 1884, pp. 265-66.

3 *Globe*, December 16, 1916.

4 DSR, *Telegram*, June 24, 1944.

5 *City Council Minutes*, April 5, 1880; July 19, 1880; August 30, 1880; and October 25, 1880.

6 *Ward's Island Weekly*, July 11, 1931.

7 *Globe*, June 28, 1883. The situation was improved in 1885 when Ward was sent to purchase a new lifeboat in Goderich and bring it down to Toronto by train. The Dobbins-like boat was a self-righting and self-bailing lifeboat designed for lake service, which required a larger crew of captain and six men. From the outset the crew found she was "very easily pulled for so heavy a boat." (*Globe*, October 17, 1886.) In the summer of 1886 the enlarged crew (which included a number of familiar Island names—Capt. William Ward, John Hanlan, John Gray, Ed. Hicks, Gus Goodson, George Durnan and William Davis) performed their drills "in a manner worthy of veterans." (*Globe*, June 29, 1886.) Pressure, however, mounted to form a "permanent Life Saving Crew on the Bay for the better security of life" and, to this end, Ward and Hanlan, among others, appeared before Council. (*Globe*, July 3, 1891.) Eventually, the Island lifeboat station was supplemented by a service on the mainland. (*Globe*, August 25, 1892.)

8 1883 Hospital Report quoted by Mulvany, *Toronto Past and Present*, p. 268.

9 Report of the first day quoted in Ibid., p. 275.

10 C. H. J. Snider, *Annals of the Royal Canadian Yacht Club, 1852-1937*. (Toronto: Rous & Mann Limited, 1937), p. 53 ff.; and "Old Islander," "Early Days On the Island," *Centre Islander*, May 17, 1946.

11 *Globe*, July 5, 1888; and "R," "Early Days On the Island," *Centre Islander*, May 17, 1946.

12 *City Council Minutes*, January 14, 1887; and Mayor Howland's Inaugural Address, *City Council Minutes*, January 17, 1887.

13 *City Council Minutes*, January 13, 1888. Throughout its history Island Park was used to provide work and alleviate the harsh effects of economic depressions which periodically hit Toronto. On February 13, 1888, for example, Council voted to spend $3,000 to employ "a large number of men who are now out of employment, and who at this season of the year are entirely destitute of any means of subsistence" to drive carts of street scrapings across the frozen bay to Island Park. The cost of this was, incidentally, "one-half the cost of doing the work when the ice is out of the Bay"—a case of relief going hand-in-hand with economy.

14 Emilie Florence Jones, "Early Toronto Island Days," *Centre Islander*, June 28, 1946.

15 DSR, *Telegram*, June 24, 1944.

16 *Globe*, July 7, 1883; and Jean Sears Suydam, *Church of St. Andrew-by-the-Lake*, no date.

17 *Globe*, July 29, 1884.

18 *Ward's Island Weekly*, August 7, 1920.

19 *Star Weekly*, February 3, 1912.

20 *Mail & Empire*, May 17, 1900.

21 *Toronto Island Guide*, 1894.

22 *Mail*, January 13, 1894.

23 The Toronto Railway Company and its supporters—bribed or otherwise—were eager to introduce streetcar service on Sundays. Their opponents, known disparagingly as the "Saints," were equally determined to keep Toronto morally pure and free of the contamination of Sunday cars. See C. Armstrong and H. V. Nelles, *The Revenge of the Methodist Bicycle Company: Sunday Streetcars and Municipal Reform in Toronto, 1888-1897* (Toronto: Peter Martin Associates Limited, 1977).

24 *Toronto Island Guide*, 1894.

25 *Toronto Island Guide*, 1894. See also *Mail*, July 2, 1894.

26 *Globe*, August 21, 1894.

27 *Globe*, August 27, 1897.

28 *Globe*, January 29, 1894.

29 *Mail & Empire*, January 7, 1896.

30 *Toronto Island Guide*, 1894.

31 *Globe*, September 4, 1894. Labour Day was officially celebrated for several years on the Island before returning to Exhibition Park.

32 *City Council Minutes*, May 9, 1892; January 11, 1893; January 4, 1894; September 24, 1894; and October 22, 1894.

[33] *City Council Minutes*, January 14, 1895 and November 18, 1895. Altogether 527 men were employed during November and December of 1894. Individuals, however, were not full-time employees. In November 1895, for example, park work was restricted to Toronto residents of 6 months and limited to 3 days continuous work for any one person.

[34] *Globe*, June 22, 1897 and June 23, 1897.

Chapter 7

[1] Aemilius Jarvis saw the need; Edward Lennox designed the building; and George H. Gooderham paid part of the cost. (Austin Seton Thompson, *Jarvis Street: A Story of Triumph and Tragedy* [Toronto: Personal Library Publishers, 1980], pp. 170-71.) The RCYC, with Commodore Aemilius Jarvis at the helm, launched the new hotel with a magnificent Club Ball in May 1903. (C. H. J. Snider, *Annals of the Royal Canadian Yacht Club, 1852-1937* [Toronto: Rous & Mann Limited, 1937], p. 137.)

[2] 1906. Quoted by Frances N. Mellen, *The Development of the Toronto Waterfront During the Railway Expansion Era 1850-1912* (University of Toronto Ph.D. thesis, 1974), p. 299.

[3] Administering the Island had always been a headache for City Hall, since it involved a wide range of matters (from park and public works to property management and landlord-tenant relations) and a variety of standing committees. In an effort to improve things, the City created an Island Committee in 1902. It was composed of the mayor and six aldermen, who were to be helped by an Advisory Board of City staff and two Island residents. Together, it was hoped, they could coordinate Island development and operations better. One of the first actions taken by the new Island Committee, which operated for about a decade, was to ask Chambers to prepare a plan.

[4] *Globe*, April 20 and April 21, 1904 and *City Council Minutes*, April 25, 1904.

[5] *Telegram*, October 5, 1909.

[6] Mary Frank, *Globe*, December 16, 1916.

[7] *Telegram*, August 24, 1906, and *Ward's Island Weekly*, August 18, 1934.

[8] *Telegram*, November 22, 1906.

[9] *World*, June 23, 1900.

[10] *Globe*, August 20, 1900.

[11] In May 1902, 6 families occupied tents or shacks along the Bay Front near the old Heber property. In 1900, 26 tents or cottages were located north of the Baths; 8 cottages and 10 tents were located south of the Baths; and a revenue of $395 accrued to the City. Between 1908 and 1912, the Assessment Rolls list 84-100 residents on the Hanlan/Solman property. So, all in all, according to Assessment Rolls, 500-600 "Campers and Others" were listed on the western end of the Island. In September 1904, for example, there were 400 "Campers and Others" plus 200 "Occupants on the Sand Bar."

[12] The City charged $15-$25 for "camping privileges"; allowed only one tent or small cottage on each lot; and required cottage designs to be approved by the City. *City Council Minutes*, September 22, 1902; December 29, 1902; and February 23, 1903.

[13] *Mail*, September 3, 1894.

[14] *Star*, May 10, 1904.

[15] Assessment File, item dated September 15, 1904, City of Toronto Archives. And *City Council Minutes*, April 25, 1905.

[16] *Ward's Island Weekly*, July 20, 1918 and Assessment Department File, "List of Tenants At Wiman Baths, 1902," City of Toronto Archives.

[17] The new island was still unfinished when the Queen City Yacht Club first applied to the City for a lease there in April 1908. The QCYC did not locate on Sunfish for another dozen years. Meanwhile, Sunfish Island itself was still not finished by the spring of 1909 when Parks Commissioner Wilson issued his Island plan. Ultimately, the new island grew from the originally suggested 20 acres to about 45 acres.

[18] James B. Marshall, August 16, 1906. Assessment Department File, City of Toronto Archives.

[19] Jesse Edgar Middleton, *The Municipality of Toronto: A History*, vol. 3 (Toronto: The Dominion Publishing Company, 1923), p. 131. According to the Assessment Rolls, Robinette and his family were living at a Centre Island cottage located between the Massey and Gooderham cottages by 1914.

[20] *City Council Minutes*, April 13, 1908 and *Globe*, April 14, 1908.

[21] "Petition" dated June 11, 1908; letter to Fred Armstrong dated May 5, 1908 and letter from Fred Armstrong dated April 30, 1908; letter from Mary Venier O'Dea dated March 6, 1909, (quoted in text) and report from Assessment Commissioner dated March 19, 1909. Assessment Department File, City of Toronto Archives.

[22] Annual Report of the City Engineer, Toronto, 1908, pp. 28-30. City of Toronto Archives.

[23] Items dealing with Haney's Point dated September 21, 1909; July 17, 1911; and September 5, 1911. Assessment Department File, City of Toronto Archives.

[24] *Globe*, March 31, 1924. Solman was discussing a new attraction for his later amusement park, Sunnyside. But the principle undoubtedly was applied to his earlier ventures at Hanlan's Point.

[25] *Globe*, August 11, 1909.

[26] *Star*, August 29, 1923.

[27] *City Council Minutes*, January 6, 1911.

[28] "Collector's Item—Vivid Memories of An Island Picnic Circa 1912," *Centre Islander*, June 27, 1953.

[29] *Globe*, November 15, 1912. The nearly thousand members of the Board of Trade who gathered together the day after the unveiling, passed a motion "approving most heartily the plans so prepared." On the overtly political front, Mayor Hocken could barely contain his pleasure, saying, "The project is a magnificent one, and one the city could not refuse to accept." It did not refuse. On November 26, City Council obligingly passed the scheme with nary a squeak of dissent. And on June 10, 1913, the federal government also gave its seal of approval.

[30] For example, on February 21, 1916, City Council voted not to renew three leases at Hanlan's Point, but to acquire the houses and rent them out until they were needed for the Boulevard. By July 1924, the City had acquired at least eleven properties for this purpose. *City Council Minutes*, February 21, 1916 and July 4, 1924.

[31] For example, cottages were originally to be only 14 by 18 feet. Then the City increased this to 18 by 22 feet. And, eventually, during the war and after,

when residents continued to add to their little 4-room cottages in spite of City prohibitions, the City decided to charge additional rent for additional square footage above a 450 square foot maximum. Other regulations included: one storey height; minimum value of $450; 6-foot-wide verandahs front and back, half of the rear verandah enclosable as a kitchen; and no alternations and no subletting without City permission.

32 Yearly financial statements reveal the following pattern: 1909, 34 tent permits issued for City campsites; 1910, 50; 1911, 71; 1912, 87; 1913, 91; and 1914, 98. Each permit covered a number of campers and in some cases the camp meant a group camp, like the YMCA that first arrived on Ward's Island in 1909. (Assessment Department File, City of Toronto Archives.) Assessment Rolls put the camping population at about 600 just before the First World War.

33 Assessment Department File items dated June 30, 1911 and July 7, 1911. City of Toronto Archives.

34 This led to the City's purchasing all of William Ward's property, except four cottages owned by Frank and Clara Ward, for $27,000 in 1914. *City Council Minutes*, November 19, 1914 and January 22, 1917.

35 Assessment Department File item dated July 8, 1913. City of Toronto Archives.

36 John Withrow, *Ward's Island Weekly*, August 18, 1934. According to the Toronto Harbour Commission, however, the life station was built in 1913, not 1912. *Report of the Toronto Harbor Commissioners*, 1912-1920, pp. 55-57.

37 Letter from Dodd dated February 29, 1912 and letter to Dodd, April 29, 1912. In this letter to Dodd confirming his appointment, the Assessment Commissioner noted that "no undesirable foreigners" were to be given sites. Since many recent immigrants from Britain found their way to Ward's Island with little trouble, "foreigner" here, as elsewhere in Toronto, meant "non-English-speaking foreigner." Assessment Department File, City of Toronto Archives.

38 *City Council Minutes*, May 28, 1913.

39 Letter from Assessment Commissioner to Chambers, March 12, 1913, outlining work to be done.

Assessment Department File, City of Toronto Archives. Also *City Council Minutes*, March 27, 1913.

40 Letter to Lt. Col. H. J. Grassett, Chief Constable, June 28, 1913 and letter from Chief Constable H. J. Grassett, July 2, 1913. Assessment Department File, City of Toronto Archives.

Chapter 8

1 *Globe*, August 5, 1914.

2 *Ward's Island Weekly*, August 22, 1947.

3 C. H. J. Snider, *Annals of the Royal Canadian Yacht Club, 1852-1937* (Toronto: Rous & Mann Limited, 1937), p. 11.

4 *Globe*, August 24, 1914.

5 According to the Assessment Rolls, the number of vacant houses increased dramatically, so that in August 1917 a peak of 107 homes were vacant, almost a third of all Island buildings. For example, fifty cottages at Centre Island were vacant, leaving whole stretches of Lakeshore dark as mid-winter. The new Island incinerator even confirmed this trend: in 1916 it processed only half of the material handled in previous years, because "many former residents and owners of Island properties, presumably because of the prevailing war conditions, did not frequent their summer homes." Mayor Tommy Church's Inaugural Address to City Council, January 1917.

6 S. F. Wise, *Canadian Airmen and the First World War: The Official History of the Royal Canadian Air Force*, vol. 1 (Toronto: University of Toronto Press in co-operation with the Department of National Defence and the Canadian Government Publishing Centre, Supply and Services Canada, 1980), p. 31 ff. Most were RNAS recruits, who had to be 19-30 years old (preferably 19-23), British subjects of "pure European descent," and able to finance most of their own preliminary training. The Curtiss School charged $400 for 400 minutes of flying time. In 1916, Toronto City Council began to subsidize Toronto men at the Toronto Schools: $8 per week up to a maximum of $64. Graduates then received final training overseas. Training in the Curtiss Flying-Boat at Hanlan's Point was supplemented by training

at Long Branch in wheeled craft. Then, during the winter, Canadian pilots were trained in Texas and elsewhere in the U.S. In 1916, the Flying-Boat section was closed and the pupils took all their training in JN3's.

7 *Globe*, May 25, 1915.

8 Mayor Church was discussing the Street Cleaning Department, but his remarks undoubtedly applied to other departments.

9 Letter dated July 20, 1918, printed in *Ward's Island Weekly*, August 10, 1918.

10 *Globe*, July 3, 1917. It was also the first "dry" holiday since Ontario had declared Prohibition.

11 *City Council Minutes*, May 20, 1918.

12 Letter to Dodd dated May 13, 1915; letter from Dodd dated May 14, 1915; letter to Dodd dated May 19, 1915; memo dated May 19, 1915, re: Tate and Gaedé; and letter to Tate dated May 20, 1915. Assessment Department File, City of Toronto Archives.

13 Letter to Sam McBride dated July 8, 1914. In 1914, in fact, 65 applications for tent sites had to be refused "for lack of space." Assessment Department File, City of Toronto Archives. See also *City Council Minutes*, April 19, 1915.

14 *Report of the Toronto Harbor Commissioners 1912-1920*, pp. 9-12.

15 *Ward's Island Weekly*, August 11, 1917. Unless otherwise noted, the quotes dealing with wartime tent life are from issues of the *Ward's Island Weekly*.

16 In 1907, the Alexandra Yacht Club leased land on Fisherman's Road south of Keating Channel from the City. They operated from this location until 1914 when the THC notified them to remove their buildings so the THC could implement its grand waterfront scheme. On May 5, 1914, the club was given permission to temporarily locate their club on a site to be created "on the northwest corner of Ward's Island, 300 feet out" until "permanent sites upon the Island for yacht clubs" were created in some 3 or 4 years time. Various hold-ups delayed the filling and completion of the site; but by the summer of 1916, the clubhouse, assessed that year at $3,000, was on new foundations at Ward's. Because of the war, with thirty of its most active sailors "in the

service of the Empire'' (i.e., a third of its total membership), the club could not live up to its original lease conditions and new ones were agreed upon. Although a THC report for 1912-1920 states that the club moved to the Island in 1916, THC photographs indicate that it was there in May 1915. *City Council Minutes* May 5, 1914; May 3, 1915; December 27, 1915; December 16, 1916; and *Report of the Toronto Harbor Commissioners 1912-1920*, p.54.

[17] *Globe*, November 12, 1918.

[18] W. G. Cosbie, *The Toronto General Hospital 1819-1965: A Chronicle* (Toronto: The Macmillan Company of Canada, 1975), p. 160.

[19] Assessment Department File, items dated May 16 and June 4, 1919. City of Toronto Archives.

[20] Snider, *Royal Canadian Yacht Club*, p. 165.

[21] *City Council Minutes*, June 16, 1919; *Report of the Toronto Harbor Commissioners 1912-1920*, pp. 54-55; and *Ward's Island Weekly*, August 8, 1936.

[22] *Globe*, July 2, 1919.

[23] The highest number recorded on City lots #33,34,35,36 and 37 was 1,036 on the Assessment Roll made on August 26, 1924. This does not include hotel or Wiman Building residents or cottagers along the Lakeshore neck of Ward's Island. On the Assessment Roll made in 1929, the comparable total was still 930.

[24] *Globe*, August 2, 1921.

[25] The description of the ''Hounds'' comes from the obituary of J. O. ''Ollie'' McCrimmon in the *Star*, September 12, 1982, and the description of Island police Sgt. Miles comes from Alan Howard.

[26] *City Council Minutes*, June 16, 1924.

[27] *City Council Minutes*, November 1, 1926; February 7, 1927; and February 21, 1927. The agreement between the City and the TTC in June 1927 stipulated that the TTC would ''fix such tolls and fares as from time to time to the Commission shall seem reasonable and which, as far as possible, will provide sufficient revenue to make such ferry properties self-sustaining.'' (*City Council Minutes*, June 27, 1927.) The City's and the TTC's obsession with making the ferry service pay for itself had major consequences in the forties and fifties, leading to numerous battles with Island residents and contrib-

uting to the transfer of the Island from the City to Metro in 1956. By the end of the first year of operation, the City had contributed over $40,000 to cover the operation of the ferry—the first of many annual subsidies.

[28] *Globe*, July 2, 1927 and advertisement, June 30, 1927.

[29] *City Council Minutes*, May 28, 1929.

[30] *City Council Minutes*, June 19, 1929.

[31] The Board of Education wanted to build a new, two-room school on the Lakeshore between Manitou and Ward's Island. But on June 27, 1921, City Council rejected the proposed site between #166 and 176 Lake Front because it was a ''choice residential district.'' Crowding at the school was especially severe in spring and fall when children of summer residents joined the classes.

[32] Quoted by I. Allen et al, *Toronto Between the Wars: A Portfolio*, p. 12.

[33] *Globe*, July 2, 1929.

[34] *Globe*, July 26, 1929.

Chapter 9

[1] *Globe*, March 6, 1934 and *Telegram*, March 6, 1934.

[2] *Globe*, July 2, 1930.

[3] *Globe*, July 2, 1931 and Metropolitan Planning Board, *Report on Transportation to the Toronto Islands*, February 12, 1965. As contemporary news accounts make clear, this figure does not match the Dominion Day records set in the pre-TTC era: 56,000 in 1916; 60,000 in 1919; and 65,000 in 1917.

[4] *Globe and Mail*, August 2, 1938.

[5] *Telegram*, August 19, 1938.

[6] *Globe*, August 5, 1930.

[7] Early in the year several residents, independently of the Ward's Island Association, had trundled off to City Hall to agitate for permission to build cottages. The City Parks and Exhibition Committee, in response, toured the Island and decided not only to allow, but to require, Ward's Islanders to replace their tents with cottages and, significantly, to pay

higher rents. The WIA then felt forced to intervene and told the City that while some Ward's Islanders wanted to build permanent roofs, others could not afford to, and others actually preferred to keep their tents. The City delayed making a decision until June 29, 1931, when Council authorized, but did not require, Ward's Islanders to erect ''permanent roofs'' with either canvas or wooden sides, enclosing a maximum area of 24 by 27 feet (or 648 square feet). On December 14, 1931, City Council increased the maximum area to 840 square feet and set the following rent schedule: $35 for a tent under 720 square feet; $40 for a tent between 720 and 840 square feet; $50 for structures with ''permanent roofs and sides'' up to 720 square feet; and $60 for buildings between 720 and 840 square feet. See *Ward's Island Weekly*, June 27, 1931; *City Council Minutes*, June 29, 1931 and December 14, 1931.

[8] *Parks and Exhibition Committee Minutes*, October 21, 1937 and *City Council Minutes*, December 27, 1937. Ward's Islanders' hold on the eastern tip of the Island has always been a precarious one. The new one-year term may not have been as secure as the 21-year lease terms granted everywhere else on the Island except the Western Sandbar, but it was definitely better than the ''seasonal'' term for the license of occupation. Sense of security, after all, is a relative thing and Ward's Islanders got used to short-term security from the very beginning.

[9] *Star Weekly*, February 25, 1933. The assessed population (i.e., summer and year-round residents) for 1934 was over 4,200.

[10] For example, on January 13, 1930, Islanders' own alderman, Nathan Phillips, made his annual bridge motion at City Council. Then, as the Depression began to bite, Con. Billy Summerville led a deputation to Ottawa in search of dollars for unemployment relief works. Among the items on his shopping list were an airport and the famous link to the Island.

[11] *Star*, May 22, 1935.

[12] *Globe and Mail*, November 17, 1936.

[13] *Mail*, December 27, 1935.

[14] *Telegram*, July 13, 1936.

[15] *City Council Minutes*, June 15, 1936.

[16] *Telegram*, September 22, 1936.

[17] *West Island Drive Association Minutes*, June 27, 1937. City of Toronto Archives.

[18] *Globe and Mail*, August 27 and 28, 1937.

[19] *West Island Drive Association Minutes*, October 1, 1937. City of Toronto Archives.

[20] *City Council Minutes*, January 17, 1938.

[21] *City Parks and Exhibition Committee Minutes*, October 12, 1937; *City Board of Control Minutes*, October 13, 1937; and *City Council Minutes*, October 18, 1937.

[22] City Council approved the name "Algonquin" on November 15, 1937, when it also approved the subdivision plan for that island.

[23] *City Board of Control Minutes*, November 3, 1937.

[24] In October, the City Parks and Exhibition Committee instructed Commissioner Chambers to search for lots on Hanlan's Point. (*City Parks and Exhibition Committee Minutes*, October 7, 1937.) In November, City Council agreed to his suggestion to release the lots acquired for the Toronto Harbour Commission's cross-Island boulevard. (*City Council Minutes*, November 1 and November 15, 1937.) And the following spring, Hiawatha Avenue was extended. (*City Council Minutes*, May 9, 1937.) Those who remained on Hanlan's Point signed 21-year, compensation leases, whereas those who moved to Algonquin Island signed 21-year, non-compensation leases.

[25] *City Council Minutes*, April 11, 1938.

[26] *Globe and Mail*, July 19, 1938.

[27] The 1939 Assessment Roll (made on July 19, 1938) shows only twelve new leases, which include only two new houses under construction on Algonquin. By the following July, the total number of houses had grown by five, to a total of thirty-eight.

[28] The description of the fire and the comments about inadequate fire protection come from the *Star* and *Globe and Mail* of January 30, 1939.

[29] C.H.J. Snider, *Annals of the Royal Canadian Yacht Club, 1852-1937* (Toronto: Rous & Mann Limited, 1937), p. 20.

[30] *Globe and Mail*, September 5, 1939.

[31] *Globe and Mail*, September 9, 1939. Dorsey also made "aviation history" by flying on the first American airliner to make a commercial flight to Canada, which landed at the Island Airport.

Chapter 10

[1] *City Council Minutes*, November 8, 1940 and *Globe and Mail*, November 2, 1940.

[2] *Globe and Mail*, May 19, 1941.

[3] *Globe and Mail*, August 7, 1942.

[4] *Globe and Mail*, May 13, 1941.

[5] *Ward's Island Weekly*, June 28, 1941.

[6] *Star*, July 28, 1941.

[7] *Star*, October 7, 1940.

[8] *Globe and Mail*, June 4, 1941.

[9] *Globe and Mail*, May 22, 1941.

[10] *Ward's Island Weekly*, June 27, 1942 and July 11, 1942.

[11] *Globe and Mail*, June 19, 1941 and *Ward's Island Weekly*, July 5, 1941.

[12] *Globe and Mail*, July 2, 1942.

[13] Joe Holliday, *Mosquito! The Wooden Wonder Aircraft of World War II* (Toronto: Doubleday Canada, 1970), p. 116.

[14] *City Council Minutes*, June 16, 1947.

[15] *Globe and Mail*, August 7, 1945.

[16] *Globe and Mail*, August 15, 1945.

[17] On August 5, 1942, for example, the Board of Control asked for a survey of how many Island houses could be used in the winter. A few weeks later William Sutherland of the Manitou Hotel reported that about 80 units could be used if proper winter transportation were provided. (*Board of Control Minutes*, August 24, 1942.) But Sutherland's enthusiasm was not universal. The half-hearted City survey, which did not involve house-to-house inspections or contacting individual cottage-owners directly, only uncovered a few units on Algonquin. The City ordered the TTC to extend its service, which the TTC did, with reluctance. (Letter to City Clerk dated October 28, 1942.) Neither City nor TTC was keen to spend the $125,000 that a new winter ferry would cost to replace the City tugs which then provided service during the winter season. Moreover, grander housing schemes were put forward and not followed through, like city planner E.G. Faludi's proposal to build 100-150 prefabricated houses for soldiers' families in relatively wild areas like Mugg's Island and as replacements for dilapidated, so-called "slum cottages" (in Faludi's urban renewal view) that were despoiling "the beauties that nature has created." After the war, Faludi concluded, "Toronto would gain a *modern well planned summer resort*." (Letters to the Board of Control dated October 1 and 5, 1942.) Nothing came of this or other proposals for new housing. Ironically, after the war, Islanders hired Faludi to counter City proposals to urban-renew the Island community out of existence.

[18] *Telegram*, February 17, 1945. Estimates of the winter population vary wildly. For example, one City official estimated the 1945-46 winter population at 1,000—or double some journalistic estimates of the time. *Board of Control Minutes*, October 23, 1946.

[19] *Telegram*, February 17, 1945.

[20] The Ward's Hotel was closed for the season of 1944 when no one was interested in operating it or either of the stores. In the fall, the City decided to remodel it. The remodelling was more of a decapitation: the entire third floor was sliced off, leaving a flat-topped two-storey store and refreshment room below, with rooms above. "Minnie" Rorke, who had operated the store since the mid-1930s, returned to operate the store in the summer of 1945.

[21] Ferry statistics indicate that the biggest jump in winter (i.e., October to March) use came in 1947-48 (from 63,900 to 111,300) with an absolute peak in 1953 of 143,000.

[22] *Globe and Mail*, October 3, 1946.

[23] Bob Maginnis, *Ward's Island Weekly*, July 21, 1950.

[24] *Star*, January 7, 1948.

[25] *Telegram*, June 14, 1947.

[26] On April 14, 1948, for example, Mayor Saunders convened a conference to discuss the subject. This meeting, which reached no conclusions, provided an interesting barometer of civic opinion at the time. Some officials were beginning to talk in terms of housing *or* recreation—a simplification that ultimately characterized Metro Toronto's thinking and its plan to eliminate all the houses. Several officials expressed concern about the *cost* of maintaining and developing the Island and felt the area should be a source of revenue rather than a cause for expense. And several (with the notable exception of the TTC

representative) supported the need for a *tunnel* and *automobile access*. "Conference Regarding the Development of the Island," April 14, 1948.

[27] *Globe and Mail*, July 2, 1948.

[28] Even as he was pushing regatta improvements through Council, Alderman Lamport was also trying, unsuccessfully, to toughen the City's lease policy toward the Island. According to City officials, Lamport's proposals "would be taking too great an advantage of its legal position" with regard to Island lessees. *City Council Minutes*, June 29, 1948.

[29] *Ward's Island Weekly*, August 6 and September 3, 1948; and *Globe and Mail*, August 10, 1950.

[30] *Ward's Island Weekly*, July 1, 1949 and *Globe and Mail*, March 23, 1962. The Terrace never reopened.

[31] *Globe and Mail*, September 17 and 19, 1949.

[32] Without doubt the most controversial part of the proposed Official Plan was the section dealing with the Island, which recommended:
  (1) That the level of the Island be raised to elevation about 253 above sea level;
  (2) That the residential leaseholds be progressively eliminated and that a new residential district, composed principally of apartments and hotels, be created on either side of the centrally located shopping centre;
  (3) That a motor highway be constructed across the Island together with parking areas.
Islanders, backed by their aldermen Phillips and Freed, fought long and hard to try to prevent these sections from being included. On October 11, 1949, for example, the Inter-Island Council opened its campaign at old City Hall. Forming what the *Telegram* called "one of the largest civic delegations ever to appear at city hall," a hundred Islanders pressed into courtroom two to hear their spokesmen argue for two hours against the Planning Board proposals. Parks Committee members were sufficiently impressed by their eloquence, and their numbers, to send the offensive proposals back to civic officials for reconsideration and to see if they could develop "practical proposals for the development of the Island for the benefit of both Island residents and citizens of Toronto generally." (*City Parks and Exhibition Committee Minutes*, October 11, 1949.) The Inter-Island Council took its arguments to the

Board of Control, which, like most City politicians, was not willing to give up its pet project, the tunnel and cars; and to the public with the issuance of its own plan to improve the status quo, without demolishing the existing community or building a tunnel.

[33] *Globe and Mail*, July 26, 1951.

[34] *Star*, September 12, 1951.

[35] *Globe and Mail*, September 13, 1951.

[36] *Telegram*, September 13, 1951 and *Globe and Mail*, November 15, 1951.

[37] *City Board of Control Minutes*, November 6, 1951.

[38] *Globe and Mail*, February 21, 1952.

[39] *Star*, March 19, 1952.

[40] *Globe and Mail*, January 7, 1953.

[41] *Telegram*, April 2, 1953.

[42] *Globe and Mail*, April 6, 1953.

[43] *Star*, April 2, 1953.

[44] *Star*, April 14, 1953.

Chapter 11

[1] *Telegram*, April 15, 1953 and *Metro Council Minutes*, April 15, 1953. This ceremony provided a rare harmonious moment for the City and Suburban politicians ranged along government benches. The City and Suburbs had been squabbling for years before the Conservative government of Leslie Frost passed Bill 80 to create Metro Toronto. Even on this day of Metro days, Toronto Mayor Allan Lamport had convened a private caucus of City members in the morning; and the ceremony itself had actually been delayed for nearly an hour as City and Suburban school trustees argued over the choice of their first Chairman.

[2] Alden Baker and Michael Graham, "Big Daddy," *The Globe Magazine*, October 21, 1961, p. 4.

[3] Timothy J. Colton, *Big Daddy: Frederick G. Gardiner and the Building of Metropolitan Toronto* (Toronto: University of Toronto Press, 1980), p. 73.

[4] Colton calculated that over 90% of the 579 policy decisions made by Gardiner's Councils followed his recommendations and fully 100% of Metro Councils' decisions on parks policy supported Gardi-

ner's wishes. Moreover, in his eight years at the helm, Gardiner only had to break eight tie votes.

[5] Quoted by Frank Smallwood, *Metro Toronto: A Decade Later* (Toronto: Bureau of Municipal Research, 1963), p. 7.

[6] Quoted by Colton, *Big Daddy*, p. 82.

[7] *Telegram*, May 7, 1953. Both the *Telegram* (May 11, 1953) and the *Globe and Mail* (May 12, 1953) warmly endorsed this suggestion.

[8] *Globe and Mail*, May 7, 1953. "The primary purpose of the area should be recreation," he told the Local Council of Women on this occasion, "but I see no reason why it can't be the centre of housing development without interfering with aquatic sports."

[9] *Globe and Mail*, May 13, 1953.

[10] *City Parks and Exhibition Committee Minutes*, May 14, 1953.

[11] *Telegram*, May 15, 1953.

[12] *Globe and Mail*, June 26, 1953. Again the press endorsed the chairman's approach. The *Globe and Mail*, for example, ran an editorial entitled "Thank You Mr. Gardiner" on June 27.

[13] *Centre Islander*, July 25, 1953.

[14] *Globe and Mail*, October 9, 1953 and *City Parks and Exhibition Committee Minutes*, October 8, 1953.

[15] After gaining agreement from both the Metro Planning Board and Metro Planning and Parks Committee to take over (immediately) the Island as part of Metro's (virtually non-existent) park system, Gardiner hit a temporary snag when Metro Council voted not for immediate transfer but only for approval in principle of the transfer. Still, it was clear that the Metro Planning Board would recommend the transfer. Gardiner sat on that board; attended all its meetings; made most of the motions; and could rely on his good friend James P. Maher who served as its chairman and seldom put a foot wrong where Gardiner's projects were concerned. In fact, by August 1957, the *Telegram* was complaining that "it [was] difficult to avoid the impression that the Planning Board allowed itself to be used in whatever way Mr. Gardiner chose to use it." According to Colton, the Metro Planning Board never turned down any of "Big Daddy's" big projects.

[16] *Star*, May 13, 1982.

[17] *Star* and *Telegram*, January 7, 1955; and *Globe and Mail*, January 8, 1955.

[18] *Star*, January 7, 1955 and *Globe and Mail*, January 8, 1955.

[19] *Globe and Mail*, January 14, 1955.

[20] *Globe and Mail*, January 22, 1955. By this time, so many children had already left that one grade five classroom at the newly-expanded Island School was about to be closed. That was just the beginning. By September 1955, there were 123 fewer students than there had been in September 1954—and the bulldozers had hardly even begun to make their contribution to declining enrolment.

[21] *Globe and Mail*, and *Star*, March 23, 1955; and *Metro Council Minutes*, March 22, 1955.

[22] *Star*, May 26, 1955. When Metro Council voted on March 22, 1955, to take over control of the Island, it had not decided exactly what part of the Island would be transferred or what the fate of existing houses and businesses would be. On March 11, the Metro Planning and Parks Committee had adopted and forwarded to Metro Council a report by the Metro Solicitor, which recommended that Metro should acquire only *part* of the Island (namely, those parts of the Island owned by the City and not subject to leases), not all of it; and also recommended that Metro do a study to determine which (residential) leases, "if any," could *continue* under City jurisdiction, because they would be "consistent with" the development of the Island as a park (the others would be terminated at some unspecified point and the property transferred to Metro). The uncertainty about the future of existing housing continued until Gardiner's committee reported. This reversal of the City's earlier policy to renew leases until 1968 was adopted by Metro Council on September 20, 1955 and City Council on November 7, 1955.

[23] *Globe and Mail*, July 23, 1955.

[24] Hans Blumenfeld, "The Role of Toronto Island in the Metropolitan Recreation System," *Metro Planning Board Minutes*, November 3, 1955; and *Metro Planning Board Minutes*, November 3, 1955; and letter from M. Jones to Metro Planning Board, dated December 19, 1955.

[25] For example, "Easy Access To the Island," *Tele-gram*, January 4, 1956 and "Need A Bridge To the Island," *Star*, January 6, 1956.

[26] *Telegram*, March 29, 1956.

[27] *Globe and Mail*, January 10, 1957. On November 13, 1956, Metro Council approved Commissioner Thompson's revised proposal to clear Centre and raise its level, which he indicated would result in few park facilities being available at Centre Island during the project period of about two years. Not surprisingly, the nadir of park patronage was reached in 1956 when only 483,000 passengers travelled on the ferries. And Island patronage remained low throughout this decade and on into the next. In fact, it was only in 1966 that the magic number of one million—common in the pre-Metro era—was again reached. To accommodate his revised plan, Thompson slightly reorganized the acquisition programme to concentrate first on Centre, rather than Hanlan's, although many Hanlan's houses were also acquired. Work on raising the Island began in the spring of 1957 when tons of sand were moved from Mugg's to Centre. By this time, Metro had demolished 155 of the 650+ buildings and had acquired many more.

[28] *Metro Council Minutes*, November 5, 1957.

[29] Letter from the Inter-Island Council to Metro Council dated May 22, 1958; *Metro Council Minutes*, May 23, 1958; *Metro Planning and Parks Committee Minutes*, June 19, 1958; and *Metro Council Minutes*, July 4, 1958.

[30] *Star*, October 2, 1958.

[31] *Globe and Mail*, December 23, 1959; *Globe and Mail*, January 7 and 8, 1960; *Star*, January 7, 1960; and *Metro Council Minutes*, September 19, 1961.

[32] 1962:4; 1963:6; 1964:10; 1965:8; 1966:9; 1967:10; 1968:42; 1969:1. Sarah Duane Satterthwaite Gibson, *Sense of Place—Defense of Place: A Case Study of the Toronto Island* (University of Toronto, Department of Geography, unpublished Ph.D. thesis, 1981), Appendix I.

[33] C. Ross Anderson, letter to Metro Council dated March 29, 1962. He appeared before the Metro Parks Committee on May 3 and again on November 1, 1962. After failing at Metro, he carried the fight to City Council and the Ontario Municipal Board in an unsuccessful bid to have the City's Official Plan amended and the houses rehabilitated rather than demolished. The OMB threw his proposal out on a technicality on July 7, 1964.

[34] *Star*, June 7, 1963. See also Brief, *Metro Planning and Parks Committee Minutes*, April 11, 1963 and *Metro Planning and Parks Committee Minutes*, June 6, 1963.

[35] *Globe and Mail*, and *Star*, June 19, 1963; *Metro Council Minutes*, June 18, 1963 and September 11, 1963.

[36] *Globe and Mail*, December 18, 1963.

[37] *Globe and Mail*, July 12, 1966. The newspapers clung to their usual positions throughout the debate: the *Globe and Mail* opposed any bus tunnel, while the *Star* and the *Telegram* favoured one.

[38] *Globe and Mail*, May 15, 1965.

[39] This tactic, of course, had been used earlier, for example during high water periods in the early 1950s when Mayor Lamport declared that there was a health hazard on the Island and residents might have to be cleared. This time Chairman Allen raised the issue of poor housing conditions at a Metro Parks Committee meeting on April 21, 1966, and the two sides batted it back and forth for the next several months. While various civic officials were scurrying about collecting information, Commissioner Thompson followed his leader and suggested to the committee on June 1, 1966, that more than a third of the residences were "believed" to be without toilets—a gross exaggeration, as it turned out on June 16 when the City's Director of Housing Standards reported that only 10% of the 151 houses inspected so far lacked W.C.s and that, in fact, the houses compared "exceptionally well" with mainland houses. *Metro Planning and Parks Committee Minutes*, April 21, 1966; *Globe and Mail*, June 2, 1966; and *Metro Planning and Parks Committee Minutes*, June 16, 1966.

[40] *Globe and Mail*, September 23, 1966.

[41] *Telegram*, January 27, 1967. Alderman David Rotenberg was now the chairman of the restructured Metro Parks and Recreation Committee. At the first meeting on January 26, 1967, Rotenberg again managed to prevent the famous 1965 Expropriation Bill from going forward to Council for Third Reading. That was three strikes and out. This particular bill was never reintroduced. The Island question and

Island expropriations came up in a different guise later this spring.

42 *Metro Council Minutes*, May 30/31, 1967. The houses involved were: 7 between Hooper and Chippewa; 18 between Chippewa and Nokomis; and 19 between Nokomis and Lenore. One amendment that did carry was Alderman Tony O'Donohue's proposal that former owners of Lakeshore houses be given the opportunity to rent the houses back from Metro on a month-to-month basis.

43 *Globe and Mail*, July 1, 1967.

44 *Star*, October 25, 1967. Controller Campbell's comment at the Metro Executive Committee meeting of October 24 was a reaction to Thompson's plan which said that the "prime need" was for more open space for "general park use," like group picnics.

45 *Metro Council Minutes*, October 31, 1967. To avoid any repetition of past procedural shenanigans, a bill to expropriate the final thirty-three Lakeshore houses was immediately brought forward and attained the two-thirds majority necessary to be read three times in one day.

46 *Globe and Mail*, January 30, 1968.

47 *Telegram*, August 10, 1968.

48 *Globe and Mail*, September 3, 1968; *Star*, September 3, 1968; and *Telegram*, September 4, 1968.

49 *Star*, September 12, 1968.

Chapter 12

1 *IRA Minutes*, July 30, 1969 and *TIRA Executive Minutes*, August 28, 1969.

2 *Telegram*, August 16, 1969 and *Globe and Mail*, July 26, 1969.

3 *Globe and Mail*, September 12, 1969.

4 Quoted in Bill Usher and Linda Page-Harpa, *"For What Time I Am In This World"—Stories from Mariposa* (Toronto: Peter Martin Associates Limited, 1977), p. 196.

5 On February 25, 1971, for example, the Parks Committee was persuaded to spend $30,000 on washrooms rather than on demolitions. With this amount flushed out of the budget, only $70,000 remained. It was only on September 21, however,

that this amount was finally allocated to building a road rather than demolishing houses.

6 *Goose and Duck*, April 15, 1971. Their six main points were: "(1) There is at present no need to extend the Island Park. (2) The present transportation facilities will accommodate no increase in the number of visitors. (3) There is a critical shortage of low and medium cost housing in Metropolitan Toronto. (4) The Island Community adds to the enjoyment and safety of visitors to the park. (5) Changing Parks Philosophy and Waterfront Development [i.e., the Provincial Government's Harbour City proposal for the Airport site and the general planning approbation for mixed-use and interest in pedestrian precincts] and (6) The Island Community would welcome the opportunity to improve their properties if reasonable tenure is given."

7 *Goose and Duck*, May 30, 1971.

8 *Globe and Mail*, May 24, 1971.

9 *Star*, July 10, 1971.

10 Christina McCall-Newman, *Grits: An Intimate Portrait of The Liberal Party* (Toronto: Macmillan of Canada, 1982), p. 130.

11 "Harbourfront Park" was eighty-six desolate acres containing abandoned warehouses, a tumbledown stadium and little obvious potential as a "park"—at least in the conventional sense of the word. Local politicians, who had not been consulted by Ottawa, were understandably miffed. Several years of intergovernmental squabbling and sorting out of who should do what passed before Toronto's waterfront Renaissance was under way, with Harbourfront and the renovated Terminal Warehouse at its core.

12 Mr. Archer had not served on Metro Council since 1963, so he had not had a chance to vote for or against the most recent lease extensions for the eastern end of the Island (1967, 1970, 1971). But, in earlier votes respecting other parts of the Island, he had voted against lease extensions or delays of acquisitions of houses (e.g., June 18, 1963 and September 11, 1963). Mr. Archer later stoutly maintained that he had made his position clear to Islanders at the time (i.e., probably a five-year extension, but ultimately parkland). But his statement in the election issue of the *Goose and Duck* left some room for misinter-

pretation, because he coupled the "inevitably it will become a park" message with the "importance of having facilities for family life and a community near the Lake" message. And his canvassing, wittingly or unwittingly, left a different impression with some Island residents.

13 On March 27, 1973, Commissioner Thompson alerted the Metro Parks Committee to the fact that it had to take action by May 1 if it wanted to evict Islanders in 1973. Then, on April 13, 1973, the commissioner unveiled a report which recommended that Metro either reconfirm and proceed with its park plan *or* return the eastern residential portions of the Island to the City. No more temporary extensions. As for his own park proposals: he still favoured a golf course for Algonquin, but abandoned his former (much maligned) amusement park proposal for Ward's in favour of "quiet, natural outdoors."

14 *Metro Parks and Recreation Committee Minutes*, April 5, 1973, and *Globe and Mail*, April 6, 1973.

15 *Metro Council Minutes*, May 1, 1973.

16 The City Planning staff co-ordinated and wrote the report, while other City staff and Islanders acted largely as resource people who provided information on everything from housing conditions and park use to community aims and activities. The Toronto Island Committee, which met several times that summer, was essentially an information clearing house rather than a policy-making body.

17 In more formal language, the *Toronto's Island Park Neighbourhoods* report argued essentially:

The basic question to be answered in this Report is whether Metro, with the consent of the City, should continue implementing its initial 1955 decision to develop all of the Islands as a park, with all permanent residents removed from the area; or whether, in the light of changed circumstances, the City should reassume control of the residential areas and develop them as a permanent park community. This report contends that there are indeed many reasons for re-assessing and revising that 1955 decision. Included among the reasons are the physical changes in the waterfront [e.g., great increases in waterfront parkland], and in housing characteristics in Toronto [e.g., loss of low-cost, low-rise, family housing in the central area]; and fundamental changes in attitudes toward the definition of "good" parkland, the value of mixed [land-use] development, the importance of preserving existing communities and existing housing, and the role the City has to play in ensuring proper, equitable development which is in accord with these values. The burden of this report is that the 1955 decision should be changed, given the changes in attitudes and values that have occurred over the past 18 years. But it should also be emphasized from the outset that there is no question—as there appeared to be when the original decision was made—of destroying the natural character of the Island. It is well to remember that the present Island community occupies a very small percentage of the total land area of the Island (less than 5%); and that any future community would have to blend in with and complement its natural surroundings.

[18] The report emphasized the need for controls to prevent Islanders from possibly reaping windfall profits and the social mix of the community from tilting more toward the affluent if greater security of tenure were granted by City Hall. Most Islanders were not opposed to a goal of controlling windfall profits. In fact, a general meeting on August 29, 1973, before the report was released, passed a motion "that TIRA express to City Representatives that we are in favour of price controls or price ceilings and also ask for suggestions they can make to keep the community as it has been up to now." But they were concerned about how to accomplish that end without eliminating homeownership.

[19] For example, of the 44 presentations made to three public meetings held by the City in November 1973, 39 groups and individuals favoured retaining the residential areas, while only 3 individuals (but no groups) favoured continuing the Metro park policy. The Central Waterfront Committee and the City Planning Board passed supportive motions. And the City Executive Committee unanimously adopted the report's recommendations with only minor changes.

[20] Jon Caufield, *The Tiny Perfect Mayor* (Toronto: James Lorimer Company, Publishers, 1974), p. 82.

[21] For example, the *Star* concluded unhappily on October 17, 1973, that "our Metro park planners are sometimes so short on imagination that they can hardly conceive of anything else on the Islands but grass and more grass."

[22] For example, he wildly exaggerated the physical deterioration of the Island and Islanders' houses by reporting that 70% of the Ward's houses and 56% of the Algonquin houses would need more than $5,000 of repairs to bring them up to Toronto housing standards, whereas, in fact, only 17% of Ward's and 10% of Algonquin houses fell into this category.

[23] *Metro Council Minutes*, December 11, 1973 and tape recording of the meeting.

[24] *Star*, December 12, 1973.

[25] Islanders had to push two motions through Metro Council before the end of June. First, a motion to re-open the issue, which had to be put and seconded by people who had voted against them on December 11. And a second motion to extend their leases, which had to win at least 17 votes on Council. They had to hold their original 12 votes and win 5 more.

[26] This notice, dated January 10, 1974 and delivered later in the month, became the focus of the long legal battle launched by TIRA in the summer of 1974, which lasted more than four years, went all the way to the Supreme Court of Canada and kept Islanders on the Island in the interim.

[27] Now that Islanders had someone ready, willing and able to put a new motion before Metro Council, the burning question was: what motion? What did Islanders want? And what could they get? Spurred on by the efforts of Elizabeth Amer's Island Position Committee, Islanders hammered out the essential ingredients of their position: they wanted parity with the Island yacht clubs, that is, a lease extension to 1980; and they wanted a master lease (rather than 250+ individual leases) between Metro and an Island Non-Profit Housing Association (INPHA) that would remove the possibility of their making windfall profits on the sale of houses in the (more secure) future. *TIRA Newsletter*, May 3, 1974.

[28] *Globe and Mail*, June 19, 1974. After this defeat, City Council voted on June 27, 1974, to amend

its Official Plan in order to change Ward's and Algonquin Islands from "parkland" to "low-density residential" use. Any such amendment requires Provincial approval. Because of Metro opposition, the City's proposed amendment remained in limbo for the rest of the decade.

[29] *Globe and Mail*, July 8, 1974.

[30] On April 25, 1975, Mr. Justice John Osler of the Supreme Court of Ontario upheld the evictions, but, because of ambiguities in Metro's eviction notices, ruled that Islanders could stay an extra year beyond the original deadline, i.e., until August 31, 1975. In order to gain more time and possibly a complete victory, Islanders appealed this decision to a higher court, which would not hear the appeal for several more months.

[31] Mr. Grossman did not succeed in persuading his colleagues to bring in legislation at this time; but he introduced a Private Member's Bill in the Ontario Legislature on December 4, 1974, which would have transferred the land from Metro to the City. Although this bill suffered the fate of most Private Member's Bills (it died), it did place the idea before the Legislature and it did enable the City to go on record as favouring the move. On December 10, 1975, City Council, therefore, reconfirmed its position of November 1973 that a portion of Ward's and Algonquin Islands should be transferred from Metro to the City.

[32] *Star*, May 20, 1976.

[33] *Star*, June 25, 1977.

[34] "Troubled Waters: The Real Story Behind the Toronto Islands Siege," *Star Sunday Magazine*, October 1, 1978; and *Star*, September 2, 1978.

[35] *Globe and Mail*, October 25, 1978 and *Star*, October 25, 1978.

[36] *TIRA Newsletter*, November 1978.

[37] TIRA General Meeting, October 14, 1979. Islanders, therefore, rejected the Province's approach not once, but twice, before it was even introduced in the Legislature: once on September 30 and again on October 14, 1978.

[38] Mayor John Sewell, Press Statement Re: Toronto Islands, October 17, 1979.

[39] *Star*, February 23, 1980. The essence of the Sewell "compromise" was that Metro agree to transfer

Ward's and Algonquin Islands to the City (to preserve the existing housing and add more housing) and to set up a process for determining what compensation the City should pay Metro.

[40] Wells wanted a five-person inquiry, with Metro and the City each appointing two members. But, when Metro refused to participate, Swadron proceeded on his own.

[41] *Globe and Mail*, July 8, 1980; and Barry B. Swadron, Q.C., Commissioner, *Pressure Island: The Report of the Commission of Inquiry into the Toronto Islands* (Toronto, January 12, 1981), p. 11.

[42] Swadron Report, p. 34. In fact, 63 of the 73 (or 86%) of the oral presentations and 71 of the 101 (or 70%) of the written submissions that took a stand, for a combined total of 77%, were in favour of retaining the residential community on the Island.

[43] *Sun*, March 10, 1981 and *Star*, March 11, 1981.

[44] As recommended by Swadron, Metro would continue to own the land, but would have to lease it to the City at market value (whatever that turned out to be) and the City, in turn, would rent the land to Island residents. The legislation did not clarify who owned the houses (Islanders or Metro). But it did establish an arbitration process which would come into play if Metro and the City failed to agree on how much rent the City would have to pay Metro or on a number of other issues.

[45] *Globe and Mail*, December 10, 1981.

[46] *Sun*, February 14, 1982. Residents would have to pay not only $600+ per month to rent the land and the houses—the houses that they resolutely maintained they owned and would therefore not pay rent for—but they would also have to pay substantial amounts to renovate their houses and pay for such new services as sewers. Some members of the community would now face not physical eviction, but what they called "economic eviction" if Metro succeeded.

[47] *Star*, April 10 and September 26, 1982.

[48] The arbitration process was established to answer two fundamental questions: first, who owned the homes (Metro or Islanders) and, based on that finding, how much rent should the City (and Islanders) pay Metro. On December 2, 1982, the gravely ill Mr. Robinson released the first part of his decision: Metro, he found, owned the houses. According to his reading of the law, the houses had become fixtures to the land and were therefore Metro's. He based his decision on general law, not on the wording of Island leases; and he fully expected his decision to be appealed. "The question of ownership is understandably an emotional one," he wrote, "and it is a relief to know that if I come to a wrong conclusion I could be put right upon a stated case to Divisional Court." Islanders voted on December 12, 1982, to appeal the arbitrator's decision, but Mr. Robinson's death in late December temporarily stalled this process. In May 1983, Gordon Atlin was appointed arbitrator and soon ruled that Metro owned the houses, though, unlike his predecessor, he based his decision on the wording of the leases. Islanders went ahead with the appeal process. In the first stage of this process, the Ontario Divisional Court, on April 25, 1984, upheld the arbitrator's ruling on home ownership. As a result, Islanders voted to seek leave to appeal this ruling before the Ontario Court of Appeal. The arbitrator, therefore, was expected to delay the second, crucial stage of the arbitration process—i.e., determining the rent that the City would have to pay Metro—until at least September, perhaps later, depending on the result of the appeal process.

[49] *Globe and Mail*, June 18, 1983.

[50] *Globe and Mail*, June 22, 1983. After the Divisional Court ruling of April 25, 1984, the City repeated this stand. On April 30, 1984, City Council confirmed its long-time support of Island residents, called on the Province to restore home ownership to Islanders and reiterated its request that the Province transfer the residential portions of the Island from Metro to the City.

Index

Numbers in *italics* refer to picture captions.
Numbers preceded by n refer to notes.

Ada Alice, 96, 117
Adams, Bert, 177
Aikenhead, Thomas E., 130
Aikens, Dr. W.T., 100
Ainslie, H.F., *53*
Aitken, Alexander, 11, 15, *16*
Aitken, Alice, 192, 221, 275
Aitken, Catherine, 249
Aitken, Harold, 219, 241-2
Alexander, F.G., *131*
Alexander, Sir J.E., *50*
Alexandra Yacht Club, *159*, 162, 165
Algonquin Bridge, 200, *260, 265*, 290-1
Algonquin Island, 134, 197-201 *passim* (1937-38), 218, 222, 242-3, 245, 247, 252, 253-9 *passim* (1962-68), 263, Chapter 12 *passim* (1969-84). *See also* Sunfish Island
Algonquin Island Association (AIA), 222, 264
Algonquin Island Association Clubhouse, 222, 268, 279, 280, 285
Allan's Wharf, 33
Allen, Robert Thomas, 182, *257*
Allen, Metro Chairman William, 253-63 *passim*, 267
Amer, David, 281
Amer, Elizabeth (née Coleman), 234, *281*, 281n27, 291
American Civil War, 68-9
Amusement parks. *See* Centre Island Amusement Park, Coney Island, Hanlan's Point Amusement Park, Peninsula Pleasure Grounds, Scarboro Beach, Sunnyside
Anderson, C. Ross, 253, *256*
Anderton & Palin, 40, 42n9
Andrews, Captain, 92, 93
Anglin, Judge Frank, 129
Ann Bell Chambers, 78, 89
Anthony, Mrs. Tony, 230
Anti-communism, 228, 229
Anti-Semitism, 189-90, 229

Arbitration between City and Metro, 293-4
Archer, Alderman William, 273, 275, 276, 284
Argonaut Rowing Club, 106, 114, *117*, 143
Arlington, 114
Armstrong, Fred, 131, 136-7, 151
Armstrong, Fred, Jr., 155, 156
Armstrong, William, *57*, 59, 60, *61, 65, 66*, 68, *71*, 77n22, *87, 89*, 95, *97*, 98
Arthur, Eric, 252
Arthur, Sir George, 46
Ashbridge's Bay, 79, 104, 145, *154*
Athenia, 202
Atkinson, Peter, 283, 284, 286, 290
Atkinson's Baths, 143. *See also* Turner's Baths
Atlin, Gordon, 294
Attrition, 269-70, 289
Automobiles, proposals for access of, 138 (1909), 145-6 (1912), 192-4 (1935), 195-6 (1937), 199 (1938), 225 (1947), 226 (1948), 228 (1949), 230 (1951), 235 (1953), 245, 248 (1955-56), 257 (1965-66). *See also* Island highway, proposals for
Avenue of the Islands, 252

Baez, Joan, 266
Baldwin, Mary Warren, 26, 28
Baldwin, Dr. William Warren, *24, 25*, 27, 30-1, 33
Balmy Beach Canoe Club, *250*
Band, C.P., 174
Barker, Billy, *176*
Barnes, Mrs. J.W., 230
Barnett, Barry, 202
Barrett, Richard, 254
Barry, Chris, 272
Bartlett, W.H., *48, 54*
Base, Ric, 215
Baseball, 134, 160, 162, 166, 171, 185, 212, 214, 217, 224-5; Inter-Island, 162, 171, 185, 207, 214, 224, 240; professional, 108, 140, 142, 152, 157, 159, 168

Batten, Jack, 275
Bathurst Street Wharf, 105
Beach, William, 88
Beasley, Warren, 259, 262
Beaty, Mayor James, 88, 93
Beavis, Alderman Fred, 274
Bell, Marilyn, 242
Belle Isle, Detroit, 121, 245
Belyea, Alderman Roy, 241
Bennett, Eldon, *294*
Bennett, Prime Minister R.B., 180, 192
Bernou, Claude, *4*
Berry, Robert, 67, 74, *75*
Besley, Gordon, 214
Bessborough, Governor General Lord, 180
Best, Michael, 270, 278
Bicycling, 104, 106, 108, 116, 182, 211, 219
Birmingham, Les, 289
Bishop, Billy, *176*, 195, 197
Bishop-Barker Airways, 195
Blackstock, Mary, 104
Blair, Mayor Willis, 283
Blake, Edward, 66
Blake, Samuel, 66
Blaver, Colin, 210, 215, 217
Blockhouse, Gibraltar Point, 12, 19-20, 29-30, *31*, 32
Blockhouse Bay, 36, 47, 77, 79, 80, 98, 198, *199*, 200
Bloor, Joseph, 55
Bluebell, *121*, 124-5, 180, 203, 214, 249
Bluenose, *183*
Blumenfeld, Hans, 248
Board of Health, 175
Boarding houses, 114, 128, 181
Boardwalk, 195
Bob Moodie, 60
Bonnycastle, Sir Richard H., *38*, 40, *41*, 42-3, 48
Bosley, Toronto Harbour Commission Chairman, *231*
Boswell, Mayor Arthur R., 90, 93, 94, 98
Bouchette, Captain Jean Baptiste, 10-11

Bouchette, Lieutenant Joseph, 12, 15, 21
Boulton, D'Arcy, 22
Bouquet, 70, 71, 72, 76
Bowes, Mayor John George, 57
Boyd, John, *99*
Boytchuk, Alderman William, 284
Bradley, Jack, 170, 199, 217, 290
Brant, Chief Joseph, 10
Breakwater, 103-4, 195, 224, 230, 232
Brébeuf, Jean de, 3
Bremner, Acting Sheriff Joseph, 291
Brewin, M.P. Andrew, 259, 267
Bridges over Don River, 22, 23, 29, 32, 42, 43
Bridges over Gaps, proposals for, 109, 145-6, 168, 192, 235, 248
Brindle, Augustus, 108, 142
Brock, Sir Isaac, 25, 26
Brookes, Air Commodore George E., 204, *205*
Brown, George, 48
Browne, J.D., *51*
Browne, James, 53
Bruce, Harry, 255
Bruce, Alderman Hugh, 257
Brûlé, Étienne, 2, *3*
Bulmer's, 158, 162, 171
Bundy, Metro Parks Commissioner Robert, 293
Burgess, Alderman Alfred, 146, 168
Burrill, William, 243
Butler, Colonel John, 11
Butler, Captain Walter, 9
Bye, Allan, 209, 210

Caccia, Alderman Charles, 257
Callaghan, Morley, 142
Callaway, Fen, 214
Campbell, Metro Chairman Ab, 258, 267, 268
Campbell, Controller Margaret, 259, 261
Campbell, Chief Justice William, 33, 35-6
Canada, *112*
Canada's Cup, *112*, 113, 266, 272
Canadian, 96

Canadian Canoe Association, 183, 266
Canadian Legion, 220
Canadian National Exhibition (CNE), 91, 121, 152, 176, 180, 197, 202, 266. *See also* Exhibition Park
Capital, 12, 15, 16, 28, 47
Caribana, 260, 266, 283
Carleton, Sir Guy. *See* Dorchester, Sir Guy Carleton, first Baron of
Carr, Harbour Master John, 84
Carroll, John, 269
Cassels, Hamilton, Q.C., 254
Cassels, Robert, 129
Cassels, Walter, 58
Catto, John, 100
Caufield, Jon, 276
Cayley, Frank, 100
Cayuga, 154
Centennial Marina, 260
Centre Island, 55, 57, *67*, 70, 88, 89, 96-101 (1880s), 105, *107*, 111-9 *passim* (1890s), 122, 127-9 (Edwardian boom), *135*, 136, 137, 138, *139*, 144, *151*, 154n5, 160, 161, 171, 172, 173, 178, 179, 182-4 (1930s), 190, *195*, 207-15 passim (World War II), 217, 218, 219, 224, 226, 227, 230, 233, 240, 243, 249-52 *passim* (demolitions), 255-63 *passim* (Lakeshore Avenue battle), 266, *267*, 272. *See also* Centre Island Amusement Park; Long Pond; Island Amateur Aquatic Association; Island Park; Island Park development; Main Drag; Manitou Road; Metro Toronto Island Park development; Residential development, Centre Island; Royal Canadian Yacht Club
Centre Island Amusement Park, *253*, 259, 262, 271
Centre Island Association (CIA), 213, 214, 218, 219, 226
Centre Island Association Clubhouse, 218, 226, 240, 252
Chambers, Parks Commissioner C.E., 177, 197, 198, 199, 200, 201
Chambers, Alderman Frank, 240
Chambers, Parks Commissioner John, 97, 98, 118, 119, 121, 131, 134-6

Champlain, Samuel de, 2
Chapman, Captain W.E., 148, 163, 165
Charles A. Reed, 175, 201, *228*
Chauncey, Commodore Isaac, 28
Cherkoff, Buzz, 268
Chetwood Terrace, 221-2. *See also* Lakeside Home For Little Children
Chicora, 68, 69, 85
Chief Justice Robinson, 48, 57-8
Children, 101, 128, 261-2, 282, 291. *See also* Island Public School
Children's camp, proposals for, 255, 257, 258, 276
Chippewa, 154
Chippewas, 22
Choate, Jack, 213
Cholera, 36-7, 40, 55
Church, Mayor Tommy, 154, 157, 182, 192
Citizen, 60
City Dairy, 127, 173, 182, 183.
City of Toronto, 50, 69, 72, 76, 81, 85
City of Toronto, incorporation of, 37
City of Toronto Committee on Wharves and Harbors, 54, 55, 56, 62, 72, 77-8
City of Toronto Council, 37 (1834), 40, 42, 43, 48, 52-5 *passim* (fishing 1830s-40s), 56 (1847 license of occupation), 62, 71 (1867 Island transfer), 72-8 *passim* (1870s leasing), 79, 82, 83, 84, 86, 88 (1880 establishment of Island Park), 90, 96, 97, 98, 102-3, 109, 110, 114, 116, 130, 131, 134, 143, 144, 145, 146, 150, 154, 155, 159, 161, 164, 168 (1926-27 take-over of ferry service), 177, 184, 187, 192-4 (1935 tunnel proposal), 195-201 *passim* (1937-38 Island Airport and Algonquin Island), 202, 203, 209, 216, 224, 227, 229, 235, 239, 241-6 *passim* (1956 transfer of Island to Metro Toronto), 253n33, 267 (1969 election), 273 (1972 election), 276 (1973 report), 279, 283n28, 285n31, 287, 294n50. *See also* Transfer from Metro to City, proposals for

City of Toronto Executive Committee, 276
City of Toronto Parks and Exhibition Committee, 187n7, 190, 199n24, 203, 228n32, 239-41
City of Toronto Property Committee, 86
City regulations, 128, 129, 130, 146, 151, 187
City-Suburban Split, 236, 239, 241, 245, 277, 279, 284
Clapp, Jack, 216
Clarke, 85
Clark, William, 101, *107*, 119
Clarke, Alured, 12
Clarke, Mayor Ned, *112*
Clarkson, E.R.C., 100, 102, 111, 155
Clarkson, G.T., *100*
Clayton, Thomas, 127
Clayton's Meat Market, 183
Clegg, Thomas, 129
Cobourg, 46
Cockburn, Bruce, 266
Colborne, Lieutenant Governor Sir John, 36-7, 40, 42, 43
Colton, Timothy, 236, 236n4, 241n15
Compensation settlements, 247, 250, 263
Conboy, Mayor Fred J., 209
Coney Island, 147
Confederation, 69, 71-2
Confederation of Residents and Ratepayers Associations (CORRA), 264
Connaught, Duke of, 148
Copping, Mr. and Mrs. George, 155
Cosgrove, Mayor Paul, 281, 282
Coulson, Arthur, *150*, *157*
Courtney, Charles, 82
Cove Fleet, 216-7, 271, 272
Cox, Arthur, *74*
Cridland, Peter, 267
Croll, M.P. David, 240
Crombie, Mayor David, 267, 272-8 *passim*, 283
Cronkwright, James E., 137
Crystal Palace, 84
Cull, John, 43-4
Curling, *50*

Curtiss flying-boat, *153*, *156*
Curtiss flying school, *153*, 155-6, *163*

Dalhousie, George Ramsay Earl of, 18
Daniel Lamb, 134
Darling, Robert, 100
Davidson, Reeve True, 255
Davis, Premier William, *265*, 269, 271
Day, Alex, 128
Day, Mayor Ralph, 196, 201, 202, 203, 204, *205*
Dean, W.A. "Billy", 156, 163
Dearborn, General, 29
Defence fortifications, 12, 17. *See also* Blockhouse, Gibraltar Point; Fort York
Demolitions, 97 (Mead's first Hotel), 201 (Hanlan's Point Stadium), *237*, 249-52 (Gardiner years), 253, 256, 258, 261-3 (Lakeshore Avenue, 1960s), 269 (1971)
Demolitions, opposition to, 250 (1958-59), 253, 254-55 (1963 plan), 255-63 *passim* (Lakeshore Avenue battle, 1964-68), Chapter 12 *passim* (1969-84)
Demolitions, threat of, 138 (1909), 146 (1909), 193 (1935), 195-201 *passim* (1937-38), 225 (1947), 228 (1949), 235 (1953), 239, 247-8 (1955-56), 254-5 (1963), Chapter 12 *passim* (1969-84)
Dempsey, Lotta, 227
Dendy, William, 116
Denison, Arthur R., 101, *106*, 129, 136
Dennison, Mayor William, 248, 258, 267, *268*, 270, 271, 272
Depressions, 69, 83, 97n13, 118, 119n33, 164, Chapter 9 *passim* (1930s)
Dewdney, Peter, 293, 294
Dick, Captain, 50
Dick, Norman B., 116
Dickens, Charles, 46
Dillon, David, 202
Dillon, Eddie, 171, 188, 189
Dillon, Mrs. Eddie, 207

Dilworth, R.J., 155

Dinghy sailing, 113, 124, 157, 162, 169

Dixon, Canon H.C., 108, 174

Dodd, Blatchford, 202

Dodd, Walter, 102, 149, 151, 159, 168, 172, 188

Dominion Day, 76 (1873), 84 (1879), 118 (1893), 120 (1900), 142 (1910), 156-9 (World War I), 165 (1919), 175 (1927), 176-7 (1929), 179 (1921), 180 (1930-1), 194 (1936), 196 (1937), 201 (1938), 208 (1940), 211 (1942), 214 (1944), 226 (1948), 240 (1953), 289-90 (1980). *See also* Dominion Day Regattas

Dominion Day Regattas, 105-6 (1894), 143 (1904), 157 (1915), 165 (1919), 175 (1927), 176 (1929), 180 (1930), 183 (1930 and 36), 196 (1937), 201 (1938), 207 (World War II), 216 (1946), *217*, 226 (1948), 228 (1950), 240 (1953), 260 (1967), 266 (1969), *287* (1982)

Dorchester, Sir Guy Carleton, first Baron of, 10-11, 16

Dorsey, Tommy, 202

Doty Family, 96, 116

Doty Ferry Company, 105

Douglas, Lieutenant William O'Shaunessy, 156

Dovercourt Beanery Boys, 227

Downing, John, 277, 278

Downman, J.T., *49*

Draper, Chief Constable, 184

Drownings, 67-8, 93, 96, 115, 142, 219, 248, 258

Duel, 25

Duggan, George W., 164

Dunfield, Ross, 207

Dunkelman, Ben, 190, 213, 229

Durham, John George Lambton, first Earl of, 46, 47

Durie, Lieutenant Colonel William, 66

Durnan, Bill, 250

Durnan, Eddie, *106*, 120, 136

Durnan, George, 52, *73*, 89, 114, 139

Durnan, James, 22, 37, 43, 46, 52

Durnan, Johnny, 165

Durnan, Katherine, 114

Durnan's Boathouse, 106

Durnan's Hotel, 105

Durnan's water taxi, *233*

Dylan, Bob, 271-2

Eagleson, Alan, 292

Eastern Gap, 40-1, 62-3 (creation of), 71, 78, 84, 89 (1880), 102-4 (1880s-90s harbour works), 109, 113, 126 (*Reuben Dowd* and *Resolute* wrecked near), 130, 145 (1912 plan), 148 (1913 Lifesaving Station at), 172, 185, 195 (1937 breakwater), 206 (Norwegian fliers crash at), 209, *247*, 248 (Hurricane ''Connie'')

Eastern Point, *83*, 90, 91, 92, 114. *See also* Ward's Island

Eaton's, 147, 171, 182, 192, 220, *227*

Eayrs, Alderman Elizabeth, 277

Eggleton, Mayor Art, 284, 292, 293, 294

Elections, federal, 272 (1972), 283-4 (1974)

Elections, municipal, 267 (1969), 272-3 (1972), 284 (1974), 292 (1980)

Elections, provincial, 271 (1971), 285 (1974, 77), 292 (1981)

Elgin, James Bruce, Earl of, 57

Elgin, Lady Mary Louisa Lambton, 57

Eliza, 63

Elizabeth II, 230

Elliott, William, 84

Emmanuel Church, 129, 204, 222, 252

Empress of India, 80, 85

Emslie, Percy, 245

English's Boathouse, 117, 127, 144

Esperanza, 90

Esplanade, the, 57, 62, 66, 68, 74, 76, 82, 90, 101, 106

Evans, Henry, 52

Evans, Terry, 183

Exhibition Park, 119, 154, 167, 180. *See also* Canadian National Exhibition

Expropriation Bill of 1965, 258

Falconbridge, Judge William G., 98

Faludi, Dr. E.G., 218n17, 254-5

Far Enough Farm, 252, *253*

Farmer's Dairy, 127, 173, 183

Farming and pasturage, 11, 21, 23, 32, 38, 51, 101, 136

Fearless, 79

Fenians, 69

Ferry boats, 38, 41-2, 50, 51, 60, 64, 70, 96, 101, 105, 125, 142, 194. *See also* individual boat names

Ferry deficits, 175n27, 197, 225, 230, 235

Ferry fares, 159, 168, 175, 243-4, 247

Ferry service, 102, 105, 168 (1926 sale to City), 171, 175, 252 (1962 transfer to Metro)

Ferry statistics, 123 (1905), 142 (1910), 157 (1915-16), 158 (1917), 159 (1918), 165 (1919), 176 (1927, 29), 180 (1931), 208 (1940), 214 (1944), 220n21 (winter), 249n27 (1956), 258 (1966), 268 (1970)

Ferry terminal, 271

Filgate, 85

Filtration Plant, 143-4, 155, 178, 190, 203, 208, 216, 223-4

Fire Fly, 64

Fire hall, 175, 201, *251*, 252

Fire protection service, 121, 138, 163, 175, 195, 201-2

Fires, 57 (1849 downtown), 102, 116 (1896 RCYC), 120-1 (1903 Hanlan's Point), 122-3 (1904 downtown), 124 (1904 RCYC), 126, 138 (1909 Ward's lifeboat station), 138-9 (1909 Island Public School), 140-1 (1909 Hanlan's Point), 146, 155 (1915 Lakeside Home), 163 (1918 RCYC), 165 (1919 Ward's life saving station), 201 (1939 IAAA), 227-8 (1949 *Noronic*)

Fishermen, *6*, 46, 52-5 *passim* (1830s-40s), 60n42, 64, 67, 70, 72, 74, 75, 79, 81, *104, 149*. *See also* Fishing

Fishing, 7, 17, 19, 22, 42, 44, 52-5 *passim* (1830s-40s), 90, 101, 104, 125, 128, 148-9 (1912 Ward's Island), 268, *269*. *See also* Fishermen

Fish market, 22, 52, *54*, 55

Fitzgerald, James P., 183

Fitzgibbon, Colonel James, 45

Flavelle, Sir Ellsworth, *217*
Fleming, M.P. Donald, 242
Fleming, Ralph, 245
Fleming, Mayor Ralph, 109, 113
Fleming, Sandford, 62
Flooding, 77, 136-7 (1908), 212, 218
　(1943), 221, 224-5 (1947), 230-4
　passim (1951-52), 273-4 (1973)
Flora and fauna, 17, 22, 49, 89
"Floreat", *111*
Flynn, Mayor Dennis, 274
Folley, Joan, 245
"Foreigners", 147, 149n37, 164
Forest, Sarah, 115
Fort Frontenac, 3, 4, 5, 7, 8
Fort Niagara, 8, 9, 12
Fort Rouillé, 7, 8, 9, 28
Fort York, *20*, 22, *27*, 28, 30, 32, 35,
　36, 46, 49
Frank, Mary, 88-9, 100, 101
Fraser, John A., 100
Freed, Alderman Norman, 228
French, William, *241*
Frise, Jimmy, 172
Frobisher, Benjamin, 10, 11
Frontenac, 31
Frost, Premier Leslie, 236
Fur trade, 3-7 *passim*, 16, 21, 31-2

G.R. Geary, 223
Gage, William, 98
Gagen, Robert F., 100, *154*
Gala Day, 169-70 (first, 1921), 186,
　210, 216, 224, 263, 266, 285, 286,
　293
Gardiner, Metro Chairman Frederick
　G., 235, 236, 239-52 *passim*, 257
Garner, Hugh, *220*
Gaudaur, Jake, Jr., 201
Gay, Art, 176
Geddes, William, 52-5, 60n42
George VI, 202
George Cup, 152
Gibraltar Point, 12, 17, 18, 19, 20, 21,
　22, *34*, 79, 80
Ginn, Frederick, 127, 173
Ginn's Casino, 173, 182, 194, 213,
　220, 247, 249
Ginty & Dick, 79

Givens, Mayor Phil, 236, 254, 255
Glass, Alderman J.J., 190
Glendinning, John, 60, 61
Goad, Charles E., *107*, 111, 112, *122*
Godard, Freya, 269
Godfrey, Metro Chairman Paul, 270,
　276, 277, 278, 286, 288, 289, 292,
　293
Gooderham, Colonel Albert E., 153
Gooderham, George, 85, 95, 96, 100,
　101, 102, 105, 113
Gooderham, George H., 111, 120n1,
　124, 157, 167, 179
Gooderham, Grant, 155
Gooderham, Norman, 113, 124, 167
Gooderham, William, 35, *40*, 42n9
Gooderham, William G., 95, 113
Gooderham family, 113, 114, 116, 182,
　247, 249
Gooderham-Worts windmill, *35*
Goodwin, Captain Joseph, 98, 117,
　126, 138, 139
Gordon, Colonel H.D.L., 155
Gordon, Captain Leslie, 155
Gordon, Captain Maitland Lockhart,
　155
Gordon, W.H. Lockhart, 102, *112*,
　113, 125, 155
Gordon Jarry, 126
Gore, Lieutenant Governor Francis, 22
Goss, Arthur, *143*
Goulding, George, 206
Grasett, Lieutenant Colonel H.J., 90
Gray, Constable John, 101, 115
Gray, Henry, *103*
Gray, Patrick, 70, *71, 73*
Gray's Hotel, 70, 86
Gray's Wharf, 70, 77
Grimsby, 184
Greene, Barbara, 277
Grieg, Velma, *255*
Grossman, M.P.P. Allan, 230, 232,
　245, *280*, 285
Grossman, M.P.P. Larry, 285, 287, 288
Guest, Jack, 165, 175, 183, 184-5
Guillet, Edwin, 22
Gwynn, Justice, 101
Gzowski, Casimir, Jr., 102
Gzowski, Peter, 264, 265, 271

H.J. Dixon, 244
Haas, Stephen, 124
Hacker, Lieutenant Richard Henry,
　164
Haggart, Ron, 257, 276
Hale, Elisabeth Frances, *19*
Hall, Lieutenant Francis, 18
Hall, Mark, 91, 93
Hallam, Alderman John, 114
Ham, George, 115
Hamilton, Ontario, 46, 50, 80, 227,
　240
Hamilton, Controller Fred, 212
Hamilton, Waterworks supervisor, 98
Haney & Miller, 137-8
Haney's Point, 126, 138, 147, 148
Hanger, Frank, 207
Hanger, Wendi, 233, 260
Hanlan, Emily (Mrs. Durnan; Mrs. Lol
　Solman), 105
Hanlan, John, Sr., 52, 64, 69, 70, *73*
Hanlan, John, Jr., 86, 98, 117
Hanlan, Ned, 64, *65*, 66, 70, 75, 80,
　81 (Philadelphia Centennial Regatta,
　1876), 82, 84 (Champion of England,
　1879), 85, 86 (Hanlan's Hotel,
　1880), *87*, 88, 90, 93, *106*, 108, 115
Hanlan family, 99, 114, 129
Hanlan's Hotel (first), 69, *70*, 81
Hanlan's Hotel (second), 86, *87*, 88,
　98, 105, *106*, 140-1 (1909 fire)
Hanlan's Island Association, 196, 199,
　209
Hanlan's Island Association Clubhouse,
　222, 252
Hanlan's Memorial Park, 129
Hanlan's Memorial Regatta Course,
　176
Hanlan's Point, 64, 70, 74, *80*, *85*, 86-
　8 (1880), 93-4 (Lakeside Home),
　96, 98-9 (1880s), 101, 105, 106 (1894
　expansion), *107*, 108 (1897 baseball),
　116, 118, 120-1 (1903 fire), *122*,
　123, 129-30 (1900s tents and
　cottages), 136, 138, 139, 140-2
　(1909 fire), 143, 146, *153*, 155-60
　passim (World War I), 168, *169*, 175
　(1927 transfer to City), 176, 177,
　179, 180-5 *passim* (early 1930s), *189*,

190, 195-201 *passim* (1937-38),
205-15 *passim* (World War II), 219-
23 *passim* (winter 1940s), 224,
227, 233, 244, 248-56 *passim*
(demolitions), 258, 293. *See also*
Filtration Plant; Gibraltar Point;
Hanlan's Point Amusement Park;
Hanlan's Point Stadium; Island
Airport; Island Public School;
Lakeside Home For Little Children;
Lighthouse; Residential
development, Hanlan's Point;
Turner's Baths; Western Sandbar
Hanlan's Point Amusement Park, 88
(1884), 96 (1888), 105 (1894
expansion), 108 (1890s), 116, 120,
121 (1903 fire), 123, 125, 139-42
(1909 fire), 156-7 (1915), 175 (1927
TTC takeover), 176, 180-2 (1930s),
196, 201 (1937-38 demolitions), 233
Hanlan's Point bridge, 83, 84, 143
Hanlan's Point Stadium, 108, 120-1,
140, 142, 156, 157, 159, 181, 182,
201
Hanlan's Wharf, 69
Harbour Commission, 62 (established
1850), 71. *See also* Toronto Harbour
Commission
Harbourfront Park, 272
Harbour Square, 271
Harbourworks, 57 (The Esplanade),
62, 63, 103-4 (1880s-90s), *103*, 113-
4, 145-6 (1912 plan). *See also*
Breakwater; Waterfront development
Harman, Mayor Samuel B., 79
Harmon, S. Bruce, 90
Harris, David, 280, 281
Harris, Mayor Gus, 271, 275, 277,
278, 288
Harrison, Mark, 264, 265
Hawdon, John, 84
Head, Lieutenant Governor Sir Francis
Bond, 43, 44, 45, 46
Health, 17, 21-2, 23, 32, 40, 93-4. *See
also* Lakeside Home For Little
Children; Red Cross Outpost
Health menace, threat of, 212, 232,
258n39, 274
Heap, Alderman Dan, 273, 276

Heathcote, George, 40n6, 41
Heber, Charles, 99, *131*
Heber's Hotel, 96, 98, 129, 130. *See
also* Gray's Hotel
Helliwell, Thomas, 38, 42
Henderson, Paul, *217*, 271, 272
Hennepin, Father Louis, 4
Hewitt, Ernie, 209
Hiawatha, 116, 157, 167
Henry, Dr. Walter, 35-6
Heriot, George, *13*
Highland Chief, 63
Hillock, Wing Commander Frank,
207, 212, 213
Hind, Henry Houle, 62
Hobson, Gren "Hobby", *233*, 245
Hodgson, Tommy, 215, 233
Holloway, William, 22, *36*
Holt, Sir Herbert Samuel, 77
Home and School Association, 221
Hood, Hugh, 182, 203
Hooper, Charles E., 100
Hooper, Emilie Florence, 100-1
Hopkins, Frances Ann, *5*
Hopkins, Reverend Paul, 257
Hopp, Mrs. Lillian, 218, 242-3
Hopp, Tony, 223, 224, 229, 243
Horse boat, 38, 41, 50, 51
Horse riding and racing, 16, 17, 19,
23, 24, 32, 43, 76
Horticultural Gardens, 81
Hospital For Sick Children, 93, 94
Hotels, 38 (O'Connor's), 50 (Privats'),
55 (Parkinson's first), 60
(Glendinning's and Quinn's), 68
(Mrs. Moodie's), 69 (Hanlan's first,
Gray's, Parkinson's second), 76
(Mead's first), 83 (Ward's first), 86-
8 (Hanlan's second), 92 (Ward's
second), 97 (Mead's second), 105
(Durnan's), 127-8 (Pierson's), 129
(Clegg's), 190 (Manitou Hotel). *See
also* individual hotel entries
Housing shortage, 218-20 *passim*
(1940s), 258, 259 (1967), 281 (1974)
Howard, Alan, 173, 179, 181, 192,
230, 235, 239, 250
Howard, John George, *42*, 48, 52, 55,
56, 57, *78*

Howard, Dr. Norman J., 179, 219
Howe, C.D., 229
Howland, Mayor Oliver Aiken, 77
Howland, Mayor William, 86
Huard, Ethel, 258
Hughes, P.C., 218
Hughes, Minister of Militia and
Defence Sam, 154
Hunt, Controller Paul, 268
Hunter, Lieutenant Governor General
Peter, 21, 22
Hunting, 22-5 *passim*, 34-6 *passim*, 48-
9, 83, 89
Hurons, 2, 3, 4
Hurricane Connie, 247-8
Hurricane Hazel, 242-3, 247
Hutchinson, James, 136
Hyland, James, 230

Iceboating, 49, 75-6, 149, 192
Images: "home", 215; "island", 23,
38; negative, 218n17, 245, 258, 261,
267-8, 273-5. *See also* Health menace,
threat of; positive, 267-8, 274-5,
276-7
Indians, *6*, 21-2, 26, 28, 33, *34*, 37, 46-
7. *See also* Chippewas; Hurons;
Iroquois; Mississaugas; Mohawks;
Senecas
Influenza, 164
Innes, Controller, 222
Inter-Island Council (IIC), 225, 226,
228, 235, *238* (1953 plan), 239, 240,
241, 250 (1958-59 lease extension)
International Picnic, 260, *261*, 266,
283, *284*, 290
Ireland, Aubrey, Jr., 183
Iroquois, 3, 4
Iroquois Avenue, 128
Iroquoise, 8
Irvine, Robert, *31*
Irwin, Alderman John, 97, 111, 118
Island, creation of, 2, 63
Island Airport, 155-6 (World War I),
177 (1929 proposal for), 192-4 (1935
proposal for), 195-201 *passim* (1937-38
creation of), 202, 204-5 (World
War II), 219, *242*, 247, *252*, 288

(1980 STOL proposal for). *See also* Norwegian Fliers
Island Amateur Aquatic Association (IAAA), 114, 127-9 (pre-war), 152, 173, 174, 183, 201 (1939 fire), 218, 242
Island Campers Association, 99
Island Canoe Club, 183, *217*, 226, 228, 233, *250*, 286, *287*
Island Committee, 121, 148, 164
Island Constable, 62n45 (John Roddy), 69-70 (John Hanlan, Sr.), 77 (George Warin), 90 (William Ward), 104, 125-6
Island firemen, 121, 123, 163, 165, 201
Island highway, proposals for, 138 (1909), 145 (1912), 146, 199n24, 225-6 (1947-48), 228 (1949), 230 (1951), 245 (1955). *See also* Automobiles; Bridges over Gaps, proposals for; Tunnel, proposals for
Island Homeowners Association, 259
Island of Hiawatha, 109
Island Park, 88 (1880), 97 (1888), 99, 102, 111, 114, 116 (1894), 118 (Labour Day 1894), 121 (1902), 137 (1908 flooding), 144 (Edwardian era), 157 (World War I), 172-3 (1921), 179 (1929), 182 (1930s), 194. *See also* Island Park development; Island Park Pavilion; Metro Toronto Island Park development
Island Park development, 88n1, 96-8 (1880-88), 116-9 (1890s), 138 (1910), 184 (1930s depression projects), 249 (1950s redevelopment). *See also* Metro Toronto Island Park development
Island Park Ferry Company, 101, 105
Island Park Pavilion, 97, 113, 173
Island Public School, 114 (1888), *115*, 125, 138 (1909 fire), 139, 179 (1920s), 215, 219, 234-5 (1952 expansion), 242 (1954 expansion), 245 (1955 classroom closed), 249 (1956, ten classrooms closed)
Island Queen, 124
Island Residents Association, 109, 113

Island Ratepayers Association (IRA), 195, 202, 213
Island Theatre, 220, *233*, 243, 252
Island Yacht Club (IYC), 190, 229

J.C. Beard, 61-2
J.C. Stewart, 223
Jackson, Dr. Gordon, 212
Jacobs, Jane, 289
Jaffary, Alderman Karl, 267, 273, 276, 277, 283
James, William, *110, 123, 126, 132, 138-9, 140, 143, 144, 149*
Jameson, Anna, 44, *45*
Jarvis, Aemilius, 111, 112, 113, 116, 119, 120n1, 152, 153, 157, 167, 169, 174
Jarvis, Fanny, 45
Jarvis, Mary, 45
Jarvis, Samuel Peters, 33
Jarvis, W.P.D., 152, 155
Jarvis, William, 24
Jarvis, Sheriff William, 45, 46
Jarvis, William (son of Sheriff William), 49
Jessie McEdwards, 101
Jim Crow Pond, 77, 90
John Hanlan, 142, *175*, 177, *179*
Johnson, Art, 233
Johnson, Sir William, 9
Johnston, Franz, 207
Johnston, M.P.P. Richard, 288, 292
Jolliet, Louis, 4
Jones, Chris, 282
Jones, Jimmy, Sr., 182, *191*
Jones, Jimmy, Jr., 182, 190-1, 199-200, 227
Jones, Reverend Trevor, 221
Jopling, Frederic Waistell, *37*
Junction Gang, 227
Jury, Alfred, 118

Kane, Paul, *6*, 7, 70
Kareda, Urjo, 275
Kashuba, Deputy Sheriff Boris, 291
Kathleen, 96
Keating, City Engineer E.H., 98, 109, 137
Keens, Jack, 155

Kellog, Walter, 160
Kennedy, Mayor Warring, 118
Ketchum, Jesse, 48
Kemp, Penny, 286
Kilbourn, Reverend Elizabeth, *178*
Kilbourn, William, 40, 43, *178*, 267
Kilbourn family, 197
Kimmings, David, 97, 114, 115, 136
King, Prime Minister William Lyon Mackenzie, 180, 193
Kingston, Ontario, 28, 32, 46, 47, 50. *See also* Fort Frontenac
Kingston, 64
Kirkpatrick, Lieutenant Governor George, 118
Knapp's Roller Boat, 110
Knott, Benjamin, 38, 40, 42n9
Korean War, 228, 229

Labour Day, 118, 221
Labroquerie, Pierre Boucher de, *9*
Lacrosse, 120
LaForce, René-Hypolite, 8, 11
Lady Elgin, 60
Lakeshore Avenue, 57 (1850 plan), 83, 102, 104, 134 (1906 plan), 127-8, 162, 177, 225 (1947 plan), 255-63 *passim* (1960s demolitions)
Lakeside Home For Little Children, 93-4 (1883), *109*, 115, 129, *139*, 146, 155 (1915 fire), 174, *175*, 204 (World War II), 221
Lamantia family, 171, 245, 251
Lamport, Mayor Allan, 197, 226, 228, 230, 232, 234-6 (1953 plan), 239, 240, 242, 244, 248, 252, 255
Landmann, George, 21
Langley, Henry, 102
LaSalle, René-Robert Cavelier, Sieur de, 4, 5
Lastman, Mayor Mel, 279, 282
Lease extensions, 242 (1954), 250-1 (1958-59), 259-60 (1967), 264-8 *passim* (1970), 268-70 *passim* (1971), 273-9 (1973 campaign for), 279-83 *passim* (1974 Spring Campaign for), 284 (1975 campaign for), 285-93 *passim* (1975-81 campaign at provincial level for)

Lease policy, 110 (1891 review), 222 (Algonquin Island 1940s), 226-8 (1948-49 review), 242 (1954), 246-7 (1955 change). *See also* Lease extensions
Legal battle, 280n26, 283-94 *passim* (1974-1984)
Lemon, Harry, 208
Lennox, E.J., 111, 120n1
Léry, Chaussegros de, 8-9
Leslie Street spit, 284, 293
Lewis, David, 283
License of occupation, 55, 56, 71
Life saving, 68, 72-4, *75*, 78-9, 92, 93, 125-7. *See also* Life saving system
Life saving system, 78 (1872), 89-90 (1880), 93, 138 (1909 fire), 148 (1912-13), 165 (1919 fire)
Lightfoot, Gordon, 271
Lighthouse, 22 (1808-09), *23*, 28 (War of 1812), 31, 36 (1815 murder at), 44, 46, 78, 102, 104, 114, 155, 254. *See also* Lighthouse Keepers; Lighthouse Keepers' cottages
Lighthouse at Eastern Gap, 206
Lighthouse Keepers, 22, 36, 37, 139. *See also* Durnan, George; Durnan, James; Holloway; McSherry, Patrick; Rademuller, J.P.
Lighthouse Keepers' cottages, 22, 43
Lillie, Beatrice, 147
Lind, Jennie, 57-8
Liquor: ban on, 86, 93, 106, 129, 173; bootlegging, 81, 90, 93, 136; licensing and consumption of, 38, 43, 52, 86-8, 106, 112
Little Norway, 204, *205*, 206. *See also* Norwegian fliers
Livingston, Barclay, 271
Long Pond, 114, 117, 119, 129, 144, 152, 183, 201, 216, 226, 260, 266
Longboat, Tom, 140, 164
Loudon, Captain Brian Melville, 164
Loudon, Professor James, 98
Loudon, Thomas, 80
Love, Parks Commissioner, 232
Lowry, "Dad", 90
Luella, 91, 94, 96, 114

Lusitania, 155
Lye, John, 98, *197*
Lye, Ted, 216

Macaulay, Theodore C., *163*
McBride, Mayor Sam, 131, 134 (1906 plan), 150, 151, 158, 162, 177 (elected mayor), 185, *189, 192,* 193-4 (opposes 1935 tunnel)
McCallum, Mayor Hiram E., 228, 229
McClelland, Jack, *174*
McClelland, John, 174
McClure, Tom, 171, 188
Macdonald, M.P. Donald, 272
Macdonald, Prime Minister Sir John A., 71, 72, 95-6
Mcdonald's Wharf, 43
Macdonnell, Attorney General John, *24,* 25
McGill, Betty, 210
McGill, George, 210
McGillevray, William, 21
McIntyre, Peter, 93
Mackenzie, Sir Alexander, 21
Mackenzie, William Lyon, 32, 33, 37, 40, 43-6
Mackie, James, 88
McLaughlin, Mary, 249, 255, 263
McLaughlin, Murray, 262
McLaughlin, Paul, 249, 255
McLaughlin, Terry, 249
McLean, T.W., *20*
Maclean, Wallace, 98
McMaster, Elizabeth Janet, 93
McMaster, Samuel T., 98
McMaster, Captain W.F., 69
McMaster, William J., 98
MacNab, Allan Napier, 46
McNaught, William K., 153
McNeil, Archbishop, 174
McSherry, Captain Patrick J., 139
McTavish, Simon, 31
Madrick, Frank, 260
Madrick, Mary, 220, 224
Magasin Royal, 6
Maher, James P., 241n15
Main Drag, 127 (1914), 182 (1930s), 208, 209, 212 (1943 flooding),

213, *214,* 215, 218, 220 (winter 1940s), 222, 224 (1947 flooding), *240,* 247-8, *250* (demolitions 1950s), 252. *See also* Manitou Road
Maitland, Lieutenant Governor Sir Peregrine, 32, *33*
Maitland's Wharf, 51, 60
Mallon, Albert, 209
Mallon, James T., 165
Mallon, Mary, 127, 141, 152, 153, 160, 165, 171, 173, 207, 209, 215
Mallon family, 197
Malton Airport (Lester B. Pearson), 197
Manitou, 266-7
Manitou Bridge, 119, 127, 184, 240, 252
Manitou Hotel, 190, *191,* 194, 207, 218, 220, 227, *233,* 245
Manitou Road, 83, 97, 101, 119 (1894 development of), 127-8 (pre-war), 138, 173 (1920s), 175, 182, 184, 190, 201, 208, *224* (1947 flooding), 225 (1947 plan), 226, 227, 233, 252 (demolitions at). *See also* Main Drag
Maps, 4 (c.1680), 9 (1757), 29 (1816), *38* (1833), *41* (1835), *51* (1851), *73* (1868), *107* (1890), 111, *122* (1903), *246* (1955). *See also* Plans; Surveys
Maple Leafs baseball team, 108, 140, 142, 152, 159, 168. *See also* Baseball
Mariposa Folk Festival, 262, 266, 268, 271-2, 275, 283
Marks, Alderman June, 267, 268, 270, 273
Marsh, Lou, 185
Marshall, James B., 131, 133, 136, 147, 149
Marshall's Drug Store, 183
Massey, Arthur L., 111
Massey, John, 101
Massey family, 182
Maxwell, Davie, 263
Mayflower, 105, 116, 125
Mazza, Fred, 222
Mazza, Pam, 285
Mazza, Ron, 261, 276, 288, 291

Mead, Mrs. Mary A., *73*, 96, 97, 101.
See also Mead's Hotel
Mead, Robert, 76. See also Mead's
Hotel
Mead's Hotel, 76, 78, 83, 84, *88*, 97,
100
Mead's Wharf, 96
Merrick, James, 151
Metcalfe, Bill, 279
Metro Toronto, 226n26, 235, 236
(creation of)
Metro Toronto bureaucracy, 276-7
Metro Toronto Council, 236 (April 15,
1953 creation of), 239, 241 (1954),
244, 245 (March 22, 1955), 247n22,
248, 249n27, 251, 253, 255 (June
18, 1963), 257, 258, 259 (May 30/
31, 1967), 261, 262, 267, 268 (April
21, 1970), 270 (June 29, 1971),
273 (1972 election to), 274-5 (May 1,
1973), 278-9 (December 11, 1973),
281, 282-3 (May 31, 1974 and June
18, 1974), 284 (April 8, 1975),
285, 288 (February 26, 1980), 289
(June, 1980), 290 (and Swadron
Commission), 292 (March 17, 1981)
Metro Toronto Executive, 246, 255,
274, 277
Metro Toronto Island Park
development, 240, 248-*59 passim*
(1955-67), 268, 271, 273, 275. *See
also* Avenue of the Islands; Far
Enough Farm; Plans
Metro Toronto Parks Commissioner,
239, 247 (established 1955), 252. *See
also* Robert Bundy; Tommy
Thompson
Metro Toronto Parks and Recreation
Committee, 254-5, 258n39, 258n41,
259, 267-8, 269, *270*, 273n13, 274,
277. *See also* Metro Toronto Planning
and Parks Committee
Metro Toronto Parks Department, 239,
247 (established 1955), 252, 269, 293
Metro Toronto Planning and Parks
Committee, 241n15, 247n22. *See also*
Metro Toronto Parks and Recreation
Committee

Metro Toronto Planning Board, 241,
245, 248
Metro Toronto Social Services
Committee, 281
Micklethwaite, F.W., *96*, 98, *103, 111*
Middleton, Jesse Edgar, 160
Miller, Percy, 250
Mills, Nathan, 131, 151, 162
Milne, David, 209
Minstrel shows, 171, 189, 210, 215,
234
Mississaga, 12, 15, 17
Mississaugas, 6 7, 8, 10, 11, 12
Mitchell, Joni, 262, 266
Mohawks, 2
Monarch, The, 61, 71
Montessori school, 285
Montreal, Quebec, 7, 9, 11, 19, 21
Moodie, Captain Bob, 60, 64
Moodie, Mrs., 68
Moodie, Susanna, 58
Morphy, George, 83
Morris, Ephraim ''Evan'', 82
Morris, James H., Q.C., 76, 77, 79
Moss, Charles, 98
Moss, Dr. G.W.O., 274
Mugg's Island (also Mugg's Landing),
55, 98-9, 117, 196-8 (1977 plan to
develop), 201, 218n17, 225 (1947
plan), 229 (Island Yacht Club),
249n27, *197, 229*
Mulock, William, 164
Mulvany, C. Pelham, 86, *87*, 88, 91-2,
100
Murder, 36, 208-9
Murray, Gordon, 213
Muskoka, 127

Naylor, Ralph, 202, 207, 210, 215
Ned Hanlan, 191, 223, 242, 252
Nellie Bly, 126, 138, 139, 140
Newark, 12, 15, 26. See also Fort
Niagara; Niagara
Newell, Aune ''Spooky'', 208-9
Newell, Hugh ''Bill'', 208-9
Niagara, 7, 19, 30, 46, 50, 58, 85, 95
Niagara Falls, 40, 44, 46, *55*, 72,
76, 122, 136

Niagara frontier, 26, 69
Nordheimer, Albert, 98
Noronic, 227-8.
North West Company, 6, 10, 16, 21,
31-2
Norton, Anna, 200
Norton, Earl, 200
Norwegian fliers, 204-6, 209.

O'Brien, D.C., 67
O'Brien, Lucius, *83*
O'Connor, J.C., 105
O'Connor, Michael, 38, 40
O'Dea, Mary, 137
O'Donohue, Alderman Tony, 259,
272, 284, 287
Oen, Major, 204
Official Plan, City of Toronto, 228
(1949), 253n33 (1960s), 283n28
(1974)
Ogetonicut, *20, 21*, 22
Oldershaw, Bert, *217*, 226, 233
Oldershaw, Charlie, 213, 214
Oldershaw, Dick, 213, 215
Oldershaw, Tom, 213
Oldershaw family, 213, 260
Olive Branch, 78-9
Olmsted, Frederick Law, 121
Olympic Island, 138, 262, *266*, 271.
See also Toothpick Island
Olympics, 183, 206, 226, 233, *217*,
271
Onondaga (also *Anandoga*), 15, 17, 18
Ongiara, 261
Ontario Court of Appeal, 285, 291,
292, 294n48
Ontario Divisional Court, 294n48,
294n50
Ontario Municipal Board, 253n33
Ontario Place, 269
Ontario Supreme Court, 284n30, 286,
290
Open Circle Theatre, 275
Oriole I, 85, 95
Oriole II, 95, 96, 113
Oriole III, 167, 168
Osborne and Naylor, 173
Osgoode, Chief Justice William, 19

Oshawa, Ontario, 22
Osler, Sir Edmund Boyd, 105, 142
Osler, Justice Featherston, 94, 98, 105

Pacific, 78
Palin, 40, 43. *See also* Anderton & Palin
Palmer, H.S., *174*
Parish Hall, 221, 252
Parkinson, Mrs. Emily, *61*, 70, 72, *73,* 76
Parkinson, Reuben, 55
Parkinson, Captain William, 70, 76
Parkinson's Hotel, 55 (first); 70, 72, *76* (second)
Parkinson's Wharf, 70, 76
Peninsula, 2-63 *passim*
Peninsula Hotel, 40, 43, 51-2, 60, *62,* 89
Peninsula Packet, 50, 51
Peninsula Pleasure Grounds, 50, 51
Pequegnat, Dr., 232
Perkins, Dale, 280, 282, 283
Phillips, Mayor Nathan, 144, 190, 192n10, 196, 202, 228, 242 (elected mayor), 244, 248
Phillips, A.J. "Plug", 124
Pickford, Mary, *205*
Picnics, 7 (1749), 16-7 (1790s), 48-9 (1840s), 72 (1867), 144 (1912), 172-3 (1921), 179 (1929)
Pierce, Lieutenant Albert, 156
Pierce, Lieutenant George, 156, *157*
Pierson's Hotel, 127-8, 173, 183, 194, 212, 247, *250,* 252. *See also* Mead's Hotel
Pike, General Zebulon, 28, 29
Plaisted, Fred, 81, 82
Plans, 11 (1788), 15, *16* (1793), 56-7 (c.1850), 72-*3* (1868), 118-9, 121-2 (1903), 130, 131 (1903), 134 (1906), 138 (1909), 145-6 (1912), 225-7 (1947-48), 228 (1949), 230-*1* (1951), *234-5* (Lamport 1953), *238*-40 (IIC 1953), 245 (1955), 248 (1956), 249n27, 254-5 (1963), 256 (1964), 257, 273n13, 275-7 (1973 City and Metro), 292 (1981 Swadron). *See also* Maps; Surveys

Playter, Ely, 28
Plewman, William R., 174, 215
Plumptre, Adelaide, 196
Police Games, 181
Police Station, 184, 208, *250,* 252
Polio, 197
Politicians' tours, 97 (1888), 113-4 (1894), 196-7 (1937), *253,* 254 (1962, 63), 259 (1967), 262 (1968), 267-8 (1970), 274 (1973)
Polson's Iron Works, 110, 125, 142, 154, 164
Population, 102 (1888), 110 (1890s), 114, 129, 139, 146n32, 150, 161, 165, 168, 170, 190 (1930s winter), 190n9, 218-21 (1940s winter), 234, 249, 252
Port Dalhousie, 184
Portage, 6, 9-10, 32
Powell, Chief Justice William Dummer, 36-7
Powell, Mrs. William Dummer, *30*
Pressure Island report, 292
Primrose, 105, 116, 121, 123, 125
Prince Louis of Battenberg, 124
Prince of Wales, 64-66 *passim* (1860), *166*-67 (1919), 176 (1927)
Prince of Wales Cup, 66, 74, 155, 167
Princess of Wales, 70
Princess Patricia, 148
Privat, Louis, 50. *See also* Privat brothers
Privat, Louis Joseph, 50, 51. *See also* Privat brothers
Privat brothers, 50, 51, 60, 154
Privats Hotel, 55, 59
Provincial, 60, *66*
Provincial legislation, 288-93 *passim*
Public opinion, 276n19 (1973), 292 (1980)
Putt, Ruth, 262, *282,* 286

Queen City Yacht Club (QCYC), 134n17, 164, *169,* 199, 260
Queen's Own Rifles, 147-8
Queen Victoria, 46
Queen's Cup, 112
Queen's Wharf, 57, 115

Quinn, Jenny, 63
Quinn, John, 60, *62,* 63
Quinn's Hotel, 60, 62, 63

R-100, 186
Rademuller, J.P., 22, *36,* 51
Railroads, 57, 90, 101, *125,* 171
Raise Island's elevation, 228, 248, 249
Randall, Al, 186
Randall, Bruce, 212, 215
Randall, Wally, 188
Rebellion of 1837, 43-46 *passim*
Receptions on waterfront, 46 (1838), 57-8 (1851), 64-6 (1860), 81 (1876), 82 (1878), 85 (1879), *166*-8 (1919), *183* (1933)
Rectory, *256*-7, 268
Red Cross Outpost, 174, 175, 194, 207, 212, *214,* 216, 217, 234
Rees's Wharf, 36, 59, 60
Reeve, Bishop, 174
Regattas, 50 (1842), 60 (1854), 61, 65-6 (1860), 66-7 (1866), 72 (1867), 99 (1888), 102 (1888), 105-6 (1894), 114 (1894), 128-9 (1900), *129,* 165 (1919), 166-7 (1919), 183 (1930s), *250* (1957), 266 (1969). *See also* Dominion Day Regattas
Regatta courses, 143, 157, 183, 196-200 *passim* (1937-38), 201, 226
Reistad, Lieutenant Colonel Ole, 204, 205
Residential development, general, 56-7 (1847), 72 (1868), 76 (1872-3), 77, 78n23, 109-10 (1890s), 174 (1920s)
Residential development, Algonquin Island, 201n27, 222. *See also* Algonquin Island; Sunfish Island
Residential development, Centre Island, 99-102 (1880s-90s), 110-3 (1890s), 127 (pre-war), 128, 218-21 *passim* (winter). *See also* Centre Island
Residential development, Hanlan's Point, 76 (1872-73), 98-9 (1880s-90s), 129-30 (1900s), 192 (1930s), 196-201 *passim* (1937-38). *See also* Hanlan's Point; Western Sandbar

Residential development, Ward's
Island, 104 (1880s), 130-4 (1900s),
146-52 *passim* (1910-13), 161 (1915),
162, 168-72 *passim* (1920s), 177-8,
187-8 (cottages, 1930s), 219-23
passim (winter), 228 (1950). *See also*
Ward's Island
Residential development, winter
community, 114-5 (1880s-90s), 125
(1900s), 139 (1909), 178-9 (1920s),
190-2 (1930s), 201-2, 218-24 *passim*
(1940s), 235. *See also* Winter;
Winter Carnival; Winter
transportation
Responsible government, 46
Retreat on the Peninsula, 38
Reuben Dowd, 126
Richardson, Harbour Master Hugh,
62, 63
Richardson Cup, 152
Riel, Louis, 95
Ripple, 70
Roach, Justice W.D., 209
Robbins, Mayor William D., 197
Roberts, Percy, 174
Robertson, John Ross, 20, 22, 43, 46-
7, 50-1, 55-6, 60, 64, 66, 69, 72,
105, *109* (Lakeside Home), 114 (St.
Andrew's-by-the-Lake), 125, *139*,
155 (Lakeside Home)
Robinette, John J., *135*, 286
Robinette, Thomas Cowper, 135
Robinson, Bruce, 230
Robinson, Chief Justice John Beverley,
45
Robinson, Percy J., 7, 15
Robinson, Robert, 294
Rocheblave, Sieur de, 11
Roddy, Bill, 250
Roddy, Duggan, 210
Roddy, Margaret, 210
Roddy, John, 62n45
Rogers, Elias, 111, *112*
Rogers, Major Robert, 9
Rolph, Joseph T., *67*, 100
Ronald, William, *256*, 257
Rorke, Minnie, 220n20, 228
Rosamond, Mrs., 243
Rosenbaum, Linda, 290, 294

Ross, Alexander, 274
Ross, Wallace, 81-2
Rotenberg, Alderman David, 253-9
passim (1963-67), 262, 267-70 *passim*
(1969-71), 272-3 (1972 election),
277 (1973)
Rothesay Castle, 67, *68*, 69, 72, 85
Rouille, 180
Rousseau, St. Jean Baptiste, 10, 15
Rowing, 80 (1870s). *See also* Argonaut
Rowing Club; Dominion Day
Regattas; Durnan, Eddie; Guest,
Jack; Hanlan, Ned; Regattas;
Toronto Rowing Club
Roy, Thomas, *41*
Royal Canadian Yacht Club (RCYC),
58-9 (1850s), 60, 65-6 (1860), 69,
72, 74, 90-*1* (Island clubhouse 1880s),
94-5, 99, 112, 113-9 *passim* (1890s),
122, 124 (1904 fire, new clubhouse),
136, 148, 152, 155, 157, 163 (1918
fire), 165, 167-8 (1919), 173-4 (1922
clubhouse), 179, 183-4 (1930s),
207, 213, 216, 230, 232 (RCYC
centennial), 266-7, 272
Royal Floating Baths, 43
Royal Norwegian Air Force. *See*
Norwegian fliers
Russell, Elizabeth, 19, 30-1
Russell, Peter, 17, 18, 19
Rust, City Engineer C.H., 136
Ruth, Babe, 142
Rutledge, John, 207

Sabot prams, 216, 271
Sadie, 99
Sagar, Arthur, 198, 199, 200
Sailing, 183-4, 216, 266-7, 270-1. *See
also* Canada's Cup; Cove Fleet;
Dinghies; Gooderhams; Island Yacht
Club; Jarvis, Aemilius; Queen City
Yacht Club; Royal Canadian Yacht
Club; Sabot prams
St. Andrew's-by-the-Lake, 101-2
(1884), 114 (1890s), 174 (1920s),
213, 221, 222, 249, 252 (moved),
257, 269, 275, 279
St. Jean Baptiste, 85, 89

St. Catharines, Ontario, 57
St. Lawrence Seaway, 240
St. Louis, 127
St. Rita's, 174, 201, 252, 269
Salmon, J.V., *240*
Sam McBride, 194, *203*, *206*
Sand excavation, 31, 55, 62
Sankey, City Surveyor Villiers, 98, 121,
136
Satterthwaite Cottage, 86
Saunders, Mayor Robert H., 197, 215,
223, 226n26
Saunders, Mayor Leslie, 242
Saywell, Art, 184
Scadding, Dr. Henry, 15, 19, 21, 22,
31-2, 34-5, 42
Scadding, John, 42
Scarboro Beach, 140
Scarborough Bluffs, 2, 3, 26, 28
Sceviour, Mr. and Mrs. Bill, 206
Schoenborn, Albrecht, 222, 244
Schoenborn, Luise, 222
Scott, Alderman Reid, 276
Senecas, 4
Sewell, Mayor John, 224, 230, 267,
282, 288, 289, 292, 293
Sewell, Marion, 230
Sewell, William, 210, 224
Sheaffe, Major General Sir Roger, 26,
28-9
Sheard, Dr. Charles, 98, 136
Sheppard, Thomas, 46
Sheriff, *265*, 290-1
Shiels, George, 212, 215
Shipwrecks, 22-*3 (Toronto)*, 61
(Monarch), 62 *(J.C. Beard)*, 72-5 *(Jane
Ann Marsh)*, 78-9 *(Ann Belle
Chambers, Olive Branch, Fearless)*, 78
(Pacific), 89 *(Ann Bell Chambers)*,
125-7 *(Reuben Dowd)*
Short Take-Off and Landing service
(STOL), 288
Shuttleworth, Professor Edward B.,
100
Simcoe, 26
Simcoe, Mrs. Elizabeth, 7, 12-8 *passim*,
22
Simcoe, Lieutenant Governor John
Graves, 2, 12, 15-18 *passim*, 22, 31

Simpson, Mayor Jimmy, 192
Simpson's, 171, 182-3, 187, 192, 220
Sinclair, Alec, 152, 207
Sinclair, Controller Bruce, 276
Sinclair, Kate, 207
Singer, Charles, 245
Sir Isaac Brock, 25-30 *passim*
Sir John of The Peninsula, 38
Skating, 8, 16, 34, 271
Slaves, 58
Sleighing and carioling, 17, 19, 49
Small, Ambrose, 120
Smallpox, 32
Smellie, Robert, 100
Smith, Cameron, 227, 262
Smith, David W., 22
Smith, George, 213
Smith, Jamie, 288
Smith, Larratt, 48, 49, 50, 77
Smith, Maureen, 264, 267, 268, 269,
    270, 273, 275, 277, 279
Smith, Alderman Stewart, 196
Smyth, Coke, 47
Smyth, Sir James Carmichael, 18
Snake Island, 216, 257
Snider, C.H.J., *21, 23, 27, 56, 68,* 95,
    113, 116, 122, 152, 155, 168, 183
Solman, Lawrence "Lol", 105, 117,
    120 (TFC manager), 121 (1903 fire),
    123, 129, 136, 139, 141 (1909 fire),
    142 (1910), 146, 168 (Sunnyside, sale
    of TFC to City), 177, 182
Southern Belle, 69
Spanner, Oliver, 127
Speedy, 21, 22
Spragge, Dr. E., 100
Spremo, Boris, *291*
Spring Campaign, 1974, 279-83 *passim*
Stanfield, M.P. Robert, 283
Sproat & Rolph, 124
Staneland, Frank "Daddy Frank", 132-
    3, 148, 151, 161, 168, *178,* 187, *189*
Stanley Barracks, 46, 69
Stanley, Governor General Lord, 112
Staples, Owen *27,* 174
Stein, George, 271, 272
Steinhoff, 104
Stevenson, William, *217,* 226
Stewart, Ian, *229*

Stewart, Mayor William J., 180, 181,
    182, 184, *189*
Stiff, Thomas, 130
Stockwell, Controller Winfield H.
    "Bill", 277, 278, 288
Storms, 2, 19, 52, 61, 63 (1858 creation
    of Island), 64, 72-*5,* 78-9, *83-4*
    (1878), 86, 90, 93, 100, 125-7 (1906),
    130, 136, 165, 183-4, 192, 195,
    206, 219, 230 (1951), 232 (1952),
    242-3 (Hurricane Hazel), 245, 247-8
    (Hurricane Connie)
Strachan, James, *36*
Strachan, Archbishop John, 26, 28, 29,
    32, 36, 40
Stretton, Lieutenant Sempronius, *20*
Strowger, William, 52, 53
Sturgeon, Ralph, 202
Sullivan, Mayor Robert Baldwin, 42-3
Summerville, Controller Billy, 192n10
Sunday streetcars controversy, 109
Sunfish flying-boat, 163
Sunfish Island, 104, 134 (1906 plan),
    151, 163, 166 (YMCA camp, 1919),
    164 (QCYC, 1920), 170-1, 185,
    197-201 *passim* (1937-38). *See also*
    Algonquin Island
Sunnyside, 28, 105, 168, 177, 180,
    209, 211-2, 215, 230, 242
Supreme Court of Canada, 284, 285
Surveys, 11 (1788), *15* (1792), 52
    (1846), 55 (1847), 56-7 (c.1850), 77.
    See also Maps; Plans
Sutherland, William, *191,* 194, 201-2,
    245
Swadron, Barry, 289, 290, 292, 293
Swain, Mabel, 158
Swallwell, Tommy, 215
Sweatman, Bishop Arthur, 101, 102
Sweny, Colonel George, 98, 102
Swimming, 83-4, 90-2, 93, 117, 162,
    184, 242. *See also* Atkinson's Baths;
    Turner's Baths; Wiman Baths
Sydenham, Charles Poulett Thompson,
    first Baron, 47
Sykes, Lieutenant "Davie", 163-4

Talbot, Lieutenant Thomas, 16
Tate, Mrs. Rose, 159

Tax strike, threat of, 230, 232
Tecumsehs, 120, 121
Teiaiagon, 4, 5
Temple, Edmund, 103
Temple, Alderman Mary, 259
Tenting at Hanlan's Point, 98-9, 129-
    30. *See also* Western Sandbar
Tenting at Ward's Island, 102 (1890s),
    126, 130-4 (1900s), 146-52 *passim*
    (1910-14), 159, 160-3 (World War
    I), 168-72 *passim* (1920s), *178,*
    185-6 (1930s), 228 (1950). *See also*
    Ward's Island
Terminal Warehouse, 272n11
Thompson, Gordon, 230
Thompson, George, 212
Thompson, Ivan, 212
Thompson, Prime Minister Sir John,
    113-4
Thompson, Metro Toronto Parks
    Commissioner Thomas W.
    "Tommy", 247 (hired 1955), 248
    (1956 plan), 249n27, 252, *253,* 254-5
    (1963 plan), 256 (1964 plan), 257,
    258, *259,* 261, 262, 263, 267, 268
    (1970), 271, 273-8 *passim* (1973)
Thomson, William J., *51, 88*
Thorne, Horace, 100
Tinning, Thomas, 60, 78-9, 80, 89
Tinning's *Cigar Boat*, 55-6
Tinning's Wharf, 60, 70, 78
Toothpick Island, 122. *See also* Olympic
    Island
Toronto. *See* City of Toronto
Toronto (yacht), 19, 22, *23*
Toronto (steamferry), 41-2, 43
Toronto Canoe Club, 98, 106, 114,
    117
Toronto Carrying Place, 2-11 *passim,*
    15
Toronto Centennial, 180, *181,* 184
Toronto City Planning Board (TCPB),
    225-6 (1947 plan), 228 (1949 Official
    Plan), 229, 230-*1* (1951 plan), 239
Toronto Ferry Company (TFC), 105
    (formed 1890), 106 (1894), 108, 109,
    116, 118, 120 (1900), 123 (1904),
    124-5 *(Bluebell),* 139, 142 *(Trillium),*
    159, 168 (1926 sale to City)

Toronto Harbour Commission (THC), 145-6 (1912 plan), 148, *160*-1 (expansion of Island), 169, 177, 180, 192, 199, 229, 230-1 (1951 plan), 239, 284 (1974). *See also* Harbour Commission

Toronto Harbour Police, *164*, 244, 268, 272, 288, 293

Toronto Island Committee (1973), 275

Toronto Island Canoe Club. *See* Island Canoe Club

Toronto Island Residents Association (TIRA), 264-5 (1969 creation of), 268-70 *passim* (1971), 274-5 (1973), 280, 284, 285, 288 (1979), 293, 294 (1983). *See also* Toronto Island Residents Association Executive; Spring Campaign 1974

Toronto Island Residents Association Executive, 267 (1970), 268-9 (1971), 272 (1972 elections), 273, 276, 279-80 (Spring Campaign 1974), 291 (1980). *See also* Toronto Island Residents Association; Spring Campaign 1974

Toronto Purchase, *10*, 11

Toronto Railway Company, 109

Toronto Rowing Club, 67, 72, 75, 80-1 (1876), 105-6 (1894), 140 (1909), 143

Toronto Semi-Centennial, 94, 138

Toronto Trades and Labour Council, 110

Toronto Transportation Commission (TTC), 168 (1927 ferry service), *169*, 175, 176, 180 (1931), 214 (1944), 218, 225, 226n26. *See also* Toronto Transit Commission; Winter transportation

Toronto Transit Commission (TTC), 242, 243-4 (Tugboat Mutiny), 252 (ferry transfer to Metro). *See also* Toronto Transportation Commission; Winter transportation

Torrence, Bob, 216

Townsend, Lieutenant Alan Jarvis, 157

Toy, Samuel M., 111

Transfer from Crown to City (1867), 71

Transfer from City to Metro, 236-247 *passim*

Transfer from Metro to City, proposals for, 258 (1966), 273, 274, 275, 276 (1973), 278, 285, 287 (1978), 288 (1980), 293 (1982), 294 (1983-84)

Trees, Alexander George, 164

Trees, Samuel, 129

Trees, Christopher F., 164

Trickett, Edward, 86, 88

Trillium, 142, 186, 214, 248-9, *257*, 285, 293

Trudeau, Margaret, *284*

Trudeau, Prime Minister Pierre Elliott, 266, *267*, 272, 283, *284*

Tugboat Mutiny, 243-4

Tully, Kivas, 62

Tunnel, proposals for vehicular, 138 (1909), 192-4 (1935), 195-6 (1937), 225-6 (1947), 226n26 (1948), 228n32 (1949), 229, 230-1 (1951), 245, 248 (1955-56), 257 (1965-66)

Tunnel, water, 137-8

Turner, John, 93

Turner family, 99

Turner's Baths, 129, 130, 196. *See also* Atkinson's Baths

Tymon, Captain Andrew, 101, 105

Tyson, Ian and Sylvia, 266

Ullmann, Liv, 204

Underground Railway, 58

Union Station, 76, *82*

Unwin, Charles, 72, *73*, 78

Vale, Bruce, 216

Varley, Frederick, 146

Vaughan, Ross, 212, 214

Veterans, 203, 217, 220, 222. *See also* Red Cross Outpost

Victoria, 46-7 (1838), 119 (1897)

Victoria, 51, 58, 60

Victoria Park, 89

Vigneault, Gilles, 262

Voyageurs, 5, 7, 21, 32

Wabukanyne, Chief, 11

Walker, Kay, 279, 286, 290

Walsh, Mary, 262

War of 1812, 21, 23, 25, 26-31 *passim*

Ward, Ann, 100

Ward, Bill, 202

Ward, David, Sr., 52, 60n42, 60, 64, 67, 68, 72, *73* (1868 map), 77, 78, 79

Ward, David, Jr., 80, 84, 148

Ward, Fram, 134, 149, 163, 165, 168, 177-8, 191, 219, 222

Ward, Frank, 148, 163, 168

Ward, Fred, 148-9

Ward, John, 52, 60n42, 72n15, 77, 115

Ward, William, *61*, 67-8 (1862 sisters drown), 74-5 (1868 rescue), 78-9 (1875 rescue), 83, 89 (1880 lifeboat), 90, 92 (hotel), 93, 104-5 (1890s), 118, 125-7 (1906 rescue), 130, 138, *147*, 148

Ward family, 101, 114, 133, 148-9

Ward's Hotel (first), 83n28

Ward's Hotel (second), 92, 104, *149*, 162, 171, 220, 229

Ward's Island, 90 (1880), 102, *103*, 104, *107*, 126, 130-7 *passim* (1900s), 146-51 (1910-14), 155-63 *passim* (World War I), *165*, 166, 168-72 (1920s), 177, 178, 179n31, 182, 184-90 *passim* (1930s), 202, 206-17 *passim* (World War II), 219-23 *passim* (winter community), 224-5, 227, 228, 230, 233-4, 240, 245, 247, 248, 249, *251*, 252, 253, 254, 255-63 *passim* (Lakeshore Avenue battle), Chapter 12 *passim* (1969-84). *See also* Eastern Point; Haney's Point; Residential development, Ward's Island; Tenting at Ward's Island; William Ward; Ward's Hotel (second); Wiman Baths; Wiman Building; Wiman Shelter; Wiman Terrace

Ward's Island Association (WIA), 151, 158, 162, 165, 166, 169, 170, 177, 184, 187, 188, 227, 264, 280. *See also* Ward's Island Association Clubhouse

Ward's Island Association Clubhouse, 186, 188-9, 207, 209, 223, 264, 269, 272, 275, 276, 282, 285, 286, 290
Ward's Island beach, 186, 284
Ward's Island Leaseholders Association, 188
Ward's Pond, 68
Warin, George, 77
Waterfront development, 271, 272n11, 293. *See also* Harbourworks
Water quality, 36 (1832), 40-*1* (1835), 48 (1840s), 71 (1860s), 79-80 (1870s), 98 (1880s), 137 (1908)
Waterworks, 79-80 (1870s), 98 (1880s-90s), 137-8 (1908), 143-4 (1911). *See also* Filtration Plant
Webster, Harry, 130
Webster, Mardi, 199, 200, 223
Weedcutter, *122*, 137
Welland, 60
Wells, M.P.P. Tom, 288, 289, 292
Wemp, Mayor Bert S., 156, 182, 184, 185
West Island Drive Association, 192-4 (1935), 195-201 *passim* (1937-38)
Western Gap, 62, 80, 85, 109, 115, 126-7 (1906), 145 (1912 plan), 168, 191, 192-4 (1935 tunnel), 225, 227, *231*, 257
Western Sandbar, 84, 93 (baths), 99 (tenting), 126, 129-30 (cottages),

140, 143, 146, 155-6 (Curtiss flying school), 164, 177, 180 (1934), 190-1 (winters), 192-4 (1935 tunnel), 195-201 *passim* (1937-38 airport), 201
Whelan, Ray, 275
Wilkinson, Frank, 160
Wilkinson, Harold, 160
Wilkinson, Reverend J.W., 131, 162-3
William Inglis, 194, 207, 258
William Lyon Mackenzie, 285
Williams, John, 281
Willinsky, Dr. B., 229
Wilson, Mayor Adam, 71
Wilson, Parks Commissioner James, 136, 137, 138 (1909 plan), 144, 145, 146
Wilson, Jim, 165, 177
Wilson, Isaac, 28, 31
Wiman, Erastus, 90, 91
Wiman Baths, 90, 91, 92, 93, *107*. *See also* Wiman Building
Wiman Building, 131, 136, 138, *149, 159*, 249. *See also* Wiman Baths
Wiman Shelter, 92, 136, 151, *158*, 159, 160, 162, 170, 177, 184, 185, 186, 249
Wiman Terrace, 131, *158-9*, 249
Winchester, Judge, 134-6
Winslow, Alf, 206
Winter, 40, *42*, 46, *49*, 51-2, *57, 76, 97, 138-9, 164, 172*, 175, 178-9, 245,

261, 267, 271, 272, 279. *See also* Residential development, winter community; Winter Carnival; Winter transportation
Winter Carnival, 273, 280-1, 286
Winter transportation, *191*, 192 (1930s), 218, 219, 223-4 (1940s), 243-4 (early 1950s), 252 (1960), 261 *(Ongiara)*
Winters, M.P. Robert, 248
Withrow, John, 84, 91
Withrow, Norman, 104
Woodburn, John, 269, 274
Woods, Michael J., 100, 102, *103*
World War I, 152-66 *passim*, 208
World War II, 202-20 *passim*
Worts, James, 35
Wright, Dorothy, 189

YMCA, 166, 170, 185, 199, 201
YWCA, 173, 210
Yacht club leases, 281n27, 286, 290. *See also* Island Yacht Club; Queen City Yacht Club; Royal Canadian Yacht Club
Yonge Street, 6, 16, 19, 31, 32, 45, 46
Yonge Street Wharf, 57, 69, 72, 81, 85, 105, 120, 125
York, 2, 11, 12-37 *passim*
York County Court, 286
Young, Thomas, *35*

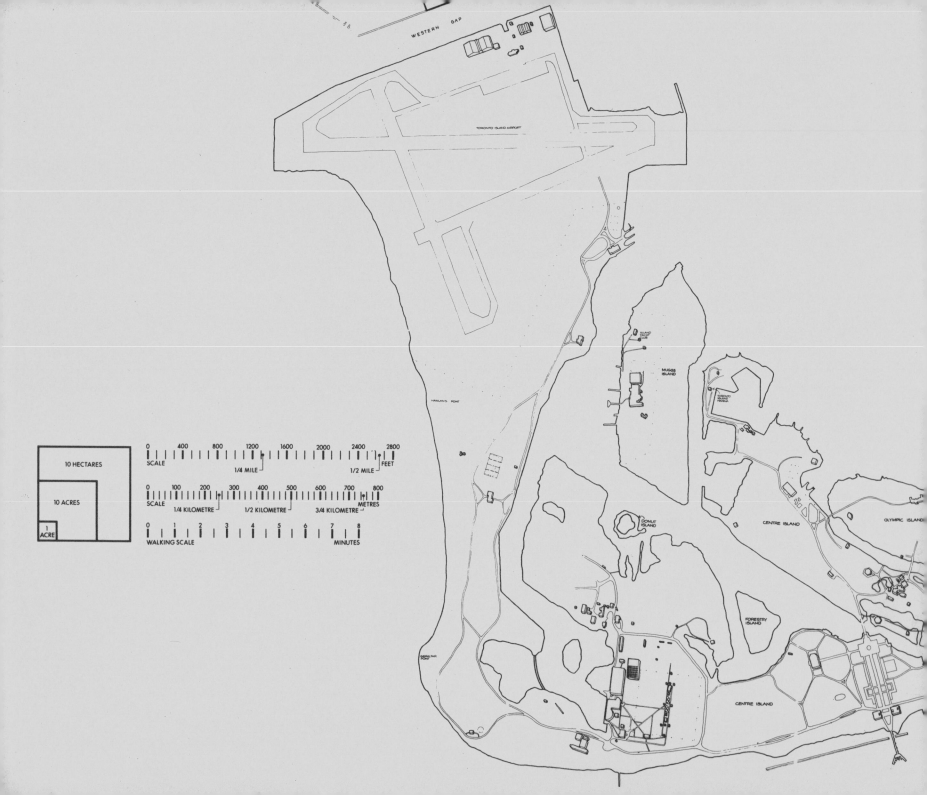

WESTERN GAP

TORONTO ISLAND AIRPORT

HANLAN'S POINT

ISLAND YACHT CLUB

MUGGS ISLAND

TORONTO ISLAND MARINA

DONUT ISLAND

CENTRE ISLAND

OLYMPIC ISLAND

FORESTRY ISLAND

GIBRALTAR POINT

CENTRE ISLAND

| 10 HECTARES |
| 10 ACRES |
| 1 ACRE |

0   400   800   1200   1600   2000   2400   2800
SCALE   FEET
        1/4 MILE   1/2 MILE

0   100   200   300   400   500   600   700   800
SCALE   METRES
    1/4 KILOMETRE   1/2 KILOMETRE   3/4 KILOMETRE

0   1   2   3   4   5   6   7   8
WALKING SCALE   MINUTES